THE CAMBRIDGE COMPANION TO
VYGOTSKY

CW00673601

L. S. Vygotsky was an early twentieth-
ogist whose writing exerts a significan.
opment of social theory in the early twenty-first century. His
nondeterministic, nonreductionist account of the formation of
mind provides current theoretical developments with a broadly
drawn, yet very powerful sketch of the ways in which humans
shape and are shaped by social, cultural, and historical conditions. The dialectical conception of development insists on the
importance of genetic or developmental analysis at several levels. *The Cambridge Companion to Vygotsky* is a comprehensive
text that provides students, academics, and practitioners with a
critical perspective on Vygotsky and his work.

Harry Daniels is the director of the Centre for Sociocultural and
Activity Theory Research (Bath) at the University of Bath, UK. He
is also adjunct professor, Centre for Learning Research, Griffith
University, Brisbane, Australia, and research professor, Centre for
Human Activity Theory, Kansai University, Osaka, Japan. Harry
Daniels is the author of *Vygotsky and Pedagogy* and the editor
of *An Introduction to Vygotsky* and *Charting the Agenda: Educational Activity after Vygotsky*. His books have been translated
into Japanese, Portuguese (in Brazil and in Europe), and Spanish.

Michael Cole is the University Professor of Communication, Psychology, and Human Development and the director of the Laboratory of Comparative Human Cognition at the University of
California, San Diego. He also holds the Sanford Berman Chair of
Language, Thought, and Communication. He is the author and
coauthor of several books and many articles on culture and development. He is a member of the National Academy of Education,
the American Academy of Arts and Sciences, and the Russian
Academy of Education.

James V. Wertsch is a professor in the Department of Anthropology in Arts and Sciences at Washington University in St. Louis.
He holds joint appointments in Education, the Russian Studies Program, and the Program in Philosophy, Neuroscience, and
Psychology, all in Arts and Sciences. He is the director of the
McDonnell International Scholars Academy. His topics of study
are collective memory and identity, especially in Russia and other
countries of the former Soviet Union, as well as in the United
States.

The Cambridge Companion to

VYGOTSKY

Edited by

Harry Daniels
University of Bath, UK

Michael Cole
University of California, San Diego

James V. Wertsch
Washington University in St. Louis

CAMBRIDGE UNIVERSITY PRESS
Cambridge, New York, Melbourne, Madrid, Cape Town, Singapore, São Paulo

Cambridge University Press
32 Avenue of the Americas, New York, NY 10013-2473, USA

www.cambridge.org
Information on this title: www.cambridge.org/9780521831048

First published 2007

Printed in the United States of America

A catalog record for this publication is available from the British Library.

Library of Congress Cataloging in Publication data

The Cambridge companion to Vygotsky / edited by Harry Daniels, Michael
Cole, James V. Wertsch.
  p. cm.
Includes bibliographical references and index.
ISBN-13: 978-0-521-83104-8 (hardback)
ISBN-10: 0-521-83104-0 (hardback)
ISBN-13: 978-0-521-53787-2 (pbk.)
ISBN-10: 0-521-53787-8 (pbk.)
  1. Vygotskii, L. S. (Lev Semenovich), 1896–1934. 2. Psychologists – Soviet
Union. I. Daniels, Harry. II. Cole, Michael. III. Wertsch, James V.
IV. Title.
BF109.V95C36 2007
150.92 – dc22   2006029810

ISBN 978-0-521-83104-8 hardback
ISBN 978-0-521-53787-2 paperback

CONTENTS

Applications of Vygotsky's Work

LIST OF CONTRIBUTORS

Amelia Álvarez has a Ph.D. in psychology from the Universidad Autónoma de Madrid. Her research is on the role of cultural contexts in the development and the education of young generations from a Vygotskian approach. She is coeditor of the journal *Cultura y Educación* and is a member of the editorial board of *Mind, Culture, and Activity*. She coedited *Explorations in Socio-Cultural Studies* and *Sociocultural Studies of Mind*. She edited *Hacia un currículum cultural. La vigencia de Vygotski en la educación*, and she is a coauthor of *Pigmalión, Informe sobre el impacto de la televisión en la infancia*.

David Bakhurst is the John and Ella G. Charlton Professor of Philosophy at Queen's University, Kingston, Ontario. His research interests include Russian philosophy and psychology, epistemology, and ethics. He has published many articles in books and journals. He is the author of *Consciousness and Revolution in Soviet Philosophy* and coeditor of *The Social Self* and *Jerome Bruner: Language, Culture, Self*. He holds an honorary Chair at the University of Birmingham, UK.

Michael Cole is the Sanford I. Berman Chair in Language, Thought, and Communication at the University of California, San Diego, where he is also University Professor of Communication, Psychology, and Human Development. His work focuses on cultural–historical, activity-centered approaches to human development and their accompanying mediational theories of mind. He spent 30 years as the editor of the journals *Russian and Eastern European Psychology* and *Soviet Psychology* and has translated Russian psychology into English. He is the founding editor of *Mind, Culture, and Activity*, where he retains the role of managing editor. He is author or coauthor of several books on issues of culture and cognitive development, including: *The Cultural Context of Learning and Thinking, Cultural Psychology,* and *The Development of Children*.

Harry Daniels is professor of Education: Culture and Pedagogy and is the director of the Centre for Sociocultural and Activity Theory Research at the University of Bath, UK. He holds honorary chairs at Kansai University in Japan and Griffith University in Australia. He is the author of *Vygotsky and Pedagogy* and editor of *An introduction to Vygotsky*. He coedited *Mind, Culture, and Activity* from 2001 to 2006. His current research is concerned with expansive learning in the development of interagency in children's services.

Pablo del Río is a professor in the Faculty of Humanities, Communication, and Documentation at the University Carlos III, Madrid, Spain. He is undertaking research on historical changes in the cultural architectures of mind and on the genetic cultural impact of media on the mind, especially on children. He is associate editor of *Culture and Psychology*. He coedited *Explorations in Socio-Cultural Studies* and *Sociocultural Studies of Mind*. He authored *Psicología de los medios de Comunicación* and coauthored *Pigmalión. Informe sobre el impacto de la televisión en la infancia*.

Anne Edwards is professor of Educational Studies, director of Research, and director of the Oxford Centre for Sociocultural and Activity Theory Research (OSAT) in the Department of Educational Studies at the University of Oxford. She is a Fellow of St. Hilda's College, is a former president of the British Educational Research Association, and is the former editor of the *British Educational Research Journal*. She coedited *Mind, Culture, and Activity* from 2001 to 2006. She has drawn on Cultural Historical Activity Theory in her work on teacher education, early education, and the prevention of social exclusion. Her current research projects focus inter alia on interprofessional working, particularly the idea of relational agency as a capacity to align one's interpretation and responses with those of others to enhance one's action, and on how research-based knowledge is mediated in the work of policy and practice in communities.

Yrjö Engeström is professor of Adult Education and director of the Center for Activity Theory and Developmental Work Research at the University of Helsinki, Finland. He is also professor emeritus of Communication at the University of California, San Diego. Known for his theory of expansive learning, he applies and develops cultural–historical activity theory in interventionist studies of work and organizations. His most recent book is *Developmental Work Research: Expanding Activity Theory in Practice*.

Natalia Gajdamaschko is a limited-term lecturer and adjunct professor at the Faculty of Education, Simon Fraser University, Canada. She is a Vygotskian psychologist, trained in Moscow, Russia. In North America, she has served as a visiting research Fellow at the Vinson Institute of Government and the Torrance Center for Creative Studies at the University of Georgia (US). As the 1993 recipient of an Advanced Scholars Award by the International Research and Exchange Board (IREX), she spent an academic year at the University of Connecticut's School of Education conducting research on topics in gifted education and educational psychology. Dr. Gajdamaschko has presented papers at numerous European, North American, and world congresses in the fields of educational theory, gifted education, and educational psychology.

Boris Gindis received his doctorate in developmental psychology at the Moscow Academic Research Institute of General and Educational Psychology and his postdoctoral training in School Psychology at the City University of New York. He is a licensed psychologist and a nationally certified bilingual (Russian/English) school psychologist. Dr. Gindis specializes in clinical work and research in the field of international adoption. He is the chief psychologist and director of the Center for Cognitive-Developmental Assessment and Remediation located in Nanuet, NY. The center provides bilingual psycho-educational evaluations and other services for internationally adopted children in cooperation with a network of bilingual mental health and education specialists. He is the author of more than 40 scientific articles and book chapters, has served as a guest-editor for psychology journals, and has been a keynote speaker at national and international conferences. He is a full professor (retired) and former director of the Bilingual Program at Touro College Graduate School of Education and Psychology.

Mariane Hedegaard is professor of psychology at the University of Copenhagen. Her research focus is on child development from a cultural–historical perspective and the formation of personality (i.e., motives, concepts, and identity) through school teaching and learning. She has researched children from migrant families in Danish schools and has documented their learning, development, and conceptions about school life. She has also taught social science to minority children. She has started a new project about children's learning and development by researching children's everyday life and the projects that children engage in within their families, schools, and related institutions.

Dorothy Holland is the Cary Boshamer professor of anthropology at the University of North Carolina at Chapel Hill. She is a former president of the Society of Psychological Anthropology. She is the coauthor of *Identity and Agency in Cultural Worlds* and *Educated in Romance*. Her coedited books include: *History in Person: Enduring Struggles, Contentious Practice, Intimate Identities; Selves in Time and Place;* and *Cultural Models in Language and Thought*.

Vera P. John-Steiner is a psycholinguist whose work includes developmental, sociocultural, and creativity studies. She is a coeditor of Vygotsky's *Mind in Society* and is the author of *Creative Collaboration* and *Notebooks of the Mind: Explorations of Thinking* (winner of the 1990 William James Book Award from the American Psychological Association). She has taught and lectured in Europe, South America, and throughout the United States, and she is a Regents' Professor of Linguistics and Education at the University of New Mexico. Her most recent award is for lifetime achievement as a scholar in Cultural–Historical Activity Theory.

Alex Kozulin is the research director of the International Center for the Enhancement of Learning Potential in Jerusalem. He also lectures at Hebrew University and Tel Aviv University.

William Lachicotte, Jr., is research assistant professor of social medicine, adjunct assistant professor of anthropology, and research associate of the FPG Child Development Institute at the University of North Carolina at Chapel Hill. He is coauthor of *Identity and Agency in Cultural Worlds* and author of chapters and articles on identity in social practice, including "Intimate Powers, Public Selves: Bakhtin's Space of Authoring," in *Power and the Self*.

Boris G. Meshcheryakov graduated from Moscow State University in 1975 with a first degree in psychology. He received his Ph.D. in 2001. He has been professor in the department of psychology at "Dubna" State University for Nature, Society, and Mankind since 1998. He is deputy editor of the *Journal of Cultural Historical Psychology*. He has authored *An Introduction to Human Sciences* and *Psychology of Memory*, and he coauthored the *Dictionary of Modern Psychology*.

René van der Veer is a professor of education at Leiden University, The Netherlands. His research interests include the history of developmental psychology and education, cultural psychology, and philosophy of science. He has published numerous articles and a dozen books, including *Understanding Vygotsky* (coauthor) and *The Social Mind* (coauthor).

James V. Wertsch is the Marshall S. Snow Professor of Arts and Sciences at Washington University in St. Louis. He received his Ph.D. from the University of Chicago in 1975 and has been on the faculty of Northwestern University (1976–1985), the University of California, San Diego (1985–1987), Utrecht University (1987–1988), Clark University (1988–1995), and Washington University (1995–present). His publications include *Vygotsky and the Social Formation of Mind*, *Voices of the Mind: A Sociocultural Approach to Mediated Action*, *Mind as Action*, and *Voices of Collective Remembering*. His research is concerned with language, thought, and culture, with a special focus on text, collective memory, and identity.

Vladimir P. Zinchenko graduated from Moscow State University in 1953 with a first degree in psychology. He received his Ph.D. in psychology in 1966. He has been a member of the Russian Academy of Education since 1992. In 1998, he was a founding member and the head of the Psychology Department at "Dubna" State University for Nature, Society, and Mankind. He is an honorary member of the American Academy of Arts and Sciences. He has been a professor in the Department of Psychology at the Higher School of Economics (HSE) since 2004. His major fields of interests are cultural–historical, developmental, general psychology, and experimental psychology. His most recent research projects have been concerned with creativity and visual thinking. He has written and contributed to more than four hundred publications, including *The Thought and Word of Gustav Shpet* and *Psychological Paedagogics*.

THE CAMBRIDGE COMPANION TO
VYGOTSKY

HARRY DANIELS, MICHAEL COLE,
AND JAMES V. WERTSCH

Editors' Introduction

L. S. Vygotsky was an early twentieth-century Russian psychologist whose writing exerts a significant influence on the development of social theory in the early years of the twenty-first century. The greater part of his legacy was produced in the 10 years that preceded his death in 1934. It now influences a wide range of disciplines and professions. His nondeterministic, nonreductionist account of the formation of mind provides current theoretical developments with a broadly drawn, yet very powerful sketch of the ways in which humans shape and are shaped by social, cultural, and historical conditions.

As David Bakhurst notes in Chapter 2, Vygotsky insisted that in order to understand the mature human mind, we must comprehend the processes from which it emerges. These ideas were originally forged at a time of rapid and intense social upheaval following the Russian Revolution. They were developed by a scholar who was charged with developing a state system for the education of "pedagogically neglected" children (Yaroshevsky, 1989, p. 96). This group included the homeless, of which there were a very large number. Thus, he was working at a time of profound social change (which was influenced by the Soviet adaptation of Marxist theory to social and political practice) and also working with a group of people who had profoundly different cultural experiences from "mainstream" members of society. He sought ways of intervening in the lives of these young people that would either compensate for or ameliorate their experience of marginalization. Consequently, it is, in some way, unsurprising that he should have attempted to develop a theory of social, cultural, and historical formation of the human mind.

A major element in Vygotsky's thesis, that human mind must be understood as the emergent outcome of cultural–historical processes. was the suggestion that methodology in social science was itself in need of profound transformation. He argued that history had presented social science with a crisis formed by the failures of the methodologies of introspectionism and reflexology that predominated in early twentieth-century Europe (Vygotsky, 1997). The latter part of his short life witnessed his struggles with enduring philosophical, methodological, and conceptual issues, such as the identification of an appropriate unit of analysis.

A close reading of Vygotsky's work shows how his ideas developed and were transformed over a very brief period of time. It is difficult to reconcile some of the writing from the early 1920s with that which was produced during the last 2 years of his life. These rapid changes, coupled with the fact that his work was not published in chronological order, make synthetic summaries of his work difficult. It is our intention that this book will make Vygotsky "easier to read" by discussing his work in terms of the cultures in which it arose and developed; seek to clarify aspects of the intellectual legacy that he left; and then discuss subsequent applications of this legacy.

There is a growing interest in what has become known as "socio-cultural or cultural–historical theory," and its subsequent close relative "activity theory." These traditions are historically linked to the work of L. S. Vygotsky and attempt to provide an account of learning and develop-ment as mediated processes. These traditions are, in themselves, broad theoretical frameworks, which defy complete descriptions to the satis-faction of all concerned. Vygotsky maintained a particular interest in the relationship between speaking and thinking. The mediational role of speech was brought to attention through the publication of *Thinking and Speech* which, in various guises, remains his most popular text. In some dialects of contemporary theory inspired by Vygotsky, the empha-sis is on semiotic mediation with a particular emphasis on speech. In this book, cultural artifacts, such as speech, serve as tools that both shape possibilities for thought and action and, in turn, are shaped by those who use them. In other accounts, more emphasis is placed on the analysis of participation and the ways in which individuals function in communi-ties. In activity theory, it is joint-mediated activity that takes the center stage in the analysis. This broad grouping of approaches has different strands emanating from the original differences in emphasis established by Russian writers such as Rubinshtein (1957), Uznadze (1961), Basov (1931), and Leont'ev (1972) as well as the physiologist Bernshtein (1966, 1967).

Contemporary approaches attempt to theorize and provide method-ological tools for investigating the processes by which phylogenetic, social, cultural, and historical factors shape human functioning. None resort to determinism because they acknowledge that in the course of their own development, human beings also actively shape the very forces that are active in shaping them. As Michael Cole has noted:

> The dual process of shaping and being shaped through culture implies that humans inhabit "intentional" (constituted) worlds within which the traditional dichotomies of subject and object, person and environment, and so on cannot be analytically separated and temporally ordered into independent and dependent variables.   (Cole, 1996, p. 103)

This mediational model, which entails the mutual influence of individual and supraindividual factors, lies at the heart of many attempts to develop our understanding of the possibilities for interventions in human learning and development. All these arguments, along with many others drawn from Vygotsky's writing, have been influential in the development of branches of social theory. Researchers and scholars working in diverse fields, such as education, psychology, sociology, communication, philosophy, sociotechnical systems design, and business studies, draw on Vygotsky's work and its subsequent developments.

The book is made up of three sections. The first section is titled "Vygotsky in Context." In the opening paragraph of Chapter 1, Rene van der Veer applies Vygotsky's theory to the analysis of Vygotsky's own work. He suggests that to understand the work we need to be guided by Vygotsky's insight: in order to comprehend the inner mental processes of human beings, we have to step outside of the mind to look at these human beings in their sociocultural context. He cites Vygotsky's close colleague Luria who argued that:

> We should not look for the explanation of behavior in the depths of the brain or the soul but in the external living conditions of persons and most of all in the external conditions of their societal life, in their social-historical forms of existence.   (Luria, 1979, p. 23)

It is this argument that drove us to open the book with these chapters. The second section, "Readings of Vygotsky," is concerned with interpretations of Vygotsky's legacy. This section allows our contributors to bring an early twenty-first century perspective to this enduring contribution. The third and final section, "Applications of Vygotsky's Work," is concerned with understandings of how the work is being applied in our current cultural historical circumstances.

VYGOTSKY IN CONTEXT

In considering the work of Lev Vygotsky in relation to its context, it is worthwhile to pause at the outset to consider the two dimensions of his writing. It is tempting, for example, to adopt a conventional understanding of context as a synonym for environment and, in turn, to interpret environment narrowly as a set of objectively specifiable set of contemporaneous surrounding social and physical conditions. However, as van der Veer notes in Chapter 1, Vygotsky argued that the individual and the environment mutually constitute each other; "the environment" cannot be specified independently of the organism (in this case, person) who lives in and through that environment, changing it even as he (in this case, Vygotsky) interprets and acts on it. We should keep in mind that when speaking of Vygotsky in context, we are speaking of two different historical eras and multiple social milieus – the context of Russia and the Soviet Union in the first half of the twentieth century and other parts of the world in the first decade of the twenty-first century. Each author in this volume is engaging in an act of interpretation that is constitutive of our own context as Vygotsky's life and work were constitutive of his.

We emphasize these complicating circumstances because recognition of these circumstances should help us to ward off the temptation to arrive at a single truth about the man, ideas, and events about which we write. The facts of Vygotsky's life and the truth about his work are a matter of continued research and reconsideration that are best viewed in that light. The conclusions that different authors reach vary within and across historical time as well as within and across national and disciplinary contexts.

Few authors have contributed as much to our attempts to understand Vygotsky in context than René van der Veer and his colleague Jaan Valsiner, who have written the most extensively researched monograph on this topic (van der Veer & Valsiner, 1991). In that volume they treat the development of Vygotsky's ideas from his early life in Byelorussia in the years preceding, accompanying, and following World War I through his move to Moscow and until his death in 1934. Drawing on a wide array of sources, they portray the life of a Jewish Russian intellectual living in tumultuous times who participated as an activist in the transformations occurring in his own country and who incorporated into his life's work an astonishing knowledge of the history of world philosophy, social theory, literature, psychology, and evolutionary biology.

In Chapter 1, van der Veer focuses on a range of contemporary Russian thinkers whose work is closely associated with psychology, although they might have identified themselves as physiologists (Pavlov) or evolutionary biologists (Severtsov). From van der Veer's account, it seems clear that from early on Vygotsky wished to create a psychology that was rooted in the tradition of the natural sciences but that reached into the laws of society, a psychology that bridged between Darwin and Marx.

As he developed his ideas through the 1920s and early 1930s, he did so in dialogue with his Russian colleagues, all of whom were wrestling the long-standing issues of how to reconcile *idealism* and *materialism,* and all of whom were required, like it or not, to do so under conditions of the growth of the Soviet state and its Marxist–Leninist ideology that resulted in the deaths of many of his colleagues.

It seems entirely fitting that van der Veer should end his account of Vygotsky in context by concluding that although "we must step outside the researcher's mind(s) and take their environment into consideration. . . . we must not forget that that environment is no absolute entity but becomes refracted in the researchers' mind(s)."

In Chapter 2, David Bakhurst forcefully requires us to attend to the uncertainties that arise when we focus on the historical nature of context and attempt to interpret a scholar's work from a different historical and sociocultural position than that in which the work was conducted. A philosopher himself, who had the opportunity to work in Moscow with several leading Soviet philosophers interested in the work of Vygotsky, Bakhurst makes clear Vygotsky's long-standing interest in, and knowledge of, the history of philosophy on which he drew repeatedly. Although Spinoza, Hegel, Marx, and Engels figure prominently in Vygotsky's writings, so do philosophers ranging from the Greeks to his European and American contemporaries.

Bakhurst is particularly interested in making the argument that Vygotsky's psychological research is best interpreted within the philosophical tradition of rationalism, a belief, as he puts it, in the "priority of reason." To make his argument, he constructs a composite picture of what he terms "Vygotsky's western followers," who, in his interpretation, wish to reconstruct and improve on Vygotsky's ideas by expunging the ideas of what is considered to be their unfortunate rationalist elements (adherence to realism, scientism, universalism, Eurocentrism and progress, didacticism and individualism) – the demon's of Bakhurst's argument. He then sets out to exorcise the demons he has summoned.

Drawing on a combination of Vygotsky's own texts and the views of a number of contemporary Anglo-American and Russian philosophers, Bakhurst takes up and sets out to exorcise each of the presumed errors in Vygotsky's thinking. His examination of the issues leads to the conclusion that "contemporary philosophy . . . promises to strengthen Vygotsky's [rationalist] position." At the same time, he urges those currently interested in the relation of culture and mind to learn from Vygotsky's deep understanding of the process of mental development. Through dialogue between Vygotsky's time and our own, Bakhurst argues, deeper understanding is attainable.

In Chapter 3, Anne Edwards takes up a topic that has been much discussed by those interested in Vygotsky – the relationship of his ideas to those of his American contemporaries associated with the philosophical school of *pragmatism*. It is well known that Vygotsky read and admired the work of William James, and there has been a good deal of speculation about the relationship between Dewy and Vygotsky, but it is George Herbert Mead on whom Edwards focuses.

Edwards notes both similarities and differences in the circumstances and ideas that characterized Mead and Vygotsky's lives and work. Just as van der Veer placed Vygotsky within the social, intellectual, and historical circumstances of his time and place, Edwards places Mead in his: America in the post–Civil War era rather than in Russia in the middle of a revolution. Mead lived in America, a nation of immigrants, where individual initiative and opportunity were wellsprings of philosophy, rather than in a nation straddling Europe and Asia, where collectivism was a reigning ideology organizing social life and opportunity. Vygotsky could experience these circumstances after the revolution that occurred when he was approaching adulthood.

Given these contrasting experiences, it is fascinating to consider, as Edwards does in detail, the similarities and differences in the ways that Vygotsky and Mead sought to understand and supersede such fundamental dichotomies as self and society, consciousness and behavior, lower and higher mental processes, and metaphysics and science. Edwards' comparative analysis of the development of Mead and Vygotsky's ideas leads us back to the question of the contexts within which Mead and Vygotsky worked and are being selectively appropriated by scholars in different countries. Why, for example, do some of Vygotsky's ideas find favor in the United States but not others (a question that invites us to reconsider Bakhurst's chapter, which raises similar issues, although, appropriately enough, with somewhat different ends in mind)? How do the two scholars in question enter into and change the contexts in which they participate? (This is a question that leads us back to van der Veer's insistence on the mutual constitution of person and environment.)

There is a sense that the cultures formed within the categories by and through which academies are structured to do their own work on the shaping of artifacts such as texts. In the Chapter 4, Dorothy Holland and William Lachicotte, Jr., whose intellectual roots are to be found in anthropology, also discuss Mead in relation to Vygotsky. Here we have Vygotsky and Mead in another context. Holland and Lachicotte draw attention to the particular place of identity as a key concept in many different fields, including psychology, anthropology, sociology, linguistic, and cultural studies. They explore this concept from the two broad perspectives proposed by Mead and Erikson in a way that reflects the authors' own anthropological priorities. In the discussion of Mead's contribution, his emphasis on the outcomes of sociogenesis in terms of links between self and society is contrasted with Vygotsky's concern for the development of mind and personality through sociogenesis. Baldwin and Royce are introduced and discussed in terms of their influence on Vygotsky and Mead's sociogenetic accounts of self and mind. Holland and Lachiotte reiterate the fundamental importance of *mediation* for the study of identity and move to a discussion of *agency*. This leads to an examination of identity formation in trajectories of participation across activities. At the close of the chapter, they return to the central underlying tension between Erikson and Mead's theories with respect to the existence of multiple identities and the degree of integration of such identities. They question the extent to which a person may seek to maintain some level of integration of self across multiple contexts, or, at least, may be distressed by their contradictory demands. They suggest that Mead and Vygotsky share a belief in *active internalization* (self authoring), *dialogic selves* (self-other dialogues), and the semiotics of behavior. They proceed to argue that when enhanced by Vygotsky's notions of semiotic mediation, higher psychological functions, and agency, these jointly held views "constitute a powerful sociogenetic vision of how individuals come to be inhabited by, and yet co-construct, the social and cultural worlds through which they exist."

In Chapter 5, Vera John-Steiner raises, in still another form, the issues surrounding a consideration of Vygotsky in context. As she notes at the outset, Vygotsky's (1934/1962) work first came to wide attention in the United States through the publication of a book titled *Thought and Language*. In that year, the United States and the then–Soviet Union came frighteningly close to thermonuclear war; the text of Vygotsky's *Myishlenie I Rech* (published in 1934, the year of Vygotsky's death) had been purged of most of its references to Marx and Engels, as well as many of its references literary works. When it appeared again in 1987, now translated as *Thinking and Speech*, American readers were prepared to consider the possibility that perhaps the references to Marxism were not a political charade and that the poet, Osip Mandelshtam's insights ("I forgot the word I wanted to say, and thought, unembodied, returned to the hall of shadows") might be a fitting starting point for understanding the relationship of the mental and the linguistic in human nature.

John-Steiner's examines and updates the question of the relation of Vygotsky's ideas to those of his American contemporary, Benjamin Lee Whorf. In addition, she includes some of her own, fascinating work that expands on several of Vygotsky's key ideas such as his characterization of inner speech. Interestingly, just as Vygotsky's work experienced a long period of neglect in Russia, Whorf's underwent a long period of disfavor in the West. However, albeit for different reasons related to their different sociopolitical contexts, Whorf has begun to find favor once again among contemporary scholars interested in the relationship of language and thought (Gentner and Goldin-Meadow, 2003).

The juxtaposition of these two thinkers, in conjunction with the juxtaposition of the two different renderings of the title of Vygotsky's *Myishlenie I Rech* at different historical eras, and their differing socio-cultural–political contexts is especially apposite to the topic of Vygotsky in context. *Thinking and Speech* clearly adheres more faithfully to the original text in terms of content. But the change in titles also bespeaks the changing context within Russian psychology at the time and the influence of third-generation Vygotskian-inspired psychologists on their American colleagues. By the time *Thinking and Speech* appeared, there was a far deeper appreciation in the United States of Vygotsky's deep commitment to the idea that the human mind must be studied in *the process of becoming*, the theme with which Bakhurst ends his chapter. Fittingly, this different set of understandings is accompanied by a different way of expressing the underlying concept in words. John-Steiner makes this point emphatically by ending her chapter with Vygotsky's declaration that "the historical study of behavior is not an auxiliary aspect of theoretical study, but rather forms its very base."

READINGS OF VYGOTSKY

At the beginning of Chapter 6, Boris Meshcheryakov reminds us of Dostoevsky's famous speech in 1880 in which he said, "Had Pushkin lived longer, there probably would be fewer discussions and misunderstandings between us than we see today. But God judged differently. Pushkin died at the peak of his powers and, undoubtedly, took some great mystery to his tomb. And now we are solving this mystery without him."

The mysteries that grew out of Vygotsky's early death do not compare with those associated with Pushkin, but Dostoevsky's comment does apply to Vygotsky. Because Vygotsky wrote so much so quickly, because he lived in a contentious and dangerous political context (see Cole and Gajdamaschko), and because he died in the middle of a brilliant career, he took some great unanswered mysteries to his tomb. This has been the source of confusion and frustration for those of us who have tried to understand Vygotsky during the last several decades, but it has also given rise to a great deal of generative debate.

The many productive readings one can make of Vygotsky stem from many sources. In our view an important starting point in this regard is that he was an "ambivalent Enlightenment rationalist" (Wertsch, 1995). In some of his writings, he seems to be deeply committed to the kind of abstract reasoning and social engineering that would be a credit to the strongest advocate of the Enlightenment. But at other points in his oeuvre he sounds like someone devoted to German Romanticism, or even mysticism. This is not simply a matter of stages in his career – the deep and abiding struggle among these grand traditions characterized his writing throughout his life.

So who was the "real" Vygotsky? In our view the only reasonable answer to this is to say he that like just about everyone in the modern West, he was a child of these two grand traditions, and his great contribution was to draw on them and others in unique ways to come up with a powerful amalgam of ideas. Instead of insisting on reading him in one or another way in isolation, however, the best way to appreciate Vygotsky is to recognize how generative this seeming contradiction has been in spawning all sorts of innovations in theory and practice.

This is not to say that we can make anything we wish out of Vygotsky's writings. Any claims about "Vygotsky said..." or "Vygotsky thought..." should be backed up by close reading, a practice that continues to be extremely rewarding in his case. However, to believe that there is a single, coherent dogma that one can derive from such reading is to miss the point in our view. In fact, Vygotsky foresaw the dangers of orthodoxy and insisted that he wished his ideas to be used, transcended, and even refuted, rather than serve as a sort of monument on which the dust of subsequent years would settle.

All this amounts to saying that one of the most important things that Vygotsky scholars can do is read his writings carefully and repeatedly – each time with a fresh eye. Given the richness and range of his thought, such readings are likely to yield continuing insight and inspiration, and the chapters by Meshcheryakov, Zinchenko, Cole and Gajdamaschko, del Rioand Alvarez, and Hedegaard offer a great deal of food for thought in this regard. These chapters differ in their focus and conclusions, but this is more a matter of complement than contradiction. The authors have used the lenses of various theoretical traditions to guide their interpretation, and they focus primarily on Vygotsky's own writings. In each case there is something new to learn.

In Chapter 6, which focuses most on Vygotsky's writings, Boris Meshcheryakov outlines a systemic, conceptual framework for gaining an overview of Vygotsky's writings (all 274 titles!). He does this with the help of "Logico-Semantic Analysis" (LSA). Meshcheryakov provides a major service – and insight into Vygotsky's thinking, a task made all the more challenging because the influences on this thinking range "from the philosophy of Spinoza and Marx to the American behaviorism of Watson and the linguistics of Sapir" (see Chapter 6, this volume).

Meshcheryakov's analysis reveals a couple of general, underlying tendencies. The first is that "Vygotsky sought to present mental development on several conceptual 'screens,' each corresponding to a particular domain of development: biological phylogenesis, sociocultural 'phylogenesis,' ontogenesis (both normal and abnormal), microgenesis ('actual genesis'), and pathogenesis" (see Chapter 6, this volume).

The second tendency Meshcheryakov identifies is the role of "systematicity" in Vygotsky's writings, a tendency noted by other authors in this volume as well. Vygotsky's discussions of functional systems, the structure of functions, interfunctional connections, and functional development all reflect an analytic stance concerned with this issue. For example, in reviewing Vygotsky's account of interiorization, Meshcheryakov notes that the key to understanding this construct is the systemic structure of consciousness, rather than some kind of relocation of processes from an external to an internal plane.

Meshcheryakov also touches on the issue of systematicity is in his summary, where he identifies issues that remain open, and he also compares Vygotsky's account of developmental stages with that of Piaget. He readily admits that he is not certain how many stages should be included in an account of Vygotsky's position, but he is clear on the nature of these stages. Instead of representing a "modular" approach, Vygotsky's account is shown to involve a "multi-lineal process," and the only way to create coherence out of this "rather odd and undifferentiated mix" of components is to recognize their contribution to a systemic approach to human consciousness.

In Chapter 9, Vladimir Petrovich Zinchenko generates another perspective on Vygotsky by reading him through the lens of the Russian philologist and philosopher Gustav Shpet (1879–1937). Vygotsky studied with Shpet and was deeply influenced by him, yet as Zinchenko points out, "Vygotsky and his whole scientific school (Aleksandr R. Luria, A. N. Leont'ev, Aleksandr V. Zaporozhets, and others) ignored Shpet's works." He notes several possible motivations for this, including the political forces of repression aimed at Shpet, forces that eventually resulted in his imprisonment and brutal torture and execution. But as Zinchenko and Wertsch (in press) have outlined, there is little doubt that Vygotsky's debt to Shpet was profound, especially when it came to *inner speech*.

Interpreting the relationship between Vygotsky and Shpet, Zinchenko goes well beyond documenting that the latter indeed did influence the former. Specifically, he goes into ideas missed or underdeveloped by Vygotsky because he did not take advantage of Shpet's ideas. In particular, Zinchenko points out that Vygotsky failed to build on Shpet's neo-Humboldtian ideas about the "inner form of language" – as opposed to the notion of "inner speech." Although Shpet clearly influenced Vygotsky's ideas on this topic, Vygotsky ended up missing an opportunity to do something more profound in Zinchenko's view.

For Shpet, the inner form of the word is unique to every language, and it distinguishes one language community from another, just as the external, grammatical form does. This does not mean that this inner form can be reduced to a static essence, or "ergon." Instead, Shpet insisted that the inner form of the word or of language must be viewed as dynamic energy ("energeia"). Up to this point, much in Shpet's analysis parallels Vygotsky's. But Shpet emphasized that the dynamic logic of the inner form of the word is a fact about the language system and language collectivity, as opposed to a fact about inner speech, which is primarily concerned with mental processes in the individual. Vygotsky seems not to have recognized this collective level of systemic organization, and in Zinchenko's view the result was that he did not take advantage of the possibilities offered by Shpet.

To be sure, Vygotsky's account of inner speech yielded some extremely productive outcomes. For example, it laid one of the foundations for Luria's brilliant and innovative typology of aphasia. However, by failing to take full advantage of Shpet's analysis, Vygotsky was left with an account that said less than it could have about the insights of hermeneutic phenomenology concerning the nexus of social and individual planes of human consciousness. In Zinchenko's view, Shpet was more true to some aspects of Vygotsky's fundamental project than was Vygotsky, and this amounts to a set of intriguing questions about what untapped potentialities there may still be in this project.

In Chapter 8, Cole and Gajdamaschko provide another perspective for reading Vygotsky, a perspective concerned with theories of culture. Much has been written about culture in the decades since Vygotsky's death, and recently his ideas have been enthusiastically embraced by a range of scholars who are providing new insight. Some may find this surprising or ironic because Vygotsky employed notions of culture that would seem to be deeply incompatible with contemporary thinking in fields such as cultural anthropology. Others, are drawing on different segments of Vygotsky's writings where he looks more in tune with contemporary thinking.

Is one of these parties right and the other wrong? Again, it all depends on the reading one makes of Vygotsky's works, and this is why Cole and Gajdamaschko's contribution to this volume is so valuable. As they note, a systematic review of Vygotsky reveals the use of several different meanings of culture. His ambivalent attitude toward Enlightenment rationalism is reflected in the distinction that Cole and Gajdamaschko make between a "hierarchical" and a "Herderian" approach to culture. On the one hand, Vygotsky and his colleagues, including Luria, sometimes wrote about culture as if it is possible to have more or less of it. This approach led them to contrast "uncultured" (or "primitive") peoples with "cultural peoples." On the other hand, however, Vygotsky was also a child of the tradition that grew out of the German Romanticism of Herder and others. From this latter perspective, the issue is difference rather than deficiency, and this is a better starting point for dialogue with many contemporary scholars.

Cole and Gajdamaschko are clearly proponents of a perspective grounded in difference and squarely against "value-laden, hierarchical notions of culture," but they provide a reminder that we are all shaped by forces of history and culture – forces of "context." In the end this means that we, along with Vygotsky, are likely to manifest remnants of now largely rejected hierarchical notions of culture.

Cole and Gajdamaschko also note another reflection of Vygotsky's historical positioning. He lived and wrote at a time when it was not unusual to be an "armchair anthropologist." To be sure, Vygotsky did participate in some research in the field, namely, the empirical studies he, Luria, and others conducted in Central Asia in the late 1920s. A wonderful photo of Vygotsky working with subjects in Uzbekistan in 1929 reminds us of this (Vygodskaya & Lifanova, 1996, p. 130). As this photo reflects, Vygotsky approached such cross-cultural studies more as relocated laboratory settings for conducting testing and laboratory psychology than as a site for rich ethnographic analysis.

This approach to fieldwork distinguished Vygotsky's comparative study of culture from that of Boas, Sapir, and other founders of modern cultural anthropology in the US. In contrast to Vygotsky's notion of a relocated laboratory, these other scholars sought to develop a more comprehensive ethnographic picture of a cultural setting and its associated aspects of mental life. Furthermore, Vygotsky's field practices reinforced his tendency to interpret culture in what Cole and Gajdamaschko call a hierarchical fashion. As he sat in Tashkent testing those subjects in 1929, he and Luria (1976) were largely involved in assessing whether they demonstrated forms of thinking widely found among subjects educated in the Western tradition. To the extent these subjects did not reveal such abilities, they were viewed as being at a lower, earlier stage in a hierarchy of consciousness. This means that Vygotsky's efforts at cultural comparison are better viewed as cross-historical research than what we now routinely take to be cross-cultural research. Cole has spent much of his career identifying the potential pitfalls of this sort of research, and his insights, in part, are the result of engaging with the ideas of Vygotsky and Luria.

Furthermore, the reading provided by Cole and Gajdamaschko goes well beyond criticizing the weaknesses we see from today's perspective in Vygotsky's notion of culture. Their analysis of the insight he provided by approaching culture from the perspective of *tool mediation* reminds us of the continuing contribution Vygotsky is making to today's discussions. By focusing on the need to keep tool use and cultural practice in mind, they remind us of the advantages of expanding the picture to what Cole has called "cultural historical activity theory." By incorporating the ideas of Evald Il'enkov, one of Vygotsky's intellectual descendents, into the picture, they take this one step further. Il'enkov's analysis of the dialectic between the ideal and material is an elaboration of Vygotsky's ideas that is still largely unfamiliar to Western readers.

In Chapter 11, Del Rio and Alvarez give us another angle from which to interpret not only Vygotsky's ideas, but those of some of the other authors in this section of this volume. Namely, their "ecofunctional reading" provides further insights into how Vygotsky's ideas can be understood. The authors make their case by examining several issues having to do with Vygotsky's "zone of proximal development," a term and idea that has perhaps received more attention in the secondary literature on Vygotsky than in any other of his writings. In an intriguing reflection on this zone, del Rio and Alvarez argue that it provided a "sort of theoretical ZPD for [Vygotsky] himself," a "frontier concept of his own theory on development."

Del Rio and Alvarez provide a complementary picture to Meshcheryakov on Vygotsky's "general genetic law of cultural development." This "law," which provides a sort of covering formulation for the zone of proximal development asserts that higher mental functioning appears twice, on two planes. First it emerges between people, on the intermental plane of functioning, and then it appears within the individual, on the intramental plane. As del Rio and Alvarez note, this means that "development takes place both inside and outside the skin, and above all, on the skin, at the border, that is, at the interface connecting the two regions." For these authors, the zone of proximal development (ZPD) is an intersection of several essential forces in Vygotsky's thinking. The ZPD is not just where intermental and intramental planes of functioning come together, but as Vygotsky so insightfully noted, where learning and development meet. In the words of these authors, the ZPD is a "frontier territory where: situated-embodied mind and the cognitive mind, the individual mind and the social mind, the development already attained and the development to be attained." (See Chapter 11.) Among the many interesting dimensions of the ZPD explored by del Rio and Alvarez is *agency*. As they notes, an ecofunctional approach challenges the view of the autonomous agent, or the "subject as self-sufficient, in favour of a subject who continues to use and borrow external operations and operators through life." Such thinking is a first cousin to analyses of "distributed cognition" in contemporary cognitive anthropology and in cognitive science, but del Rio and Alvarez introduce some unique ideas. In part, this is due to the influence of Rene Zazzo on their thinking.

Alhough he is not widely cited outside of French-speaking circles, Zazzo is a figure whose ideas in psychology and related fields deserve greater recognition. Based on their reading, as well as their personal discussions with Zazzo, del Rio, and Alvarez provide several additional insights on the issue of agency in social and mental life. Zazzo's comments about "personal intelligences," for example, lead them to propose that "each developmental process is idiosyncratic, that cultural operators and operations appropriated by each child define a complex of behaviors of which he is or is not capable himself, but above all, of viable functional loans in the ZPD, which he may or may not receive in different activity environments" (See Chapter 10.). This amounts to going a step further in specifying what it means to argue that development takes place, "both inside and outside the skin," an assertion that avoids the pitfalls of focusing exclusively on individuals or on the social and cultural contexts into which they are socialized.

Mariane Hedegaard brings most the chapters in this section of the volume down to a more concrete level – or as Davydov used to say, she "rises to the concrete." By examining preschool children's concept development from the perspective of how it is shaped by the institutional settings in which these children function, Hedegaard brings several strands of Vygotsky's ideas together. She starts with the observation that "cultural-historical developed tools mediate the child's relation to the world" (Chapter 10), a point that runs throughout Vygotsky's writings, but she spends a great deal of effort in examining ways in which activity settings involving collaboration with adults shape tool use and the associated socialization processes. By expanding on these basic starting points, Hedegaard takes a systemic approach to the issues involved, a point where she subscribes to some of the basic theoretical commitments in Vygotsky's writings that provide the focus of Meshcheryakov's Logico-Semantic Analysis.

Hedegaard's particular emphasis is on concept formation, but rather than exploring this topic in the controlled setting of a laboratory, she insists on examining the "interconnection between the child's conceptual development in different developmental periods and different institutional practice traditions and knowledge." By pursuing this issue in a systemic manner, she keeps the interrelationships between everyday and scientific concepts in view. Indeed, this is part of the classic issue of interfunctional relations as outlined by Vygotsky.

Hedegaard approaches these issues from the perspective of what she has termed "societal knowledge," which transcends specific institutional practices such as those found in preschool settings. By drawing in ideas on issues such as event representation as developed by Katherine Nelson (1996), Hedegaard is able to extend and update the interpretation of Vygotsky on several fronts. In keeping with her broad ranging systemic analysis, she outlines a series of developmental stages in such a way that she ties together a "societal perspective" and a "personal perspective" (Figure 10.2), emphasizing all the while that "there is no one to one relation between knowledge form and institutional practice."

Hedegaard ends by drawing all this together through an empirical illustration based on an instructional play setting for preschool children. This allows her to revisit several of the theoretical claims she raises while also introducing the powerful idea of "leading activities."

APPLICATIONS OF VYGOTSKY'S WORK

The fields of application that are discussed in this section are the study and analysis of pedagogy, the education of children with special needs, studies of cultural influence, and identity formation and studies of work.

In Chapter 12, Harry Daniels considers the pedagogic implications of Vygotsky's assertion of the primacy of social influence in the formation of mind. He maintains a specific focus on three elements of the Vygotskian thesis: (1) the general genetic law of cultural development, (2) the zone of proximal development, and (3) concept formation as an outcome of the subtle interplay between scientific and everyday concepts. He examines differences in the extent to which the analysis of the content of instruction (as against forms of pedagogic interaction and participation) is grounded in recommendations for pedagogic practice that claim a Vygotskian root. As part of this analysis, he maintains a concern for the cultural–historical circumstances in which these recommendations have arisen and have been implemented. In this respect, he draws on Vygotsky, who was well aware of the extent to which pedagogic practice is subject to social, cultural, and political influence.

> Pedagogics is never and was never politically indifferent, since, willingly or unwillingly, through its own work on the psyche, it has always adopted a particular social pattern, political line, in accordance with the dominant social class that has guided its interests.   (Vygotsky, 1997b, p. 348)

In Chapter 13, Alex Kozulin and Boris Gindis question whether Vygotsky actively chose to work with young people with special needs or whether he benefited from an opportunity that arose at a particular moment in time. Whatever the answer is to this question, Kozulin and Gindis note that Vygotsky's engagement with special-needs education continued from the time of his work as a teacher in the early 1920s until his death.

Kozulin and Gindis discuss the meaning of the somewhat unfamiliar term "defectology" and grounds their discussion in Vygotsky's general cultural–historical theory of human development as well as his special theory of "disontogenesis," or different/distorted development. Here, the natural and cultural determinants of development are discussed with reference to the major cultural upheaval that was taking place through the conflict and the mass migration in Russia at the time. It is in this context that Vygotsky discusses the distinction between cultural difference and cultural deprivation. This distinction leads to concepts of primary and secondary "handicapping conditions" where secondary conditions are those that arise in the social world of a child with an impairment give rise to difficulties that are social rather than biological in origin. The development and application of this work references the studies of Feuerstein and his colleagues, as well as that of contemporary Russian educators. Kozulin and Gindis call for more work to be done to explore issues such as the possibility of disability-specific ZPDs as well as forms of intervention such as disability-specific sets of psychological tools and disability-specific mediation techniques.

In Chapter 14, Yrjö Engeström returns to one of Vygotsky's major theoretical and methodological contributions – the method of double stimulation. He argues that this method can be used to design formative interventions in workplaces. Engeström suggests that by studying problem solving that is supported by providing artifacts that have the potential for adaptation and development as problem solving tools, one is able to understand how human groups can learn to control their own behavior from the outside through Engeström argues such research involves making subjects masters of their own lives in the workplace. He provides a description of the Change Laboratory that he and his colleagues have developed in Finland. This application of double stimulation is contrasted with Design Experiments, which Engeström depicts as research designs that provide settings in which researchers make designs for practitioners to implement. In the context of studies of schooling it is assumed that researchers make the grand design, teachers implement it (and contribute to its modification), and students learn better as a result. Engeström provides a robust critique of this linear view of implementation, which he suggests ignores the contestation and resistance that actually takes place in such workplaces. By way of contrast, he presents the Change Laboratory method as one in which work practices are developed by the practitioners in dialogue and debate among themselves, with their management, with their clients, and with the interventionist researchers. He concludes with an account of three challenges that such research presents to those concerned to develop the Vygotskian legacy in interventionist research. The first challenge concerns the understanding of tools and signs that are in play. Engeström argues for an analysis of a constantly evolving whole interconnected *instrumentality* of multiple means of mediation rather than the separate analysis of individual means of mediation. The second challenge concerns the understanding of causality that is deployed in such research. He calls for the analysis of an agentive layer of causality as well as the more familiar interpretative and contradictory layers. The third challenge emerges from the second. If there is to be more emphasis on an agentive layer of causality, then researchers need to learn new ways to listen to and amplify the voices of the subjects who are marginalized, underprivileged, or in other ways silenced. This is as much a challenge for those who advocate a dialogic basis for decision making in welfare services as it is for researchers concerned with the Change Laboratory method.

VYGOTSKY IN CONTEXT

1   Vygotsky in Context: 1900–1935

It is a fundamental tenet of Vygotskian theory that in order to understand the inner mental processes of human beings, we must look at human beings in their sociocultural context. We should not look for the explanation of human behavior in the depths of the brain or the soul but in the external living conditions of persons and, most of all, in the external conditions of their societal life – in their social–historical forms of existence (Luria, 1979, p. 23).

By accepting this tenet and generalizing it to the understanding of the creative work of investigators, we might say that in order to more fully understand the work of a specific thinker, we should step outside of that thinker's mind and take a look at the broader socioeconomic and sociocultural background in which he or she worked. The researcher's private abilities and preferences undoubtedly play a role in the creation of major theories, but the shaping of character, inclinations, and abilities of the researcher takes place in a specific sociocultural context, and every scientist is dependent on the ideas and tools available in his or her time. There is no true understanding of an investigator's theories, then, without an assessment of the broad context in which the theories were created (cf. Van der Veer, 1997).

PERSON AND CONTEXT

What do we mean by context? It is obvious that we should not just think of the physical and socioeconomical environment with all the possibilities and tools that it affords but also of the intellectual environment in the sense of available ideas, traditions of thinking, and so on. The physical, technological, socioeconomical, and intellectual environments and their complex interdependency determine the individual's possibilities.

However, individual (or organism) and environment cannot be defined independently (cf. Gesell, 1928, p. 357). What constitutes an inhospitable environment for one organism may be an *El Dorado* for another. A playground offers plenty of affordances for the young child but few for the elderly. A green meadow is food for the herbivore, money for the farmer, a playing field for the child, and a pretty landscape for the artist. A deep-pile carpet can simultaneously be a meeting-place for romantic lovers and a forest replete with healthy food for the glycypha-gus. It all depends on one's size, age, and capacities. In other words, we are always speaking about the *environment for some organism*. We cannot define the concept of environment independently from the organism living in that environment.

In 1933, Vygotsky delivered a lecture on the relationship between the individual and his or her environment in which he elaborated on this issue and applied it to the relationship between the child and his or her physical and social environment (Vygotsky, 1994). Vygotsky argued that individual and environment should not be viewed as distinct, separate factors that can in some way be added up to explain the individual's development and behavior. Rather, we should conceive of individual and environment as factors that mutually shape each other in a spiral process of growth.

Vygotsky argued that the environment is not an absolute entity that plays the same role for every child regardless of his or her age or mental capacities. What constitutes the environment is to a large extent dependent on the child. The very same object, for example, a book, will mean different things to children of different ages and capacities. At first it can only be seen, later on it can be grasped and torn apart, still later it can be read and enjoyed. In other words, there is no such thing as an objective environment with absolute meaning irrespective of the child that lives in that environment. That physical environment can remain objectively the same (although it will often become much larger as the child grows up), but it will always be interpreted in different ways as the child grows older.[1]

A similar thing can be said about the child's social environment. Depending on his or her age and temperament, the child will interpret the social environment in different ways, and the social environment will change as a function of the child's age. And, to make things even more complex, the social environment will change as a function of the child's development. Adults will adjust their demands of children as the children grow older.

---

[1] Of course, the concept of "sensitive periods" in development (a certain kind of experience at one point of development has a profoundly different impact on the organism than having that same experience at any other point in development) is only a specific example of this rule (Bailey et al. 2001).

We can conclude that for human beings it is difficult to define the environment if only because human beings attach meaning to aspects of their environment and because this environment is partly a social environment that changes in response to the person's actions, capacities, age, and so on.

Returning to Vygotsky, we may conclude that in order to understand his writings we need not study the scientific works, novels, and pieces of art of his time in any objective sense. Rather, we should analyze how Vygotsky reflected on them and see how they influenced his own conception. It is through the prism of Vygotsky's preferences and tastes that we will look at his sociocultural and intellectual background. So, what was the larger sociocultural background?

SOCIOCULTURAL BACKGROUND

All quiet scientific careers resemble one another, but each eventful career is eventful in its own way. Vygotsky's life and career were quite eventful. As a child he may have witnessed pogroms in his native town Gomel'; later on he certainly experienced several revolutions, World War I, the German and Ukrainian occupations, the civil war, famine, and political repression (Valsiner & Van der Veer, 2000; Van der Veer, 2002b). These events had repercussions for Vygotsky's personal life but also caused problems that he had to deal with professionally. One result of the upheavals was that millions of children lost their homes (the so-called *bezprizorniki*) and roamed the streets, causing inconvenience in the form of begging, theft, and prostitution (Stevens 1982). Vygotsky was involved in finding a solution for this major social problem. Another problem was that, as a result of the October Revolution, about 2 million Russians fled their country and others were expelled in the subsequent years. Naturally, these Russians left vacancies in all layers of the society that could not always be filled by competent candidates. The result was often chaos and improvisation. Vygotsky would be among those who tried to fill the gaps in the educational system by, for example, teaching evening courses to laborers (Valsiner & Van der Veer, 2000).

The social upheavals went hand in glove with an outburst of creativity in cultural life that was truly remarkable even by Russian standards. In Moscow and St. Petersburg, and also in the émigré circles in Berlin, Paris, and Prague (Raeff, 1990), Russian artists, musicians, and writers created works of art that are still being admired as outstanding achievements at a world-class level. The number of new and brilliant novelists in early-twentieth century Russia (subsequently the Soviet Union) was quite astonishing. Among Vygotsky's contemporaries we find such world-famous writers as Babel, Belyj, Bulgakov, Gorky,

Nabokov, Paustovsky, Platonov, Sholokhov, and Zamyatin. Outstanding poets such as Akhmatova, Blok, Esenin, Khodasevich, Mayakovsky, Mandel'shtam, Pasternak, and Tsvetaeva wrote unforgettable poems. The composers Prokofiev, Shostakovich, and Stravinsky created extraordinary new music. Chagall, Kandinsky, and Malevich produced masterful paintings. Eisenstein single-handedly originated a new style of filming with his *Battleship Potemkin* (1926). The stage directors Meyerhold, Stanislavsky, and Tairov staged unique performances of classic plays. And the list goes on. The Russian avant-garde with all its *-isms* (e.g., acmeism, constructivism, formalism, futurism, rayonnism, symbolism, suprematism) produced a bewildering avalanche of works of art that stunned and shocked contemporary consumers.

And Vygotsky was not a bigoted intellectual who knew only his own favorite discipline and pet hypotheses. On the contrary, he was a man of immense culture who kept abreast of the recent developments in literature, drama, the fine arts, and music. Above all, Vygotsky absorbed the new theater performances and the new poems and novels. He reviewed, for instance, Belyj's famous novel *Petersburg*. He was also personally acquainted with the poets Mandel'shtam and Ehrenburg and the film director Eisenstein. He frequented Tairov's Chamber Theater and Meyerhold's and Stanislavsky's Art Theater. From about 1920 to 1923, he worked in Gomel as the local cultural official. In this capacity, he traveled all over Russia to bring the best theatrical companies to Gomel'. He also wrote weekly reviews of their performances for the local newspapers and cofounded a literary journal and a publishing house, both enterprises were rather short-lived (Valsiner & Van der Veer, 2000). Vygotsky knew dozens of poems by heart, and in his psychological writings he often referred to passages from poems, novels, and plays. In sum, before turning to psychology, Vygotsky's world was that of poems, novels, and plays and to a lesser extent that of graphic art and music.[2] He took active part in the cultural events of the time both as a popularizer and as a critic, and his thinking was shaped by them.

THE OLDER GENERATION OF PSYCHOLOGISTS

Vygotsky's turn to psychology took place gradually (Van der Veer & Valsiner, 1991); his first acquaintance with psychology was through the

---

[2] Vygotsky wrote an interesting introduction to a book with drawings by his acquaintance, the artist from Gomel', A. Ya. Bykhovsky (Vygotsky 1926), but in general, he seems to have had much more of an affinity with poetry and prose than with music and the graphic arts.

reading of the well-known psychologists of that time, including James, Wundt, Thorndike, and Watson, and in Russia Pavlov, Bekhterev, and Chelpanov. Judging by Vygotsky's references, few psychologists escaped his attention.

The case could be made that the researchers who most influenced Vygotsky's thinking were German-Austrian thinkers such as Bühler and Werner and the founders of the Gestalt schools in Berlin and Leipzig (e.g., Goldstein, Koffka, Köhler, Krueger, and Lewin). In fact, this is what Vygotsky's contemporary critics observed and highlighted as a major shortcoming (Van der Veer, 2002b).

However, in this chapter we will limit ourselves to Vygotsky's Russian/Soviet colleagues. Among the older generation of Russian psychologists we can distinguish – following Vygotsky's (1926) distinction in his analysis of the crisis in psychology – objectivists and subjectivists. We must keep in mind, however, that behind these epithets were a bewildering variety of theories and currents. Moreover, in the increasingly intolerant scientific climate of the Soviet Union such words as "objective," "materialist," "subjective," "idealist," and "dialectic" lost much of their meaning and were used as invectives by researchers to discredit their scientific rivals and promote their own systems.

Having said that, we can still with some difficulty distinguish between the adherents of a rigorous experimental approach with a reductionist mind-set, on the one hand, and the proponents of introspection or hermeneutic understanding of irreducible spiritual phenomena, on the other hand. In short, with Vygotsky we can arrange the Russian psychologists along the dimension (or dichotomy?) of *erklärende* and *begreifende Wissenschaften* and highlight proponents of the opposing camps.

The Objectivists: Pavlov and Bekhterev

Attempts to reduce human mental processes to physiology or neurology have a long tradition in Russia. I. M. Sechenov (1829–1905), who studied with Müller, Helmholtz, Du Bois-Reymond, and Bernard, speculated in his *Reflexes of the Brain* (1866) that the brain was a reflex organ and that our private thoughts are no more than speech reflexes interrupted two thirds of the way through the process The afferent and central parts of the speech reflex are there, but the third, efferent, part is being inhibited (Sechenov, 1866/1965, p. 86). Sechenov did not so much deny that mental processes exist but he sought their materialist explanation (Mecacci 1977). The socialist reformer Chernyshevsky (*What Is to Be Done?*, 1863) and the novelists Turgenyev (*Fathers and Sons*, 1862) and Dostoevsky

(*Notes from the Underground*, 1864) elaborated on the theme of physiological materialism and the moral nihilism that it might or might not entail in their brilliant novels.

It was I. P. Pavlov (1849–1936) and V. M. Bekhterev (1857–1927) who would take up Sechenov's challenge to work out the physiological basis of the mind. Both were remarkably successful when they stuck to careful laboratory work, and both failed when they tried to extend their approach to more complex phenomena outside the laboratory. Pavlov, with rare exceptions, stuck to his dogged attempts to lay bare the laws of conditioning in *canis lupus familiaris* in the laboratory, and his ultimate claim that these laws might explain higher human behavior as well came as a bit of a surprise. Bekhterev, as a medical doctor, psychiatrist, hypnotizer, and societal reformer, had always transcended the confines of the laboratory, and his later reductionist claim that reflexes are the alpha and omega of personal and social life could not do justice to his own personal and scientific achievements.

PAVLOV. Ivan Pavlov, at the age of 21, was inspired by the writings of Sechenov and the progressive literary critic Pisarev, so he abandoned a religious career and joined the faculty of physics and mathematics of the Military Medical Academy of St. Petersburg to take a course in natural science. He became fascinated with physiology and neurology and eventually wrote his doctoral thesis on the nerves of the heart. He spent his training years as an apprentice at the laboratories of Heidenhain in Breslau and Ludwig in Leipzig. In 1890, Pavlov became the head of the Department of Physiology at the Institute of Experimental Medicine in St. Petersburg. It was there that he made his major discoveries in the physiology of digestion that would bring him the 1904 Nobel Prize in Medicine. Among other things, he developed the technique to use fistulas to study the functions of various organs in vivo, making vivisection unnecessary. This technique allowed him to infer the role of the nervous system in the regulation of the digestive process.

This was the same technique that led him to his theory of conditional reflexes. While studying the activity of the digestive glands of dogs, Pavlov noted the phenomenon of "psychic secretion"; that is, dogs would salivate not just when food was placed in their mouths but also when food was at a distance or even when they heard the sounds that normally preceded the arrival of food. Now, naïve persons would assume that the dog somehow "expected" or "anticipated" the lab worker to bring food, but Pavlov dismissed such hypotheses about the animal's innermost feelings as unscientific speculation and, in accordance with

Sechenov's idea that mental activity was reflexive, he set out to explore the laws of what was to be called *classical conditioning.*

Without any foundation (Kozulin, 1984), Pavlov subsequently claimed that the conditional reflex was the clue to the explanation of the most highly developed forms of reactions of both animals and humans to their environment and that it made the objective study of all human mental activity possible. In distant America, Watson would embrace that grandiose claim and use it to develop his brand of behaviorism.

Meanwhile, in Russia, politicians and psychologists were impressed as well. In 1921, Lenin, in a special government decree, noted "the outstanding scientific services of Academician I. P. Pavlov, which are of enormous significance to the working class of the whole world." This official endorsement by the highest authorities of Pavlov's alleged materialistic underpinning of the human mind lasted for decades and would make it increasingly difficult to openly criticize Pavlov's ideas. Subjectivist psychologists might not like it, but reflexes, both unconditional and conditional, were said to lie at the foundation of all behavior and mental activity.

It is not surprising, then, that young Marxist psychologists like Vygotsky and his coworkers at first enthusiastically turned to Pavlov's teachings. Luria (1979, p. 41) remembered that "Pavlovian psychophysiology provided a materialist underpinning to our study of the mind." He and Vygotsky were initially quite impressed by Pavlov's work. In a preface to a psychology book published in 1925, for example, Vygotsky stated that acquired reactions (conditional responses) develop on the basis of innate reactions (unconditional responses) and that the nature of these acquired reactions is fully determined by the environment. In his own words:

> The decisive factor in the establishment and formation of conditional reflexes turns out to be the environment as a system of stimuli that act upon the organism. It is the organization of the environment that determines and causes the conditions on which depends the formation of the new connections that form the animal's behavior. For each of us the environment plays the role of the laboratory that establishes the conditional reflexes in the dog and that, by combining and linking stimuli (meat, light, bread + metronome) in a certain manner, organizes the animal's behavior in a way that is each time different. In this sense, the mechanism of the conditional reflex is a bridge thrown from the biological laws of the formation of hereditary adaptations established by Darwin to the sociological laws established by Marx. This very mechanism may explain and show how man's hereditary behavior, which forms the general biological acquisition of the whole animal species, turns into man's social behavior, which emerges on the basis of the hereditary behavior under the decisive influence of the social environment. Only this theory allows

> us to give a firm biosocial footing to the theory of the behavior of man and
> to study it as a biosocial fact. In this sense, academician Pavlov is quite
> right in saying that his theory must form the foundation of psychology:
> psychology must begin with it.   (Vygotsky, 1925/1997, p. 59)

This lengthy quote demonstrates that Vygotsky initially considered
the conditional reflexes a unique link between nature and culture. Conditional reflexes supposedly linked Darwin's biology with Marx's sociology and formed the foundation of all acquired behavior. Vygotsky's fascination with Pavlov's discoveries lasted for several years and resulted
in positive references to the similar writings of behaviorists such as
Thorndike, Watson, and Lashley and reactologists such as Kornilov. But
after a while, Vygotsky realized that although Pavlov's theory might provide the beginning of a scientific objective psychology, it was certainly
not its end.

Vygotsky now dismissed Pavlov's claim that the formation of conditional reflexes could ultimately explain higher mental processes. In
its place, the theory of classical conditioning was very fruitful, but elevated to the rank of a universal law it was pure metaphysics (Vygotsky,
1926/1997, pp. 245–246). Moreover, Pavlov's theory was inadequate to
study the typically human forms of behavior. This was a conclusion that
others, such as Chelpanov (1926b), had reached as well. But Vygotsky
added his own theoretical reasons. One characteristic of Pavlov's theory
is the claim that the foundation of behavior is *signalization,* that is, the
fact that organisms are able to learn that certain stimuli signal others.
However,

> Human behavior is distinguished exactly in that it creates artificial sig-
> naling stimuli, primarily the grandiose signalization of speech, and in
> this way masters the signaling activity of the cerebral hemispheres. If
> the basic and most general activity of the cerebral hemispheres in ani-
> mals and man is signalization, then the basic and most general activity
> of man that differentiates man from animals in the first place, from the
> aspect of psychology, is *signification,* that is, the creation and use of signs.
>   (Vygotsky, 1931/1997, p. 55)

With the concept of *signification,* Vygotsky introduced the fundamental idea into psychology that human beings are not passively reacting to environmental stimuli but actively determine their own behavior through the creation of stimuli of a specific nature, namely, *signs.*
This idea both fit in with Marxist ideas about the fundamental distinction between human beings and animals and strongly restricted the
applicability of Pavlov's theory; classical conditioning failed to explain
typically human behavior.

BEKHTEREV. Vladimir Bekhterev enrolled at the Military Medical Academy in St. Petersburg in 1873, 3 years after Pavlov, and graduated as a medical doctor in 1878. Like Pavlov, Bekhterev had been inspired by such progressive thinkers as Pisarev, Dobrolyubov, and Chernyshevsky, and he embraced Sechenov's materialist reflexological approach. Bekhterev held teaching positions in neurology and psychiatry and specialized in the field of the anatomy and physiology of the brain.

Like Pavlov, Bekhterev spent several years abroad working with the leading psychologists and physiologists of his time (e.g., Charcot, Flechsig, Meynert, Du Bois-Reymond, Westphal, Wundt), but in the early 1890s, he settled in St. Petersburg: first, as the professor and head of the department of psychic disease of the Military Medical Academy, and later as the head of the Psychoneurological Institute, which he founded. This became a highly progressive academic institution with excellent collaborators, including the zoopsychologist Vagner, the psychologist Lazurskiy, the philosophers Losskiy and Frank, and the linguists Shcherba and Baudoin-de-Courtenay (cf. Kozulin, 1984; Valsiner, 1994).

After the October Revolution, Bekhterev became chair of the Department of Psychology and Reflexology at the University of Petrograd. Unlike Pavlov, throughout his adult life Bekhterev was active not only as a scientist – publishing more than 600 books and papers and founding dozens of institutions and scientific journals – but also as a medical doctor and psychiatrist[3] and a proponent of social reforms. He pointed out the devastating results of poverty, argued against quotas for Jews in universities, informed the general public about matters of health, and suffered a predictable defeat in his bitter campaign against Russia's national vice, alcohol abuse (Brushlinskiy & Kol'tsova, 1994; Kozulin, 1984; Lomov, Kol'tsova, & Stepanova, 1991).

Bekhterev's sudden death in 1927, at the age of 70 and in apparently excellent health, came immediately after a visit to the Kremlin and has been attributed to Stalin's henchmen. Persistent rumors have it that he diagnosed Stalin as suffering from "acute paranoia," which clearly was not what the dictator wanted to hear.

Bekhterev's main contribution to science was in the description of brain morphology and a number of reflexes and diseases. Quite a number of structures, reflexes, and diseases carry his name, including

---

[3] As a psychiatrist, Bekhterev made abundant use of hypnosis. He apparently learned how to hypnotize while visiting Charcot in Paris but defended a view of hypnosis that had more in common with that of Bernheim (cf. Bekhterev, 1998; Van der Veer, 2002a).

Bekhterev's nucleus (of the vestibular nerve), Bekhterev's reflex of the heel, and Bekhterev's disease (a chronic and progressive disease that results, among other things, in numbness of the spine). He also did interesting research in the area of the localization of psychological functions in the brain and showed, among other things, that this localization is dynamic in the sense that it can change after brain damage. In the field of psychiatry, Bekhterev became one of the principal figures to lay bare the neurological background of many mental diseases (Lomov, Kol'tsova, & Stepanova, 1991).

In psychology, however, Bekhterev became known as the founder of *reflexology*. His methodological credo was that all human behavior, whether individual behavior or social behavior, consisted of complex combinations of reflexes. Reflexes were the "vital atoms" (*zhiznennye atomy*), the most elementary behavioral acts that could be observed. However, Bekhterev combined the wish to use a natural scientific approach analyzing all phenomena in terms of reflexes with the urge to understand highly complicated psychological and social phenomena such as mental disturbances and social revolts. He was too much of a clinician to reduce patients to bundles of reflexes, and he did not deny the existence of complicated mental phenomena such as consciousness. Yet this combination of a reductionist methodological approach and an almost boundless scientific curiosity created a tension that Bekhterev could not solve. Yes, we may term eye blinks, chess moves, and threats to launch nuclear missiles all "reflexes" but only at the cost of stretching the meaning of this concept too far.

In the same vein, Bekhterev attempted to show that well-known natural scientific laws such as the law of inertia or the law of conservation of energy hold for social psychological phenomena as well. The law of inertia, for example, was supposedly valid for societies because social customs are very difficult to change[4] but, once changes have been established and a process of reform has begun, it is very difficult to stop (Bekhterev, 1994, pp. 247–259).

The law of the preservation of energy was likewise valid for social life: the social collective or group receives energy in the form of food or other external influences, and this energy can be transformed or spent but it will never be lost. Neither individuals nor groups disappear without leaving a trace, and the energy exchange between individual or group

---

[4] Bekhterev (1921/1994, p. 247) noted, as an example, that "the most tempestuous revolutions often result in no more than a change in the name of institutions." This was indeed what would happen several years later when his contemporary Chelpanov was replaced by Kornilov.

and the surroundings can never be unequal in the long run (Bekhterev, 1994, pp. 193–196).

In the same spirit, Bekhterev argued the validity for social psychology (or collective reflexology) of another two dozen natural laws. Like in the case of the reflex, we can see that in his efforts to find unifying principles for brain physiology, individual psychology, and group behavior, Bekhterev was stretching the meaning of these natural laws too far and ended up with mere terminological similarities. With Kozulin (1984, p. 51), we might conclude that the superficial unity of his reflexology went to pieces under the force of his own humanistic orientation.

Vygotsky (1926/1997) was quite critical of Bekhterev's eclectic approach. To Vygotsky, the very fact that Bekhterev's theory could encompass so many facts and principles of widely different origins proved its vacuous nature. For Bekhterev not only "showed" how natural scientific laws were applicable in social psychology, he also argued that the findings of all his major theoretical opponents were easily explicable in terms of his reflexology. The findings of the Würzburg school, the theories of Freud, Jung, and Adler, in the end, could all be explained in terms of reflexes. Vygotsky (1926/1997, p. 245) observed that for Bekhterev "Anna Karenina and kleptomania, the class struggle and a landscape, language and dream are all reflexes." But how could these researchers with their supposedly inadequate methods, with their reliance on introspection, with their allegedly false presuppositions arrive at the same objective truth as the wonderfully exact reflexology, Vygotsky wondered. "No problem," he concluded sarcastically, "we live in the world of pre-established harmony, of the miraculous correspondence, the amazing coincidence of theories based on false analyses with the data of the exact sciences" (Vygotsky 1926/1997, p. 260).

In fact, Vygotsky concluded, Bekhterev's system had little to offer in the area of the study of the higher mental processes. In this he concurred with Chelpanov (1926a), who likewise concluded that Bekhterev's treatment of higher mental processes was no more than prescientific rubbish in reflexological disguise. Yes, it can be claimed that higher mental processes depend on reflexes, but that claim is an article of faith and cannot be proven in laboratory research. Like in the case of Pavlov, the claim that reflexology could contribute to our understanding of higher mental processes had little or no foundation.

The Subjectivists: Chelpanov

In Russia, just like in other countries, psychology as a separate discipline emerged toward the end of the nineteenth century. Following

Wundt's example, psychologists founded laboratories all over the country: in Odessa, Tartu, Kiev, Kharkov, and other cities (Umrikhin, 1994).
In 1885, the Moscow Psychological Society was founded on the initiative of the philosopher M. M. Troitsky, an adherent of the British school
of empiricism, and it closed in 1922 (Zhdan, 1995). The society published the journal *Problems of Philosophy and Psychology*, and its meetings were dedicated to discussions about the most recent psychological
investigations and methods, in Russia and beyond. Among its members
in different periods were Grot, Lapshin, Lopatin, Losev, Solov'ev, Chelpanov, and Blonsky. Only the last two names sound familiar to those
interested in Russian psychology; Chelpanov as the principal proponent
of a subjective, "idealistic" psychology, and Blonsky as one of the first
psychologists to suggest a Marxist psychology. All the other names and
the rich history of prerevolutionary psychology in Russia are not widely
known (Botsmanova & Guseeva, 1997; Nikol'skaya, 1997).

CHELPANOV. Georgiy Chelpanov (1862–1936) studied philosophy in
Odessa; physiology under Du Bois-Reymond, Hering, and Köning; and
psychology under Wundt and Stumpf. He was appointed professor of
philosophy at Kiev University in 1897 and lectured about psychological and philosophical topics and published numerous papers and books
(Bogdanchikov, 1998; Ekzemplyarskiy, 1992). In 1898 he founded a psychological laboratory in Kiev where Pavel Blonsky and Gustav Shpet
were among his students. Chelpanov soon became a prominent figure
of the *intelligentsia* in Kiev. He and his wife held open house on Satur-
days and debated topical issues with the intellectual *fine fleur* of Kiev.
Among the regular visitors were future important philosophers such as
Berdyaev, Bulgakov, and Shestov.

In 1907 Chelpanov moved to Moscow University to succeed to the
philosophy chair formerly held by Prince E. N. Trubetskoy (Berdyaev,
1930). There he began a modest Psychological Seminary consisting of
three rooms, where he taught psychology to several dozen students and
conducted some experiments (Rybnikov, 1994a, 1994b). In 1910 a gen-
erous gift of 120.000 rubles from the wealthy merchant S. I. Shchukin
allowed the construction of a separate building and the installation of
a laboratory (Chelpanov,1992a; Nikol'skaya, 1994a). The new laboratory was equipped after the finest laboratories in the world[5] and the

---

[5] In order to acquaint himself with the latest equipment Chelpanov visited about
fifteen of the most important American and German universities. He discussed his
plans with, for example, Wundt, Stumpf, and Marbe in Germany, and Titchener,
Cattell, Münsterberg, and Judd in America. As a result, the new laboratory became

experiments conducted there allowed Chelpanov (1915) to write a text-book on experimental psychology. The Shchukina Institute of Psychology of Moscow Imperial University (later called the Moscow Institute of Psychology) began functioning in 1912 and was officially opened in 1914 (Kozulin, 1984; Yaroshevskiy, 1985). In his opening address, Chelpanov (1922b) argued psychology's importance for disciplines such as criminology, linguistics, and pedagogics and emphasized that the primary task of modern universities was not teaching but the creation of science. Among Chelpanov's first students in Moscow we find persons who would later become known as proponents of a Marxist psychology, such as Kornilov, Blonsky, and Leontiev.

Immediately after the October Revolution things in academia hardly changed: after several years of social turmoil, Chelpanov was reappointed head of the Moscow Institute of Psychology in 1921. Unlike his former students Blonsky and Kornilov, he did not immediately embrace the Marxist worldview and criticized all forms of materialism in psychology. For several years, it seemed that such normal scientific disagreements were tolerated by the authorities. However, in 1922 and 1923, a first and shocking wave of imprisonments, dismissals, and forced exiles occurred. Many intellectuals were forced to leave the country, among them such close friends of Chelpanov as Berdyaev, Frank, and Shpet.[6] Chelpanov himself was fired as director of his Institute of Psychology in November 1923 and replaced by Kornilov,[7] whose views better suited the authorities (Kozulin, 1984).

Chelpanov's dismissal seemed to signify an abrupt end to his ongoing debate with Blonsky and Kornilov, who attempted to formulate a psychology on materialist foundations. However, rather surprisingly,

---

one of the finest and most modern psychological laboratories of the world (Chelpanov 1992a). On occasion of the Institute's official opening, Cattell, Marbe, Titchener, Wundt, and others sent congratulatory letters.

[6] Chelpanov's student Gustav Shpet was also on Lenin's list of persons to be exiled, but he successfully appealed to Lunacharsky, the minister of education, and was allowed to stay (Nemeth 2003). However, in 1937 Shpet was arrested, accused of counterrevolutionary activities, and shot (Myasnikov 2002).

[7] It is ironic that it was Chelpanov, who had gone out of his way to appoint Kornilov *privat-dotsent* at the university despite the fierce opposition of his colleagues, who considered that Kornilov lacked all academic qualities. In fact, after Kornilov twice failed his final university examinations Chelpanov gave him an unheard of third opportunity and when the minister of education refused to appoint Kornilov at Moscow University because of his poor credentials, Chelpanov successfully intervened (Gordon, 1995). And the pattern of teachers betrayed by their students repeated itself. In 1931 Kornilov was dismissed after vehement ideological attacks by his student A. A. Talankin (Luria, 1994; Kornilov, 1994; Talankin, 1994; Umrikhin, 1994).

Chelpanov did not lay down arms, and he continued to publicly criticize the attempts to formulate a materialist psychology (Bogdanchikov, 1996; Chelpanov, 1924, 1925, 1926b). That this was at all possible is characteristic of that confusing period in Soviet psychology when public disagreement with the highest authorities and ideological gatekeepers did not yet have serious consequences and discussants could harbor the illusion that scientific debates are meant to discover the truth.

After his dismissal, Chelpanov found refuge at the State Academy of Aesthetic Sciences (GAKhN) where his former student Shpet had become vice president (Martsinkovskaya & Yaroshevskiy, 1999; Mayasnikov, 2002). He lectured and published on aesthetic perception, "primitive" creativity, children's drawings, and related themes. When the academy closed in 1930, Chelpanov again lost his job and income. This event and other circumstances (one of his daughters died, another emigrated, and his son was arrested and shot) had a bad effect on his health, and in 1936 he died a poor and bitter man (Martsinkovskaya & Yaroshevskiy, 1999).

Contemporaries had rather mixed opinions about Chelpanov's qualities: Some claimed that he was a brilliant lecturer and an erudite and cordial person (Berdyaev, 1936; Ekzemplyarskiy, 1992; Rybnikov, 1994a, 1994b), while others emphasized that he was a second-rate figure who had no views of his own (Bogdanchikov, 1998; Gordon, 1995; Umrikhin, 1994). Perhaps both views can be defended: Chelpanov did not develop any new theoretical ideas of significance, but he seems to have been a good popularizer and an efficient organizer and administrator (Bogdanchikov 1994; Botsmanova & Guseva, 1997; Nikol'skaya, 1994a).

In histories of Russian philosophy, Chelpanov is mentioned sometimes as one of the Neo-Kantians (together with Vvedensky, Lapshin, Gessen, and others). Supposedly, Chelpanov defended a realistic conception of the *thing-in-itself*, a view he called *critical realism* that opposed Kant's *transcendental idealism* (Gordon, 1995; Nemeth, 2003). In psychology, Chelpanov's views were rather traditional: Throughout his career he seems to have avoided radical views and made attempts to reconcile opposite views (Bogdanchikov, 1998). Luria (1979, p. 29) remarked that the psychological laboratories Chelpanov founded were no more than faithful copies of those of Wundt and Titchener, and the research practiced there was meant to simply replicate the content of Wundt's and Titchener's textbooks.

Throughout the first decades of his career, Chelpanov published articles and books against materialism, a fact that he must have regretted in the later years of his life. In his popular book *Brain and Soul* (Chelpanov, 1912), he argued that it is in vain to try to find a materialistic approach to the study of mind, and he defended a Wundtian version of psychophysical parallelism.[8] In Chelpanov's view, brain studies cannot reveal anything of value for understanding the workings of the mind, but *introspection* can further our understanding. Chelpanov (1913) regarded psychological experiments to be important insofar as they could make introspection more accurate. With Wundt, Chelpanov first considered that introspection should be confined to the lower mental processes, but, later on, he embraced the Würzburg approach, which involved introspection of higher mental processes, for example, thinking (Umrikhin, 1994). Chelpanov's claim – which he shared with many of the Russian philosophers of that time – that the mind has a unique quality of its own and cannot be reduced to material processes – made him a dualistic or "idealistic" thinker of the type that the new Soviet generation of psychologists deemed obsolete (Ekzemplyarskiy, 1992). Psychology had to be monistic and materialist, although what that meant in theory or practice remained decidedly unclear.

To Chelpanov's dismay, it was Blonsky and Kornilov, his beloved former students, who suddenly dismissed their earlier views about the subject matter and methods of psychology and turned toward Marxism. (Chelpanov did not usually tolerate students with independent views.) Fierce public debates followed, both at conferences and at the university (Gordon, 1995). Newspapers, such as *Pravda* and *Izvestiya*, reported about the debates at the conferences (Bogdanchikov, 1996), and both parties feared the intervention of the authorities. Eventually, Kornilov's shameless self-advertisements (Gordon, 1995) proved successful with the authorities, and Soviet historians of psychology have subsequently written that the "materialist" Kornilov scored a devastating theoretical victory over the "idealist" Chelpanov.

In fact, Chelpanov turned out to be quite apt at pointing out the weaknesses in the theories of the young Marxist radicals (Bogdanchikov, 1996). In his *Psychology or Reflexology* (Chelpanov, 1926a), he exposed Blonsky, Kornilov, Bekhterev, and Pavlov as vulgar materialists who did not know their Marx and who could not explain the higher psychological processes. According to Chelpanov, their discussions of these processes were based on prescientific experience translated into the newly

---

[8] That scientific differences of opinion did not exclude civilized behavior in the older generation of Russian psychologists is proved by Pavlov who on occasion of the opening of Chelpanov's Institute wrote his colleague the following lines: "he who fully excludes any mention of subjective states from his laboratory sends his cordial congratulations to the Institute of Psychology and its founder" (Luria, 1979, p. 29). Pavlov also explicitly condemned Chelpanov's dismissal and offered him to head a psychological section in his own laboratory (Umrikhin, 1994).

prescribed and tedious jargon of reflexes or reactions. That there was much truth in that observation can be gathered from Luria's memory of the institutional changes: he remembered that after Kornilov took over Chelpanov's Institute all laboratories were renamed to include the term *reactions*. This relabeling was meant to eliminate any traces of subjective psychology in favor of what Luria, in retrospect, called "a kind of behaviorism" (Luria, 1977, p. 31). In the end, however, it turned out that Chelpanov was fighting a lost war: The authorities strengthened their control over scientific debates and from then on decided who held the right views. It was Kornilov who carried the day only to be dismissed several years later.

Chelpanov was definitely Vygotsky's bête noire. It is easy to find pejorative and emphatic commentaries about Chelpanov in Vygotsky's writings. Thus, in his analysis of the crisis in psychology, Vygotsky (1926/1997) wrote that the choice of scientific terms does not matter "for a psychologist of Chelpanov's kind... who does not investigate nor discover anything new... who has no view of his own" (p. 283). Vygotsky also noted that "now Chelpanov is publishing much about Marxism. Soon he will be studying reflexology, and the first textbook of the victorious behaviorism will be compiled by him or a student of his. On the whole, they are professors and examiners, organizers, and 'Kulturträger,' but not a single investigation of any importance has emerged from their school" (p. 292). Elsewhere, Vygotsky commented on Chelpanov's "extreme ignorance or the expectation that others would be so ignorant" (p. 337). And he observed that "in his current polemics he implores us to believe him that psychology is a materialistic science... and does not with a single word mention that in the Russian literature the idea of two sciences belongs to *him*" (p. 303).

Reading Vygotsky, one gets the impression that what annoyed him most was not so much that Chelpanov, for decades, defended a nonmaterialist view in psychology – indeed, Vygotsky frequently quoted idealistic philosophers such as Frank – but the fact that Chelpanov , in his later writings, opportunistically changed his views. Feigning to believe in Marxism and materialism, Chelpanov exposed the weak points in the writings of the younger generation who were creating a Marxist psychology. That must have been extremely irritating indeed.[9] In addition,

---

[9] Of course, psychologists such as Blonsky and Kornilov also experienced rather sudden conversions to Marxism – not every contemporary believed they were sincere (Gordon, 1995). And Chelpanov's move was to claim that he had never been against materialism per se but only against vulgar materialism or reductionism. Indeed, he valued the materialism of Marx and Spinoza (Martsinkovskaya & Yaroshevskiy, 1999).

Vygotsky clearly did not value Chelpanov's scientific production. Vygotsky obviously preferred principled opponents, such as Pavlov, who made their own original contribution to science and invented their own scientific vocabulary to mediocre university professors, such as the present writer, who can only summarize what others have discovered.

THE YOUNGER GENERATION OF PSYCHOLOGISTS

It is impossible to give a full overview of the psychologists of the younger generation, that is, those of about the same age category as Vygotsky. Here I will restrict myself to the work of Basov, Blonsky, and Kornilov, leaving separate the work of Bernstein (1896–1965), Reisner (1868–1928), Rubinstein (1889–1960), Shpilrein (1891–193?), Uznadze (1986–1950), Zalkind (1888–1936), and many others. What is characteristic of this generation, of course, is that they all, in one way or the other, had to take the officially endorsed views into account, in their choice of topics, in the methods they used, and, above all, in their theoretical analyses. The work of Vygotsky and Luria is a good example. From about 1931, their work was repeatedly criticized in both the official journal of the communist party, *Under the Banner of Marxism,* and in the scientific press (Van der Veer, 2002b). Several critics made attempts to discredit Vygotsky and Luria and to paint them as "harmful elements" in the developing communist society.

Basov

Each researcher in the Soviet Union of the 1920s and 1930s found his own way to deal with the social demands of that time. Mikhail Basov (1892–1931) seems to have been successful in steering his own course until his untimely death from accidental blood poisoning. A few months before his death, ideological criticism of his work had begun, but Basov seemed not prepared to yield. However, like in the case of Vygotsky, his works were posthumously banned after the Pedology Decree of 1936.

Basov had been trained at Bekhterev's Psychoneurological Institute where he worked in Lazurskiy's Psychological Laboratory. Lazurskiy advocated the use of the "naturalistic" experiment as a means to study behavior in everyday-life settings. After Lazurskiy's death, Basov and his colleagues developed a research program with the emphasis on the observational and experimental study of children's behavior. This resulted in a large number of publications on a variety of children's activities and ideas (Valsiner, 1988; Valsiner & Van der Veer 1991a, 1991b).

Although he was trained in Bekhterev's Psychoneurological Institute, and although he accepted Bekhterev's emphasis on the active nature of the individual, Basov was far from accepting Bekhterev's or Pavlov's claim that the alpha and omega of human behavior is the (conditional) *reflex*. Like Vygotsky, Basov accepted the relevance of conditioning for lower processes but denied that it could illuminate higher mental processes and consciousness. Intellectually, Basov seems to have been influenced more by Russian evolutionary thought and by foreign thinkers such as Claparède, Köhler, Lewin, and Piaget (Valsiner, 1988).

Basov shared a number of ideas with Vygotsky. These include the emphasis on the active nature of the child; the importance of the distinction between lower and higher mental processes in relation to the animal–human distinction; the emphasis on finding appropriate units of analysis; the attention given to the topic of consciousness; an analysis of the internalization process; and more. The similarities in their thinking can be attributed to their roots in European psychology and to direct knowledge of each other's writings.

Unlike Vygotsky, who developed the innovative *double-stimulation method*, in his gathering of research data Basov relied heavily on traditional observation and the clinical interview. Children were observed in their natural habitats (e.g., while playing or solving Köhler-like tasks) and questioned about their ideas, goals, plans, and so on. Thus, Basov accepted the usefulness of both introspective data and data based on observation or "extrospection" (Valsiner, 1988).

Perhaps Basov's most original contribution to psychology is his elaborate description of the development of different structures in children's thinking. In his view, children's behavior at different ages can be characterized in terms of structural qualities. Very young children, for example, show simple temporal chains of acts, that is, they react to different stimuli, and these stimuli and the reactions to the stimuli are not in any way related to each other in the children's mind. In older children, however, the different behavioral acts are tied together by the presence of an overarching goal that guides the behavioral process in different directions. Valsiner (1988, pp. 188–203) has given a detailed analysis of Basov's structuralist approach. A clear example of the way these thought structures were derived from children's actions can be found in an article by Basov's colleagues (Shapiro and Gerke, 1991), in which they analyze how children of different ages try to reach a toy train that is hanging on the wall (a task that was directly inspired by Köhler's experiments).

Given the similarities with Vygotsky's own research it should come as no surprise that Vygotsky welcomed Basov's contribution to psychology. He favorably mentions Shapiro and Gerke's investigation (Vygotsky, 1930/1994, p. 104), notes that Basov advanced the idea of the human being as an active agent in the environment (Vygotsky, 1997, p. 87), and concludes that Basov's theory was the first and the clearest to combine an analytic and a holistic approach to personality (Vygotsky, 1997, p. 66). All in all, there are remarkable similarities both in Vygotsky's and Basov's life course and in their theorizing. That Vygotsky was rescued from oblivion and Basov remains relatively unknown once more demonstrates Clio's capricious nature.

Blonsky

Pavel Blonsky (1884–1941) was one of Chelpanov's philosophy students who moved with his teacher from Kiev to Moscow. His original interests were in the history of philosophy – notably the work of Aristotle, Plato, Plotinus, and Hegel. Later, he became interested in pedagogy and read the classic authors in this field. The views he developed on the need for educational reform in Russia were inspired by the leading advocates of educational reform, for example, Kerschensteiner, Montessori, Pedersen, Tolstoy, and, above all, Dewey (Kozulin, 1984; Petrovsky & Danil'chenko, 1979).

Shortly after the October Revolution, Blonsky suddenly embraced the new worldview (cf. Gordon, 1995) and wrote a letter to the local newspaper in which he condemned his striking university colleagues for their "sabotage" urging them to return to work (Petrovsky & Danil'chenko, 1979). After that public statement, he became involved in the implementation of new educational ideas in Soviet schools. He also began a rather erratic search for the creation of a new materialist psychology. Neither of these endeavors proved particularly successful: in the early 1930s, the educational experiments were condemned as "leftist deviations," and Blonsky's program for the new psychology remained rather schematic. After the Pedology Decree of 1936, Blonsky was criticized and his work moved toward traditional psychology (e.g., on children's sexuality, memory development, and thinking) (Blonsky, 1979).

Blonsky's educational ideas were developed in close collaboration with Lenin's wife Krupskaya (1869–1939) and minister of education Lunacharsky (1875–1933). His ideal was that of a labor school where children would develop their cognitive, aesthetic, and moral capacities while devoting part of their time to productive work (cf. Marx's ideal of *polytechnic education*). In that new school, children would not be passive receivers of knowledge but would be actively participating in the acquisition of new ideas. To encourage active participation in the classroom, new methods, for example, projects, learning-by-doing, and flexible curricula were introduced. For some time it seemed that such ideas fitted the situation in the Soviet Union, but Kozulin (1984) has convincingly argued that Blonsky's progressivist ideas emphasized creativity and individuality in a society that demanded strong discipline and uniformity of thought. Indeed, one may try to bring school into society or society into the school, one may advocate child-centered, individualistic methods, but only if these new ideas fit the demands of that society and, therefore, the leaders of that society. In 1931 a government decree put an end to all progressivist experiments in education and restored the old prerevolutionary subjects and methods in the Soviet school (Bauer, 1955).

Blonsky's search for a new psychology began with the condemnation of philosophical idealism that he – the specialist in Plato and neo-Platonism – now considered to be clearly irreconcilable with "normal common sense" (Blonsky,1920). Psychology had to be the psychology of behavior, it had to be Marxist, it had to be a biological science, and it had to take into account that all human behavior was social. Furthermore, Blonsky reminded us that man is a tool-making animal, and, in order to understand his behavior, we should study the history of his behavior. In his own words: "scientific psychology is first of all genetic psychology" and "behavior is intelligible only as the history of behavior" (quoted by Petrovsky & Danil'chenko, 1979). These claims may now seem programmatic, but it is fair to note that they all became incontestable truths in Soviet psychology and that they were shared by Vygotsky and other progressive psychologists of that time.

Blonsky's emphasis on the study of observable behavior and his enthusiasm for observation and experiment led him to take positions that were quite close to those of Pavlov, Bekhterev, and American behaviorism. Introspection he considered to be of questionable value. His interest in hard data is also evident in his research on the specifics of different age periods in child development. Blonsky distinguished the different age periods by the number of teeth, endocrine changes, and so on. Soviet historians of psychology have subsequently pointed out that this regrettable approach was characteristic of that period when Soviet psychologists had not yet realized that child development is above all influenced by societal factors (e.g., social class) and schooling.

To make things worse, Blonsky had become involved in pedology, the then-fashionable discipline in the Soviet Union that sought to study the child from the perspective of a variety of disciplines. In agreement with the new religion of hard data, pedologists were fond of testing and measuring children and of subjecting their findings to elaborate statistical techniques. According to the authorities, the pedologists overestimated the importance of innate factors and absurdly underestimated the reforming influence of the new socialist society.

In 1936, the Pedology Decree put an end to pedology and the work of its adherents.

It is abundantly clear that Vygotsky appreciated Blonsky as one of the founders of Marxist psychology. Vygotsky referred to Blonsky's writings dozens of times and mostly in a neutral or positive way. This is not to say that Vygotsky agreed with each and every statement Blonsky made or with his whole approach – he clearly did not – but one senses that Vygotsky valued Blonsky as a serious researcher. Vygotsky often referred to Blonsky's plea for a developmental or genetic approach in psychology ("behavior is only intelligible as the history of behavior"). It is clear that he shared Blonsky's ideas about the need for educational reform. In his 1926 book *Pedagogical Psychology*, Vygotsky, just like Blonsky, advocated all the progressivist ideas about education that the 1931 decree would eventually condemn; that is, he defended the labor school, the project method, learning-by-doing, the need to tear down the walls of the school, and so on. Thus, Vygotsky and Blonsky shared many goals and interests. The principal difference between the two psychologists is that Vygotsky, to a much greater extent, succeeded in creating a coherent system of ideas. Blonsky's work, despite interesting investigations and the formulation of valuable principles, remained too schematic to be of lasting value.

Kornilov

For some, Konstantin Kornilov (1879–1957) was an extremely narrow-minded, malicious, and abnormally touchy person who attacked his former teacher and patron like a predator and produced no interesting ideas of his own (Gordon, 1995; Umrikhin, 1994; cf. Lipkina, 1994). For others, Kornilov was a hero figure who fought the "reactionary opinions" of his teacher (Petrovsky 1984) and, in developing his reactology, made a decisive step toward a Marxist psychology (Yaroshevsky 1985). The facts are that Kornilov was Chelpanov's favorite student and assistant who, just like his teacher, worked, for a number of years, in the tradition of Wundt and the Würzburg school (Rybnikov, 1994a). However, from 1921 to 1923, and following the example of his colleague Blonsky, Kornilov made a quick conversion to Marxism and advanced his own theory as the new Marxist psychology (Nikol'skaya, 1994; Van der Veer and Valsiner, 1991).

What was Kornilov's reactology about, and why could it be advanced as a Marxist psychology? For many years, Kornilov dedicated his research time under the supervision of Chelpanov to the study of reaction times to stimuli of different complexity. However, unlike other researchers, he was not just interested in the speed of the reactions but also in their form and intensity (cf. chapter 6 in Van der Veer & Valsiner, 1991). To Kornilov, reactions were whole acts that encompassed both an internal part and an external part. These internal and external parts were part of an energetic exchange process between subjects and their environment. In fact, the reaction was "nothing other than the transformation of energy and constant violation of the energetic balance between the individual and the surrounding environment" (cf. Van der Veer & Valsiner, 1991, p. 114). Internal energy was transformed into external movements and, therefore, the strength of the internal, mental energy could be derived from the force of the external movement. As Kornilov put it: "the more complex and intense the thinking process becomes, the less intense the external expression of movement" (Van der Veer & Valsiner, 1991, p. 115).

Thus, assuming that the amount of "energy" is fixed and that it is "expended" either in internal processes (thinking) or in movements, Kornilov tried to retain the wholeness of the human reaction. It is true that he considered the external part as primary and as ontogenetically older; thinking was an inhibited process that did not result in external action (cf. Sechenov notion of thinking as inhibited speech) – hence his affinity with a behaviorist type of psychology.

Kornilov distinguished seven types of reactions of different complexity, ranging from simple, "natural" reactions to complex, "associative" reactions. The "associative" reaction, for example, involved that the movement only followed after the stimulus had triggered a first association in the mind (free association), or after the stimulus had evoked an image that stood in a specific logical connection with the stimulus (logical association) (Van der Veer and Valsiner 1991, p. 115).

Kornilov's theory of reactions seemed an unlikely candidate for a Marxist psychology. However, Kornilov did his utmost to connect his theory with the social developments of that time and with Marxist theory. First, he claimed that his seven types of reactions corresponded with seven levels of professional occupation. Therefore, his approach might be useful in revealing the nature of certain professions and, perhaps, in selecting personnel. Intellectual work, for example, would involve more complex reactions and less energetic expenditure in movement. Kornilov extended his ideas to education as well: the school should strive for a synthesis of mental and physical work in line with Marx's polytechnic education (cf. Blonsky's labor school). Kornilov also tried to link up with Engels's philosophy of nature (first published in 1925) by pointing out the workings of dialectical laws in psychology. Thus, according to Kornilov we can observe "qualitative leaps" in the development of emotions: "we can observe, for instance, that the feeling of [self]-praise, when it reaches a certain key point, transforms into the feeling of self-admiration; the feeling of self-worth into a feeling of pride, economizing becomes stinginess, bravery becomes impudence, etc." (Van der Veer & Valsiner 1991, p. 121).

In addition, Kornilov's concepts of "reaction" and "energy" were flexible enough to incorporate the findings of psychoanalysis. In his view, cognitive and affective processes both played a role in reaction tasks, psychic energy might be observed. From here it was but a small step to Freud's analysis of psychic energy that leads to somatic disorders, that is, to conversion phenomena. Therefore, it should come as no surprise that Kornilov appointed several young psychoanalytically oriented enthusiasts at his institute, with Luria as the best-known example.

What to say about Kornilov and his reactology? The concept of reaction was sufficiently flexible to incorporate rather diverse findings, and it also seemed less reductionist than Bekhterev's and Pavlov's reflex notions because it claimed to involve both lower and higher processes, cognitive and affective aspects, and psychic and somatic energy. Like Bekhterev and Pavlov, Kornilov emphasized the observable part of behavior and disregarded subjective evidence through introspection, which made his approach akin to the then-popular brands of behaviorist psychology. However, a characteristic of such psychologies was that the organism was depicted as passively reacting to stimuli, which was a notion that ultimately would not prove acceptable in the Soviet Union. Also, Kornilov's reference to *dialectical phenomena* in psychology seemed poorly linked to his theory of reactions. One may doubt whether Kornilov's categorization of reactions and his notion of energy exchange led to new fruitful research questions. Even Soviet historians of psychology have concluded that Kornilov's reactology did not lead to very much because of his inadequate knowledge of dialectics and Lenin's theory of reflection (Petrovsky, 1984, pp. 92–93).

Meanwhile, Kornilov was instrumental in bringing Vygotsky to Moscow. In 1924, at Luria's suggestion, he decided to appoint the young Vygotsky as a "scientific coworker of the second rank" at the Institute of Psychology. This invitation was no doubt motivated by some theoretical affinity between Kornilov's reactology and Vygotsky's ideas of that time. Like Kornilov, Vygotsky rejected Pavlov's and Bekhterev's systems as reductionist. With Kornilov, Vygotsky accepted the importance of the inner world of the subject, but, again with Kornilov, he toyed with a behaviorist approach.

Fairly soon, however, Vygotsky developed his thinking further and began to see the limitations of Kornilov's reactological approach (cf. Luria, 2003). In his essay on the significance of the crisis in psychology, we can clearly see the aspects of Kornilov's work Vygotsky (1926/1997) that he valued.

First, Vygotsky appreciated the fact that Kornilov did not ignore subjective factors in psychology. His measurements of the energetic budget formed an indirect means to study the mind (Vygotsky, 1926/1997, p. 278). Second, Vygotsky valued the introduction of the concept of reaction as including both subjective and objective processes. He mentions Kornilov's argument that the reflex is a physiological (and therefore objective) concept, whereas the reaction is a biological (and therefore subjective objective) concept, with some sympathy (Vygotsky, 1926/1997, p. 285).

Third, Vygotsky repeatedly praised Kornilov for his principled choice for new terms in psychology. In Vygotsky's opinion, the creation of new concepts and new terms must go together.

In this sense, those who wish to create a new, Marxist psychology have to follow in Kornilov's footsteps (Vygotsky, 1926/1997, p. 332). But as interesting as Kornilov's attempt to create a new psychology was, it nonetheless failed at the meta-theoretical level. In his attempt to avoid both an idealistic psychology and a reductionist psychology, Kornilov introduced the concept of reaction that supposedly encompassed both the mental and the physical. But how can there be one science about two categories of being that are fundamentally and qualitatively heterogeneous and irreducible to each other? How can they merge into the integral act of the reaction? In Vygotsky's (1926/1997, p. 314) opinion, Kornilov could not answer these questions. Kornilov included the immaterial world of the subjective mind and the material world of the organism into the reaction, but inside that reaction, they remained two separate worlds. Hence, Kornilov just replaced the problem: He rejected the purely materialist approach, and he rejected the approach that solely relied on subjective accounts but in bringing the subjective and the objective together in the concept of reaction he retained their irreconcilable, qualitatively different nature. Therefore Vygotsky concluded that Kornilov failed to develop a psychology that bridged the gap between the explanatory and the hermeneutic sciences. Although Kornilov's approach was a promising first step, on the meta-theoretical level, it retained the errors of the older psychologies. Vygotsky (1926/1997, p. 290) concluded that although Kornilov rejected mind–body dualism, his new psychology, in essence, retained it.

BIOLOGISTS AND COMPARATIVE PSYCHOLOGISTS

The relevance of Darwin's legacy for psychology is evident and both the older and the newer generations of Russian psychologists (and biologists) attempted to incorporate Darwin's ideas into their thinking (Valsiner, 1988). However, as the influence of the authorities on science increased in the 1920s, the new task became to reconcile Darwin's ideas with those of Marx and Engels, and this led to a number of problems.

Vygotsky was among those who grappled with Darwin's legacy. In different writings in the late 1920s, he dealt with the evolutionary viewpoint (Vygotsky, 1929a, 1929b, 1929c, 1930). One major problem that he addressed repeatedly was that of continuity and change (Valsiner & Van der Veer, 2000). Evolutionary theory implies continuous (gradual) change, but its results seem fundamentally distinct. How can we explain qualitatively distinct products (e.g., humans and apes) on the basis of tiny (quantitative) changes? What is the distinguishing characteristic of human beings? Is it the capacity for tool-use and labor as Marx had suggested or something else? In order to address these questions, Vygotsky attentively followed the work of the major Western researchers Karl Bühler, Guillaume, Koffka, Köhler, and Yerkes and also the research of his compatriots Borovsky, Ladygina-Kohts, Severtsov, and Vagner. We now turn to the work of Borovsky, Ladygina-Kohts, Severtsov, and Vagner (cf. Valsiner & Van der Veer, 2000).

Ladygina-Kohts

The work of Nadya Ladygina-Kohts (1889–1963) is little-known in contemporary psychology. Yet she was one of the pioneers in the field of comparative psychology together with Köhler, Yerkes, and the Kellogs. Ladygina-Kohts finished her studies in comparative psychology at Moscow University in 1917 and became head of the Laboratory of Zoopsycholology of the Darwin Museum in Moscow, which had been founded in 1907 by her husband Alexander Kohts.

Working at the Darwin Museum she studied the behavior of monkeys and apes and published her findings in both Russian and Western journals (Ladygina-Kohts, 1923, 1928a,1928b, 1930, 1937). These publications drew the attention of Yerkes (1925; Yerkes and Petrunkevich, 1925) who was sufficiently impressed to pay a visit to her laboratory in Moscow in 1929.

But Ladygina-Kohts's most remarkable publication was her magnum opus, *The Chimpanzee Child and the Human Child: Their Instincts,*

Emotions, Play, Habits, and Expressive Movements (Ladygina-Kohts 1935) in which she related how she raised the chimpanzee Joni and her own son Rudi together. This book was recently rediscovered and published in English as *Infant Chimpanzee and Human Child* (Ladygina-Kohts, 2002).

The writings of Ladygina-Kohts contained a wealth of observations on the mental and physical development of apes and human beings. One of her fundamental research goals – which she shared with Vygotsky – was to establish whether, and if so how, the mental development of ape and child differed. To this end she confronted both ape and child with endless practical problems such as boxes that had to be unlocked by means of bolts, keys, and so on. It is characteristic of that time that Ladygina-Kohts (1928) considered her work to yield the experimental proof of Marx's and Engels's claims about the distinguishing characteristics of humans. On the basis of her observations, she concluded that "on the ground of the present research mainly devoted to the monkey's manual labor (which labor, in fact, underlies every working process) [we must say] *that the monkey ... is incapable of work"* (Ladygina-Kohts, 1928b, p. 351).

This was a conclusion that seemed directly relevant for Vygotsky and other Marxist psychologists who desperately tried to reconcile the findings of modern comparative psychology with the texts of the Marxists classics. Rather surprisingly, however, Vygotsky never once referred to Ladygina-Kohts's writings although it is beyond doubt that he knew them very well (Valsiner & Van der Veer, 2000). One may surmise that Vygotsky shared the opinion of his close colleague Borovsky that Ladygina-Kohts's work was too subjective and anthropomorphic, but this remains no more than an educated guess.

Borovsky

Vladimir M. Borovsky was Vygotsky's colleague at the Institute of Psychology, where he headed a small section for the study of animal behavior. In his appraisal of the newest comparative psychological findings, he followed the line advocated by Vagner: Borovsky resisted both the reductionist approach of Bekhterev and Pavlov who claimed that the behavior of all species is based on reflexes and the anthropomorphic approach that without foundation ascribed human-like abilities to animals. Borovsky's criticism of Pavlov brought him into ideological difficulties (Valsiner & Van der Veer, 2000), and he eventually moved to a university at the Crimea.

In his criticism of both the reductionist and the anthropomorphic approaches, Borovsky (1926, 1927a, 1927b) was quite similar to Vygotsky (1929c). Where they differed was in their assessment of the seminal work of Köhler. Whereas Vygotsky at first attributed human-like abilities to Köhler's chimpanzees, Borovsky resisted this claim from the start. Under the influence of the arguments of his friend and colleague Vagner, Vygotsky would eventually come to share Borovsky's judgment.

Severtsov

Aleksey N. Severtsov (1866–1936) was professor of biology at Moscow University. His writings gained him an international reputation as a leading scholar in the field of evolutionary morphology. His writings also exerted considerable influence on Russian developmental psychology (Valsiner, 1988; Vucinich 1988).

There was one book by Severtsov that was particularly relevant for psychology. In this book, he addressed the role of individual behavior in evolution and concluded that "From a very early stage of his evolution, man begins to replace new organs by new tools. Where the animal, to adapt to new life conditions, elaborates new structural capacities ... man invents ... new tools ... man creates for himself so to speak an artificial environment, – the environment of culture and civilization" (Severtsov, 1922, pp. 52/54). Thus, according to Severtsov human beings are qualitatively different because they have the ability to change their environment with the help of tools. This was a conclusion that was in wonderful agreement with the statements made by Marx and Engels, and one that was eagerly accepted by Vygotsky.

Severtsov's theory was very useful to highlight the animal–human being distinction, but his writings lacked detailed analyses of cross-species differences in behavior and cognitive abilities. However, it was exactly these differences that became a hot topic in the psychology of the 1920s and 1930s. Behaviorists claimed that all species were similar because their behavior was based on reflexes; others distinguished reflexes from instincts and instincts from intellect. The waiting was for comparative studies that could actually show – rather than claim – that there is more to life than (conditional) reflexes. It is here that the ideas of Vagner become relevant (cf. Valsiner & Van der Veer, 2000).

Vagner

Vladimir A. Vagner (1849–1934) had been a professor of comparative psychology at Bekhterev's Neuropsychological Institute, but, by the time

Vygotsky first met him, he had already retired. Vagner advocated the comparative study of closely related species, the use of natural-science methodology, and a consistent historical perspective. His idea was that animal behavior represented an adaptation to different selective environmental pressures.

Vagner and his student Boris Khotin believed in careful observation of different species in their natural habitat complemented by experimental manipulations. Through such studies they wished to establish the phylogeny of specific phenomena, for example, nest-building behavior. The next step was to proceed to the ontogenetic study of the same behavior by studying it at different ages of the organism. By combining the findings of both the phylogenetic and the ontogenetic approach, Vagner and Khotin wished to avoid superficial cross-species comparisons and unwarranted generalizations.

The research tradition originated by Vagner, and continued by Khotin, ended rather abruptly. Vagner failed to create a school and shortly after his death in 1934 his most important student, Khotin, was exiled to Central Asia. Vagner's attempts to persuade Vygotsky to pursue his line of research had failed even earlier because Vygotsky felt he lacked the required training.

Theoretically, Vygotsky's and Vagner's ideas were quite close. Vygotsky shared Vagner's antireductionist stance and his criticism of the reflexologies of Bekhterev and Pavlov. With Vagner, he accepted that one can distinguish qualitative different levels of behavior (e.g., reflex, instinct, intellect) that cannot be reduced to each other. Vagner's claim that morphological and psychological changes can take place independently was very welcome to Vygotsky. It allowed him to think about developmental changes without having to think about corresponding structural (brain) changes.

In general, we can conclude that Russian comparative psychology was important to Vygotsky in three respects. First, comparative psychology provided phylogenetic and ontogenetic data that fitted into Vygotsky's historical approach. Second, by distinguishing qualitatively different levels of intellectual functioning, comparative psychology provided Vygotsky with arguments to single out human beings as a unique species. Third, the findings of comparative psychology allowed Vygotsky to fight the reductionist and simplistic claims of the "physiologists" Pavlov and Bekhterev. In sum, the findings of Russian comparative psychology could be used by Vygotsky as a necessary antidote against reflexology, much like decades later the findings of Tinbergen's and Lorenz's ethology could be used to fight the simplistic claims of American behaviorism.

CONCLUSIONS

In this chapter, I have discussed a number of Vygotsky's Russian colleagues in psychology and related areas from the period of 1900 to 1935. It is important to note once more that the restriction of the discussion to *Russian* colleagues is somewhat arbitrary because for Vygotsky national boundaries played no role whatsoever in science. Also, the demarcation of a historical period itself raises questions. Should we confine ourselves to persons living in that period, or should we include persons who were intellectually relevant in that period but had already died? Moreover, even when one limits the discussion to Russian colleagues living then and there, there remain some decisions to be made, if only for space reasons. In this chapter, I have left out of consideration, for example, the influence of discussions within Russian linguistics (Van der Veer, 1996, 1999), and I did not say anything about the discussions that took place on the "philosophical front" during Vygotsky's lifetime. In general, I have left out elaborate discussions of the larger societal changes that took place in the Soviet Union of the 1920s and 1930s (Van der Veer & Valsiner, 1991).

However, the most fundamental question, perhaps, that one may raise after having read a chapter such as this one is the following: Can we explain the phenomenon of Vygotsky's creativity? Can we explain his work on the basis of a let-it-be exhaustive analysis of influences on his person and work? Can we find some equation of the form Köhler plus Durkheim plus Marx plus Vagner equals Vygotsky? To this question, the answer can only be "no." On the basis of the writings of his predecessors and contemporaries, Vygotsky created his own unique synthesis. True, Vygotsky cannot be fully understood without a thorough study of his intellectual environment but neither can his theory be fully explained on the basis of our knowledge of that environment. To quote Baldwin (1906, p. 12), on "truly genetic" development, "that series of events is truly genetic, which cannot be constructed before it has happened, and which cannot be exhausted backwards, after it has happened." Scientists, like children, create fundamentally novel things that cannot be predicted beforehand nor be exhaustively explained afterward.

Yes, we must step outside of researchers' minds and take their environments into consideration in order to understand them, but at the same time, we must not forget that that environment is no absolute entity because it becomes refracted in the researcher's mind.

2 Vygotsky's Demons

This chapter examines the philosophical dimensions of Vygotsky's legacy. Vygotsky was a profoundly original thinker, but he was not one whose independence of thought caused him to neglect the ideas of others. On the contrary, Vygotsky was exceptionally well-read. He had an impressive command of the European psychological literature and considerable knowledge of adjacent fields, such as anthropology and educational theory. His appreciation of literature and literary theory is well-known and justly celebrated. Less often remarked upon, however, is his debt to philosophy. In this field, too, he was well-versed, having majored in philosophy and history at the Shanyavsky People's University. Vygotsky was much influenced by the philosophical vision of Marx and Engels: Almost all of the many references to their writings in Vygotsky's *Collected Works* are to philosophical themes.[1] He was also inspired by a number of philosophers who had influenced Marx and Engels, notably Hegel (whom Vygotsky had read in high school), Spinoza, and Feuerbach. Marxism and its antecedents, however, by no means exhaust Vygotsky's philosophical interests. He cites numerous other philosophers, including Aristotle, Bergson, Brentano, Descartes, Dewey, Dilthey, Fichte, Hobbes, Husserl, James, Kant, Lichtenberg, Malebranche, Nietzsche, Neurath, Plato, and Scheler.[2]

---

[1] There is no credibility in the once-popular idea that Vygotsky's references to Marx and Engels are simply the obligatory lip service demanded of Soviet scholars. It is true that Vygotsky was critical of the idea of "Marxist psychology," but this was not out of contempt for Marxism. On the contrary, he felt that Marxism should inform all psychological inquiry, just as Darwinism informs all biology (Vygotsky, 1927, pp. 338–341 [*SS* 1, pp. 431–435]). Vygotsky's most extended discussion of Marxism is his "The Socialist Alteration of Man" (1930a/1994).

[2] The only Russian philosopher regularly cited by Vygotsky is Semyen Frank, whose *Filosofiia i zhizn'* (1910) and *Dusha cheloveka* (1917) clearly impressed him. Vygotsky also alludes to Lev Shestov (Vygotsky, 1927, p. 266 [*SS* 1, p. 336]). As for the

It would be wrong, however, to treat the study of the philosophical elements of Vygotsky's thought merely as an archaeological exercise designed to uncover some of the sources of his ideas. This is because Vygotsky warrants consideration as a philosopher in his own right. What endures most in his legacy are not the results of his empirical inquiries, but the portrait he paints of the mind and its development, together with his reflections on the nature of psychological explanation. The contemporary significance of Vygotsky's work resides, to a significant extent, in its philosophical content.

In what follows, I begin by setting out Vygotsky's vision of the mind and his attendant conception of the obligations of psychology. I proceed to argue that his vision is steeped in the tradition of philosophical rationalism. I then consider the argument that the fecundity of Vygotsky's insights depends on liberating them from this rationalist perspective, which, it is claimed, has a deleterious, indeed reactionary, influence on his thought. In response, I argue that Vygotsky's ideas draw much of their power from their rationalist heritage. Their contemporary import cannot be properly appreciated without due recognition of this fact.

VYGOTSKY'S VISION

Vygotsky saw himself as responding to a crisis in the psychology of his times. He argued that psychology was typical of a young science: It comprised a variety of schools each with its own distinctive concepts and methods (e.g., Behaviorism, Reflexology, Stern's Personalism, Gestalt Psychology, Psychoanalysis). Each school illuminated certain phenomena, but their respective insights were incommensurable. Moreover, they each had colonial ambitions, stretching their central concepts to the point of vacuity in an effort to encompass the whole of the discipline. Psychology was thus far from discharging its obligation to provide a comprehensive scientific account of the human mind. The discipline's shortcomings were particularly evident in the study of consciousness. Although subjectivist psychology saw consciousness as

---

Russian Marxists, Vygotsky discusses Plekhanov (e.g., Vygotsky, 1927, pp. 313–315 [SS 1, pp. 397–400]; 1930b, pp. 178–180 [SS 1, pp. 214–217]) and Lenin, especially the latter's notes on Hegel (Vygotsky, 1931a, pp. 79n, 119–120, 147; 1934, p. 88 [SS 2, p. 75]), and in *Thinking and Speech*, he takes a swipe at Bogdanov's view of truth as socially organized experience (1934, pp. 85, 87 [SS 2, pp. 71, 75]). It seems that Vygotsky, no doubt wisely, paid little attention to the Soviet philosophical scholarship in the 1920s and 1930s, but he does cite V. F. Asmus's fine book on early modern philosophy (1929) in his treatise on the emotions (Vygotsky, 1933a, 124, 199 [SS6, pp. 166, 269]).

accessible only by introspection, thereby placing it outside the realm of scientific inquiry, the dominant scientific schools, premised on such concepts as "reflex" or "stimulus-response," lacked the resources to capture consciousness altogether. Indeed, some proposed to make a virtue of their ineptitude by explicitly advancing a "psychology without consciousness." Vygotsky, in contrast, held that consciousness was "an indisputable fact, a primary reality" (Vygotsky, 1924, p. 47 [SS 1, p. 59]).[3] No plausible science of the mind could fail to address its nature.

That Vygotsky was scornful of the prevailing approaches to consciousness is plain. His own view, however, is much less clear. He certainly does not think of consciousness as a kind of "mysterious flame" or "inner light" illuminating the theater of the mind. Rather, he takes a broadly functionalist approach that identifies consciousness with a certain set of capacities. In his early works, he invokes the notion of "doubled" (udvoennyi) experience (Vygotsky, 1925a, p. 68 [SS 1, p. 85]). When I perceive an object before me, I am aware of the object, but I am also aware, or can become so, of my perceiving the object. Human beings are able to have "experience of experience": We have reflexive awareness of our own mental states and act in that light. Vygotsky identifies consciousness not just with such multilayered awareness, but with the function of selection and control that it enables. For him, the problem of consciousness is one of "the structure of behavior," not of phenomenology or subjectivity, and despite his wariness about the explanatory pretensions of the reflex concept, he suggests in his early papers, that "consciousness is merely the reflex of reflexes" (1925a, p. 79 [SS 1, p. 98]; see also 1924, 46 [SS 1, pp. 57–58]).

In his later writings, Vygotsky takes a broader view, using the term "consciousness" as a synonym for "mind."[4] He maintains that there is a profound distinction between the infant and the mature human mind. Normal children are endowed by nature with certain "elementary mental functions" (e.g., prelinguistic thought, preintellectual speech, associative memory, basic forms of attention, perception, volition). These are modular in character and fundamentally explicable within the causal framework of stimulus and response. The mature descendents of these functions, in contrast, represent a holistic system of interfunctionally related capacities. Each "higher mental function" (e.g., linguistic

---

3 Where I refer to writings of Vygotsky's that appear in the six-volume *Collected Works of L. S. Vygotsky*, I cite the English translation and give the reference to the appropriate volume of the original Russian edition in square brackets (e.g., [SS 3, p. 32] = *Sobranie sochinenie, vol. 3*, p. 32). Note that the numbering of the volumes of the English version differs from the Russian original.

4 In keeping with the Russian word *"soznanie,"* literally "with knowledge."

thought, intellectual speech, "logical" memory, voluntary attention, conceptual perception, "rational" will) is what it is in virtue of the relations it bears to the others. Memory, for example, does not simply serve up material for thought, it is permeated and organized by thought, for remembering the past involves reconstruction and narrative; we "think through" past events to make sense of them. By the same token, memory provides the constant background for thought and reasoning: each act of thinking takes place in the context of our awareness of the past. Similarly, perception and attention are structured by concepts and categories from language and thought, the will is directed to objects represented as desirable, and so on.

The cornerstone of Vygotsky's "dialectical method" is the idea that everything in time must be understood in its development.[5] Accordingly, he argues that to understand the mature human mind, we must comprehend the processes from which it emerges. The higher mental functions, he argues, are irreducible to their primitive antecedents; they do not simply grow from the elementary functions as if the latter contained them in embryo. To appreciate the qualitative transformations that engender the mature mind, we must look outside the head, for the higher mental functions are distinguished by their mediation by external means.[6] Vygotsky's first and most straightforward example of such mediation is the tying of knots to assist memory. Although elementary memory is simply a causal process in which stimuli evoke an idea of some past happening, higher forms of memory deploy artificial devices intentionally to call forth the past. Such "mediational means" are described as "psychological tools" that enable human beings to master and control their own mental functions (Vygotsky, 1931b, pp. 61–62 [SS 3, pp. 86–90]).

It is important that such mediational means are fundamentally social in nature. The development of the child's higher mental functions thus rests upon her appropriation of culture. Following Janet, Vygotsky formulates the "general genetic law of cultural development":

> [E]very function in the cultural development of the child appears on the stage twice, in two planes, first, the social, then the psychological, first between people as an intermental category, then within the child as an

---

[5] Vygotsky writes, "To encompass in research the process of development of some thing in all its phases and changes – from the moment of its appearance to its death – means to reveal its nature, to know its essence, for only in movement does a body exhibit what it is" (1931b, p. 43 [SS 3, pp. 62–63]).

[6] Vygotsky writes, "[T]he central fact in our psychology is the fact of mediation" (1933b, p. 138 [SS 1, p. 166]).

intramental category. This pertains equally to voluntary attention, to logical memory, to the formation of concepts, and to the development of will.   (Vygotsky, 1931b, p. 106 [SS 3, p. 145])

Here, the leading idea is that the child first grasps external mediational means – for example, the practice of tying a knot in a handkerchief as a reminder – and then she "internalizes" such techniques, coming to deploy mnemonic devices in thought. Internalization, Vygotsky explains, is not a matter of merely transplanting a social activity onto an inner plane, for the internalized practice is transfigured in the act of internalization. Nevertheless, the developmental roots of the higher mental functions lie in the mastery of social practices: "genetically, social relations, real relations of people, stand behind all the higher functions and their relations... [T]he mental nature of man represents the totality of social relations internalized" (Vygotsky, 1931b, p. 106 [SS 3, pp. 145–146]).

Two points of clarification. First, each higher function has its own specific developmental story. Although concept acquisition and volition are the fruit of internalization, their genetic roots are very different. The former emerges from practices of grouping, categorizing, and from the development of early language; the latter from the internalization of the social expression and mediation of preferences, and the acquisition of techniques that enable the child to cope with the frustration of her preferences and to reflect critically on her wants. Second, Vygotsky does not see the child's appropriation of culture simply in terms of facility with discrete mediational means. From his earliest works, Vygotsky invokes the phenomenon of cumulative cultural evolution: human beings transmit vast amounts of knowledge across generations not biologically, but culturally (Vygotsky, 1925a, p. 68 [SS 1, p. 84]).[7] The child inherits whole traditions of thought and experience. In addition, the cognitive powers of individuals are greatly expanded by their relations to culture and community. Much of an individual's knowledge rests on the testimony of authorities, and much inquiry is collaborative.

As his position developed, Vygotsky increasingly gave pride of place to the concept of meaning.[8] Although he initially portrayed mediational

---

[7] The term "cumulative cultural evolution" is Michael Tomasello's (see Tomasello, 1999).

[8] There is an intriguing passage in Vygotsky's "The Problem of Consciousness" (which is in note form), where Vygotsky seems to set his position, premised on the concept of meaning, in contrast to an approach based on activity: "'In the beginning was the deed (but not: *the deed* was in the beginning), at the end came the word, *and that is most important of all* (L. S.). What is the significance of what has been said? 'For me, I'm content with the knowledge', i.e. it's enough that the problem

means as artificial stimuli triangulating the basic stimulus-response model (e.g., Vygotsky, 1930c [SS 1, pp. 105–108]), he later recognized that mediation undermines the whole reflexological framework. Mediational means are not simply intervening causes. They influence us in virtue of their significance, and their significance depends on how they are understood or interpreted by human subjects (see Vygotsky, 1933b, p. 137 [SS 1, p. 166]; Bakhurst 1990). By the time Vygotsky wrote his masterpiece, *Thinking and Speech* (1934 [SS 2]), *meaning* [*slovesnoe znachenie*] had become his fundamental "unit of analysis," the key to the relation of thought and speech and, thereby, the essence of the whole system of higher mental functions. In this work, Vygotsky argues that thought and speech have different developmental roots; thought is grounded in basic problem-solving activities, speech in primitive communicative utterances. The critical point is when the two lines of development merge and the child relates to her own utterances as meaningful and employs them to communicate in virtue of their meaning. At this point, thought becomes linguistic and speech rational. This is a developmental moment of enormous significance for, with meaning as their common currency, thought can permeate all the higher mental functions (Vygotsky, 1932, p. 324 [SS 2, p. 415]).[9] Even perception becomes an essentially meaningful process (Vygotsky, 1932, p. 295 [SS 2, p. 372]; Vygotsky, 1933b, pp. 136–17 [SS 1, pp. 164–165]): the child experiences a world of objects that have meaning for her. Such a world influences her, not just causally, but normatively in virtue of its significance. The child thus enters a distinctively human mode of engagement with reality.

We can now see Vygotsky's rationale for identifying consciousness with mind, understood as the system of higher mental functions. Vygotsky's view of the relation of mind and meaning leads him to a sophisticated successor to the notion of "doubled experience." Mental phenomena take as their objects meaningful states of affairs in the world or representations thereof and any mental state can itself become the object of another: my thought can become the object of attention, reasoning, memory, volition, and so forth. Any being capable of such reflexive mental acts is conscious. With this, consciousness is fundamentally related to meaning and Vygotsky concludes that "consciousness as a whole has a semantic [*smyslovoe*] structure" (1933b, p. 137

---

has been posed." (1933b, p. 138 [SS 1, p. 166]). I have modified the translation, which suffers from a serious error ("deed" is mistranslated as "thing"). The passage contains allusions to Goethe's *Faust* and Pushkin's *Covetous Knight*.

[9] I discuss Vygotsky's view of the relation of thought and speech at length in Bakhurst (1991), pp. 68–81.

[*SS* 1, p. 165]). We might say that a conscious being occupies the space of meanings.[10]

Vygotsky's is a vision of the social constitution of mind: "through others we become ourselves" (1931b, p. 105 [*SS* 3, p. 144]). We owe our very mindedness, our personhood, to our appropriation of culture, and our mental lives are lived in communication and activity with others, either directly or through the mediation of culture. Education in the broadest sense makes us what we are. Vygotsky's pedagogical and "defectological" writings are premised on this vision. He argues, for example, that the significance of a disability such as blindness is that it inhibits the child's acquisition of culture. The task therefore is not to compensate for a specific physical defect (Vygotsky urges us to shun the very notion of defectiveness[11]), but to create conditions in which culture becomes accessible to the child. To this end, Vygotsky puts special emphasis on the disabled child's development of language.[12] He insists, however, that the *"principles and the psychological mechanism of education are the same here as for a normal child"* (Vygotsky, 1925b, p. 112 [*SS* 5, p. 104], Vygotsky's emphasis). And for Vygotsky, the ultimate aim of all educational practice is the same: to promote the full and active life of an intellectually and morally accomplished social being.

---

[10] What, then, is the relation between the idea of a conscious being as an inhabitant of the realm of meanings and the idea of consciousness as the possession of "an inner life"? After all, as Vygotsky admits, one can navigate the realm of meanings with greater or lesser awareness. I do not think Vygotsky would have held that his "semiotic" view of consciousness displaces the need for an account of phenomenal awareness, of *what it is like* to be conscious. The latter account, however, will be subservient to the former.

[11] He writes: "Education must, in fact, make a blind child become a normal, socially accepted adult and must eliminate the label and the notion *defectiveness* which has been affixed to the blind" (Vygotsky, 1928a, p. 108 [*SS* 5, p.100]).

[12] Vygotsky therefore urges that deaf children learn to lip-read and, if possible, speak the natural languages of the hearing culture(s) in which they live. Thus, his view is at odds with the contemporary received opinion that sign languages of deaf people are not primitive protolanguages but possess all the syntactic complexity necessary for full semantic efficacy and that sign languages can and do sustain deaf culture, initiation into which is sufficient for the development of higher mental functions and full and flourishing personality (see Padden & Humphries, 1988, 2005; Sacks, 1989). Were he alive today, I do not think it would be hard to persuade Vygotsky of the power of sign languages and the reality of deaf culture (see Vygotsky, 1928b, p. 168 [*SS* 5, p. 171], where he writes: "Speech is not necessarily tied to the sound apparatus; it may be embodied in another sign system, just as the written language may be transferred from the path of vision to the path of touch"). He would never have granted, however, that deaf people should confine themselves to their own culture, on the grounds that the members of any minority culture should have the wherewithal to engage with a wider cultural milieu.

Vygotsky's vision thus has a profoundly normative dimension. His cultural–historical theory of mind is perfectionist – in that it strives to understand and promote the conditions in which minds can flourish – and egalitarian, in that he sought that flourishing for all.[13] He hoped that the new psychology would prosper in the Soviet Union, where its insights would contribute to the creation of a new and more just society that would facilitate the well-being of all.

RATIONALISM

In presenting Vygotsky's vision as "philosophical," I do not mean to suggest it is a purely a priori conception. On the contrary, it is informed by extensive empirical inquiry and stands or falls to the extent to which it can inspire psychological theories that are empirically corroborated and vindicated in practice. It remains the case, however, that Vygotsky's brilliant portrait of the mind's place in nature far outruns the empirical data that prompted it. It is the fruit of much speculation, in the best sense of the term. Vygotsky's writings are less presentations of "results" as injunctions to *think of the issue in these terms*, to *see things this way*. The "general genetic law of cultural development," for instance, is not so much a law as a piece of advice about how to represent the relation between the "inner" and the "outer"; between the psychological capacities the exercise of which is constitutive of our inner lives and the social practices that constantly mediate our engagement with the world. It could remain good advice even if Vygotsky had the empirical details of internalization wrong. In this sense, his legacy endures as a kind of prolegomenon to empirical psychology rather than an instance of it. Not that Vygotsky merely offers us some helpful ways of thinking. The significance of his contributions resides in his relentless interrogation of the theoretical framework of psychological inquiry. He appreciated very well that "science is philosophical down to its ultimate elements, to its words" (Vygotsky, 1927, p. 291 [SS 1,p. 369]) and that the methods and theoretical vocabularies of any science must be constantly subjected to critical reflection.

How, then, should we characterize Vygotsky's philosophical cast of mind? When I conducted research in Moscow in the early 1980s, I was fortunate to be able to discuss Vygotsky's ideas with a number of Russian philosophers and psychologists, among them V. S. Bibler. Bibler maintained that Vygotsky's work should be seen against a philosophical

---

[13] I am inspired to describe Vygotsky as an egalitarian perfectionist by Christine Sypnowich's writings in political philosophy (see Sypnowich, 2000a, 2000b).

tradition he called "high rationalism" [*vysokii rationalizm*, a tradition that originates with the Ancient Greeks and that numbers Descartes, Leibnitz, Spinoza, Kant, Hegel, and Marx as its most prominent modern representatives.[14] At the time, Bibler's view struck me as eccentric. I was anxious to portray Vygotsky as a post-Cartesian, post-Enlightenment thinker, so it seemed puzzling to associate him with rationalism. Over the years, however, I have come to see the wisdom of Bibler's suggestion.[15]

I am not the only Western philosopher to endorse such a view of Vygotsky's legacy. Jan Derry has recently argued forcibly for a similar position.[16] But ours is a minority opinion. It is not difficult, however, to find the roots of prominent Vygotskian ideas in the thinkers of this tradition. For example, Vygotsky's conception of development through qualitative transformation is profoundly Hegelian,[17] as is his vision of the emergence of the individual intellect through the appropriation of culture as the repository of collective wisdom. Vygotsky, of course, endorses Marx's attempt to provide a naturalistic reading of such Hegelian insights. Indeed, his cultural–historical theory can been seen as an attempt to give content to Marx's Feuerbachian assertion that the essence of man is "the ensemble of social relations" (Marx, 1845/1968). The key notion of mediation is also Hegelian (Vygotsky, 1931b, p. 61 [*SS* 3, p. 89]). Spinoza's idea that free, creative activity presupposes, in Vygotsky's words, the "intellectualization of all mental functions" (1932, p. 324 [*SS* 2, p. 415]) is a crucial influence on the latter's view of the mastery of the intellect through the creation of psychological tools.[18] Vygotsky's conception of freedom is also indebted to Kant, albeit Kant refracted through Hegel. In addition, Vygotsky's method of "unit analysis" owes much to *Das Kapital*, where Marx deploys the commodity

[14] See Bibler, 1975 (pp.137–161), where he describes the "high rationalist" tradition and explores the affinity between Vygotsky and Hegel. See also Bibler's contribution to the seminar transcribed in Bakhurst (1995).

[15] My initial resistance was no doubt born of an uncritical acceptance of the kind of sharp cultural transitions that people attempt to mark with the prefix "post."

[16] Derry makes the case in her doctoral dissertation, written at the University of London (Derry, 2003). The dissertation is as yet unpublished, but Derry has begun to develop some of its ideas in article form (see Derry, 2004).

[17] In their peerless book on Vygotsky's thought, van der Veer and Valsiner find the roots of Vygotsky's conception of development in Hegelian dialectics. They are rather too quick, however, to characterize dialectical transformation in terms of a simple "thesis-antithesis-synthesis" model, which is, I believe, far too formulaic to capture the nuances of Vygotsky's conception of qualitative transformation (see van der Veer and Valsiner, 1991, p. 26).

[18] I have modified the translation better to reflect the original (Vygotsky, 1982, p. 415).

form as the key concept in explicating the development of capitalism. Indeed, Vygotsky's constant preoccupation with questions of method was inspired by Marx's methodological sophistication. Finally, Vygotsky appreciated Descartes' significance in defining the questions that psychology still struggled to address, especially the mind–body problem. "The tragedy of all modern psychology," Vygotsky writes, "consists in the fact that it cannot find a way to understand the real sensible tie between our thoughts and feelings on the one hand, and the activity of the body on the other hand" (1933a, pp. 196–197 [SS 6, p. 265]).[19] He was also well aware of the shadow Descartes' dualism cast over the history of psychology. Many attempts to develop a monistic picture had failed, Vygotsky argued, because they had allowed Descartes to define the terms of debate and tried to reduce mind to matter conceived mechanistically.[20] This was a further reason Vygotsky believed that psychology could learn from Spinoza, whose response to Descartes, he felt, represented a far superior variety of monism.

I contend that we must recognize the extent of Vygotsky's debt to these thinkers. They profoundly influenced his conception of the problems of psychology and the style of thinking with which he addressed these problems. Moreover, Vygotsky repaid the debt by making a genuine contribution to the rationalist tradition. No attempt to understand his psychology, or to develop his ideas, can fail to appreciate this.

SUMMONING THE EXORCIST

Many of Vygotsky's contemporary followers will be skeptical. They will grant that an appreciation of Vygotsky's favorite philosophers is sometimes relevant to understanding his ideas, just as it is also important to know something about the many psychologists he discusses. But it would be a mistake, they will argue, to emphasize the rationalist tenor of Vygotsky's thought.

The antirationalist will argue, first, that it is misleading to portray Vygotsky as a philosophical rationalist, and second, that insofar as there

---

[19] I have followed the translation used by van der Veer and Valsiner when they quote the passage in their book, *Understanding Vygotsky: The Quest for Synthesis* (1991, p. 335).

[20] See Vygotsky (1925a, p. 65 [SS 1, p. 81]), where Vygotsky argues that Reflexology's "basic assumption that it is possible to fully explain all of man's behaviour without resorting to subjective phenomena (to build a psychology without mind) is the dualism of subjective psychology turned inside out" (also cf. 1924, p. 46 [SS 1, p. 57]), and the extensive discussion of the Cartesian elements of the James–Lange theory of emotion throughout Vygotsky (1933a) [SS 6, pp. 91–328].

are rationalistic elements in his thinking, these are better purged rather than celebrated. As a cursory perusal of the relevant entry in any reputable philosophy encyclopedia will show, "rationalism" is a rather vague appellation. Rationalists, it appears, are committed to what we might call the priority of reason. They are thus united in their hostility to the traditional empiricist idea of the individual subject constructing a conception of the world out of materials provided exclusively by sense experience. There is little unanimity among rationalists, however, about the nature of reason's "priority." Rather, there are a variety of overlapping themes that are given contrasting expression by different philosophers. Yet, our antirationalist will insist, none of the themes most commonly associated with rationalism is found in Vygotsky. For example, he is not a devotee of a priori knowledge. He does not think that philosophical speculation can establish substantive truths about the nature of reality prior to or independently of scientific inquiry. Nor does he believe in innate ideas: what innate structure the infant mind possesses is radically transformed by enculturation. Nor does Vygotsky subscribe to the Hegelian thesis that the real is rational and the rational is real. Nor does he think the course of history is dictated by laws that might be discerned by reason. Nor is he a friend of teleological explanation. Spinoza and Hegel impressed Vygotsky, as they did Marx, but both Vygotsky and Marx are thoroughgoing naturalists. Human beings are part of the natural world, the character of which is to be disclosed by scientific inquiry. If there are laws of development – historical, cultural, or psychological – they must be established by attention to the facts, not discerned by speculation. It thus serves no purpose, the antirationalist concludes, to portray Vygotsky, or Marx for that matter, as a contributing member of the rationalist tradition.

Of course, the antirationalist will concede, there are themes in Vygotsky's work that are "rationalistic" in the conventional sense of that term: he was, as it were, a "small-r rationalist." As Nadezhda Mandel'shtam observed, "Vygotsky was fettered to some extent by the rationalism common to all scientists of that period" (Mandel'shtam, 1970, p. 241). What the antirationalist will insist, however, is that such rationalistic elements must be eliminated from Vygotsky's thought if cultural–historical psychology is to flourish on the contemporary scene. These elements are demons that distort the real content of his insights. As such, they should be exorcised, not extolled. Harping upon Vygotsky's links to philosophical rationalism only threatens to make them stronger.[21]

---

[21] A number of Vygotsky's Western followers have made such a case, focusing on one or more of the six elements discussed here. In this chapter, I prefer to work with a

The antirationalist invites us to consider the following six demons:

Realism

Vygotsky, the antirationalist begins, suffered from a naïve acceptance of the concepts *truth* and *reality*. He never doubted he was engaged in the search for truth. "What can shake a person looking for truth!" he wrote, "How much inner light, warmth, support there is in this quest itself."[22] Psychology, he imagined, aspires to disclose the true nature of mind. But surely, the antirationalist continues, a genuinely cultural–historical psychology should recognize that what we take truth and reality to be – and, indeed, the very concepts of truth and reality themselves – are a cultural inheritance. What presents itself to us as "reality" is the outcome of our culturally forged modes of conceptualization as they organize and structure the deliverances of experience. A thinker like Vygotsky, who appreciated the extent to which our methods and vocabularies determine the objects we study, should have perceived that cultural–historical psychology is better served by admitting that reality is a social construct and that "truth" is simply a compliment we pay to views currently accepted within the community.

Scientism

The antirationalist proceeds to argue that Vygotsky, in harmony with his realism, uncritically privileges scientific knowledge. This emerges in his preoccupation with psychology's status as a science. But it is also evident in his conception of psychological development, which he portrays as an ascent from spontaneous, fragmented, and particular forms of awareness to integrated and general modes of theoretical knowledge. Thus, for Vygotsky, a major pedagogical ideal is the transformation of the child's intellect through the assimilation of scientific concepts. However, a truly cultural–historical psychology ought to recognize that cultures contain a plethora of contrasting tools for engaging with reality of which science is only one, useful for certain types of explanatory and technical projects pertaining to the manipulation and control of nature, but inept in other respects.

stylized antirationalist opponent than to complicate matters by associating points with particular commentators. Derry (2003) contains a helpful discussion of some of the relevant Western literature.

[22] The passage is from a letter to Levina in which Vygotsky describes how his work lends meaning to his life. It is quoted from van der Veer and Valsiner (1991, p. 16).

Universalism

In keeping with his privileging of science, Vygotsky commends abstract and universal modes of cognition. For him, it is a virtue of cognitive abilities that they can be disengaged from particular contexts and transferred to others. He takes the sophistication of our concepts and other psychological tools to be directly proportional to the degree of their "decontextualization." Yet, the antirationalist argues, a theory that emphasizes the relation of cognitive development and enculturation should recognize that there are powerful ways of knowing that are culturally situated and context-bound. Failure to appreciate this has a number of unfortunate consequences. It results, for instance, in the privileging, in educational contexts, of abstract modes of reasoning that are remote from everyday practice and it obscures the significance of effective local solutions to culturally specific cognitive tasks.

Eurocentrism and Progress

Vygotsky's universalism is part of an elitist, Eurocentric conception of historical progress. In his view, cultural evolution proceeds on a linear scale from primitive to scientific, and individual psychological development undergoes a similar progression. Just as the spontaneous, untheoretical modes of conceptualization characteristic of "primitive" peoples give way to the sophisticated cognitive and technological powers of scientific cultures, so a child's psychological development moves from elementary forms of mental functioning to the full-blown rationality of a self-conscious subject of scientific knowledge. Once again, the antirationalist concludes, this is at odds with what a cultural–historical approach ought to say. For once we admit the intimate relation of culture and mind, proper recognition of cultural difference suggests that there is no single path of psychological development from ineptitude to rationality. It is therefore absurd to classify individuals or cultures as "primitive" or "advanced." Psychology and educational theory need to recognize the diversity of intelligences and eschew altogether the idea of psychological "progress."

Didacticism

Consistent with his elitism, Vygotsky advances a profoundly "top-down" conception of child development. His view that the emergence of mind depends on the child's assimilation of the collective wisdom of her elders suggests an extremely instruction-based, teacher-oriented conception of learning. This might seem surprising because Vygotsky's emphasis on collaborative cognition is often celebrated. Yet consider the famous "the zone of proximal development," which is defined by the difference between what a child can accomplish unaided and what she can achieve in collaboration with others. Its outer limits are determined by adult instructors who lead the child through the zone. The child is pictured as absorbing antecedently existing information, rather than building concepts and constructing knowledge. Surely, the antirationalist insists, a properly cultural–historical approach would acknowledge our agency in the creation of culture and portray the child as an equal partner in meaning making with others.

Individualism

Despite his emphasis on the sociocultural foundations of psychological development, Vygotsky's thought remains centered on the individual subject conceived as a discrete, autonomous person. A cultural–historical approach, however, ought rightly to stress the dialogical character of the self. We do not just become persons through out interaction with others; we *are* ourselves only in relation to others. Selves are sustained through communicative practices, and our identities are forged through the negotiation of meaning. The growing appreciation of the significance of the semiotic that marks Vygotsky's later work should have led him to dialogism, for if consciousness is a semiotic phenomenon, and if meaning is a cultural product, then the very content of consciousness is fixed in social space (just as the meaning of an author's words is not determined by her say-so). A psychology that grasps this insight will attend more to the negotiation of meaning in public contexts and focus less on events in individual minds. Vygotsky, the antirationalist laments, could never shake free of the idea that the individual is the primary unit of psychological analysis.

These are the demons that the antirationalist would have us exorcise so that the real potential of cultural–historical psychology may be unleashed. From this perspective, situating Vygotsky's legacy squarely in the rationalist tradition is a profoundly reactionary move.

THE DEMONS CONFRONTED

Let us consider the antirationalist's first claim: that Vygotsky is not, in any meaningful sense, a member of the tradition of philosophical rationalism.

In my view, the critical factor is that, for Vygotsky, the distinctive characteristic of human minds is their responsiveness to reasons. Our engagement with our environment expresses our mindedness insofar as our thoughts and actions issue from an appreciation of reasons. Human beings are not mere playthings of causal forces. We do not simply react to stimuli, however complex and multilayered those stimuli may be. Rather, we think and act in light of what there is reason to think and do. Perception is not just a matter of the world impinging causally on the subject.[23] The world beyond the mind is a meaningful terrain, a "space of reasons," that is disclosed to us in experience. Our relation to the meaningful is a normative, rational relation, rather than a merely causal one.

The idiom in which I have expressed this point is not particularly Vygotskian.[24] So let me develop the point with reference to an issue Vygotsky often discusses: freedom (1932, pp. 351–358 [SS 2, pp. 454–465]; 1933a, pp. 168–172 [SS 6, pp. 226–237]). Vygotsky subscribes to a thesis endorsed by many within the rationalist tradition: freedom is identical with the recognition of necessity (1931b, pp. 209–210, 218–219 [SS 3, pp. 277–278, 290–291]; 1933a, p. 172 [SS 6, p. 232]). This thesis seems paradoxical. After all, it is common to *contrast* freedom and necessity; surely a person is free only if her actions are not necessitated but issue from her will. Thus, those familiar with the thesis only in its Marxist version often see it as a piece of Orwellian "double speak," urging us to acquiesce before the inevitable triumph of communism. But although the thesis did take on this sinister dimension under Stalin, Vygotsky (who was no fan of dogmatic Marxism[25]) was faithful to its

---

[23] In the *Lectures on Psychology*, Vygotsky writes of "the meaningful nature of perception": "It has been shown experimentally that we cannot create conditions that will functionally separate our perception from meaningful interpretation of the perceived object. I now hold a notebook in front of myself. I do not perceive something white with four corners and then associate this perception with my knowledge of the object and its designation, that is with my understanding that this is a notebook. The understanding of the thing, the name of the object, is given together with its perception" (1932, p. 295 [SS 2, p. 372]).

[24] The notion of "responsiveness to reasons" is drawn from the work of John McDowell (1994), who also deploys the metaphor of "the space of reasons" (which he takes from Wilfred Sellars). I have argued for many years that there is an interesting affinity between McDowell's work and the ideas of members of the Russian cultural-historical tradition, such as F. T. Mikhailov and E. V. Ilyenkov (see Bakhurst, 1981, 1997, 2001b). Derry deploys McDowell's work to illuminate Vygotskian themes in Derry (2003).

[25] See, Vygotsky (1927, pp. 228–332 [SS 1, pp. 417–423]), where he writes: "I do not want to learn what constitutes the mind for free, by picking out a couple of citations, I want to learn from Marx's whole method how to build a science, how to approach the investigation of the mind" (p. 331 [p. 421]).

original point, which can be stated like this: Freedom pertains to actions (including mental actions, such as the making of judgments). Something is only an action if it can be represented as done for a reason: the difference between something an agent does and something that simply happens to her is that her actions can be portrayed as issuing from her awareness of reasons. Reasons stand in a normative relation to actions; that is, they determine what we *ought* to think or do. It follows that acting for reasons involves attunement to a certain sort of necessity: the recognition of what one must, or must not, think or do. For the rationalists, rational necessitation is not just compatible with freedom; it is constitutive of it.[26] The contrast is between the autonomous, self-determining agent, who acts out of recognition for what she has most reason to think or do, and the heteronymous agent, whose actions are not motivated by reason, but by error, weakness, passion, or emotion. Autonomy does not reside in acts of will that transcend necessitation; it is a matter of how our actions are necessitated. This position left its mark on Vygotsky.

The notion of the maximally rational person – the person who thinks what she should think for the reasons she should think it and does what she should do for the reasons she should do it – is an ideal. Real human beings are less than wholly rational and subject to all kinds of contingent influences and distractions. But fidelity to this ideal lends Vygotsky's psychology a certain teleological dimension. For him, human beings are not born responsive to reasons, but become so only through enculturation. The example of the free, rational agent becomes a norm to guide our educational practices. We must endeavor to create the conditions in which our children can, as they mature, reach as close as possible to this ideal.

Vygotsky's conception of freedom and rationality is linked to an idea that is a cornerstone of his thinking: the idea that reason must conquer nature. As Vygotsky puts it, "Man overcomes nature outside himself, but also in himself, this is – isn't it – the crux of our psychology and

---

[26] There is an important subtlety here that complicates matters. Not all reasons necessitate some particular belief or action. Some reasons permit us to act in such-and-such a way, or to think so-and-so, without requiring that we do; some reasons require us to bring about an act of a certain kind but allow a variety of ways of doing so, and so on. Because permissibility is not necessity, the proper way to state the rationalist thesis is this: the notion of free action can be elucidated only with reference to the way in which reasons necessitate, determine, constrain, or license action, and that the degree of our freedom is not inversely proportional to the extent to which reasons limit what we ought to think or do. On the contrary, we are free beings precisely because we are influenced by reasons, even if those reasons leave no rational option about what to think or do.

ethics."[27] We are free insofar as we are authors of our lives and not the playthings of external forces and this demands the mastery of nature. Although some see the conflict between reason and nature as a matter of the individual intellect subordinating the bodily promptings of emotion and desire, Vygotsky works with a more refined notion of "the mastery of nature in our own person." For him, the very development of the higher mental functions rests on the mastery of nature through the creation of psychological tools to control our own psychological processes. Because this involves the creation of external technology – in the form of symbolic systems established in the environment – the task of mastering ourselves is one with project of the control of nature outside us. We can find this theme in Marx's philosophical anthropology, but it is taken to a higher level by Vygotsky's sophisticated vision of psychological development.

The idea of human mindedness as constituted by responsiveness to reasons, the identification of freedom and rational necessitation, the ideal of the maximally rational agent, and the vision of reason's mastery of nature are classic themes of the rationalist tradition, even if they are given very different expression by different thinkers. It is on this basis that I believe Vygotsky should be seen as heir to the rationalist tradition. But, in addition, a number of other rationalist ideas appear in his work, albeit ingeniously transformed. Consider, for example, innate ideas and a priori knowledge. Vygotsky does deny that children are born with innate ideas. The elementary mental functions with which we are endowed by nature enable only a prerational engagement with the world; the child's mind develops insofar as she appropriates "forms of thought" (psychological tools, conceptual structures, and common knowledge) that are borne by the child's culture. In a sense, however, these forms of thought represent a kind of "cultural a priori." What Kant saw as forms of thought innate in each individual mind, Vygotsky saw as a cultural legacy.[28] In both cases, the forms of thought

---

[27] Vygotsky writes this in a letter to Morozova, quoted by van der Veer and Valsiner (1991, p. 17); see also Vygotsky (1926/1997, pp. 51–52, 350–351).

[28] This view is explicitly endorsed by Ilyenkov (1991, p. 250). It should be noted that although Kant is often read as supposing that our fundamental (categories) are innate, he is in fact only committed to the view that these concepts must be possessed by any being that can experience the world. This leaves open the possibility that these concepts are acquired.

The whole question of innateness is a vexed one. As David Wiggins has pointed out to me, it is superficial to think that Vygotsky would have entirely embraced Locke's famous critique of innate ideas (Locke, 1690/1975). Although he would have had no time for the view that the mind is endowed with ideas by the deity (one of Locke's main targets), Vygotsky would have found much to admire in Leibniz's

are antecedent to experience. For Vygotsky, as for Kant, the child is not a subject of experience in the full sense of the term until she possesses them.

Let us now confront our demons.

Truth and Reality

Vygotsky was certainly a realist, in the philosophical sense of the term. His inquiries assume that we are inhabitants of a world that is, for the most part, not of our making. He took it that thought is accountable to reality in that we are beholden to bring our conception of the world into line with how things actually are. Although Vygotsky appreciated that our research methods, language, and other conceptual tools influence our conception of the objects of our inquiries, he never lost confidence in the idea that those objects are independent of our forms of understanding them. He does not argue for this conviction. He takes it as a presupposition of inquiry.[29]

In all of this, I believe that Vygotsky was absolutely correct. Suppose someone invites a seminar group to consider the proposition, "There is a child in the courtyard." Lengthy discussion might ensue about the boundaries of the concept "child," the mutability of the child/adult distinction, the historical contingency of the idea of "childhood," and so on. The seminar might conclude that there is no "fact of the matter" about who is or is not a child: childhood is "socially constructed." Now imagine that a frantic parent interrupts the seminar to ask whether her missing child has been seen in the courtyard onto which the seminar room looks. Here, all the niceties of constructionism evaporate. Given that we define the concept *child* in a certain way, there is a fact-of-the-matter whether something answering to that concept has been in the courtyard. Our natural assumptions are entirely realist. Only someone in the spell of an extravagant philosophical theory could possibly take a different attitude.[30]

There is nothing demonic about Vygotsky's realism. To believe that there are facts of the matter is not a recipe for arrogance, intellectual conservatism, or similar sins; it is perfectly consistent with a proper

---

critique of Locke, especially where Leibniz enjoins us to see innate ideas not as representations but as the fundamental predispositions of mind that influence how we think, reason, form conceptions, and so forth (Leibniz, 1705/1981).

[29] I do not mean that he merely assumes realism on pragmatic grounds. Rather, the reality of objects is treated as a precondition of the possibility of our cognitive relation to the world.

[30] I develop this example further in Bakhurst (2001a).

appreciation of the difficulties of inquiry and our proneness to error and fallibility. No exorcism necessary.

Science

It is beyond doubt that Vygotsky admired science. The key issue, however, is what he understood by science. His writings suggest that he took scientific explanation to have three distinguishing marks (see Vygotsky, 1927, chapter 15, section 2 [SS 1, pp. 291–436]). Scientific explanations are (1) *naturalistic* in that they invoke only phenomena that are constituents of the natural world; (2) *causal* in that they explain events by showing how they are necessitated by prior conditions; and (3) *systematic* in that their intelligibility depends on a background system of theoretical knowledge. It is crucial to note, however, that Vygotsky did not take a narrow view of nature, cause, and system. His conception of causation is not mechanistic, and he was consistently hostile to reductive modes of explanation, as is evident from his dialectical conception of development through qualitative transformation. He understood well that any naturalistic monism must admit diverse forms of causal interaction and adopt relaxed, open-minded strategies to integrate the various elements in our conception of the world to reflect the unity of nature.

It is also important that Vygotsky did not disparage "nonscientific" modes of understanding. He was not the kind of rationalist who preferred to see human beings as cold, abstract reasoners. On the contrary, he insisted on the importance of the emotions in guiding and informing cognition. In his early book, *Educational Psychology*, he wrote:

> The ancient Greeks said that philosophy begins with wonder. Psychologically, this is true with regard to all knowledge, in the sense that every bit of new knowledge must be preceded by a certain sense of craving. A certain degree of emotional sensitivity, a degree of involvement must, of necessity, serve as the starting point of all educational efforts.
> (Vygotsky, 1926/1997, p. 107)

And in his late work, *Thinking and Speech*, he goes so far as to argue that consciousness involves "*a unity of affective and intellectual processes. Every idea contains some remnant of the individual's affective relationship to that aspect of reality which it represents*" (1934, p. 50 [SS 2, p. 22], Vygotsky's emphasis; see also 1935, pp. 238–240 [SS 5, pp. 254–256]). There is no inconsistency between this view and the idea that reason must master the emotions. The latter entails only that unreflective affective responses should not dictate our thoughts and actions. Emotion may nonetheless be essential to our responsiveness to reasons, in part because it facilitates the intellect, and in part because some reasons can be discerned only by beings with the appropriate emotional sensitivity. Consider, for example, our understanding of music or poetry and our appreciation of the subjectivity of other people.

Vygotsky's admiration for scientific inquiry, and his general conception of rationality, were far from myopic or one-dimensional. Once again there is nothing demonic to exorcise.

Context, Concepts, and Cognition

Those critical of Vygotsky's affection for science, also tend to disparage his apparent admiration for abstract and general forms of cognition. Vygotsky did believe that psychological tools are more potent the less they are tied to specific contexts. The power of ordinary linguistic concepts, for example, derives from their generality. The concept "dog" can refer to all and any dogs; "water" to any instance of water, and so on. One of the miracles of language acquisition is that the child effortlessly learns to "decontextualize" such concepts from the specific settings in which she encounters them. Though the child may at first, to the amusement of listeners, use the word "dog" as if it were a proper name of a particular dog, or as if it referred only to dogs of a certain sort, she soon catches on to its universal character. Mathematical concepts and techniques exhibit similar generality. We use number systems capable of counting any discrete objects; we design systems of measurement that apply as universally as possible. And in science, we construct theories that aim to subsume as much as possible under the minimum possible number of scientific laws with maximum generality. Generality is linked to transferability: the more general a concept or technique, the greater its sphere of application.

In themselves, these observations are innocuous. It would be a mistake to conclude that someone who acknowledges their truth must embrace a view of the subject as a disembodied reasoner and disparage forms of situated knowledge. A talented footballer, for example, has sophisticated knowledge of how to read and play the game that is both uncodifiable and extremely context-sensitive (though, of course, it had better be transferable from game to game and from situation to situation within a game). An experienced salesperson at a street market might have impressive abilities to estimate quantities and calculate prices in ways that are unlike techniques taught in school mathematics. There are many examples of such situated knowledge. But they are hardly inconsistent with an appreciation of the significance of the abstract and the universal. It is not "either-or."

It is important to understand that Vygotsky does not applaud abstraction and generality for its own sake. On the contrary, his conception of abstraction is informed, I believe, by Hegelian–Marxist accounts of cognition as an "ascent from the abstract to the concrete" (see Vygotsky 1927, pp. 310–332 [SS 1, pp. 386–423]; 1931c, pp. 204–205 [SS 5, p. 214]).[31] By way of illustration, consider his view of concepts. Vygotsky offers a sophisticated typology of concepts (see van der Veer and Valsiner, 1991, pp. 264–266), but one basic distinction he draws is that between "everyday" and "scientific" concepts. The child's initial "spontaneous" concepts are formed in relation to concrete experience; they sort entities into kinds according to criteria formed by abstraction from the entities' surface characteristics. In contrast, scientific concepts unite the kind in question by establishing a principle of its unity, a principle that explains why members of the kind are what they are. So although the everyday concept *tiger* individuates tigers by their characteristic appearance and behavior, the scientific concept individuates them as members of a certain species, the criteria for membership of which are established by biological theory (which might, for example, hold that something is a tiger only if it has a certain genetic makeup). Because such scientific concepts are verbally articulated, theoretically embedded, and tightly related to many other concepts, they seem abstract, general, and remote from concrete experience. But appreciation of such concepts, properly integrated into a system of knowledge, actually facilitates the understanding of objects in their particularity (e.g., to understand exactly why *this* tiger has developed in just *this* way). Therefore, abstraction allows us to ascend to a detailed understanding of the concrete and particular.

It is thus misleading to deploy a sharp distinction between abstract, general, universal forms of cognition, and concrete, specific, situated ways of knowing. Vygotsky, who had a deep feeling for poetry, understood brilliantly how language, in virtue of its generality, enables us both to commune with infinity and to glimpse the fleeting and particular. Words allow us to express thoughts that span the whole of logical space and to say just how things are in the unrepeatable here and now. The trick is not to disparage the abstract and general but to acknowledge the subtle relation of the universal and the particular in the life of the mind.

---

[31] The present discussion merely touches on what is a most complex issue. Its point is simply to argue that abstraction and generalization are movements of thought that serve our understanding of the concrete and particular. The best Russian discussion of the dialectic of the abstract and the concrete, considered as a model of both scientific knowledge and individual cognition, is Ilyenkov (1960); see Bakhurst (1991, chapter 5). Ilyenkov had an enormous influence on one of Vygotsky's later followers, V. V. Davydov (see Davydov, 1972).

Progress

Vygotsky was a child of his time. He believed in progress. For him, humanity was on a path of intellectual, scientific, and social evolution issuing in ever more powerful knowledge and technology and in the emergence of ever more just forms of social organization. Unlike doctrinaire Marxists, he did not think that progress was guaranteed by the laws of history; but he believed in it nevertheless. Because he saw enculturation as the source of mind, he naturally held that an individual's potential is constrained by the level of sophistication of the mediational means offered by his or her culture. This prompted him to draw parallels between the child's elementary mental functioning and the forms of representation and reasoning typical of so-called primitive societies.

Such a linear notion of historical development no longer carries conviction. The key question, however, is how to reject it without embracing a vapid cultural relativism. We must appreciate the rich varieties of local knowledge in cultures remote from our own without conceding that it is senseless to speak to their respective strengths and weaknesses. Of course, we should not be so arrogant as to suppose, for example, that cultures whose members have no grasp on theoretical science have nothing to teach us about the natural world or human life. However, we should also not conclude that the radical differences between such cultures and our own make our respective conceptions incommensurable, so that they cannot be explained and appraised in a common discourse. One can excise the linear view of cultural evolution from Vygotsky's psychology while leaving a position recognizably his own; no Vygotskian, however, can hold that the recognition of cultural difference requires us to forsake our confidence in the unity of nature and the possibility of genuine intercultural understanding.

The pernicious influence of Eurocentrism in Vygotsky's works must certainly be countered. We should not, however, exorcise the idea of progress as such. After all, progress in the search for truth, well-being, and moral excellence was a guiding idea of Vygotsky's scholarship and a central constituent of his understanding of the ideals of education. It may be essentially contestable where truth and flourishing lie, but we cannot forsake the ideal of movement toward them.

Enculturation and Pedagogy

It is natural that a theory of psychological development giving pride of place to enculturation should embrace "top-down" conceptions of upbringing and education. It is not fair, however, to accuse Vygotsky of representing the child as a merely passive recipient of culture. One problem is that Vygotsky's Western critics often look for agency in the wrong place. They want to portray the child's acquisition of knowledge as a matter of negotiation rather than assimilation. Much of Vygotsky's account, however, focuses on the child's acquisition of basic linguistic and conceptual structures and fundamental psychological tools and techniques. It makes little sense to think of these as negotiable, for until the child acquires a repertoire of concepts and forms of thought and reasoning, she lacks the wherewithal to negotiate anything. At the same time, not much of this repertoire is explicitly taught to the child; she "picks it up" through her engagement in various practices that are, of course, initiated or scaffolded by caregivers. It is important, however, that such a picture must nonetheless acknowledge the child's agency, for our criterion of the child's acquisition of some concept or technique is her ability actively to deploy it. For Vygotsky, the child who has "internalized" a psychological tool has "made it her own." The child may inherit rather than construct her basic concepts, but she possesses them only when they become a vehicle of her activity.

When we turn from infancy and the kindergarten to consider, say, the education of an 11-year-old child, the situation looks rather different. Now we have a child equipped to engage actively in her own education, and it seems appropriate to ask whether Vygotsky's vision of the zone of proximal development represents an unduly teacher-centered view of learning. After all, he argues that "instruction must lead development" (1934, pp. 208–214 [SS 2, pp. 246–255]); that is, to encourage intellectual growth, instructors should teach at a level somewhat ahead of the child's actual ability. The dictum that *"the teacher must orient his work not on yesterday's development in the child but on tomorrow's"* (1934, p. 211 [SS 2, p. 251]; Vygotsky's emphasis) is wonderfully forward-looking, but does it not hand too much initiative to the teacher to direct the educational process?

It is important, however, to set Vygotsky's view of instruction against his broader vision of education. For Vygotsky, educators must encourage in their students a critical, independently minded appreciation of whatever subject matter is before them, for the aim of education is not the assimilation of received wisdom, but its critical interrogation by each new generation. In his earliest writing on education, he asserts:

> The student educates himself ... For present-day education, it is not so important to teach a certain quantity of knowledge as it is to inculcate the ability to acquire such knowledge and to make use of it ... Where he [the teacher] acts like a simple pump, filling up students with knowledge, there he can be replaced with no trouble at all by a textbook, by a dictionary, by a map, by a nature walk ... Where he is simply setting

forth ready-prepared bits and pieces of knowledge, there he has ceased to
be a teacher.   (Vygotsky, 1926/1997, p. 339)

Vygotsky never abandoned this position, and his subsequent reflections
on teaching and learning must be read in this light. The assimilation
of culture is thus not the absorption of some fixed, stable collection of
facts, but the internalization of traditions of thought and inquiry that are
essentially open to reflection, contestation, and development. Although
the child initially confronts the knowledge embodied in her culture as
something external, the appropriation of that knowledge is, or ought to
be, a voyage of discovery on which she makes that knowledge her own
and emerges as a creative voice in its expansion and development.

The Autonomous Individual

As should be clear from these reflections, Vygotsky does indeed treat
the individual as the ultimate focus of psychological inquiry. What he
seeks to explain is the development of the individual human mind, conceived, in its mature form, as conscious, self-aware, rational, creative,
and autonomous. Vygotsky appreciates, perhaps better than any other
thinker, the social preconditions of this development. We owe our very
being to others, and we are what we are only in relation to others. In this
sense, our essence *is* dialogical: "The individual becomes for himself
what he is in himself through what he manifests for others" (Vygotsky,
1931b, p. 105 [*SS* 3, p. 144]).

There are constraints, however, on how far these ideas can be taken.
They cannot be allowed to undermine the very idea of the autonomous
self; that is, of a self that is the subject of an integral mental life and
the author of its own utterances. My conception of the world may be
the product of my initiation into traditions of thinking; my very way
of expressing myself may be structured by speech genres embodied in
my culture. Yet, even if the words I speak are the product of numerous influences, the voice in which I speak is nonetheless *mine*. I speak
these words; they do not speak me. This is even true of a work such
as this chapter, which is easily detached from any specific context of
utterance. But it is especially clear of the paradigm of utterance: where
one speaker addresses another. In an encounter between persons, mediated by language, the assumption is that the encounter is one between
autonomous, integral selves. Where language makes possible a meeting
of minds, such selves are brought into contact with one another, but
they do not thereby meld, fuse, or dissolve. You and I are, and remain,
ourselves.

In cultures dominated by political individualism, it can appear that people have become atoms divided from and closed to one another. Those who lament this sometimes yearn nostalgically for lost community, and that yearning prompts interest in thinkers who, like Vygotsky, celebrate the sociocultural foundations of the self. It can then seem puzzling that Vygotsky never loses confidence in a robust sense of the individual. But the divisiveness of individualist politics is not best countered by denying autonomy in favor of romantic images of "relational" selves. The idea that we are autonomous individuals is a deeply entrenched aspect of our understanding of ourselves. This is evident if we consider, for example, our conception of the ideals of education. What we seek for our children is that they should become independent, critical, and responsible, and that they should be the authors of their own identities. Vygotsky's brilliance is that he sees both the significance of autonomy and how we owe our status as autonomous selves to history, culture, and society. The creation of the conditions in which we may attain genuine autonomy is therefore a social project that requires the political commitment of community. It is precisely this idea that political individualism – for all its interest in autonomy understood as freedom of choice – fails to discern.

IN LIEU OF A CONCLUSION

I have sought to defend the view that Vygotsky's legacy should be set against the tradition of philosophical rationalism. I have also argued against those who would seek to purge his thought of various rationalistic tendencies. Apart from Vygotsky's Eurocentrism and his linear vision of historical progress, none of these elements is threatening. They are not demons that must be vanquished if the true potential of Vygotsky's legacy is to come forth. On the contrary, if Vygotskian psychology is to flourish, we must let loose these ideas. If there is anything demonic about them, it is the havoc they threaten to wreak simultaneously on much mainstream psychology and on the ideas of many who attack it from the margins.

It is certainly the case that a heightened appreciation of the philosophical content of Vygotsky's legacy will enable a fruitful dialogue between his ideas and contemporary philosophical developments. Let me conclude by briefly mentioning two possible avenues of inquiry. One problem that haunts Vygotsky's work is the exact form nonreductive monism is to take. In recent Western philosophy, it is common to develop such a position by appeal to different modes of explanation. Although all events are events within the natural world, mental events are rendered intelligible by explanatory principles different in kind from natural laws. An event described using psychological terms is to be "rationalized" by appeal to normative principles that express what it is appropriate for the subject to believe, desire, infer, or do in the circumstances in light of their existing mental states. Events described in physical events, in contrast, are explained by appeal to causal laws. These two modes of explanation are fundamentally different in kind.[32] Is such a position available to a Vygotskian? Its advocates sometimes invoke Dilthey's famous distinction between the natural and the human sciences. Yet Vygotsky is consistently critical of Dilthey and strongly resisted the idea that psychology should be divided into, on the one hand, a descriptive or hermeneutical discipline dealing with the higher mental functions and, on the other, a causal-scientific discipline treating the underlying physical mechanisms of behavior. It is important, however, that Vygotsky treats descriptive psychology as a throwback to the Cartesian idea of mind as a special subjective realm. This is very different from those contemporary invocations of Dilthey that view psychological explanation as one among several irreducible modes of understanding the activity of an embodied being. Recently, Yaroshevsky (1984/1999) has suggested that Vygotsky worked with three levels of causal explanation: physical, biological, and sociohistorical.[33] It seems possible that such a reading, if suitably developed, might bring Vygotsky's position into fruitful dialogue with contemporary nonreductive materialism.

Attention to developments in contemporary philosophy thus promises to strengthen Vygotsky's position. There is also the possibility of a reciprocal influence. For example, the view that initiation into social or cultural practices is a precondition of the development of mind is a position that has been voiced by some prominent philosophers (e.g., McDowell, 1994, lecture 6). But all too often the philosophers write as if the acquisition of conceptual capacities occurs at a discrete point in the child's development, usually identified with the acquisition of language, as if we all undergo a kind of cognitive baptism. Prior to this moment the child is not a minded being in the full sense; after it she is a full-fledged inhabitant of the space of reasons. There is something absurd about such a view, which seems to treat a complex developmental

---

[32] Examples of such a view are Davidson's famous "anomalous monism" (see Davidson, 1970/1984), and McDowell's contrast between explaining events by placing them in either "the logical space of reasons" or "the realm of law" (McDowell, 1994). The distinction between hermeneutical and scientific-causal explanation is also prominent in Jerome Bruner's cultural psychology (Bruner, 1990).

[33] See van der Veer and Valsiner (1991, pp. 356–359).

process as if it were a single all-or-nothing transition. Vygotsky saw the *Bildungsprozess* as drawn out in time, extending across the life of the subject, and, as such, his vision offers an antidote to these austere philosophical renditions of enculturation. His interest in development made him ever alive to the not-quite-present, to shades of grey, to twilight and dusk. Philosophical accounts of the relation of culture and mind would do well to reflect on his sophisticated appreciation of the circumstances of mind's becoming.

3   An Interesting Resemblance

Vygotsky, Mead, and American Pragmatism

Vygotsky is an original. It is a disservice to him to either find his significance solely in developing Soviet conceptions of man or to render him by gloss translation into language of functionalism or to see only his kinship to George Herbert Mead, to whom he has an interesting resemblance.

(Bruner, 1962, p. vi)

INTRODUCTION

Bruner's description of Vygotsky in his introduction to *Thought and Language* sets out the challenge to be faced when examining his work alongside that of Mead and of James, Peirce, and Dewey. Vygotsky's unique genius is beyond dispute and Bruner was right to warn against a seductive assimilation of his ideas into the prevailing schema of Western social science.[1] Neither, I would suggest, that Vygotsky's work be tested according to the pragmatic principle of its use to a particular field of study.

Therefore, in this chapter there will be some resistance to assimilation by association and to judgments of utility. I will focus on Vygotsky and Mead, separately, as distinct contributors to enduring schools of thought that have much in common but which have developed quite differently. The comparison will, ultimately, lend support to the premise so central to the reflexive form of social science that both espoused: that ideas and, therefore, minds are socially formed and shape the ways in which we act in and on the world.

The discussion of North American pragmatism will center on Mead, primarily because of the "interesting resemblance" to Vygotsky's work

---

[1] Interestingly, the title of the 1978 selection of Vygotsky's work, *Mind in Society*, edited by Cole, John-Steiner, Scribner, and Souberman was chosen not by the editors but by Harvard University Press (personal communication, Cole, 2004). Who can say whether it was a knowing nod in the direction of the collection of Mead's work in *Mind, Self, and Society* (1934)?

There will some glancing across to the influences of William James, Charles Sanders Peirce, and John Dewey on Mead in order to identify his place within pragmatism and to trace similarities between strands in pragmatism and Vygotsky's work. However, Mead will be at the core of the comparison so that we might tease out the extent of the resemblance and the detail of the difference. This process is designed to assist our understanding of the historical construction and contemporary relevance of both Mead and Vygotsky. When examining Vygotsky's writings, I will focus on points of possible similarity with elements of pragmatism and particularly those represented in Mead's work. Consequently, topics covered include relations between mind and world, interpretations of the social and collective, consciousness, the use of cultural tools, and methodology. The chapter will conclude with a discussion of what can be learned from this kind of comparison.

At first glance, our two protagonists have much in common. They were working in countries still reeling from the shock of civil war. Although the U.S. war was long over by the time Mead was lecturing, the aftermath continued to reverberate through U.S. intellectual life and, arguably, still does. A consequent dislike of dogmatism informed their quests for a social science that could help to shape new versions of the common good in emerging systems of modernity. Their work, however, was not in line with developments in mainstream psychology in that period, which aimed at supporting modernizing governments' need for certainty, prediction, and control (Edwards, Gilroy, & Hartley, 2002). Both, despite the respect of students and colleagues, were therefore working against the grain of the establishment for part of their professional lives, and both were far less influential from the mid-1930s to the 1950s, or even later, than they perhaps should have been.

Their responses to modernity aimed at offering a reflective version of a problem-solving human science with profound implications for understanding dynamic interrelationships between people and their worlds. Their styles of argumentation reveal them as dialectical thinkers, who were attempting to tackle the complexities of social systems by creating new intellectual tools in order to transform how humans work within them. These tools, although focused on the formation of mind in action in the world, reflected the multidisciplinary resources both men could draw on and the scope of their curiosity. Both Vygotsky and Mead are, at times, difficult to interpret and to categorize, and their work has, as a consequence, often been oversimplified.

But there are also differences in their histories and their development as intellectuals that finally place them firmly in their own communities with, in activity theory terms, very different objects to work on and improve. For Vygotsky the object was ultimately a Marxist, transformational psychology, which would explain how people acted on and changed their worlds. His focus was the study of socially meaningful activity as a key to understanding consciousness. Mead, as we will see, worked at a different level of analysis. For Mead, as a theorist, the object was an account of the formation of reflectively aware and socially responsible individuals.

In brief, Vygotsky, in the latter part of his life, was working as a psychologist, continuously battling against what he saw as entrenched intellectual strongholds within the field and aiming to turn it into a discipline that might make a difference. Mead, despite his background in psychology, did not tackle the discipline head-on and instead offered an unappreciative field a rich line of enquiry, which it failed to take up.

MEAD AND AMERICAN PRAGMATISM

Vygotsky's personal position and background are discussed at length in other chapters in this volume. Therefore, the focus here will be on Mead. Born in 1863, he was brought up in an academic and Puritan family in Massachusetts and studied at Harvard, where he was also briefly a tutor in the household of William James. He subsequently spent three years, between 1888 and 1891, as a student in Germany. For the first few months he was in Leipzig, where he listened to Wundt lecture. From the the spring of 1889, he settled in Berlin where he was taught by, among others, Dilthey and Ebbinghaus.

While living in the newly united Germany he became interested in the socialism he heard discussed. The growth of industrialization and the dynamics of local social reform that he saw there revealed the limitations of the individual-focused liberalism that was encapsulated in the romanticism and nationalism of the German professional classes. These discussions, as Valsiner and van der Veer (2000) suggest, helped him to interpret the history of the US as a dynamic, which owed a great deal to the European roots of early immigrants. It was a complex dynamic that linked Puritan individualism and Calvinist probity with revolutionary self-government that, in turn, reduced the importance of social class and emphasized responsible citizenship at a local level. Mead emerged as community-centered in his political thought, but in a particularly North American way, which emphasized the responsibility of the individual to the community and the seeking of community homogeneity.

His questioning attention to the making of the human psyche and, in 1891, his own connections took him to Ann Arbor to lecture in psychology. There he met with Charles Horton Cooley, started his lifelong friendship with Dewey, and became part of the broader group of social scientists, which included James, who were to shape U.S. sociology over the next decades. In 1894, he went with Dewey to the University of Chicago and stayed there until his death in 1931, despite Dewey's move to Columbia University in 1904. Our access to his work is mainly, though not only, through the collection of his lectures and papers edited by Charles Morris and published in 1934 as *Mind, Self, and Society.* While in Chicago he put into practice his beliefs about reconfiguring the environment to improve the lives of the socially excluded and underprivileged in the city. That he did not have a huge practical impact was more an indication of how his communitarianism was at odds with prevailing political discourses than of his commitment to the effort.

It is all too easy to cast what is commonly labeled "American pragmatism" as merely a way of thinking about an individual as a unity of beliefs and actions with a focus on the social good in those actions. But his belief contains several assumptions and responses to these marked out slightly different lines within pragmatism that enable us to question the homogeneity of the label and to try to place Mead within the area of social sciences so frequently described in this way.

Here we need to connect Mead's own biography with the emergence of pragmatism in the late nineteenth century in North America. *Pragmatism,* as a label applied to a broad approach to self and action, originated in the cauldron of conflicts and contradictions in U.S. social and economic history that led to the Civil War.[2] Unsurprisingly therefore, the label has been given to strands of thought that were sometimes contradictory. These contradictions led to different approaches to countering the separation of mind and world. These differences, however, are sometimes blurred in the writings of the main protagonists because of their friendship, mutual respect, and influence on each other.

One origin of the differences between James and Dewey in their approaches to the dualism of mind and world is their startlingly different starting points as philosophers. James was influenced initially by the British empiricists, Locke, Hume, Berkley, and, particularly, John Stewart Mill, and clung to the primacy of individual experience as the key to overcoming a separation of mind and world. In James's individual constructivism, mind and the material world were simply different aspects of the same phenomenon, and thoughts were part of direct experience. This is a complex point, which we will take up later. In brief,

---

[2] Menand (2001) provides a wide-ranging yet succinct overview of the origins of pragmatism in the fissures in American demographics that led to the Civil War and shaped its aftermath.

he argued that thoughts and things are both parts of the same stream of consciousness and therefore part of experiencing the world.[3] Dewey, in contrast, was formed intellectually in the dialectical tradition of Hegel even though he later rejected Hegelianism. Hegel's notion of "Being" nonetheless seems to have remained a core concept, enabling Dewey to examine the adaptation of individuals to their worlds in their actions on it, while not espousing overtly a separation of mind and world.

James, it seems, used what came to be labeled as pragmatism as a way of looking back and preserving the unity of mind and spirit against the growing power and reductionism of rational science in the late nineteenth century. Although for Dewey and Mead it enabled a looking forward to a better social future. Indeed perhaps too much has been made of possible connections between Vygotsky and Dewey in this regard with debates over whether they actually met and influenced each other in Moscow in 1928 (Gredler & Shields, 2003; Prawat, 2000,[4] 2003). However, the fault lines in pragmatism are most clearly seen when we examine the influence of Peirce.

The term pragmatism was first used in the context of U.S. philosophy by Peirce in a paper he gave to the last meeting of the Metaphysical Club[5] in late 1872. In later papers, which built on this informal presentation, he recognized his debt to Kant's notion of pragmatic belief.[6] In summary, this set out that our actions are contingent on what we believe will best achieve the outcome required. In other words, any action is contingently the best and, therefore, all actions are a best bet with regard

---

[3] In his paper, "Does Consciousness Exist?" (James, 1971), he argued that consciousness is not a separate entity but is an important function. Thinking agents cannot exist independently of thought and vice versa. This argument enabled him to transcend the mind world dualism.

[4] In this paper, Prawat proposes that there was both a physical meeting between Dewey and Vygotsky and a meeting of minds in their work in the late 1920s where Vygotsky was influenced by Dewey. There is no doubt that Vygotsky knew Dewey's work and that Dewey was influential on some Russian pedologists. However, Gredler and Shields argue that the meeting was unlikely and that Dewey's influence on Vygotsky was limited "his few references to Dewey were brief and non-laudatory" (p. 181). Prawat also argues for similarities between Dewey and Vygotsky in his 2002 critique of a 2001 paper by Glassman on the differences between the two scholars.

[5] This is the name given to the group who met in Cambridge, Massachusetts, in the early 1870s. They included, James, Peirce, and Oliver Wendell Holmes, among others. (See Menand [2001] for an overview of the impact of the group on U.S. thought.) The original paper has not survived, but the term "pragmatic maxim" later appeared in an essay by Peirce titled "How to Make our Ideas Clear" in *Popular Science Monthly* in January, 1878.

[6] See also the influence of Alexander Bain's definition of "belief" as "that upon which a man is prepared to act" on Peirce's use of the term pragmatic (Scheffler, 1974).

to the desired outcome. However, for Peirce, unlike James, the focus in the analysis of actions was not to be placed on the flow of personal meaning making. Instead he suggested that we should attend to the collective, but not a collective that produced the overweening authority of social determinism. Science could prevent this occurring. Our beliefs and interpretations may draw on those of others, but the prime purpose of science is to inform these beliefs by reference to external permanencies, which should be held against human construals.

His was a realist position, which acknowledged the social nature of knowledge construction and looked to what he termed the *community* for the continuity and development of knowledge. But his position also admitted of an external reality that we might one day come to understand. In Peirce's work, we see that pragmatism cannot simply be equated with the individual constructivism of James or with the individual actions that preoccupied Dewey. As we will see, it was Mead who most clearly picked up Peirce's legacy of attention to the mind-forming powers of the social and the need for a form of scientific enquiry could relate to it.

At times pragmatism seems to be a flag of convenience that enables scholars to trace interactionist lines of thought through a period in the development of U.S. social sciences and that disguises important differences within the group so labeled. Indeed, Menand reports that at the time of the Metaphysical Club meeting James would have preferred the term "humanism" for what Peirce was describing. He introduced the term "pragmatism" to a public audience in 1898[7] simply to relaunch the failing career of his friend Peirce who was no longer employed as an academic. This act of friendship masked differences between Peirce and James, differences of which Peirce was certainly aware.

Lewis and Smith (1980), for example, have argued that because of his friendship with Peirce, James was unable to see the fundamental differences between them. These differences they saw lying in what they described as James's nominalism, by which they meant his emphasis on the individual construction of knowledge and in a belief in the reality of that construction, what we would now call "radical constructivism." This tendency toward nominalism in some of James's work was at odds with Peirce's position as a social realist who acknowledged the social construction of mind and could admit of both community and universals. More nuanced differences can be found in the belief systems of

---

[7] James employed the term *pragmatism* in a talk at the University of California, Berkeley, in August 1898 and credited Peirce as the originator of its use within U.S. philosophy.

Dewey and Mead. These differences are difficult to discern because of the way the two men mutually informed each other's work and certainly cannot be addressed in any detail here (see Garrison, 1995, 1996; Lewis & Smith, 1980). Like James, Dewey would not have selected pragmatism as the term to describe his work preferring "instrumentalism." Whether he was in the end a nominalist or admitted of a preexisting reality is still open to debate given the contradictory statements in his work and the development in his thinking over his long working life. Prawat argued that Dewey turned to the realism of Peirce in the final phase of his career (Prawat, 2001).

Dewey's writings on psychology do not give much of a clue to his belief system. They are not always entirely clear, nor are they his central concern. Nonetheless, his functional psychology did focus on explaining how we control, as individuals, our means of existence. His psychology primarily centered on individuals as actors who coordinate their behaviors to fit with the possibilities for action available to them. The same amount of attention was not given to the mind-shaping dynamics of the group or collective and their influence on individual behaviors. In crude summary, in Dewey's attempts to bridge the dualism of mind and world, he appeared to attend more to individual action on the world rather than to the action of the world on the individual. Consequently, there is a strong temptation to follow the Lewis and Smith argument, that it was Mead who most evidently picked up the Peircean emphasis on the seeking of universals and mind-shaping powers of the social.

Under the flag of convenience of pragmatism we therefore find a field of debate and a striving for understanding. These encompassed the fin de siècle concerns of the humanism of James, the engagement with modernity that is represented by the versions of social action associated with Dewey and Mead together with tensions over dualism brought about by attempts at working out how mind and world interact. We now turn to Mead and his route through this bumpy terrain and start our direct comparisons with Vygotsky's own intellectual journeying.

RELATIONSHIPS BETWEEN MIND AND WORLD IN THE WORK
OF VYGOTSKY AND MEAD

One important resemblance in the work of these two men is that in bridging the dualism of mind and world they started not with the individual but with society. However, there were considerable differences in how they examined the relationship. They produced different interpretations of the dynamic between mind and society.

They also saw society differently, with Vygotsky working within Russian notions of a historically and materially constructed collective and Mead with more benign U.S. interpretations of homogenizing community.

For Vygotsky, the focus was the continuous dialectic between mind and a world that was both social and material and was being changed as it was acted in and on. For Mead, although he clearly acknowledged the dynamic of self and society, he attended more to the impact of the world on individual performance and did not examine, in any detail in his academic life, the relationship between the material and the social. In addition, as we will see, for Vygotsky the psychologist, the devil was in the detail of the formation of the mind. He wanted to understand the processes of individual sense-making, broader social meaning-making and their interactions. In contrast, as Valsiner and van der Veer (1988) note, Mead's focus was more the interaction between the self and social roles than on the development of that interaction and the formation of mind.

Wertsch (1985a) has observed that, given Vygotsky's mission to produce a Marxist psychology, he paid relatively little attention to Marx or indeed to social theory more generally. Nonetheless, his cultural–historical premise, that human nature is not fixed but arises out of changing social conditions that it in turn produces, placed his psychology within contemporary interpretations of Marx and the power of the collective in the organization of consciousness. Mead certainly paid more attention to social theory,[8] and it was doubtless far safer for him to do so than was the case for Vygotsky. He was also more explicitly engaged as a social activist during his lifetime, but had longevity and better health on his side. Strangely therefore, for the modern reader, Mead's idea of community, in relation to the development of self lacks a theorizing of differential social power and reads as benign.

> The order of the universe we live in is the moral order. It has become the moral order by becoming the self-conscious method of the members of a human society . . . the world that comes to us from the past possesses and controls us. We posses and control the world that we discover and invent. And this is the world of the moral order. It is a splendid adventure if we can rise to it.   (Mead, 1923, p. 247)

His optimism for the "splendid adventure" shines through in his version of the American Dream, which appears as a counterblast to the fragmenting forces of modernity he would have witnessed in Chicago. His focus,

---

[8] See, for example, sections 36, 37, 39, 40, and 41, in Mead (1934).

therefore, was far more on the impact of the social on the individual, than on the potentially problematic nature of the social.[9] The greater danger was that one might find oneself without a social world to call forth one's identity, than that a version of the social might be deemed alienating.

Modernity demands the accomplishment of variations of the self in different social situations. Our reactions at work, for example, are different from those at home. Mead's description of self helps explain the phenomenon. For Mead, the self was a dynamic between the unpredictable and intentional "I," which "gives the sense of freedom and initiative" (Mead, 1934, p. 177) and the "me," which represents a "definite organization of the community there in our own attitudes" (Mead, 1934, p. 178). By describing the dynamic, he gave primacy to the social without espousing determinism. The "old self" (Mead, 1913) may find that it needs to adapt to new expectations.

> In the reflective analysis, the old self should enter upon the same terms whose roles are assumed, and the test of the reconstruction is found in the fact that all the personal interests are adequately recognized in a new situation. The new self that answers to this new situation can appear in consciousness only after this new situation has been realized and accepted. The new self cannot enter into the field as the determining factor because he is consciously present only after the new end has been formulated and accepted.   (Mead, 1913)

The dynamic and the process of reflection he described capture the qualities of freedom and initiative so central to historical constructions of the American psyche and appear to deny social determinism. Although one may exhibit different selves, one does not become the situation. Indeed, the social world may also need to adjust "by the construction of a new world harmonizing the conflicting interests into which enters the new self" (Mead, 1913). Equally, one is not imprisoned by past selves because of the way in which new social roles are called forth by new situations. It is tempting to see Mead's analyses as reflections of the making of new identities within new communities that would have been evident in the US in the early twentieth century; while at the same time, he incorporated an emphasis on the ultimate homogeneity of the community.

---

[9] In section 36, "Democracy and Universality in Society" (Mead, 1934), he seeks examples of universals in social interactions and paints an idealized picture of a self-abnegating socially focused community, despite a historical analysis which sees conflict as the source of new forms of society. He concludes that with "the full development of such organization we should get a higher spiritual expression in which the individual realizes himself in others through that which he does as peculiar to himself" (Mead, 1934, p. 289).

We can see the influence of James[10] on self-esteem and Cooley on the looking-glass self on Mead's analyses of self. For Mead, the sustaining of self, as sets of behaviors that are acceptable to others, becomes the object of our activities as humans. The presence of the "I," which is always different from "what the situation itself calls for" (Mead, 1934, p. 178), prevents us from seeing Mead's "self" as simply a social construction and a set of learnt behaviors. However, we are not led further into the "I–me" dynamic to have revealed to us, either its workings, or the long-term development of the "I." The self-producing dynamic appears to continue because in the end it is likely to result in the greater good of most people – a rationale derived from pragmatism.

Vygotsky, although at times as much a historian as a psychologist, in his argumentation was not, as we have already observed, a social theorist. Instead, he saw himself as a methodologist. His particular contribution to both Marxism and the history of science was as a psychologist who sought to transform the discipline. The object of his activity was therefore a psychology that could explain both human development and transformational practice.

> In the future society, psychology will indeed be the science of the new man. Without this the perspective of Marxism and the history of science would not be complete. But this science of the new man will still remain psychology. Now we hold this thread on our hands. There is no need for this psychology to correspond as little to the present one as – in the words of Spinoza . . . – the constellation Dog, corresponds to a dog, a barking animal.   (Vygotsky, 1997a, p. 343)

When working on mind–world interactions Vygotsky's focus was the explanation of cognitive processes: the making of mind. He explained these processes in terms of the relationship between the intermental (collective and external) plane of activity and the intramental (personal and internal) plane[11] and the consequent development of mental structures. His examination of the relationship between mind and world ultimately called for an account of consciousness, which we will look at a little later. Here we will focus on what Bruner has since described as growth "from the outside in" (Bruner, 1966, p. 21). Development for Vygotsky was evident in an increase in "the complexity" of an infant's "relation

---

[10] Here the reference is to James's work on identity and the concept of self-esteem (James, 1890). There self-esteem is described as the outcome of the relationship between success and pretensions.

[11] Vygotsky's concern here is the process of the construction of the individual plane. This does not mean that these processes occur only when the learner is alone, rather that they are processes that are internal to the individual.

to things," which are external (Vygotsky, 1998a, p. 234) and, as the child matures and learns, in the development of higher mental functions. By these he meant the development of the capacity to organise one's relationship with that external world in increasingly complex ways.

Like Mead, Vygotsky saw the external plane as preexisting and separate from individual mentality: when we are born, we enter a world that is not of our making. To that extent both were concerned with development as a movement "from the outside in." Mead's focus was a self-oriented reflexiveness. Vygotsky's concern was to reveal the laws and create the science that enabled an explanation of how the external was first assimilated by the individual and then, in turn, enabled the organization of an increasingly complex relationship with the external.

Vygotsky's analysis of double stimulation and the role of mediation provide the key to his work on the formation of mind and qualitative differences in mental functioning. His analysis of how people become competent actors in their worlds is therefore worth explaining. Vygotsky distinguished between what he termed "stimuli-means" and "stimuli-objects." The first form of stimuli, to which we respond in a behavioral manner, he termed "stimuli-means." Stimuli-means differ from stimuli-objects, such as someone telling us to complete a particular task, because they are to be used to assist our performance. Stimuli-means may include, for example, a knot in a handkerchief to help us remember, a map, a gesture, a word, a rhyme, or a picture. They have in common that they are all cultural artifacts that are available to us as tools to assist our performance as actors in and on our worlds and to mediate what is culturally significant. A picture may help us attend to a particular set of words. However, these artifacts ultimately become, as A. N. Leont'ev put it, "ingrowing" (Leont'ev, 1997, p. 22). By that he meant that we begin to take control of and use the tools ourselves, for example, we might select and match pictures and words without help and then find we can operate without the pictures and use the words in other tasks.

Vygotsky explained the impact of the changed relationship with the external world in the following way, "The adolescent who has mastered algebraic concepts has gained a vantage point from which he sees arithmetical concepts in broader perspective" (Vygotsky, 1962, p. 115). In the 1962 translation of the book, *Thought and Language* Vygotsky was describing the use of what he was there somewhat confusingly translated as calling "higher concepts" (elsewhere these are "scientific concepts"[12]).

---

[12] In *Crisis in Psychology* (Vygotsky, 1997a), he described the development of scientific concepts as a process of close iteration between concept and fact: "we need to analyze both fact and concept" (Vygotsky, 1997a, p. 251). In other words, we need

These differ from "everyday" or "spontaneous" concepts because of the analytic power they offer us (see Daniels, in this volume).

For Vygotsky, the mediational function of these cultural tools and our control of them as stimuli meant that the mental processes themselves were changed. New mental structures, which allowed us to move beyond instinct and take control over our worlds, were produced. Importantly, Vygotsky's focus was the change in the mental structures and not simply the performance. The formation of a new concept, he argued, was "qualitatively new" and "cannot be reduced to more elementary processes that characterize the development of the intellect at earlier stages" (Vygotsky, 1998b, p. 40). That is, the structure of the internal plane has been reconfigured.

Moreover, what is salient in the social is not only incorporated into the new mental functions but is found in the ways in which the functions are formed and transformed. Put simply, our minds are formed by the ways of thinking and concepts in use that are available to us in our social worlds. As Wertsch (1985a) particularly noted, Vygotsky was also preoccupied with speech as a representational system, which is a mind-shaping tool.

Vygotsky demonstrated a distinction between himself and Mead by examining not simply socially responsive behavior. He also looked at the processes of the reconfiguration of mental structures, which, in turn, guide action on the world. Mead was, of course, interested in the shaping of mind, and the role of language in it, but at a different level of analysis. He recognized the culturally symbolic nature of language but described it as follows:

> A person learns a new language and, as we say, gets a new soul. He puts himself into the attitude of those that make use of that language...He becomes in that sense a different individual. You cannot convey a language as a pure abstraction; you inevitably in some degree convey also the life that lies behind it. And this result builds itself into relationship with the organized attitudes of the individual who gets this language....
> (Mead, 1934, p. 283)

For Mead, therefore, because one inhabited the social worlds of that speech community, one assumed a socially constructed identity within

---

to endeavor, in Marxist terms, to break though the limitations of false consciousness. Here he was describing a reflective social science, but the same processes can be applied to the development of scientific concepts for the individual use of, for example, the adolescent who is learning algebra. A. N. Leont'ev (1997, p. 28) suggests that Vygotsky did not get very far with these ideas at the individual level, rather they were taken forward in the work of Shif, his student (see Vygotsky, 1987, chapter 6, "The Development of Scientific Concepts in Childhood").

it, and the analysis remained at the level of social role. He argued that one acts into the practices of the community. The organism is "a set of acts which carry out the processes which are essential to the life of the form" (Mead, 1934, p. 60). What makes us human is the capacity to act reflectively into society and to absorb the social into the individual.

The influence of Dewey's concern with the coordination of individual and world to form the individual is seen in Mead's explanation of the formation of mind.

> The evolutionary appearance of mind or intelligence takes place when the whole social process of experience and behavior is brought into the experience of any one of the separate individuals implicated therein, and when the individual's adjustment to the process is modified and refined by the awareness or consciousness which he thus has of it. It is by means of reflexiveness – the turning-back of the experience of the individual upon himself – that the whole social process is thus brought into the experience of the individuals involved in it . . . Reflexiveness, then, is the essential condition, within the social process, for the development of mind.   (Mead, 1934, p. 134)

For Mead, a capacity for "reflexiveness" bridged mind and world and that capacity was enabled by an ability to communicate. "The ability to pick these meanings out and to indicate them to others and to the organism is an ability which gives particular power to the human individual" (Mead, 1934, p.133). As Valsiner (1998) observed, there was a place for inner speech in Mead's description of reflexiveness as a state of "self-oriented dramatization of conduct" (p. 170). But this internalization of expectation was part of a process of coordinating individual development and social expectation, and Mead's focus was not so much on the mechanisms as on the outcomes.

Therefore, despite his interest in language and its symbolic function, the interaction between brain and world and the social nature of mind Mead did not make the cognitive turn that Vygotsky grappled with. Instead, he remained working at the level of socially shaped behavior, even when thinking developmentally and when invoking consciousness as an explanatory principle.

THE DEVELOPMENT OF CONSCIOUSNESS

Luria and Leont'ev have described the period of Vygotsky's influence in Moscow (from the late 1920s to the period immediately after his death in 1934) as the time when "the battle for consciousness raged" (Bruner, 1962, p. v). That battle, for Vygotsky and his immediate colleagues, consisted of freeing oneself from both "vulgar behaviorism" and the subjectivity of introspection. In the United States, in the same period, vulgar behaviorism ruled and, like Vygotsky, Mead tried to move beyond the limitations it presented.

At first sight there are similarities between the Dewey–Mead interest in the relationship between practical activity and consciousness where mind and self arise in the social act, and Vygotsky's concern that the analysis of consciousness should start with the analysis of practical activity.[13] Mead was not a vulgar behaviorist; neither was he taking refuge in any spiritual or unobservable physiological account of consciousness. He was interested in the meaning inherent in the act. Although Mead proposed that social acts were a precondition of consciousness, he went on to suggest that consciousness emerged from such behavior.

> the social act, in its more elementary forms, is possible without, or apart from, some form of consciousness.   (Mead, 1934, p. 18)

In a similar vein, Vygotsky argued that

> ... development based on collaboration and imitation is the source of the specifically human characteristics of consciousness that develop in the child.   (Vygotsky, 1987, p. 210)

As Wertsch (1985a) has observed, the line taken by Mead shows considerable similarities with Vygotsky's attack on the separation of behavior and consciousness.

Vygotsky's concern with consciousness as the organizing feature of mind arose from his assault on Russian psychology's focus on reflex and reaction[14] and its inability to deal with will or intention except as mystical constructs. Here too, he had much in common with Mead's criticism of the capacities of physiological and behavioral psychology to deal with consciousness (Mead, 1934).[15] For Mead the human ability to attend to particular stimuli appeared to be one key to understanding consciousness. But he did not, as a social psychologist, pursue it: "the physiology of attention is a field which is still, a dark continent" (Mead, 1934, p. 25). Yet, again, Vygotsky went much further than Mead. This was in part because he was concerned with the mechanisms of development at the level of the individual and "the scientific study of consciousness" (Rieber and Wollock, 1997, p. ix). But it was also because he did not interpret practices and the acts that constitute simply as patterns of

---

[13] See Vygotsky's experimentation using double stimulation as his experimental design, in Vygotsky (1997c).

[14] Van der Veer and Valsiner (1991) outline Vygotsky's relationship with Kornilov and reactology during his first few years in Moscow (1924–1928).

[15] See, for example, Mead (1934, pp. 21–24).

behavior in preexisting worlds we acted into. Instead, he argued that by acting in and on the world, we transform it by understanding it better.

In Vygotsky's emphases, we can therefore also observe the development of consciousness in cultural–historical terms, which show the construction of mind by linking the phylogenetic formation of mental structures with the social organization of cultural practices. Mead too undertook historical analyses but, as has already been suggested, was more concerned with seeking universals in behavior than with phylogenetic analyses of cultural change and human development. Vygotsky did not, of course, confuse *phylogenetic change* with *ontogenetic development* – they operated on different time-scales. His prime concern was ultimately the ontogenetic level of analysis,[16] that is, the development of individual consciousness and particularly the intersection between consciousness and behavior (Vygotsky, 1997b).

Several of the contributors to Wertsch's seminal collection of papers on Vygotskian perspectives on culture, communication, and cognition (Wertsch, 1985b) observed that although Vygotsky took forward the analysis of consciousness, he did not have at his disposal the conceptual tools that would allow him to go as far as A. N. Leont'ev was able to do later. As Wertsch noted that the key concept available to Leont'ev was "activity."

Vygotsky certainly saw consciousness as deeply problematic both conceptually and methodologically.[17] He was clear that he did not want a reductionist account of consciousness as a result of isolating it as one element of mind, nor did he want to see it simply as a form of subjective stream of consciousness in the nominalist style of James. Instead, as we will see, he tried to access its cohering structure through semiotic analysis as "the only adequate method for the study of the semantic structure of consciousness" (Vygotsky, 1997b, p. 137).

Davydov and Radzikhovskii (1985) usefully distinguished between Vygotsky's approach to consciousness as (a) an explanatory psychological construct and (b) the centrality of it to his methodology. They argued that his methodology made consciousness the object of study and opened up new ways of understanding the space between the material and the mental where consciousness could be found. They referred to James's use of consciousness as a function (James, 1971) and suggested that the difference James drew between essence and function was very important for Vygotsky who agreed with James's emphasis on the functionality of consciousness.

---

[16] Van der Veer and Valsiner (1991) suggest that although Vygotsky gave intellectual support to Luria's work in Central Asia and saw it as important, he regarded it as Luria's project (1991, p. 242).

[17] See Vygotsky on 'The Problem of Consciousness" in Vygotsky (1997b).

They suggested that the semifunctionality of consciousness became an object of inquiry for Vygotsky. It enabled him to examine consciousness as the salient feature of coordinated activity that linked the external and material with the internal and mental. This interpretation of consciousness therefore did not see it simply as a way of explaining behavior instead it was a feature of activity and worthy of examination. Kozulin (1986) has argued that the making of this distinction between consciousness as an explanatory principle and as a subject of study was Vygotsky's "major achievement" with considerable implications.

> If consciousness is to become a subject of psychological study, some other layer of reality should be referred to in a course of explanation. Socially laden activity, then, may serve as such a layer and as such an explanatory principle. Vygotsky thus broke the vicious circle of explanation of consciousness through consciousness, and of behavior through behavior, and established premises for the unified theory of behavior and mind.
>
> (Kozulin, 1986, p. 265)

Leont'ev acknowledged that Vygotsky got close to making the link between activity and consciousness not long before he died in a 1933 lecture on play where he tried to show how an external activity (play) "determines the formation of . . . thinking" and become a "leading activity" (Leont'ev, 1997, p. 32). However, it was Leont'ev's subsequent development of the concept of activity, which enabled Vygotskian ideas on consciousness to enter more thoroughly into explanations of the dynamic between mind and world (Kozulin, 1986; Wertsch & Stone, 1985).[18]

Unsurprisingly, given the broad influence of James on understandings of consciousness in pragmatism, Mead also saw consciousness as inseparable from the interaction of mind and environment (Mead, 1982). As we have already noted, he saw it emergent in action as an indication of a normally functioning organism. However, Mead's quest was at this point quite different from Vygotsky's. He was exploring the nature of the self-conscious when the self becomes an object to itself. The self is aware of the roles of others within the social act and able to act into a role by taking into account the attitudes of the generalized other. Mead's improvable object was ultimately self-conscious social behavior, which emerged in interactions, and it was not the detailed articulation of mind and world. By not attempting to explain the processes of the dynamic of

---

[18] A. N. Leont'ev (1981) outlined the contribution of the work of Vygotsky and those who survived him as an account of how internal activity arises out of external, practical activity and "retains its fundamental two-way connection with it" (1981, p. 58). This is not a matter of transferal of the external to internal but of the formation of the internal.

the "I" and the "me" he did not need to invoke a concept of consciousness as an object of study in the way presented by Vygotsky.

When Mead did attempt to explain the relationship of mind and world, it was in the language of the social psychologist who was trying make sense of the biological self using the frameworks of behaviorism and pragmatism – the explanation was clearly not his central concern.

> The higher centers of the central nervous system are involved in the... behavior by making possible the interposition, between stimulus and response in the simple stimulus response arc, of a process of selecting one to another of a whole set of responses to the given stimulus.

> Mental processes take place in this field of attitudes as expressed by the central nervous system; and this field is hence the field of ideas; the field of the control of present behavior in terms of its future consequences; or in terms of future behavior... (Mead, 1934, p. 117–118)

THE USE OF CULTURAL TOOLS

As Cole (1996, p. 114) observed, the argument that changes in culture go hand-in-hand with changes in tools and in the "mediational potentials" they offer, which in turn have an impact on changes in thinking, was part of the North American and European intellectual Zeitgeist by the 1930s. Cole's point was that the phylogenetic analyses of Vygotsky and his colleagues, and particularly Luria, were in line with one element of the broad set of ideas that was influencing social scientists, including Dewey, in the early twentieth century. Clearly, Mead would have been aware of these ideas. But given his focus on social behavior, his contribution to symbolic interactionism, and his strong connection with Dewey, Mead surprisingly paid little attention to the historical production of cultural tools. It was Blumer who turned to these concerns in symbolic interactionism.[19]

As a set of concepts, these phylogenetic analyses provided different affordances to Vygotsky and to Dewey in their quite different social and political environments and with their different intellectual agendas. Glassman (2001) characterizes the differences between these agendas as Dewey's focus on instrumentality and Vygotsky's focus on cultural–historical development. Glassman suggested that, for Dewey, tools were instruments, which enabled the adaptation of the individual to the

[19] Mead's legacy was taken up by Blumer who took forward symbolic interactionism in a 1937 chapter on "Social Psychology" and in his 1969 book *Symbolic Interactionism: Perspective and method.* Blumer was a doctoral student at Chicago. There he was supervised by Ellsworth Faris and not by Mead, but he acknowledged that he constructed symbolic interactionism from his interpretations of Mead.

social.[20] Hickman's descriptions of the "productive pragmatism" of Dewey (Hickman, 2001, p. 4) take us further into the processes of that adjustment. There, Hickman explains that Dewey's concern with looking forward led him to focus on the need to produce new knowledge tools to enable us to deal with both the irritations and dangers that we encounter as we move forward and to create stable conditions to support human well-being.

Culturally saturated tools were, for Vygotsky, far more than a means of assisting the adjustment of person to the world. Again, he was focusing as much on the processes of cognition as on the impact those processes might have on the world. Ultimately, the prime function of tools was to shape minds and tools were in turn shaped by the minds that worked on and with them. Vygotsky also differed from Dewey, and those influenced by him, in the attention he and his colleagues paid to the detail of the processes involved in tool use and changes in thinking. A focus on tool-mediated action, as we have seen, was central to his understanding of the formation of mind and the analysis of tool use was, of course, a sensible starting point for a Marxist psychology.

In order to deal with the detail of the processes Vygotsky demanded some precision in the use of term "tool." We know that he was critical of what he read (erroneously) as the literal meaning that Dewey gave to the term and also of the use of tool as metaphor (Vygotsky, 1978). Instead, he aimed at precision by recognizing the mediating functions of both tool and sign by distinguishing between them. He argued that tools are "externally oriented" and "serve as the conductor of human influence on the object of activity" and signs are "internally oriented" for the self regulation of the actions we take on an object (Vygotsky, 1978, p. 55). Mead did not make the distinctions that Vygotsky did. However, he similarly regarded language, and following Wundt, also gesture, as symbols that originated in our social worlds and that acted as tools because they enabled reflexive awareness and the self-regulation of behavior.

Vygotsky's use of sign resonated more obviously in its detail and orientation with Peirce's analysis of the relationship between sign and interpretation. For Peirce, signs did not represent objects but enabled some acknowledgement of an object, and importantly called forth a more developed sign or interpretant that may lead to action.[21] There is

---

[20] Glassman refers to Eldridge (1998) for an explanation of Dewey's instrumentality.

[21] Lewis and Smith (1980, p. 39) provide the following useful illustration of the relationship between sign and interpretant. If we tell a cook that that his pie is burning, that statement is a sign, and its object is the burning pie. The sign may cause the cook to think "remove the pie from the oven" and this thought is the interpretant of the sign and may lead to action.

no indication that Vygotsky was influenced directly by Peirce's system of semiotics. However, there are resemblances between the schema that both employed.

These similarities, in part, have their root in their very similar epistemological positions. Both admitted of an external reality, both acknowledged the role of culture in shaping our interpretations of the real, and both looked to an ever improvable science as a way of approaching that reality. Therefore, for both of them the sign, as partial representation of reality,[22] was open to improvement, socially constructed, and led to action. One should not make too much of these similarities; they were again part of the intellectual Zeitgeist,[23] and Peirce's influence on the field was wide-ranging. But again, Vygotsky stands out for going further. By focusing on connecting the regulation of the world with the regulation of the self through the link between tool and sign his analysis of the psychological realm was placed very clearly at the point of action.

However, Vygotsky's turn from both decontextualized mentalism and from behaviorism toward mediated action did not simply involve finding better, more sensitive methods to use within current procedures. It involved a rethinking of methodology and therefore also the philosophical foundations of the processes of psychological enquiry. As we have seen, in taking the issue of consciousness as his central line of inquiry, Vygotsky needed a methodology that would enable him to reveal consciousness in an examination of practical activity.

METHODOLOGY

Again, at first glance there are considerable resemblances between Mead and Vygotsky. Both respected systematic scientific enquiry, but demanded that it should itself be open to reflective development. Mead saw it as a way of avoiding the subjectivism of James's nominalism and the intuitions on which dogmatism might rest. For Vygotsky it was also an important underpinning for the new psychology he was hoping to

---

[22] In Vygotsky's work we can see connections between pseudo-concepts that are the result of our reasoning with what is available to us and the idea of the improveable sign. Valsiner, however, has argued that Vygotsky "overly idealized" the role of more developed concepts in human reasoning and he suggested that instead we should see pseudoconcepts as the "highest form" of "human psychological functioning," which would be more in line with Peirce on this topic (Valsiner, 1998, p. 279).

[23] See Chapter 6 "Semiotic Regulation of Psychological Processes" in Valsiner (1998) for an overview of the field, including the contributions of Peirce, Dewey, and Vygotsky.

create. Equally, for both of them, the systematic enquiry they sought was not reductionist. It needed to capture the flow of iterations of self and social role for Mead and of mind and society for Vygotsky. The fluidity of those iterations and the interest of both men in the adaptations of organism and environment meant that units of analysis needed to contain the dynamics under examination.

Both wanted to move beyond descriptions of complex phenomena to explanations of how they arose, though as we have seen, at different levels of analysis. To that end, they were both concerned with the building of theory and were therefore accepting of universals. Both also valued a form of reflectiveness, which made the conceptual tools used available for scrutiny and revision. But both were also products of their time and place, and perhaps this is most evident in their approaches to methodology and their legacies to it.

Although Mead valued the scientific enquiry he observed, he was also critical of its narrowness and lack of reflection.[24] In one of his discussions of science (Mead, 1982) he revealed his concerns. He criticized "research scientists" for their lack of interest in consciousness or a "metaphysical object" (1982, p. 179) and argued that, "The problem is ... to explain immediate experience in terms of objects whose existence must lie outside of human experience" (1982, p. 182). His seeking of universals within the social world as commonly accepted interpretations of complex phenomena was his way out of the impasse of the mind–world separation. For Mead the building of these universals was the purpose of science.

> Research defines its problem by isolating certain facts which appear for the time being not as the sense-data of a solipsistic mind, but as experiences of an individual in a highly organized society, facts which, because they are in conflict with accepted doctrines, must be described so that they can be experienced by others under like conditions. The ground for the analysis which leads to such facts is found in the conflict between the accepted theory and the experience of the individual scientist.
>
> (Mead, 1964, p. 196)

This is a statement about the social psychology of scientific research and in the end this is where Mead's interest lay. Kozulin reminded us

---

[24] In Mead (1982) he argues that "neo-realism with its symbolic logic ... proceeding by a ruthless analysis ... conceives its task not to be that of relating objects in immediate experience with metaphysical objects, but of taking everything to pieces." He goes on to point out that this does not seem to concern scientists. This criticism of a lack of reflection resonates strongly with Vygotsky's attack on psychology in "The Crisis in Psychology" (1997a).

(Kozulin, 1986) that methodology has a rich meaning in Russian where it refers to the philosophical study of the methods used in a particular science.

Mead's approach seems very much in line with this richer interpretation. His position has been described as metaphysical rather than scientific, and there is little evidence of actual empirical enquiry in the work available to us. Certainly statements such as the following one suggest that he was neither exploring, nor talking from evidence, rather he was aiming at providing a structure for the "adventure" of creating a moral order.

> The gestures thus internalized are significant symbols because they have the same meanings for all individual members of a given society or social group, i.e., they respectively arouse the same attitudes in the individuals making them as they arouse in the individuals responding to them: Otherwise the individual could not internalize them or be conscious of them and their meanings. (Mead, 1934, p. 47)

Mead's analysis provided the groundwork for the symbolic interactionism of Blumer and the understandings of social meaning making and action informed by that branch of sociology – a fascinating topic for a society that regarded itself as a cultural melting pot. That groundwork therefore should not be underplayed as a result of contrasting him with Vygotsky.

Vygotsky's methodology was, unsurprisingly, informed by Marx. In brief, his uncovering of the movement from spontaneous to scientific concepts, together with his metatask of creating the conceptual tools for a new transformational psychology, demonstrate both his realism and his commitment to scientific method, albeit one that was socially constructed and open to improvement. That scientific method had as its object the transcending of false consciousness. Vygotsky's realism therefore marked him as taking a somewhat different line from Mead's version of social constructivism. Instead, the route back to Marx and the transforming power of scientific tools is clear. In *Thinking and Speech*, Vygotsky wrote:

> The essence of any scientific concept was defined in a profound manner by Marx:

> If the form in which a thing is manifested and its essence were in direct correspondence, science would be unnecessary.
> (Vygotsky, 1987, p. 193)

As we have already suggested, Vygotsky's quest, the analysis of consciousness, was more ambitious than Mead's. Vygotsky needed to capture the sociohistorical genesis of mental structures and of higher or scientific concepts and to do so during the processes of concrete tool mediated action. He was clear that existing methods would not reveal the object of his study because they were not premised on the same conceptualization of consciousness,[25] that is, as a feature of the interaction between mind and world.

His response was to turn to the process of double stimulation outlined earlier in order to reveal not just the "final effect of the operation, but the specific psychological structures of the operation" (Vygotsky, 1999, p. 59). By structuring tasks so that there were incremental changes in difficulty over a period of time, he was able to observe the developing sense-making processes of the child. It is interesting to note that here Vygotsky was at pains to present the tasks within carefully controlled settings. His examination of practical action involved the contriving of conditions which highlighted cognitive processes in tool mediated action. His methodological legacy here,, subsequently extended by A. N. Leont'ev and later by Engeström,[26] was the focus on action.

Unfortunately, there are few examples of detailed reports of Vygotsky's studies of tool mediated action in his surviving work. Bruner, in his introduction to *Thought and Language* (Bruner, 1962) observed that the book is "is at times distressingly swift in coming to conclusions," but then he reminded us that Vygotsky's analyses were derived from "incessant observation of children learning to talk and learning to solve problems" (1962, pp. viii–ix). Vygotsky's second legacy, developed initially by Bruner and by Wertsch, was his recognition that semiotic analysis provided the clue to consciousness. Proposing that a "change in the word's sense is a basic factor in the semantic analysis of speech," he went on to argue that the meaning of the word "is nothing more than a potential" to be "realized in living speech" (Vygotsky, 1987, p. 276). His linguistic turn, aimed at revealing consciousness, opened up a rich vein of enquiry that is still underway.

Mead also was aware that consciousness emerged in action and was evident in the language used as we acted into roles and responded to others, but finally his interest was the formation of socially responsible behavior. Their respective approaches to the making of mind and

[25] See Chapter 5, "Methods of Studying Higher Mental Functions," in Vygotsky (1999) for his account of the challenges presented by his new psychology to existing methods of enquiry. In this chapter, he also explains in some detail the use of double simulation as a research method.

[26] See, for example, Engeström (1987, 1999) and Kozulin (1986) for the development of activity theory.

to the societies in which those minds were produced also, therefore, had an impact on the scope of the methodological groundwork they undertook.

THE INTERACTION OF THE LEGACIES OF VYGOTSKY AND MEAD

Following Peirce, the signs we use as we attempt to engage with the object are necessarily partial representations and the interpretants that lead to action are shaped by what is possible for us to do. In this chapter, I have presented distinctly partial representations of the work of Vygotsky and Mead and have filtered those representations through my own position. That position includes a background in social history, social psychology, and the study of pedagogy, as I am an English speaking European, old enough to have witnessed the later fortunes of the legacies of both Vygotsky and Mead at firsthand, and now working on analyses of activity. Such processes of personal sense making and public meaning making are experienced by all of us. These processes are part of the social psychology of theory building.

A comparison of the intellectual journeys of Vygotsky and Mead, therefore, is not simply a matter of intellectual stamp-collecting. It should also take us forward toward a better and critical understanding of why, following Mead's analyses, some universals capture the social imagination and others do not. Why, for example, in the US and the UK, is the notion of community of practice almost ubiquitous and distressingly distanced from its origins in the cognitive anthropology of Lave and Wenger (1991)? Often misleadingly seen as synonymous with a sociocultural analysis, it seems to have become a way of arguing that coherent communities have been formed. Are we, in the throes of late capitalism, still in need of evidence of Mead's benign socially responsible communities?

Why is the semiotic strand of Vygotsky's legacy carried forward most vividly in the U.S. and areas where U.S. intellectual influence is strong? Is it because this version of the analysis of consciousness most closely resonates with the broader constructivist legacy of James and the linguistics of Peirce? Is it also because, following both Mead and Dewey, it focuses finally more on individual than cultural change? Why is it taking so long for Vygotsky's pedagogical influence to be felt in the West? Does his realism clash too strongly with constructivism, and his Marxism disturb those who might share his belief in a knowable world? Why is Marxism, as a force for social transformation, played down in so many current activity theory analyses? Is it simply that the systems theorists and psychologists who have appropriated activity theory lack the constructs of social history that allow for such analyses,or is it because it is antithetical to both corporate capitalism and individual liberalism? If we are to develop Vygotsky's legacies in the reflective manner valued by both Vygotsky and Mead, we need to continue to ask these questions.

4 Vygotsky, Mead, and the New Sociocultural Studies of Identity

INTRODUCTION

Identity is a key concept in many different fields including psychology, anthropology, sociology, linguistics, and cultural studies. At the intersection of these fields, *sociocultural research* – a recent name for the interdisciplinary approach inspired by the cultural historical work of L. S. Vygotsky and others – is developing its own integrated perspective on identity. In his brief life, Vygotsky wrote down only rudimentary ideas about personality or self. Still, those he did offer, when combined with his general notions of semiotic mediation and higher-order psychological functions, formulate an important nascent understanding of identity formation and its significance for processes of social and cultural change. This chapter examines developments in relevant research and theory that have appeared, for the most part, since William Penuel and James Wertsch's key 1995 article. By adopting an expanded definition of identity, we include a wide range of research, from case studies of individual identity development to analyses of the centrality of identities in mediating response to state projects and to social movements.

Concepts of identity are often (although not in Penuel and Wertsch) promiscuously mingled, producing a good bit of confusion and ambiguity. Because we concentrate on the approach to identity associated with George Herbert Mead, rather than following Penuel and Wertsch's focus on Erik Erikson's better-known concept, our first task is to clarify the differences between these two major conceptualizations. Those who are tempted to move directly to the review of empirical studies in the "Sociocultural Studies of Identity" section in this chapter should consider first reading the clarification that follows.

TWO LINES OF THEORIZING IDENTITY: ERIKSON AND MEAD

Despite its current ubiquity in the social sciences, the humanities, and in everyday talk, the concept of identity is relatively recent. Gleason's (1983) "semantic history" dates its appearance as a popular social science term to the 1950s, when Erik Erikson put it into circulation. Thanks to his choice of topics, and to the coincidental rise of the social sciences to prestige in those years, Erikson won a Pulitzer and several other notable prizes, received extensive journalistic coverage, and saw his ideas reach wide audiences. His and others' writings, such as David Riesman's *The Lonely Crowd*, resonated with the disquiet many postwar Americans felt as they lived through the vast expansion of mass-produced consumer goods in the 1950s, and the political and cultural turmoil of the 1960s. Many were searching for answers to the core questions Erikson associated with an integrated self-concept providing a sense of continuity and sameness over time: Who am I? Where do I belong in today's society? Summarizing the interpretations engendered by Erikson's writing, Penuel and Wertsch (1995, p. 83) defined *identity* as "...a sense, felt by individuals within themselves, and as an experience of continuity, oriented toward a self-chosen and positively anticipated future...." Another frequently cited conception, inspired by Erikson, sees identity as "a process 'located' in the core of the individual and yet also in the core of his communal culture..." that answers questions of who one is and what one stands for (Erikson, 1968, p. 22 quoted in Gleason, 1983, p. 914; see also Erikson, 1980, and Sökefeld, 1999).

Although Erikson saw identity as profoundly shaped by historical circumstances, his emphases have made his concept of identity most attractive to those interested in psychological well-being and in the psychodynamics that achieve or impede it. Interpretations of Erikson's work have proliferated, and his concerns have been extended to ethnicity, the consequences of disrespect for ethnic groups, and many other topics; some that Erikson considered and others that he did not. Still, questions of belonging and of locating oneself in society continue to be core aspects of the concept. Because Erikson considered achieving a *stable, consistent,* and *enduring* answer to the core questions to be an important psychodynamic task; "identity" continues to invoke coherence and continuity of self as fundamental to mental health.

Other trends in early twentieth-century social science resulted in alternative concepts of identity. These ideas were more clearly oriented toward sociological and anthropological interests in the dense relations between *identities as aspects of self* and *identities as social and cultural objects.* Perhaps the best known of these variant notions of identity developed in the American school of social psychology, which claims G. H. Mead (1910, 1912, 1913, 1925, 1934) as its founder. Mead's conception of the "I–me" dynamic grounded self-formation in the social coordination of activity through symbolic communication. It highlighted the importance of everyday encounters with people generalized as social "types." Although the Meadian concept has been expanded to include master statuses (such as race and gender) and culturally defined persona (such as an aggressive person or, along the Southwest Border of the United States and Mexico, the narcotrafficer (Edberg, 2004; Stryker, 1987; McCall, 1978), it was originally developed to account for self formation by relation to the linguistically recognized social positions and other roles crucial to the conduct of social activities and relationships.[1] Today, the extension of this idea is that people form senses of themselves – identities – in relation to ways of inhabiting roles, positions, and cultural imaginaries that matter to them (e.g., as a skater, a punk, a radical environmentalist, a theoretically sophisticated anthropologist, a stylish dresser, a good father, a third-wave feminist, a black activist, a moderate Republican).[2]

The theoretical school, which became identified as symbolic interactionism in the 1940s, did not at first use the term "identity." Mead and Charles Horton Cooley, the founders of the approach, used "self" instead. During the 1960s, their usage shifted from "self" to "identity." Erving Goffman's popular books, *The Presentation of Self in Everyday Life* (1959), and *Stigma* (1963) gave this alternative meaning of identity a more widespread circulation.

Gleason (1983, pp. 917–918) helps explain how the emergence of this distinctive sense of identity managed only to complicate, or muddy, the more casual use of "identity." Strands of the Meadian or "symbolic interactionist" usage became conflated with the more dominant Eriksonian meanings. Although there are clear ways that studies of Eriksonian

---

[1] See Stryker, Owens, and White (2000, p. 6) who refer to a 1980 definition: identity "refers to an internalized set of meanings attached to a role played in a network of social relationships, with a person's self viewed as, in important part, an organization of the various identities held by the person."

[2] We use "Meadian" to describe such identities for the purposes of this chapter. Other names for theories that build on the symbolic interactionist school include "identity theory," "structural identity theory" (e.g., Burke & Reitzes, 1991), and, from anthropology, "social practice theories of identity" (e.g., Holland & Lave, 2001). The majority of anthropological writing on identity treats ethnic and other identities as cultural and social objects that create subjects. These writings show less interest in the relation of identities to self (Sökefeld, 1999). Social practice theory of identity is an exception to this generalization.

"identity" can be brought into conversation with studies of Meadian "identities," the two notions are oriented to different phenomena. An Eriksonian "identity" is overarching. It weaves together an individual's answers to questions about who he or she is as a member of the cultural and social group(s) that make up his or her society. A Meadian identity, on the other hand, is a sense of oneself as a participant in the social roles and positions defined by a specific, historically constituted set of social activities. Meadian identities are understood to be multiple – one's important identities can include "radical environmentalist" *and* "good father" *and* "American," and they may reflect, for example, contradictory moral stances. Eriksonian approaches, in contrast, attribute psychodynamic significance to achieving a coherent and consistent identity that continues over the course of adulthood. Thus, to the extent that one emphasizes consistency and continuity, the two definitions can be in tension with one another. Penuel and Wertsch (1995) use the term "analytic primacy" to describe how theorists give priority to one aspect of phenomena over others. At the very least, the analytic primacy of Eriksonian orientations differ from Meadian ones. The questions of the Eriksonian orientations have to do with processes of and obstacles to achieving an integrated, enduring, and consistent identity/self in social life; those of Mead have to do with the means by which individuals form senses of self – identities – in relation to roles, statuses, and cultural persona, and how these identities organize affect, motivation, action, and agency.

In the next section, we discuss how Vygotskian concepts contribute to the study of what we call "Meadian" identities and present research that develops this theoretical formulation. In the final sections, we return to Eriksonian approaches. For now, we will use "identity" to refer to Meadian identities, which we define as a self-understanding to which one is emotionally attached and that informs one's behavior and interpretations: "People tell others who they are, but even more important, they tell themselves who they are and then try to act as though they are who they say they are. These self-understandings are what we ... refer to as identities" (Holland et al., 1998, p. 3).

CONCEPTUALIZING IDENTITY FORMATION: MEAD AND VYGOTSKY

L. S. Vygotsky, to the limited extent he wrote about personality, was like Mead in his view of self as a complex emergent phenomenon, continually produced in and by individuals in their interchanges with others and with the culturally transformed material world. The two theorists shared ideas about this sociogenetic formation of self. They were both interested in the ways in which social interaction, mediated by symbolic forms, provided crucial resources and ever-present constraints for self-making. They both emphasized *active internalization,* internalized *self-other dialogues*, and, in their respective ways, paid attention to the *semiotics of behavior*. Valsiner and van der Veer (1988, pp. 127–128), however, point out an important difference between the two. Mead gave analytic primacy to the *outcomes* of sociogenesis, the resulting linkages formed between self and society through the dynamic "I–me" system, while Vygotsky emphasized *how mind and personality*, as sociogenetic products, *develop* over time.

There is no record that the younger Vygotsky (1896–1934) crossed paths with Mead (1863–1931), or that either read the other's work. Nonetheless, they drew on several of the same intellectual sources, and their ideas are sufficiently compatible to augment one another. Vygotsky's importance to the line of research spawned by Mead is, if anything, even greater than his significance for Eriksonian studies of identities. Semiotic mediation is crucial to the formation of Meadian identities. In turn, Meadian identities can be considered to constitute what Vygotsky referred to as "higher psychological functions." Conceived as such, these identities influence behavior in everyday life and, very importantly, enable a modest form of agency. A brief sketch of Vygotsky and Mead's commonalities helps to explain the value of convening their separate interests.

Active Internalization

Mead and Vygotsky each developed their respective sociogenetic accounts of self and mind in relation to the writings of the psychologist, James Mark Baldwin, and the moral philosopher, Josiah Royce. One influence was Baldwin's rendering of the proclivity of humans to imitate the behavior of others in ways that produce individually distinctive behavioral formations. Baldwin provided a nuanced conceptualization of the ontogeny of imitation: Embedded in a context of ongoing social suggestions, a child, as she becomes able, imitates the behavior of others. At first, her *own* performance serves as a stimulus for her subsequent behavior. She reiterates her own behavior regardless of its mistakes as judged against the model. Then, at some point, as the child matures, she stops focusing on her own original imitation, attends instead to the model, and produces novel variations on it, including even oppositions to it.[3] On their own, neither the model nor the novel variant excite her. Instead, her focus shifts to *the relationship between the two.*

For Baldwin, individuals are attracted to collective activities, forms, and patterns, and copy them, but much more goes on than straightforward copying. Rather, they learn to assemble their own, "novel patterns of personality, still within the frame that is provided for them by society." In response to ongoing social demands, "The individual becomes a law unto himself, exercises his private judgment, fights his own battles for truth, shows the virtue of independence and the vice of obstinacy" (Baldwin, 1898, pp. 19–20, quoted in Valsiner & Van der Veer, 1988, p.122). This productive pattern of imitation, "makes the person an active agent in the internalization process" (Valsiner & Van der Veer, 1988, p. 121).

Today, many scholars would amend Baldwin's position by insisting that the social suggestions coming to the child are associated with varying amounts of power. Power relations, in particular, are thought to shape a person's self (or a group's identity) through "positioning" – distinguishing and treating a person or group as gendered, raced, classed, or other type of subject. Regimes of power shape knowledge of normative categories (e.g., the "disabled," "troubled youth," or "attractive women"). A person or group is "offered" or "afforded" a social position when a powerful body, such as a governmental agency, proposes a particular sort of subject – a "felon," "sexual harasser," or "at-risk" student – and calls on an individual to occupy the position (Bourdieu, 1977b; Davies & Harré, 1990; Foucault, 1978, 1988; Harré & Van Langenhove 1991). Baldwin's conceptualization of "imitation," however, fosters the idea of active internalization *even* in the face of social power. Acts of positioning must be answered, even if studiously ignored, but self-authoring is nevertheless a part of the process of positioning (Holland et al. 1998, p. 272; Holland & Leander, 2004).

Dialogic Selves: Self-Authoring in Relation to Others

It is key to *active internalization*, for both Vygotsky and Mead, that one's behaviors elicit reactions from others, so that, over time, one develops an inner sense of the collective meanings and social judgments that may meet one's behavior. A self–other split, with associated tensions, is a

---

[3] For important details about the progenitor of each aspect of these shared ideas, consult Valsiner and Van der Veer, (1988), from whom this account of Baldwin and Royce is primarily drawn.

feature of both theoreticians' sociogenetic views. Vygotsky (and Luria) developed this theme in their accounts of word meaning, which contrasts the *meaning* attributed to the word by (official) others to personal *senses* of the terms (Vygotsky, 1986; Luria, 1981). For Mead, an internalized self–other relationship was clearly personified. His central conception of the "I–me" self system developed during the period that he was citing Baldwin and Royce, and his conception of the "I" (as agent) and the "me" (as [social] object) bears similarities to Royce's ideas. Royce accepted Baldwin's general thesis about imitation, but he stressed that social judgment is internalized in *association* with others (van der Veer & Valsiner, 1988, p.123).

Mead, whose interests inclined to what we now associate with sociology's version of social psychology, placed more emphasis on the internalization of others as integral to one's inhabitation of the *positions and roles afforded us by society* than did Vygotsky, who was more interested in cognitive and affective development. We actively internalize a sense of our own behavior as compared to the behavior of others acting in related roles and positions. We develop an inner sense of the collective regard that society is likely to have for our performances. Then, we craft our own way of being in roles and positions in relationship to this "generalized other," the collective sense that we gradually develop from those who evaluate us. In Mead's terms, the "I" is simultaneously the actor *and* the observer in the ongoing flow of practice. The "I" as actor, with less than total control of the mind–body, responds to manifold stimuli. The "I" as an observer evaluates and infers "me's" from its own acts (as stimuli) which, in the next instance, become memory traces affecting "I," the actor. Contemporary notions of "identity" in identity theory owe much to Mead's conceptions of this "I–me" dynamic.

Recent anthropological works that develop Meadian identity concepts, especially those inspired by Bakhtin's dialogic approach,[4] rely heavily on this decentralized view in which self becomes a self-other relation carried out through inner dialogue over difference in social position or claims about cultural personae (Holland et al., 1998; Holland & Lave, 2001; Satterfield, 2002). (Approaches of a more Eriksonian bent have also begun to emphasize the importance of the self-other dialogue, for example, Tappan, 1999, 2000; and Sarbin, 2000.)

---

[4] The dialogical quality of self-authoring has been raised to prominence by the works of Bakhtin (1981, 1990) and on Bakhtin (see, e.g., Holquist, 1990; Wertsch, 1991), but it was first noted by Mead (1911, 1913) and (by extension from inner speaking) Vygotsky (1986). See also Lee, Wertsch, and Stone 1983.

The Semiotics of Behavior: Signs of the Other, Signs of the Self

Another important element shared by Mead and Vygotsky is their focus on the semiotics of behavior. Both stress the transitivity of signs for self and other. In Vygotsky's version, words, gestures, artifacts, and acts are initially signs in interaction, either directed by the self toward the other or received by the self from the other. At some point, however, the self takes itself as the object of the gesture. *The self comes to use the signs, once directed to others or received from others, in relation to the self.*[5] Vygotsky credits Baldwin for his recognition that self is understood through applying one's understanding of others to oneself, "We are conscious of ourselves because we cognize . . . others, and in the same way which we use to cognize others – since we are the same in relation to us that others are in relation to us. We are *aware* of our self only to the extent that we are *the other* for our self, i.e. in so far as we can perceive our own reflexes again as stimuli" (Vygotsky, 1982, p. 52, quoted in Valsiner & van der Veer, 1988, p. 129; cf. Vygotsky, 1997, p. 77, which has a variant translation).

In Mead's version of the transitivity of symbolic behavior, one's own behavior comes to call out the same meaning for, and thus be a stimulant for, *self*, as it is for the *other*. Mead, who emphasized coordination of behavior even more than imitation in shaping the social self, placed great stress on this transitivity (Mead 1912, 1913, 1934). As we develop maturity in society's activity systems, we, as *individuals*, begin to experience our own behavior as signs of who we are. We become objects of our own gaze, and we experience our own behavior – and by association ourselves – *in relation to the meanings of the group* and so become liable to receive admiration and respect or disapproval and condemnation, according to *the values practiced by the group.*

These foundations – active internationalization, dialogic selves, and the semiotics of behavior – underlie the Meadian approaches of identity theorists such as Goffman (1959, 1963), McCall and Simmons (1978), and Stryker (1968, 1980). They understand identities as the means by which "individuals infuse self and subjective meaning into roles" and develop a desire for being in society (Burke & Reitzes, 1991, p. 241). Identities motivate action. One pursues opportunities to enact one's claimed identities and thereby validates them for oneself and for others. "[W]hen an individual is committed, he gambles his regard for himself on living up

---

[5] Conversion experiences constitute dramatic episodes of taking oneself as the object of meaning.

to this self conception" (Burke & Reitzes, 1991, p. 241, see also McCall & Simmons, 1978).

Burke and Reitzes (1981; 1991, p. 242) sum up five aspects that Meadian theorists attribute to identities. (Here we amend Burke and Reitzes's list, to bring it in line with an integrated sociocultural approach to identity.) Identities are simultaneously (1) *social products*, that is, collectively developed and imagined social categories; (2) *self-meanings*, developed through a sociogenetic process that entails active internalization; (3) *symbolic*, when performed they call up the same responses in one person as they do in others; (4) *reflexive*, providing a vantage point from which persons can assess the "implications of their own behavior as well as of other people's behaviors" (1991, p. 242); and (5) a *source of motivation for action*, "particularly actions that result in the social confirmation of the identity." In an integrated sociocultural approach to identity that builds on Vygotskian interests in development, researchers are also encouraged to pay attention not only to the end product of commitment, but to how identities form in practice and other time, both as social products and as personal formations.

VYGOTSKY AND IDENTITY DEVELOPMENT

While Mead explored how persons creatively inhabit and are motivated by the roles, positions, and cultural personae that are ubiquitous features of human societies, Vygotsky's interests led him to the general developmental processes affecting human cognition, emotion, and motivation. He was more interested in the general, but related, process in which collective signs deployed in social activities become the means for complex, volitional behavior on the part of the individual. His developmental perspective is provocative for theorizing about how persons construct their personal versions of the social identities that mediate their behavior and interpretations of the world. Vygotsky's ideas about semiotic mediation clarify the role of culture in the formation of identities and envision how actively internalized identities enable one to control one's behavior and, thus, have agency.

Vygotsky's key to human existence was the capacity to escape enslavement to whatever stimuli humans happened to encounter, whether from within or without. The way that they accomplished this was (broadly) linguistic, that is, through the active construction and use of symbols. Just as humans can modify the environment physically – thanks to their production of, and facility with, tools and symbols – humans can also modify the environment's stimulus value for their own mental states.

A typical mediating device is constructed by assigning meaning to an object and then placing it in the environment so as to affect mental events. It is important to remember that Vygotsky saw these tools for the self-control of cognition and affect as, above all, social and cultural. "Assigning meaning" and "placing in the environment" are not just individual acts. Rather, mediating devices are part of collectively formed systems of meaning and are products of social history. As simple examples, he cited techniques drawn from cross-cultural accounts – from the elaborate mnemonic objects used by messengers in traditional cultures, to the Westerner's string around her finger or knot in her handkerchief (1993, pp. 102–104) – to claim that humans' use of mediating devices signaled a turning point in human cultural history – the transition from the *use* of one's memory to *active control* over it (Vygotsky, 1978, p. 51; 1993, p. 101). Vygotsky referred to these complexes, which extend natural abilities through cultural means, as "higher psychological functions" (Vygotsky, 1978).[6]

Identity as a Higher Order Mental Function

Although Vygotsky exemplified the construction of "higher psychological functions" in experimental situations of recall or problem solving, he and his associates considered mediating devices to be important to human activities beyond control over memory, problem solving and inferencing. Luria (cited in Cole 1985, p. 149), for example, gives a case

---

[6] In a 1929 manuscript unpublished in his lifetime, Vygotsky puts the social origin of higher psychological functions in no uncertain terms: "Genetically, social relations, real relations between people, underlie all higher functions and their relationships . . . the mechanism of such functions is a copy of the social. *They are internalized relations of a social order, transferred to the individual personality,* the basis of the social structure of the personality. Their composition, genesis, and function (mode of action) – in a word, their *nature* – are social. Even transformed in the personality into psychological processes, they remain quasi-social. The individual and personal are not in opposition, but a higher form of sociality" (Vygotsky, 1989, pp. 58–59; italics in the original).

Vygotsky grasped the relationship of the social and the personal in this manuscript so literally, that he argued that the relations between psychological functions, their organization into personality, take the form of a drama, and can only be apprehended by a method of personification. The words remind us of Royce, but Vygotsky follows Marx's dictum that humans must be understood concretely, that is, as the totality of their social relationships and social histories. It is this entire person who thinks, speaks, and acts, and whose behavior can therefore only be explained genetically, as a function of social history and development. Psychology was a science to be sure, deploying laws of behavior, but it was also a historical science. The instance of law in psychology was refracted by social conditions and circumstances.

of the mediation of will, and Vygotsky (1984a, p. 379; 1998, pp. 291–292) discussed the development of a "logic of emotion." Children learn, through signs and words, to objectify, talk about, compare, and classify, and thus, through semiotic mediation, learn to manage their own emotions. These ideas (popularly expressed as self-control) inform recent studies of human artifices for modulating emotion.

Arlie Hochschild's book *The Managed Heart* describes the training of flight attendants and the devices that these women were taught to control their anger at obnoxious passengers. They learned to imagine, for example, that something traumatic had happened in the passenger's life, or to remind themselves that the irritating passenger was behaving childishly because of his fear of flying (1983, pp. 24–27). Hochschild shows how these devices were carefully inculcated and continually reproduced in practice, under a regimen of training that was instituted and maintained by the airline company and supported as well by a popular tradition of such means of self-control. This training was so effective that flight attendants often began to lose any sense of their own anger on, and even off, the job.

Most of Vygotsky's suggestions about the development of personality concern self-management. These abilities are important in the self-regulation of emotion and behavior called for in the performance of roles, such as flight attendant, and especially roles that have become elaborated into identities. Vygotsky also hints, in other writings, at more comprehensive processes of self-organization for the purpose of carrying out socially recognized acts. In fact, he describes a self-reorganization that emerges as a child matures and becomes capable of occupying a new role or position in an activity. Vygotsky writes about a child trying to solve a problem put to him in an experiment. The child could not solve the problem on his own, but he could solve it by directing speech about the solution to an adult. Vygotsky thought that the child had not yet transfigured the necessary references into inner speech and so could not organize his *own* behavior:

> The big change in the child's development takes place when the speech becomes socialized, when, instead of turning to the experimenter with a plan for a solution, the child turns to himself. In the latter case, the speech that takes part in the problem-solving process, turns from being in the category of the inter-psychical into that of an intra-psychical function. The child, *organizing his own behaviour along the lines of the social type*, applies to himself that means of behaviour that he previously applied to others. Consequently, the source of the intellectual activity and control over one's own behaviour in the process of practical problem-solving lies *not in the invention of a purely logical act*, but in the *application to one's*

self of a social relationship, in the transfer of a social form of behaviour into one's own psychic organization. (Vygotsky, 1984b, pp. 33–34; quoted in Valsiner & van der Veer, 1988, pp. 130–131, authors' translation, our italics; cf. Vygotsky, 1999, p. 23, again with a variant translation) [7]

In a later paper, Vygotsky (1978, pp. 92–104) described processes reminiscent of self-organization in the name of an identity. In this paper, one sees Vygotsky's usual fascination with humans' ability to manipulate their imaginative worlds, and themselves, by means of symbols. The paper analyzed young children's play and their later abilities with games.

Early in their lives, children begin a type of play in which the everyday meaning of objects is suspended, and new meaning is assigned to objects, others, and self. Behind the couch becomes the bad guy's hideout, under the table becomes the jail. One's playmate becomes the sheriff; oneself, the outlaw. Or perhaps a certain set of everyday meanings is retained and highlighted, and other features drop away. Vygotsky, for instance, describes two sisters playing at being sisters. In either type of play, meanings are manipulated to point to another (absent or distilled) social setting, and one's motivations and feelings are geared to participation in the imagined scene. A piece of candy is used to represent something else – a jewel that robbers have stolen, perhaps – and is treated as a jewel. The temptation to eat it is resisted. Likewise, one is treated and treats oneself as acting out of a position in the play scene. The words of one's playmates are heard as words toward one's character in the play. Being called a "bad guy" is not taken to heart when the play is finished. Immediate sensations of pain and fatigue may also be ignored for the purpose of continuing play. When a race is run, the goal of winning the race, or at least reaching the finish line, overcomes any desire to stop, to sit down from fatigue. Of course, children sometimes do stop before the race is over; eat the candy, take personal offense, or tire of playing sister, wandering away to watch TV. The remarkable point is how often they do not. They learn to detach themselves from their reactions to immediate surroundings, to enter a play world – a conceptual world that differs from the everyday – and come to react to the imagined actors, objects and events of that world.[8]

Games with more explicit rules and less concrete fantasy become more prominent as the child grows older. Still, the child must shift himself or herself to a conceptual world beyond his or her immediate

---

[7] Vygotsky (1989) puts the point even more pithily, "I am a social relation of me to myself." The phrasing echoes Mead.

[8] This description and the next few paragraphs are adapted and reprinted from Holland et al. (1998, pp. 49–51) by permission of Harvard University Press.

surroundings in order to become an actor who submits to the premises of the game and treats events of the game as *real*. Her desires and motivations become related to "a fictitious 'I,' to her role in the game and its rules" (Vygotsky (1978, p. 100). It is this competence that makes culturally constituted – or what Holland et al. (1998) call "figured worlds" – possible and, consequently, the range of human institutions. Lee (1985) points out the definite link between play worlds and institutional life. Fantasy and games serve as precursors to participation in institutional life, where individuals are treated as "scholars," "bosses," or "at-risk" children – whatever the institutional role – and events such as the granting of tenure, a corporate raid, or the "self esteem" of at-risk children are taken in all seriousness. The identities one develops in those worlds (e.g., "activist scholar," "competent boss," "top student") become identities or senses of self that one can evoke. In Vygotskian terminology, an *identity* is a higher-order psychological function that organizes sentiments, understandings, and embodied knowledge relevant to a culturally imagined, personally valued social position. Identities formed on personal terrain mediate one's ability to organize and perform the intention of one's activity in the locales and "occupations" of cultural worlds.

Identity Development and Semiotic Mediation

The ability to organize oneself in the name of an identity, according to a Vygotskian perspective, develops as one transacts cultural artifacts with others and then, at some point, applies the cultural resource to oneself. Holland et al. (1998, chapter 4; see also Cain, 1991) provide examples of mediation devices explicitly related to the development of an identity, for example, that of a nondrinking alcoholic. This is an identity that one develops in activities sponsored by Alcoholics Anonymous (AA). In AA meetings, participants are drawn into telling stories about their lives before joining the organization and encouraged to take up symbols of their journey to sobriety (e.g., collect tokens to mark periods of time spent sober). They are drawn into a world of cultural meaning where these devices have a particular symbolic value and an emotional valence. Cain (1991) identified these stories and tokens as mediational devices that were important in the formation of members' personal identities as nondrinking alcoholics. They came to name themselves, and often to see themselves, as "alcoholics" and not just as social drinkers. These elements of AA were meaningful in, relevant to, and valued in relation to a frame of meaning, "a virtual world" – a world that had been figured. When Cain did her research, the chips used in AA meetings to mark length of sobriety were the same plastic chips sold for playing poker. In the world of AA, these chips were not won by holding a straight flush. Rather, the chips were meaningfully revalued to a world where the stake, the thing waged, was staying sober; the chip became an emblem of a different achievement, another kind of success. On the store's shelf, a poker chip is worth little, but within the world of AA, the significance of a chip, color-coded for length of time without a drink, is great. The difference between being able to pick up a chip and having to forgo the act becomes, for some, the difference between a self that is recovering and desired, and one that is not.

The stories that AA participants learned to tell of their former lives and current temptations signified an experience and place in a world that signally differs from that of the nonalcoholic. Cain followed newcomers through their participation in AA activities. She recorded stories and noted a gradually developing ability on the part of some, not all, newcomers to recount the various segments of their lives in the genre of AA stories. The stories became, as Holland et al. (1998) argue, the primary cultural resource that semiotically mediated members' senses of self and their abilities to organize themselves as "nondrinking alcoholics" – even in the face of powerful urges to continue their older patterns of drinking and drinking activities.

Culture and Identity Formation

Penuel and Wertsch (1995, p. 83) advise researchers "to study identity in local activity settings where participants are actively engaged in forming their identities; to examine the cultural and historical resources for identity formation as empowering and constraining tools for identity formation; [and] to take mediated action as a unit of analysis." Although they found their notion of identity in Erikson's work, their list is also a good start for researchers interested in Meadian concepts of identity. Accommodating Meadian "identities," however, requires making additional features explicit: Identities are social and cultural products through which a person identifies the self-in-activity and learns, through the mediation of cultural resources, to manage and organize himself or herself to act in the name of an identity. Identities are personally significant, actively internalized, self-meanings, but first and foremost, in contrast to Erikson's view, they are formed in relation to collectively produced social identities.

Culture is vital for Meadian identities in two respects. First, cultural genres (e.g., the stories told in Alcoholic Anonymous meetings) and cultural artifacts (e.g., the poker-chips-turned-into-markers-of-sobriety) are the means to the semiotic mediation of self as a recognized social type (e.g., a nondrinking alcoholic). Second, and even more significant, identities are part of more encompassing cultural constructions.

Wertsch (1991) and Holland et al. (1998), among others, have pointed out that identities are associated with activities understood against a horizon of cultural meaning. Social types make sense only within the richly developed imaginings of the worlds in which they exist. Holland et al. (1998, p. 52) use "figured worlds" or "cultural worlds" interchangeably to refer to socially and culturally constructed realms of interpretation and performance in which particular characters and actors (e.g., "nondrinking alcoholics," "gifted and talented student," "radical environmentalist") are recognized. Significance is assigned to certain *activities* (e.g., AA meetings, field trips, direct actions), and the *acts* that compose them (e.g., picking up a chip, scoring in the top 10 percent, engaging in a lock down) and particular *outcomes* (e.g., staying sober, being accepted at Harvard, realizing the "wild within") are valued over others.[9] People develop selves in relation to social identities and cultural persona and, in their name, perform and create or re-create the activities meaningful to those worlds. The acts and artifacts become evocative, to participants, of the meanings relevant to those worlds, and the genre of the worlds (e.g., AA stories) become personalized. Unorganized sentiments are orchestrated in relation to tools of self authoring (e.g., names for social types in the world, poker chips, or other tangible signs) and eventually the person is able to organize himself or herself as, say, a nondrinking alcoholic, and in the process, contribute to the performance of the cultural world. Culture is integral to self formation: in the absences of cultural resources and cultural worlds, such identities are impossible.

Vygotsky's Concept of Agency and Its Significance

We need to reiterate one of the more important implications of Vygotsky's theory before turning to particular lines of research. Vygotsky argued that, without semiotic mediation, people would be buffeted about by the stimuli they happened to encounter as they went about in the world. Instead, semiotic mediation provides the means for humans to control, organize, and resignify their own behavior. As Hochschild

---

[9] The idea of figured worlds as a horizon of meaning for Meadian identities is related to studies of framing process, drawing on Goffman's (1974) frame analysis, and sociological studies of social movements (e.g., Hunt, Benford, & Snow 1994). Moreover, see Wertsch (1991) for analogous concepts. There he deploys "genre" and "sociocultural setting" (cultural, historical, and institutional setting), which together approximate the intent of figured world (a narrative genre of activity in situ).

observed for Delta flight attendants, by first relying on "training wheels" of a symbolic sort, one can learn to ignore aspects of situations to which one would have previously responded. One of the convincing points about this tool of agency is its appropriate modesty. It is an indirect means – one modifies one's environment with the aim, *but not the certainty*, of affecting one's own behavior – and it requires a sustained effort. Self-control and self-organization are enabled by semiotic mediation but by no means entailed. Mead's "I" is an unruly character, whose actions are always uncertain, always unfinished. In addition, newly generated cultural resources, because they usually permit many readings, may elicit unanticipated behavior. Therefore, a Vygotskian approach values the cultural production of new cultural resources as a means, albeit a contingent one, of bringing about social and cultural change. People, banded in communities of practice, can author, intentionally or unintentionally, new selves and new cultural worlds and try to realize them. As Valsiner (1998, p. 388) writes in *The Guided Mind*: "This break – the capability to transcend a present situated activity context and *create a new one* – is made possible by the human capacity for semiotic regulation of one another and of oneself" [italics our emphasis].

As a higher-order psychological function, identities constitute a relatively organized complex of thoughts, feelings, memories, and experience that a person can, more or less, durably evoke as a platform for action and response. A person who has developed an identity through Alcoholics Anonymous as a "nondrinking alcoholic," for example, can narrate, and otherwise project, himself as a recovering alcoholic. He can evaluate actions through the lens of AA and care about how he appears through those lenses. He predicts and takes responsibility for the outcome of his actions in the world of AA. He has identified with the cultural world of Alcoholics Anonymous and developed a self sensitive to that world. He observes, interprets, and values himself and others in terms of that world and especially important, interprets the past and plans future action in those terms. An identity is a key means of escape from the tyranny of environmental stimuli. Just because one is offered a drink, one doesn't have to take it – as long as one can imagine otherwise.

These possibilities for agency make identity and identity processes important not only in the lives of individuals, but in the course of social change.

SOCIOCULTURAL STUDIES OF IDENTITY

We searched the literature since 1995 for sociocultural studies of identity formation that draw upon a Vygotskian approach. The empirical studies that we found included Eriksonian and Meadian approaches to identity, and most were directed to the ethnographic study of identity processes in practice. The studies favor cases of identity formation and reformation in response to social and cultural change and other life-altering events (mimicking Vygotsky's genetic method). Despite the relatively recent emergence of a sociocultural perspective on identity, these studies help illuminate how identities form and the role that they play in mediating personal experience and motivating personal action and in shaping social life and its transformations. We briefly describe examples of the more suggestive research along six different lines.[10] The last one addresses issues of the universality of identity, and so it returns the focus from Meadian identities to Eriksonian identity.

Identity Formation and Its Complications

In the account of identity development in Alcoholics Anonymous, we emphasized the importance of several processes: interacting artifacts of the cultural world, directing the meaning of the markers of sobriety toward oneself, and learning to narrate oneself as a nondrinking

---

[10] For reasons of space, we have had to forgo many tantalizing ideas and studies. Davies (1999, pp. 23–24), for example, suggests that a Meadian concept of self formation can help resolve vexing challenges to the possibilities of studying selves across cultural differences. Another omission involves an influential vein of work centered around dialogism. This cultural psychological tradition, set out most fully in Hermans and Kempen (1993), shares many sources and correlates with Vygotskian research on the self and identity. Its strongest inspiration, however, lies in the writings of Mikhail Bakhtin. Hermans and Kempen describe a distributed, multicentric self composed of many "I-positions" that are related dialogically. That is, the self is composed as a dialogue among voices – those socially identifiable "speaking personalities" or consciousnesses that Bakhtin conceived as characteristic of the concrete life of human speech and thought. This dialogically composite self is similarly a dynamic and open system intimately and necessarily tied to cultural forms and social activity. Its semiotically mediated, historical, and developmental quality has obvious connections to the sociocultural tradition, as Valsiner (2002) and Ingrid Josephs (1998, 2002; see also Josephs, Valsiner, & Surgan, 1999) have made clear. It is also clearly related to contemporary concepts of identity, especially the multiple, culturally differentiated identities that are signaled through voice and invested in I-positions. Hermans (2001), Hermans and Kempen (1998), Josephs (1998, 2002), Bhatia (2002, 2003), Bhatia and Ram (2001, 2004), and von Meijl (2003) also make clear that dialogical selves and multiple identities reflect the changing conceptions of culture and social action that poststructuralist and postmodernist social theory articulates. These works share this connection to social theory with social practice theories of identity (Holland et al. 1998; Holland & Lave 2001), though Holland and Lave's work draws more intimately on Bourdieu's emphases on embodiment and the constructive, practically (rather than symbolically) mediated, force of power (as social position).

alcoholic. Several studies make clear that these tasks of identity formation – participation in cultural activities, mastering cultural artifacts, identifying with and figuring oneself in a cultural world – often encounter complications. From the AA research, for example (Holland et al. 1998; Cain, 1991), we learned that newcomers to AA meetings typically resisted the idea that they had a problem with alcohol consumption. In the popular imagination of the time, the "space of the imaginary drunk" was filled by images of skid row bums. To the ears of newcomers, AA's insistence that *they* were alcoholics appeared as attempts to position them as inebriated derelicts. Part of their process of identity development in AA involved reimagining what a person with a drinking problem might be like.

Studies of people who had recently come to the environmental movement revealed a similar complication in the development of their identities as environmentalists. Many outside the movement tended to have a negative image of environmentalists. For outsiders, the space of the imaginary environmentalist was filled by young, "hippy looking," wild-eyed, tree-huggers or the more sinister tree-spiker. Giving voice to these images affiliated outsiders with the imagined community of reasonable, middle-class folks who favor compromise and avoid conflict. They disdained "environmentalists," thinking of them as either immature people who carry their environmental sentiments too far or as privileged whites: somewhat wealthy, well-educated people who belong to the Sierra Club. The latter sort has the wealth and the leisure time to engage in activities like flying off somewhere to save whales. Both the hunters our research team followed and (especially) our African American consultants found this class-marked image off-putting. Becoming environmentalists in the face of these widespread popular images meant coming to peace with the fact that other sorts of folks and types of people could become environmentalists despite these popular images (Holland, 2003; Allen et al. in press).

Another complication in identify formation flows from the nature of self-authoring as a social, dialogical process. Identity is an achievement of the person's activity – but only within the contexts and events of social interaction. One's identities are social products drawn from social history, actively internalized, and redrawn as one's expressions of these identities enter into new circumstances and new activities. They are complicated by the ongoing dialogue of many actors in many activities, and the continual interplay of personal and interpersonal negotiations of their meaning and effects. At times, identity development becomes intermeshed in the strategic involvement of self-authoring, as a means to organize activity and gain a better footing with specific audiences.

William Lachicotte (2002) provides an account of Roger, a person with mental disorders caught up in the kind of interpersonal politics familiar to us all. Roger is remarkable, Lachicotte argues, not just because he forges different senses of himself – different identities – through the behavioral profiles of the two differing psychiatric diagnoses given him (manic-depressive and borderline), but also because he improvises these identifications (and the scenes that evoke them) in order to create a legitimate place for himself as a son, husband, and worker – as well as a patient.

Roger calls on the authoritative medical discourse of psychiatry to give force to his own actions and does so through different figures, according to his partners or audience. With his parents and coworkers, who charge him as "lazy" and lacking will power, he forefronts his identity as a manic-depressive; with his wife and psychiatrist, who believe in his illness, he organizes himself as the willful figure of the "borderline." In both cases, these different identities respond to the specific history of interaction, perceived personally and interpersonally. They answer different problems by organizing Roger's acts toward different goals.

Another study hints at the complicated processes that occur in response to striking events that invite the articulation of new identities. Cheryl Mattingly and her colleagues in the Collective Narrative Group (Mattingly et al., 2002) had been facilitating group meetings of African American, primarily working-class, women caring for children with disabilities when the events of September 11 occurred. Their article describes how this group of women understood and narrated the events of September 11 in group meetings, as the event became "experience," both in African American communities and personally for African Americans. The authors observed that the women's identities as African Americans, as Americans, and as working-class people affected how they interpreted the events of September 11.

Initially, the women responded as Americans in a figured world of international politics whose dangers had been made all too clear: as the targets of "terrorism." Mattingly et al. (2002), however, insisting upon the "incomplete," "in process," and "multiple" quality of identities, paid attention to the *continuing* process of storytelling through which women in the group recast their positions in the "9/11 world." Participants in the media and in other sites of discussion continued to elaborate the social identities of terrorists, and of Americans as victims of 9/11 and as potential victims of future attacks. The participants of the Collective Narratives Group did not automatically embrace the discourses served up by the media. Instead, they inflected these common identifications through the lens of their own histories. Together, as the weeks passed, through their dialogue, they turned "9/11" toward the activities and contexts of more immediate concern to them (and to the focus of their group on the problems of caring for children with disabilities). In these discussions, "9/11" came to be less imposing, less a transfiguring rupture in "reality" than yet another life-threatening "challenge" in a social world that, even before 9/11, was dangerous and stressful. From their standpoints – as poor women, as African American women, as mothers of children with "multiple challenges," as Americans long lacking the privileges that had protected others from a sense of endangerment – the events of 9/11 took on the cast of the everyday. During group discussions, the authors noted, "[the women's] position as blacks became the most salient characteristic of their cultural identity" (2002, pp. 748). Their "active internalization" of the discourse about 9/11 recast the meanings and possible identities framed there. (For additional cases of challenges to identity formation, see Blackburn, 2003.)[11]

Identity Formation in Trajectories of Participation across Activities

Another exciting line of research productively attends to identity formation in and across cultural activities *over time*. These studies search out and analyze trajectories of engagement and withdrawal from cultural worlds. They document common life paths of participation and identity formation.

Studies of schooling, education, and literacy have produced several longitudinal analyses of the formation of Meadian identities. Boaler and Greeno (2000), for example, draw on the ideas of *situated cognition* and *situated learning* (Lave, 1988, 1993; Lave & Wenger, 1991) to analyze identity formation in the activity systems organized in math classrooms – understood as the site of performance in a figured world – as an integral part of mathematical knowing. They argue that the senses of self that students fashion in relationship to mathematics strongly affect their continuing engagement with its learning (Boaler & Greeno, 2000, p. 173). That is, these identities shape students' subsequent orientation and choices regarding math activities and the possibilities of math careers.

Boaler and her research assistant interviewed members of Advanced Placement (AP) math classes in a number of northern California high

---

[11] This study could have also been used as an example of the later section, "Identities and Popular Consciousness." The categories are not meant to be exclusive.

schools. They discovered that the roles of students and their relationship to math learning were constructed in two different ways. One group of classrooms was organized around collaborative discussion; the remaining ("traditional") group around the teaching of procedures and individual mastering of math problems. Most of the students described themselves as (being positioned as) active learners in the first case; as passive learners in the second. "In discussion-oriented figured worlds, [for example,] connections between learners are emphasized as students are positioned as relational agents who are mutually committed and accountable to each other for constructing understanding in their discourse" (Boaler & Greeno, 2000, p. 178). The differences in the positional identities thrust on them correlated with students' desires to continue the study of math. Students in the traditional classroom tended to dislike being treated as passive learners. They were less likely than students in the discussion-oriented classrooms to want to continue in math activities. Boaler and Greeno (2000, p. 172) refer to a "trajectory of participation in the practices of mathematical discourse and thinking." Students' trajectories through math learning activities resulted (or not) in identities as "math students," and for the few who went on, as "mathematicians." [For other studies that trace the formation of social identities in classroom activities over time, see Leander (2002) and Wortham (2006).]

Another study, based on in-depth interviews, revealed an interesting longitudinal relationship between participation and identification in schooling activities. Urrieta (2003, 2005) presents the histories of twenty-four individuals, self-identified as Chicanos/Chicanas, drawn from intensive interviews about their lives and their "trajectories of participation" across educational activities. He sampled undergraduate and graduate students, primary and secondary school teachers, and university professors. Although they differed in truly striking ways, the detailed narratives of these Chicano/Chicana activists describe their social identification as "good students" in their early school careers. Their anecdotes told of being positioned as *good students*, often in invidious comparison to other Latina/Latino students. During this early period of schooling, their identities as "good students" were salient to them; their sentiments as Latina/Latino students were not.

Urrieta's analysis found another commonality in his participants' life histories. They told of becoming, usually at college, more conscious of the negative positions "offered" Latino/Latina people, including themselves, in the past and the present. They were gradually drawn, via informal and formal groups, into activities figured against the cultural world of Chicano/Chicana activism. In these communities of practice, they developed senses of themselves as activists.[12] This empirically identified common path of participation in cultural activities that first identified them as good students and then cultivated identities as activists raises interesting questions about the extent to which histories and qualities of participation become bases for subsequent identities.

Peter Demarath's (2003) research on Manus Island, Papua New Guinea, underscores the historically contingent, yet potent, nature of the relationship between trajectories of participation across cultural activities and identity formation. His research depicts a point in history when the identity of "villager" became resignified for many students, providing them a basis of action quite different from their predecessor villagers. In the article, Demarath analyzes the role of peer culture among high school students – and of the identities crafted there – in mediating the changes affecting local Papuan communities. In a time of extended economic "downturn," when the opportunities supposedly afforded by the "modernizing" projects of the Papuan government and transnational corporations had diminished, Manus Islanders were coming to doubt the benefits of (Westernized) education. Students of the local high schools began to identify themselves as "villagers," even at school, revalorizing the communal relationships and egalitarian ethos through which that social order is imagined and enacted – and, yet, as students who valued the experience of high school. Behind the peer group's aggressively egalitarian ethos, where teasing and gossip policed any action that smelt of the school (and its counterpart, the town), students expressed, only to their intimates, personal goals: "private" dreams that escaped the bounds of the village. Their identification as "villager," as it evoked a traditional (un-Westernized) cultural world, signified disengagement with the mission of the school and the content of its curricula. Yet, this identity and the relationships it mediated did not have the obligatory character of the "traditional" community. They were instead posed as a choice against a framework of "modernity" – instituted in the school – and organized an alternative stance in that world. In their trajectory though historically shifting activities they had transformed and were transformed by their sense (as Vygotsky uses the term) of "villager." Through their active internalization of "villager" across their trajectories of participation in school and village activities, Manus youth developed new textures of the identity.

---

[12] Urrieta's discussion features the most important of several ways in which unorganized sentiments about being Latina/Latino become organized around particular identities: participation in communities of practice that regularly produce cultural activities and events.

Identities and the Fortunes of State and Institutional Projects

This line of research explicitly considers the importance of identities in mediating responses to state and institutional projects. Bartlett's (2005; Bartlett, 2007) contribution to the field of literacy studies, approaches the problem of response to such projects from a Vygotskian angle. The analysis employs the *concepts of figured world*, *semiotic mediation*, and *identity* to analyze adult literacy programs that Bartlett studied in Brazil. There, identification as an "educated person," or its complement, the uneducated or illiterate, mediates one's activity even beyond the field of education. Bartlett found the figured world of the "educated person" to be virtually coterminous with the space of public activity and discourse. The educated person was more than learned. He or she was also marked as the emblem of well-mannered sociability. To be *educacao* was to know how to converse, how to make entrances, how to depart with grace, and generally how to deal with the civil and political world. To lack educacao was to feel socially inept, crude, ill-spoken, invisible and ashamed in the public world. Illiterate "donkeys" learned a kind of linguistic *habitus*, in Bourdieu's term (1977), which the analyses borrow, that disposed those who considered themselves illiterate to silence and withdrawal: to disengage from the public world that exposed them to contact with members of other classes.

This stigmatized sense of self was enforced by practices of linguistic and literacy shaming – a kind of symbolic violence in which dialectical patterns differing from "standard" (Brazilian) Portuguese were denigrated, and the inability to read and write marked one as like an animal. Bartlett (2005) recounts a story told by a woman whose registering to vote was plagued by fear that she would not be able to reproduce her newly learned signature. The process required either that one sign one's name to the registration forms or that those who were illiterate use a thumbprint as identification. The ink pad used to make the thumbprint was tellingly called the *father of donkeys* (*pai de burros*). It was an artifact that evoked for registrants the demeaning and silencing world of the "educated person" – even though it enabled them to vote.

Maria, a rural immigrant to the provincial capital where Bartlett did the research, described her feelings of vulnerability to everyday symbolic violence:

> I'm ashamed to talk to people who have studied, because I don't speak Portuguese correctly. There are words whose meaning I don't know, and I 'swallow letters' when I'm speaking. . . . Some people pay no attention. But others like to show off and correct you. Wherever there's a group of people, I always avoid speaking. I have a complex, a trauma, from this

thing of people correcting each other. I've heard people do it since I was little and it stayed with me. They do it to undermine others, to show their defects. (Bartlett, 2007)

The practice of literacy or linguistic shaming positioned one as inferior and literally "of no account" in company. Maria, through her participation in literacy training, learned to articulate explicitly this positional form of identity. Overcoming its behavioral and affective consequences was another issue.

Such an achievement depended on the creation of a world in which public spaces and public life could be refigured. This refiguring was in fact the objective of one of the adult literacy projects Bartlett studied. It was based on the work of Paolo Freire. Freirean consciousness-raising involves the redescription/reinscription of the public world in the egalitarian terms of relations among peers. Bartlett's study shows the complications of teaching literacy in the cultural and social context of Brazil. Literacy programs needed both to help their students refigure the public life of the civic world and to enable them, through new artifacts, to refigure themselves in such a world against the symbolic violence of shaming. Although the programs worked for some adult literacy students, they failed for most. Consciousness-raising was not easily effected. Unlike the successful students that Bartlett portrayed, many could not identify with, or find themselves in, the newly figured world in which they would be literate because the training program failed to produce the meaningful artifacts, or semiotic devices, that would have "powered," given force and form to that identification (Bartlett, 2007).

Elizabeth Brumfiel (2005) provides another, though radically different, case in which identity formation and state projects are intertwined through artifactual media. Brumfiel is an archaeologist of Aztecan Mexico who argues that coercion was the principal means of integration in the Aztecan state. That is, populations were subjugated by conquest and maintained as subjects of the Aztecs by military force. The military, the body of warriors, was the indispensable tool of statecraft, and it is the bond that unites this social body that interests Brumfiel. State "ideology" or belief played only a small role in making civic order for the population at large, Brumfiel suggests, but it was essential to the state cadres. Warriors were bound to the rulers and to themselves by their identification within a cosmological system. Only through ritual sacrifice of captives (who were themselves warriors of conquered polities) were the sun, the life that it sustains, and the rulers who apportion life's bounty to the human world, preserved from darkness, chaos, and death. Warriors were implicated in the very preservation of the cosmos, and the everyday performances of military life were filled with commemorations of that central role.

Brumfiel draws upon the notion of the "figured world," especially the place of "artifacts" – material-semiotic mediators – within figured worlds, to show the potency of this identification for warriors. Virtually every item of military life – even the ceramic dishes and bowls recovered through archaeological excavation – depicted and, thus, materialized and kept before their users the cosmic divisions of sun (life, order) and dark (death, chaos), which the warriors served to mediate through conquest. Therefore, each activity performed with these everyday implements "pivoted" warriors into the figured world and into identities of the Aztecan political cosmos. They were, through common usage, continually replicated, drawn to each other as servants of sun and ruler, and given personal value through that identification with the sources of human life. Brumfiel argues that it is the personal and interpersonal force of such identities that powers "ideology" as the bonds of institutional (here military) life. To call it *ideology* would be a misnomer, if we were to conceive it without the material forms that draw meaning out to observable, literally figured, social or cultural worlds. These objectified and, thus, perceptible and meaningful fields of activity are what Vygotsky called "real worlds." They are the landscapes that humans inhabit and that, in turn, inform "people" as social beings.

Identities and Popular Consciousness

Another, interrelated strand of research is characteristic of the interdisciplinary field of cultural studies; it regards the place of identity in what we might call "popular consciousness." Popular consciousness refers to common modes of representing and accounting for the social world, expressed not only in popular media, but in everyday speech. Peter Hervik's research on Danish neoracism (2004) shows how identities of popular consciousness can be retooled and extended to new situations. Hervik considers the ways Danes responded to the influx of Muslim refugees during the 1990s, first from Bosnia and then from Somalia. This was the first substantial immigration of peoples that contemporary Danes considered to be quite different from themselves in heritage and culture, and the Danes struggled to settle their position in society and polity. Hervik found that his interviewees drew on a popular, domestic analogy to interpret their relations with Muslim refugees. They conceived the nation, Denmark, as their home and figured the refugees as guests within the home. This discourse of "guest/host" has precedents in Europe (cf. the term "gastarbeiter") and in the transnational discourse on immigration (which speaks, for example, of "host societies"). Hervik found that "guest/host" was something more than a convenient analogy. The identification – of Muslim refugees as guests, and Danish nationals as hosts – was widespread, not only in all his interviews, but in the reports of popular media. As guests, Muslims were subjected to a domestic etiquette that denied them the standing of member even as it extended them hospitality (aid), which met their needs during the "visit." Guests were expected to show gratitude, to interfere as little as possible with the conduct of "household" (national) business, and to behave in accordance with household rules (Danish customs). And, as a matter of course, guests were expected to leave once the crisis in their homeland(s) was settled and the "purpose" of their visit was fulfilled.

Of course, guests are sometimes taken-in permanently. And a liberal "home" (as Danes have long perceived their nation to be) has room for many ways of life. So it was not clear to Hervik why Muslim refugees were considered to be such problematic guests that could not be assimilated. In order to explain this puzzle, Hervik described a second discourse, the second figured world noted in part of his title: the cultural world of unbridgeable differences. Here popular consciousness intersects with institutional projects. European scholars have noted the continent-wide revival, during the last quarter of the twentieth century, of racialized accounts of human difference in neoconservative discourse. However, the revival did not use the notion of race except in the (dis)guise of culture.[13] Parties and governments of the right, through their organs of publicity, have fostered an understanding of cultural difference – non-European, nonmodern, fundamentalist, and (most common of all) Muslim – as inalterable. In this figuring, culture-become-temperament resists the liberal (rational) tolerance of civil societies and finds the interplay of democratic multiculturalism anathematic. In the public sphere of Denmark, this cultural world of unbridgeable difference dovetails with the domestic world of guest/host.

In this case, Danish popular sentiment is that people (refugees) raised to radically *other* manners of life cannot be adopted or naturalized. These people do not recognize or respect the rights and lifeways of others. They remain religiously apart from the consensus of a liberal home. They, in effect, remain guests, and disliked ones at that, by their own choice. Therefore, as the cultural logic runs, any claim they make to civil and political rights is presumptuous misbehavior that arrogates a position

---

[13] Of course, the fusion of people and culture is a long-standing inheritance of nineteenth-century continental romanticism, whether in Germany, England, or Denmark. See, for example, Steiner, 1973.

no guest should have. Instead of a history of cultural politics that gives rise to the current, ethnicized civil and political relations, neoconservatism finds only the exclusionary ground of unbridgeable differences. The power of this figured world in popular discourse perpetuates the identification of refugees as (misbehaving and arrogant) guests and of Danes as (naïve, foolish, and wronged) hosts. It guarantees an enduring struggle based on identities that only reproduce their opposition. (For other relevant articles in this line of research, see Fields, 1995.)

Identities, Social Movements, and Other Social Transformations

Identities, the cultural worlds that ground these senses of self, and the discursive and practical activity of positioning that realize them, pervade the social contests of politics and social change. This line of research brings processes of identification onto the center stage of social transformation. Terre Satterfield's rich ethnographic study (2002) shows clearly how the controversy over logging in the forests of Oregon during the 1980s and 1990s was mediated through the articulation and deployment of identities. Here, senses of self not only served as a touchstone for action (what would a logger or an environmentalist do?). They also united actors into solidarity (grassroots) groups that are as much imagined as bound by interchange. Participants in this struggle also located *selves* as loggers and environmentalists within histories and futures that projected activity and self into practical continuity and regenerated their durable value. Satterfield's work and the various studies collected in Holland and Lave (2001) also continue a theme raised by Mead as early as his article, "The Social Self" (1913) – the interplay of social change and the sense of self. This theme has become an important part of contemporary social theories of political change, especially theories associated with so-called new social movements that insist on the profoundly cultural character of political action.

There is too much in Satterfield's work to summarize here. For purposes of this article, we will simply point out two aspects of her argument that are important for understanding identity formation. First, Satterfield's depiction of the struggle of "environmentalists" and "loggers" over the proper relationship of humans to forest lands explores the inevitably dialogic quality of the self that both Vygotsky and Mead posit. Loggers' actions – mental, verbal, and practical – were posed with environmentalists in mind and responded to the actions of environmentalists that put "loggers" in question. Satterfield's transcripts and observations show, over and over, the active tie, imagined as the active voice, which directs one side to the other in speech and action. For either side to gain political "capital," both in the state and in relation to federal authority, they had to figure themselves as representatives of "environmental" values. Loggers realized that they must somehow claim to provide a vision, a figured world of human interaction with the natural world, that placed (identified) them in a positive light and laid claim to environmental value through their stewardship of forests and forest inhabitants. Even "environmentalists," who began with a closer public identification with widespread environmental value, had to articulate a framework that concretely figured them, through their actions, as the promoters of environmental preservation. Both groups posed a vision that valued their ways of life and devalued their opponents', but these were two divergent paths over the same territory. The contentious dialogue was kept alive and identifiable by the fact that neither loggers nor environmentalists could divorce themselves from the activities in which they were opposed, or resolve the divergent visions through which they construed these fields.

Satterfield's study exemplifies a second point. Contention and conflict are characteristic of contemporary notions of culture. Social movements construct new figured worlds thereby giving meaning and value to action and actors, as well as recruiting converts, in the interest of political objectives broadly conceived. Identities are not byproducts of social change; identities are the means by which change acquires agents and becomes effective.[14] Cultural worlds do not "diffuse"; instead culture works by transforming who we are. Vygotsky's developmental social psychology provides, in semiotic devices, the clearest model for how this transformation comes about.

Meadian identities also offer a means to conceptualize seemingly rapid, radical shifts from which social movements and their adherents emerge. Marianne Gullestad (2003) has analyzed processes of identification among Muslims in Europe in a suggestive article. She posits that Muslims in European societies are cast into cultural worlds so contradictory that they are likely to develop multiple selves, some of which she calls "sleeper" identities. By and large, these first and second generation immigrants have left their native societies behind, literally and figuratively. Either they have chosen the "modernism" of European societies, adopting the liberal ethos and politics of the E.U., or, by taking advantage of economic opportunity, they have been assimilated to the

---

[14] Cf. Mead (1913), which clearly conceived social change in terms of transformations of self, but only as self is always figured in Mead – in relation to social objectifications.

cultural politics of "Europeanism." That is, they have been cast, as Peter Hervik (above) clearly shows for Denmark, into the role of perpetual guest among host societies. As guests, Muslims are subject to a domestic etiquette that denies them the standing of member and invalidates their claims to civil and political rights even as it sanitizes [by transfiguring] the discrimination practiced upon them. This disguised racism is founded on their "cultural identity": differences in linguistic, familial, and religious heritage are somehow regarded as inalterable by European "hosts." Yet, that is not the experience of European Muslims. They know that these features change, that they do not live as they were "accustomed" in the societies they left, and as they were supposed to live by their European consociates. They are left in a kind of limbo, a political–cultural state of misidentification. They are denied standing in both their "native" and "host" societies.

Gullestad (2003) argues that it is in this displaced condition that "radical Islam" has appeal for some European Muslims. The continual turning back to "tradition" that European reaction forces on them forges an hypostasized and exaggerated form of practice: a fantasy Islam that is necessarily the antithesis of "the West," as no actually existing Islamic practice is. This fantasy Islam is the counterpart of the simplified cultural world assigned them by European prejudice. Yet, a personal identification with "radical Islam" is not ordinarily acknowledged to others. Drawing on the writings of Nazneen Khan, a Norwegian Muslim of Afghan heritage, Gullestad defines this as a "sleeper" identitiy – one that is created within one's intimate repertory as sympathy, presentiment or possibility, and as an unformed sense of self. Only the networks of activists provide the affirmation and the "project-world" that shapes and empowers this identification with the force that organizes action.

Kahn, in her writings, conveys how sleeper identities emerge. Once Mohammed Atta and his cohorts exist and become publicized, Khan realizes that she knows him intimately. He sleeps within her, just as he once slept within the city planning student who was Atta before Al Quaeda. Atta has become an emblem, a semiotic device, through which Khan recognizes the part of her self which disowns "the West" that disdains her. As Mead insists, we know ourselves – we identify ourselves – with others, and only with figures of otherness. Yet, the preconditions for that self-awareness, the unorganized sentiments, and the raw materials of its production, exist beforehand as a social history of positioning. (Interestingly, Gullestad also attributes to the "hosts," to the equally fantastic European counterpart, a sleeper identity – the presentiment of a new racism that she fears may be realized in the Europe produced by global neoliberalism.)

Are Identities Universal?

A final line of research concerns the debate over the universality of identity. It is important to stress that this line addresses Eriksonian conceptualizations of identity *not* Meadian ones. The occasional anthropologist asks us why we bother to pursue studies of identity when post-structuralist and postmodernist assaults have successfully debunked the modernist, Western assumptions that undergird the concept. These critics are referring to the normative aspects of an Eriksonian approach that construe stability, consistency, and coherence of identity across contexts as the standard for psychological health. These interlocutors fail to realize that Meadian approaches to identity make no such normative claims. Identities, in the Meadian framework, are not only multiple and open, there is also no expectation that they will be well-integrated. Nor are these critics aware that the emerging sociocultural perspective on Eriksonian identities, presented by Penuel and Wertsch (1995), Tappan (1999, 2000), and others, is moving away from the prescription of consistency and stability. Examination of developments in the dialogue about Eriksonian identities is useful in another respect: it suggests a conceptual bridge between Meadian notions of identity and the emerging sociocultural understanding of Eriksonian ones.

Over the past 30 years, poststructuralist and postmodernist scholars have recast anthropology's core concept of culture and refigured the significance of discourses and practices of the self. Notions of coherent, stable cultures equally embraced by all, regardless of social position, have been replaced by attention to plural cultural imaginaries and institutions shaped by relations of power that favor some social positions over others. Research has pursued the ways that gender, class, race, and other social divisions refract day-to-day experiences and the selves that take shape within them. Heterogeneity, power, and struggle have gained visibility as the formative context of cultural resources and representations.[15] To the extent that Eriksonian identity had been adopted by anthropology to conceptualize collective (and therefore the individual's[16] stances on morality, social worth, and belonging, it, too, underwent a shift. "Self" and "identity" (and other aspects of subjectivity) were deconstructed alongside ideas of homogeneous "culture," "community," and "tradition/history" in poststructuralist and postmodern critiques. "Identity" (coherent, consistent, integral identity) became yet

---

[15] See reviews in Holland et al. (1998) and Holland and Lave (2001).
[16] Van Meijl and Driessen (2003) provide an overview of the long elision of self and person in anthropology.

another "master narrative" to be discarded. Rather than finding the integration of difference (which modernist "identity" achieved) into self-persistence, postmodernists saw only the pastiche of multiple selves, multiply identified with multicultural others (e.g., Clifford, 1988; van Meijl & Driessen, 2003; Sökefeld, 1999).

In response to these critiques, many of the articles reviewed in this section, both empirical and theoretical, explicitly recognize the existence of multiple, contradictory contexts of identity performance and explicitly rejected expectation of a fixed and coherent Eriksonian identity. Still, they expect the individual to be at work maintaining some level of integration of self across multiple contexts, or, at least, to be distressed by their contradictory demands (e.g., Marx 2002; van Meijl & Driessen, 2003; Lowe, 2002).

Nicole Marx (2002) provides an example. She draws on studies on second language acquisition and adopts the device of "inflection" – accent – as a marker or index of the psychosocial process of "self-translation" that characterizes the second language learner's Eriksonian identity. Her own autobiography as an immigrant to Germany who later returned to her native Canada serves as her case. Marx describes six stages through which she shifted identities (and levels of membership) from first language/first culture (L1/C1), to second language/second culture (L2/C2), and then back. Although her account is valuable, we will not detail these stages. What is interesting for our argument is the kind of "postmodern" reading of Eriksonian identity that Marx exemplifies. She breaks up the integrity of identity as Erikson conceived it by accepting identity's relation to different communities and different frames of self-activity. "Because a person may affiliate himself with more than one culture or language, it is possible to hold multiple identities, and these dynamic identities must in some way be reconciled within one unified self in order to maintain this self across boundaries" (2002, p. 266). If the first part of this quote marks her (poststructuralist) departure from Erikson, the second part – the "problem" of multimembership, as she calls it – points to her continuity with Erikson. Marx and others like her move the integrity of the social person from identity to self, but the impetus of that integrity is inherent and unavoidable, or at least recurrent. The unified self, inherently it seems, must be maintained across boundaries. The relation of person–society must be stabilized.

Van Meijl and Driessen (2003), in their introduction to a set of articles on multiple identities, draw on Kathy Ewing's (1990) well-known argument that peoples' *actions* do not demonstrate continuity of the self across contexts, but that "wholeness" is a comforting "fable" that people tell themselves. Van Meijl and Driessen argue that the play of multiple identifications (multiple selves) is best understood as managed dialogically and in awareness that relations of power continue to forge authoritative forms of subjectivity, which give significance to the illusion of continuity. Selves are themselves composites of various "I/me's" drawn against various sets of "others," and all related practically – in activity, but still there is a sense of continuity that people find important. Elsewhere, van Meijl (n.d.), for example, describes the distress that Maori youth feel when confronted with alternative representations of Maoriness that clash with their own.

Other researchers attend to the effects of contradictory expectations about ways of acting and comporting oneself. Lowe's (2003) research, for example, examines the relationship between identity formation and psychosocial stress (leading to destructive behaviors) among adolescents and young adults on Chuuk Island in the Federated States of Micronesia. Lowe is interested in how stress is socially produced as these young people try to negotiate multiple cultural worlds. Conflicts arise because the cultural worlds of young people on Chuuk are valued differently in wider society (where the family world is more valued than the peer group world), and because behaviors and spaces important in the creation of one cultural world may damage a youth's place in another. These conflicts have increased over the past few decades since Western influences (e.g., economics and schooling) have become more prevalent, and young people are spending more time away from their families. For Lowe, identity construction is restitutive, "the ongoing project of forming an emotionally engaging self-concept and a valued social position both within and across the multiple settings of everyday activity." The process is impelled by the "negative emotions," and the stress that Chuuk youth feel as they struggle to negotiate multiple identities that often come into conflict with one another.

These different studies recognize that people often face conflicting social demands and opportunities within and across social contexts, but they maintain Eriksonian concerns by presuming the stress of multiple identification – individuals are troubled by "self-discrepancies" between contexts. One of us (Holland, 2003) has suggested, in the analysis of a case, that contradictions experienced as stressful need not be inherently stressful. Contradictions may pose problems in the minds of some actors, but dilemmas of multiple affiliation and identification become significant when they are *socially* problematic.[17]

---

[17] Also relevant to the debate are studies of ethnosocial psychologies (e.g., Hermann, 2003) that find no problem with multiple cultural identities.

Eriksonian approaches posit the universal importance of such questions as: Where, with whom, do I belong? Am I (are we) good? What is my (group's) place in society? Do I (do we) deserve respect? Am I acceptable as a person? Am I true to myself, whatever the situation? The research cited in this section suggests that these *are* questions that individuals often become embroiled in answering. And the answers people come up with affect their subsequent actions and understanding of the world around them. But, research is equivocal about the source of these questions: Do they come (unbidden) from within or from questions and challenges lodged by dialogic partners? Are they psychogenetic or sociogenetic or both?

Eriksonian perspectives give analytic primacy to the psychological origins and psychodynamic significance of identity formation, Meadian approaches, to the sociocultural origins, and social psychological consequences. In Eriksonian conceptualizations, the individual strives to resolve questions that define one: affiliation and allegiance to a culturally identifiable group, claims to social worth, ideological commitments, and moral stance. In Meadian frameworks, one makes and remakes one's selves in relation to figures in society, through processes of active internalization described originally by Baldwin. One may be sensitive to charges that one is not a "real American," for example, or to questions about the morality of the actions of American officials overseas, but one's identities are centered around historically contingent collective imaginaries and actual examples of social types, rather than around sets of answers to general questions about morality, belonging, and social worth. Or, in another example, a person who has participated in a community of environmental practice and developed a sense of herself as an environmentalist in that community disdains owning a Sport Utility Vehicle, not because she has developed an Eriksonian moral identity whose generic principles dispose against excessive gasoline consumption, but because SUVs and SUV ownership have acquired distinctly negative values in the world of environmental action in which she has formed a self. In yet another example, as part of the struggle over the old-growth forests of Oregon, loggers were portrayed by environmentalists as acting with inappropriate anger (Satterfield, 2002). In the context and in Eriksonian terms, the loggers authored an emotional identity, but the impetus for the identity and for its consistency and stability clearly arose *in the contingencies of the struggle*. To the extent that (Eriksonian) questions of identity are socially posed, identifications are brought into conflict historically, through activities, and not universally by the nature of human psychology. Moreover, in a Meadian framework, consistency, coherence, and stability in and among one's multiple identities are not attributed the significance they are in the Eriksonian approach. If such characteristics are found they are attributed to *social* demands and *social* stability first, and only secondarily to any drive of individuals to achieve a consistent identity.

SUMMARY AND CONCLUSIONS

In this chapter, we have furthered an integrated sociocultural perspective on identity formation by reviewing developments that postdate Penuel and Wertsch's (1995) assessment. A striking aspect of the newer literature is its incorporation of what we refer to as "Meadian" identities. We use the term to distinguish them from Eriksonian approaches to identity. In the Meadian scenario, identities are culturally imagined and socially recognized types – social and cultural products – that are actively internalized as self-meanings (treating one's own behavior reflexively as symbolic) and serve as motivation for action. People identify themselves with (and against) these socially constructed types in the various domains of their everyday lives.

Vygotskian concepts are helpful in formulating the development of Eriksonian identities, but they are even more useful in formulating that of Meadian identities. The latter are social and cultural products that people transact in practice and at some point begin to direct to themselves. Vygotskian developmental concepts help us to understand how people come to be able to organize themselves in the name of an identity. Communities of practice identify, by correlating the usage of a variety of cultural artifacts or *emblems*, sets of characters in interaction that participants learn as the organizational means for their own activity. They figure (and prefigure) their actions as "nondrinking alcoholics," "global justice activists," "progressive faculty members," "good mothers," or "rigorous scientists." That is, they develop a higher order psychological function – an identity – which personalizes a set of collectively developed discourses about a type and cultivates, in interaction with others, a set of embodied practices that signify the person. They creatively direct the sets of collective meanings to their selves. Through this orchestration, they come to be able to organize and narrate themselves in practice in the name of an identity, and thus achieve a modest form of agency.

The concepts Mead and Vygotsky share – active internalization (self-authoring), dialogic selves (self–other dialogues), and the semiotics of behavior, coupled with Vygotsky's notions of semiotic mediation, higher psychological functions, and agency, constitute a powerful sociogenetic vision of how individuals come to be inhabited by, and yet are able to co-construct, the social and cultural worlds in which they exist. At times, we take the observable behavior of others as models – acts emblematic of roles and positions of activity systems – for our own behavior. Yet, we engage with the models *as belonging to others*. By relating ourselves to, joining in dialogue with, or even opposing the models, we produce personalized variants that are purposefully not the same as what we observed. We develop identities in the manner of jazz musicians rather than player pianos (cf. Eisenhart [1995] for a slightly different metaphorization of this point). People have to create selves that (in the metaphor of residence) inhabit the (social) structures and spaces (cultural imaginaries) that collectivities create, but they produce selves that inhabit these structures and imaginaries in creative, variant, and often oppositional, ways. Mead's "I," in fact, generates unexpected behavior. And, in the circuits of emerging communities of practice, innovation may play out and regularize the semiotic means for new identities and activities that lie beyond existing structures of power.

Vygotsky's notions of development and agency empower Mead's formulation of the relationship between self and society. They help us appreciate not only the ways in which identities mediate individual behavior and interpretation, but the ways in which they inform the development of social movements and mediate popular responses to state projects, institutional projects, and to changing social and economic conditions. The research reviewed in the chapter explores various complications of identity formation and expands our ideas of how identities are of key importance in social change. Vygotsky's stamp on this growing body of research is not always made explicit, but it is our conviction that his work is a crucial component of its foundations.

5   Vygotsky on Thinking and Speaking

Vygotsky's most popular book in the English-speaking world, *Thought and Language*, was first published in English in 1962. (It was originally published in Russian in 1934.) When retitled *Thinking and Speech* in 1987, it captured a more active notion of these interrelated processes. They are seen as activities rather than entities and the book explores the developmentally changing relationship between intellectual and verbal processes. Vygotsky viewed speaking and thinking as dynamically related and approached their connection as

> The complex movement from the first vague emergence of the thought to its completion in a verbal formulation.... Thought is not expressed but completed in the word.... Any thought has movement. It unfolds.... This flow of thought is realized as an internal movement through several planes. As a transition from thought to word and from word to thought.   (Vygotsky, 1987, pp. 249–250)

Thinking and Speech presents important distinctions between communicative language and language used for conceptual representation. By addressing such broad themes, Vygotsky's work was grounded in philosophical, psychological, and linguistic traditions that have influenced Western students of language. Within these disciplines, the relationship between thinking and speech was forged, and it is still of great concern to contemporary thinkers. Part of what is so interesting about revisiting this relationship is that it emerges repeatedly across disciplines and informs every aspect of the human sciences.

By focusing on this relationship, Vygotsky chose to revisit controversial philosophical ideas that have been debated since the beginnings of Western thought. For instance, Aristotle suggested that we think and remember through the use of images. Such a stance is shared by the psychologist Rudolph Arnheim who maintains that the dynamics of thought are visual (Arnheim, 1971). In contrast, the philosopher Hannah

Arendt has elegantly expressed her belief that we think in words, "The sheer naming of things, the creation of words, is the human way of appropriating, and as it were, disalienating the world into which, after all, each of us is born as a newcomer and a stranger" (Arendt, 1977, p. 100).

Vygotsky rejected the Cartesian dichotomy between thought and language. He saw the two processes as developmentally woven together. His analysis focused on the need to simplify and generalize experience before it can be fully expressed in words and symbols. He considers word meaning as the unit that expresses both thinking and speaking.

> Word meaning is a unity of both processes (i.e., both thinking and speech) which cannot be further decomposed... the word without meaning is not a word but an empty sound. Meaning is a necessary, constituting feature of the word itself.... It is the word viewed from the inside. In psychological terms, however, word meaning is nothing other than a generalization, that is a concept... Thus, word meaning is also a phenomenon of thinking... it is a unity of word and thought.   (Vygotsky, 1987, p. 244)

Vygotsky's own process began with studying the work of his contemporaries (which he frequently translated into Russian) and while working through their ideas he generated and refined his theoretical approach. In *Thinking and Speech*, he developed his ideas by critically examining Kohler's research on problem solving and communicative expressions; Jean Piaget's developmental theory of cognition; and William Stern's studies on speech development in children. Vygotsky suggested that before thinking and speaking are unified in word meaning, children learn about their world by nonverbal exploration to which he referred to as the prelinguistic stage. During the first two years of life, children also engage in conveying their feelings through crying, laughing, social contact, and response. He referred to this as the preintellectual stage of speech development. And then, he wrote, "At a certain point, the two lines cross: thinking becomes verbal and speech intellectual" (Vygotsky, 1987, p. 112). The internalization of communicative interaction, which becomes possible once children use language to express their needs, to describe their world, and to plan their actions with others, leads to the transformation of communicative language into inner speech and verbal thinking. But as he further suggests, "the structure of speech is not a simple mirror image of the structure of thought. It cannot, therefore, be placed on thought like clothes on a rack. Speech doesn't merely serve as the expression of developed thought. Thought is restructured as it is transformed into speech. It is not expressed but completed in the word" (Vygotsky, 1987, p. 251).

In *Thinking and Speech*, Vygotsky examines concept development as a long process that starts with *heaps* (i.e., the way in which objects are thought by the child to belong together), through *complexes* where the connection is functional, for example, saucers and spoons and progresses to *conceptual thinking* that requires the full analysis of generalized understanding. The mastery of concepts, such as "justice," is a slow process that is scaffolded by teaching as well as by children's social activities in their daily lives. The meaning of a fully developed concept involves cultural and intergenerational transmission, verbal thinking, and practical application.

Vygotsky traces the development of conceptual thinking and relates it to the internalization of language. By the time children enter school, they use language not only for communicative purposes, but also for thinking and planning. This function first appears overtly in children's use of language for the self. Such "private speech" contributes to the structuring and preparation of young learners' activities. Alex Kozulin describes further developments in this process in his book *Vygotsky's Psychology*, "Next comes the realization of thought in the form of verbal meanings which take place in inner speech" (Kouzulin, 1990, p. 187).

In this chapter, I will first present Vygotsky's notions of private and inner speech to be followed by a discussion of linguistic relativity and the cross-linguistic and developmental comparisons of "thinking and speaking." I will end the chapter with a short analysis of metaphors.

PRIVATE AND INNER SPEECH

In his examination of the multiple connections of thinking and speaking, Vygotsky developed his ideas by closely examining the psychological writings of his contemporaries. Although the phenomenon of "self-talk" or egocentric speech was identified by Piaget, it was in Vygotsky's work that its role in planning and problem solving emerged as vital. "Private speech" is particularly powerful when children confront challenging tasks. When a child relies on audible speech while struggling with hard problems, the child develops a form of language that is somewhat different from speech addressed communicatively to others. "Egocentric speech . . . is speech on its way inward, intimately tied up with the ordering of the child's behavior, already partly incomprehensible to others, yet still overt in form . . . " (Vygotsky, 1986, p. 86).

Around the age of seven, audible speech moves inward to become the basis of inner speech, a condensed rapid form of language in which the speaker and the listener are the same person. At this inner level,

Vygotsky wrote that, "meaning is a dynamic, fluid, complex whole, which has several zones of unequal stability" (Vygotsky, 1986, p. 245).

One of the ways we know that inner speech differs from communicative language is that it takes many words and several minutes to elaborate on a single thought. In a well-known metaphor, Vygotsky suggests that, "a thought may be compared to a cloud shedding a shower of words...Precisely because a thought does not have its automatic counterpart in words, the transition to thought from word leads through meaning" (Vygotsky, 1986, p. 251).

There are many more studies on private speech, learning, and problem solving than there are on the hidden processes of inner speech. A number of investigators have established that the more complex the task, the greater the usefulness of private speech (Berk, 1992; Ramirez, 1992; John-Steiner, 1992). As Vygotsky and Luria (1994) state:

> The more complex the action demanded by the situation and the less direct its solution, the greater the importance played by speech in the operation as a whole. Sometimes speech becomes of such vital importance that without it the child proves to be positively unable to accomplish the given task.   (Vygotsky & Luria, 1994, p. 109)

Some of the early studies of private speech found no relationship between the amount of language produced and the child's proficiency in solving the task. It is when children were studied over time that the associations between the amount of private speech and the accuracy of solutions became clear. Easy tasks require very little language, as routine solutions are already available to the child. But simple correlations of task difficulty and the use of private speech do not effectively test Vygotsky's hypothesis; it is when the method of study is aimed at observing improvements in memory, attention, and strategic thinking that this relationship is successfully demonstrated.

Laura Berk studied schoolchildren from the first grade through the third grade:

> Every child we observed talked to himself or herself on average 60% of the time...as in previous studies, many children whose remarks described or otherwise commented on their activity received lower scores on homework and achievement tests taken that same [first] year. Yet private speech that was typical for a particular age predicted gains in math achievement over time. Specifically, first graders who made many self-guiding comments out loud or quietly did better at second grade math.
> (Berk, 1994, p. 81)

Azmitia addressed a related question in her study of expertise in private speech in which she compared two groups of children who were copying a Lego model. She worked with them for four sessions, where participants, for the first three sessions, were assigned to complete the task alone, with other experts, or with other novices. Following these sessions, children received an individual posttest in which they, once more, copied the pretest model.

> The differences between experts' and novices' use of private speech suggest that children must have sufficient understanding of a problem before they use private speech to regulate their problem solving behavior.... Novices may acquire problem solving skills by observing competent peers and being the recipient of explanations and guidance; in turn this increase in competence may allow them to talk themselves through the problem, i.e. to use private speech to regulate their behavior.
>
> (Azmitia, 1992, p. 112)

For the researcher, the recording of spontaneous self-directed speech is useful as it provides "a direct window into the child's thought processes as they occur without reliance on retrospective accounts" (Matuga, 2004, p. 270). In a recent study of children's drawings and private speech, Matuga discovered that first- through fifth-grade schoolchildren used more private speech when engaged in drawing make-believe objects than realistic ones. This increase can be related to the greater challenge implicit in make-believe drawings, which "require more cognitive resources for planning, monitoring, and adjusting" (Matuga, 2004, p. 269). Private speech provides focus for these more challenging tasks as the children generate more novel solutions.

Although most of the studies of private speech have been conducted with children, there is another area in which its usefulness has been established in the acquisition of a second language. Most of these studies have been conducted with adult learners (Lantolf, 1994).

One of Lantolf's collaborators, McCafferty (1994), found that English as a Second Language (ESL) students engaged in a picture-narration task relied on self-regulatory private speech. Participants used labeling, counting, self-directed questions, and self-corrections to guide their work. He noted that these verbalizations are produced in greater number by students categorized as "low intermediates" compared to "advanced" subjects acquiring a second language. McCafferty suggests that learners experiencing greater difficulty in communicating in a second language produce more self-regulatory speech than advanced learners, supporting Vygotsky's theoretical framework.

In an interesting study combining questionnaires with interviews focusing on inner speech, de Guerrero worked with a large sample of second-language learners. She identified a group of students who relied on internal rehearsal of their target language to a great extent and contrasted those with students who almost never, or only sometimes, used covert rehearsal as a learning method. Among the practices that the high rehearsers followed was repeating new words to acquire them, as well as attempting to match word pronunciation to that of native speakers. They also attempted to covertly construct sentences as part of their attempt to master a new language. Author de Guerrero suggests that inner speech is used as an aid to memory, both to store and retrieve verbal data; inner speech is also seen as a tool for self-teaching, for correcting errors, to clarify thought, and to create, organize, and experiment with the forms of the target language. In addition, some participants imagine conversations with others and use inner speech to talk to themselves (Lantolf, 1994, pp. 90–91). In this study, an increase in proficiency level correlated with the frequency of inner speech. Exploring further, the researcher found, in the interviews with the participants who were students in the ESL courses, that the students' inner speech lexicon was highly related to the thematic context and that it was drawn from dictionaries, books, and other people. Their internal activity was not limited to the target language. Sometimes the students mixed Spanish and English, and they also relied on images while trying to translate visual stimuli into words. Lantolf found that, "Without doubt, inner speech emerged from the study as a necessary medium for verbal thought in L2" (Lantolf, 1994, p, 101).

The concept of inner speech formulated by Vygotsky has been of theoretical interest to many researchers, but it is a topic about which it is difficult to gather data that is direct rather than self-reported. There are exceptions, however, when people plan a lecture, they frequently make a list of the topics they wish to cover. These brief planning notes reveal the same abbreviation of thinking about which Vygotsky wrote. Another context in which semantic shorthand (a form of inner speech) can be encountered is in the study of writers' diaries and journals. Passages in which ideas are jotted down in an abbreviated manner correspond to Vygotsky's characterization of inner speech. "Inner speech is to a large extent thinking in pure meanings. It is a dynamic, shifting unstable thing" (Vygotsky, 1989, p. 249). Virginia Woolf's diary provides interesting illustrations of this process; one of which occurs as she was planning the next chapter of her biography of Robert Fry.

> Give the pre-war atmosphere. Ott. Duncan. France Letter to Bridges about beauty and sensuality. His exactingness. Logic.   (Woolf, 1953, p. 292)

In order to understand these jottings, the reader of this passage needs to examine the finished biography to see how Woolf expands on her rapid "inner speech-writing." This use of a telegraphic style captures the speed with which clusters of thoughts emerge. "The pressure the writer feels when relying upon such jottings of the mind may, in the case of an accomplished craftsperson, arise from a sense of a newly realized pattern of order, a pattern allowing more complete realization of his or her artistic endeavor. In such cases of intuitively comprehended pattern, the sense of its significance is powerful" (John-Steiner, 1992, p. 292). It is from this inner speech, or mental shorthand, that written expression is constructed.

It is interesting to note that inner speech writing also occurs in some of Vygotsky's plans for his own presentations. In a chapter on the "Problem of Consciousness," many condensed ideas are presented. This material was found in A. N. Leontiev's private archives, and, therefore, it is difficult to differentiate which are Vygotsky's own condensed jottings and which are Leontiev's notes on the lectures. An example from this chapter is, for instance, "The development of meaning = the development of generalization" (Vygotsky, 1997, p. 136). This idea is more fully developed in the text of *Thinking and Speech*, and this parallels Woolf's inner speech journal entries that are later expanded in her fully crafted writing. The movement between inner and outer meaning represents both self-development and external communication.

Further elaborating on these ideas, Vygotsky proposed that written speech is a separate linguistic function that requires a high level of abstraction. One of the problems for children when acquiring literacy is that they need to address an absent or imaginary person, and they do not always know why they should be *writing* when interactional speech is so much more immediate and gratifying. In addition, Vygotsky explains some of the cognitive challenges that the complexity of writing presents: "Written speech is deployed to its fullest extent, more complete than oral speech. Inner speech is almost entirely predicative because the situation, the thinker always knows the subject of thought. Written speech, on the contrary, must explain the situation fully in order to be intelligible. The change from maximally compact inner speech to maximally detailed written speech requires what might be called deliberate semantics – deliberate structuring of the web of meaning" (Vygotsky, 1986, p. 182).

Educator James Moffett (1981) uses this concept as the basis for his writing assignments as he sees, "[T]he whole shift from inner speech to outer speech...occurs continually as people verbalize their experience for others. [Writing assignments are] designed to show students how to tap off and verbalize what is going on at any moment in their sensations, memories, thoughts, and feelings.... Both talking and writing may be usefully regarded as a revision of inner speech" (Moffett, 1981, p. 29).

The relationship between language and thought has been of great interest to scholars and researchers throughout the centuries. Vygotsky's strong emphasis on the centrality of inner speech in thought is paralleled by some influential linguists such as Benjamin Whorf and Edward Sapir. They have written extensively about the reciprocal relationship between language and thought. I now turn to an examination of the Whorfian hypothesis and its connections to the cultural historical thinking of Vygotsky.

LINGUISTIC RELATIVITY

In the first half of the twentieth century, the American anthropologist Edward Sapir wrote:

> Language is not merely a more or less systematic inventory of the various items of experience which seem relevant to the individual, as is so often naively assumed, but is also a self-contained, creative symbolic organization, which not only refers to experience largely acquired without its help, but actually defines experience for us by reason of its formal completeness and because of our unconscious projection of its implicit expectations into the field of experience.   (Sapir, 1931, p. 578)

In a similar vein Benjamin Lee Whorf, who was deeply influenced by Sapir, wrote extensively about "the linguistics of thinking," emphasizing the rapport between words, which contributes to "linguistic patterning operations" that effectively structures thinking (1964).

These anthropological linguists examined the connection between thinking and speech by using comparative methods. As the interest in the study of indigenous languages increased, field anthropologists continued to be motivated by questions surrounding how language influences thinking. For instance Harry Hoijer, in his study of Navaho verbs explains how "Navaho emphasizes movement and specifies the nature, direction, and status of such movement in considerable detail... these words permeate the Navaho lexicon" (Hoijer, 1950/1964).

Following in Hoijer's tradition, the anthropologist Gary Witherspoon further documented the crucial role of motion in Navajo[1] language and culture. He identifies verbal prefixes which differentiate between successive and repetitive actions. He also views as important the patterns viewed in Navajo rugs where movement and activity are expressed through diagonal and zigzag lines [lightning] and diamond shapes (Witherspoon, 1997).

---

[1] Witherspoon uses "j" in his spelling of the proper noun "Navajo," which reflects more modern scholarship and the preference of the Navajo Nation.

Whorf's linguistic relativity hypothesis is still a source of study and debate. According to George Lakoff, Whorf's concern was to examine "the heart of our conceptual systems: space, time, causation, event structure, aspect, evidentiality, fundamental classification of objects, and so on" (Lakoff, 1999, p. 71).

In a comprehensive examination of the linguistic relativity hypothesis, John Lucy clearly summarizes some of the main themes in Whorf's thought.

> First Whorf argued...that a language can unite demonstrably different aspects of reality by giving them similar linguistic treatment. The importance of such linguistic classifications is that the meanings of elements that are grouped together influence each other, that is, they are analogically interpreted as the same....Second, Whorf argued that such linguistic analogies are used in thought as guides in the interpretation of and behavioral response to experienced reality.   (Lucy, 1992, p. 45)

Whorf maintained that thought is shaped or influenced by the grammar of a particular language providing salience to some features of that which is observed. However, some linguists and psychologists strongly oppose Whorf's ideas; for instance, Steven Pinker (1995) advocates that language and thought are entirely independent from one another. His position is in stark contrast to Vygotsky's stance of the developmental interconnection of thought and language. In Pinker's view, there is a "language of thought" which he refers to as "mentalese"; it is preprogrammed and continues to exist independently of the structures and lexicons of any particular language. Consequently, he challenges the Whorfian hypothesis, and refers to experimental support as "banal and weak" and the hypothesis itself as a "conventional absurdity."

But researchers who view language and thought as interdependent have collected important cross-linguistic data that supports Whorf's hypothesis. In Lucy's research among the Yucatec Maya (1996), he specified differences in the way their language and English encode objects. They differ in the way in which they signal plurals: In English, number marking is obligatory for both animate and inanimate objects, but in Yucatec, number marking is less frequent. In Yucatec as well as in other indigenous languages, the shape or properties of the object are reflected in the classifier used. As opposed to the English "one candle," Lucy uses the object "candle" as an example that in Yucatec refers to "long thin wax." These two groups of speakers varied in their performance in memory and classification experiments reflecting these grammatical differences.

Recent comparative studies conducted by the MIT linguist, Lera Boroditsky, further reformulated the Whorfian hypothesis. Her studies support the importance of language categories in the analysis and interpretation of nonverbal experiences. Boroditsky compares English and Mandarin speakers and how they describe time concepts. In Mandarin, speakers represent time vertically, whereas in English speakers represent time horizontally (Boroditsky, 2001). She found that when stimulus materials were represented horizontally and vertically, English speakers answered time questions faster after exposure to horizontal primes rather than after vertical primes. The reverse held true for Mandarin speakers. She suggests that language is most powerful in influencing thought for those abstracts domains that are not fully determined by sensory experience, such as time. In another experiment, English speakers more rapidly verified that March comes earlier than April after having seen a horizontal array of objects, and again, for Mandarin speakers, the vertical array of objects was more helpful in visualizing the sequence of months. In addition, when she tested English-Mandarin bilinguals, she found that those who acquired English at a younger age showed less vertical bias than those who acquired English later in life. When discussing these experiments while teaching, I moved my hand horizontally when referring to time, much to the amusement of my students.

In a subsequent study, when Boroditsky collected adjectives by Spanish and German speakers for objects that had opposite genders in their native languages, for instance, the word "key," which is masculine in German and feminine in Spanish, she found, "German speakers described keys as hard, heavy, jagged, metal, while Spanish speakers said they were golden, intricate, and lovely" (Boroditsky et al., 2003, p. 70).

Interestingly, Vygotsky was aware of the possible implications of grammatical gender because he had worked with Russian translations of many psychological works from French, German, and English languages. In his analysis of the external and the semantic aspects of speech, he refers to two different translations of Heine's poem, "The Fir and the Palm":

> In German, "fir" is masculine in gender. Thus, in German, the poem symbolizes love for women. To preserve the sense of the German text, Tiutchev substituted a cedar for the fir, since in Russian "cedar" is masculine. In contrast, by translating the poem literally, Lermontov lost this sense. As a consequence, his translation gives the poem a fundamentally different sense, one that is more abstract and generalized. Thus, a change in a single, seemingly insignificant, grammatical detail can lead to a change in the whole meaningful aspect of speech.
>
> (Vygotsky, 1987, p. 253)

In a recent study of linguistic gender in the Chinese language (Tong, Chiu, & Fu, 2001), participants were asked to rate nonsense Chinese characters on semantic differential scales including activity which ranged from very active to very passive. The researchers included *radicals*, that is, a shared form that represents a basic concept or activity, including combinations that are not part of the Chinese language. "Nonsense characters with the radical 'woman' were rated to be less active and less potent than nonsense characters with the other radicals" (Lau et al., 2004, p. 84). They attribute these findings to cultural representations that are the result of existing social evaluations of psychological genders.

In a related study, Lau et al. endorse Whorf's basic hypothesis and add that the activation of shared meanings and communication contributes to "the cognitive accessibility of shared meanings in the communicators" (Lau et al., 2004, p. 82). Lau et al. examine the use of pronouns, such as the differentiation between the formal and informal choice in French, or the obligatory use of "I" and "you" in English. They contrast these linguistic practices with other languages where such obligatory use is absent and suggest that the use of pronouns varies between individualistic and collectivist cultures. The dynamics of shared representation are supported by communicative practice in which idiosyncratic expressions and a reliance on low frequency words are avoided. Communities, thus, strengthen their understanding by co-constructing their perception of reality. They suggest that some of the ambiguous findings obtained when testing Whorfian notions are due to a deterministic view of culture, which they contrast with their own view, "which emphasizes the interpersonal processes that create, activate, maintain, and modify shared representations" (Lau et al., 2004, p. 97).

In a similar vein, Vygotsky addressed some issues concerning speech intentions. He argued that motivation (intention) engenders thought, which at that stage is devoid of specific linguistic form:

> The motive gives birth to thought, to the formation of thought itself, to its mediation in the internal word, to the meanings of external words, and finally, to words themselves . . . However, it would be a mistake to imagine that the single path from thought to word is always realized.
>
> (Vygotsky, 1987, p. 283)

A contemporary of Vygotsky's, the literary theorist Mikhail Bakhtin, also held that language is central to human consciousness. Although there is no evidence that Vygotsky and Bakhtin ever met, they did belong to overlapping intellectual circles, and there has been much interest in the parallels between Bakhtin's and Vygotsky's writings (Van der Veer,

1991, p. 371). In a famous quote, Bakhtin wrote of the ways in which speakers appropriate the words of others:

> The word in language is half someone else's. It becomes "one's own" only when the speaker populates it with his own intention, his own accent, when he appropriates the word, adapting it to his own semantic and expressive intention. Prior to this moment of appropriation, the word does not exist in a neutral and impersonal language (it is not, after all, out of a dictionary that a speaker gets his words!), but rather it exists in other people's mouths, in other people's contexts, serving other people's intentions: it is from there that one must take the word and make it one's own.   (Bakhtin, 1981, pp. 293–294)

There are many similarities between Vygotsky, Whorf, and Bakhtin in their emphasis on the interdependence between language and thought. Although the strong, or deterministic, version of Whorf's hypothesis has been challenged, recent research supports his notion that habitual thought is shaped by specific forms and interactional uses of language. Bakhtin and Vygotsky also shared a view of language that emphasized the dialogic nature of learning. Bakhtin accentuated the sharing of speech through conversation and the analysis of literary texts and Vygotsky approached the sharing of speech developmentally.

THE DEVELOPMENT OF SPEAKING AND THINKING

Vygotsky's approach to language acquisition has become more prevalent in the last three decades as Chomsky's and Pinker's nativist theories have been increasingly challenged. His legacy stands in contrast to those who place syntax – Chomsky et al. – at the center of linguistic study. In cultural historical theories of language acquisition, the *social sources of development* and the *central role of meaning* are emphasized. The developmental psychologist Tomasello has been effective in documenting the impact of meaningful joint attention as the basis of imitation, dialogue, and linguistic intentions. "A variety of studies have shown that after children have begun progressing in language acquisition they learn new words best in joint attentional scenes that are socially shared with others; often ones that are recurrent in their daily experience such as bathing, feeding, diaper changing, book reading, and traveling in the car" (Tomasello, 1999, pp. 109–110).

In *Thinking and Speech*, Vygotsky proposes that in the earliest periods of development children experience language and cognition somewhat separated from each other. Following Vygotsky's line of reasoning, Tomasello studied how in infancy, children rely on sensory-motor schemes, but as they acquire language "the social nature of linguistic symbols" transforms their participation in interpersonal exchanges (Tomasello, 1999). Tomasello traces the subsequent internalization of communicative and symbolic means by children.

Tomasello's research documents the process of language development starting at an earlier age than what Vygotsky had described, but it follows a similar line of argument. "Following Vygotsky and many other cultural psychologists, I contend that many of the most interesting and important human cognitive achievements, such as language and mathematics, require historical time and processes for their realization – even if most cognitive scientists largely ignore these historical processes" (Tomasello, 1999, p. 48). He further wrote that, "Acquiring a natural language [also] serves to socialize, to structure culturally, the ways in which children habitually attend to and conceptualize different aspects of their worlds" (Tomasello, 1999, p. 166).

Vygotsky proposed that meaningful communication between children and their caretakers occurs as they engage in dialogue and social interaction. "Meaning is . . . what is lying between the thought and the word. Meaning is not equal to the word, not equal to the thought. This disparity is revealed by the fact that their lines of development do not coincide" (Vygotsky, 1997, p. 133). But Vygotsky further suggests that it is through the unification of thinking and speaking that consciousness develops and that meaning becomes central to this synthesis.

Although Vygotsky's impact may have been slow to be realized, his vision inspired a generation of linguists and psychologists whose interest in placing "meaning" at the center of language is now coming into prominence. One example of this trend is Michael Halliday who wrote:

> A child learning his [her] mother tongue is learning how to name; he [she] is building up a meaning potential in respect of a limited number of social functions. These functions [instrumental, regulatory, interactional, personal, heuristic, and imaginative] constitute the semiotic environment of a very small child, and may be thought of as universals of human culture (Halliday, 1978, p. 121).

Halliday continues to greatly influence cognitive and functional linguistic theories which conceive of language as a dynamic system.

In studying the acquisition of language from a perspective shaped by Vygotsky and Halliday, Paul Tatter and I wrote:

> From birth, the social forms of child-caretaker interactions, the tools used by humans in society to manipulate the environment, the culturally institutionalized patterns of social relations, and language operating together as a socio-semiotic system are used by the child in cooperation with adults to organize behavior, perception, memory, and complex

mental processes. For children, the development of language is a development of social existence into individuated persons and into culture.

(John-Steiner and Tatter, 1983, p. 83)

The social, linguistic, and cultural contexts of language acquisition are documented in a large-scale cross-linguistic study by Dan Slobin and his collaborators. They examined texts generated by children and adults from picture books without words. Children from five speech communities were asked to create a story based on *Frog, Where are You?* (Mayer, 1969). The languages were English, Spanish, German, Turkish, and Hebrew. A grammatical distinction that emerges when comparing descriptions across these different languages is the contrastive salience of a completed activity versus an ongoing activity. This contrast is selectively "favored" according to the grammatical categories in one's native language: "Our data – across a number of story episodes and languages – suggests that categories that are not grammaticized in the native language are generally ignored, whereas those that are grammaticized are all expressed by children as young as three" (Slobin, 1996, p. 83).

For example, in describing the act of falling, Spanish grammar provides for a completion of the activity, but in German and Hebrew an understanding of actions can be inferred without being grammatically marked. Slobin refers to this phenomenon as "thinking for speaking." Namely, "that the language or the languages that we learn in childhood are not neutral coding systems of an objective reality. Rather, each one is a subjective orientation to the world of human experience, and this orientation affects the ways in which we think while we are speaking" (Slobin, 1996, p. 91).

Conceptions of space are also influenced by grammatical categories that vary across languages. For example, there are three categories in Dutch for "on": *op, aan,* and *om. Om* is like the English for "around," which means "encirclement," that is, like a ring on a finger. *Aan* is used to express hanging – as in an apple from a tree – and indicates support from above. *Op* is used to describe support from the ground, for instance, a cup on a table. In Finnish the distinction revolves around the degree of contact between an object and a surface. "These examples show that if you are a child learning Dutch or Finnish, you will have to learn to attend to rather different aspects of topological relationships then if you are a child learning English" (Bowerman, 1996, pp. 152–158).

An interesting grammatical distinction is provided in Turkish which requires a differentiation between witnessed and nonwitnessed events. In one of the pictures from *Frog, Where Are You?* we see a boy, who is the story's main character, lying on the ground in a position suggesting that he just fell from an adjacent tree. In this same picture, we see a dog running from pursuing bees. Turkish-speaking children used the progressive-witnessed form when they spoke of the dog "running." But for the boy they used the nonwitnessed past that would translate into English, "The boy (apparently) fell" (Slobin, 1996, p. 332). These studies illustrate how a particular language channels the speaker's attention according to the categories provided by the native language. They support Slobin's theory that part of acquiring a native language is learning particular ways of thinking for speaking.

The field of language acquisition is one of the most fertile in contemporary social science. The impact of Vygotsky, Whorf, and Bakhtin is significant as they have influenced lively theoretical debates which characterize this domain of inquiry. Research and debate on early semantic development, the language of adults when addressing young children, the acquisition of sign language, language socialization in diverse cultures, syntactic theory in language acquisition, and discourse processes are growing.

An important contribution to this field is the emerging cultural–historical model of language development. This is not the work of any single theorist or researcher. Psychologists and educators, including Jerome Bruner, Courtney Cazden, Toni Cross, Kris Guitierrez, Vera John-Steiner, Katherine Nelson, Eleanor Ochs and Bambi Schieffelin, Catherine Snow, Michael Tomasello, and Gordon Wells, and linguists James Gee, John Gumperz, Michael Halliday, Shirley B. Heath, William Labov, Jay Lemke, James Wertsch, and Stanton Wortham, jointly construct it. These authors have emphasized that children develop the structures of their language in recurrent settings and activities (Nelson, 1986) while relying upon "a shared and familiar context to aid the partners in making their communicative intentions clear to each other" (Bruner, 1983, p. 128).

The interdisciplinary quality of this field of study is akin to Vygotsky's own development as a scholar who used literature, psychology, linguistics, philosophy, art, and cinema to inform his own discourse. His writing, as drawn from so many diverse sources, is frequently synthesized and expressed through his effective use of metaphors. In the epigraph to chapter 7 in *Thought and Language*, he quotes Mandel'shtam's poem "Swallow":

> I forgot the word
> I wanted to say
> And thought, unembodied
> Returns to the hall of shadows

METAPHOR

Vygotsky uses metaphors to enrich his own writing. Many of these reflect his interest in movement. For instance when describing inner speech, he writes of "speech turning inward" (Vygotsky, 1934/1997, p. 86). This movement is also conceptualized dynamically when he writes, "It is at this point that the lines representing the development of thinking and speech, lines that up to this point have moved in isolation from one another, cross and begin to coincide" (Vygotsky, 1987, p. 110).

In an insightful paper, Clay Beckner (2003) wrote of Vygotsky's metaphors "as fluid and complex." He mentions, in passing, Vygotsky's famous metaphor involving water: "The evaporation of speech into thought" (Vygotsky qtd. in Beckner, 2003, p. 4). Two other well known metaphors also involve water: "A thought can be compared to a cloud shedding a shower of words" (Vygotsky, 1986, p. 251), and "Consciousness is reflected in a word as the sun in a drop of water" (Vygotsky, 1986, p. 256).

There are many examples of the way in which Vygotsky writes metaphorically in order to describe language and thought as dynamic and interactive. In differentiating between a word's sense and meaning, he writes of the former as "fluid" and the latter as "stable, unified, and precise" (Vygotsky, 1987, p. 276).

It is not surprising that many of Vygotsky's descriptions are metaphorical. The challenge of conveying complex relationships invites alternative ways of expression. As the cognitive sciences move away from reductionism and address the complexity of human psychological processes, the study of metaphor has become exceedingly popular. George Lakoff and Mark Johnson (1999) are among those who have raised this interest to the level of cultural and philosophical study.

> Our most important abstract philosophical concepts...are all conceptualized by multiple metaphors....What each philosophical theory typically does is to choose one of those metaphors as "right," as the true literal meaning of the concept.   (Lakoff & Johnson, 1999, p. 71)

In our own work on artistic and scientific collaboration, Christopher Shank, Teresa Meehan, and I found that in the narrative co-construction of joint experiences, partners frequently use metaphorical language to recount their activities. One of the participants in our study of collaborative narratives related:

> You know, go back to this point, or that point. And then you take everything you've learned with you with something that happened before and

you go and it's not like a clean circle, but maybe it's more like some kind of arching and then twisting back and picking up.

(Shank & Meehan, 2005, p. 186)

This participant was one of many who used kinesthetically oriented metaphors that dealt with touch, motion, and manipulation in their conceptualization of collaboration and their own mental processes. At the beginning of our research, we focused on visual and verbal figurative speech and did not anticipate the prevalence and richness of kinesthetic metaphors. However, it is interesting to note that when comparing metaphors across gender, men tended to produce more visual metaphors while women favored those with relational qualities. In these co-constructed narratives of joint endeavors, we learned of the collaborators' internal processes through their figurative expressions. This study is one of many contemporary investigations which aim to implement Vygotsky's commitment to the linguistic exploration of mental processes and the dynamics of change.

CONCLUSIONS

The relationship of thinking and speaking has remained of central concern to scholars in the human sciences. In this examination of Vygotsky's impact upon this domain of inquiry, different approaches have emerged. They include cross-linguistic comparisons of "thinking for speaking," developmental analyses of language and thought, studies of language acquisition, private and inner speech, and metaphoric representations of collaborative processes. As the diversity of these methods illustrate, no single discipline can claim definitively to have explained this crucial relationship. Vygotsky acknowledged the nature and complexity of his own thinking when he said,

> To encompass in research the process of a given thing's development in all its phases and changes – from birth to death – fundamentally means to discover its nature, its essence, for "it is only in movement that a body shows what it is." Thus, the historical [that is, in the broadest sense of "history"] study of behavior is not an auxiliary aspect of theoretical study, but rather forms its very base.   (Vygotsky, 1978, pp. 64–65)

Vygotsky's bold model of possibility and the very power of his analysis continue to drive these interdisciplinary explorations.

Author's Note: I wish to thank Mera Wolfe and Valerie Clement for their contributions to this paper.

READINGS OF VYGOTSKY

6 Terminology in L. S. Vygotsky's Writings

THE NEED FOR LOGICO-SEMANTIC ANALYSIS (LSA)

There are many reasons why it is difficult for readers to analyze and to understand Vygotsky's terminology. He developed his psychology in a direct and indirect dialogue with many other authors. In doing so, he absorbed and processed all the ideas and terms that he believed could be useful. These ideas ranged from the philosophy of Spinoza and Marx to the American behaviorism of Watson and the linguistics of Sapir. However, when one meets a seemingly familiar term borrowed from some predecessor in Vygotsky's writings, one should keep in mind that he was likely to have modified the term's meaning.

Another motivation for a logico-semantic analysis of Vygotsky's writings is the quantity, variety, and nature of his scientific heritage. A 1960 bibliography of Vygotsky's works includes 274 titles (Vygotsky, 1960). Excluding nonscientific articles and notes devoted for the most part to the events of literary and theatrical life (1916–1923), there remain around 190 works in psychology, written from 1924 until Vygotsky's death (June 11, 1934): a period of only ten years. Many items from this decade were written very quickly, in almost telegraphic style. Some works remain unfinished. It is certainly possible that some of the works that were published posthumously were not yet intended for publication (unfortunately, the editors of contemporary editions do not always warn the reader about the state and nature of the original texts). Therefore, when reading Vygotsky's works one needs to remember his own words (from a letter to A. N. Leontiev dated July 31, 1930), "our writings are imperfect but there is great truth in them. This is my symbol of faith...." (Vygotsky, 1960, p. 169).

In this regard, we are reminded of Dostoevsky's famous speech of June 8, 1880 about the Russian poet and writer Alexander Pushkin. In this setting, Dostoevsky used words that are applicable to many geniuses who died at a young age: "Had Pushkin lived longer, there probably would be fewer discussions and misunderstandings between us than we see today. But God judged differently. Pushkin died at the peak of his powers and, undoubtedly, took some great mystery to his tomb. And now we are solving this mystery without him."

Vygotsky's conceptual approach is very complex and multifaceted, and it certainly cannot be scraped from the surface of the author's texts. He had too little time to follow through on all the implications of his theory, to systematize and present them in an extended academic fashion. Therefore, we must not expect to find finished and complete conception in all of his texts, although these texts may be used as an implicit, internal form for reconstructing a more comprehensive conception.

The path to understanding Vygotsky is through study of the scientific language he employed, through a reconstruction of the most essential instrument and grounding of any creative idea: its conceptual and terminological system. It is impossible to lay out the full scope of my ideas on this topic in one chapter, and, therefore, I will limit myself to a schematic presentation of the overall results from a logico-semantic analysis (LSA) of Vygotsky's published works.

The principal purpose of this LSA is to identify and systematize the conceptual and terminological apparatus of Vygotsky's theory of the development of higher mental functions, or, as it is often called, the "cultural–historical theory of the mind" (Leont'ev & Luria, 1956, p. 7), the "cultural–historical theory of the development of the mind" (Leont'ev, 1982, p. 19), or the "theory of cultural–historical development" (Leont'ev, 1983, p. 103). Hereafter, for brevity's sake, I will refer to this theory as "Vygotsky's conceptual framework." (I will refer to the Russian editions of Vygotsky's works.)

Of course Vygotsky's early death was not the only (and not even the main) reason for the absence of detail in some works and the general incompleteness of his conceptual framework. The most important reason was the complexity of the problems that he wanted to solve; problems whose resolution could only emerge in the future. Even now, these problems seem to be extremely complicated and beyond the grasp not only of one person, but for the whole of psychology.

This raises the issues of Vygotsky's methodology and style of thinking. Two characteristic features of this thinking style stand out. The first can be called "developmental multiscreening." Vygotsky sought to present mental development on several conceptual "screens," each corresponding to a particular domain of development: biological phylogenesis, sociocultural "phylogenesis," ontogenesis (both normal and abnormal), microgenesis ("actual genesis"), and pathogenesis (psychological and neuropsychological disturbances). In general, this first feature cannot be considered to be original; its use was quite typical for the psychology of the first half of the twentieth century, although different scholars brought different inclinations and levels of imagination to bear on developmental and interdisciplinary multiscreening.

The second peculiarity of Vygotsky's style of thinking can be called its "systematicity." There are various forms of textual evidence of his constant striving to construct and connect at least four planes (e.g., projections, points of view, or representations) when describing mentalnctions (or more precisely, the mind) and forms of behavior. I consider these four planes to be four sections of Vygotsky's conceptual and terminological system (Meshcheryakov, 1998, 2000).

From this point of view, Vygotsky cannot be understood in any narrow sense (or in either/or terms) as a functionalist *or* a structuralist *or* a developmentalist (evolutionist). Long before the official birth of systems theory, Vygotsky had developed his own systemic approach. It was oriented toward understanding the wholeness of an object: establishing connections among systematization (taxonomy), structure (of mental processes, meaning, and brain mechanisms), function, and development. It was aimed at the integration of these different perspectives into a unified theoretical scheme. Vygotsky was one of the first psychologists to use original notions systematically and meaningfully, notions such as "functional system," "structure of functions," "interfunctional connections," and "functional development." Incidentally, Vygotsky did not resist the notion that the *concept of a system* was used for the first time by behaviorists and, at the same time, prophetically foresaw that this concept would make behaviorism "abandon a mechanistic conception of behavior." (Vygotsky & Luria, 1993, v. 3, p. 11). The developmental multiscreening and the systematicity of Vygotsky's thinking do not exhaust the originality of his methodology, but for the sake of simplicity, we may limit ourselves to these two concepts.

THE SYSTEMIC CLASSIFICATION OF MENTAL FUNCTIONS: THE RESULTS OF LSA

To present Vygotsky's views and conceptions, while avoiding contradictions and semantic distortion, one must first construct the total schema of concepts, take one of the alternatives as a basis, and then perform the necessary "deciphering." The classification schema I propose is shown in Figure 6.1.

Vygotsky's principal criterion for dividing forms of behavior into natural and cultural categories, at least in this particular context, is the

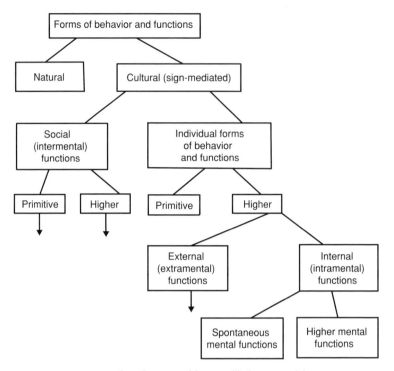

FIGURE 6.1. Classification of forms of behavior and functions.

mediated structure of behavior: the use of instruments (tools and/or signs). It is inherent in this notion that instruments are borrowed from culture, and culture acts as the social repository of human inventions.

Intermental functions are those which Vygotsky sometimes called "collective forms of collaboration." They are the subject of the general genetic law of cultural development (the law of sociogenesis) in which, " ... collective forms of collaboration precede individual forms of behavior which grow on their basis, and they also are the direct ancestors of individual forms of behavior and the sources of their appearance" (Vygotsky & Luria, 1993, v. 5, p. 203). Apparently, the main distinction between intermental (social) and individual functions is that in the intermental functions, a subject uses sign mediation to direct the behavior and mental processes of another subject, whereas, in the case of individual functions, such direction is carried out reflexively, on and for oneself.

The term *intermental function* should perhaps be used only for early stages of development. In its classic form, an intermental functioning is one aspect of joint or quasi-joint activity engaged in by adult and child (here "primitive" means at a preverbal stage and "higher" means at a verbal stage). It should be noted that this approach views each point of differentiation as involving a process whereby the previous form does not die away (symbolized by the arrows in Figure 6.1) and does not remain unchanged. Instead, it is reorganized under the impact of new formations.

The notion of a primitive function should be interpreted in a slightly different way when speaking of individual mental functions and forms of behavior. In most cases, when Vygotsky used this concept, it was in the context of psychological analysis of ethnographic material (e.g., Danzel, Lévi-Bruhl, Thurnwald, Tylor, Weule). When speaking of primitive forms of behavior, Vygotsky usually was referring to those shared by representatives of so-called nonliterate peoples ("traditional" cultures).

In these cases, "primitive" is a very imprecise term, not only from an ethical but also from a logical standpoint. Nonetheless, it played an important role in Vygotsky's writings. By all appearances, he was aware that this term was rather shaky, but he at least tried to provide the requisite clarification. (Lévi-Bruhl seemed to have had something similar in mind in his foreword to the 1930 Russian edition of *Primitive Thought*, where he wrote, "In the strict sense of the word, primitive man does not exist anywhere today, and the human type that is represented by these primitive peoples can be called only relatively primitive" (Wertsch, 1991, p. 68). The notion of primitiveness with respect to ontogeny is just as arbitrary (see Vygotsky & Luria 1993, v. 3, p. 79).

In some of his writing, especially in his "Studies in the History of Behavior" (Wertsch, 1991), Vygotsky unfortunately contrasted "primitive" with "cultural." This corresponds to the dichotomy of cultural and primitive peoples, a dichotomy that was widely used at the time. The title of one of the books of the German ethnologist Weule, *The Culture of Uncultured Peoples* (Russian edition, 1924) is symptomatic of this.

Unfortunately, Vygotsky did not provide unambiguous criteria for defining primitive peoples. In some cases, their reactive and passive nature is underscored; in others, their incomprehension of the psychological function of signs (the stage of "naive psychology," magical function); and in still others, the distinctive feature involves the signs employed (e.g., nonlinguistic, multifunctional, signs that are not capable of being internalized). In any case, this concept has developmental overtones, that is, it applies to an initial and/or transitional form in "the history" of the development of cultural behavior.

This unmanageable variety of criteria follows directly from the fact that the various forms of sign-mediated functions found in a "traditional" culture do not form a unified or homogenous set. Therefore, the term *primitive* in Vygotsky's texts requires extremely cautious treatment. Depending on the context, it requires "terminological reciphering," that is, replacing it with a term for one or another higher form of behavior. However, in order to maintain the notion of a stage of naïve psychology, which Vygotsky considered to be one of the phases of the development of higher mental functions, terminal reciphering is required. It is needed when speaking of the so-called magical use of signs and of the use of signs without understanding of their psychological functional meaning (i.e., the facts of erroneous and vague metacognition). In Vygotsky's formulation these are primitive forms of individual behavior and functions proper (as presented in Figure 6.1). The situation is analogous to the the closely related concept of rudimentary functions.

According to Vygotsky, the concept of rudimentary mental functions comprises "mental functions that have been preserved down to the present, but have played no essential role in the behavior of the individual at all and are vestiges of more ancient systems of behavior" (Vygotsky & Luria, 1993, v. 3, p. 60). Therefore, "primitive" refers to something that often surfaces in traditional culture, whereas "rudimentary" is a remnant (in Taylor's cultural-anthropological evolutionism sense) of the primitive. For example, tying a knot in one's handkerchief (the Russian equivalent of trying a string around one's finger) when one has an opportunity to use an alarm clock or a cell-phone is a rudimentary behavior. I presume that some of Vygotsky's examples characterizing primitive and rudimentary forms of behavior can be validly classified not only as "cultural" but even as higher forms of social and individual behavior and mental functioning.

Vygotsky placed "extramental" functioning – a higher form of individual behavior (for instance, egocentric speech) – at an intermediate stage of development between intermental and intramental functioning. However, he used this term only once: "Any system about which I speak goes through three stages. First, intermental – I command, you carry out; then, extramental – I begin to speak to myself; and then intramental" (Vygotsky & Luria, 1993, v. 1, p. 130). In the developmental sense, intramental functioning, which is a higher form of individual behavior, results from the internalization of extramental functioning.

An important result of LSA is that it reveals the distinction between two types of intramental functioning: spontaneous and voluntary (the latter being a higher mental function in the narrow sense). Vygotsky provided detailed accounts of spontaneous speech and spontaneous thinking in children, which, like Piaget, he considered it to be involuntary and a relatively unconscious intramental processes.

Unfortunately, Vygotsky never provided a rigorous definition of the basic concept of his theory – higher mental functioning. A month and a half before his death he wrote:

> One might think that, in exploring the question of higher mental functions, it is necessary to begin by giving a clear definition of higher mental functions and indicating what criteria enable us to distinguish them from

elementary functions. But it seems to me that a precise definition is not something that belongs to the beginning phase of scientific knowledge. Instead, I believe I can limit myself initially merely to empirical and heuristic definitions." (Vygotsky, 1982–1984, pp. 367–368)

Luria attempted to solve this problem. His definition fits in well with Vygotsky's notions and gives to the these notions a distinct – one could even say classic – formulation. Higher mental functions are "complex and self-regulating, and are social in origin, mediated in their structure, and conscious and voluntary in their mode of functioning" (Luria, 1980, p. 31). One can also add another qualification essential for Vygotsky's conception: higher mental functions are not simply "mediated," but are "mediated by signs."

Vygotsky wrote that the concept of the "development of higher mental functions" embraces "two principal branches, two currents of development of the higher forms of behavior that are inseparably connected, but never merged completely into one. These are, first, mastering the external means of cultural development and thought – language, writing, calculation, drawing; and, second, unique forms of development in higher mental functions that are not demarcated or defined precisely in any way. In traditional psychology, the results of this development are called voluntary attention, logical memory, concept formation, and so forth. All of these together form what we provisionally call the process of development of higher forms of behavior in the child" (Vygotsky & Luria, 1993, v. 3, p. 24).

It is evident from this formulation that Vygotsky used the term *higher mental functions* in two distinct ways: (a) in a broad sense, roughly equivalent to the meaning of higher forms of behavior and (b) in a narrow sense – "special (or strictly speaking) higher mental functions."

LAWS AND STAGES OF DEVELOPMENT OF HIGHER
MENTAL FUNCTIONS

This section will examine Vygotsky's laws describing the ontogenetic stages of higher mental functions (HMF). Vygotsky repeatedly formulated these laws; moreover, he used different terms and expressions when referring to some of them. In most cases, he confined himself to a single law, which he called different things at different points in his writings. He variously referred to it as "the general genetic law of cultural development," "the law of the sociogenesis of the higher forms of behavior," "the fundamental law of the construction of HMF," "the general law for construction of all HMF," "the law of double appearance of HMF in the history of the child's development," and "the most important and basic of genetic laws."

This law is frequently cited in works devoted to Vygotsky's theory, and the wording used most frequently comes from the "History of the Development of HMF." According to this formulation, "any function in children's development appears twice or on two planes. First, it appears on the social plane and then on the psychological plane. First it appears between people as an intermental category and then within the individual child as an intramental category."

There are other laws that apply to the development of HMF in Vygotsky's work. In *The Pedology of the Adolescent*, the law mentioned in "History of the Development of the HMF" is included as the second law in a list of three. These laws are:

1. The law of the transition from natural forms of behavior to cultural forms of behavior (i.e., mediated by tools and signs). This can be called the law of mediation. (Vygotskii & Luria, 1993, v. 4, p. 221).

2. The law of sociogenesis. This concept involves the transition from social (intermental) to individual forms of behavior. Because of it, the mediational means of social forms of behavior become the means of individual forms of behavior. (Vygotskii & Luria, 1993, v. 4, pp. 221, 223).

3. The law of transition of the functions from without to within. "This process of transition of operations from without to within, we call the law of ingrowth" (Vygotskii & Luria, 1993, v. 4, p. 140; see also, *Interiorization*).

Later, in the volume *Thinking and Speech*, Vygotsky formulated a fourth law that supplements and completes this list. (Vygotsky actually introduced this law without specifying its position in the list of the others.) In this case he wrote:

4. "The common law of development is that realization and acquisition are peculiar only to the highest level of the development of a function. Obviously, this law can be called the law of realization and acquisition" (Vygotskii & Luria, 1993, v. 2, p. 217; see also, *Intellectualization*).

It should be noted that in Vygotsky's texts some wordings of the laws conflate different levels of genetic transition in an almost syncretistic way.

Are there any criteria for checking the precision of the wordings and terms Vygotsky used? In other words, is there an inner logic in this canon

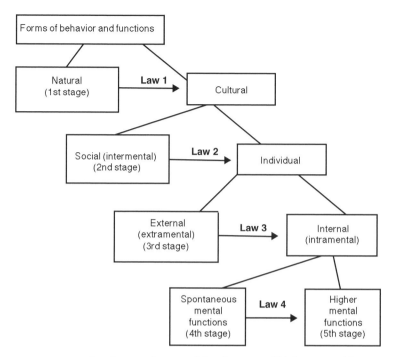

FIGURE 6.2. Laws and stages of development of higher mental functions.

of laws? Is it possible that the four laws given constitute the full set? If we assume that these laws are the laws of transition describing the evolution from one stage of development to another, then the number of laws obviously should be one less than the number of stages. Answering these questions is connected with revealing stages of development in Vygotsky's writings.

In Vygotsky's works, reader most frequently encounter four-stage schemas (less often – three-stage schemas) of "cultural development" both on the social–historical and ontogenetic plane. The first version of this schema appeared as early as in his article "The Problem of the Cultural Development of the Child" (1928). In later works, it was repeated with relatively minor changes in the names of the stages. Obviously, within the four-stage schema the maximum number of the transitional laws is three. However, the four laws suggest a five-stage scheme, as shown in Figure 6.2.

The stages presented in this figure belong to Vygotsky's more or less explicit formulation. At the same time, by means of a LSA of Vygotsky's works (Meshcheryakov, 1998, 2000), two more stages can be identified, which belong to the implicit content of his conceptual system. Therefore, in this system the following seven stages can be identified:

1. natural functions,
2. primitive social (intermental) functions,
3. higher social (intermental) functions,
4. the stage of primitive individual functions (or the "stage of naïve psychology," also the magic stage),
5. extramental functions,
6. spontaneous intramental functions,
7. voluntary intramental functions (or HMF in a narrow sense).

From this, we can conclude that the number of the transitional laws should be equal to six.

The following issue deserves clarification: how is it possible that after the stage of "higher intermental function," we encounter the "stage of naïve psychology," which Vygotsky always described as "primitive" and "lower"? One way to overcome this perplexity was proposed by Vygotsky when he stated, "The transition from collective forms of behavior to individual forms of behavior at first lowers the character of the whole operation, incorporates it into the system of primitive functions... Social forms of behavior are more complex, they are developed in a child earlier; as they become individual, they become lower forms in order to function according to the simpler laws" (Vygotsky & Luria, 1993, v. 6, p. 16).

An example of such a regression is *egocentric speech*, which is obscure to the external observer, and it may be treated like a form of regression, or decollage in Piaget's terms, in comparison to social (communicative) speech. Another possibility is to assume that the "magical attitude" toward signs is also present in the previous stages. Using speech in communication with adults does not exclude, for example, children's use of speech toward animals, plants, and even inanimate objects. According to Vygotsky, "Sometimes speech, no matter how paradoxically it sounds, is directly addressed to an object of activity." (Vygotsky & Luria 1993, v. 6, p. 32; see also, v. 3, pp. 323–324)

Finally, it is necessary to bear in mind that the appearance of the new formations in the course of development does not presume the automatic disappearance of previous forms. In Vygotsky's account of psychological development, the idea that genetically older forms of behavior are reconstructed by the influence of newer ones and continue their development is quite clear. For example, he wrote that "not only do absolutely new complex synthetic forms that are unknown in a three-year-old appear in the mind of an adolescent, but those elementary primitive forms which a child acquired at the age of three are reconstructed on new bases during the transitional period."

This expanded schema of the stages of development of HMF should be taken as an explicit specification of Vygotsky's position without forgetting its hypothetical and approximate nature (which the author emphasized). It is important that the schema has heuristic value, that is, it can help organize new research and systematize a larger set of concepts and facts.

By way of concluding this section, let me turn to several genetic terms. The first two belong to Vygotsky's own thesaurus; the other two are offered by contemporary authors in the spirit of a deeper exploration of Vygotsky's ideas.

Interiorization (from Latin "interior") literally means the transition from without to within. In psychological usage, it is a term that refers to the formation of stable structural–functional units of *consciousness* through the mastery of external actions with objects and the mastery of external sign means (e.g., the formation of inner speech from external speech). Sometimes it is interpreted more broadly as any mastery of information, knowledge, roles, and attitudes. In his theory, Vygotsky wrote primarily about the formation of the inner means of mental activity out of the external means of communication in joint activity. In other words, Vygotsky used the concept of interiorization to refer to the formation of the "systemic" structure of consciousness (as opposed to the "meaning" structure). However, interiorization does not by itself constitute the formation of HMF (because spontaneous functions are also the result of interiorization). For that, intellectualization is needed.

In Vygotsky's works, one may encounter the following synonyms of "interiorization," or ingrowth, "becoming interiorized." He called the fourth stage of his original scheme of the development of HMF "the stage of ingrowth." The term *interiorization* is often is missing in English. It is close in sound and meaning is "internalization," which is rather loaded with psychoanalytical connotations.

Intellectualization is an important concept in the thesaurus of Vygotsky's psychological conceptual system. According to his definition, intellectualization occurs when children start to treat their mental activity rationally. As a result, functions that were formerly spontaneous and not conscious may become conscious and voluntary in their further development. This transition is called *intellectualization*. Different functions become intellectualized at different times. The order of their intellectualization probably coincides with the development of self-consciousness. Vygotsky claimed that all of the intellectual functions (such as perception, attention, and memory), except intellect itself (i.e., discursive thinking in this context), become intellectualized before the onset of adolescence.

Decontextualization is a historic and/or ontogenetic process of generalizing meanings and skills (semiotic actions) and their transformation into more abstract actions that do not depend on concrete conditions. Wertsch (1991) believes that Vygotsky recognized an important principle of development, which may be called "the principle of the decontextualization of mediational means." The decontextualization of mediational means is a process in the course of which the meaning of signs (e.g., numbers, words in natural language) becomes more independent of the unique context of space and time in which they were originally used. (This is illustrated very clearly in the cultural development of the concept of number and the procedure of counting.)

Prolepsis is one of the most important mechanisms of individual psychological and personal development. It occurs when an individual, by himself herself, or through the help of someone else "sees" something that is yet to be developed. This definition suggests the terminological division of prolepsis into two types: heteroprolepsis and autoprolepsis. It is important to emphasize that the process is certainly not limited to just "seeing." Instead, it is assumed that a certain type of activity is systematically organized in accordance with the "seeing" (i.e., an idea).

Cole (1996/1997) defines prolepsis as a "cultural mechanism that brings 'end to the beginning.'" Prolepsis is usually defined as, "the treating of a future event as if it had already happened." In Vygotsky's conceptual system, prolepsis plays the role of the "origin of development" and is called "ideal form" (this concept has its roots in the linguistic conception of Humboldt and even more ancient roots in Plato's theory of ideas).

An example of heteroprolepsis can be normal parents' attitude to their infant as a person. From this perspective, speech addressed to the infant treats him or her as a subject with whom it is possible and necessary to coordinate one's action to act together. This amounts to a kind of personification of an infant. Moreover, even in a newborn, adults sometimes "discover" clear signs of future outstanding abilities (music, sports, invention, leadership). Such overtures (or myths) may have an enormous impact on children's development. Because of the overestimation built into these overtures, adults strive to saturate joint activity not only with emotional means of communication but also genuine signs (including language).

Joint activity always appears to be sign-mediated. Because of this, it becomes an environment encouraging the maturation of the first intermental functions, which, according to Vygotsky, are the beginning of the road of development leading to individual activity and higher mental functions. Simultaneously, joint activity includes objects and often tools as well. That is why we can already see here a specifically human environment for the development of activity. This activity (as well as its subject) objectively appears to be mediated in three different ways: (1) by an adult (mediator), (2) by the sign (semiotic artifact), and (3) by the tool (technological artifact). This "holy trinity" contains the basis (framework, skeleton) of the original genetic unit of development. As M. Lisina writes movingly, "She [the mother] sees something that is not there yet – and that is how she virtually sculpts a child's new behavior. She starts to communicate with her child when the child is not yet capable of communicative activity, but because of that the child in the end is drawn into this activity" (Lisina, 1978, p. 276). Another example of heteroprolepsis can be seen in Vygotsky's widely admired and widely used description of the transformation of an infant's unsuccessful grasping movement into an indicatory gesture.

An example of autoprolepsis is a toddler's role-play when he or she imagines him or herself in various adults' roles (hunter, mother, teacher, etc.), imitating the elements of cultural forms of behavior. It is possible to assume that in early ontogenesis there is a shift from heteroprolepsis to autoprolepsis. In the early years of life, heteroprolepsis plays the main role in development and later autoprolepsis becomes more important.

EMPIRICAL REFERENTS OF THE STAGES
OF THE DEVELOPMENT OF HMF

Whatever noble and important dimensions we envision in the reconstruction of Vygotsky's conceptual system, it is even more important in the end that this system should comply with empirical reality and help predict and understand it. However, systematic comparison with facts can be used for further reconstruction and can revise the conceptual system.

In any case, I am far from offering the schemes I have presented as precise and final representations of Vygotsky's conceptual system. That is why the examples presented here will be used not only for the purposes of illustration but also to provide further specification of Vygotsky's conceptual system and verification of its heuristic value. However, we will limit ourselves to the first five stages because the whole spirit of Vygotsky's approach was aimed at proving the existence of the precursors of the last two stages (intramental functioning).

The Stage of Natural Functions and Forms of Behavior

Empirical referents of the concepts "natural function" and "natural forms of behavior" can be found in animal psychology, where innumerable investigations have been made of the behavior of species ranging from amoebas to higher primates.

The list in its generalized form includes such phenomena as instincts, unconditional and conditional reflexes, and the practical intellect of apes. This list should be supplemented with the so-called elementary psycho-physiological functions (lower mental functions) that are interpreted as processes independent of consciousness and learning (i.e., genetically conditioned), emerging as a reaction to the influence of extrasomatic and intrasomatic (outer and inner) signals.

Such processes have a forced, automatic nature; usually they are explained by the influence of the environment and anatomical–physiological mechanisms. An illustrative example is the process of dark/light adaptation, which proceeds regardless of whether we know anything about it or not and regardless of our will; it is connected with the external stimulus conditions. It is common to refer to sensory functions and involuntary attention as elementary psycho-physiological functions. It is somewhat unexpected that Vygotsky included in this list such complex phenomena as associations (including verbal associations), eidetic memory, and even so-called natural arithmetic (Wertsch, 1991, pp. 108–111).

Regardless of the specifics of this stage, the main point is that the theoretical scheme of developmental stages for higher mental functions takes as its beginning point natural, genetically determined processes. This is a major feature of Vygotsky's thinking: higher mental functions are viewed in terms of their unity and their mutual connections with lower mental functions.

The Stage of Primitive Social (Intermental) Functioning

There is no specified understanding of the "primitive" in higher mental functioning (HMF) in a broad sense. In the case of intermental functioning, we consider the preverbal, prespeech level of communication (Meshcheriakov, 2000) to be a more fundamental and heuristic criterion; however, this does not exclude the use of other criteria as supplementary characteristics of stages and for distinguishing between substages. For example, when examining the positioning of a child in joint activity, notions of positional–passive and positional–active intermental functioning might be employed. Therefore, we claim that primitive intermental functioning is carried out by means of protolanguage (non-verbal signals), whereas higher intermental functioning is carried out mainly by means of verbal messages that the partners understand in an approximately equivalent manner.

However, this criterion is by no means completely clear or unproblematic. All one has to do to see this is to note well-known facts such as the use of verbal commands to direct the behavior of pets or infants who have not mastered speech. We must admit that in Vygotsky's work we will not find a detailed analysis of such facts. Nevertheless, without going into detail, he still indicated his point of view. He considered the mechanisms of animals' submission to verbal commands based on conditioned reflex and the mechanisms of directing an infant's behavior to be identical; both are explained by the "passive creation of a connection to sound signals" (Vygotsky & Luria, 1993, v. 3, p. 83; see also, pp. 166, 319). Vygotsky's point of view can be understood in the following way: although language is used in directing animals and infants, these phenomena do not constitute real verbal communication.

The paradox is that the preverbal (prespeech) level of communication is absolutely saturated by verbal signals (see *Prolepsis*). As Vygotsky writes, "other people direct a child's attention by means of words distracting a child from some elements of the visual field to others or even directing a child toward internal processes of thinking. The means here remains external; the operation itself is still shared between two different people. Attention directed in such a way, objectively, is already voluntary directed attention, but as of yet involuntary from the point of view of the child" (Vygotsky & Luria, 1993. v. 4, p. 139). Here is another example:

> At first a child perceives the milieu diffusely, but as soon as the mother points at a certain object and names it, distinguishing it from the whole environment, the child pays attention specifically to this object. At first the process of attention here becomes a cultural operation. However, it truly becomes a cultural operation only when the child herself masters the way of creating such additional stimuli, using them for concentrating on some parts of the situation and distinguishing them from the rest of the background.   (Wertsch, 1991, p. 178)

Among nonverbal signals characteristic for this stage, the most noticeable role are indicative gestures and gestures prompting action. Based on a well-known study by Wolfgang Köhler (1921), Vygotsky had to admit that at least chimpanzees use mimicry and gestures to express not only their emotional states, but also "both desires and drives directed to other apes or other objects" (Vygotsky & Luria, 1993, v. 2, p. 93).

Does it follow that the primitive social (intermental) function exists in animals as well as humans? Vygotsky does not give a direct answer to this question. At the same time, he admits that in children who do not possess language analogous ways of communication can be found:

> In the descriptions of chimpanzees' social behavior many examples are given in which one animal influences another either by action or by instinctive automatic expressive movements. The contact is established through a touch, through a cry, through a glance. The entire history of early forms of a child's social contacts is full of examples of this sort. Here we also see the contact, established by a cry, by grabbing a sleeve, by glances.   (Vygotsky & Luria, 1993, v. 3, p. 143)

Evidently, the answer to this question should be in the affirmative because primitive social (intermental) functioning is not exclusively human. However, the fundamental fact is that animals do not develop toward higher mental functioning. The main obstacle to this is the absence of language. Subsequent mental development in humans occurs in close connection with the development of speech. Language is the main and universal means of regulating behavior and mental processes, but this does not suggest that there is no place for nonverbal mediational means in the subsequent stages in the development of higher mental functions. On the contrary, we believe that it is language that creates the foundation and opens the way for activity to become saturated with various mediational means – graphic, figurative, and so forth. It is not accidental that Vygotsky included practical action in the assortment of higher mental functions, however it is only under the condition that such action is regulated by language. Therefore, it is not the tool that makes practical action a higher mental function (in a broader sense); attaching the regulating verbal-thinking function to the practical action makes it a higher function.

We can also find marvelous examples of this stage in a journal of the well-known Russian psychologist D. B. El'konin who described his grandchild Andrei, about 1 year old, inviting his grandfather to continue an activity that Andrei liked.

> The first example is from the time when Andrei could neither walk by himself, nor use words in an appropriate way. Andreika [diminitive from Andrei – translators' note] straddles my knees and I move my knees so that he jumps, and I accompany these jumps with the words, "Whoop! Whoop!" Suddenly, I stop these movements. Andreika watches me intently, and then starts the jumping movements himself and pulls me, as if inviting me to continue the activity. I start moving my knees again and stop them again. He renews his appeals.

An analogous picture takes place in the other cases. Andreika lies down, and I tap on his feet and keep saying, "Shoe the hoof. We'll go on the road..." ['Kuj, kuj nozhku. Poedem po dorozhke...' is a little child's rhyme; translator's note]. And at the end of the procedure I tickle him gently, and he laughs. After I finish this 'game,' he takes my hand and directs it to his foot, inviting me to continue the 'game.' The facts given indicate that very early (before one year old) a child already can try to involve an adult in continuing joint activity that is pleasant for him.

(El'konin, 1995, p. 93)

The Stage of Higher Social (Intermental) Functioning

Wertsch provides an illustration of "intermental" recollection: "A 6-year-old child has lost a toy and asks her father for help. The father asks where she last saw the toy; the child says, 'I can't remember.' He asks a series of questions: 'Did you have it in your room? Outside? Next door?' To each question the child answers, 'No. When he says, 'In the car?' she says 'I think so' and goes to retrieve the toy" (Wertsch, 1991, p. 27, quotation from Tharp & Gallimore, 1988, p. 14).

Commenting on this situation, Wertsch notes a characteristic peculiarity of intermental functioning: "In such cases, we cannot answer the question 'Who did the remembering?' A dyad as a system performed the function of recollection on the intermental plane" (Wertsch, 1991, pp. 38–39).

An important question to ask when analyzing such situations is whether both parties in a dyad really understand the psychological meaning of the dialogue, and whether they both really strove to use it in full measure. Vygotsky often used an illustration that suggests that a child sometimes is not ready yet for higher intermental functioning. In this example, a little girl (about 4 years old) asked an adult to repeat the instructions for a task and immediately ran away, without listening to them until the end.

> The mother gives a child a task, analogous to the one from Binet's test, to go to another room and carry out three little operations. In giving the task, the mother sometimes repeats it several times; at other times she states it just once. The girl notices that in those cases when her mother repeats the instructions several times, she can accomplish the task. The child remembers that and, finally, starts to understand that the mother needs to repeat the order several times. When the mother gives her a new task, the girl says to her, "Repeat it one more time," but she runs away without listening. The girl notices the connection between the repetition of the instruction and the success in accomplishing it, but she does not understand that it is not repetition by itself that helps. Instead, the key

is that she needs to listen to the repetition, learn it clearly, and only then will it become easier to accomplish the task. (Vygotsky, v. 3, p. 157). In another account, a girl asks her mother not just to repeat the instruction but to repeat it three times.   (Vygotsky, v. 3, p. 154).

This is similar to Wertsch's example. The child in this case addresses an adult with a request for help (to recall, in one example, to remember in the other), but the child's behavior shows that she yet "does not understand the connection between repetition and remembering, does not have sufficient psychological experience regarding the real conditions of her own reaction and uses this experience in a naïve way" (Vygotsky, 1982–4, v. 3, p. 158). It is possible to say that in these cases there was simply an attempt to use an intermental function, but the child is not yet capable of exercising it adequately. In terms of the stages of development, it is possible to say that the development of the "mnemonic function" has hardly risen to the level of higher intermental functioning. However, intermental functioning is situated in the zone of proximal development.

Later studies of communication between children of preschool age[1] indicate that 4-year-olds are capable of directing the attention of adults and other children, including younger children. For example, when 4-year-olds were asked to tell 2-year-olds how a toy is constructed, they employed a whole array of verbal means for directing attention: they spoke slowly, used short phrases, often used words that helped to draw attention, such as "look" and "here," and repeated the child's name [Shatz & Gelman, 1973].

It is difficult to render in English, but let me give an example from Russian history. Long ago, illiterate recruits in the Russian army who mixed up the commands "Right turn!" and "Left turn!" had straw tied to one leg and hay to the other. While moving in line formation, they were given the commands "Hay!" or "Straw!" From this example, we can also see that mediational means of different nature are combined in the directing of behavior.

The psycholinguist Brudny describes an interesting example from American military history: "President John Kennedy, who was in command of a torpedo boat during WWII, often liked to tell how he suddenly heard the shout of a lookout, 'Japanese at two o'clock!' before a Japanese torpedo-boat destroyer emerged from the night darkness and hit his boat in the side. The lookout, a professional sailor, precisely [but too late – although it was not his fault; author's note] indicated where the danger

---

[1] Children before 6 to 7 years of age [translator's note].

was coming from. Imagine that you are in the center of a gigantic clock-face facing 12 o'clock and it will be clear for you where the destroyer was coming from" (Brudny, 1998, p. 44).

In this episode, the verbal indication is mediated by a specially constructed and interiorized scheme of a clock face. This illustrates the point that human mental processes are saturated not only by verbal signs, but also by artificial schemes/representations (e.g., topographic maps, local maps, clock-face schemes, schemes of a tree, an eye, a reflex curve).

THE STAGE OF PRIMITIVE INDIVIDUAL FUNCTIONING (ALSO TERMED THE "MAGIC STAGE" OR "THE STAGE OF NAÏVE PSYCHOLOGY")

This and the following stages are ones where external mediational means start to be used for regulating one's behavior and one's own mental processes. According to Vygotsky, "this stage does not last very long in a child" (Vygotsky, 1982–4, v. 3, p. 159). However, "in subsequent life, we can observe the echoes of this naïve phase very widely" (Vygotsky & Luria, 1993, p. 201).

Sometimes, it is possible to reveal this stage through experimentation. In "Studies in the History of Behavior," Vygotsky and Luria provide a description of an experiment with 5- to 10-year old children. (Vygotsky, 1982–4, v. 3, pp. 109, 155; Vygotsky v. 6, pp. 44–45). This experiment was described more than once in their writings, but one will not find the following detailed description of the procedure and of quantitative results anywhere else. The idea, the method, and the results are generally clear (and deserve verification with more strict observance of the norms of empirical research).

A little preliminary explanation: in the Russian tradition of psychology this type of method is called "the method of dual stimulation." In the works of Vygotsky and his colleagues, this method is represented by a variety of particular techniques, the common principle in each technique is that it is a test a subject's ability to use the external auxiliary means (stimuli–means, psychological tools) to solve a problem (of remembering, practical action, concept formation, and so forth). The essence of the method is that the analysis of higher mental functioning of HMF is carried out by using two types of stimuli: the first type, stimulus–object, is the object of the subject's activity and the other type, stimulus–means, is the mediational means (signs) by which the subject's activity is organized.

In this particular experiment, children had to press different keys on a toy piano (a well-known technique when studying choice reactions) in response to different pictures shown to them one-by-one (e.g., an ax, an apple, an envelope, a table; the number of stimulus-objects should exceed the capacity of short-term memory). Each picture corresponded with a particular key. The researchers were interested in the process whereby children came to remember the rules of correspondence (how did the children remember the rules of correspondence between the pictures [stimulus–object] and the keys). Therefore, this technique can be considered to be a version of the *technique of paired associations*. The main question was whether children could efficiently use the stimulus–means (pictures or objects, stimulus–means) that were chosen (sometimes by the researcher, sometimes by the child) from a separate set and put in front of the keys. By introducing these stimulus–means into the procedure, an ordinary technique for studying the formation of paired associations was transformed into a test on mediated remembering.

It appears that children below 6 years old do not, or cannot, use stimuli–means, even in cases involving rather simple relations between SO and SM (e.g., apple–pear, beetle–butterfly). (Vygotsky & Luria, 1993, p. 200). Children of 6 to 7 years of age already show signs of understanding that the stimuli–means facilitate solving the problem. Some of the children chose helpful versions of associations, but the majority of children still did it in a rather naïve, not very deliberate way. For example, a description of typical behavior includes:

> . . . becoming convinced, from the individual cases, that auxiliary signs may really help in a child's problem solving, but the child does not understand exactly why the signs help and decides that it is sufficient to carry out the task successfully to do something like putting a sign in front of the keys in order to solve the problem, so that it will be remembered on its own when it is necessary to press the particular key. After placing the sign in a particular position, the child does not care any more about remembering; he is naively sure that 'the sign will do the remembering for him,' and one of our little subjects put a nail in front of the key and said that surely 'the nail will remember' and that now there is nothing for him to do to fulfill the task.   (Vygotsky & Luria, 1993, p. 201).

Vygotsky summarized and interpreted the results of these experiments in the following way:

> The stage described above proceeds differently in different children, but the main thing in all children's behavior is that they turn to the pictures not understanding yet how the picture works; they do remember that somehow "a horse" helped to find "a sledge." A child considers internal complicated connections merely superficially, associatively; she feels that certainly the picture ought to help her make a choice, though she cannot explain the internal connection on which it is based. (. . .)

It is interesting that a similar phenomenon, observed in primitive people, is often called magical thinking. Magical thinking appears because of limited knowledge of the laws of nature and because primitive persons mistake the connection between ideas for the connection between objects. (. . .)

For a child at this stage the opposite phenomenon occurs: the connection between objects is mistaken for the connection between ideas; the connection between pictures is mistaken for the psychological connection. In other words, what happens is not the true usage of the law but its superficial, associative usage. This stage can be called the stage of naïve psychology. The name "naïve psychology" is given by an analogy with the name "naïve physics," introduced by Lipmann, Bogen, and later Köhler.   (Vygotsky, 1982–4, v. 3, p. 157)

EXTRAMENTAL FUNCTIONING

The extramental function stage is the "stage at which an external sign, an external operation, provides the means by which a child solves some internal psychological task. This is stage well known to us by counting with fingers in the child's arithmetic development, and the stage of using external mnemonic signs in the process of remembering. In speech development the corresponding stage is the one of egocentric speech" (Vygotsky, 1982–4, v. 2, p. 109). In order to illustrate this stage, involving other so-called rudimentary functions, Vygotsky liked to refer to tying knots in a handkerchief in order to remember.

Vygotsky also participated in a psychopathology review of a patient (a 51-year-old, dentist, diagnosed with Pick's disease) with rather distinct disturbances in the realm of extramental functions (Samukhin, Birnbaum, & Vygotsky, 1934). For example, the patient was capable of memorizing four words if these words were repeated several times, but he was not capable of remembering the same number of words with the help of picture cards that could be very easily connected with the words. Instead, he responded using the word for the object on the card rather than the word from the list with which it was supposed to be connected. Vygotsky's biggest interest, however, was age differences in the success at carrying out extramental functioning and the efficiency of employing various kinds of mediational means.

We will not linger on the rather well-known set of Vygotsky's ideas and investigations on egocentric speech (here we refer to a very well-written description in Crain (2002). Unfortunately, his rather keen observations of counting operations in children was not further developed. According to him, "During this stage a child calculates mainly with her fingers (and also by means of words, which denote numbers; author's note), and if a child is given a task like 'Here are seven apples. Take two away. How many will be left?' a child will turn from apples to fingers. In this case fingers play the role of signs. The child puts out seven fingers, then removes two, five is left. In other words, the child solves the problem by means of external signs. As soon as you forbid a child to move the hands, she becomes unable to fulfill the corresponding operation." (Vygotsky, 1982–4, v. 3, p. 162).

Vygotsky gave significantly more attention to the ontogenetic development of memory. This was the area where he organized the main line of his experiments, attacking several issues at one time. We have already mentioned his pilot study of mediated reaction with the toy piano. The other two experiments worth mentioning had the same pilot nature.

Vygotsky and Luria report interesting results from experiments on children's "invention" of ways to remember the names of numbers, when they were given various objects such as paper, a rope, shavings, and an abacus to help them remember (Vygotsky & Luria, 1993, pp. 165–169; 19, v. 3, pp. 251–252). Vygotsky concluded from this study:

> During the experiment, the child creates the labels, i.e., a way of writing down numbers that is widely used among people who cannot count... This provides an opportunity, first, to trace the very moment of transition, the moment of inventing written language, and second, to immediately discover the deep changes that occur when a child makes the transformation from unmediated remembering to mediated remembering.   (Vygotsky, 1982–4, v. 3, p. 252)

Vygotsky's student Roza E. Levina (1968) (8, experiments of 1938) also studied children's abilities to make drawings that could help them remember phrases (the pictogram method), but her data are limited to three protocols of children from 4 to 6 years of age. She also provided vague references to experiments with 8- to 10-year-old children. She concluded that: the child of 4 to 5 years of age is incapable of creating a pictogram for remembering phrases (like "a girl is listening," "a boy is deaf," "a teacher is angry"), success for the 5- to 6-year-old depends on how pronounced egocentric speech is, and children of 8- to 10-years old successfully fulfill the task without using external speech.

Undoubtedly, it was A. N. Leont'ev, who studied voluntary mediated verbal memory and compared it with voluntary unmediated memory, who achieved the greatest success in this area of research (Leont'ev, 1983, first edition 1931). His study has been given a rather detailed and critical account in the book of van der Veer and Valsiner (1991, pp. 230–234). It is worth noting, that all the studies mentioned above used the method of double stimulation developed by Vygotsky.

SUMMARY

In conclusion, I wish to focus on two questions. The first is whether the account provided here attributes too many stages of development to Vygotsky's conception. The seven-stage scheme presented in this chapter can obviously be structured into four phases: natural functions, intermental functions, extramental functions, and intramental functions. I have proposed dividing each of the last three phases into two. The logic of this separation follows that of Vygotsky who emphasized the difference between the stage of naïve psychology (magical stage) and the stage of using external signs (extramental functioning), but the majority of the examples for the stage of naïve psychology obviously belong to the stage at which extramental functioning has not yet formed. I believe it makes sense to apply the same approach to the earlier and the later stages because this allows Vygotsky's conception to be more precise and differentiated.

The other question has a more common, fundamental, and problematic nature. What general type of approach does Vygotsky's analysis represent? Is it a theory of the same type as Piaget's stage analysis? Should we consider the various stages as sequential steps in the synchronized and parallel development of all mental functions?

At this point, I will simply express a hypothesis. It seems to me that from a Piagetian perspective Vygotsky's concept of stages is a rather odd and undifferentiated mix. Instead of representing a modular approach, it qualifies as a multilineal process; different lines pass through roughly the same stages, but not in a synchronic manner. This involves a sort of symbiosis in which psychological development, from the point of view of its moving forces, is a polyfactor process. The term *factor* is used by Vygotsky as often as, say, the term *law*. It is also necessary to take into account that he attributed to the category of the developmental factors such concepts as "moving forces," "origins," "bases," "reasons," "determinants," "presuppositions," "conditions," and so forth. This "side" of Vygotsky's conception also deserves a thorough logico-semantic analysis.

7 Mediation

Mediation is a theme that runs throughout the writings of Lev Semë-novich Vygotsky. In his view, a hallmark of human consciousness is that it is associated with the use of tools, especially "psychological tools" or "signs." Instead of acting in a direct, unmediated way in the social and physical world, our contact with the world is indirect or mediated by signs. This means that understanding the emergence and the definition of higher mental processes must be grounded in the notion of mediation.

Mediation also provides the foundation for another of Vygotsky's theoretical goals, namely, building a link between social and historical processes, on the one hand, and individuals' mental processes, on the other. It is because humans internalize forms of mediation provided by particular cultural, historical, and institutional forces that their mental functioning sociohistorically situated.

The importance that Vygotsky attached to mediation is reflected in a lecture he delivered near the end of his life, where he asserted, "A central fact of our psychology is the fact of mediation [oposredovanie]" (Vygotsky, 1982, p. 166). But this is an issue that concerned him from the beginning of his career onward. In a 1930 report on "The Instrumental Method in Psychology," for example, he focused on the importance of signs as "artificial formations...[that] are social, not organic or individual" (Vygotsky, 1981, p. 137) and he included under this heading: "language; various systems for counting; mnemonic techniques; algebraic symbol systems; works of art; writing; schemes, diagrams, maps, and mechanical drawings; all sorts of conventional signs" (Vygotsky, 1981, p. 137).

The writing of this chapter was assisted by a grant from the Spencer Foundation. The statements made and the views expressed are solely the responsibility of the author. Not for quotation.

In the analysis of the instrumental method that he provides in this article, Vygotsky outlined a mediational triangle for "artificial (instrumental) acts" (Vygotsky, 1981, p. 137). With regard to memory, for example, this meant that

> In natural memory, the direct (conditioned reflex) associative connection A-B is established between two stimuli A and B. In artificial, mnemotechnical memory of the same impression, instead of this direct connection A-B, two new connections, A-X and B-X, are established with the help of the psychological tool X (e.g., a knot in a handkerchief, a string on one's finger, a mnemonic scheme). (Vygotsky, 1981, p. 138)

It is no accident that this formulation bears striking similarities to the "basic mediational triangle" that Michael Cole (1996) places at the foundation of cultural psychology or to the elaborated set of triangles within triangles that Yrjö Engeström (1987) has employed in his writings. The ideas that Vygotsky developed have been elaborated in a variety of ways by other theorists to yield several productive lines of inquiry.

Vygotsky harnessed a developmental, or "genetic," method (Wertsch, 1985) when analyzing mediation, and for him this meant emphasizing qualitative transformation rather than quantitative increments. From this perspective, the inclusion of signs into human action does not simply lead to quantitative improvements in terms of speed or efficiency. Instead, the focus is on how the inclusion of tools and signs leads to qualitative transformation, a point Vygotsky made when he wrote, "By being included in the process of behavior, the psychological tool [i.e., sign] alters the entire flow and structure of mental functions. It does this by determining the structure of a new instrumental act just as a technical tool alters the process of a natural adaptation by determining the form of labor operations" (Vygotsky, 1981, p. 137).

In short, *mediation* is a central theme that runs throughout Vygotsky's thinking. However, this does not mean that he gave it a single, unified definition. Instead, mediation emerged in his texts in a variety of ways, and in the process, somewhat different meanings arose. I begin by presenting a basic opposition in the meanings that the term "mediation" took on in Vygotsky's writings. After outlining the two general types of mediation I see in his texts, I will return to some overarching themes that show how they can be understood as part of a larger picture.

VYGOTSKY'S TWO PERSPECTIVES ON MEDIATION

It is possible to find order in what otherwise might appear to be a varied, indeed contradictory, picture in Vygotsky's writings by distinguishing between two basic types of mediation. This distinction has as much to do with the different disciplinary lenses through which Vygotsky approached mediation as it has to do with the actual differences in the forms it takes.

During the last decade of his career, Vygotsky was busy speaking to psychologists, teachers, and professionals concerned with children and adults with disabilities and difficulties, and, in doing so, he employed the professional language of the psychology and physiology of his day, a form of speaking that qualifies as what Bakhtin (1986) called a "social language." At the same time, however, Vygotsky continued to employ the theoretical framework and social language he had acquired in his early study of semiotics, poetics, and literary theory. These two social languages need not be viewed as entirely distinct or mutually unintelligible, but in many instances, they led Vygotsky to take somewhat different perspectives on a range of topics, including mediation.

When employing the first of these social languages, Vygotsky spoke in the idiom of psychology, especially about what we would today view as a form of behaviorism, or perhaps cognitivism, to come up with an account of what I will call "explicit mediation." The mediation involved is explicit in two senses. First, it is explicit in that an individual, or another person who is directing this individual, overtly and intentionally introduce a "stimulus means" into an ongoing stream of activity. Second, it is explicit in the sense that the materiality of the stimulus means, or signs involved, tends to be obvious and nontransitory.

Explicit mediation continues to be a topic of study in contemporary psychology and cognitive science. For example, in his analysis of "how a cockpit remembers its speeds," Edwin Hutchins (1995) examines human agents' uses of various "sociotechnical systems" to organize their memory and cognitive processes. As part of his argument, he makes an explicit call for cognitive science to go beyond its focus on isolated individuals and to take into account the role of cultural tools such as airplane gauges and instruments in remembering and human action in general.

Standing in contrast to explicit mediation is "implicit mediation," which tends to be less obvious and, therefore, more difficult to detect. For examples of *implicit mediation*, consider Vygotsky's discussions of the role of social and inner speech in mediating human consciousness. Because of the ephemeral and fleeting nature of these forms of mediation, they are often "transparent" to the unwary observer and are, therefore, less easily taken as objects of conscious reflection or manipulation. Furthermore, implicit mediation typically does not need to be artificially and intentionally introduced into ongoing action. Instead, it is part of an already ongoing communicative stream that is brought into contact with other forms of action. Indeed, one of the properties that characterizes implicit mediation is that it involves signs, especially natural language, whose primary function is communication. In contrast to the case for explicit mediation, these signs are not purposefully introduced into human action, and they do not initially emerge for the purpose of organizing it. Instead, they are part of a preexisting, independent stream of communicative action that becomes integrated with other forms of goal-directed behavior.

EXPLICIT MEDIATION

Comments about what I am calling explicit mediation can be found at many points in Vygotsky's writing and in the work of his students and colleagues. For example, explicit mediation underpins his approach to concept development (e.g., Vygotsky, 1987, chapters 5 and 6), as well as the study of memory development in the "Forbidden Colors Task" used by Aleksei Nikolaevich Leont'ev in research he conducted in Vygotsky's Laboratory (cf. Leont'ev, 1932; Vygotsky, 1978, pp. 38–51).

Explicit mediation is usually at issue in discussions of the "functional method of dual stimulation," a notion that Vygotsky outlined in "An Experimental Study of Concept Development," in chapter 5 of *Thinking and Speech*. There he wrote:

> In using this method, we study the development and activity of the higher mental functions with the aid of two sets of stimuli. These two sets of stimuli fulfill different roles *vis-à-vis* the subject's behavior. One set of stimuli fulfills the function of the object on which the subject's activity is directed. The second functions as signs that facilitate the organization of this activity. (Vygotsky, 1987, p. 127)

In studies involving dual stimulation, Vygotsky's basic procedure was to encourage subjects to use a set of artificial stimuli, or signs that are overtly introduced into a subject's activity by an experimenter. For example, in the Forbidden Colors Task, subjects engaged in a task that required them to remember a list of color terms. They were given a set of colored cards and told that these cards could help them remember what color terms they had already mentioned and, according to the rules of the game, were not to mention again. In this case, the first set of stimuli, which "fulfill the function of the object on which the subject's activity is directed," was the set of color terms used by the subjects as they responded to the experimenter's questions. The second set of stimuli that were to function "as signs that facilitate the organization of this activity" were the colored cards introduced by the experimenter.

The basic aim of the Forbidden Colors Task study was to document how children use the signs provided by the experimenter (i.e., the colored cards) more effectively with age. Most 5- and 6-year-olds did not seem to realize that the signs had anything to do with their performance on the task, whereas 10- to 13-year-olds clearly did. The developmental path involved is one that moves from a point where the stimuli had very little meaning and functional efficacy to a point where subjects came to appreciate their significance for organizing their performance.

The following summary of the general point to be derived from this study frames this claim in terms of Vygotsky's genetic method, with its focus on qualitative transformation.

> We have found that sign operations appear as the result of a complex and prolonged process subject to all the basic laws of psychological evolution. *This means that sign-using activity in children is neither simply invented nor passed down from adults;* rather it arises from something that is originally not a sign operation and becomes one only after a series of *qualitative* transformations.
> (Vygotsky, 1978, pp. 45–46; emphasis in the original)

At this and other points where Vygotsky dealt with explicit mediation, he focused on how signs can be introduced to facilitate its organization. On the one hand, he presented his points in a social language of stimuli and responses, a language that would suggest there is little room for talk about the meaning or functional significance of signs. It would appear that one of his reasons for formulating things in this way was to join an ongoing intellectual discussion that employed this social language. On the other hand, his emphasis on the qualitative transformation of stimulus signs as they are employed at higher levels of development suggests that their meaning is undergoing change, a claim that lies outside the boundaries of this social language, which tends to eschew notions such as meaning or signification. In my view, the fact that Vygotsky introduced meaning into this discussion reflects his continuing concern with the poetic and semiotic issues that had been at the core of his studies since his earliest years, a concern that emerges more clearly in his writings that deal with the second general category of mediation.

IMPLICIT MEDIATION

Ideas about what I am calling implicit mediation emerge at numerous points in Vygotsky's writings, but perhaps the most elaborate rendition can be found in chapter 7 of *Thinking and Speech* (Vygotsky, 1987), a text he completed near the end of his life. The title of this chapter is "Thought and Word" [Mysl' i Slovo].

The two terms in this chapter title represent poles of an opposition in Vygotsky's view. He formulated this opposition in order to highlight a conceptual problem he saw in much of the existing literature on thinking and speech. This was the "tendency to view thought and word as two independent and isolated elements" (Vygotsky, 1987, pp. 243–244). His account of verbal thinking – an account in which opposition, tension, and dialectic characterize the relationship between the two terms – was an attempt to overcome this tendency.

In his critique of the kind of false and misleading isolation of thought and word that he saw in the research of his day, Vygotsky proposed taking "word meaning" as a unit of analysis, something that allows us to recognize that it is "a phenomenon of both speech and intellect" (Vygotsky, 1987, p. 244). Throughout this chapter, Vygotsky emphasized the need to focus on the dialectic between thought and word. He viewed this dialectic as a sort of developmental struggle and asserted that this was "the primary result of this work [and]...the conceptual center of our investigation" (Vygotsky, 1987, p. 245). In his view, "The discovery that word meaning changes and develops is our new and fundamental contribution to the theory of thinking and speech" (Vygotsky, 1987, p. 245).

Vygotsky saw this claim about the developmental relationship between thought and word as applying to *microgenetic*, as well as *ontogenetic* processes, a point that is reflected in his assertion that word meaning "changes during the child's development and with different modes of functioning of thought" (Vygotsky, 1987, p. 249). Regardless of which "genetic domain" (Wertsch, 1985) is at issue, the general picture Vygotsky presented was one in which thought is posited to be an inchoate, "fused, unpartitioned whole" (Vygotsky, 1987, p. 251) that comes into contact with words, which involve generalization and discrete, sequential representation.

With regard to the latter realm of words, generalization, and discrete, sequential representation, Vygotsky posited "two planes of speech and argued that "the inner, meaningful, semantic aspect of speech is associated with different laws of movement than its external, auditory aspect" (Vygotsky, 1987, p. 250). This provided the foundation for an account of inner speech that was used by Luria (1975), Akhutina (1975), and others in their analyses of "dynamic aphasia." The general line of reasoning is one in which inner speech, with its peculiar properties such as *predicativity* (the tendency to drop "given" information or the "psychological subject") and *agglutination* (the tendency to combine surface forms into single units – see Wertsch [1985] on predicativity and agglutination) differs from the grammatical organization of external, auditory speech.

In this account, inner speech imposes the first round of segmentation and sequential organization on thought as it makes its way to overt expression.

In chapter 7 of *Thinking and Speech*, then, the story line is one in which two types of representation collide and mutually transform one another. One type – "thought" [mysl'] – is relatively inchoate, fused, unpartitioned, and nonsequential, and the other – "word" [slovo] introduces segmentation and sequence. For my purposes, what is important in all this is that the mediation involved is not explicit, that is, not the object of conscious reflection and not externally or intentionally introduced. Instead, mediation is something that is automatically and in most cases unintentionally built into mental functioning.

In developing his line of reasoning on this issue, Vygotsky was heavily indebted to one of his mentors, Gustav Gustavovich Shpet (1879–1937). In chapter 7 of *Thinking and Speech*, Vygotsky did not cite Shpet (although he did cite him in earlier work), but the reasons for this probably stemmed from political necessity. As Martsinkovskaya (1996), Nemeth (1997), and Zinchenko (2000) discuss, Shpet's problems with Soviet authorities, problems that would eventually lead to his brutal interrogation and execution in 1937, were already starting to emerge in the early 1930s. Recent accounts of Vygotsky's political acumen by Cole and Levitin (2006) make it clear that he would have been aware of what was, and was not permissible in the political atmosphere of the early 1930s in the USSR.

In any event, we know that Vygotsky was a student in Shpet's seminars for two years (Vygodskaya & Lifanova, 1996), and the themes that were discussed there undoubtedly included those outlined by Shpet in his writings, especially in his 1927 monograph, *The Inner Form of the Word: Studies and Variations on a Humboldtian Theme* (Shpet, 1999).

Building on the conceptual groundwork laid by Wilhelm von Humboldt, Shpet emphasized that,

> Language is not completed action, "ergon," but protracted activity, "energeia," that is, as Humboldt explained, "perpetually repeated work of the spirit, directed at making articulate sound the means for expressing thought." ... Synthesis in this case does not consist of tying together two abstracted units: pure thought and pure sound, but two members of a unified concrete structure, two terms of relationship: object oriented sense content ... and the external form of its verbal expression-embodiment ... in sensory perceptible forms. These forms are transformed through a relation to sense from natural forms combined in the "thing" to social signification specifically in the signs of cultural meaning.
>
> (Vygotsky, 1996, p. 94)

Shpet's insistence on language as activity is quite consistent with
Vygotsky's focus on speech, as opposed to language. And Shpet's argument that the dialectic or synthesis involved is not between pure thought
and pure sound is consistent with Vygotsky's critique of investigators
who mistakenly viewed "thought and word as two independent and isolated elements." Instead of focusing on such elements as if they can be
considered separately, Vygotsky, like Shpet, insisted on examining them
as part of a unit of analysis that is inherently complex and dynamic. In
Vygotsky's terms:

> This central idea . . . can be expressed in the following general formula:
> The relationship of thought to word is not a thing but a process, a move-
> ment from thought to word and from word to thought. Psychological
> analysis indicates that this relationship is a developing process which
> changes as it passes through a series of stages . . . The movement of think-
> ing from thought to word is a developmental process.
>
> (Vygotsky, 1987, p. 250)

From this perspective the dialectic involved is between a material sign
form – what Charles Sanders Peirce (1960) called a "sign vehicle" – and
the object-oriented intentions of speakers or listeners. It always involves
an element of collision and conflict between a sign vehicle, whose meaning tends to abstract and generalize and belongs to a preexisting semiotic
community, on the one hand, and the unique, spatiotemporally located
intention of the individual, on the other.

These points can be used to help summarize some of the differences
between implicit and explicit mediation. Explicit mediation involves
the intentional introduction of signs into an ongoing flow of activity. In
this case, the signs tend to be designed and introduced by an external
agent, such as a tutor, who can help reorganize an activity in some way.
In contrast, implicit mediation typically involves signs in the form of
natural language that have evolved in the service of communication and
are then harnessed in other forms of activity. Because the integration of
signs into thinking, remembering, and other forms of mental functioning
occurs as part of the naturally occurring dialectic outlined by Shpet and
Vygotsky, they do not readily become the object of consciousness or
reflection.

SIGN MEANING DEVELOPS

The distinction I have drawn between explicit and implicit mediation in
Vygotsky's writings might appear to take the form of a neat, even polar
opposition, but this would be to oversimplify. The fact that these two

forms of mediation are part of a broader conceptual framework means that they share several common features, which can be appreciated by returning to Vygotsky's basic maxim that "sign meaning develops."

Throughout his writings Vygotsky emphasized the importance of using a developmental method to understand human mental functioning, and this applied to mediation in all its forms no less than any other topic. In this connection, he argued that a hallmark of the relationship between sign and behavior, as well as between word and thought, is that it undergoes fundamental change.

The general line of reasoning Vygotsky employed in this respect grew out of his critique of theorists who assumed that the relationship between word and thought remains constant. In contrast to this, he began with the assumption that signs first emerge in social and individual action without their users' full understanding of their meaning or functional role. What then follows is a process of coming to understand the meaning and functional significance of the sign forms that one has been using all along. In an important sense humans use signs before understanding what they are doing, or demonstrate "performance before competence," as Courtney Cazden (1981) succinctly and elegantly put it.

Vygotsky's line of reasoning on this issue rests on crucial assumptions about signs and their use in social and mental processes. In particular, it rests on ideas inherent in the semiotic triangle mentioned earlier, which distinguishes between sign form and sign meaning. In his account of phenomena ranging from the stimulus signs used in the Forbidden Colors Task to the regulative function of social, egocentric, and inner speech, Vygotsky assumed that a material sign form is involved and that this is crucial for understanding how its meaning can develop. The key to this is the insight that material sign forms make it possible to initiate communication and self-regulation, at least at primitive levels, even when the agents involved do not understand their full significance.

From this perspective, the general goal of instruction is to assist students in becoming fluent users of a sign system. The outcome is a new level, often a qualitatively new type, of "distributed cognition" (Salomon, 1993). Namely, it involves distribution between signs and the active agents employing them. In this approach, instruction amounts to a sort of "taming," or "domestication," of novices' actions in the world. This domestication has both benefits and costs because cultural tools inevitably bring with them "constraints" as well as "affordances" (Gibson, 1979; Wertsch, 1998). For example, learning how to deal with a set of data from empirical observations by employing a particular graphing technique provides insight into patterns that would otherwise remain undetected, but it also entails being less able to see other patterns that could be revealed by employing different means.

From a Vygotskian perspective, the process of mastering a semiotic tool typically begins on the social plane, though it of course has individual psychological moments and outcomes as well. In his "general genetic law of cultural development," Vygotsky made this point by arguing that higher mental functioning appears first on the "intermental" and then on the "intramental" plane. When encountering a new cultural tool, this means that the first stages of acquaintance typically involve social interaction and negotiation between experts and novices or among novices. It is precisely by means of participating in this social interaction that interpretations are first proposed and worked out and, therefore, become available to be taken over by individuals.

An interesting property of the sign systems that are at the heart of instruction is that they are incredibly robust in that they can allow interpretation and understanding at many different levels, and yet still support some form of the intermental functioning required to move learning and instruction along. It often seems to be possible to use these sign systems to communicate even with a very low level of shared understanding of their full implications. Indeed, most of us probably speak, calculate, and carry out other semiotic actions most of the time without understanding the full power of the sign systems we are employing. In the famous image provided by Edward Sapir (1921), it is as if we are harnessing a dynamo capable of generating a huge amount of electricity to power a simple doorbell.

This approach suggests that the act of speaking often (perhaps always) involves employing a sign system that forces us to say more (as well as perhaps less) than what we understand or intend. We say more in the sense that our interlocutors may understand us to be conveying a higher level message than our mastery of the sign system would warrant. This is so in everyday communication, even when we are speaking about topics on which we have developed real expertise, but it has particularly important implications when it comes to how novices participate in intermental functioning in instructional settings.

In order to see how all this works, it is useful to invoke a notion of "intersubjectivity" such as that proposed by Ragnar Rommetveit (1972, 1979) in connection with human communication in general and Barbara Rogoff (1980) in connection with human development and socialization in particular. Recently, Rommetveit has provided the following illustration of this phenomenon:

> Imagine the following situation: A lady who is a very knowledgeable amateur auto mechanic discovers that there is something wrong with the carburetor of her car. Her husband, who is notoriously ignorant about car engines and does not even know what a carburetor looks like, offers to drive the car to a garage to have it repaired. He tells the car

mechanic at the garage: "There is apparently something wrong with the carburetor." This saves the latter considerable time in searching for the problem.

For Rommetveit, the point is that the husband in this case may have attained only a very minimal level of intersubjectivity with the mechanic when it comes to understanding the idea and function – and even the referent – of "carburetor." However, he was still capable of passing along the message from his wife because he was harnessing a sign vehicle that did part of the work for him. As Rommetveit notes, instead of assuming that the husband possessed the understanding that could fully back up this utterance, he was involved in an episode of "ventriloquation" that allowed him to say more than he understood.

The point of Rommetveit's example is not to encourage us to go about using expressions for which we have only a minimal understanding. Indeed, his example is clever precisely to the degree that it manages to do something unusual in this regard. In socialization, learning, and instruction, though, the point of many exercises may be to put us in a position not unlike that of the husband in this illustration. The standard situation in many instructional settings involves students' saying and doing things that they only partially understand. This raises what might appear to some to be a paradox of how it is possible to say more than one understands, but it makes sense if one recognizes that the material form of sign vehicles allows us to function at a level that is "out ahead" of our current mastery.

But the point for instruction goes beyond this. Not only may it be possible, but it may be *desirable* for students to say and do things that seem to extend beyond their level of understanding. This is because such a possibility means they can enter into a basic form of intersubjectivity with more experienced teachers and experts and thereby leverage their way up through increasing levels of expertise. What might at first appear to be a failure to communicate is often the key to entering into a new area of instruction.

To illustrate how these ideas are instantiated in an instructional setting, I turn to a recent analysis by Wertsch and Kazak (in press). This has to do with a teacher speaking to a group of students about organizing and presenting data from observations they had made about what conditions foster the most growth in plants. Specifically, they had grown plants under various conditions of light. By discussing the date the students had collected in this exercise, this teacher introduced both explicit mediation and implicit forms of mediation. The explicit mediational means he introduced was a piece of graph paper that the students were to use for presenting their data. The implicit mediation in this case arose in connection with his use of a few basic terms. In addition to telling the students "to organize the data in some way," he asks the students to "try to determine what's the typical fast plant," using the term "typical" on several occasions, and he tells them that they should asking "how spread out" the data are.

For anyone familiar with statistical analysis, terms such as "typical" and "spread out" are tied to a standard set of procedures and measures. Namely, the typicality about which the instructor was inquiring has to do with central tendency, and a concern with how spread out the data are reflects an interest in what is called variation in the language of statistics. This instructor did not employ technical terms like "central tendency" or "variation" into the discussion, but he was introducing expressions intended to get students to start thinking about these issues. Furthermore, he provided them with graph paper, which would "help them" in some way, such as plotting the data in the form of a histogram. From the perspective of analyzing mediation, then, he was introducing three material sign vehicles into the *intermental* and *intramental* functioning that had only minimal meaning or functional significance for the students.

In the discussion that followed, it became quite clear that, at least initially, the students' understanding of how to use graph paper to organize the data, as well as their understanding of the terms "typical" and "spread out" had little overlap with that of the instructor. The group first proposed to put one number from their data set in each square on the paper. This seems to have been their initial attempt to respond to the directive to "organize the data." To be sure, they were using the material sign vehicle (i.e., the graph paper) provided to them, but they clearly did not know how to use it as an expert would. In contrast to expert performance, they were using this tool at a very low level of sophistication, one that indeed might simply be termed inappropriate. In this sense, their use (misuse?) of the cultural tool bears a striking resemblance with young children's use of cards as memory cues in Leont'ev's "forbidden colors task" (Vygotsky, 1978).

Well into this instructional session, the instructor clearly understood that the students still were using the graph paper in a way that had little to do with how it would be employed by an expert user, and she asked them to reflect on what they were doing. She pointed out, "So, we have these numbers from 30 to 255. What would be a good way of showing our data to make sense?" This increasingly direct form of "other-regulation" (Wertsch, 1985) still did not result in the students' using the graph paper in a way that would organize the data into something like a histogram, and the instructor switched from using questions and other forms of indirect other–regulation to a concrete proposal for how the graph paper should be used. Specifically, she suggested, "It would be possible to group the numbers in one square, like from this to this, and then put an X there for each value in that range, like a frequency table or histogram."

This seems to have generated a new insight in the students as to how the graph paper could be used as a cultural tool to get at the issues of central tendency and variation. They eventually turned to grouping their data in such a way that their presentation on the graph paper suggested – at least to the expert eye – central tendency and distribution. At the end of this session, the students were clearly much closer to an expert's perspective than they had been at the beginning of the session.

For a Vygotsky-Shpet approach to learning and instruction, the goal is to encourage students to master the use of cultural tools. Becoming more expert means being socialized into an existing social order, characterized by an existing set of cultural tools, and expertise is reflected in the ability to use these tools flexibly and fluently. Given that the goal is to socialize students to use socioculturally provided and sanctioned semiotic means, the issue is how to engage them in a way that will lead to increasing levels of expertise, and this is where material sign vehicles as entry-level mechanisms come into play. Thanks to these, it is possible to create initial levels of intersubjectivity when interlocutors have much different levels of understanding of what the task is and how to leverage that to higher levels of intersubjectivity and expertise.

The illustration involving students and instructors discussing ways to present data from a science experiment provides an example of this and also is revealing of how explicit and implicit mediation operate. What is perhaps most striking about this interaction is the degree to which the teacher and students were able to enter into a superficial level of intermental functioning on the basis of very limited agreement on the meaning of sign forms. Just as in Rommetveit's example of the man talking about carburetors with very little understanding of what the term means, the students participated in an exchange on the basis of very minimal understanding of what the teacher's words mean and what the graph paper was for.

In all the cases examined in this chapter the material sign vehicle is an essential part of the story. This sign vehicle could take the form of spoken words ("typical," "spread out"), graph paper, colored cards, and so forth, and it provided the foundation on which intersubjectivity and the mastery of sign meaning could grow.

CONCLUSION

Mediation is such a central category in Vygotsky's writings that it deserves careful scrutiny for anyone interested in his general approach. This is no easy task, however, given that Vygotsky seems to have had somewhat different thoughts at different points in his extensive writings. In some cases, he dealt with mediation as an issue of stimuli, stimulus means, and other terms from psychology, and in others he formulated it in terms of meaning, sense, and other semiotic constructs. In the former case, he seems to have been casting his analysis in a social language of the psychology of his day, and in the latter, he was harnessing a social language that belonged to a tradition of semiotics that can be traced to Shpet, Husserl, and Humboldt.

In an effort to bring some clarity to this complex picture, I have distinguished between two main categories of mediation in Vygotsky's writings: explicit and implicit. The former is explicit in the sense that it is intentionally and overtly introduced into problem solving activity, often by an outside party, and the materiality of the signs involved (e.g., colored cards in Leont'ev's Forbidden Colors Task or graph paper in the classroom illustration) tends to be obvious and nontransitory. In contrast, the latter is implicit in that it typically involves spoken language, whose materiality is transitory and seemingly ephemeral. The transparency of the signs in this case is exacerbated by the fact that they preexist in communication and are often not consciously or intentionally introduced into a problem solving or memory task setting as mediational means.

The two distinct theoretical traditions and social languages on which Vygotsky drew when developing his claims about *mediation means,* show that he discussed a range of quite disparate forms of sign processes under this general heading. However, the two forms of mediation can be seen as part of a larger theoretical framework when one considers some commonalities in the way he treated these forms. In particular, he viewed both forms of mediation under the general dictum that sign meaning develops.

As I have emphasized, this dictum rests on the separation of material sign form from sign meaning, and this semiotic insight is what motivated Vygotsky's critique of psychologists who failed to understand the dynamics of the relationship between these two elements. From his perspective, the development of mediated action involves a dynamic transition from minimal appreciation of the meaning and functional significance of a sign form to ever increasing levels of sophistication.

The distinction between explicit and implicit mediation that I have developed in this chapter is not so much a critique as an explication of Vygotsky's ideas. However, it is an explication with a mission, namely, to clarify discussion of these ideas and, hopefully, reduce the incidence of bogus disagreement as we seek to harness Vygotsky's conceptual system.

8 Vygotsky and Culture

Vygotsky's ideas about culture are of special interest because he attributed such an essential role to culture in human psychological processes. However, any attempt to provide an adequate account of his ideas about culture and human nature faces formidable obstacles. To begin with, the term "culture" is virtually absent from the indexes of his published works. When we delve deeper into his texts, we find *culture* appearing in three distinctive forms.

First, *culture* defined as artistic products and the processes of creation, appears in such works as *The Psychology of Art*, as part of Vygotsky's long-standing interest in literary and cultural criticism. This early involvement of culture in Vygotsky's writings (which engaged him in debates with Russian formalists) appears later in his extensive use of literary examples to illustrate the operation of important psychological functions. Tolstoy, Dostoevsky, and several Russian poets provide important material for his arguments in *Thinking and Speech*.

Second, when we turn to Vygotsky's better-known works on the development of higher psychological functions, *culture* appears in two related forms. We find it appearing in terms such as "cultural–historical" and "cultural development," which apply to the way in which the mediation of action through culture is a defining property of human psychological functioning.

Third, we find *culture* used in terms such as "cultural people," in relation to the term "primitive" peoples. Both his use of terms such as "cultural–historical" and his reference to cultural people (with its clear implication that there are people who lack culture) reflect the fact that at the time Vygotsky was writing dominant Western European traditions regarding the relation of culture and thought assumed that both culture and mind evolve and that they evolve in close connection with each other (Cole, 1996; Jahoda, 1999; van der Veer, 1996). Vygotsky often refers to writers representing these traditions. Therefore, a good deal of what we can conclude about his conceptions regarding culture must be induced from these references and the uses he makes of them.

A final complication to keep in mind is that twenty-first century notions of culture, both in Europe and elsewhere, differ in a number of important ways from those that were prevalent during Vygotsky's life-time; because we are creatures of our own times and places, we need to be as clear as possible about when we are projecting our own conceptions of culture onto the writings of Vygotsky and of his colleagues.

To deal with these complexities, we begin this chapter by seeking to understand issues of culture and cultural change as they were under-stood in European thought at the time Vygotsky and his colleagues for-mulated cultural–historical psychology, and how Vygotsky drew upon these understandings. This effort will take us back to German, French, and English scholars of the nineteenth and early twentieth centuries as well as to other Russian followers such as Potebnya and Shpet.

Next we will summarize the way that these conceptions of culture influenced theoretical and empirical research carried out by Vygotsky and his colleagues as they sought to understand the relationship between culture and psychological processes and the reception that this research encountered in the USSR at the time.

We end by evaluating Vygotsky's notion of culture and its role in human development from a contemporary viewpoint, seeking to high-light aspects of his approach that invite modification and those that are likely to be of central importance to those who seek to use his ideas as a basis for their own attempts to understand culture and human psycho-logical processes.

CULTURE AND CULTURES: DIFFERENCE AND DEFICIENCY

Since the time of Herodotus (484–425 B.C.E.) (Herodotus, 1945), the term "culture," as applied to human groups, has been used in two different senses that share a common core.[1] The first sense is to be found in the descriptions of the lifeways of the many peoples Herodotus visited as expressed in their religion, art, and beliefs about the gods and their everyday practices. The second sense of "culture" involves the impor-tant dimension of evaluation that arises when descriptions of specific

---

[1] The earliest known uses of the term "culture" in Latin referred almost exclusively to the process of raising crops, as seen in such terms as agriculture and horticulture. This meaning survives and has interesting heuristic value for developmentalists, but it is not relevant to understandings used in the social sciences in the early twentieth century (cf. Cole, 1996, ch. 4).

lifeways are compared. Very often, this second sense leads to notions of one culture being superior to another, a superiority attributed to users of the culture as well. This evaluative dimension can be seen in the shifting meaning of the term "barbarian" that Herodotus used to describe the subjects of his inquiries. In early fourth-century Greece, barbarian was a descriptive term; for Herodotus, barbarian meant "people who are different," and his *History* is an inquisitive catalogue of human variability that is relatively free of strong value judgments.

However, it was not long before difference became deficiency. Later Greeks used "barbarian" to mean "outlandish, rude, brutal." Both the senses of barbaric as different and as deficient were retained when the term was appropriated into Latin. Subsequently, it came to mean "uncivilized," or "uncultured," and later "non-Christian." The increasingly unflattering meanings attached to barbarian reached their apex when the word was taken into English, where it is equated with "savage, rude, savagely cruel, and inhuman" (*Oxford English Dictionary*, 2nd ed., 1987).

When the modern social sciences were beginning to take shape in the eighteenth and nineteenth centuries, this same duality between descriptive, relatively nonjudgmental versus value-laden, hierarchical notions of culture was very much in evidence (Jahoda, 1999). Some authors emphasized sociocultural evolution as a natural accompaniment of history and putative progress; others emphasized the uniqueness of cultural characteristics to current circumstances in their historical context; and some adopted mixed views.

On the relativistic, nonjudgmental side of this issue one encounters, for example, the ideas of Johann Herder (1744–1803) (Herder, 1966) who argued that traditions coded in language and custom constitute an organic unity that gives each human group its own sense of identity. Herder introduced the notion of *Völk*, a community of people with shared language and historical traditions. He is often credited with the earliest formulation of the modern concept of cultural relativism, for he believed that the diversity of *Völk* is to be valued, and he explicitly asserted that each social group should be evaluated in terms of its own circumstances: "Thus nations change according to place, time, and their inner character; each carries within itself the measure of its perfection, incommensurable with others" (1785/1969, vol. 4, p. 362).

But Herder's was a minority view. As documented in detail by Jahoda (1999) and Hodgen (1964), at least since the period of European exploration and colonialism, Europeans have considered the people they met to be either at a lower cultural level or not entirely human; the humanity of non-Europeans was brought into sufficient doubt on the grounds of their putative barbarous or uncultured state to serve as justification for genocidal wars of expropriation, slavery, and annihilation.

Even if we exclude what appear now as the most ludicrous of these views, which served as the foundations of scientific racism (e.g., that people of African descent are a species somewhere between apes and humans judging by the nature of their cultures), the view that cultures differ by levels, and that the European educated classes represent the highest level yet attained, was extremely widespread when the social sciences were taking shape. This view is reflected, for example, by the poet Mathew Arnold who defined culture as "the best that has been known and said in the world" (Arnold, 1874/1924). From this perspective, culture was associated with characteristics such as refinement of taste or qualities associated with an educated European person.

E. B. Tylor, often considered the "father of anthropology," mixed together the core and evaluative notions of culture in a manner designed to account for what he perceived to be the social–evolutionary changes in culture revealed by the historical record and by the accounts of missionaries and explorers. In *Primitive Culture* (1871), he defined culture as "that complex whole which includes knowledge, belief, art, morals, law, custom, and any other capabilities and habits acquired by man as a member of society" (Tylor, 1871/1958, p. 1). Here we have the core notion. But note that it is used in the singular; Tylor assumed *culture* to be a property of human life in any society but the "amount" of culture characteristic of any specific human group was assumed to differ. Using the term *civilization*, a virtual synonym for *culture* in Tylor's lexicon, he made his belief in sociocultural evolution quite explicit:

> We may fancy ourselves looking on Civilization, as in personal figure she traverses the world; we see her lingering or resting by the way, and often deviating into paths that bring her toiling back to where she had passed by long ago; but, direct or devious, her path lies forward, and if now and then she tries a few backward steps, her walk soon falls into helpless stumbling. It is not in her nature, her feet were not made to plant uncertain steps behind her, for both in her forward view and in her onward gain she is of truly human type.   (Tylor, 1958, p. 69)

Lewis Henry Morgan, on the basis of his experience living among the Iroquois, as well as his reading of Tylor and his understanding of historical sources, divided the evolution of human culture into three basic stages (*savagery, barbarism*, and *civilization*). Each stage was distinguished by technological developments that were correlated with development in patterns of subsistence, marriage, family, and political organization. In *Ancient Society* (1877), Morgan explicitly linked levels of culture/civilization to history:

> As it is undeniable that portions of the human family have existed in a state of savagery, other portions in a state of barbarism, and still others in a state of civilization, it seems equally so that these three distinct conditions are connected with each other in a natural as well as necessary sequence of progress.   (Morgan, 1877, p. 3)

Morgan is an important figure in considering the sources of Vygotsky's ideas because he had a major influence on Marx and Engels, whose ideas are frequently cited by Vygotsky.

An important manifestation of the view that degrees of culture differentiate social groups is that various scholars on whom Vygotsky drew used the terms *naturvölk* and *kulturvölk* ["natural people"/"cultural people"] that became common in German in the nineteenth century. These terms have the unfortunate connotation in English that there are human societies devoid of culture in comparison with those have acquired it. Wilhelm Wundt, who developed a *völkerpyschologie* in addition to his well-known version of scientific psychology, adhered to the distinction between naturvölker and kulturvölker. However, he maintained that although there were vast differences among societies in their level of Kultur, there were, strictly speaking, not human beings who could be described as entirely devoid of culture.[2]

Toward the end of the nineteenth century, the notion of culture as the lifeways of people conditioned by their unique historical circumstances forcefully reentered anthropological and psychological thought through the writings of Franz Boas and his students. Boas noted that the various constituents of culture identified by writers such as Tylor did not adhere in any neat way to permit the attribution of different overall levels of culture to one social group vis à vis another. For example,

---

[2] "Naturvölk" (from http://naturvolk.adlexikon.de/naturvolk.shtml) is a term for the people who inhabit the unchanged nature area isolated from the industrialized civilization and are, to a large extent, free of technology. Mostly. The term refers to relatively small groups of peoples in remote regions of the world, for example, in the savanna in Africa or in the rain forest of South America. Many "nature peoples" are threatened by penetrating the "civilization" in their own culture or in their existence.

The one exception to this generalization were people of African descent who were, collectively, viewed as transitional between nature and kulturvölk, but individual Africans were viewed, literally as "naturmenchen," or raw children of nature (see Jahoda, 1992, pp. 172–173). Confusion between cultural and biological sources of social group variation was common in the nineteenth century and became the basis for "scientific racism" in the twentieth century.

although the industrial technology of a group might be considered to be rudimentary, its artistic achievements (such as those of the peoples of the American and Canadian northwest) might seem unusually high. Consequently, rather than thinking of culture in the singular, a characteristic of a social group that varied in level or amount, Boas, much in the spirit of Herder, viewed a society's culture as a kind of collective response to the conditions of its history, which, by producing a unique set of resources for every human group, made cultures incommensurate with respect to any general criterion of level of achievement. Each culture needed to be taken on its own terms. Significantly, this turn toward discussion of cultures and their internal coherence as modes of life coincided with a marked change in the practice of anthropologists, who, instead of depending on the reports of explorers, missionaries, and colonial administrators, began to make it a practice to live among and learn the language of the people about whom they wrote. This practice helped to legitimate ethnographic fieldwork as the source of primary data about the nature of culture in human life.

However, the Boasian turn, with its accompanying practice of extensive ethnographic fieldwork, was not part of the Russian scholarly tradition on which Vygotsky drew, and it remains a very small part of Russian scholarly research to this day. Consequently, when we turn to definitions of culture in Russian, we see a combination of attributes that place it in the tradition that focuses on a conceptual core constituted of accomplishments inherited from the past and differentiated according to levels, especially with respect to "the best that has been known and said." In the official dictionary of the Soviet Academy of Sciences for 1958, for example, the primary (what we have referred to as "core") definition identifies culture as "the entirety of accomplishments of human society and manufacturing, social, and spiritual life." But next in line we learn that culture also refers to "the level of such accomplishments in a given epoch for one or another specific people" followed by "enlightenment" and "educatedness" (1958).

CORE AND COMPARISON IN VYGOTSKY

It should be clear that develop in developing a cultural–historical theory of human development, Vygotsky came upon his cultural–historical theory while deeply immersed in an academic and social tradition that assumed a close link between sociocultural evolution and history. He, like most of his German, French, English, and American contemporaries, assumed that all human beings lived in a manner akin to that of contemporary peoples in small, face-to-face societies where the technologies appear relatively simple and life is mediated primarily through oral language. This orientation to culture as a historical phenomenon is central to the comparative aspect of Vygotsky's theory.

In addition, he, like most of his contemporaries, believed that there was an intimate link between culture and mind. As he and Luria put it, "technology and social organization, which stem from a definite stage in the development of this technology, are the basic factors in the development of primitive man" (Vygotsky & Luria, 1993, pp. 92–93). This statement points us toward Vygotsky's understanding of the common "core" of culture characteristic of all *Homo sapiens*: the intertwining of their use of tools, signs, language, and the distinctive core of their technologies, with the special forms of social life that the technologies mediate.[3] Consequently, the core and the comparative aspects of his theory are also intimately related. In what follows, we will distinguish these core and comparative aspects to the extent possible.

The Core

Writing several decades after Vygotsky's death, Alexei A. Leontiev summarized the assumptions, attributable to the writings of Marx and Engels that constitute the core of a cultural–historical understanding of culture:

> The evolution of the species, "homo sapiens" . . . has proceeded in some other different sphere than the biological, the species characteristics being accumulated not in the form of morphological changes, but in some other form. It has been a sphere of social human life, a form of the fixation of the achievements of human activities in the social and historical experience of humanity. . . .
> (Leontiev, 1970, pp. 123–124, quoted in Wertsch, 1985)

It is difficult to overestimate the influence of the idea that tool making and use is the core of human beings' cultural (and psychological) nature among European and American intellectuals at the time Vygotsky was writing. A few examples here will suffice.

Henri Bergson, representing in this case the French sociogenetic perspective wrote,

> If we could rid ourselves of all pride, if, to define our species, we kept strictly to what the historic and prehistoric periods show us to be the constant characteristic of man and of intelligence, we should say not *Homo Sapiens* but *Homo Faber*. In short, *intelligence, considered in*

---

[3] In his prescient introduction to the 1962 edition of *Thought and Language,* Jerome Bruner (1962, p. vii) notes Vygotsky's fondness for Sir Francis Bacon's declaration that, "Neither the naked hand nor the understanding left to itself can effect much. It is by instruments and helps that the work is done" (Bacon, 1620/1960, p. 39).

> *what seems to be its original feature, is the faculty of manufacturing*
> *artificial objects, especially tools for making tools, and of indefinitely*
> *varying their manufacture.*   (Bergson, 1911/1983, p. 139)

The American psychologist, C. H. Judd (1926), who is best known for his work on transfer of training but who had studied with Wundt, put the matter as follows:

> The tools which man has invented are powerful influences in determin-
> ing the course of civilized life. Through the long ages while man has been
> inventing tools and learning to use them, his mode of individual reaction
> has been undergoing a change. He is no longer absorbed in direct attack on
> prey which furnishes him his food. He does not develop more skill in the
> use of claws and teeth in order that he may cope with his environment.
> He has adopted an indirect mode of action. He uses instruments which
> he has devised or borrowed from his forefathers or from his neighbor.
>   (Judd, 1926, pp. 3–4)

What distinguishes Vygotsky and Luria's approach is that they insist that what is crucial in human development, and distinct from the development of other creatures is not the existence of tool use or communication considered in isolation, but their fusion such that what are ordinarily considered separately as tools, signs, and symbols are unified.

> As soon as speech and the use of symbolic signs are included in this
> (tool mediated) operation, it transforms itself along entirely new line,
> overcoming the former natural laws and for the first time giving birth to
> authentically human use of implements...speech and action are in this
> case one and the same psychological function.
>   (Vygotsky & Luria, 1930/1993, pp. 108–109)

It is especially important to realize that the consequences of this new form of behavior, associated with biologically evolved human beings living in a culturally organized environment, change people's relationships not only to themselves (they are now capable of more effectively controlling their own behavior) and their relationship to the nonhuman world (they think about it and act on it through the medium of the accomplishments of the past), but with other people who constitute their social group as well. As Vygotsky and Luria note (1930/1993), from the earliest days of life "the road from object to child and from child to object lies through another person." They explained the process as follows:

> As children acquire language the fact that language, action on the world,
> and action involving other people are all part of a specifically human
> mode of life means that changes in one part of this system of inter-
> relations ineluctably brings about changes in the others. In Marxist

terms, changes in modes of production and relation of production are inextricably linked.   (Vygotsky & Luria, 1930/1933, p. 116)

CULTURES AND CULTURAL COMPARISONS

When it came to the issue of comparing cultures, the Western European traditions and dominant Russian beliefs on which Vygotsky drew adhered to a family of ideas that posited a succession of social-evolutionary stages in human development from the emergence of biologically modern, but culturally primitive humans, some tens of thousands of years ago to "modern, civilized" humans of whatever era and society the writer lived in. In the cases we have examined, the writers were part of the Euro-American society of the eighteenth through the twentieth centuries. In all but a few instances, Vygotsky denied the existence of human beings without culture – after all, he considered culture and culturally mediated thought/action to be the hallmark of the emergence of human beings as a distinct species.[4] So, for example, when Vygotsky and Luria make a point of noting that in speaking of "primitive man," they are talking about an abstraction or "the starting point of historical development." Yet, they argue, data about prehistoric humans ("the lowest rung of cultural development") and people from different contemporary cultures can both provide evidence about the psychology of primitive man. On both theoretical and empirical grounds, they argued that there are no *biological* differences distinguishing different human groups:

> ... from the point of view of the elementary physiological activity at the base of our perceptions and our movements, that is, all the components of the simplest reactions forming out behavior, no substantial difference exists between primitive man and cultural man.
>
> (Vygotsky & Luria, 1930/1993, p. 91)

Nevertheless, it is clear that like many before him, Vygotsky distinguished between "uncultured" (e.g., primitive) and cultural peoples. The underlying logic for the study of historical changes in culture and thinking could be summarized roughly as follows: All human beings share a common pool of elementary, or natural, psychological functions as a result of their common phylogenetic heritage. However, from the time

---

[4] As Mescheryakov (2000) notes, it is possible to find passages in Vygotsky's writings where he refers to primitiveness as somewhere intermediate between the cultural and the natural, but these appear to be cases where he is repeating the views of others rather than expressing his own view.

of their emergence as a species, human beings merged the creation of language and tools, and thereby remediated their relations to the natural world, themselves, and their social group. Because of humans' ability to build on past accomplishments, culture has, in general evolved, that is, increased in quantity and become more complex in quality (although, under some circumstances, devolution has also occurred).

Two kinds of psychological change vis à vis culture and its relationship to thought occur in tandem with each other over the course of cultural history. First, there is a greater and greater tendency to rely on cultural modes of behavior rather than natural modes of behavior. In their survey of evidence concerning the memory in "primitive" peoples, Vygotsky and Luria pointed to reports of extraordinary memory feats that they attributed to "natural," unmediated, memory, for example, Australian Aborigines were said to be able to recognize the footprint of everyone they knew and African tribal people were able to relay messages with uncanny accuracy. Vygotsky and Luria related this form of natural memory to what Jaensch (1925/1930) referred to as "eidetic imagery," the ability to reproduce a picture or page of text immediately after seeing it.

Second, they emphasized evolution of the mediational means of behavior, that is, the increased complexity of signs and tools. Well-known in this respect is their invocation (following Thurnwald, 1922) of the Inca quipu as a means of arithmetic calculation and devices that served as mnemonic devices for aiding in the sending of messages.

Vygotsky believed that this process of evolution/development in mediational means applied not only to specialized psychological tools such as arithmetic notation systems and writing but also to language itself. He assumed, based on the work of von Humboldt and Levy-Bruhl, as well as the writings of his Russian contemporaries Potebnya and Shpet, that primitive languages were relatively simple with restricted, often concrete vocabularies lacking in superordinate terms and simple grammars (Levy-Bruhl, 1910/1926; von Humboldt, 1836/1988). (For a discussion of Potebnya and Shpet's influence on Vygotsky's work, see van der Veer [1996].) According to this view, over the course of history, owing to the press of new forms of activity needed to deal with increasingly complex socioeconomic life, linguistic complexity, like the complexity of other technologies, increased, and so did the thought processes that it mediated.

Vygotsky and Luria summarize the overall process as follows:

> Paralleling a higher level of control over nature, man's social life and his labor activity begin to demand still higher requirements for control over

his own behavior. Language, calculation, writing, and other technical means of culture develop. With the aid of these means, man's behavior ascends to a higher level.   (Vygotsky & Luria, 1930/1993:, p. 139)

Commenting on this monograph, James Wertsch provides an appropriate summary of its place in studies of culture and thought that can serve to introduce modern attempts to build on, amend, and improve on, Vygotsky's approach to culture in relationship to human psychological processes.

> Thus, although some of the specifics of the claims of Vygotsky and Luria about culture may be outdated, this does not call into question the basic genetic approach that they were seeking to outline. We still have not come to grips with how one accounts for the complex structural properties of cultures and language on the one hand, and genetic transitions on the other. For example, as Wertsch and Tulviste (in press) note, there is very little attention paid in contemporary developmental psychology to historical factors and historical change. One manifestation of this general state of affairs is that, at a time of increasing traffic between psychologists and anthropologists, there still continues to be little productive contact between psychologists and historians. For all of these reasons, the attempt by Vygotsky and Luria to outline a "new genetic psychology" touching on multiple domains of development retains great contemporary relevance.   (Wertsch, 1993, pp. xi–xii)

There are ample excuses, should one wish to focus on them, to ignore Wertsch's advice about taking seriously the contemporary relevance of Vygotsky's ideas about culture, phylogenesis, and ontogeny. For example, there is a good deal of current evidence pointing to more prevelant tool use, communication abilities, and forms of practical intelligence in nonhuman primates and other animals than Vygotsky could have been aware of (e.g., de Waal, 2001). There is also a growing literature on socially acquired behavioral patterns that many consider evidence of culture among nonhuman primates. This literature contains evidence of the existence of patterns of behavior characteristic of a group that are acquired postnatally, which suggests that culture and tools use are not unique to humans (see Cole [2006] for a review). Bergson, Judd, and Vygotsky and his students, can be seen as naïve and mistaken in their invocation of tool use and manufacture, or the presence of culture, as uniquely human characteristics.

Reading Vygotsky's treatment of these materials based on the then-extant work of Köhler and others indicates that such a conclusion would be quite misleading. His evidence may have been deficient, but his treatment of the question of continuities and discontinuities in human evolution does not assume an either/or position. For example, he quotes the Marxist theorist Plekhanov to argue that evidence such as Köhler's probably justifies Darwin's arguments for the continuity of human and nonhuman primates. To characterize changes between humans and nonhuman primates, Vygotsky (following Engels) introduces the idea of the transformation of quantity into quality:

> However, we must not forget that *quantitative differences may transform into qualitative ones.* What may exist as *a rudimentary form* in one animal may become *outstanding signs* (in other species). We have to say that this is particularly true when it comes to the use of tools. An elephant breaks branches and uses then to swish flies. This is interesting and instructive. But using branches to battle flies probably played no substantial role in the history of "the elephant" species. Elephants did not become elephants for the reason that their more or less elephant-like ancestors swatted flies.

> This is not the case with man. The entire existence of an Australian aborigine depends on his boomerang, just as the entire existence of modern England depends upon her machines. Take the boomerang away from the aborigines, make him a farmer, then out of necessity he will have to completely change his life style, his habits, his entire style of thinking, his entire nature (Vygotsky & Luria, 1930/1993, p. 74).

CONTEMPORARY PERSPECTIVES INSPIRED BY VYGOTSKY

Over the past quarter century, many research programs and a large literature have grown up around the ideas of Vygotsky and his students. We restrict ourselves here to developments that highlight work that is most focused on the questions of culture discussed above, recognizing that questions of mediation cannot be entirely divorced from them (see Wertsch, Chapter 7, in this volume). Both the "core" and comparative aspects of Vygotsky's approach have been subject to collegial modification and not-so-collegial criticism both in Russia and abroad.

Concerns over Vygotsky's conceptions relating to the notion of culture were obvious from the initial proposal for a cultural–historical psychology. Vygotsky and his students were attacked in the 1930s as presenting inauthentic representations of a Marxist psychology, for their ideas about close linkages between the sociocultural–economic evolution on the one hand and the evolution of mental functioning on the other (for a summary, see Valsiner, 1988; van der veer, 2002). These criticisms are difficult to interpret with respect to their academic motivations because of the then-intensely xenophobic atmosphere in the USSR and the ongoing purge of Bolsheviks in all walks of life (Graham, 1972).

An article written for a 1966 symposium on Soviet psychology by Jeffrey Gray indicates the difficulties of interpretation that such conditions created even for those not living directly under Soviet control.

> The official status of Marxism-Leninism has had the result that philosophy intrudes in scientific research and writing in a way that is totally unexpected for a Western scientist. It is a shock to discover in a text ostensibly concerned with the empirical investigation of psychology that there are frequent references to Marx, Engels, Lenin and even – not so long ago – Stalin. One's first reaction is to dismiss this as a necessary obeisance in the direction of the political powers-that-be – as no doubt, in part, it is; and, in any case, one feels that philosophy has no place in the conduct of scientific research. However, a more sympathetic consideration of the use to which these philosophers are put reveals that there is something of more importance, and perhaps even of real value, going on. In the first place, the Russian habit of making the philosophical background plain for all to see is not such a bad one; above all, it becomes clear that, with different philosophical assumptions, there would be different research and different favoured forms of expression – and this connection is not to be broken simply by keeping the philosophical assumptions out of sight (and out of mind) as the Anglo-Saxon psychologist tries to do. Secondly, there is a good case to be made for the particular assumptions of Marxist philosophy as a reasonable starting point for a scientific psychology – provided, of course, that we are ready to abandon them if our data suggest that other assumptions would make a better starting point. In particular, it can be argued that Marxist assumptions are more consistent with the results of recent psychological and neurophysiological research than are the assumptions contained in the extreme associationist-behaviourist point of view identified with the names of J. B. Watson and C. L. Hull; and that the recent retreat from this extreme position in Anglo-American psychology has made it possible to attempt a rapprochement between the views of human nature held in the East and the West.
>
> (Quoted in Graham, 1972, p. 428)

The demise of the Soviet Union and the passage of time have made possible the kind of reevaluations that Graham called for several decades ago.

THE CORE

With respect to the core elements of the theory, two issues concerning Vygotsky's theory of culture seem to be of continuing importance. First, beginning in the early 1930s, a group of Vygotsky's students and colleagues, prominent among whom was A. N. Leontiev, began to criticize Vygotsky's focus on word meaning as an appropriate unit of analysis for the understanding of the relation of human thought to language on the grounds that it focused too much on mediational means and not enough on the activities that these means were mediating. Citing the first of Marx's "Theses on Feuerbach" ("The chief defect of all hitherto existing materialism [that of Feuerbach included] is that the thing, reality, sensuousness, is conceived only in the form of the *object or of contemplation*, but not as *sensuous human activity, practice...*"), Leontiev (1981, p. 46) proposed that psychological analysis be based on a unit of analysis he called "activity," which he claimed is "the nonadditive, molar unit of life for the material, corporeal subject." "Human psychology," he wrote,

> ...is concerned with the activity of concrete individuals, which takes place either in a collective – that is, jointly with other people – or in a situation in which the subject deals directly with the surrounding world of objects – for example, the potter's wheel or the writer's desk. However, if we removed human activity from the system of social relationships and social life, it would not exist and would have no structure. With all its varied forms, the human individual's activity is a system in the system of social relations. It does not exist without these relations. The specific form in which it exists is determined by the forms and means of material and mental social interaction (*Verkher*) that are created by the development of production and that cannot be realized in any way other than the activity of concrete people.   (Leontiev, 1981, p. 47)

In the highly charged ideological context of the USSR, this statement and others of Leontiev's writings have been seen as a repudiation of Vygotsky and the substitution of activity for mediation as a unit of analysis. It is certainly plausible that Leontiev, like many others, sought to distance himself from ideas and associations that had led to the deaths of colleagues and friends. However, given the evidence, it seems more plausible to see his reformulation as an effort to place mediation in its cultural context, extending culture's actual presence both within a Vygotskian framework and in human life. From a contemporary point of view, however, not only mediational means but also the cultural practices of which they are a part constitute culture.

This point of view is compatible with the position, formulated by Leontiev's student, Vladimir Zinchenko and his colleague, James Wertsch, who have sought to overcome what has been seen an over-reliance on word meaning as a unit for the study of human consciousness by proposing mediated action in its cultural context as an alternative unit (Wertsch, 1998; Zinchenko, 1985). Following Engeström (1993), insofar as activity and context are treated synonymously, the idea that the emphases found in both Vygotsky and Leontiev's writings are compatible is perfectly plausible. This inclusive position is now referred to as "cultural–historical activity theory" (Cole, 1996).

Another issue that has received attention with regard to the "core" notion of culture in a Vygotskian perspective is the relation of the ideal and material in culture. Here the work of the philosopher Evald Ilyenkov has been central. First, Ilyenkov makes the strong claim that the ideal and material in human life are created in the process of specifically human activity, that is, activity mediated by the products of past human activity:

> The ideal form is a form of a thing, but outside the thing, and is to be found in man as a form of his dynamic life activity, *as goals and needs*. Or conversely, it is a form of man's life activity, but outside man, in the form of the thing he creates. "Ideality" as such exists only in the constant succession and replacement of these two forms of its "external embodiment" and does not coincide with either of them taken separately. It exists only through the unceasing process of the transformation of the form of activity into the form of a thing and back – the form of a thing into the form of activity.   (Ilyenkov, 1977, p. 140)

As David Bakhurst notes, a general designation of the "things that humans create" is the term *artifact*, a term that refers to more than a purely physical form within the framework proposed by Ilyenkov.

> Rather, in being created as an embodiment of purpose and incorporated into life activity in a certain way – being manufactured for a *reason* and put into *use* – the natural object acquires a significance. This significance is the "ideal form" of the object, a form that includes not a single atom of the tangible physical substance that possesses it.
> (Bakhurst, 1990, p. 182)

In this way of thinking, mediation through artifacts applies equally to objects and people. What differs in the two cases are (1) the ways in which ideality and materiality are fused among members of the two categories of being and (2) the kinds of interactivity into which they can enter. It is relatively easy to recognize that a table or a pencil is a material artifact. It is less obvious to realize that, as anthropologist Roy D'Andrade put it, "A table is just an idea, reified in a different medium" (D'Andrade, 1986, p. 22). Reciprocally, humans are so used to language as the bearer of meanings that the materiality of human vocal sounds, or the artificial ways in which sound waves are packaged to create words and utterances, that the materiality of language is often difficult to keep in mind.

In our view, Ilyenkov's formulation usefully expands on Vygotsky's conceptual duality of "tools/mediators," which simultaneously operate to modify the world external to the individual and the organization of the individual's own actions, providing the material/ideal medium of human existence, for example, culture. In addition, Ilyenkov's approach argues for a synthesis of the views of Vygotsky and Leontiev, treating them as complementary, not contradictory.

A third emphasis in modern work using the conception of culture as the artifact-saturated environment of human life is that because no individual comes in contact with the entire pool of artifacts and practices that constitute the social life of the group human thought processes need to be conceived of as distributed among and across the constituents of activity – they occur both "within" and "between" individuals and their partially held-in-common cultural tool kits (Cole & Engeström, 1993). At the same time, it becomes useful to think of each person as acquiring their own personal culture, or personal cultural tool kit, made up of that part of the common pool that they have come in contact with and appropriated (Valsiner, 1998).

Finally, a balancing of mediational means and activities, which recognizes them as interwoven and mutually constituting, makes contact with contemporary emphases on the domain specificity/context specificity of cultural contributions to human thought. Culture is not a random array of artifacts, but rather a heterogeneously, dynamically changing set of practices and resources that require constant active engagement for their continued existence (Cole, 1996).

Cultural–Historical Change and Processes of Comparison

Contemporary views concerning the plausibility of Vygotsky's treatment of cultural differences have secured less enduring support and elaboration than his core propositions about culture and the culturally mediated nature of human life. We will discuss three areas of current interest and controversy.

NATURAL VERSUS CULTURAL LINES OF DEVELOPMENT. First of all, there has been criticism of Vygotsky's conception both of the relationship between what he termed *the natural and cultural lines of development* and the content of the phylogenetic underpinnings of human nature. With respect the natural and cultural lines of development, Vygotsky adopted what Geertz referred to as the "critical point" theory of phylogeny-cultural history relations. According to this view, phylogeny progressed to a certain point at which culture made its appearance; subsequently sociocultural evolution proceeds more or less independently of any changes in the phylogenetic foundations of behavior (Geertz,

1973; Wertsch, 1985). Contemporary evidence appears to demonstrate conclusively that for at least the past 5 million years, cultural evolution and phylogenetic evolution have been part of a dialectically constituted process as both cause and effect of the evolution of modern *Homo sapiens* (Plotkin, 2001).

Second, contemporary evidence suggests that there is more conceptual structure present in the natural (phylogenetic) foundations of human nature than Vygotsky realized (Medin & Atran, 2004). Cross-cultural studies of classification as well as studies of infants and young children strongly suggest that humans everywhere are born possessing at least skeletal, innate mechanisms for parsing the world in ways that enable them to make correct inferences about a variety of physical and biological phenomena.

Third, attempts to verify the idea that cultural forms in both cultural history and ontogeny *replace* natural forms of cognition have generally failed. For example, a considerable amount of research on memory among nonliterate, nonschooled populations or among children in industrialized countries has failed to find evidence that eidetic imagery, a major example used by Vygotsky and Luria, is differentially prevalent in either population. It is rare in general. Nor is evidence of rote recapitulation, another candidate for a natural memory process, generally found among either nonliterate adults or children (see Cole & Scribner, 1977, for a summary of modern evidence).

SOCIOCULTURAL EVOLUTION. The issue of sociocultural evolution and a corresponding evolution in mental capacity is more contentious, but some matters are relatively clear. For example, although there is no disagreement that the mediational means at humans' disposal have increased in complexity astronomically over the past forty thousand years (Donald, 1990), there is no support for the notion that human languages have become more complex in any general way (Nettle & Romaine, 2000). Modern linguists point out that all human languages possess the essential property of recursion and that grammatical complexity appears in all languages. What differs appears to be the size of vocabulary that has developed to deal *with different domains of life* and the particular aspects of a grammar that are more or less complex. No general "concrete to abstract" or general simple–complex change over history is discernable from the record of living languages.

The picture becomes more complicated when we turn from the claims made by Luria and Vygotsky on the basis of secondary accounts of data collected by a mélange of generally nonprofessional observers, to data that Luria collected during a project in Central Asia. In this work, Luria studied cognitive performance on a variety of tasks among pastoralist peoples, some of whom continued to live in a traditional fashion, others of whom had been drawn into Soviet-style modern forms of industrialized agriculture and schooling. These studies included examination of both the tendency to use "natural" versus "cultural" modes of thought and changes in the level of cultural modes of thought. They interpreted the outcome as a confirmation of the theoretical proposals they had published earlier. With respect to certain perceptual phenomena, for example, Luria reported that traditional peasants were not susceptible to visual illusions, a result he attributed to their "natural modes" of perception. With respect to various kinds of classification and verbal reasoning problems, he interpreted the findings as support for the general position of a historical shift from more context bound, functional-graphic modes of thought to more theory-like, conceptual modes of thought.

This research ran into a firestorm of criticism at the time, the essence of which was that Luria and Vygotsky were claiming the Central Asian builders of socialism thought like children (van der Veer, 2002). On the one hand, this criticism might seem odd because the result would appear to provide justification for a Marxist view linking modes of production to levels of civilization and cultural modes of cognition. On the other hand, it seems perfectly understandable insofar as, in their prior writings, Vygotsky, Luria, and Leontiev had all quoted evidence from Levy-Bruhl, Thurnwald, and other non-Russian authors (which, ipso facto, made the ideas suspect) and used examples from this literature that made adults appear conspicuously childlike.

Luria did not publish results from this work until the 1970s and at that time only reported some of them (Luria, 1976). At this later time, he offered two explanations for the results contrasting traditional and "modernized" people from the same social group. First, he invoked the differences in social and cultural development that were a part of the legacy of his work with Vygotsky in the 1920s and 1930s. Second, he suggested that the nonschooled subjects were only involved in practical activities, so they had no opportunity to acquire theoretical thinking.

Non-Russian researchers involved in cross-cultural studies have extensively cited this work as evidence for the positive impact of literacy and/or schooling on cognitive development – mechanisms of change that can be interpreted as changes in both mediational means and activity (e.g., Goody, 1977). However, it has also been subject to criticism by those who point out that Luria never observed the activities to which he attributed the change and his experimental procedures derived almost exclusively from research with educated European children and adults that patently involve forms of activity with which nonschooled people could not be expected to be familiar (Cole, 1996).

Peeter Tulviste (1999), an Estonian student of Luria's who replicated some of his experimental procedures in the Soviet far east in the 1970s, has offered a bridge between these interpretations by narrowing his claims to a category he calls *verbal thinking* and focusing on the idea of the heterogeneity of thinking existing in all societies as a function of the activities that people engage in. This approach and the cultural practice approach proposed by Scribner and Cole (1981) appear to offer a way to deploy a cultural–historical activity theory using data from different societies without falling into a general, progressivist–historical perspective.

In her article devoted to Vygotsky's uses of history in the analysis of development, Scribner (1985) interprets Vygotsky in a manner compatible with an emphasis on cultural practices that are heterogeneous with respect to "level" within societies. In her view, Vygotsky did not "represent higher systems as general modes of thought" or as general structures of intelligence in a Piagetian sense. Vygotsky addressed the question of general processes of development of particular functional systems (Scribner, 1985, p. 132).

SUMMARY

As we remarked at the outset, it is an oddity that a scholar currently viewed as one of the inspirations for attempts to put culture on an equal footing with phylogeny and individual human actions at the center of his theory should have so little to say, explicitly, about his conception of culture. The process of inferential reconstruction that we have used to illuminate these issues is clearly problematic, but it does succeed in illuminating both why it is justified to consider Vygotsky's ideas about culture to be important, and why these ideas are generative of continued development by his successors.

In effect, the very fact that he insists on the mutual interlacing of cultural mediation and human cognition is both the source of inspiration for current scholars and a major impediment to separating culture from history and ontogeny. In Vygotsky's view, and in ours, these different "genetic domains" are interlaced in complex, mutually constituting ways rendering separations between them difficult and problematic. So it is natural for there to be disagreements about matters of fact as well as specific theoretical claims. Squarely facing these disagreements and seeking to overcome them in continuing dialogue appears necessary both for obtaining a clearer idea of Vygotsky's ideas and for discovering the best ways to carry them forward usefully into the future.

9   Thought and Word

The Approaches of L. S. Vygotsky and G. G. Shpet

These two scholars were more than a little acquainted: Vygotsky was Shpet's student at the Shanyavsky People's University, and he attended Shpet's seminar for two years. At the beginning of the 1920s, Vygotsky started to work at the psychological institute where, as Aleksei N. Leont'ev has noted, Shpet was the most famous professor. At the end of the 1920s, Shpet and Vygotsky both taught at the Pedology Department of the Second Moscow University.

Despite all these connections, there is only one reference to Shpet in Vygotsky's works (in *The Psychology of Art*), and even this is only in passing. And Shpet's books *Phenomenon and Meaning* (1914), *Aesthetic Fragments* (1922), and *The Inner Form of Word* (1927), in which he discussed thinking and language, thought and word, meaning and sense, and external and inner forms of a word were all published significantly earlier than Vygotsky's *Thinking and Speech* (1934).

Today, it is hard to guess why Vygotsky and his whole scientific school (Aleksandr R. Luria, A. N. Leont'ev, Aleksandr V. Zaporozhets, and others) ignored Shpet's works. It could have been fear or caution born out of Shpet's style of behavior and writing. This style was characterized by freedom and dignity and the independence of his thought from Marxist–Leninist ideology, which at the time was growing stronger and stronger. The Bolsheviks felt this independence, dismissed Shpet several times from his academic positions, and, in the end, arrested and shot him in 1937.

Unlike Shpet, Vygotsky accepted Marxism and became infected with its ambitions to reform not only society but science as well. As early as in *The Psychology of Art*, written in 1923, Vygotsky seriously asserted that

---

The order of the names in the title of this article is neither alphabetical nor chronological. Gustav Gustavovich Shpet (1879–1937) was older than Lev Semenovich Vygotsky (1896–1934).

even "physics, chemistry, mineralogy ... can be Marxist or anti-Marxist" (Vygotsky, 1987, p. 17). Boris Meshcheryakov (2000) has written very interestingly about Vygotsky's reformist intentions, having discovered the parallels in the biographies and social attitudes of Martin Luther and Lev Vygotsky. In the end, however, Vygotsky's commitment to Marxist beliefs did not save him from criticism. His works were banned, denounced, and declared to be vicious and even evil. He was lucky to have managed to die in his own bed in 1934.

Another reason for the absence of references to Shpet in these scholars' writings could have been a lack of understanding of his thought, which, indeed, was ahead of its time. I will proceed from the fact that many of Shpet's ideas about thought and word, being more hermeneutic than psychological, were lacking in psychological context. This context was only to be created later, and not only in Vygotsky's writings. Had he lived longer, Vygotsky might have connected his ideas with those of Shpet. This possibility was missed by Vygotsky's apprentices, who shifted their interest from the analysis of the word and its meaning and sense in the studies of thinking to the analysis of activity and action. The works of Vygotsky themselves provided the foundation for such a shift of interest.

In the end, however, my goal is not to place the approaches of Vygotsky and Shpet in opposition, but to present them as mutually complementary. Because ss the views of Vygotsky are significantly better known than those of Shpet, for the sake of didactics, I will start with the Vygotsky's and supplement the discussion with Shpet's approach. This is why Vygotsky's name appears first in the title of this chapter.

The problems of thinking and language and thought and word are among the eternal issues in the human sciences. Vygotsky, usually not known for his modesty and inclined to rather categorical opinions, wrote at the end of *Thinking and Speech*, "We did not have any intention to exhaust all the complexity of the structure and dynamic of verbal thinking. We only wanted to give an elementary idea of the vast complexity of this dynamic structure ... " (Vygosky, 1982, v. 2, p. 359).

Thinking, of course, is the *movement of thought*, but one should not underestimate the complexity of defining and studying thought. Thought, regardless of truth or falseness, is manifested sometimes in a word, sometimes in an image, sometimes in an action or a deed, sometimes in all of these as well as something else, or as something elusive and mysterious. Perhaps, this elusive nature is the most interesting thing about thought. What thought is and how it emerges are not the most important questions. Instead, the presence of the intention to learn, understand, and see *something* standing behind a *thought* is important

The emergence of such an intention is a sign of a genuine thought, which is different from something that just "comes into someone's head," say, from another's opinion. *To see behind* . . . is thinking, and *to see behind a thought* . . . is a reflection about thought. To see behind a thought is the second act, the *post scriptum* to a thought, as Joseph Brodsky has called it, and the beginning of its proof.

Shpet and Vygotsky were neither the first nor the last to offer an answer to the question: What is behind thought? Rene Descartes *saw* behind thought something of obvious necessity, namely, the necessity of his own existence: *cogito ergo sum.* William James *saw* behind thought a stream of raw sensory experience. Ivan Sechenov *saw* behind thought not only a sensory background but also a background of individual action. The psychoanalyst Wilfred Ruprecht Bion *saw* behind thought a frustration born from ignorance. Merab Mamardashvili *saw* behind thought personal feelings. Albert Einstein *saw* behind thought visual images and even muscular sensations (evidently, besides all the rest, Einstein was also a genius of self-observation). Edouard Claparede *saw* silence behind thought. The mathematician Jacques Hadamard, who was especially interested in the creations of the famous physicists of the twentieth century, confirmed that, "the word is absolutely absent from my mind when I really think." Rainer Maria Rilke spoke about it in his own way: "The wise men turned their lips into hearing."

Andrew Bely *saw* movement and rhythm behind thought. Mikhail Bakhtin *saw* emotion and will behind thought, and he saw intonation in thought, "the truly acting mind is a mind of emotion and volition, a mind of intonation, and this intonation essentially penetrates all the significant moments of thinking." (Bakhtin, 1994, p. 36). He also saw behind thought another person – an interlocutor, or participant in a dialogue, "Human thought becomes a true thought, an idea, only under conditions of live contact with someone else's thought, embodied in someone else's voice, which is, someone else's mind expressed in words. . . . The idea is a *living event*, occurring in a point of dramatic meeting of two or more minds. In this regard, the idea is similar to word, with which it is dialectically united" (Bakhtin, 1994a, p. 294). Vygotsky expressed a similar idea about thought as a unity of communication and generalization.

Joseph Brodsky *saw* thought behind thought: People think not in some language, instead they think by thoughts. Aleksandr Pushkin remarkably said about one of his heroes, "He develops thought by thought." Osip Mandel'shtam explained some surprising claims about poets, "Now, for example, while I am stating my thought as far as possible in precise but not at all poetic form, in essence, I am speaking with a mind, not with a word" (Mandel'shtam, 1987, p. 168). Let us note, however, *speak* with a *mind.*

The philosopher Mamardashvili talked about it in a different way: Thinking is always more than what was thought. And that is why it is possible to think what was thought. Soul and word are also not forgotten. As Plato describes in "Tête-à-tête," the soul has a dialogue with itself about what it considers; while thinking, it indeed talks with itself, asks itself, claims, denies. Jose Ortega-Gasset *saw* the depths of the soul behind thought; "the pupils of my eyes look with curiosity into the depths of the soul, and facing them, the energetic thoughts rise" (Ortega-Gasset, 1997, p. 93)

Vygotsky *saw* the word behind thought, and he saw emotional and volitional tendencies behind verbal thinking as a whole. Shpet *saw* thought behind the word, the word behind thought, and the word in thought, and he certainly understood that not all words have meaning or thought.

It is highly unlikely that these differing ideas – sometimes in polar opposition – about what can be found behind thought are simply errors or illusions of self-observation; and I hope that you will be convinced of this by the end of this chapter. The most surprising thing is that all the thinkers, scholars, and poets we have mentioned are right. Vygotsky would have subscribed to his own version, namely: "The thought itself is born not from another thought but from the motivational sphere of our consciousness which encompasses our drive and mind, our needs, our interests and intentions, our affections and emotions" (Vygotsky, 1983, v. 2, p. 357).

Because he was a product of the discipline of psychology, Vygotsky proposed an ontological status for thinking and thought. Much earlier, Shpet talked about meaning as being deeply rooted in being, and agreed with Parmenides that "thinking and being are the same." Or, as Parmenides said even more clearly: "thinking and what thinking is directed to are the same, and one will not find thinking without existence, with regard to which a thought is expressed." Thus, not only is an object of being an object of thought for philosophy, but it is necessarily a thought about an object. A thought "about nothing," therefore, does not exist.

Here philosophy as a system of knowledge provides a firm and durable beginning (Shpet, 1994, pp. 233–234). Let us add psychology as well. Georg Hegel and later Evald Il'envkov and Karl Popper claimed the identity of thinking and being. Bakhtin extensively wrote about participation of thinking in being; Mamardashvili's reasoning followed in a similar way.

The birth of thought, regardless of what stands behind it, remains a miracle and a mystery. Johann Goethe certainly was being clever when he said that thoughts come to him like the children of God and tell him, "Here we are." Einstein was more sincere in saying to Max Wertheimer, "I am not sure if it is really possible to understand the miracle of thinking" (Wertheimer, 1987, p. 262). This did not keep him from talking with Wertheimer for hours about the dramatic events that resulted in the creation of the theory of relativity.

Thought and word are no less polyphonic than mind. Yet, there is a long way to go to arrive at this conclusion. And it is hard to overestimate the input of Shpet and Vygotsky, along with Aleksandr Potebnya.

Out of all the polyphony of mind and thought, out of all the various possible origins, Shpet and Vygotsky gave their preference to the word, although they understood it differently. Let us start from Vygotsky's metaphorical description: *What is simultaneous in thought is successive in language.* It would be possible to compare a thought with a cloud that showers a rain of words. That is why the transition from thought to language is a very complicated process of dismemberment of a thought and its recreation in a word (Vygotsky, 1987, p. 356). On the next page, Vygotsky wrote, "continuing this picturesque comparison, we should liken the motivation of thought to the wind that sets the clouds in motion" (Vygotsky, 1987, p. 357). If something can *pour itself,* it means that it already exists. Therefore, we can understand the given metaphor as saying that thought, already existing, *is expressed* in a word.

In his earlier work, Vygotsky (1926) wrote that thoughts are expressed in inner motions, a special group of which are speech-locomotion reactions, that is, internal or mute speech (Vygotsky, 1991, p. 196). According to Vygotsky, "External speech is a process of transformation of thought into words, its materialization and objectification. Inner speech is a process of the reverse direction going from without to within, the process of evaporation of speech to a thought" (Vygotsky, 1983, v. 2, p. 316). Such *vapors,* evidently, constitute the cloud, which later *pours itself with a shower of words.* In Vygotsky's works, there are other places where thought is considered as if separate from word, but this does not accord with his no less categorical claims that "thought is not expressed by language but takes place in it" (Vygotsky, 1983, v. 2, p. 356).

Of course, as is true for any other author, Vygotsky can be read in various ways. For example, Luria did not seem to find any contradiction when he wrote, "According to Vygotsky, thought is simply primary and insufficiently differentiated, which reflects the general tendency of a subject, and which is *not embodied but is occasioned by, and formed in the word.* By this description Vygotsky gives to the word a new function that has not been described before, and the process of giving birth to thought as an utterance acquires a more complex, dynamic and change-able character" (Luria, 1982, pp. 474–475).

However, Vygotsky's formulations did have contradictory elements. Sometimes these contradictions appear not just on the same page, but in the same phrase. Consider, for instance, his statement: "we were interested in one thing – the discovery of the relation between thought and word as a dynamic process, as a way from thought to word, the creation and embodiment of thought in a word" (Luria, 1982, p. 358). If thought was not created in the word, then it is not there, and never has been; and if thought was not embodied, then it was there and, as Mandel'shtam would say, "returned into the palace of shadows."

Vygotsky cited the lines from another poet as well; "we get tired soon in heaven." In this case, he was talking about the evaporation of speech into thought, but immediately adds, "Mind does not evaporate at all and does not dissolve in a pure spirit" and again contradicts himself, saying that "the word dies in internal speech, giving birth to a thought. Inner speech is to a large extent thinking with pure meanings" (Vygotsky, 1982, p. 353). If the word dies while giving birth to a thought, then the latter remains wordless and therefore unembodied. If inner speech is not completely, even *to a significant extent*, thinking with pure meanings, then why is it speech? In Vygotsky's works the two versions – creation and embodiment – alternate, although the object of his investigation is exactly the embodiment of thought in word – in inner and external speech, a discussion of which will follow.

Such a situation is not new in the study of thinking and language. In Plato's dialogue "Cratylus," Socrates sometimes talks about a word as an organ for learning and for recognizing an essence and sometimes as an icon of truth, and he advises us to look at the truth instead. The same can be found in Saint Augustine. In the first half of the dialogue "About a Teacher," he claims that we cannot give an idea of an object without a sign, but in its second half, he argues that it only appears that words teach. What teaches is truth itself (see Bibikhin, 1996).

In Shpet's formulation, which appeared before Vygotsky wrote *Thinking and Speech*, if you consider thought as abstracted from word, there is an oscillation – from thought to word and back again (Shpet, 1996, p. 143). Shpet objected strongly to the notion that unembodied thought exists. He doubted the unexpressed nature of mystic consciousness and doubted that there exists "a monster – a dumb thought with no word." After all, a thought is a cultural act, the essence of which is in the sign-giving. There can be no cultural act without any sign.

The notion of such an "oscillation" can be found in Vygotsky's formulation but certainly not in Shpet's. The latter clearly rejected even the possibility of an *unembodied thought*. When he said that the *cause* of thought is anything given in sensations, he characterized it as a trampoline from which we toss ourselves toward the "pure object," but it is only pure from sensation; otherwise, we would have to admit that we think sensibly, too.

> An object pure from the substance of words is a different matter. This issue should not be solved in an analogous way to the previous one. Pushing itself off the trampoline, thought has not just to overcome the material resistance, but also to use it as a supporting environment. If it dragged all its material baggage, it would not fly high. But also without an expedient adjustment of its form to its environment, it would be incapable of staying in an ideal sphere. It would be either in absolute emptiness or in absolute shapelessness. Its image, form, appearance, ideal body is a *word*.
>
> Feeling-less thought is normal; this is thought raised above animal sensation. Wordless thought is pathology; this is thought that cannot be delivered; it would be stuck in an inflamed womb and would be decomposing there...Words are not the swaddling clothes of thought; they are thought's body. The thought is born in a word and together with it. Even this is not a sufficient formulation. Thought is begotten in a word. This is why there are no stillborn thoughts, there are only empty words, there are no thoughts that shake the world, there are only words. Nothingness, grandeur, vulgarity, beauty, stupidity, insidiousness, indigence, truth, shamelessness, treachery, love, intellect – all these are predicates of words, not thoughts, i.e., I understand them to be real concrete predicates rather than metaphorical ones. All the qualities of the word are ascribed to thought in only a metaphoric way.
>
> (Shpet, 1989, pp. 397–398)

In Shpet's view, "strictly and seriously, without romantic diversions – wordless thought is a meaningless expression. On earth, on waters, in the skies, the word rules everything."

> There is a short conclusion to everything that has been said above: a pure object thought, considered without the word form as part of its ontology, is an *abstraction*...Taken out of the word, it is a part of a whole, and, therefore, it maintains concreteness; but it does not have its own life outside words, and, therefore, it is an abstraction.
>
> (Shpet, 1989, pp. 397–398)

Shpet's position on the impossibility of unembodied, completely intangible thought is expressed clearly and categorically. A thesis on the concreteness of the word, and, therefore, thinking and thought is presented just as clearly. Shpet talked not about a sensory object but about a *sensory carcass*; about the concept of object, a *pure object*, which is part of the structure of a word. It is to this kind of "object," as opposed either to sensibility or object, that he gives the credit for the form and form-making origin of the material content that is denominated, or named, in a word, and then participates in creating full, living *concepts of objects.*

It is significant that, for Shpet, the concreteness of a thought, like a concrete object itself, is not connected to a concrete object the way it is given (e.g., perceptions of participants in communication and thinking process). It is a meaningful image as an object that possesses genuine concreteness in its quality of object and transmits its concreteness to thought and word, as it were. The concreteness of thought, of course, can be called a quasiconcreteness or an abstraction, but it is necessary to remember that it is generated by us on the basis of actually perceived (or even imagined) concrete objects. (see also, Portnov, 1999).

Therefore, for Shpet there was no "oscillation" between a word and a thought. He warned against this from the outset by taking as an epigraph his *The Inner Form of a Word*, Plato's statement, "Aren't mind and speech the same – except that we call mind an internal dialogue of a soul with itself, performing it all in silence" (Plato, 1984, p. 263e).

Despite his severe attitude toward psychology, Shpet admitted that it is not incorrect to study *language* and *thinking* as activities, but he recommended not forgetting about their amalgamation; "we divide intellectuality and language but in reality such division does not exist. The spiritual *peculiarities and setting* of the language [Sprachgestaltung] of people are so intimately connected that if one is given, the other can be derived from it, since intellectuality and language tolerate and support only mutually useful forms. Language is an external manifestation of spirit, as it were – a people's language is their spirit and their spirit is their language" (Shpet, 1996, p. 55).

So, language and word "rule" not only thinking, but also sprit and mind: "Indeed, analyzing our consciousness, we cannot escape noticing that the 'word' lies in it as a special, but absolutely universal layer..." (Shpet, 1994, p. 294). Shpet considered *pointing* (denoting) as an original function of consciousness, and the sense and role of this function are to be discovered in the analysis of consciousness itself. (Shpet, 1999, p. 265). But even this is not enough. Shpet glorified the *word* to an extent that made him ready to remake the good old principle of cognition: our knowledge comes from *experience,* in the broader sense of the word – from a *feeling.* In Shpet's opinion, this formula is too crude for the cognoscendi principle. He offers his version: "*word is* principum cognoscendi of our knowledge" (Shpet, 1999, p. 265).

Consider for a moment Shpet's arguments: "We call a word 'the beginning of cognition' in the literal sense of the origin of cognition, that *first*
which emanates in our utterances" (Shpet, 1999, p. 271). He was not sat-
isfied with considering the word as a "third thing" after "experience"
and "reason" in the origins of cognition. Shpet reminded us of Plato's resolution of the conflict between experience and reason: Both sources are
right, because "experience" only becomes a source for cognition when
reason is discovered in it.

Having made this decision, Shpet wrote, "It is not hard to find a
place for the 'third' source, which is the word. It is a part of an entity
of experience and reason because just as reason permeates experience as
the source of cognition, word which is correlative to reason, gives this
saturation constant true form." And again we reproduce the ancient
idea of *logos:* the realm of thought constituting anything that should be
achieved by word (Aristotle, 1996, p. 145a).

Word, therefore, is not a "third" source of cognition in the true sense.
We talk everywhere about one and only one source, as a *cognitive* whole.
Of course, it is possible to think of emotional experience, which is not
cognitive, and it is possible to think of word and reason in various functions. But their entity is cognition: In it a feeling finds its reasonable
base in the logical form of a word. A word as a *sign*, therefore, embraces
in itself all three moments of cognition, as its meaning, and at the same
time serves as the symbol of their close unity" (Shpet, 1999, p. 273).
Running slightly ahead, we will say that understanding the word and
its meaning as a logical tool, logical form, or "term" could have served
Vygotsky as a foundation for using meaning as a unit of analysis of verbal
thinking.

Additionally, for Shpet, a word was an archetype of culture. It is also an
embodiment of reason, its organ, and its nurturing environment. Such a
"load" on a word is not a declaration; rather, it is a summation of Shpet's
many years of work on the structure and functions of the word. We will
turn to his interpretation of the structure of the word later, but now we
return to Vygotsky.

Despite the contradictions I have noted in Vygotsky's account of the
relation between thought and word (the "oscillation"), at least in the conception of his book *Thinking and Speech* (especially chapter 1), he strove
to present thinking in words as a whole, insisting on the existence of a
living unity of sound and meaning, which contains , like a living cell, the
main characteristics of verbal thinking. According to Vygotsky, "By
the unit of analysis we mean such a product of analysis, which unlike
the elements of analysis possesses all the main characteristics of the
whole . . . " (Vygotsky, 1982, v. 2, p. 15). And, in contrast to the statement

noted earlier that claimed that such a cell of thinking with words is a word, Vygotsky offered to look for such a cell in the internal side of a word – in its meaning (Vygotsky, 1982, p. 16). He distinguished meaning from unmediated sensations and perceptions and identified meaning with generalization.

Finally, Vygotsky asserted that the meaning of a word is the very act of thinking in its true sense. The meaning of a word is an inseparable part of a word as such, and it belongs equally to the kingdom of speech and to the kingdom of thought (Vygotsky, 1982, p. 17). But this is not enough. Vygotsky considered meaning not only as *the unity of thinking and speech*, but also as *the unity of communication and generalization.* Both unities are included in a complex dynamic system, constituting one more *unity of affective and intellectual processes.*

It is relevant to pose a number of questions at this point. What is the unit of verbal thinking? A word as a whole or its internal side – meaning? If it is meaning, which other characteristics does it have except for generalization (which, by the way, is true for perception, too)? A word, indeed, represents a unity of the sound (external) and meaning (inner) sides of language. As for the meaning, Vygotsky envisaged the existence of "pure meanings," meanings that would not satisfy his demands for the unit of analysis.

However, pure meanings still might satisfy the demands, formulated by Shpet some twelve years earlier: "Indeed, whatever *concrete* part we would single out of the whole of human language, it contains, at least virtually, the characteristics, functions and relations of the whole" (Shpet, 1989, p. 402). And even earlier, he rather strongly objected to explanations that had been introduced into psychology that begin with psychological atom-like elements: "Many have proposed a future synthesis of the whole from decomposed elements, but this synthesis may only be an abstraction; whatever complicated whole it provides, it will not be alive. Chemical synthesis may provide water, but only chemically pure water, and no synthesis would provide a drop of real, 'living' water with its plentiful flora and fauna" (Shpet, 1996, p. 32).

Speaking of units of analysis, Shpet chose the *word* for one, presenting it as a functional structure, grandiose in its complexity, in all the variety of its external and internal forms. In the internal forms, he was looking for the "place" for a thought.

In spite of the frequent identification of thought and meaning in his works, Vygotsky did not find such a place in the structure that he offered. When analyzing the underlying theme of speech (regardless of whether it is external or internal), he believed it necessary to distinguish in verbal thinking a new plane of verbal thinking. Note that the new plane of verbal thinking is not a unit of verbal thinking, but a plane that he, however, thought is firm. It is not a cloud.

I do not mean to reproach Vygotsky's position on this issue. On the contrary, it is completely reasonable: Thought should be firm and operate in accordance with laws. Descartes in his time told us that only a strong thought is a true one. Alexander Blok talked about the muscles of consciousness, and Mamardashvili talked about the muscles of thought.

> The new plane of verbal thinking is thought itself. The first task of our analysis is distinguishing this plane, distinguishing it from the unity in which it is always situated. We already mentioned that each thought strives to connect something to something else, it has movement and development, it establishes relationships between something and something else; in short, it serves some functions, performs some task, solves some problem. This flow and movement of thought does not correspond directly to the emergence of speech. The units of thought and speech do not coincide.   (Vygotsky, 1982, v. 2, pp. 354–355)

At the end of *Thinking and Speech*, Vygostky (1987) was talking about *units*, not *planes*. The plane of thought is distinguished from the unity of verbal thinking, and a new yet-to-be-named unit of thought is introduced, not a unit of verbal thinking as it was before. Then the plane of thought is called a process, and finally, he said: "those processes [of thought and speech; author's note] show unity but not identity" (Vygotsky, 1982, p. 355). Unity, but not identity, is a sort of magic spell of dialectic materialists that usually serves as a cover for a lack of understanding. Later, Vygotsky wrote again about the interweaving of the units of word and thought, and even made a heuristically useful hint on their complex transformations, but his previously postulated unity of verbal thinking falls apart.

The reason for Vygotsky's vacillation on this issue might be a lack of a detailed idea about the structure of the word as a whole and a tendency to ignore the concept of "the inner form of the word," which was introduced by Humboldt and variously interpreted by Potebnya and Shpet. Except for a few rare instances, Vygotsky did not use the concept of "the inner form," as it was discussed by Humboldt, Potebnya, and Shpet; rather, he preferred to talk about the "internal side" of the word, defining it as meaning, identifying it with thought, and in the end tearing it apart from word. The "pure meanings" Vygotsky discussed are thoughts with no words attached.

This view was reproduced by Vygotsky's followers. For example, Petr Ya. Gal'perin outlined the following stages in the formation of mental actions: action with an object, overt speech, inner speech, and "pure thought." It remains unclear what the meanings and thoughts were "purified" from. If they were purified from the word, what were they embodied in? Of course such doubts concerning "pure meanings" and "pure thoughts" do not devalue the studies of the ontogenesis of thinking and speech, including the research on concept development in children, carried out by Vygotsky, and the meaning of functional genesis of mental actions, carried out by Gal'perin. I will follow Vygotsky's lead and make a paradoxical statement. Although he separated thought and word, he gave an account concerned with *embodying* and *expressing* thought in word. In the present context, the results of Vygotsky's studies of the functions and interrelations between egocentric and internal speech are very significant. Here the problems of thought and word stand out with particular salience.

In his well-known critique of Piaget, Vygotsky considered egocentric speech as a developmentally intermediate, transitional form in the development from external to internal speech. He perspicaciously observed that a child's egocentric speech "easily becomes thinking in the true sense of the word, that is, takes on the functions of a planning operation, solving a new problem that emerges in activity" (Vygotsky, 1982, v. 2, p. 107). In his view, egocentric speech "becomes psychologically internal earlier than it becomes physiologically internal. Egocentric speech is speech internal in its function; it is a speech for oneself, moving towards going inside, speech already half unclear for the environment, speech that is already deeply rooted in a child's behavior . . . " (Vygotsky, 1982, p. 108).

Thus, for Vygotsky, "egocentric speech is a number of steps preceding the development of internal speech, it fulfills a number of intellectual functions. It does not die away, as Piaget claimed, rather it is one of the phenomena of transition from intermental functions to intramental functions. The fate of egocentric speech is conversion into inner speech (Vygotsky, 1982, v. 2, pp. 317–320).

Unfotunately, Vygotsky was not always consistent with this reasonable logic. Having not allowed egocentric speech to die away, he did allow this fate for internal speech – and, therefore, it would seem, for its ancestor, egocentric speech. It turns out that Piaget was right in the end. However, his conclusion about the transition of egocentric speech into inner speech allowed Vygotsky to accomplish a transition of a whole series of distinctly observable characteristics of egocentric speech into inner speech.

Certainly, questions about such transitions still remain. Can this transition be an ascription of the characteristics of one object of research to another? Later this methodological technique was widely used by Vygotsky's followers not only in the realm of cultural–historical psychology but also in the context of the activity approach to psychology. For example, A. N. Leont'ev according to the same logic, talked about *the fundamentally common structure* of external and internal activity. Some (e.g., N. F. Talyzina) even claimed that they are identical. In order to claim this, one needs to have the external activity, on the one hand, and the internal activity, on the other. Moreover, it is necessary to have measures and instruments for comparing them.

Such a research technique appears to be very treacherous. If one closely analyzes the numerous characteristics that Vygotsky gave to internal speech, one will find that they describe its external characteristics: abbreviated, shorthand, telegraphic style, a fragmentary, predicative, agglutinative, idiomatic, antigrammatical nature, and the other signs of speech for oneself. In sum, this resembles talk with a smart, understanding person with whom it is nice to sit even in silence. Because of the peculiarity of the syntax of inner speech, Vygotsky believed that the semantics of internal speech changes as well: The speech becomes more and more context bound and idiomatic, and it includes not only objective meanings of the word but also all the intellectual and affective content connected to them. This, in turn, leads to predominance in the internal speech of a deeply contextualized sense of words rather than their object-oriented meanings.

Reading Vygotsky, one can see how his own thought struggles because it cannot express itself in a noncontradictory way:

- The thought does not find room in a word.
- Thought and word appear to be cast not from the same mold from the outset.
- There is more contradiction than harmony between thought and word.
- Speech in its structure is not a mirror image of thought.
- Thought cannot put on speech as a garment.
- Speech does not serve as expression of thought.
- The grammar of the language does not coincide with the grammar of thinking (as if the latter is already well-known!) and so forth.

And, finally, the crowning phrase, "Thought does not express itself in a word but takes place in a word," which is followed by a discouraging (and tautological) claim, " . . . oppositely directed processes of the development of the meaning and sound sides of speech form a true unity precisely because of this opposite orientation" (Vygotsky, 1982, v. 2, p. 307). This claim is discouraging because the meaning side, also the inner side, develops from whole to parts, from sentence to word, and the external side of speech goes from parts to wholes, from word to sentence (Vygotsky, 1982, v. 2, p. 306).

Let us try to understand what may be hiding behind these statements. Is the whole a certain internal meaning (or maybe a thought)? Potentially, this meaning could have been expressed by a sentence, but a child cannot do it yet and only expresses it with one word. That may happen to an adult, too. An individual is looking for a word in order to express a meaning or a thought. The question is what was this initial, original meaning (or a thought) embodied before that word?

A poetic answer to this question was given a long time ago by Osip Mandel'shtam, when he said, "It *is a whisper before it meets the lips.*" In 1919, approximately when Shpet was working out his analysis of the structure of the word, Mandel'shtam, in his philosophical way, wrote: "slowly arising of 'the word as such.' Gradually, one after another, all the elements of the word were drawn into the concept of form, only the conscious meaning, Logos, up till now had mistakenly and arbitrarily been considered to be the meaning of the word. However, Logos lost out in this account. Logos demands parity with the other elements of the word. A futurist, who could not manage to deal with conscious meaning as material for creativity, thoughtlessly threw it overboard... For acmeists (the group of poets, part of the so-called Silver Age of Russian poetry; author's note) the conscious meaning of the word, the Logos, is as much of a beautiful form, as is the music of the word for the symbolists" (Mandelshtam, 1987, pp. 168–169).

Let us note for future purposes that the poet saw meaning (Logos) rather than an image behind poetry. It is hard to deal with meaning, not only in art but in psychology. After all, Vygotsky postulated the unity of word and thought, and he should not have digressed from this unity. His tortuous search was no accident. It reflected the real complexity of the problem.

Let us digress, for now, from the question of the material form that the initial meaning takes, the question of what sort of flesh it has (verbal or otherwise). We should note that meaning is not just a property of thinking. It is not only a structural component of motor, perceptual, or mnemonic activities directed at solving a motor, perceptual, or mnemonic problem; it penetrates the structure of these activities. Using Vygotsky's language, meaning provides their unity, sometimes including contradictions in this unity.

At the same time, meaning is a force that directs the activity. And solving a motor or thought problem is realizing, embodying, or expressing this meaning. If the problem is solved, it will be a second embodiment of the meaning, although we do not know what the initial, original meaning or conception was embodied in. Its second embodiment is objectification, if you wish, signification, of the first meaning in perceptual, motor, operational, and verbal meanings (depending on the nature of the problem). In these meanings or images, that is, in the second embodiment of meaning, the initial meaning reveals itself for the individual for the first time; the thought about meaning emerges in the individual, and he realizes what he wants, what he is really looking for, and what the reason for his frustration is. It may turn out to be an image, an action, or a thought. The latter will be expressed in a word, even if only awkwardly. Only after this expression, after objectification, will it become available for analysis, transmission, and so forth. This very difficult point about the second embodiment of the first meaning, which itself was embodied in an unknown way, is possible to illustrate with Mandel'shtam's poetic metaphor: "yesterday has not been born yet."

Thus, Vygotsky operated with thought and word as if they were two things, trying in many different ways to fit each to the other. However, when he talks about the inner side of a word, its meaning, his eloquence betrays him. Sometimes he identifies the inner side of a word with generalization, sometimes with a thought, sometimes with the road to a thought, and sometimes even with consciousness: The meaning of a word grows into the consciousness and develops depending on the changes in consciousness (Vygotsky, 1982, v. 1, p. 164).

Sometimes one encounters definitions of meaning that are diametrically opposed to these. Let us cite the most detailed one, "Meaning is not the sum of all the psychological operations that define a word. Meaning is something more definite – it is the internal structure of a sign operation. This is what lies in between a thought and a word. Meaning does not equal a word, it does not equal a thought either. This inequality is revealed in the noncoincidence of the lines of development" (Vygotsky, 1982, v. 1, p. 160). This comment was taken from Leont'ev's notes on a presentation by Vygotsky titled, "The Problem of Consciousness." Let us take the last quote from the same source: "Meaning is related not to thinking, but to the whole of consciousness" (Vygotsky, 1982, v. 1, p. 167).

At the beginning of Thinking and Speech, Vygotsky outlined a characterization of meaning that is not particularly rich. The most interesting aspect of this characterization comes in the context of the problem of thought and word and concerns the internal structure of a sign operation. Here Vygotsky revealed the role of meaning as a mediational means between thought and word. Later, Zaporozhets would call this a signifying operation (or operational meaning) and view it as a crystal of learning.

Vygotsky returned to the concept of meaning at the end of Thinking and Speech. There he cites F. Paulhan's account of the relationship between sense and meaning and drew conclusions from his own studies.

The main point he made has to do with the predominance of sense over meaning. "Meaning is just one of the zones of the sense that a word acquires in the context of event of speaking, and it is the most stable, unified and precise zone. It is well known that a word may easily change its sense in different contexts. Meaning, on the other hand, is that immovable and invariable point that remains stable no matter how the sense of a word changes in different contexts" (Vygotsky, 1983, v. 2, p. 346). Or, in other words, "meaning is simply a stone in the edifice of sense" (Vygotsky, 1983, v. 2, p. 347).

This was not an accidental slip of the tongue. It corresponds to the modest role that *meaning* plays in Vygotsky's book. Vygotsky presents a formal-sounding thesis on the double mediation of thought: first, by meanings, then by words. "Meaning mediates thought on its way to verbal expression, that is, the way from thought to word is an indirect, internally mediated one" (Vygotsky, 1983, v. 2, pp. 356–357). Thus, the main unit of analysis of thought and word appeared only in the role of one of the two mediators, even the most stable one, so inert that it was compared with a stone. It is not very clear how such a heavy meaning can be transformed into a "cloud," into "pure meaning." How can a stone evaporate?

Perhaps, this was not very clear to Vygotsky. That is why on the very last pages of the book he elegantly *parts* with *meaning*: "In the problem of thought and speech we attempted to examine its internal side [internal side of what? of a problem? (author's note)] hidden from direct observation. We attempted to analyze word meaning, which for psychology had always been the dark side of the moon, unstudied and unknown. *The semantic and internal side* [italics added] of speech, the side by which speech is directed not outward but within, to personality, until the most recent times remained a Terra Incognita for psychology . . . There is nothing in our wish to differentiate the external and the *semantic* [the meaning has disappeared; author's note; italics added] side of speech, thought and word, except a desire to present a more complicated view and finer connections of the unity of verbal thinking" (Vygotsky, 1983, v. 2, pp. 358–359).

In a comparison to the moon and its sides, *meaning* is closer to the visible side of this body and sense is closer to the dark side, which is mentioned by Vygotsky in the next phrase. Objects, items, words, and their meanings are given, sense is to be found. It is possible to find it, but it is difficult and not directly accessible.

A good image for the mutual relationships of meaning and sense is a Mobius strip. In the processes of understanding or thinking, we encounter oppositely directed *acts of making sense of meanings and giving meaningful signs to senses*; author's note], which are transformed into each other. In Russian, "meaning" ["znachenie"] and "sign" ["znak"] have a common root and, hence, the untranslated italicized phrase sounds like a Russian pun. On the outer side of the strip may be meaning, which is transformed into sense as a result of the act of making sense, and this becomes the internal side of the same strip. Assigning a meaningful sign to sense makes an analogous transformation. Anyway, it was highly productive for Vygotsky to change the focus from "*meaning*" to *sense*. Such a change brings his views closer to those of Shpet.

My teachers, Zaporozhets, Luria, and A. N. Leont'ev, told me how Vygotsky was seriously ill and dictated the last chapter of *Thinking and Speech* on the eve of his death. It was already too late to return to the beginning of the book and compare it with what he was dictating. But the changes that emerged represent the creativity of thought in word, as is the case for the entire book. Perhaps foreseeing one's own end makes one think about sense rather than meaning. Thinking about sense at such a point is more important than thinking about meaning.

Luria had a different reading of this book by his teacher than I do. He did not see the change of meaning to sense. Instead, he saw sense as only complementing meaning. "Up to this point we were talking about two components of the word (or utterance): *its object orientation and its meaning* . . . there is, however, a third functional side of the word, one that is as important as the correspondence to an object and its meaning. This is the meaning that the word has to the speaker, and it constitutes the underlying theme of the utterance" (Luria, 1982, p. 475).

In any event, the concluding phrase of Vygotsky's entire book, "The word full of sense is a microcosm of human consciousness," would have made a good beginning for what could have been new book about the word. But such a book (and not only this one!) had already been written by Shpet. However, it is a difficult book to read, and perhaps neither Vygotsky nor many other psychologists from later generations read it.

It is not my task to answer the question: What is the unit of analysis of verbal thinking? The answer could be meaning, or sense, or sensible meaning, or, finally, co-meaning, which is a particular, *intimate* sense of the word with its own intimate forms (Shpet, 1989, p. 470). Shpet saw the object of psychological research to be subjective comeanings rather than objective senses and meanings: "Not sense, not meaning, but co-meaning, subjective reactions and feeling *accompanying* the accomplishments of history and expressing individuals' relations to it are the subject of psychology" (Shpet, 1989, p. 480). Discussing the unit of analysis, it is necessary to take into account that Shpet was talking about meaning as the "*substance*" of word and that he talked about a special class of operative meanings and their differences from objective meanings.

Let us turn to Shpet's interpretation of the structure of the word. Particular attention should be paid to meaning and sense, which Vygotsky called the "internal side of the word." Shpet, following Humboldt, distinguished the external and inner forms of the word. But this was not all. In the structure of word he separated external, *pure* (or "ontic") form, on the one hand, and *internal* form, on the other. Morphological forms are external forms of the word. Shpet added a pure ontic form that carries objective reference because of his commitment to the difference between *theme* and *object*.

A nominative, or indexical, sign of an existing or a remembered object is a word. When we talk about an object, there is a sensory moment presented in the word, and when we talk about a theme, the new moment in the structure of the word is an intellectual one, and the word becomes related to intellectual reality rather then sensory reality: "Word now indicates something present, possible to reach not by the index finger but by intellectual intuition. What the word is pointing at now is now *meant* by it, the word implies a theme" (Shpet, 1994, p. 399). Furthermore: "The 'theme' that is implied is only a certain item for attention, 'something,' a given topic. Carrying it out, realization (in terms of content), elaboration is a further matter, implying new realities, new functions, new depths and 'steps.' Theme is only a question, even a mystery, an X, and the word problem for discovering this X is yet to be given and comprehended in some other way" (Shpet, 1994, p. 194). And, finally: "Any really, empirically really *existing* objects, real persons, real characteristics, actions are *objects*. Themes are the possibilities; their ontology is ideal" (Shpet, 1994).

Shpet distinguished between factual being ("being in the world") and "being in an idea." It is important to emphasize that "being in an idea" is intentional being, and, moreover, is concrete being, carrying a concrete meaning. Such thematic (or ideal) being is presented in pure (or ontic) forms of the word. Thus, the meaning of a word is situated exclusively in *ontological* spheres: "wherever and whatever theme we name (whether that theme is an object or a relation), we cannot limit the word to its nominative function, we have to ascertain its *meaning* function as well, i.e., whatever we name, we also utter or *ascertain* with our utterance *its* content and sense – perceive them" (Shpet, 1999, p. 280).

Proceeding to the internal form of word: "The interweaving of new forms, *logical* forms, wedges itself between the ontic forms with their formal content and morphologic forms (with the same content as the ontic forms have) as a *system of relations between them*" (Shpet, 1989, p. 398). Logical forms are the forms of meaningful sense. (I will not dwell here on Shpet's objections to formal logic.) Internal logical forms are as concrete as forms of semantic content. They are "relations," the terms of which are empirical linguistic forms of the word and the principal ideal ("relational") meaning.

Shpet brought specific arguments concerning the strict correspondence between logic and ontology, the possibility of translating from the language of logic to the language of ontology and vice versa. This provides almost unlimited possibilities for interaction between morphological, ontic, and logical forms. If one looks for analogies to Shpet's internal logical forms in the psychological literature, Piaget's ideas of operational structures may be the closest, but this is an issue that goes beyond the bounds of our present analysis.

Let us supplement what we have already learned from Vygotsky with the ideas of Shpet:

> Reason is a function concerned with understanding sense . . . In the structure of the word, its content, or sense possesses a particular place compared with the other members of the structure. Sense is not separable from this structure as, using an analogy with the structure of a living organism, the bone system and muscular systems might be separable. Rather, it is more reminiscent of blood, which is a carrier of nutrition throughout the entire organism and makes possible both the normal logic of its brain-psyche and the logic of its sensory organs.
>
> On the other hand, semantic content may be compared with matter that fills in spaces, with revolving movement around its own center of gravity and condensation creating chaotic nebulae. The living vocabulary of a language is chaotic, and the meanings of isolated words are always only scraps of thought, undefined nebulae. Only in the process of distribution among the various forms discussed above does sense acquire meaningful and organic being.   (Shpet, 1989, pp. 416–417)

Therefore, unlike Vygotsky, Shpet considered sense not as a mere mediator substituting for meaning. *Sense* is a thought, which is understood as coming into being. Shpet constantly talked about it when he discussed the forms of the word, the content of these forms, and the word as being full of sense as well. Such an interpretation of sense may be considered to be the fulfillment of Mandel'shtam's wish about the parity of sense, Logos, with the other elements of the word. The metaphor of sense as the blood system compares with Weber's (1978) metaphor: Man is a beast suspended in a web of senses which he has woven by himself. Perhaps, we can add "woven from his own being" (p. 188).

As if in anticipation of the suggestion of the possible existence of "pure meanings" (Vygotsky) or "pure thought" (Gal'perin), Shpet wrote, "Pure sense, the pure content of thought, literally and figuratively, is an impossibility, in the same way that pure sensory content is ... Pure content as a subject of analysis is a content with an increasingly small meaning of the form" (Shpet, 1999).

Finally, on the impossibility of a pure thought, Shpet wrote that no matter how "vague and elusive" a thought is

> It is "given" in pure sense in forms of consciousness, perhaps undefined. Thought is always directed to something; even if this something would seem like the most blurred "something," it is already a minimum of a natural form without which we cannot consider a thought. This minimum of form suggests by its ontological existence at least the same minimum of a logical form. And, therefore, the minimum of thought postulates a minimum, a fetus of verbalization. That is why attempts to depict a wordless thought are so childishly hopeless. They present a thinker as some *deaf and dumb being*, immersed into "pure" thinking as if in puffs of tobacco smoke, and not an empirical alive deaf and dumb being which always possesses its own means of embodiment and transition of thought. Such an imaginary thinker would have to be an ethereal deaf and dumb being – either an angel or a demon."
>
> (Shpet, 1999, pp. 417–418)

We have only to add that according to Shpet, sense is rooted in being, and it is a cothought not only etymologically (Shpet, 1999, p. 455). The characteristic of sense as a co-thought is remarkable in itself. In this chapter, I have referred to the sense of motor, perceptual, and mnemonic problems. I will now discuss the sense of the actions directed at solving these problems in a corresponding way. A side result of successfully solving these problems is building corresponding objective, operational, and perceptual meanings, Therefore, meanings are preceded by sense, or co-thought that looks for its embodiments and finds it there.

When characterizing the inner form of the word, Shpet paid particular attention to the dynamic nature of logico-semantic forms. I will illustrate this dynamic nature by a description of the emergence of poetic speech from Shpet's like-minded colleague (be this by design or happenstance), Mandel'shtam. They had in common not only their thought but also fate. Mandel'shtam perished in the Gulag a year after Shpet's murder.

Describing Dante's poetry, and distinguishing it from its external imagery, Mandel'shtam wrote:

> Semantic waves-signals disappear, having fulfilled their job: the stronger they are, the more yielding they are and the less they are likely to linger

on ... The quality of poetry is defined by the speed and decisiveness with which it inculcates its intentions or orders into the purely lexical quantitative nature of word-formation. It is necessary to forge the whole width of a river, crowded by Chinese junks moving actively in different directions – that's how the sense of poetic speech emerges. It cannot be restored, like our route, by surveying the boatmen: they won't tell us how and why we jumped from junk to junk.

(Mandel'shtam, 1987, p. 109)

Shpet expressed his position clearly and energetically. The reader is free to treat it as either a supplement to Vygotsky's position or as a forestalling critique and a warning not to accept Vygotsky's ideas. In 2001, Bibikhin used the same image of "oscillation," analyzing Potebnya's thought about thought and word. He carried out the analysis without mentioning either Vygotsky's contradictory position or Shpet's limiting position. When he completed his project, Bibikhin exclaimed, "Will there be an end to these oscillations?"

Potebnya's views are very edifying, first of all from the perspective of his influence on Vygotsky, who invoked the concept of inner form only once and only in the context of his thoughts on the psychology of art. Using this concept when interpreting Potebnya rather than Humboldt and Shpet, Vygotsky wrote: "In each word, as shown by the psychological system of linguistics, we distinguish three main elements, first, the external sound form, then an image or an inner form, and finally, meaning. The inner form is the closest etymologic meaning of a word by means of which it acquires a possibility to actually mean the content that is put into it. In many cases, this inner form has been forgotten and pushed under the influence of the ever-widening meaning of word" (Vygotsky, 1987, p. 29). Vygotsky criticized Potebnya for his inclination toward associationist and sensualist trends in psychology and objected in the spirit of the previously cited protest by Mandel'shtam against the reduction of poetry to external imagery. Subsequently, Vygotsky lost interest in the image as an element involved in the contruction of inner form, which is what Potebnya was talking about. After displacement of inner form, there was something like a short circuit between sound form and meaning. The concept of inner form lost its constructive sense, and Vygotsky forgot it and never came back to it again.

Vygotsky probably does not deserve reproach for his treatment of Potebnya's interpretation of the inner form of the word. From Shpet's perspective, by reducing the inner form of the word to an image and etymology, Potebnya compromised "the concept of the inner form of language" (Shpet, 1989, p. 447). Potebyna also lured himself into an interesting trap. As Bibikhin describes it [the phrases in single quotations inside the longer quote belong to Potebnya; author's note]:

> Potebnya, having said that only the concept and word bring order to the world, starts to look at the word as a "strange and arbitrary sign"...A developing thought absorbs concepts and images, its speeding rush whips itself up and reinforces itself. A pure thought strives to freedom. "With the creation of a concept, the inner form disappears, as in the most part of our words, mistaken for the natives...Words become a pure indicator to a thought, nothing between its sound and content remains for the consciousness of the speaker." It would seem that the disappearance of the inner form of the word and a clear way from the word's sound to what it is about should have saddened the poetic Potebnya; however, it did not. On the contrary, the ability to discard all the garlands of inner form and other overtones of meaning is seen by Potebnya as a virtue of language. "It would be unjust to reproach language for slowing down the flow of our thought." The highest virtue lies in lightening-fast thought. In the moment of important decisions, a pure thought like an arrow is aimed at the heart of the matter and the admixture of appendages, the plume of inner forms would burden it. There is no need for that. "There is no doubt that the actions of our thought, which do not need assistance from language in the moment of their happening, happen very fast."

> Let us take note: the actions of thought do not need assistance from language. Therefore, thought gets by without language at all. "Under circumstances that demand an immediate grasp of the situation and action, for example, in cases of unexpected questions, when a lot depends on the answer, during the indivisible moment before the answer, one is able to think over a lot of things without words." Let us note this "think without words," because here is the next phrase, "But language does not take this ability away from the person, just the opposite, if it does not give it then at least it strengthens it."

> We might call this a brilliant absurdity. Language does not take away from a person the ability to think without language but strengthens it, and maybe even provides for it. It is not hard to understand this. Language gradually trains thought, teaching it how to get by without using language's crutches; the word brings thought to lightning fast wordlessness. But Potebnya says something different: "The word, fragmenting simultaneous acts of the soul into sequential vectors of acts at the same time [!] serves as a basis of humans' innate striving to embrace everything with one indivisible rush of thought." So the word exists both in the slow composition of thought from images and in fast "indivisible" flight, that is not marked up by verbal images.

> Put another way, the word is even where there is no word but where there is only an indivisible goal-oriented thought, having to do directly with the heart of the matter. A word can exist in such a way that it cannot

exist. It does not exist for the rush of thought and still it is a "basis" for such a thought. But excuse me, the "basis" of the pure thought that "does not need assistance from language" and thinks "without words," is the naked heart of the matter – the objects themselves. Where did the word come from if we said that it is not there? What is Potebnya suggesting here? Is he suggesting freedom from language given by language itself? We are impatient, nearly irritated. And as if wavering between word based action and object-based action were not enough, we are given a barefaced contradiction: there is no word in the "rush of thought" and it is still there, creating or strengthening this rush.

We could not follow Potebnya if we had not thought about the same things ourselves, if the landscape had not been clarified for us at least partially, with regard to the main questions and mysteries. Potebnya's attempts to untangle the skein thought-object-world-word-language make it worthy to persevere ourselves." (Bibikhin, 2001, pp. 90–92)

I do not know if there was a text in Bibikhin's impatient rush of words, but there is definitely energy and expressiveness. Although Shpet seemed to remove the problem of "oscillations," which Vygotsky did not notice or did not want to notice, Bibikhin, with the help of Potebnya, reintroduces it for discussion and recommends that we persevere. Let us follow his recommendation.

On the issue of the relation between thought and word, Vygotsky was a determined adherent of Potebnya. Willingly and repeatedly, he quotes Potebnya's "formula," which is as beautiful as it is mysterious: "The ability to think in a human way but without words is given only by the word" (Vygotsky, 1984, v. 4, p .101; v. 6, p. 18). Where do the words go? This is a question for both Potebnya and Vygotsky. Underlying Potebnya's paradox (this is what we would call his "formula") there are two circumstances. The first is the notion of the instantaneous, simultaneous nature of thought, the speed of which is said to be incomparable with anything else. The second, which stems from the first, is a false or extremely poor characterization of the inner form of word, its role, and its fate in the act of giving rise to a thought. Let us start with simultaneity, keeping in mind that our senses of sight and touch may be simultaneous.

The problem of the richness and fullness of an indivisible moment is not new. One remarkable example of an instantaneous representation of the external world can be found in the Bible: "And the devil took him up, and showed him all the kingdoms of the world in a moment of time... " (Luke 4:5). No less amazing is the speed of representation of our own experience. Although the capacity of our memory does have clear limits, it is characterized by instantaneous readiness. This is also true about verbal memory. Not only poets, as Brodsky said, but all of us at any given moment possess language in all its fullness. However, a poet also has strophic structure and syntax. Brodsky once noted that he and Akhmatova knew all the rhymes in the Russian language.

Language is not only a means of communication and thinking. It is a whole world in and of itself, whole and instantaneously available (and it seems, available without the devil's assistance). It is the world that we carry in us, with us. Of course, Freudian slips happen, as well as repression, but such exceptions only reinforce the rule. In the study of motor control, motor units have been discovered to be within the quanta of action and, by definition, indivisible. These motor units last for 40–50 milliseconds and react to external stimuli in different ways (Gordeeva &, Zinchenko, 2001). It is striking that in spite of their indivisibility and minuteness, they have individual features. A decisive role is played by semantic wave-signals, not only washing over the discrete motor control of performance but also inculcating in it its intention-orders (compare this with Mandel'shtam's description).

The question still remains, What embodies drives, intentions, and senses before they are realized? Vygotsky agreed that the word dies in thought. Shpet categorically objected to this notion. Potebnya left us with an ambiguous answer: it both dies and lives. Where do we need to look for an answer to this?

Perhaps, turning to the concept of inner form may help us find it. The easiest thing to do is to *lose* or *discard* all the ballast of the inner form of the word in order not to *slow down* the flow of our thought. This is Potebnya's variant, and Vygotsky agreed with it. Is this the version that pushed Shpet, in his day, to make his disparaging remark about Potebnya's interpretation of the concept of inner form? However, Shpet did not go into detail on his negative critique, which, in my opinion, is not fully justified.

Shpet denied the possibility of including an image in the inner form of the word. The only exception he made was for the poetic word, in which an image could be present as an inner form. I would think that Potebnya's position on this issue is more grounded that Shpet's. For the latter, who knew as many as seventeen, even nineteen languages according to the evidence, word, sense, and logic were self-sufficient and did not need any crutches. That's why Shpet, in a way, encapsulated the inner form in language and word. Let us turn to the origins of the concept of inner form.

Not wishing to go deep into antiquity, we start with Humboldt. Initially he used the notion of the inner form of the word as a characteristic of the person or work of art, and only later of language. Humboldt substituted the concepts of inner and external form for the rather indefinite terms "internal" and "external," which are still widespread in psychology. Let us try to extend this substitution into psychology.

Nikolai A. Bernstein considered human action as a functional organ of a reactive, evolving, biodynamically grounded materiality. Zaporozhets added to this list the characteristic of the perceptibility of movement, its sensibility. Bernstein was the author of the metaphor, "Action is a living being" (compare this with what I noted earlier about Shpet's similar metaphor as it is applied to word). This provides a foundation for considering action, or its biodynamic substance, as external form, which has an inner form (or internal picture, as Zaporozhets used to say).

The inner form of action contains an image of the situation in which the action is being carried out – the image of a necessary future, that is, the image of the situation that is to be achieved as a result of the action – and an image of the actions that have to be carried out in order to achieve the desired result. In other words, image is intentional. Descartes referred to the images of action as passions. The inner form of action contains the word as well, providing for its expediency and regulating its process. At the same time, the word may be contained with all the "fringes" of its inner forms.

In its turn the image, also considered as a functional organ, has its own external form (the substance of sensory forms) and inner forms. The inner form may contain perceptual actions that lead to its creation and the word, with the help of which the image may be actualized, aroused, and so forth. Interpreting the image as a functional organ implies that "from the very beginning an emerging image of an object is a certain heuristic projection of reality, which is subsequently checked and restructured repeatedly for its practical connection to reality" (Ukhtomsky, 1978, p. 274).

Finally, the word (which is also a functional organ), considered as inner form, may contain, in addition to all the ontic and inner forms described by Shpet, image and action. Let us not forget that the word itself may become an action – a performative: "Words stop the Sun, words ruin cities," said the poet Nikolai Gumilev (1989, p. 33).

In all of the cases considered so far, the inner form seems to be insubstantial, and the external form seems to be rather real. It is easy to notice that words, actions, and images sometimes play a role in the inner form and sometimes play a role in the external form, allowing for the general conclusion of the reversibility of internal and external forms. Invisible inner form turns into visible form, and the visible form, in turn, becomes invisible.

Something similar happens with action and passion, thought and word, sense and meaning. The Mobius strip metaphor, used to characterize the interrelation of the sense and meaning is good for any external and inner forms. According to such logic, inner forms do not disappear, but rather continue to participate in perception, memory, thinking, and action.

Action, image, word, feeling, thought, and will – in other words everything that is united by the concepts "mental processes," "mental acts," or "forces of the soul" – are living forms. And because they are living, they are, therefore, active, meaningful, unfinalized, and restless . . . Like a soul! Each one of them is not "pure culture." One form contains in itself the others. The ancient principle of "All in one, one in all" is at work, and this does not interfere with their relatively autonomous existence. But even while they maintain their autonomy, they "remember" their origins and remain heterogeneous forms.

The heterogeneity of images, words, and actions is noted in various poetic metaphors: "eyes of the soul," "poetic senses," "organs of sense as theoreticians," "kinetic melody," "picturesque idea," "reasonable eye," "sighted mind," "soul in flight" (about ballet), "shame of sighted fingers," and so forth. The internal forms of action and image have their own dynamic forms subordinated to the sense of movement or perceptual (or perhaps thinking) tasks. We know that we can play out action before action, and after action (if it is not too late!), we can manipulate an image, mentally rotate it, and so forth.

The dynamic forms of words, images, and actions enrich each other. Images and actions, like words, perform operational functions, which, as in the case of word, may be separated from meaning. Shpet paid attention to meaning. The instantaneousness of thought may be related to the simultaneity of image, and perhaps the internal playback of action. Finally, the interchange of function is possible between word, image, and action, perhaps, including intellectual functions. Don't we talk about visual or musical thinking? Doesn't the experienced conductor play the whole symphony in the internal plane in one or two minutes?

I have said enough here to come back to the "wordless impulse," or "unembodied intention," to the situation, paradoxically presented by Potebnya and Bibikhin when they say: "there is word even where there is no word." The word does not die in thought. More likely, thought dies by drowning in words. After all, truth may be born and regenerated in discussions, but it may degenerate as well. Perhaps, thought has its own internal form, and this has to become a subject of serious reflection. It is no accident that the beginning of this chapter contains the whole gamut of answers on what stands behind thought. And if, for example, the internal form of thought contains images, the internal form of images contains the word.

The same happens with action, and with passion: Descartes said that action and passion are one. The similar logic may be considered as a first approximation to solving the paradox "word is where it is not." Both in the underlying bases and on the peaks of consciousness and in the entire mind, there is the word. And there is no miracle that can take us back to our wordless past.

Let us try to approach the problem of thought and word from the side of the birth of thought. What happens in the process of creating the new? Let us look at this problem through the lens of the concepts of external and inner forms. The torture of embodying the inner form in creative work is connected with the fact that something was given or was glimpsed "inside," as an image and as an idea. At least it seems that way, but it is not possible to express it, to embody it. What is embodied does not correspond to the "internal perfection," which is felt, but which may be an illusion. We have come right up to the mystery of creativity. The task is not to discover it but at least to understand where it lies and how it is hidden.

Let us turn to the division of forms into external and inner, of course, not denying that they may be more or less substantial. Let us listen to Shpet: "It is possible to say that in idea *form and content are united.* This means that the more deeply we go into the analysis of what is given, the more we will be convinced that it is an infinite amalgamation, interweaving of substances of forms, ad infinitum. And this is the very law of method: each task is solved through the resolution of the given content into the system of forms" (Shpet, 1989, p. 425).

But this content is already expressed through the language of some forms, which might not be realized – at least not easily verbalized or visualized. Without that, language simply does not exist. The task may be in releasing it, expressing it in a different form, and therefore realizing it, seeing it, and showing it to others. In other words, we do this by resolving (embodying) the content in the form of a word, an image, or an action. I have already mentioned that action, word, and image constantly "grow" into each other, and interweave and enrich each other, creating the fringes of forms. This is the basis; this is where the semantic unity that cements words, actions, and images together is constructed.

If we use the customary division of mental processes, the substance of sensory forms is important for perception, biodynamic substance is important for action, and affective substance is important for feeling. This is only partially true because all of these substances participate in the formation of image, feeling, and action. Similarly, the word is also characterized by the interweaving of the substance of sensory forms, bio-dynamic substance, and affective substance. Psychology knows different ways to thought: from action, from image, from word, from feeling. All this heteroglossia is explained by the fact that thought, like a work of art, which, of course, is a thought as well, does not have the "talking footprints" (an expression of N. N. Volkov) that mark the artistic process of its creation.

Bakhtin wrote about the origins of thought: "The meaningful content of potential feeling and thought does not enter into my head accidentally, like a meteor from another world, remaining there closed and impenetrable. It is intertwined with the whole fabric of my emotional, voluntary, active, living thought-feeling as its essential moment" (Bakhtin, 1994, p. 36). So, despite the possible, sometimes striking depth and transparency of thought, it is heterogeneous and syncretistic in its origins. All the forces of the soul participate in its birth. The same applies to other creations of the person, including works of art that are so striking in their perfection. Let us try to imagine, at least schematically, what happens during their creation.

Let us place the word, image, and action at the angles of a triangle – a favorite figure for philosophers, linguists, and psychologists. In our version, the word, the action, and the image are mutually reflected, entailed, and mediated, and they essentially develop and construct each other. This is in a sense functional polyphony and polysemy. They imply the emergence of a distinct leading tone or voice, a dominant form. If such an explanatory image is necessary, such an emergence may be imagined as a mental rotation of the triangle clockwise or counterclockwise.

As a result of rotating (or "oscillating), any of these functional organs can serve as means for solving the problem and may become the triangle's peak. (The image of "oscillation" haunts me; it is very difficult to escape it.) The dominance of one or the other of these is defined not only by the concrete content and the sense of the problem solved, but by the arsenal of dynamic internal forms. This may be logical, in Shpet's way, or subordinated to the peculiar logic of perceptual actions (handling and manipulating, for example, a visual image or the logic of concrete action – from manipulative to tool-mediated).

Let us return once more to the story that Einstein told Wertheimer about seven years of work on the theory of relativity. During this entire period, according to Einstein, the main thing was the "feeling of being oriented, the feeling of movement directed toward something concrete. Of course, it is very difficult to express this feeling in words, but it was definitely present and it should be distinguished from later reflections on the rational form of decision making. Undoubtedly, behind such directedness there always stands something logical, but I have it in a form of some visual image" (Wertheimer , 1987, pp. 263–264).

Such oscillation is a rule and a norm; it amounts to trying out a means to solve a problem (a task), the search for a language in which the problem has a solution. Dominance does not exclude collaboration; rather, it implies it. Let us not forget that whatever language is chosen to formulate a solution, it contains the rest as its internal form. The relations between word, action, and image imply the interdependency as well. Karl Lashley (1964) would call it equipotentiality, which of course has certain boundaries rather than being absolute.

The "triangle" is a relatively limited metaphor. What is going on resembles more of a spiritual and intellectual crucible, in which the internal forms of word, action, and image meld together, mix, and divide. In this crucible, "the inner fire flames up now brighter, now more muted, now more lively, now less so, and usually melds with the expression of each thought and each set of images rushing out" (Humboldt, 1984, p. 105). The external expression of thought *melds* as well. For each form participating, this "melding" is not "pure culture." Being intertwined with each other, and with their content, too, they are what the poet Anna Akhmatova (1977) called sweeping out, a process in which *"poems grow free of shame."*

Pasternak, who was educated in philosophy, expressed it in a more academic way: "The most complicated is chaos. Art is the overcoming of chaos, as Christianity is the overcoming of pre-historic masses of time. Pre-historic chaos does not know the phenomena of memory: memory is history, and memory is art. The past does not exist outside memory. History and art are the children of the same mother – memory. Art is simplification that takes the form of rising rather than lowering: it is reality crystallized out of chaos, which is anti-real due to its nature. It is there, but it does not exist, i.e., it only exists through art and history, through the faces in defiance of the facelessness of chaos..." (1990, p. 533).

Without going into the discussion between Pasternak and Shalamov about the permissibility of incomplete, inexact assonating rhyme in poetry, I will cite Shalamov's ideas about his understanding of poetic creation: "...rhyme is not only the castle of a poem, not only the main tool, the key to the harmony of sound. It is – and this is its main role – an instrument for searching for comparisons, metaphors, thoughts, turns of speech, images – a strong magnet that sticks out into the darkness and the whole universe flies past it, leaving in the poem only a tiny part of what was tried. It is an instrument of choice, a tool of poetic thought, a tool of learning about the world, the fishing hook of the net of the poem, and it seems to me that there is no need solely for the sake of harmony of sound to cut off part of the net from the very start. The catch will be poorer" (Pasternak, 1990, p. 535).

In this reasoning, the flying universe is the same as Akhmatova's sweepings or the fringes of the internal forms, floating above spontaneously or under the influence of the current impressions. And the rhyme serves the function of a searching image and a determining tendency defining the choice of what is needed. Taken together, the "net" and the "hook" provide for the semantic unity (seine) and external perfection-euphony (hook).

And still, the main mystery is how the multiple heterogeneous forms in the end give birth to the purest forms, how they entail, or "meld," a *style* as a result of their interaction. The style at issue may be of the word, painting, sculpture, dance, or form of thinking, and it entails, for example, "geometric eloquence," and finally, a style of behavior. Style, which is deeply individual, "transparent" or "dark," is impossible to confuse with anything else. No matter how far we move toward unraveling this mystery, we need to realize that there is an element of magic in the creative act. According to Pasternak, this act is "the tangible sorcery or alchemy, which makes the work of art seem to be an accidentally broken off piece of the very density of being or form making essence of being rather than reflection or descriptions of life" (Pasternak, 1990, pp. 366–367).

It is a different question whether we can see this sorcery, whether we will be able to penetrate, *see* behind these purest forms the fringes of their internal forms, their sense and meaning. This is already an issue of our aesthetic culture or taste, an issue of the richness or poorness of our own inner form.

In the external forms that were created and behind them, there are hidden layers of invisible inner forms. *"Under the surface of each word bottomless darkness hides"* said the poet Zabolotsky. "Pure form" is a double-edged sword. When, for example, verbal culture is not nurtured by image, action, affection, and volition, it will be transformed into the purest absence of culture. The same applies to image and action. Then we receive a hollow word, a cliché, a reflex, a motor perseveration, mechanical movement, dull image, sealed symbol, or generally a "dead point of view." If there is no intertwining, no fringes of the inner forms, the external form becomes meaningless, senseless.

The concept of "inner form," despite its long existence, has only slowly entered the conceptual apparatus of psychology. In order to facilitate its acceptance, we will provide some needed clarification. Today, it is commonplace to consider the world as a text that we gradually learn how to read, and to consider the person as a text that we read even more poorly. Is it possible to present each form of the word, including image, action, and feeling as the word, sometimes a verbal word, more often nonverbal word? *"Nonverbal internal word"* is a notion belonging to Mamardashvili. Or present it as an *"embryo of verbalzation"* (Shpet) rather than its ashes (Potebnya, Vygotsky)?

Of course, I understand that calling an inner form a nonverbal word does not alleviate the tortures of its verbalization or embodiment in a different medium – a text. But still it seems to me that at least the poets who talk about "poetic matter" will feel comfortable with such a clarification. Let us start with Pushkin's questions:

> Fate's womanlike mumble
> Fluttering of the sleeping night
> Life's mouse-race . . .
> Why do you trouble me?
> Dull whisper, what do you mean?

Mandel'shtam comments about the unintelligible *whisper*, which is both *music and word, and silentium*, appears before it reaches the lips:

> Perhaps, the whisper was born before the lips
> And the leaves were spinning in treelessness
> And those to whom we devote our experience
> Were featured before experience.

And finally an anthem to the silent word by T. S. Eliot:

> If the lost word is lost, if the spent word is spent
> If the unheard, unspoken
> Word is unspoken, unheard;
> Still is the unspoken word, the Word unheard,
> The Word without a word, the Word within
> The world and for the world;
> And the light shone in darkness and
> Against the Word the unstilled world still whirled
> About the centre of the silent Word.
> (T. S. Eliot, *Ash Wednesday V*, 1930)

Of course, empirically we feel the nonverbal inner word as sensations, images, signs, symbols, and thoughts about something, hardly expressible in words. At the same time, we can distinctly observe a temporal gap between the emerging feeling and its verbal articulation, of course, if the latter is successful at all.

Based on detailed differentiations of activity of the "speech center" or speech constellation in the centers, Ukhtomsky came to the following generalization:

> During the first orienting analysis of the process of speech it is easy to distinguish psycho-physiologically two main devices with distinctly different original speeds of operation. In the most common way they may be named as a) *components of word-realization* and b) *components of thought*. In the course of introspection it is easy to report on how quickly

thought runs and takes shape while it waits to be uttered, and how relatively slowly and with friction the initial utterance is accomplished.

Discrepancies between words and tempos often make for difficult, halting attempts to express thought in word and put off the flow of thought, and this results in inhibited speech process. This is experienced by any beginning, or novice teacher or orator. Thus, components of speech processes may appear in conflict with each other as a result of the discrepancy of the intervals and speeds... Only by mutual co-tuning to a certain medium "sympathetic" speed (i.e., partially lowering the higher speeds of activity, partially speeding up the higher speeds of activity in other components), does the speaker reach the uniform march of excitement in the speech constellation of the centers.

(Ukhtomsky, 1978, pp. 152–153)

Here the most interesting things are the concepts of "sympathetic rhythm" and "uniform march" in the intense flow of work. Ukhtomsky gave this psychological–practical analysis of the embodiment of thought in word in 1937. After several years he came back to it and introduced the concept of "chronotope":

A specific correspondence in time between "the flow of thought" and speed of putting thought in speech is a necessary condition for well-organized, smooth speech. The discipline of speech processes requires restraining the overly full flow of images and thoughts in accordance with the speed of word-composition... the coordination in time, speed, rhythm of action, and therefore in times of completion of the separate mechanisms of a reaction, for the first time creates a functionally defined "center" out of spatially separated ganglion groups. Here a well-known reminder from Herman Minkovsky comes to mind: space alone just like time alone are "shadows of reality," whereas real events take place in an undivided way in space and time, in a chronotope. Both in our milieu and inside our organism concrete facts and dependencies are given to us as sequences and connections in space and time between events."

(Ukhtomsky, 1978, pp. 268–269)

Such a "chronotopic" interpretation of psychological and physiological events as applied to "putting thought into speech" and to other similar occurrences studied by psychology and physiology, provides us with an opportunity to remove or significantly limit the opposition between external and internal. Let us remember that such a limitation can also be provided by the introduction of concepts of the external and inner forms discussed above. If the inner form is born outside and external form is born inside, this not only removes the opposition between external and inner, but limits the problem of the beginning and the end which is out of place in the logic of an active chronotope. The question of thought before word or word before thought no longer makes sense:

> What we call the beginning is often the end
> And to make an end is to make a beginning.
> The end is where we start from. And every phrase
> And sentence that is right (where every word is at home,
> Taking its place to support the others,
> The word neither diffident nor ostentatious,
> An easy commerce of the old and the new,
> The common word exact without vulgarity,
> The formal word precise but not pedantic,
> The complete consort dancing together)
> Every phrase and every sentence is an end and a beginning,
> Every poem an epitaph. And any action
> Is a step to the block, to the fire, down the sea's throat
> Or to an illegible stone: and that is where we start.
> (T. S. Elliot, Little Gidding, 1942 V.)

This poem, along with reasoning of Ukhtomsky, may be taken as a recommendation (aesthetically and ethically colored rather than formal) of reasonable practical psychology. If we put them together with the excerpt from *Ash Wednesday* cited above, we will see that the problem of the originality of Word and Thought was as relative as the whole problem of beginning and end:

> In my beginning is my end...
> In my end is my beginning.

The poet was anxious about us having received a freedom of choice, to oscillate

> Between fruitless thought and thoughtless action.

Let us come back from a set of metaphors from poetry to the one of philosophy and psychology. According to Shpet, signs and symbols may serve the function of being a *verbal embryo* standing behind thought. Proper nouns that are the symbols of what is "unspoken" may be such signs and symbols as well. Shpet saw the only way to understanding them "in the pure disclosure of symbols, in their revelation, and therefore in opening what is secret" (Shpet, 1994, p. 112).

The situation is similar for *idea*, eidos in Plato's meaning of the word: we look at the very essence as at a sign, says Shpet. "Transition from sign to sense" is not a "conclusion" but at least in its basis is an original and primary act of "seeing" sense. In its originality, we find it. Semasiologic acceptance of the very essence eo ipso makes us look in it for the *sense* which is opened in front of us as *reasonable basis* built into the very essence; essence in its content comes from reason as its origin.

In the end it is possible to say that the object here performs not the role of a "problem" but as a *sign* that *here* is a problem, and therefore its conditions are not given directly yet but "will" be found in the process of deciphering its sign" (Shpet, 1994, p. 316). Here Shpet thought not about an abstract thought but of thought in action. He was interested in philosophical thinking when the object of thought is mind. And in these extreme situations of idealistic theoretical world, discovered by Parmenides in antiquity, thought is not unembodied. Behind it if there is not a word, then there is a symbol, a sign, a meaningful image that is to be deciphered, revealed, understood, and re-created, embodied in word, image, or action.

Once again, let us return to the analysis of a hypothetical creative act. If we put a symbol in the beginning of "wordless impulse," distracting ourselves from the fact that symbol itself is an object and an idea, and therefore a word, then what is needed is its deciphering, or penetration into its mysterious inner form. Once this is done, handling the outcome takes place directed by the certain criteria of *internal justification*. And finally, the clothing, the adorning of the obtained result in the new form is directed by criteria of *external perfection*. If we talk about a genuine work of art, in addition to the perfection of external forms including the perfection of their intentional (and inspired by ugliness, like Goya or Dostoevsky), it is an invitation into its internal space, created by the web of its internal forms, an invitation to enter into its internal layers of meanings and senses, and to finally penetrate into its inner word regardless of whether this word is verbal or not.

Then, what is the origin of the internal form of a person? Is it possible to present it in a more concrete way? My hypothesis is that in the course of lively, active, or contemplative penetration into inner forms of the word, symbol, another person, a work of art, or nature, including one's own nature, a person is building his or her internal form and expanding the internal space of his or her soul. Without such work, a person turns out to be *hollow*. But this is already a beginning of a different story.

10 The Development of Children's
Conceptual Relation to the World,
with a Focus on Concept Formation
in Preschool Children's Activity

Two of Vygotsky's (1997) central theoretical points are that cultural–historically developed tools mediate the child's relation to the world and that the competence to handle such tools is acquired in social settings through guidance from others. His theory of concept formation for preschoolers, schoolchildren, and adolescents explains how the practice of institutional activities influences children's concept formation (Vygotsky, 1987, 1998a). Small children participate in the everyday activities at home; schoolchildren meet the academic world in school, which he points out as a necessity for schoolchildren's development of scientific concepts; and adolescents get acquainted with the activities in work life, a necessity for their development of dialectical concepts.

Vygotsky describes how very young children appropriate concepts of tools and objects through interaction with their caregivers and, as an example, he exemplifies this with how a child learns to use a spoon in interaction with his caregivers (Kravtsov & Berezlizhkaya, 1999). In his theory, Vygotsky characterizes small children's and preschool children's concepts as everyday concepts developed spontaneously in collaboration with others through everyday activities. He contrasts these concepts to schoolchildren's concepts, which he characterizes as scientifically developed through systematic school instruction.

Although Vygotsky describes the concept learning of preschool children as inscribed in the social practice of everyday activities, what he primarily draws on when describing preschool children's concept formation is an experiment with the double-stimulation method (Vygotsky, 1987 p. 130ff). In this experiment, children's task is to sort blocks that vary in form, size, and color, gradually finding the sorting principle because a meaningless label is attached to the bottom of each block that is turned over each time the child has chosen one. The two types of stimuli in the double stimulation method are designed to be as far as possible from everyday practice. Vygotsky characterizes four steps in the small child's concept formation based on the results of this experiment.

As Davydov (1998) notes, Vygotsky's experiment has led to the misunderstanding that the child's appropriation of everyday concepts is a natural process and not a cultural process. This is easy to understand because this experiment dominates the description in one of Vygotsky's first translated and perhaps best-known works, *Thought and Language* (1962).[1] Instead, as Davydov points out, Vygotsky's theory about concept formation and the formation of individual consciousness has to be understood within the following process: "collective activity-culture-the ideal-sign or symbol-individual consciousness" (Davydov, 1998, pp. 92–93).[2]

Systematic analysis of small children's and preschool children's concept development within everyday activities at home and in the community is an area that must be developed in relation to Vygotsky's theory. Vygotsky was aware of this and suggests that the domain of preschool children's concept formation must be one of the areas for future research:

> We know that the relationship between instruction and development differs with each developmental stage – we will merely assert that future researchers must remember that the unique character of the child's spontaneous concept is entirely dependent on the relationship between instruction and development in preschool age, we will refer to this as a transitional spontaneous-reactive form of instruction since it constitutes a bridge between the spontaneous instruction characteristic of early childhood and the reactive instruction common to the school age.
>
> (Vygotsky, 1987, p. 238)

In this article, I will build on Vygotsky's ideas of how collective activity is the foundation for children's concept formation – and explore what these ideas about the interconnection between the child's conceptual development in different developmental periods, in different institutional practice traditions, and in knowledge traditions mean for small children's and preschool children's concept formation.

VYGOTSKY'S THEORY ABOUT PRESCHOOL AND
SCHOOLCHILDREN'S CONCEPT FORMATION

Vygotsky's characterization of the development of small children's and preschool children's concept formation from the results of the double-stimulation experiment can lead to the misunderstanding that the visual

---

[1] This title was later translated as *Thinking and Speech* (1987).
[2] See also, Davydov, 1993, pp. 14–15.

world is the foundation of the child's everyday concepts and that concepts reflect the objective characteristics of the world,[3] an interpretation of concepts that Iljenkov points out is problematic (Iljenkov, 1977, p. 83). Rather, concepts should be understood as the idealized activity that is expressed in all objects as results of human activity (Iljenkov, 1977, p. 92). This implies that by perceiving, handling, or acting in relation to objects, a person relates to the way previous generations have perceived, handled, and acted with these objects.

Vygotsky saw everyday concepts as connected to a child's activity in everyday settings and the scientific concepts as connected to a child's activity in settings with systematic symbolic systems that the child becomes acquainted with in school. The difference between everyday and scientific concepts can be found in the spontaneousness or, respectively, consciousness of the child's conceptual competence.

According to Vygotsky, the difference between these two conceptual modes[4] lies both in the difference in structure and content and in the processes by which they are acquired. For the child, everyday concepts are connected to family and community life and are appropriated through the child's experience with objects outside an integrated system of knowledge. The scientific concepts are about academic matters and are appropriated in relation to other concepts within a system of knowledge. The appropriation of concepts within a system of knowledge gives the child a possibility to use them consciously and intentionally. The various subjects in school are the systems within which the child can come to act consciously and intentionally with concepts. Vygotsky shows that there is both a difference in the learning process and in the developmental process during the child's appropriation of the two conceptual modes.

Learning

For the preschool child, the learning of everyday concepts is spontaneous and takes the form of imitation in a broad sense which means imitating what a more competent person demonstrates in social situations. In school-age children, the learning activity is based on conscious

---

[3] Vygotsky theory of concept formation is only outlined in *Thinking and Speech* (*The Collected Works of L. S. Vygotsky. Volume 1*, 1987). The theory is developed further in his writings about child development (*The Collected Works of L. S. Vygotsky. Volume 6*, 1997).

[4] I use conceptual modes instead of type, because the spontaneous and scientific concepts can be seen as a differentiation of a person's appropriation of concepts within a conceptual domain.

voluntary orientation to instruction based on linguistic communication within the different subjects in school. Vygotsky writes:

> *The strength of the scientific concepts lies in the higher characteristics of concepts, in the consciousness awareness and volition.* In contrast this is the weakness in the child's everyday concepts. The strength of everyday concepts lies in spontaneous, situationally meaningful concrete applications, that is, in the sphere of experience and the empirical. The development of scientific concepts begins in the domain of conscious awareness and volition. It grows downwards into the domain of the concrete, into the domain of personal experience. In contrast, the development of spontaneous concepts begins in the domain of the concrete and empirical. It moves toward the higher characteristics of concepts, toward conscious awareness and volition. The link between these two lines of development reflects their true nature. This is the link of the zone of proximal and actual development.   (Vygotsky, 1987, p. 220)

Development

From a developmental perspective of concept formation, Vygotsky has associated everyday concepts with home and community life and scientific concepts with school life. These two modes of concept formation are also intertwined according to Vygotsky. These two modes of concept formation are preconditions of each other. Scientific concepts build on everyday concepts, but they also qualify the person's everyday concepts. It is only when the scientific concepts become integrated with the child's everyday concepts that they become a competence in the child's life outside the classroom. These two modes of conceptual activity are tightly connected processes. In early childhood, everyday concept formation dominates over scientific concept formation, but changes around school age when the scientific concept formation dominates and thereby enriches the child's everyday concepts.

The difference in age, that is, from preschool to school age, is a difference in how the psychological functions relate to each other. Vygotsky's main point is that a person's psychological functioning is a unitary process, so when a developmental change takes place in one function, such as the child's development of concepts, this will influence all the other functions and change the child's conscious relation to the world – perception, logical memory, intentional attention, abstract thinking, and scientific imagination (Vygotsky, 1987, pp. 189, 208).

Vygotsky uses the double-stimulation experiment to outline steps in the development of a structure of small children's and preschool children's everyday concepts. He outlines the following four structural steps:

syncretic concepts (which are organized by what factors and entities are together in a situation); complexes (which are organized by similarities that are not consistent, but may vary from object to object, or connect different objects to a core object based on associations only of the similarity between one object and the core object); preconcepts (which are organized by abstracted similarities between all objects); and with real concepts that are logically defined (organized by abstract similarities and differentiated into a categorical system). Vygotsky describes it this way:

> *Each structure of generalization (i.e., syncretic, complexes, preconcepts, and concepts) corresponds with a specific system of generality and specific types of relationship of generality between general and specific concepts.* Each structure of generalization has a characteristic degree of unity, a characteristic degree of abstractness or concreteness, and characteristic thought operations associated with a given level of development of word meaning.
>
> An example may help clarify this point. In our experiments, a child who rarely spoke learned the meanings of five words (i.e., chair, table, cabinet, couch, bookcase) with no particular difficulty. He clearly would have been able to extend the series. However he could not learn the world "furniture". Though the child could easily learn any word from the series of subordinate concepts, this more general word was impossible for him. Learning the word "furniture" represented something more then the addition of a sixth word to the five that the child had already mastered. It represented the mastery of the relationship of generality. The mastery of the world "furniture" represented the mastery of the child's first higher concept, a concept that would include a series of more specific subordinate concepts. This meant that the child would have to master a new type of relationship between concepts, a vertical rather than a horizontal relationship.   (Vygotsky, 1987, p. 225)

This example shows the difference between logical concepts and the three other structural forms, but it also shows how Vygotsky saw the ideal conceptual system that the child will acquire at school age to be dominated by the empirical knowledge form. Other forms of knowledge used as foundations for children's concept formation have been formulated by Davydov (1972/1990, 1988) and Bruner (1986) as theoretical–dialectical and narrative, respectively.[5]

In order to explain why preschool children's everyday concept formation is not a "natural" process and why "everyday concept formation" can led to different conceptual competencies depending of the type of

---

[5] Vygotsky's research (Vygotsky, 1998a) about concept formation in late school age and the youth period seems to build on aspects of the theoretical–dialectical knowledge traditions as specified by Davydov (1972/1990).

knowledge form that characterizes the everyday practice in the institution where the child is learning, I must sketch Davydov and Bruner's characterization of different knowledge forms.

ARTIFACTS, TYPES OF KNOWLEDGE, AND SOCIAL PRACTICE

The philosophical work of Evald Iljenkov, Marx Wartofsky, and Uffe Juul Jensen has made it possible to formulate quite clearly that knowledge about practice and traditions is not only personal but transcends the single person and becomes ideals in the form of collective societal knowledge. Iljenkov (1977, p. 92) formulates this principle of collective concepts: "The ideal form of a thing is not the form of the thing 'in itself,' but a form of social human life activity regarded as 'the form of a thing.'"

A concept in this sense always combines the idealized practice with the humanly constructed objects. This kind of knowledge is developed through the societal practice of solving pressing institutional and societal problems (Jensen, 1986), whereby both knowledge as "tools" and procedures are developed. When knowledge procedures transcend the specific institutional practice and become generalized and used in other types of institutions as is the case for empirical, narrative, and theoretical knowledge, I have called this *societal knowledge* (Hedegaard, 2002)[6] Davydov's distinction between empirical and theoretical knowledge forms can then be seen as different forms of societal knowledge. Bruner's differentiation between narrative and empirical knowledge can also be characterized as societal forms of knowledge, where Bruner and Davydov's description of empirical knowledge refers to the same form of knowledge.

Empirical knowledge is reflected in abstract concepts that are attained through observation, description, classification, and quantification (Bruner, Goodnow, & Austin, 1956; Davydov, 1972/1990, 1988). This form of knowledge presupposes that the world can be represented correctly, and correct representation gives the possibility for accurate measurement, creating factual knowledge. Empirical knowledge presupposes the use of categories for its representation. Similarities and differences are recognized, which is the foundation for the construction of categories. Categories can be organized hierarchically into super- and subcategories, and hierarchical systems and networks can be created.

---

[6] Practice, form, and content cannot be completely separated. My aim here is to illustrate how generalization of practice and content in a certain way are connected to form, and what I do in this chapter is to focus on the aspect of form.

Paradigms of classical logic are the methods for combining knowledge categories.

Empirical knowledge (or factual knowledge) influences a great deal of everyday life for people in Western industrialized societies and characterizes the educational activity of most schools today (Cole, in Davydov & Markova, 1993).

Narrative knowledge may be characterized by (a) changeableness in intentions, (b) possible mutual perspectives and goals which interact, and (c) involvement of feelings and emotions (Bruner, 1986, pp. 16–25). This kind of knowledge is created by transcending the situated descriptions and relating them to general themes of human life. Bruner describes the method as *presupposition*, the creation of implicit rather than explicit meaning; *subjectification*, the depiction of reality through a personal view; and *multiple perspectives*, beholding the world not universally but simultaneously through different views that each express some part of (Bruner, 1986, pp. 25–26). Examples of narrative knowledge are epic descriptions, novels, comedy, drama, and poetry. Narrative knowledge and thinking forms can also be seen in "folk theories" about daily life events.

Narrative knowledge characterizes the communication in a child's daily life at home and among peers. Educational theories that prefer dialogue as the primary pedagogic form can be seen as promoting narrative knowledge and dialogical thinking.

Theoretical – dialectical knowledge is related two forms of knowledge in systems where one type of knowledge is complementary to the other so that if a change takes place it will be reflected in all the central relations of the system. This kind of knowledge can be found in theories and models that can be used to understand events and situations and to organize and experiment with actions (concrete life activities). This type of knowledge can also be found in all professional work (e.g., engineering, city planning, professional cooking or nursing, steering a ship, dress designing), where persons have a theory and models for their work.

A core model is a central method of modeling within the theoretical knowledge tradition. Core models contain oppositions and complementary poles within a subject-matter area. Davydov names these form of models *germ-cells* (Davydov, 1972/1990; Davydov et al., 1982). For example, in biology a germ-cell is the relationship between *organism* and *context*. This relationship can easily be recognized in all specific biological matters. Such a core relation can be extended by a new relationship, which influences and changes the meaning of the initial concepts (see Hedegaard, 1990). In psychology, the relationship between subject and object can be seen as a germ-cell, where the various parts in this relationship define each other. In Vygotsky's theory this relationship is extended and mediated by the concept of tool, so that the "object" always has to be understood within its relation to tools and artifacts; the same is true for the "subject," who, through this relation, becomes not only active, but active within the human mode of relating to the world (Vygotsky, 1997, ch. 5).

A child is born into a world of artifacts that includes different forms of knowledge. The upbringing of a child should lead the child to appropriate competences with these artifacts that can satisfy both the child's own needs and the societal expectations of how a child should contribute to societal life at various ages. Different knowledge systems and forms of knowledge can be seen as collective conceptual knowledge. This must be differentiated from a person's conceptual knowledge. Therefore, I will now use *knowledge* to discuss collective conceptual knowledge and *concepts* to discuss personal conceptual competence. Collective knowledge and personal concepts meet and develop through a person's activity in institutional practice.

Figure 10.1 illustrates the relationships between collective (societal) knowledge (including various types), institutional practice (everyday, academic, and work practice), and personal conceptual competences. The various institutions depicted in Figure 10.1 illustrate that children can appropriate conceptual competences that are related to different practices and different knowledge systems. However, it is not the case that the knowledge systems are narrative at home, empirical in school, and theoretical at work. Institutional practice leads to increased knowledge, but this can find expression in all three forms of knowledge depending of the traditions for representing knowledge in a given institution.

Vygotsky's and Davydov's theories of concept formation are two different perspectives on concept formation in practice – a societal one and a personal one. Participation in an institutional practice leads to a child's appropriation of societal knowledge, thereby acquiring conceptual competence within specific content areas and motives that orient the child in specific ways toward these areas.

How the same type of institutional activity can be qualitatively different and result in children's appropriation of different forms of concepts even for small children and preschool children will be the next topic in this chapter.

INSTITUTIONAL PRACTICE AS THE FOUNDATION
FOR DEVELOPMENT OF PERSONAL KNOWLEDGE

Children first meet concepts in family and community practice, and, through participation in this practice, they appropriate societal or collective knowledge. This collective knowledge is transformed into personal

	Societal Perspective		Personal Perspective
Cultural Practice Traditions	**Developmental Changes**	**Competence**	**Leading Motives**
Maternity ward/ home	Crises of the newborn/infancy	Starting acquiring competence with primary artifacts Experimentation with perception	Intentional orientation toward the caregiver (attachment)
Home	Crises at age 1/ early childhood	Action representation (enactive) Competence with own body (walking) Experimentation with objects	Intentional orientation to the object and spatial world (object play)
Kindergarten	Crises at age 3/ preschool age	Imaginary representation (iconic) Beginning competence with secondary artifact Experimentation with words, objects and rules in play	Orientation toward other children and to the adult world (role play)
Primary school	Crises at age 7/ school age	Symbolic representation Beginning competence with connected system of knowledge – tertiary artifacts Experimentation with imaginations and symbols within systems	Orientation toward mastering the adult world and to academic learning
Secondary school	Crises at age 13/ age of puberty	Competence with tertiary artifact Experimentation with representational systems	Orientation to youth life and friends
Higher education/ work	Crises at age 17/ adolescence	Work profession	Societal orientation

FIGURE 10.1. Developmental stages from a societal and a personal perspective.

conceptual competencies through the child's activity. These personal competencies continue to develop as the child is introduced to new practices in school, at home, and in the community. How children's personal conceptual competencies from home and community life will be related to academic knowledge and work knowledge depends on how the situational conditions encourage him or her to develop motives for using conceptual competencies in these new situations.

I will draw on Katherine Nelson's (1974, 1977a, 1977b) research of small children's concept formation, especially her analyses of the interchange between the small child and caregivers to illustrate how this activity can lead to children's appropriation of conceptual competencies. In order to be able to take one step further than Nelson, who presupposes the child's perceptual competence in her theorizing about small children's concept formation, I will draw on Wartofsky's (1973/1979) philosophical analyses of the perception of objects as an activity that is mediated by artifacts, where these artifacts are seen as objectifications of human needs and intentions.[7] Wartofsky's formulation of the embeddedness of human intentions and needs in objects is in line with Iljenkov's ideas about concepts as collective ideals, but Wartofsky takes an important step further because, in his formulations, he integrates the emotional and intentional aspects in the child's perception of objects. Wartofsky's theory has shed light on the child's concept learning as it is interwoven with the child's intentional orientation and motives from the very beginning of life.

Furthermore, in order to transcend the conception of young and preschool children as using only one ideal form of concepts, namely, the empirical one, I will use Vygotsky's theory of children's development in play. Vygotsky has stressed the importance of play for children's cognitive development. His description of children's acquisition of symbols and rules through play activity will be important. In small children's and preschool children's play one can see how their early forms of conceptual representation can reflect both narrative and dialectical theoretical knowledge forms.

In the last section, I will outline a developmental perspective that implies qualitative developmental changes in children's concept formation related to qualitative changes in institutional practice and the forms of knowledge that dominate an institution.

This theoretical analysis of preschool children's concept formation will be illustrated by a project analyzing preschool children's play with different types of play material aimed at promoting concept formation. This illustration focuses on both the support and the restrictions that educational play materials give to children's concept learning.

---

[7] Wartofsky writes, "I take these artefacts" (tools and language) to be the objectifications of human needs and intentions that is, as *already* invested with cognitive and affective content.

KATHERINE NELSON'S THEORY OF INFANTS' AND SMALL CHILDREN'S CONCEPT FORMATION

Katherine Nelson (1995) has criticized Vygotsky's characterization of everyday concept learning as being unsystematical in contrast to scientific concept learning. She argues that small children acquire knowledge within a system, a system she characterizes as an "event structure." In her opinion, the acquisition of knowledge within an event structure system and the child's recognition of these event structures are necessary for children in order to acquire categories and language (Nelson, 1995, p. 232).

Nelson's theory describes young children's concept formation as a process of acquiring knowledge through the child's action and interaction in specific types of situations (Nelson, 1974). Such a situation is exemplified by how a 12-month-old child develops the concept of "ball" (Nelson, 1977a, p. 215). There are three main phases depicted in this process. In the first phase, the child forms a representation of the situation (an event representation – a script[8]) from his or her experience of the situation. This "event representation" encompasses all aspects of a concrete situation. In the first phase, objects in the situation are not necessarily experienced as having permanence but are recognized through the situational relationships that are established through the child's actions. In the next phase, the child begins to recognize the relationships among the objects, simply because certain objects vary while others remain constant. Then, gradually, an identity is established for the objects focused on. In the third phase, new members of the concept can be identified because the prominent and invariant traits can be identified as attributes by themselves.

In the example of the mother and child's interaction with a ball, the ball becomes the center of the child's interaction, where the following actions in the script are abstracted: mother throws; baby catches, rolls, bounces; playroom. The specific actions and relationships are altered depending on the context of the interaction, the only constant object in the series of situations with the ball rolling is the ball itself, but the ball does not exist outside these relationships in the first phase. Therefore, in order to create the idea of "ballness" instead of "ball" as many different objects in different relationships, the child must synthesize over time the various relationships into which the ball enters. This functional

---

[8] Event representation and scripts can be seen as two substages within the first stage (Nelson, 1996, p. 16).

synthesis is the core of the concept. When a functional synthesis of a series of situations concerning a given object occurs, other objects may obtain a status within the same functional synthesis (e.g., ball number two). The third phase concerns the child's ability to recognize an object outside of its context. Nelson's point is that, in order to do this, the child must employ identifiable information. The child then analyzes the entire object into relevant attributes. This process begins as soon as the functional core is created.

Nelson's contribution in relation to Vygotsky's work is her empirical and theoretical demonstration that small children's concepts must be seen within a system of knowledge characterized as event structures. The importance of language is central in Nelson's theory to explain how the child goes from event representation to categorical systems. Nelson (1995, p. 232) notes that categories (defined as recognizing similarities among members) can be demonstrated in acting, but the abstract relation of asymmetrical inclusion (e.g., a table is a piece of furniture) can only be realized in a symbolic system such as natural language, and the child is not able to use language at this level until he or she is about 7 years old.[9] This distinction is similar to Vygotsky's distinction between pre-concepts and concepts, and Nelson also refers to Vygotsky's point that even though the adult and the preschool child use the same word, the underlying structure and understanding is different for each. Although Nelson criticizes Vygotsky's conception of everyday concept formation in preschool age as taking place outside a system, she recognizes one of Vygotsky's main points:

> Although Vygotsky's discussion conveys the impression that it is only scientific concepts that represent the "cultural", whereas spontaneous concepts are products of the individual unfettered by cultural knowledge, this impression is misleading. The child's initial conceptual knowledge system derives from experience in culturally arranged activities and scenes; thus there is no sudden discontinuity in human development from the natural to the sociocultural. Rather there are a series of accommodations of the individual's organization of experientially derived knowledge to conventional knowledge systems as learning in and through language progresses.   (Nelson, 1995, p. 240)

---

[9] This connection between the two theories' depiction of the age period for establishing "true" concepts demonstrates rather that school traditions are alike in the industrialized societies, as Scribner and Cole's (1981) research in Liberia showed, and that concept formation is a "natural" developmental process that is realized when the child is around 7 years old. See also Luria's research (1976) of how school traditions influence a person's use of general categories.

Nelson regards the child's experiential meeting with the world as central rather than the educational and cultural tradition of the caregiver. So even though she recognizes that social interaction and culture contribute to children's development of concepts, her theory does not solve the problem of the child's first encounter with the world as primarily a "natural" perceptual process because, in her theory, she does not recognize objects as social constructs. Nelson's theory of concept acquisition considers empirical knowledge forms to be the ideal forms (Nelson, 1995, figure 10.1, p. 238).

Forms of knowledge and social practice need a more central place in a theory of children's concept development than Nelson's theory gives room for. Turning to Wartofsky's theory of artifacts as a mediating link between the child and the world makes it possible to integrate social practice with various kinds of artifacts more central to an understanding of the conceptual development of children.

WARTOFSKY'S CONCEPTION OF ARTIFACT AS MEDIATING BETWEEN THE PERSON AND THE WORLD

Wartofsky argues that all human functions are related to the historical changes in the form and modes of human practice. Perception is the human function that he uses to demonstrates this view, and he argues for:

> an explicit realist view of perception in two senses: *first*, that the 'objects of perception' are taken to be independent of perception, though they are mediated by the activity of perception, in that they are perceived by *means of our representation of them*. – The meditative entities, – I take to be representations – i.e. perceptual artefacts which we *do not perceive*, but *by means of which* we perceive real objects (or processes). Second: by virtue of this, perception is not simply an inward activity, directed upon some 'mental' or 'perceptual' entities 'in the mind' or 'in the brain'; but is itself a (mediated) form of outward activity, which is continuous with other forms of outward human actions in the world. Therefore, in its very genesis, perception is directly linked to that practical interaction with an external world whose qualities and structures are transformed by human action, and thus, by perception as well; but which transformations are nevertheless transformation *of* an objective and independently existing environment.   (Wartofsky, 1973, pp. 193–194)

In Wartofsky's theory, perception is a relation between the person and the world, mediated by culturally produced artifacts that are created historically through human practice. This description of practice is the same one finds within the cultural–historical traditions for activity (Leontiev, 1978). Wartofsky defines practice in the following way:

> What is this "historical human praxis" which is proposed here as the genesis of human perception? It is, in the first place, the fundamental activity of producing and reproducing the conditions of species existence, or survival. What is distinctly *human* about this activity (since *all* species fall under this injunction of reproducing the species life) is that human beings do this by means of the creation of artefacts. – In more generic terms, the 'tool' may be *any* artefact created for the purpose of successful production and reproduction of the means of existence. – The crucial character of the human artefact is that its production, its use, and the attainment of skill in these, can be transmitted, and thus preserved within a social group, and through time, from one generation to the next. The symbolic communication of such skills in the production, reproduction and use of artefacts – i.e. the teaching or transmission of such skills is the context in which *mimicry or the imitation of an action becomes a characteristic human mode of activity.*   (Wartofsky, 1973, pp. 200–201)

What is very important in this connection is Wartofsky's characterization of the artifacts (tool and language) as the objectification of human needs and intentions.[10] He stresses that the cognitive and affective content are interwoven. The "objects" are what motivates the activity, a point that is important to stress because the intentional aspect has been neglected or directly denied in research about concept formation (see (Stenild, 1978).[11]

Wartofsky distinguishes between primary, secondary, and tertiary artifacts:

> *Primary* artefacts are those that are used in the direct production; *secondary* artefacts are those used in the preservation and transmission of the acquired skills or modes of action or praxis by which the production is carried out. Secondary artefacts are therefore *representations* of such modes of actions, and in this sense are *mimetic*, not simply of the *objects* of an environment – but of these objects as they are acted upon, or the mode of operation or action involving such objects.
>
> (Wartofsky, 1973, p. 202)

In this sense, mastering secondary artifacts can be understood as symbolic conceptual competence within institutional practice traditions. The *tertiary* form of artifacts is abstracted from their direct

---

[10] A point that is very close to Leontiev's characterization of activity as motivated by its objects (1978).

[11] Within the cognitive tradition, Pintrich and his colleagues (1993) distinction between warm and cold cognition is a first attempt to relate emotion/motive with cognition.

representational function, and Wartofsky suggests that artifacts "constitute a domain in which there is a free construction in the imagination of rules and operations different from those adopted for ordinary, this worldly praxis." Wartofsky goes on to say that imagination is a derivate of "embodied representations or better embodies alternative canons of representation: embodied *in* actual artefacts, which express or picture this alternative mode. Once the visual picture can be 'lived in', perceptually, it can also come to colour and change our perception of the 'actual' world, as envisioning possibilities in it not presently recognized" (Wartofsky, p. 209).

Tertiary concepts can be seen as a mastery of theoretical–dialectical knowledge that provides a possibility for formulation of core models and exploration through experimentation with these models in concrete situations.

Wartofsky gives us a clear idea about human psychic functions as developed through participation in human practice with artifacts. One could also get the impression that primary, secondary, and tertiary artifacts can only be encountered in a developmental sequence, where competence with primary artifacts is the foundation for the child's appropriation of secondary artifacts, and so forth. However, to understand Wartofsky's theory, it is important to remember that primary, secondary, and tertiary artifacts exist as collective artifacts and my hypothesis is that, dependent on the practice it participates in, the child may become acquainted with all three types of artifacts early on and that, in line with Vygotsky's idea of the interconnectedness of everyday and scientific concepts, competence with these three types of artifacts is interwoven. Therefore, a child's competence with secondary and tertiary artifacts can enrich his or her competence with primary artifacts. Play is one way that this can happen as I will try to argue from the perspective of Vygotsky's theory of play.

PLAY AS EXPERIMENTATION WITH RULES AND MODELS

Vygotsky points out that the features of human perception of real objects are not only colors and shapes, but also meaning. He expresses this in a ratio where the object is the numerator and the meaning is the denominator (object/meaning). This ratio symbolizes the idea that all human perception is made up of generalized rather than isolated instances of perception. The object dominates the meaning, but what Vygotsky points out is that in a child's play *this ratio can be inverted* and the meaning can dominate the object, for example, when a stick can be a horse or a gun. In play, the child can operate with meanings detached from their usual objects and actions. For the small child, there is some constraint on what can function as the meaning of an object. Vygotsky characterizes this reversal of the ratio between object and meaning as an intermediate stage between early childhood and the adult's competence with meaning. For the adult, meaning can come to dominate thoughts totally free of real situations. Vygotsky says that:

> A divergence between the field of meaning and vision first occurs at preschool age. In play thought is separated from objects, and action arises from the ideas rather than from things: a piece of wood begins to be a doll and a stick becomes a horse. Action according to rules begins to be determined by ideas and not by objects themselves. This is such a reversal of the child's relation to the real immediate, concrete situation that it is hard to underestimate its full significance. (Vygotsky, 1978, p. 97)

In the same way as the object-meaning ratio, Vygotsky notes that the action-meaning ratio can be reversed in play. Vygotsky points out that, when action becomes separated from meaning in play, the rules become very explicit in play. "Thus the essential attribute of play is a rule that has become a desire. Spinoza's notion of 'an idea which has become a desire, a concept which has turned into a passion' finds its prototype in play, which is the realm of spontaneity and freedom" (Vygotsky, 1978, p. 99). The children can play the persons that do activities that they want to do or change, for example, bus driver or doctor. In addition, play enriches the child's everyday activity through developing the child's concepts and motives.

Combining Wartofsky's ideas of tertiary artifacts with Vygotsky's theory play can be seen as a step toward mastering tertiary artifacts, that is, where children can experiment with the meaning in an imagined world such as role-play. For preschool children, experimentation with objects and rules that attain "new meanings," can become aspects of play within an imagined world. This can be found when children develop the same game over time and extend and change the rules of the game. Today, this can also be found in commercial games, such as *Dungeons and Dragons* and in computer games. So the three forms of representation (primary, secondary, and tertiary) find their first form in children's play activity.

APPROPRIATION OF CONCEPTS AS CONCEPTUAL
COMPETENCE THROUGH VARIOUS TYPES OF SOCIAL
PRACTICE – A DEVELOPMENTAL PERSPECTIVE

Human practice is the key to understanding how societal collective knowledge is acquired as personal concepts. Furthermore, it is important to be aware that there is a range of institutions in society with different traditions for artifacts and practice. In Figure 10.1, I have distinguished between three institutions, namely, home, school, and work, but one could easily mention several others that influence childhood: day care, afterschool, commercial institutions, health systems, church, and several other more-specific institutions. In Western society, the central institutions for small children, preschool children, and schoolchildren are home, day care, and school.[12] A child's psychic functions are culturally created from the very first moments that he or she participates in these collective institutions. Wartofsky argues that a child's needs from the first satisfaction become cultural through the objects that satisfy them. Objects, procedures, and meanings are produced in cultural institutions. From a child's first encounter with the world, his or her biological needs are transformed into cultural needs. Therefore, the development of the child's perception and intention becomes attached to or anchored in the artifacts and knowledge systems and forms that exist and dominate in the institutions that the child becomes part of (at birth this is usually the maternity ward and the home).

A child's interaction with others is dependent on the types of artifacts (including knowledge forms) that dominate the practice of the institutions where the child lives his or her everyday life. Concepts can be viewed as action capacities with artifacts in these practice situations. Content and capacity with everyday concepts are closely interwoven in the conceptual competence of a child. The capacity aspect of a child's everyday concepts is shown in the child's readiness to use his conceptual competence in relevant settings. The content aspect is the meaning of situations and objects that a child can act on. Concepts regarded as competences to act in different situations can never be regarded as static, for each time they are used they are extended because social situations are never quite the same. Concepts must be understood in this functional connection. Therefore, the aspect of intention is of crucial importance. It is through the intentional participation in activities where communication and action are tightly interwoven that conceptual competences are acquired and manifested.

A child's relation to the world changes through developmental periods when he or she meets new artifacts and appropriates new competences and he or she thereby gets new possibilities of relating differently to the world.

Both Vygotsky (1998b) and Elkonin (1999) describe six stages in children's development. Elkonin specifies how these stages are related to

---

[12] In other types of society, work is as dominant as school for some children at 7 or 8 years old, or school is not included among the institutional practice because children function as cheap labor, and there is no time for school (see Hundeide, 2005), or that children can be valued contributors in home activities (Rogoff, 2003).

different societal practice and interconnected into developmental-age periods reflecting the dominating practice in Western industrialized society. In Elkonin's model there are three periods, each characterized by two stages. In each new developmental period, first the child's orientation, motive, and intentions develop, then the competence develops. When the child goes from one period to the next, the change takes place first through crises in the child's emotional relationship to the world by the child developing a new orientation to the world and to new motives. The educational practice that supports the child's building an orientation toward new aspects of the world and new motives is as important as the promotion of the child's appropriation of competence. One cannot be realized without the other. In Figure 10.2, I have summarized this relationship by using the two perspectives of Figure 10.1 (societal and personal) to combine Vygotsky's and Elkonin's theory of developmental stages with Davydov's theory of knowledge forms and Wartofsky's representational theory. In the diagram, I also include Bruner's (Bruner et al., 1966) distinction between enactive, iconic, and symbolic forms of representations. In Bruner's theory, the child's first competencies are connected to his or her manual and perceptual activities, which form the basis of enactive and iconic representation. Bruner argues that these forms of representation are the foundation for but are also changed by the child's development of symbolic representation when he or she enters school. This characteristic of the development of representation fits in with Vygotsky's (1978) writings about the change from perceptual orientation to imagination and, later, the child's ability to act on a symbolic level.

In the following section, I will discuss how educational "tools" can influence preschool children's appropriation of conceptual competence and motives in an educational setting. For most preschool children in Denmark and other Western countries, the educational setting is home and kindergarten. The instruction in these settings is usually adapted to how the everyday activities are structured to allow for a child's need for food, rest, and play activities. What the child learns in these everyday practices depends on the objects (artifacts) that the adults make available. Through objects and activities caregivers initiate a child's appropriation of knowledge.

In connection with Figure 10.1, I have postulated that there is not a one-to-one relation between knowledge form and institutional practice. Therefore, the question in the last part of this article is, Can everyday settings in which preschool children take part contain several forms of knowledge, and can theoretical knowledge in the form of experimentation within an imagined world be part of the everyday practices in which preschool children take part?

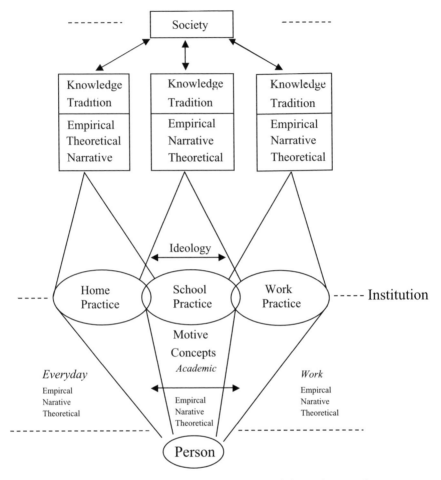

FIGURE 10.2. The model of how societal knowledge and personal concepts are created through a person's activity in institutional practice.

INSTRUCTIONAL PLAY MATERIAL
FOR PRESCHOOL CHILDREN

Preschool children appropriate competence by participating in shared activities with various cultural artifacts that the adults bring into the social situation.[13] In educational situations adults create situations in which children learn to use these artifacts. By mediating their

---

[13] In their play, children also create artifacts that they bring into the social situation and share with each other. That mainly happens independently of adults (Corsaro, 1997), but in this chapter, this does not influence the argument I am building up.

interaction with small children with cultural artifacts and by giving the child objects, adults demonstrate for children that these objects should be attended to.

In most educational material for preschool children, a child is required to participate by manual acting. When playing with puzzles, self-controlling materials, and group games the children are asked to participate by acting manually with symbolic representations, but at the same time, they also get tasks that require their reflection before acting. An important aspect of these materials is that the tasks that they set require the child's actions to be based on his or her reflection, either through visual exploration or through communication.

In the following, I will draw on my own project of studying preschool children's concept formation through play with pedagogical play material that aims at promoting children's concept learning (Hedegaard, 1984).[14] I will focus on games produced for preschool children and present three types of material that illustrate the form of concepts that are promoted by these materials.

THE PLAY GROUP PROJECT

The aim of this project was to study how educational play material with symbolic content and traditions influenced preschool children's social interaction and their appropriation of conceptual competences. In addition, the aim was to find out what kind of negative consequences some types of material could have for both children's social interaction and the type of conceptual competence children appropriated. The play group was created as an institution at the Department of Psychology at Aarhus University with children ranging from 3 to 5 years in age. The group met for three hours each week with ten to twelve children participating. This institution existed for three years with the participation over the years of twenty-four children. All children participated for at least six months, most of them for two years, and some for all three years (they were taken out when they started in first grade in school). Thirteen students participated in the project, each time with two or three present in a session together with a kindergarten teacher (she was the same throughout the whole period) and the researcher. The sequence of the activities was as follows: the children arrived and were given time to find play things and

---

[14] The usefullness of this project to argue about preschool children's encounter with knowledge systems in play material and games is not affected by the twenty years that have passed, because the principle(s) in the games can still be evaluated, and, furthermore, if one looks at play material today, many of the same types with the same content are present in kindergarten.

contact the other children and student helpers. After twenty minutes, the kindergarten teacher called everybody to sit at a big table to talk about a specific topic while she illustrated the topic with different objects for another twenty minutes. This topic was most often connected to the research activity that would follow. Then the children again had time to play with each other and with the playthings that were in the playroom,[15] while the researcher and students put out the games that they would use later. Many times some of the children came to see what was prepared and wanted to play immediately. The play with games was arranged in groups; one group was the research group (here the participant observer was placed). We took care to equalize the children's participation in the research group over time. After the games, it was snack time. After snack time the children could draw or play or the whole group went outside to play. At the end of each session, the kindergarten teacher assembled all children and read a storybook until the last parent had arrived to take his or her child home.

The educational play material was collected by contacting about fifty Danish firms producing play material for kindergartens, getting free samples, or buying material, which resulted in a representative sample aimed at Danish kindergartens of about 100 educational materials. The types of material that were examined were puzzles, games such as domino and picture lotto with conceptual content, self-controlling concept material, books with concept formation tasks for preschool children, language training materials, and materials for training children's logical reasoning.[16]

The research method can be described as experimentation with play material and making protocols through participant observation, where two researchers always worked together; the one playing with the children, the other observing. One hundred to 120 protocols were collected, the exact number depending on whether nonstructured role-play observations were included or only observations of play with educational materials, for example, games and books.

The protocols were analyzed in relation to (1) the content of the material, the competence the children demonstrated, and problems they had in the play/game activities; and (2) the children's intentions and social interaction. From this, we drew conclusions about the children's concept learning.

In the following, I have chosen two individual games and two group games: a puzzle, a picture-matching material, and two different kinds of

[15] This room was a permanent institution with tables, chairs, decoration, and play material for preschool children.

[16] None of these materials implied the child's ability to read.

lotto picture. Even though the puzzle and the picture-matching material can be seen as material for a single child, in the playgroup, we encouraged children to participate and help each other with these games.

The difference between the two lotto picture games presented demonstrates the diversity in a fairly popular game with regard to knowledge type and content as well as how differently the material contributed to the children's involvement and competence.

Content and Possibilities for Development of Competence

Many different themes can be presented in the picture of a puzzle; they can vary from fairy tales and figures from comic strips to realistic drawings or photos or geometric figures. The conceptual competence a child can acquire depends both of the content and how the puzzle is cut in relation to the thematic content. A cutting that underlines meaning and objects as wholes can direct the child toward analyzing the relation between the parts and the whole and offers the possibility for a conversation between an adult and the child about how the pieces are related.

Observation extracted from a puzzle game

Puzzle: A green grocery with cuttings that make the object the pieces

Participants: Søren: 3.9 year, Adult (A)

Søren takes out the pieces, one at a time.

Then A starts the game by asking: What is this?

Søren looks at the piece A is holding in her hand, but does not answer.

A: Do you think you can find where it belongs?

Søren: "Yes!" He smiles and starts to place the pieces

A: What is it you have put on the board?

Søren: Beers.

A points to another piece: What is this?

Søren: Bananas.

A: Do you eat bananas at home?

Søren: Yes me, my dad, and Kalle (his brother)

Søren finds another piece and A asks what it is.

Søren: Husband and wife.

A: What are they doing?

Søren: They have a basket to pick cherries in.

A remarks about a piece with a pair of scales: "I do not think you ever have seen such a thing, this is a pair of scales."

Søren: I have seen one where we buy beers and bananas.

This puzzle offers the possibility to talk about the things in a grocery store. In general, Søren does not talk very much because he is shy, but he seems interested in solving the puzzle and talking with the adult about the objects and his experience from a grocery. This type of puzzle gives him the possibility to develop narrative forms of concepts with activities and objects in a grocery store.

The content in *picture-matching material* depends on establishing a correct relation between ranges of objects. This material can be found in books or in games with boards and cards. These kinds of materials are relevant for recognizing numbers and letters and quantity matching. But when the matching material aims at a part–whole or cause–effect relation, and there is not a general theme that connects the various tasks, the child's activity has to build on his or her knowledge of these relations, and the material rarely contributes very much to extend this knowledge. With several of these materials, the children had problems because they did not know the relations beforehand, so that connections were found by trial and error without the child's understanding of the relation, as in the following example.

Observation extracted from a self-controlling matching material: matching parts with objects

Participants: Jens 4.10, Adult
Jens takes the picture of the bishop and places it on the bishops hat
Adult: What is that? (Point to the bishop's hat)
Jens: A kind of iron (seems unsure)
Adult: No, I think it is a hat. Did you only guess?
Jens does not answer but takes another picture and says: This is a paint brush
Adult: I think it is the tail of a donkey

By matching and sorting materials, the children can orient themselves toward looking for differences or likenesses or part–whole relations, but they do not get much new knowledge about the world because the knowledge is split up, atomized, and often spread in as many parts as there are tasks in each game or book. With the best tasks, a general principle guided the child's activity, that is, to sort different objects into two categories, for example, hard and soft objects, dead and living objects, objects from a bakery or a butcher, whereby the children could become acquainted with categories. Unfortunately, in most cases, the objects were drawn only in outline in order to favor the abstract variation within a category at the expense of concrete and realistic pictures of the objects. These abstractions created problems because, when the children found it difficult to see what the drawings were about, they also found it difficult to relate a category to the relevant objects.

The matching and sorting material (books, self-controlling materials), as well as several of the group games, were based on the empirical form of knowledge. These materials and the connected tasks gave associations to tasks in intelligence tests, where the material is made general and culture-independent. In the intelligence tests, it is also the general simplified drawings of objects, people, and events that dominate.

In the *group game lotto picture*, we found one case of a lotto game where the board had a general theme that could guide the children's placement of the cards and where the task could enable children to acquire narrative and theoretical concepts. In this game, the pieces with pictures of objects were to be placed on a board that depicted a general concept, so that the pieces could be seen as depicting aspects of the concept without a one to one relation (see Figure 10.3). One showed various professional activities (firemen, fisherman, dentist, farmer, doctor etc. – ten boards in total). The children who participated in this game were able to understand the general theme and could talk about the relations so that real communication took place between the participants.

The relationship between part and whole in this lotto was very meaningful for the children, and they could relate the specific aspects on the cards of this job activity to the board, and, at the same time, they liked to talk about what they saw.

The knowledge depicted in the lotto-picture game with work situations gave the children the possibility to encounter both narrative and theoretical knowledge, depending on how the material was introduced to the children. In this specific case, it was primarily the narrative knowledge form that came into the foreground. If the children had been expected to play and experiment with the relationships between the conceptual aspects, they would have been given other instructions for play and other conditions than a single play setting allows.

Social Interaction and Involvement

It is easy to see that the involvement varies with the materials used. When doing *puzzles* and solving tasks in *books*, training conceptual competence with an adult by their side, the children do not express wishes to leave the situation. The children enjoyed being together with an adult doing these activities.

They also want to play *domino and lotto games*, especially when an adult participates. The most popular games are the ones they know well. However, in several of the new educational games, they express

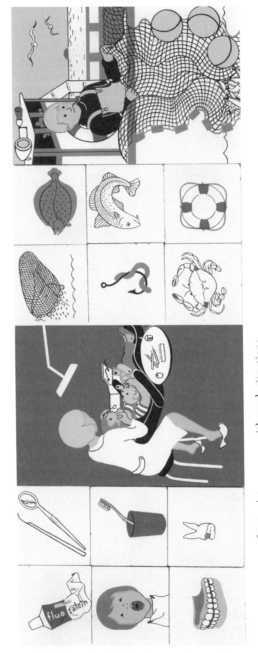

FIGURE 10.3. Lotto picture game with work situations.

their wish to leave the game if the task seems meaningless to them, for example, if they cannot see what the picture depicts or understand the relation that they are supposed to find. This is the case with *quantity-dominos* and *perspective-dominos*. Also, when the children can see that they are not winning in these educational games, they express a wish to leave the game.

Perspective Domino:

Participants: Svend 5.1, Jens: 5.3, Barbara: 5.0, Robert: 5.1, Sofie, 5.5, Adult

In this game the same object is depicted from different angles, and the children have to place their cards so the same objects touch each other.

Svend stands up when each player has one brick left and says: I know I am not going to win, and leaves

[Competition dominates over the coziness of being together and the interest in the activity. The competition can also take the form of an argument between the children as seen in the same game immediately after Svend has left]

Adult: So here is a new object (a TV from the side)
Robert: A record-player
Barbara: A television
Robert: A record-player
Barbara: A television
Robert: No, a record-player
Barbara: No, a television

This exchange between the two proceeds more and more intensely. None of the other children or the adult interrupts, and at last Roberts says in a rather calm and self-assured manner: This is a record-player.

Robert has finished his cards, and without saying anything he lets himself slide down from the chair to the floor, where he tumbles around with another chair.

Sofie is now eager to finish. She is turning on the chair and says "I will be happy when we are finished."

Barbara repeats what Sofie has just said.

Sofie puts down her last card. Stands up demonstratively and says "Now I do not care to participate any more."

In this game, the children have been very competitive though the adult has tried to keep this aspect down and the focus on the content.

What we found in general by analyzing the observation of group-play is that the activity with this type of educational material occurs on the adult's conditions. This does not mean that the children are not interested in participating or that they do not choose to play with them spontaneously, but they always invite adults to participate. In these games, the adult and the children can participate together on an equal footing if the adult takes the game seriously. However, if the adult cheats to make it easier for the child, and the child finds out, he or she will be disappointed.

As pedagogues and researchers, we had hoped to find (1) that adults and children would find solutions together, (2) that the children would help each other, and (3) that the children were interested in the content. But often what we found was (A) that the adults decide what to do and (B) that the oldest children win the games. In order to support points (1) to (3), the tasks connected to the material must be more than mere matching and sorting, and they must challenge the children in a meaningful way so that they can inspire them to experiment with the material.

In general, we found that one cannot use culturally established games to teach children something that is hidden within the game. Instead, adults should play games with the purpose of being together with children on equal terms and teach them content more directly in other situations because the children have no trouble being interested in the content when presented as tasks in books.

DISCUSSION OF THE KNOWLEDGE PUT INTO EDUCATIONAL MATERIAL AND CHILDREN'S ACTIVITIES WITH SUCH MATERIAL

In the 1980s, as a result of the cognitive traditions in psychology and education, the importance of stimulating and challenging small children's and preschool children's cognitive development led to the production of educational material, which was aimed at giving children concepts that were relevant for their development. Many of the materials were inspired by the tasks in intelligence tests or oriented toward preparing children for school. Today, many of these materials are transformed into computer material, but they are still based on the same principles as the hard cover items. This is demonstrated, for example, by the research connected to the project "5th dimension" (Cole, 1996), but this research also demonstrates how it is possible to transcend these commercial materials with task cards and communication tasks with a "wizard." It is important to transcend the training aspects inherent in several of these items by constructing materials and tasks that offer children the possibility for orientation toward play and experimentation. In this manner, it may be possible to transcend the traditions in education of presenting children with educational material that primarily leads to their appropriation of empirical concepts.

THE IMPORTANCE OF PLAY FOR THE PRESCHOOL CHILD'S DEVELOPMENT AND CONCEPT FORMATION

The social situation in which a child's play takes place is created by the child, by the other participants, and with the artifacts in the situation. The pedagogue can use play to promote children's conceptual competence. She can invite the child to play with her and with certain materials and through this participation introduce new knowledge to the child both in form and content.

Shared participation in play is a way to do this in relation to preschool children. At the same time this is a desirable activity that has social, intellectual, and emotional importance for the child's development. In play, the child both learns from other children and tries out his or her newly acquired competencies. Through play, the adult can also contact and support the preschool child in his or her appropriation of conceptual competencies because play can be the leading activity for preschool children, and, therefore, it can contribute to children's development of imaginary/symbolic relations to the world. In principle, educational materials can support the child's development of competencies with all three forms of concept: the empirical, the narrative, and the theoretical, but in practice, in the playgroup project it was unfortunately the empirical – and at best the narrative – form of knowledge that the children became oriented toward.

If pedagogues and parents do not pay attention to playthings and educational play material, but rather let commercial interest determine the choice, the child may appropriate skills and competencies that are inappropriate in relation to the child's everyday life, and this can be detrimental to the child's development of a theoretical orientation to his or her surroundings. Many educational play materials (and actually most of those in the research project described here) are constructed to train the child's functions such as discrimination and categorization of objects and not to promote a theoretical orientation to the world. Theoretical concept material can orient the child toward the relation between aspects of the world and relate this to a whole in a way that encourages the child to play and experiment with conceptual relations. Instead, though, most of the materials we analyzed trained the children to pass intelligence tests but did not allow much creative experimentation or symbolic play activity. Play materials ought not to be formalized function training materials where visual discrimination, remembering, and manipulations that dominate without a content or task that is meaningful for the child. Rather, educational material ought to be a help for children to explore and get competencies in relation to what happens in various social situations in their everyday life, and educational material should motivate them to enter new social situations and give them conceptual tools to explore these.

CONCLUSION

In the first part of this chapter, a distinction between societal knowledge and personal concepts was introduced. Societal knowledge, I argued, must be understood in relation to how it has developed through various forms of practice as both thematic and structural forms of knowledge. The thematic aspect, I argued, is connected to the objective of practice in institutions; the structural aspect is related to methodological considerations within various research traditions. Three forms of knowledge – the empirical, the narrative, and the theoretical–dialectical – were described. The empirical knowledge form dominates in school, but narrative and theoretical knowledge is also found within school education. The questions then were, Can preschool children encounter theoretical knowledge in their everyday activities? Can preschool children appropriate theoretical knowledge so that their everyday concepts may reflect the methodological aspects of this form of knowledge?

Based on a research project with educational play material for preschool children, I have argued that preschool children can encounter theoretical concepts. But most of the materials analyzed in this project did not offer these possibilities, and the few that did so, I am sorry to say, did not encourage the children to experiment as in play, so the theoretical–dialectical concepts were not promoted by this activity. However, I would still argue that an educational approach can support children's appropriation of theoretical concepts that are relevant to the child's ability to make conceptual experiments as in preschool children's role-play. Children's concepts about various forms of jobs or the seasons of the year, as well as their conceptual competence within family practice, often take the form of conceptual competences with theoretical concepts where each part is dependent on the other parts.

My theoretical arguments have opposed the idea that children's development should be regarded as a natural sequence where their appropriation of empirical concepts should be seen as a prerequisite for their appropriation of narrative and theoretical concepts. Rather, I would argue that it is the knowledge systems that dominate the practice children participate in at different ages. If we want to give children conceptual competence that is more oriented toward theoretical knowledge, we must make this part of their everyday practice. So parents and educators should change the practice traditions that the children participate in to change the conceptual competences the child will acquire. Play, as the key activity for preschool children, offers the possibility for such a development where the motivational aspect is also involved. Games can be of value if the content gives the child a theoretical orientation and possibility for experimentation and if the preschool children feel that they can participate in the games with adults on equal terms.

11 Inside and Outside the *Zone of Proximal Development*

An Ecofunctional Reading of Vygotsky

The *Zone of Proximal Development* (ZPD) has drawn attention from psychologists and educators and has oriented their research, diagnosis, and educational work toward new grounds. We hold that, rather than a term to be added to conventional psychology and pedagogy, the ZPD provides us with an instrument whose use will inevitably lead to a reappraisal and renewal of theory.

We suggest that this concept also operated as a Zone of Proximal Development in its own right for Vygotsky's theoretical thought. He focused his endeavors on the areas of conflict where his contemporaries ran into difficulties by exploring three theoretical frontiers:

1. The evolutionary and historical frontier (change and evolution of the child and individual, of the species, of cultures).
2. The identity frontier (the view of the functional system as shared, of functions as socially distributed).
3. The ecological frontier between the internal and external, the mental and the material, the organism and the medium.

A large part of the literature on Vygotsky and the research carried out on the basis of his ideas have developed his proposals with regard to the first two frontiers. Although the third frontier has received scant attention, it is in our opinion essential to a full understanding of Vygotsky's thought, especially the concept of ZPD. We will therefore pay special attention to this third frontier. Taking the ecofunctionalist influences on his thought as a framework, we will analyze the internal and external context of the ZPD and the internal and external mediation processes and conclude with a reflection on the possible future projection for Vygotskian approaches.

Currently, the ZPD is a concept of reference for education and teaching in most areas and subjects: language and second language education,
reading, writing, mathematics, science, social sciences, moral education,
and so forth. It is used in normal and in special education, with both disabled and gifted children, across age groups, from preschool to adult education, in verbal and reading–writing-based traditional education, and in
audiovisual and new technology–mediated education; higher education
in general, including teacher training, employs it, and it plays a part in
both the conventional school context and in social education and occupational therapy. As evidenced by the literature, the ZPD is Vygotsky's
best-known concept in the Western hemisphere, but although proper
understanding of the ZPD also requires knowledge of his general genetic
model, this seldom occurs: "Indeed, it is the only aspect of Vygotsky's
genetic theory of human development that most teachers have ever
heard of and, as a result, it is not infrequently cited to justify forms
of teaching that seem quite incompatible with the theory as a whole"
(Wells, 1999, p. 313).

Van der Veer and Valsiner (1991) have pointed out that in his initial
formulation of the ZPD, Vygotsky did not intend to be original. Although
they have not been able to establish the origins of the idea in great
detail, it seems that Vygotsky was trying to find an explanation, from the
ideas of his contemporary psychologists (Binet, Meumann, McCarthy),
for certain paradoxical results yielded by the application of metric scales
of intelligence (IQ). For example, the development of some children who
are initially more mature is held back when they start school, although
the opposite occurs in the case of others. Attempting to explain this fact,
Vygotsky tried to characterize the initial and terminal thresholds within
which development can take place, in order to determine the sensitive
periods for different educational goals in association with the concept of
"mental age."

Vygotsky discussed these issues concerning the ZPD at a conference at the end of 1933 (Vygotsky, 1933/1935). He continued to develop
his ideas in other writings involving reflections on and extensions of
the ZPD concept. This became a sort of theoretical ZPD for Vygotsky
himself, which worked as a heuristic or frontier concept of his theory
on development. Naturally, when Vygotsky encountered the problems
of evaluation and the impact of schooling on development, he could
hardly do anything but address them from the psychological ideas he

had already elaborated. Thus, the ZPD concept was outlined as a way of evaluating and educationally fostering development in accordance with his genetic–cultural theory of higher functions.

> When it was first shown that the capability of children with equal levels of mental development to learn under a teacher's guidance varied to a high degree, it became apparent that those children were not mentally the same age and that the subsequent course of their learning would obviously be different. This difference between twelve and eight, or between nine and eight, is what we call *the zone of proximal development. It is the distance between the actual developmental level as determined by independent problem solving and the level of potential development as determined through problem solving under adult guidance or in collaboration with more capable peers.*   (Vygotsky, 1978a, p. 86)

It must be understood that Vygotsky's thesis of the cultural formation of higher mental functions raises problems with Binet's model. It cannot be assumed that there exists, a priori, a general and normalized plan of behavior, in the nature and sequence of stages, in which only the attained *level* is to be evaluated, assuming that the rest follow a determined and general course of development. Vygotsky is therefore impelled to conceive and define the ZPD as the alternative to conventional tests and to to emphasize the *openness* of development to diverse possible *trajectories*:

> The actual developmental level characterizes mental development retrospectively, while the zone of proximal development characterizes mental development prospectively.   (Vygotsky, 1978a, pp. 86–87)

Unlike previous authors who assumed a fixed and single line of development, Vygotsky tried at the end of his career in his later work (1934/1956) to define development toward open and divergent futures. The concept of ZPD refers to the notion of developmental courses or trajectories. That is, it claims that the functional architecture and possible course of growth for a certain child, a specific group, or the infant population of a certain culture cannot be assumed in terms of such a fixed line, and that its particular course must be identified explicitly and dynamically. Vygotsky argues that externally induced (through cultural and educational action) learning determines not the *level* on the single line of development, but rather defines different lines, and the level attained on the corresponding specific line.

> The real task of analyzing an educational process is to find the emergence and disappearance of the *internal courses* of development at the point when they are verified, during school learning. This hypothesis assumes

necessarily that the developmental process is not coincidental to that of learning; the process of development follows that of learning, which *creates* the area of potential development.

(Vygotsky, 1934/1956, pp. 451–452; italics added)

Because Vygotsky conceives development as the outcome of learning and instruction, in order to anticipate a specific course or trajectory of development one would need to comprehend the cultural model a society tries to promote (in his perspective, *to develop*), and, therefore, to define the educational task. In this way, psychological diagnosis and cultural and educational design become real educational tools:

> Formerly, it was believed that by using tests we determine the mental development level with which education should reckon and whose limits it should not exceed. This procedure oriented learning toward yesterday's development, toward developmental stages already completed [...]. Learning which is oriented toward developmental levels that have already been reached is ineffective from the viewpoint of a child's overall development. It does not aim for a new stage of the developmental process, but rather lags behind this process. Thus, the notion of a zone of proximal development enables us to propose a new formula, namely, that the only good learning is that which is in advance of development [...]. We propose that an essential feature of learning is that it *creates* the zone of proximal development; that is, learning awakens a variety of internal developmental processes that *are able to operate only* when the child is interacting with people in his environment and in cooperation with his peers. Once these processes are internalized, they become part of the child's independent developmental achievement.
>
> (Vygotsky, 1978a, pp. 89–90; italics added)

When formulating his general law of psychological development, Vygotsky placed it at the junction of three dimensions that have constituted, as we mentioned above, psychology's real frontier territories: developmental, social, and ecological (to which we will return shortly).

> *An operation that initially represents an external activity is reconstructed and begins to occur internally.* [...] *An interpersonal process is transformed into an intrapersonal one.* Every function in the child's cultural development appears twice: first it appears on the social level, and later, on the individual level; first *between* people (*interpsychological*), and then inside the child (*intrapsychological*). This applies equally to voluntary attention, to logical memory, and to the formation of concepts. All the higher functions originate as actual relations between human individuals.
>
> (Vygotsky, 1978a, pp. 56–57)

Extending the implications of the Vygotskian conception leads toward a theory of psychological development more concerned with the courses open to the future than about the routes already trodden by a preconceived notion of development. A strongly cultural reading would imply the existence of culturally and individually distinctive mental models or *architectures* (del Río & Álvarez, 1995), knowledge of which is necessary for establishing the reference point for cultural and mental ages of child development. Also implied is the need for characterizing the logic of personalized functional behavior, so that a *personal functional architecture* can be described for each individual. This is what Leont'ev (1975) called *personality*, and Zazzo *personal intelligences* (personal communication, May 1975). This conception of development suggests that each developmental process is idiosyncratic, that cultural operators and operations appropriated by each child define a complex of behaviors of which he is or is not capable himself, and above all, of *viable functional loans in the ZPD*, which *he may or may not* receive in different activity environments. The functional loan by social others and by culture, and its active reception by the subject in this cultural sense, would result in what Zazzo (1968) called *functional anticipation*: the child uses a function he has not yet mastered, that is not *his* or Cazden (1981) called *performance before competence*.

This active dimension of learning as the source of development seems to be the central idea of ZPD for Vygotsky: "*Teaching should be oriented not towards the yesterday, but towards the tomorrow of child development*" (Vygotsky, 1934/1982/1993, p. 242; italics in the original).

Vygotsky formulated the concept of Zone of Proximal Development in order to deal methodologically with the need to anticipate the course of development. This appears in principle a simple idea, requiring nothing more than fixing a particular point in a general sequence of development. It conflicts, however, with another central idea of Vygotsky's system, namely, that human development is an open process, which eventually leads to the ZPD itself becoming a concept open to his entire theory and epistemologically demanding.

Therefore, different models of development and education shape different ZPD conditions, setting up the encounter between the child and the *ideal model of development* given in a cultural system (Elkonin, 1994). In this space, the child is not unarmed and exposed: He is in the ZPD, in an area that grants him access to functions new to him and placed within his reach by culture and society.

Ideally, the development work in the ZPD requires the combination of evaluation, design, and educational action or teaching; this could be carried out very technically by a developmental psychologist, or very intuitively by, for example, a father. The educator – inasmuch as education is science and art simultaneously – is at an intermediate point, which would potentially enable him to work on both planes.

We can understand, therefore, why the ZPD concept is considered as the Vygotskian system's "leading window": it addresses all the basic questions that can be posed regarding any psychological system – the subject, the object (what is developed), the mechanisms that account for development and the conditions in which this takes place (the explanatory principle):

1. *Who?* Who develops? An interrelated multiplicity of human subjects: communities and cultures, families, professional groups, and, of course, the individual subject.

2. *With whom?* The accessible and socially distributed functional systems that provide ZPDs not only afford provisional and subsequently dispensable scaffolding but are also usually permanent social structures of the distributed functional design of culture. This is because psychological functions are not always designed in human cultures to operate, in their most developed state, in a totally individualized way; rather, some psychological functions are conceived to operate always in a shared fashion.

3. *What is developed?* Higher functions, as new forms of mediated activity, evolve and change historically, and they also do so within the history of an individual (ontogenesis), of a culture, of a community, and, in a global and cumulative way, of our species. That is, they can be researched backward, as Vygotsky does, but also forward, as possible designs, as architectures open to the action of the individual and collective subjects themselves; as functional systems that "can be written." The analytical units recently proposed are therefore more "distributed" and "frontier-breaking" than those classically conceived in the Vygotskian tradition (Cobb, 1998).

4. *With what? How?* The *activity systems* (the frameworks) and *settings* (the artifacts and operator systems) of a culture are not only provisional instrumental mediators with the sole goal of producing internal development but also constitute a firm, external, functional tissue of mental activity.

5. *Where?* Development takes place both inside and outside the skin, and above all, *on* the skin, *at the border*, that is, at the interface connecting the two regions. Vygotsky stressed the external origin of every higher function, but at the same time, he seemed to consider an ideal model of development in which any function

should finally become established in the internal plane. This simplified conception today appears more heuristic than real, an idealistic modeling of the developmental genetic cultural approach, which overlooks the fact that, to a greater or lesser extent, many functions in all subjects remain partially externally distributed throughout the life cycle. (del Río, 2002.)

Thus, the ZPD should consider development not only from the inside, to reveal the *potential* of an individual's psychological growth, at a given point in the *development course*; it should also, within the general Vygotskian approach, to consider development on the outside, in the distributed bioecopsychological system. The ZPD would thus acquire cultural, social, and political implications, apart from educational ones, because an individual cannot develop without his medium. In order to justify this claim, it is necessary to examine what we earlier called the third border – the ecological border between the internal and the external, the mental and the material, the organism and its medium.

THE ECOLOGICAL FRONTIER OF HUMAN DEVELOPMENT: INSIDE AND OUTSIDE THE ZPD

Vygotsky's work could be considered as a bridge that connects the human organism to its medium, the mind to the body. It rests on the ecological, biofunctionalist and sociogenetic theories of his age, seeking within them the means of breaching the frontiers established by Cartesian thought. The concept of ZPD also seems to play a heuristic role in the approach advocated by Michael Cole (1985), which emphasizes the frontier character of Vygotskian concepts, and directs our gaze toward the intermediate area between the internal and the external, the individual and the social, the material and the symbolic, the static and the evolutionary. This no-man's land, generally left uncultivated and unexplored in dualistic approaches, was for Vygotsky the vital zone for understanding the human mind.

The Internal and External Scenario of the ZPD: The Ecofunctional Perspective

There is an inevitable tendency to read Vygotsky "retrospectively," interpreting his concepts from the perspective of the psychology that came after his death (such as cognitive and neo-Piagetian psychology), but it can actually be interpreted somewhat better from the perspective of neuropsychology, or from that of approaches contemporary to his own. However, it is more comprehensible still if approached from within the whole scientific historical framework in which his thought and the definition of the ZPD took place. Vygotsky based a substantial part of his analysis of human development on the basic concepts of the materialistic scientific tendencies prevalent in his time from biology, psychology, philosophy, and history. Therefore, his analysis of culture draws on the concepts of *activity systems* of the evolutionary biologist Jennings (1906), and of *specific environments*, proposed by von Uexküll (1909); also important was the influence of ecologically oriented Gestalt authors, such as Lewin (1926) and Koffka (1935). Vygotsky's central idea about phylogenetic change is that the prehuman biological environment is gradually transformed into a *cultural environment*, and this changes the *activity system* of humankind into a socially and instrumentally mediated activity.

Because Vygotsky borrowed his view of the mind as a system of functions from biological functionalism some fundamental ecofunctionalist concepts may help us recognize this conceptual affiliation of Vygotsky's thought, which also affects the idea of the ZPD. Let us first briefly recall the foundational concept of "functional circle" and the associated concept of *Umwelt* (Von Uexküll, 1909, 1926, 1934), as well as the later notion of *affordance* (Gibson, 1979; Koffka, 1935; Lewin, 1926, 1936).

FUNCTIONALISM AND FUNCTIONS AS BIOLOGICAL CONCEPTS. Spencer (1887) applied biological thought to psychology by proposing that the evolution of the mind is a process of adaptation to the medium. The ideas of biological evolutionism and biofunctionalism can still be perceived today in biocybernetics, ecobiology, and evolutionary psychology. This approach attempts to describe evolutionary logic as a pragmatic logic, that is, explaining structures by their function. Claparède, the proponent of biofunctionalist psychology, refers to William James and John Dewey as the first great authors of psychological functionalism (1973). Either way, the impact of biofunctionalism on the important figures of European evolutionary psychology – among them, needless to say, Vygotsky – was profound:

> The new psychology starts from the idea of an unbreakable bond between the psyche and the rest of the organism's vital processes, and seeks the sense, the meaning, the laws of evolution of that psyche, including it wholly among the rest of the organism's vital functions. The biological rationality of the psyche acts in this case as a fundamental explanatory principle. The psyche is interpreted as one of the organism's functions

that resembles the others in the most essential: in that it is also a biological adaptation to the medium, useful and vital.

(Vygotsky, 1926/1982/1990, p. 151)

With regard to the fundamental vital functions of the organism, it has been pointed out that, due to a common origin and physical structure, there is a great coherence and unity of all living beings, including humans, in relation to certain basic biological macrofunctions, such as feeding and survival; attention and perception; retention and processing; movement and action; and identity and communication (Cordón, 1990).

The Complex Organism–Medium

Von Uexküll (1909, 1926, 1934), considered to be the father of ecological thinking, proposed an interactionist view in which he tried to find a middle ground between his teachers' biological vitalism and the mechanicism dominant at the time. Vitalism invoked a nonresearchable cause – beyond the natural – for explaining the systemic unity of organisms, and mechanicism stated that all vital processes could be explained by physical–chemical processes or mechanisms. Therefore, Von Uexküll reconsidered the relations of organism and medium in a way that holds the organism to be part of the medium and the medium to be part of the organism.[1] Going beyond the Darwinist view, in which the pace of the organism's evolution's is set by the pace of adaptation to the medium surrounding it (*environment, milieu,* a medium broadly defined), Von Uexküll conceives the medium as a system of specific *media* for each organism (*Umwelt*) and the organism as a component of various *media*. According to the laws of evolution, all organisms are well adapted to

---

[1] We can understand Von Uexküll's position from what Konrad Lorenz has to say on the problem of perceptual isomorphism or the possibility of knowing things: "If the way in which we experience the external world is based on the function of internal 'receivers' that are differentiated in a definite way – and no other – adapting to that which they have to register in a clear material conflict between two equally real worlds, there exists then a material relation and, consequently, *basically apt of being investigated,* between the phenomenic and the real world; hence Kant's first premise on the absence of relation between the two worlds is false. The general character of this relation is relatively easy to understand. And an organ whose function of conserving the species *does not* consist in reproducing real things, but in mechanically confronting one of them, when adapting to its function will always turn, in a way, to an image of that thing, its 'counterpoint,' using Jacob von Uexküll's expression. The shape of an organ is, to a certain extent, the negative, the copy of the immutable data of the organic external world in the plastic matrix of organic substance" (Lorenz, 1993, pp. 65–66).

their medium. The medium is not "given to" the organism; rather, the latter acts upon the former and actively contributes to its organization. The *Umwelt* is not a background or scenario to be passed through, like a hotel room, but a flexible habitat that is occupied and remade, and on which each organism leaves its impression.

> Each living being, according to its structure, only enters into contact with a very small part of the external world, and through that relation creates its own surrounding world, in which it leads its life.
>   (Von Uexküll, 1909, pp. 52–53)

In this interaction, the basic macrofunctions of perception and motor action define the two great *media* in which the organism operates – the *Merkwelt* or perceptive medium, and the *Wirkungswelt* or action sphere of the organism. These two external media are united by a third, internal one – the *Innenwelt*. And these three components of the *Umwelt* can only explain life if there is a dynamic process from the inside out and vice versa. This articulated project for life is the *Bauplan*: "the organism, along with its surrounding world, forms a purposeful whole," so that a "planned dependence between animal and external world" is required (Von Uexküll, 1909, p. 53).

The Functional Circle

Von Uexküll (1909) thus defines the relations of the animal organism with the medium in an ecological and dynamic way, as a dialectic process, a functional circle, of combined and interdependent perception and action. The amoeba, the tick, the sparrow, or the wolf could all be defined by their functional circles and their specific contexts that determine their systems for perceiving and acting. The *activity systems specific* to each species thus configure their psychic systems (Jennings, 1906). Vygotsky takes this perspective as a starting point for trying to understand the characteristics specific to the human functional system. Higher psychological functions would be, in a sense, the counterpoint of mediated activity systems.

Vygotsky's decisive contribution to ecofunctionalism is to introduce the genetic–cultural perspective, according to which the *functional circle is at once interfered with and enlarged* (Figure 11.1). In his model, the natural flow of perception and action present at the animal level is reconstructed; by means of mediating and representing stimuli, we humans enlarge our functional circle and the *Umwelt* of our species. Perceiving and acting in the human cultural contexts – densely mediated – is

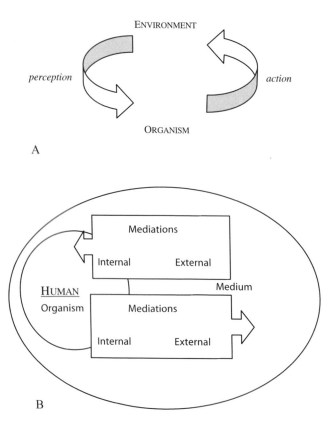

FIGURE 11.1. (A) The basic functional circle. (B) The mediated functional circle.

impossible unless we learn to make at least minimal use of mediations.[2] This *learning* is equivalent to the *development* of the human functional system.

From the Vygotskian cultural ecofunctionalist perspective, humans culturally extend their *merkwelt* and their possibilities for perception,

---

[2] The ecofunctional perspective exerts its influence over both the Vygotskian school and other tendencies in Soviet psychology. We should mention, regarding the Vygotskian perspective, the mental action and "perceptual movement" models proposed by Zaporozhets, and, associated with these, his efferent model of perception and the psychological conception of movement (Zaporozhets, 1959, 1967); or Zinchenko's proposal of sensuous-object action as a unit of analysis in living beings (Zinchenko, 1985). Regarding other Soviet approaches in psychology, we will only mention the emphasis on movement as a basic functional process (Bernshtein, 1966).

and they relearn through new, mediated sensorial systems how to take notice, how to see, how to remember, how to think and feel, and so forth. With the help of analogous devices, they extend their *wirkungswelt* and learn new mediated ways to act and engage with new activity systems. Vygotsky and Luria (1994) conceived of the perceptual field as a field in which a child's attention is enslaved by the external flow of stimuli, but in which an adult constructs voluntary attention by highlighting the structurally relevant elements. We might say that adults lend the child – enslaved to his field in his passive attention – their active attention through this process of highlighting stimuli and capturing and guiding the child's gaze toward cultural affordances. Similarly, Zaporozhets (1967) showed how the attention process is culturally reconstructed, so that the child's external gaze, mediated by culture and by the intelligence of others, becomes, in turn, intelligent: Instead of following the stimulus, it anticipates the stimulus. Through the interiorization of mediations, the externally oriented stance becomes an intelligent "interior gaze" in the same way that external action becomes mental action. Early human interaction is a complex dynamic of perception and action, or coperception and cooperation, in which the reconstructed cultural functional circle of the adult is naturally superposed on the natural circle of the child.

Lewin and Koffka, sharing this ecofunctionalist perspective, proposed that certain stimuli, in the specific context, were conferred a value that would focus and orient attention and perception. The stimuli ecologically most relevant in the specific medium of a species (*Umwelt*) were considered to be endowed with specific perceptual *potentials* for interacting with the organism. In order to define the organism-medium functional relationship, Lewin (1926) appealed to the chemical metaphor of *valency* and to the physical metaphors of *vector* and *field of forces*, as well as coined the term *Aufforderungscharakter* – Koffka (1935) later proposed replacing this term with that of *demand character*. All of these concepts are consistent with the perceptual and enactive dimensions of flow in the functional circle and continue to play a relevant role in psychology. Thus, James Gibson – one of whose mentors with was Koffka – has updated the concept of affordance and established the historical continuity of the ecological approach in the psychology of perception (Gibson, 1979). For their part, Turvey and Shaw added to perceptual affordance the complementary concept of action effectivity (Turvey & Shaw, 1977).

Vygotsky's suggestion for explaining the role played by cultural mediators in the reconstruction of perceptual and effector natural structures is also linked to the Lewinian concept of *Aufforderungscharakter*.

Vygotsky holds that thanks to the introduction of cultural elements in the functional circle, perception and action are reconstructed:

> When speech comes into play, his [the child's] perception is no longer connected with immediate impression of the whole; new centers fixed by words and connections of various points with these centers arise in the visual field; perception stops being "the slave of the visual field."
> (Vygotsky, 1930/1984/1999, p. 12)

> Here the action comes from the thing's meaning, and not from the thing itself. The *aufforderungscharakter* is transferred to the meaning of the word.   (Vygotsky, 1980, p. 273)

Vygotsky did not develop the implications of his model further in order to adjust it to functionalism and ecologism in detail; he merely used the functionalist seedbed to germinate and cultivate his own psychology. However, it would seem essential to consider the historical sources of his thought so as to ensure that his conceptions regarding ecological features are understood in both cultural and symbolic terms, as well as in terms of an extended biological organism. The ecofunctional approach speaks of how species learn, and how through their own phylogenesis they construct all their natural functions, developing at the same time their own specific activity systems. Without departing from this tradition, but nevertheless transcending it, the Vygotskian approach implies that cultures would also relearn how to see and act by designing new higher mediated functions, and cultural activity systems.[3]

From the ecofunctional perspective, the fact that humans start to act through introducing stimuli-media or cultural operators into a specific medium (*Umwelt*) artificially provokes a perceptual and active rechanneling – a crucifix, a traffic light, an alarm clock are introduced and situated in the field as *cultural affordances*, by means of cultural action. We may well refer to this type of intentional *affordances* as *cultural affordances*, suggesting that they should be distinguished from natural ones. The overall result is that culture reconstructs the natural medium and turns it into a mixed natural-cultural medium, in which an ever-larger part of our specific *affordances* or valences thus become *self-designed*.

---

[3] The thesis that each culture throughout the course of history has learned to see in a particular way has been upheld, by Vygotsky as well as by other authors in the history of art (Gombrich, 1989) or the media (McLuhan, 1964), and could well be extended to the artifactual mediations and perceptual prostheses in all areas of human activity. This view, simultaneously historical and ecological, along with the influence of the systemic perspective on biology, leads toward a current tendency of Western thought, subsequent to Vygotsky's, that understands cultures as processes of the "extension" and/or "amputation" of basic functions (McLuhan, 1964).

In this sense, human perception is a culturally *designed* function in which gaze and gesture become the thread for weaving new mediated connections.

In the framework of the functional circle, Vygotsky identifies two mechanisms through which the human species has crossed the first inside–outside frontier. The first of these involves making extracortical connections in the medium, outside the organism; the second, making intracortical connections inside the organism. Extracortical connections make use of external mediations or cultural affordances, while intracortical connections make use of internal mediations. These two mechanisms constitute the technical layout of the ZPD.

THE ECOFUNCTIONAL PERSPECTIVE
ON EXTERNAL MEDIATION

External Mediation as Situated Psychological Action

Vygotsky reproached the idealist psychology of his time as a "psychology without space" (Vygotsky, 1982, p. 104) arguing his case on the basis of three theoretical traditions: Pavlov's (1950) materialist reflexology, the ecologism mentioned above, and Spinoza's antidualism, according to which thinking and extension were not two different substances, but two attributes of one and the same substance. In this attempt to find the frontier at which the presentational and the representational meet, a material, physical and ecofunctional space can be inferred. Vygotsky gives the principal role to some physical objects referred to as stimuli-media, or psychological tools which, insofar as they are situated in this space, are clearly *res extensa*, and, therefore, are subject to the natural laws of the functional circle, exerting at the same time an action on psychological functions:

> [...] For Pavlov 'It is impossible by means of psychological concepts, which are essentially non-spatial, to penetrate into the mechanism of animal behaviour, into the mechanism of these relations.' (Pavlov, 1950, p 207). [...] 'Our facts are conceived of in terms of time and space; they are purely scientific facts; but psychological facts are thought of only in terms of time.' (*ibid*). [...] Pavlov states explicitly that it is a question not only of emancipation from psychological concepts, but also of the elaboration of a new psychology with the help of *concepts equipped with spatial references*.
>
> (Vygotsky, 1927/982/1990, pp. 262–263; italics added)

The demonstration of the materiality of signs and psychological representations is, for Vygotsky, their ability to fill a place in the physical

space of the medium and their unambiguous inclusion in the basic biological functional circle. In his endeavor to contemplate mental action
in a real physical scenario, Vygotsky conceives of the natural medium
as a sort of Pavlovian laboratory designed in terms of neural connectors:

> [...] Self-experience is formed and organized as a copy of the organiza-
> tion of the different elements in the medium. [...] The medium, as the
> source of all stimuli that act upon the organism, fulfils the same role with
> respect to each one of us as Pavlov's laboratory with respect to the dogs he
> experimented with. [...] For, after all, inherited experience is also deter-
> mined and conditioned by older influences of the medium, and, indeed,
> man himself also owes his origin and structure to the medium.
>
> (Vygotsky, 1926/1982/1990, pp. 157–158)

Through ecological connectionism, the organism externally generates
its specific external cortex, which is the cultural redesign of medium
that echoes von Uexküll's concept of "counterpoint" (see footnote 1).
This ecofunctional conception is evidenced in Vygotsky's ambivalent
and dialectic way of viewing the relations between organism and
medium. The organism weaves its neural webs, its internal mediated representations, as adaptations that evoke the medium and are directed
toward it, while the medium is seen as a laboratory where stimuli that
operate specifically upon the organism are relocated and re-presented:

> [...] the organism itself is a part of the medium, in the sense of the
> influence it exerts upon itself. The organism plays in respect to itself
> the role of medium [...] It is medium to itself [...] All human behavior
> is based on the medium multiplied by the medium. That is, the social
> squared.   (Vygotsky, 1926/1982/1990, p. 158)

Psychological Tools as Operators of External Mediation

Although still feeding off the roots of historical materialism and Marxism, Vygotsky maintains his own thinking deeply rooted in biology and
ecology, thus permitting a better understanding of historical materialism. He also shows a fearless open-mindedness regarding the revealing
contributions of several contemporary psychologists on social or artifactual external stimulation (Janet, 1937; Binet, 1903) or behaviorism. He
established an essential difference between those efficient tools destined
to transform nature, which had captured the attention of Marxists, and
the psychological tools aimed at the transformation of the mind.

> In subjecting to his will the process of his own reactions, man enters
> in this way into a substantially new relation with the environment,
> comes to a new functional exploitation of elements in the environment

as stimuli-signs which he uses, depending on external means, and directs and control his own behavior, controls himself from the outside, compelling stimuli-signs to affect him, and elicits reactions that he desires. Internal regulation of goal-directed activity arises initially from external regulation.   (Vygotsky, 1930/1984/1999, p. 63)

The fundamental quality of elemental functions is that they are totally and directly determined by environmental stimulation. The central quality of higher functions is self-generated stimulation, that is, the creation and use of artificial stimuli that become the immediate cause of behavior.   (Vygotsky, 1978b, pp. 38–39)

The functional circle, expanded by external mediation, thus places the human species in a new kind of *medium* that operates simultaneously with elements of the organism's present context – presentational – and with elements of a new context expanded by means of external mediations that enable *re-presentation*, or the presentation of absent stimuli.

Vygotsky makes frequent use of the terms *stimuli-media* and *extracortical connections*. *Stimuli-media* consist of intermediate stimulations (the immediate stimulus connects to the intermediate stimulus, and this to responsive reaction), and *extracotical connections* are neurological, even though they are made in the external *medium* and not inside the brain. In the initial steps of phylogenetic and ontogenetic development, stimuli-media are not yet signs, and belong rather to a territory neighboring the animal functional circle.[4] Vygotsky conceives the stimulus-medium initially as an operator for acting on the existing internal functions which, on activating them by means of a trigger stimulus in the environment, generates new functions *from the outside*. In this way,

---

[4] The anecdote referred to by Luria in *The Making of Mind*, about a patient with Parkinson's disease, is quite illustrative of the Vygotskian conception of extracortical connections. Parkinson's disease affects subcortical motor ganglia, so that the involuntary serial flux of gait movements is interrupted. However, curiously enough, this patient could climb stairs. Vygotsky and Luria then hypothesized that the reason for this disparity lay in that, when climbing stairs, each step represented a new signal to which the motor system readily reacted (because climbing the stairs involved not the serialized involuntary walking movement, but discrete voluntary actions). The clinical challenge was to use the motor circuit of the independent and intact connections, reconnecting them externally and enabling them to function as an articulate group of sequenced steps. Vygotsky placed a series of white cards on the ground and asked the patient to step on each of them. "A marvelous thing happened. A patient that had not been able to walk two or three steps by himself was walking through the room, stepping easily over each card as if he were climbing a stair" (Luria, 1979, p. 129). In order to understand correctly the role of the stimulus-medium, we must observe that the cards were not a sign: nobody told the patients that they were the steps of a stair, he was simply asked to step on them.

higher functions appear first as situated operation systems that define new modes or strategies for acting on the outside. More important for Vygotsky than the stimulus-medium is the "instrumental action,"and with it the reorganization of psychological functions that it implies:

> The inclusion of a tool in the process of behavior (a) introduces several new functions connected with the use of the given tool and with its control; (b) abolishes and makes unnecessary several natural processes, whose work is accomplished by the tool; and (c) alters the course and individual features (intensity, duration, sequence, etc.) of all the mental processes involved in the composition of the instrumental act, replacing some functions with others (i.e., it re-creates and reorganizes the whole structure of behavior just as a technical-efficient tool re-creates the whole structure of labor operations).   (Vygotsky, 1981, pp. 139–140)

Vygotsky approaches the analysis of the evolution of mediated functions at the points of functional change in the child. In his early work, he begins by situating the basic mechanism of the sign in two convergent frames: the ecological circle and the paradigm of stimulus-response. He calls these connections that transcend classical animal conditioning and the classical functional circle "instrumental acts":

> This "functional barrier" between perception and the motor system, which we established above and which is forced by its origin to insert a word or other symbol between the beginning and end of action, explain the separation of the impulses from the direct realization of the act; separation that in turn is a mechanism of preparation for actions postponed for the future. Specifically the inclusion of symbolic operations makes possible the appearance of a psychological field completely new in composition, not based in what is at hand in the present, but presenting a sketch of the future, and in this way creating the free action independent of the direct situation.   (Vygotsky, 1930/1984/1999, p. 36)

THE BUILDING OF THE EXTERNAL
REPRESENTATIONAL PLANE

The Vygotskian ecofunctional perspective leads to the understanding that by means of functional social loans and artifactual cognitive and directive tools, higher functions are reconstructed in a syncretic territory where natural stimuli and mediated stimuli converge.

When the use of psychological tools reaches a higher level of functioning and articulates as a system, as in language, the full maturity of this advanced functioning is achieved. From that point on, not only does it become possible to represent and include absent entities in the natural field, but an entire new representational field is created. Understanding the constitution and interplay of these two planes – the natural field and the culturally created representational plane – was one of Vygotsky's main challenges. For him, the first step, and the most obvious way of conceptualizing mediation, was to understand the implications of introducing words as external operators in auditory and visual external perceptual planes From there, Vygotsky enters into a more complex elaboration of mediation that leads him to conceive *two different planes of representation*. In addition to the external representational plane in which the mediation process begins, Vygotsky identifies the constitution of a new plane, which he calls the plane of time. Thus, Vygotsky defines two levels of impact of mediation, external and internal, which operate in harmony. In this new scenario, it is necessary to resituate the circle of perception-and-action.

Although in his early writings on mediation, Vygotsky was excited about the way external mediations work (1927/1982), later on (1930/1984) he became more concerned with internal mediations, stating for example that perception is guided and mediated by internal meanings, and not only by external artificial operators. The functional circle begins to flow in two planes:

> The more complex the action required and the less direct the path toward solution, the more important does the role of speech in the whole process become. Sometimes speech becomes so important that without it, the child is definitely not capable of concluding the task. [. . .] These observations bring us to the conclusion that the child solves a practical problem not only with his eyes and hands, but also with the help of speech.   (Vygotsky, 1930/1984/1999, p. 15)

> The child forms significantly greater potentials in words than the ape can realize in action. The child can free himself more easily from the vector that directs attention directly to the goal and he can carry out a series of complex additional actions using a comparatively long chain of auxiliary instrumental methods. He is capable of independently introducing objects that are not in the direct or in the peripheral visual field into the process of solving the problem. Creating certain designs with the help of words, the child develops substantially large circle of operations, using objects that are not at hand as tools, but he also seeks and prepares those that may become useful for solving the problem and plans further actions.   (Vygotsky, 1930/1984/1999, p. 16)

> Using speech to create, together with the spatial field, a temporal field of action that is just as visible and real as the optical situation (although perhaps somehow more vague), the child who can speak has the possibility of dynamically directing his attention, acting in the present from the point of view of a future field, and frequently referring to actively created changes in the present situation form the point of view of his past actions.

Specifically owing to the participation of speech and the transition to a
free distribution of attention, the future field of action is converted from
the old and abstract verbal formula into an actual, optical situation; in
it, all of the elements that are part of the plan of future action enter into
the basic configuration, eliminating possible actions from the general
background in this way. With the help of speech, the fact that the field
of attention does not coincide with the field of perception extracts from
the latter the elements of an actual *future field* and results in the specific
difference between the child's operation and the operation of higher animals. In the child, the field of perception is organized by the verbalized
function of attention and if, for the ape, absence of direct optical contact
between the object and the goal is enough to make the problem insol-
uble, the child easily eliminates this difficulty by verbal intervention,
reorganizing his sensory field.   (Vygotsky, 1930/1984/1999, p. 34)

If external mediations create in a first stage the external scenario of
ZPD and open the way to higher functions, internal mediation profoundly transforms the new psychological medium and the new higher
functions.

AN ECOFUNCTIONAL APPROACH TO INTERNAL MEDIATION

Reconstructing the Functional Circle

Although Vygotsky's thesis on the external origin of mediated actions
has been brought to light by Western reviews, less attention has been
paid to the fact that – as seen in the previous section – these mediated
actions are *actions*, with the physiological substratum of any action, as
Zaporozhets, Leontiev, and Zinchenko have persistently stressed. We
wholeheartedly endorse such emphasis, because, in a large part of current psychology, when research is carried out on mental actions they are
idealized and considered without the external mediations that support
them. This is partly due to the fact that current methodologies do not
approach the two articulated planes defined by Vygotsky jointly, and seg-
regate cognitive actions from observations of external and physiological
actions.[5]

---

[5] Following Zaporozhets (1967) and Bernshtein (1966), Zinchenko suggested a patent
structural analogy between internal-cognitive and motor actions: "Results showed
that the complexity of the motor act is completely commensurate with the complexity of the cognitive act [. . .] All this is evidence for the fact that the structures
of external and internal activity share not only a common genesis, but a common
functional nature as well" (Zinchenko, 1985, pp. 111–112).

In Vygotsky's model, internal mental action and external mental action, and what is more, physical and mental action, form part of the *same functional circle*:

> These observations bring us to the conclusion that the child solves a practical problem not only with his eyes and hands, but also with the help of speech. This new unit, which leads to the reorganization of the laws of the visual field, constitutes *the real and vital object of analysis* aimed at studying the origin of specifically human forms of behavior.
>
> (Vygotsky, 1930/1984, p. 23; italics added)

For Zinchenko (1985), externalization is the eventual transformation process by which internal activity, promoted formerly by interiorization, constitutes itself in turn, and somewhat differently, in external activity. If we adopt the biocybernetic and global perspective of the functional circle, Zaporozhets' (1967) "perception–action" proposal or other bio-functionalist terms present in Bernshtein, Zaporozhets, or Zinchenko's quoted works, internalization and externalization processes should not be seen as separate and one way, but rather as a new complex of frontier functions that expand the functional circle. In this circular functional perspective, internal actions mediated through meanings may therefore come to the outside, as meaning mediated by words or any kinds of psychological tool used as cultural effectivities. As Vygotsky graphically illustrates it, the meaning in clouds must find its way out as raindrops.

The initial proposal of the mediation model *implies the breaking of the functional circle*, in both the afferent-perceptual and efferent-effective cycles. Although this task occupied a large part of Vygotsky's attention, even from the beginning, he stressed the need to recompose the circle in a new plane. For Vygotsky, perceptual mediation introduces the nonpresent into the perceptual field and thus crosses the limits of the *Umwelt*. He also pointed out that in this way the human organism breaks its specific action schemes because, in animals, the organism's action is determined solely by its immediate perception. In the process of restructuring the circle, Vygotsky focuses on the psychic architecture that enables the subject, through mediations, to perceive and act on the nonpresent. In this sense, his analyses of the breaking of the circle and of the new segments that reestablish it on another mediated level are complementary:

> Two principal features make up an original form of this new layer of "motors" of human behavior: the mechanism of implementing an intention at the moment of its appearance, first, is separated from the motor apparatus and, second, contains an impulse to action, the implementation of which is referred to a future field. Neither of these features is

present in the action organized by a natural need where the motor system is inseparable from direct perception and all the action is concentrated in a real mental field.   (Vygotsky, 1930/1984/1999, p. 360)

If this approach to a less well known – or at least less widely discussed – Vygotsky is correct, the ecofunctionalist and Vygotskian theories could be recovered to bear new fruit and provide fertile soil for current work in perspectives on cognitive-embodied mind. As Michael Cole points out, "the artifacts which enter into human psychological functions are themselves culturally, historically and institutionally situated. In a sense, then, there is no way not to be socioculturally situated when carrying out an action" (Cole, 1997, p. 3).

On the basis of the analysis of "cognitive ethnographies," Hutchins (1995) argues that most complex functions could not be executed by an individual mind as modeled by current cognitive psychology, and that the real object of analysis for psychology is the functional system situated precisely "in the wild," at the boundaries of the person. Heidmets's "personal cultures" (1985) or our own "cultural ecographies" (del Río & Álvarez, 1999) and Zone of Syncretic Representation (del Río, 1990) also move in this direction.

This notion of continuity in perception and action, and in internal and external action, may prove to be the key to improving our perspective on interiorization and mental action.

MOVEMENT AND MENTAL GESTURE

The action makes sense for the first time during play; it is then that consciousness about it appears. An action replaces another action, as one thing replaces another. How does the child transform one thing into another or an action into another action? Through movement in the semiologic field. This semiologic movement is the most important thing about play: on one hand it is movement in the abstract field, but the way of moving is situational, concrete – that is, not logical but efficient. The emergence of the semantic field endowed with movement, as if it were real, is play's main genetic contradiction [. . .] The child operates in play with meanings detached from things, but attached to the real action with the real objects: [. . .] a division occurs between the meaning of horse and the real horse, and the former is transferred to the stick – which becomes an objectual fulcrum, otherwise the meaning vanishes into thin air – , upon which the child acts as if it were a horse. The child cannot separate the thing's meaning from the word that signifies it if he does not find a fulcrum somewhere else [. . .] He forces one thing, so to speak, to influence another at a semiologic level.   (Vygotsky, 1980, pp. 274–276)

As we have already noted, Vygotsky sought psychophysical and physiological relations between natural and higher functions at the borderline where words and objects, gestures and motor actions, and meanings and mental operations share space and time, presentation, and re-presentation. The Würzburg school provided with a starting point for Vygotsky. The Würzburg researchers had pointed out the motor nature of thought and the externally verifiable movements connected to mental activity, and Vygotsky assumed that voluntary mental actions (higher functions) are necessarily supported by the natural perception-and-action structures of involuntary kinesthetic actions; this link permits the external observation of the motor vestiges of natural functions on which the higher functions rest. Therefore, he called the group of movements associated with the internal or silent private speech system "phonomotor reactions" (Vygotsky, 1926). Connecting with the kinesthetic tradition of thought – also adopted by his disciples – he tried to find the mirror reflecting internal actions in external motor actions:

> In experiments on the study of the motor system linked to internal affective processes, we demonstrated that the motor reaction is so merged and inseparably participates in the affective process that it can serve as a reflecting mirror in which it is possible to literally read the hidden structure of the affective process that is hidden of direct observation.
>
> (Vygotsky, 1930/1984/1999, p. 31)

On similar grounds, Henri Wallon (1934) postulated in the same period a continuity between the tonic and postural organization of the higher processes. The traces of original motor actions remain as support and company for mental actions, and such continuity is visible for any experienced child psychologist who, for practically any mental act, should be able to identify manifested *synkinesias* – movements that accompany, in a postural complex, attentional, mnemonic or intellectual acts, for example, when a child puts his or her tongue out to write with deeper concentration. Wallon maintained that mental actions leave visible traces on external behavior. This would make it possible to track "motor biographies" as Damasio (2000) suggests.

It can be assumed, from the interiorization perspective, that "motor biographies" of mental actions are supported by external architectures that articulate neurologically with internal structures to produce a tandem of internal and external fields of mediation and representation that are idiosyncratic to each psychological personality.

THE PROCESS OF INTERIORIZATION

Vygotsky's first step forward in his theory of mediation was directed toward the analysis of the role of "outside-the-skin" mediators. However, once the elemental features of external mediation had been unraveled, Vygotsky turned to the inside of skin. His general genetic law of cultural development had already defined two aspects of the process: functional *appropriation*, or the stage in which the function, formerly socially distributed, becomes individually mastered; and *interiorization*, or the stage in which the function comes from the external plane into the internal plane. The step into the inside is, for Vygotsky, not merely a transfer, as Wertsch (1985) or Leontiev (1981) have pointed out. Interiorization is a genetic process that involves the transformation of functions, and therefore the creation of internal processes; moreover, it constitutes a veritable mental and functional revolution.

Following the idea of "interiorization as formation," much work has been done by the followers of Vygotsky to detail the process of mental formation of psychological higher operations such as calculation, reading, or spatial representations. Galperin's model of interiorization of mental operations postulates some stages and moments in educational work in the ZPD that articulate those functional dependencies between external and internal operations (Galperin, 1978/1992). Galperin's stages are as follows:

1. Creating a preliminary conception of the task (ideation, anticipation, planification);
2. Mastering the action using objects;
3. Mastering the action in the plane of private external speech;
4. Transferring the action to the mental plane (private internal speech or mental gesture);
5. Consolidating the mental action.

In our view of the staged formation of mental actions in the ZPD, the three first stages involve the process of construction and appropriation of new mental action, in the external scenario. The fourth and fifth stages involve the interiorization process of new mental actions already in the internal scenario.

THE SYSTEMIC UNITY OF EXTERNAL
AND INTERNAL MEDIATIONS

The external–internal continuity (steps 1, 2, and 3 taking place in the outside and steps 4 and 5 in the inside) proposed in Galperin's model cannot be considered a simple matter of sequencing in the execution of a procedure. As from Vygotsky's perspectives, each stage of the mediated construction of the functions' process implies that there are no functionally void (or inoperant) moments; at each moment, the functional organization modes that arise are associated with the integrated dynamism of the functional circle. At any moment, the subject is able to exercise his activity by integrating the internal and the external processes he has acquired up to that point, and which he is capable of carrying out as a dynamic whole:

> With the *revolution (vraschivanye)*, that is, with the transfer of the function inward, a complex reconstruction of its whole structure occurs. As experiment shows, the following are essential points of the reconstruction: 1) replacement of functions; 2) change in natural functions (elementary processes that form the basis for the higher function and make up a part of it); 3) the appearance of new psychological, functional systems (or systemic functions), taking on in the general structure of behavior a role that had been carried out thus far by separate functions.
>
> (Vygotsky, 1930/1984/1999, p. 55)

THE TWO DIMENSIONS OF REPRESENTATION: THE INDICATIVE FUNCTION AND THE SEMANTIC FUNCTION

Vygotsky's analysis of semiotic mediation goes through two stages, which finally leads him to identify two aspects in the process of human psychological development. The first aspect involves the use of external psychological instruments and their material appropriation by the subject together with the psychological operations they make possible. The second begins with the process of interiorization; in this process, internal mediations are associated with a new dimension of the sign:

> In our previous works we ignored the fact that meaning is inherent to the sign (and changes with it). We started out from the principle of consistency of meaning, taking it out of the brackets ... If previously our task consisted in showing what there was in common between the "knot" [Vygotsky refers to the knot as a memory artifact, and as one of the three vestigial functions representing the origins of *external* instrumental mediation] and logical memory, it now consists in pointing out how they differ [...] From our work it emerges that the *sign modifies interfunctional relations*.
>
> (Vygotsky, 1933/1982/1990, p. 121; the clarifications in square brackets were added by the authors)

In the articulated logic of the functional circle, interiorization cannot simply entail the transfer of the externally mediated function to the inside; it means that the global organism–medium structure is profoundly altered due to the specificity of organism, to its oriented nature. As can be surmised from the previous quote, Vygotsky understands that *on the outside the sign has a different function from that which it has on the inside*. Outside, its function is *indicative*; inside, it is *semantic*. Therefore, interiorization involves not only the appropriation and individuation of the indicative function of the action externally mediated by words but also the *construction of virtual mental entities and actions mediated by meanings*. Private speech may be rooted in its external origin, which enables the person to initiate internally and evoke external actions, but above all, it allows for a new type of human activity in the new internal plane. In the new plane, the referents are no longer just objects and organisms mediated by signs but are concepts and subjects mediated by meanings.

> [...] Thought is not only externally mediated by signs; it is also mediated internally by meanings. The crux of the matter is that immediate communication of consciousness is impossible not only physically but psychologically. The communication of consciousness can be accomplished only indirectly, through a mediated path. This path consist in the internal mediation of thought first by meanings and then by words. Therefore, thought is never the direct equivalent of word meanings. Meaning mediates thought in its path to verbal expression. The path from thought to word is indirect and internally mediated. [...] We carried our analysis from the most external to the most internal plane. In the living *drama* of verbal thinking, movement takes the reverse path. It moves form the motive that gives birth to thought, to the formation of thought itself, to its mediation in the internal word, to the meanings of external words, and finally, to words themselves. [...] the complex fluid connections and transitions among the separate planes of verbal thinking, arise only in process of development. The isolation of meaning from sound, the isolation of word from thing, and the isolation of thought from word are necessary stages in the history of development of concepts.
>
> (Vygotsky, 1934/1982/1987, pp. 282–284) (italics added)

The more obvious and direct product of semiotic mediation is that it allows re-presentation of the stimulus. The less obvious and transforming product of semiotic mediation is that by re-presenting re-presentations a new kind of perception emerges, that of meanings. What is now relevant is that the referent of a meaning is not a fact, but rather a concept that works as an internal percept. This explains why Vygotsky was working at the end of his life on the psychological function of concepts and on the psychological function of *drama* as the core of a specifically human form of orientation to reality.

For Vygotsky, the interiorization process implies access to a new kind of speech and re-presentation that changes not only its scenario from the outside in, but also its operators, its objects, and its very logic of orientation to reality.

READING THE ZPD FROM AN ECOFUNCTIONAL PERSPECTIVE

The ecological and functional reading of Vygotsky's ideas as an attempt to remove the barriers between organism and medium, opening up a cultural ecology that goes hand in hand with an ecology of mind, allows for a new understanding of the ZPD as a core concept for future research and educational applications. The ZPD emerges as a zone of human development, the frontier territory with which we have become familiar through the work of Vygotsky; the territory where we can find the links between the situated-embodied mind and the cognitive mind, the individual mind and the social mind, the development already attained and the development to be attained.

The conceptual and methodological development of the ZPD, in this perspective, is undoubtedly an ambitious task that goes beyond the brief of the present work. Nevertheless, we can point to some essential aspects that emerge from the ecological and functional approach, which we feel should be kept in mind when undertaking such a task.

- *The ZPD as Zone of Syncretic Representation.* The human mind always operates through the simultaneous employment, in different proportions, of natural and cultural stimuli, but above all, of external mediated stimuli, or external re-presentations, and internal mediated stimuli, that is, representations with an external origin, but incorporated into the internal private mental action. Diagnostic and educational work in the ZPD requires *the joint consideration* of all these processes, internal, and external, in order to understand how we can change the external processes and, through them, eventually the internal processes. It is important to bear in mind that in the Vygotskian psychotechnical proposal, the construction of internal mental operations requires the prior construction of external mental actions to be accessible to the learner, and that this is precisely the viable mechanism of the ZPD; in order to take the child from the immediate level of presentation, re-presentation resources are required in the ecological zone of loaned and distributed functions.

- *The distributed mind is not a merely provisional resource in the human mind.* A conception that considers the isolated individual as the only form of mental functional organization would perhaps accept the mechanisms of functional distribution – social functional loans and instrumental mediations – but it would do so only in provisional terms, so that in the adult all of the mediated operations would already be fully appropriated and internalized as typical mental functions. However, the ecological analysis of the operations present in everyday life challenges this view of the subject as self-sufficient, in favor of a subject who continues to use and borrow external operations and operators throughout life (del Río, 2002). Thus, the conception of the ZPD as scaffolding that would achieve full internalization of all mental functioning should be revised in order to consider the ZPD, and education itself, from the ecology of the mind. This involves accepting the existence of nonindividual mental subjects – communities, institutions, cultures – and the notion that an individual maintains, throughout his life, a large part of his individual functional system distributed effectively in his personal *Umwelt*.

- *Making the ZPD concept operational requires the development of the practical engineering of the mind.* Vygotsky proposed two *psychotecniques*, or psychological techniques (although a term referring to psychological *engineering* would be more appropriate today), which he called the *psychotechnique of thinking* and *the psychotechnique of feelings*. The first of these techniques refers to the ambit we consider today as related to knowledge; the second, to the ambit of moral and social action. Only the combination of the two in educational contexts will give rise to a fully developed human being, and both can be operationalized in cultural–educational designs. This "operational," Vygotsky – who shares with other authors of his time, such as Binet or Janet, the assumptions of the educational construction of mental functions – appears to have been overlooked in many current speculative approaches to the concept of mediation and to that of ZPD. Even so, instructional designs of mediated operations and specific operators can be found in various fields of education in which proponents of Vygotsky's theories have worked.

- *Development of individuals and cultures.* In the sociocultural perspective of the distributed mind, it is accepted that nonindividual functional units, such as families, institutions, communities and cultures, also develop. Thus, the ZPD is a model that can and should be applied to them as well – all the more so if we bear in mind that the development of the individual psychological functional system and the development of these entities are interdependent. Therefore, diagnosing and designing the ZPD for an individual child will imply doing the same with for the ZPD of his nonindividual functional units with which his functional system is interdependent. As several authors have asserted, with regard to educational action in the ZPD it becomes clear how important it is to have access to the community's *funds of knowledge* (Moll, 1990, 2005), and to promote *functional accessibility, participation and appropriation* (Lave & Wenger, 1988; Rogoff, 1990) in the cultural psychological systems that constitute symbiotic niches for the child

- *The ZPD as Umwelt in evolution.* Activity in the ZPD is intended to create new mediated paths and strategies for perceiving and acting, and this implies new connections on the outside – the extracortical tissue of culture- and neurological- neoformations on the inside. But if the human cultural medium and the human mind are articulated, this articulation takes place in the context of a process of development; this makes the territory in which the mediations that produce development occur into a vast work scenario of the ZPD.

- *The ZPD as a method for an epistemology.* Having reached this point, we believe it can be appreciated that Vygotsky's general conception on changing human functional systems pulls the ZPD concept forward, and converts it into a diagnostic mechanism of the emergent and unpredictable historical psychological transformations. Even more, the Vygotskian approach demands that the ZPD turn into a tool for an epistemology of human mind in permanent historical evolution, as well as for the conscious active design of educational settings sensitive to the evolution, both of the child and of the functional systems.

APPLICATIONS OF
VYGOTSKY'S WORK

12 Pedagogy

INTRODUCTION

In this chapter, I will discuss the pedagogic implications of some aspects of Vygotsky's writing. I will draw heavily on his own words and seek to develop two major strands in the range of possible interpretations of his work. The central tension that I wish to explore is between those accounts that emphasize the analysis of the content of instruction as against those which are more concerned with forms of pedagogic interaction and participation. Arguably, many of the differences in emphasis and priority that have arisen reflect differences in what are, ultimately, political preferences. Vygotsky was well aware of the extent to which pedagogic practice is subject to social, cultural, and political influence.

> Pedagogics is never and was never politically indifferent, since, willingly or unwillingly, through its own work on the psyche, it has always adopted a particular social pattern, political line, in accordance with the dominant social class that has guided its interests.   (Vygotsky, 1997b, p. 348)

Vygotsky was suggesting a process of social formation in the formation of educational ideas. He distances himself from the naturalistic or common sense pedagogic positions that pervade so much political debate, particularly when the term *back to basics* is invoked. For him pedagogies arise and are shaped in particular social circumstances. Ironically, the text *Pedagogical Psychology* from which the above quote is drawn, was considered to be so politically unacceptable to the rulers of the Soviet state that one had to have a special pass from the KGB that would admit one to the restricted reading room in the Lenin Library where the book could be read (Davydov, 1993). My intention in this chapter is to outline some of the differences in pedagogical thinking that have been attributed to the influence of Vygotsky, which may have their origins in cultural differences. An account of pedagogic practice in which large-scale factors or macrofactors are integrated with microlevels of analysis. In this discussion, I will take the general definition offered by Bernstein as the operational specification of pedagogy:

> Pedagogy is a sustained process whereby somebody(s) acquires new forms or develops existing forms of conduct, knowledge, practice and criteria, from somebody(s) or something deemed to be an appropriate provider and evaluator. Appropriate either from the point of view of the acquirer or by some other body(s) or both.   (Bernstein, 1999, p. 259)

This definition emphasizes that conduct, knowledge, practice, and criteria may all be developed. This sets it apart from definitions that attend only to matters of skills and knowledge. It suggests that a complete analysis of processes of development and learning within pedagogic practice must consider cognitive and affective matters. It also suggests that pedagogic provision may be thought of in terms of material things as well as persons.

DEVELOPMENT

At this point of departure, it is probably worth remembering Vygotsky's own account of the term "development." In an introductory chapter, Norris Minick (1987), the translator of *The Collected Works of L. S. Vygotsky. Volume 1:* Problems of General Psychology, suggests that Vygotsky's work can be understood in terms of three phases. His position on *development* witnesses these phases. In *The Collected Works of L. S. Vygotsky, Volume 3,* a previously unpublished manuscript titled "On psychological systems" (Vygotsky, 1997), which was written in what Minick (1987) describes as Vygotsky's second phase, the following position is announced:

> Its main (and extremely simple) idea is that in the process of development, and in historical development of behaviour in particular, it is not so much the functions which change (these we mistakenly studied before). Their structure and the system of their development remain the same. What is changed and modified are the relationships, the links between the functions. New constellations emerge which were unknown in the preceding stage. That is why intrafunctional is often **not** essential in the transition from one stage to another. It is inter-functional changes, the changes of interfunctional connections and the interfunctional structure which matter.   (Vygotsky, 1997, p. 92)

However, by the time Vygostky had entered what Minick (1987) refers to as his third and final stage of work, a clear difference in the degree of emphasis on the social situation in development emerges. This is witnessed in *The Collected Works of L. S. Vygotsky. Volume 5*, in which an essay on "The problem of age" contains the following:

> The neoformations (new mental processes) that arise toward the end of a given age lead to a reconstruction of the whole structure of the child's consciousness and in this way change the whole system of relations to external reality and to himself. – the child becomes a completely different being than he was at the beginning of the age. But this necessarily also means that the social situation of development ... must also change since the social situation of development is nothing other than a system of relations between the child of a certain age and social reality.
>
> (Vygotsky, 1998, p. 199)

This chapter was to be placed in a book on child developmental psychology that was being written in last years of Vygotsky's life (1932–1934). This shift in emphasis presents a challenge to those of us who attempt to read his work in twenty-first century. We have to be mindful of the moment of Vygotsky's intellectual trajectory in which specific texts were written.

Given that the relationship between instruction and development was a major preoccupation for Vygotsky, we must remember that his views on the processes of development changed from an inter-functional analysis to one which placed much more emphasis on the relation between psychological structures and the social situation of development.

KEY ELEMENTS IN VYGOTSKY'S APPROACH TO PEDAGOGY

I will initiate the discussion with a reminder of the three of the central theoretical notions within his overall account of learning and development as mediated processes. This introduction will lead quickly from the general genetic law of cultural development to the Zone of Proximal Development (ZPD) and the distinction between scientific and everyday concepts. The major thrust of the analysis will be driven by the distinction between scientific and everyday concepts. However, these notions are highly interrelated. The discussion will reflect this interrelation.

In his ofted-quoted general genetic law of cultural development, Vygotsky proclaims the primacy of social influences on development:

> Every function in the child's cultural development appears twice: first, on the social level, and later, on the individual level; first between people (interpsychological), and then inside the child (intrapsychological). This applies equally to voluntary attention, to logical memory, and to the formation of concepts. All the higher functions originate as actual relations between human individuals.
>
> (Vygotsky, 1978, p. 57)

Vygotsky discussed the ZPD in terms of assessment and instruction. Within both of these frames of reference, he discussed the relationship between an individual learner and a supportive other(s) even if the other was not physically present in the context in which learning was taking place. The second account of the ZPD is to be found in *Thinking and Speech* (1934/1987), and is embedded in chapter 6, in which he discussed "The Development of Scientific Concepts in Childhood."

> We have seen that instruction and development do not coincide. They are two different processes with very complex interrelationships. Instruction is only useful when it moves ahead of development. When it does, it impels or awakens a whole series of functions that are in a stage of maturation lying in the zone of proximal development. This is the major role of instruction in development. This is what distinguishes the instruction of the child from the training of animals. This is also what distinguishes instruction of the child which is directed toward his full development from instruction in specialised, technical skills such as typing or riding a bicycle. The formal aspect of each school subject is that in which the influence of instruction on development is realized. Instruction would be completely unnecessary if it merely utilized what had already matured in the developmental process, if it were not itself a source of development.
>
> (Vygotsky, 1987, p. 212)

As Chaiklin (2003) reminds us, the reference made by Vygotsky was to instruction that is designed to support the development of psychological functions as these functions are transformed and reconfigured through particular age periods. Chaiklin suggests that much of what has been discussed under the rubric of the ZPD misses the central insistence on instruction that leads *development*. The distinction between microgenesis and ontogenesis is missed in, what, according to Chaiklin, are misinterpretations of the original formulation of ZPD in its instructional frame of reference. He suggests that terms such as *scaffolding* should be reserved for practices that are designed to teach specific skills and subject matter concepts that are not designed for instruction but are designed to serve explicitly developmental purposes (Chaiklin, 2003, p. 59). In this chapter, I will refer to what might be called developmental teaching as well on skills and concepts. The discussion of scaffolding, which follows later in the chapter, is informed by the distinction between the analysis of the content of instruction and the learner's role within the ZPD.

From 1927 to 1934 Vygotsky and his colleague Shif were particularly interested in two types of concepts: the scientific and the everyday or spontaneous. Vygotsky referred to *scientific concepts* as those that were introduced by a teacher in school and *spontaneous concepts* as those that were acquired by the child outside of the contexts in which explicit instruction was in place. Scientific concepts were described as those that form a coherent, logical hierarchical system. For Vygotsky scientific concepts are characterized by a high degree of generality, and their relationship to objects is mediated through other concepts. According to Vygotsky (1987), children can make deliberate use of scientific concepts, they are consciously aware of them, and they can reflect on these concepts. Rieber and Carton, the editors of the most recent translation of *Thinking and Speech* suggest that when Vygotsky (1987) uses the terms "spontaneous thinking" or "spontaneous concepts," he is referring to a context of formation, which is of immediate, social, practical activity as against a context of instruction in a formal system of knowledge. Scientific concepts are, through their very systematic nature, open to the voluntary control of the child.

For Vygotsky, cooperation and collaboration are crucial features of effective teaching.

> The development of the scientific concept, a phenomenon that occurs as part of the educational process, constitutes a unique form of systematic co-operation between the teacher and the child. The maturation of the child's higher mental functions occurs in this co-operative process, that is, it occurs through the adult's assistance and participation.... In a problem involving scientific concepts, he must be able to do in collaboration with the teacher something that he has never done spontaneously...we know that the child can do more in collaboration that he can independently. (Vygotsky, 1987, pp. 168–169, 216)

Vygotsky argued that the systematic, organized, and hierarchical thinking that he associated with scientific concepts becomes gradually embedded in every day referents and, therefore, achieves a general sense in the contextual richness of everyday thought. Vygotsky presented a model of an interdependant relationship between scientific and everyday (or spontaneous) concepts in the process of true concept formation. He argued that everyday thought is given structure and order in the context of systematic scientific thought. Vygotsky was keen to point out the relative strengths of scientific and everyday concepts as they both contributed to each other.

> The formation of concepts develops simultaneously from two directions: from the direction of the general and the particular....the development of a scientific concept begins with the verbal definition. As part of an organised system, this verbal definition descends to concrete.; it descends to phenomena which the concept represents. In contrast, the everyday concept tends to develop outside any definite system; it tends to move upwards toward abstraction and generalisation...the weakness of the

everyday concept lies in its incapacity for abstraction, in the child's incapacity to operate on it in a voluntary manner...the weakness of the
scientific concept lies in its verbalism, in its insufficient saturation with
the concrete.   (Vygotsky, 1987, pp. 163,168, 169)

Vygotsky argued that scientific concepts are not assimilated in ready
made or prepackaged form. He insisted that the two forms of concept are
brought into the forms of relationship within which they both develop.
An important corollary of this model of is the denial of the possibility
of direct pedagogic transmission of concepts.

> Pedagogical experience demonstrates that direct instruction in concepts
> is impossible. It is pedagogically fruitless. The teacher who attempts to
> uses this approach achieves nothing but a mindless learning of words,
> an empty verbalism that stimulates or imitates the presence of concepts
> in the child. Under these conditions, the child learns not the concept
> but the word, and this word is taken over by the child through memory
> rather than thought. Such knowledge turns out to be inadequate in any
> meaningful application. This mode of instruction is the basic defect of the
> purely scholastic verbal modes of teaching which have been universally
> condemned. It substitutes the learning of dead and empty verbal schemes
> for the mastery of living knowledge.   (Vygotsky, 1987, p. 170)

In "Educational Psychology," Vygotsky uses the analogy of a gardener
trying to affect the growth of a plant by directly tugging at its roots with
his hands from underneath the plant when he is criticizing teachers
who directly influence concept development in the student (Vygotsky,
1997b, p. 49). If concept development is to be effective in the formation
of scientific concepts, instruction must be designed to foster conscious
awareness of conceptual form and structure and thereby allow for individual access and control over acquired scientific concepts. It must also
foster the interaction and development of everyday concepts with scientific concepts. In one of his better-known examples of learning a foreign
language, Vygotsky raises the level of development of mother tongue
speech through enhanced conscious awareness of linguistic forms. Similarly, he suggests that by learning algebra, the child comes to understand
arithmetic operations as particular instantiations of algebraic operations. The scientific concepts of grammar and algebra are seen as means
by which thought is freed from concrete instances of speech or numerical
relations and is raised to a more abstract level (Vygotsky, 1987, p. 180).

By arguing that conceptual thinking positively influences not only
the cognitive domain but also aesthetic reactions and emotions, Van der
Veer (1994) suggests that Vygotsky's view of conceptual development is
overly rationalistic. For Wardekker (1998), the development of scientific

concepts also includes a moral dimension. He argues that "scientific (or scholarly) concepts are the products of reflection in a practice that includes choices about the future development of that praxis and are, in that sense, of a moral nature" (Wardekker, 1998, p. 143). This issue is recognized if not developed in theVygotsky's writing:

> [Thought] is not born of other thoughts. Thought has its origins in the motivating sphere of consciousness, a sphere that includes our inclinations and needs, our interests and impulses, and our affect and emotions. The affective and volitional tendency stands behind thought. Only here do we find the answer to the final "why" in the analysis of thinking.
>
> (Vygotsky, 1987, p. 282)

In summary, in the general genetic law of cultural development Vygotsky establishes his assertion concerning the formative effect of social, cultural, and historical influences. The notion of the ZPD establishes his position on the way in which instruction can lead development. Importantly, he acknowledges that not all instruction will serve a developmental function. It may, for example, only serve to promote skill acquisition. With the distinction between scientific and everyday concepts, he outlines his views on the complexities of true concept development. All three ideas can be deployed in arguments that attempt to justify particular approaches to formulation of the "what" and "how" of teaching.

The rest of this chapter will consist of an exploration of the proposals that have arisen as these concepts have been deployed in specific cultural contexts at particular historical moments. I will open with a discussion of those approaches that have placed emphasis on the analysis of the content of instruction that is designed to serve a developmental function. I will then discuss the work of those who use the scaffold metaphor of to illustrate their views on the arrangement of interpersonal relationships in the presentation of the content of instruction. I will also introduce aspects of the literature that have employed "apprenticeship" and "reciprocal teaching" as the dominant descriptor of pedagogic practice. This will lead to a broader discussion of the design of contexts for learning.

SOCIAL CONTEXTS FOR LEARNING: DEVELOPMENTAL TEACHING

Davydov (1988, 1990, 1995) insisted that the tradition of teaching empirical knowledge should be changed to a focus on teaching theoretical knowledge. He developed a "Developmental Teaching" program that pursued this goal. The connection between the spontaneous concepts that arise through empirical learning and the scientific concepts that develop through theoretical teaching is seen as the main dimension of the ZPD. The process of "ascending from the abstract to the concrete," which formed the core of Davydov's early work, has been extended by Hedegaard into a conceptualization of teaching and learning as a "double move" between situated activity and subject matter concepts. When working within this approach, general laws are used by teachers to formulate instruction and children investigate the manifestations of these general laws in carefully chosen examples that embody core concepts. These core concepts constitute the "germ cell" for subsequent learning. In practical activity, children grapple with the central conceptual relations that underpin particular phenomena. In this way, the teaching focuses directly on the scientific concepts that constitute the subject matter. Hedegaard (1998) suggests that "the teacher guides the learning activity both from the perspective of general concepts and from the perspective of engaging students in 'situated' problems that are meaningful in relation to their developmental stage and life situations" (Hedegaard, 1998, p. 120). Her account makes it clear that successful applications of this approach are possible, while indicating the enormous amount of work that will be required if such practices are to become both routine and effective.

The importance of the interplay between the scientific concepts derived in theoretical learning and the spontaneous concepts formed in empirical learning is central to this account of development. If the two forms do not "connect," then true concept development does not take place. Thus, theoretically driven content-based teaching that is not designed to connect with learners' everyday empirical learning will remain inert and developmentally ineffective.

Davydov is associated with the formulation of an approach to teaching and learning within which the analysis of theoretical knowledge is central. Davydov and his group, along with the now 2,500-school strong Association for Developmental Instruction, have done much to pursue the "Marxist epistemologist" interpretation of Vygotsky's work to which Rowlands alludes:

> ..... any consideration as to the conditions necessary to evoke develop-
> ment must have, as its starting point, the content of the body of knowl-
> edge (and by content I mean logical structure, its theoretical objects and
> the way these theoretical objects speak of the world). This ... is Vygotsky
> as 'marxist epistemologist' and the ZPD ought to be seen in the context
> of this epistemology.   (Rowlands, 2000, p. 541)

As Hedegaard and Chaiklin (1990) remind us, this body of work identifies the general developmental potential of particular forms of teaching as well as its specific microgenetic function. The assertion is that teaching should promote general mental development as well as the acquisition of special abilities and knowledge.

> Good teaching develops a capacity for relating to problems in a theoretical way, and to reflect on one's thinking. Davydov develops an extensive analysis of theoretical knowledge grounded in a materialist-dialectical philosophy. This concept contrasts with the concept of knowledge and thinking used by the cognitive and Piagetian traditions because it emphasises that knowledge is constituted by the relations between the object of knowledge and other objects, rather than some essential properties or characteristics that define the object.
>
> (Hedegaard & Chaiklin, 1990, p. 153)

Ivic (1989) also insists that Vygotsky's emphasis was not on the transmission and acquisition of a body of information alone. Vygotsky was concerned with the provision through education, of the tools, techniques, and intellectual operations that would facilitate development. He was critical of many forms of education that seemed to remain content with the transmission of knowledge. Ivic argued that schools do not always teach systems of knowledge but in many cases overburden learners with isolated and meaningless facts (Ivic, 1989, p. 434). This position was clearly established in some of Davydov's later writing.

> For the contemporary reform of Russian education, the following general ideas of Vygotsky are basic, ideas that have been set forth and made more precise by his students and followers. The first idea is that education, which includes both human teaching/learning and upbringing, is intended first of all to develop their personalities. The second idea is that the human personality is linked to its creative potentials; therefore, the development of the personality in the education system demands first of all the creation of conditions for discovering and making manifest the creative potentials of students. The third idea is that teaching/learning and upbringing assume personal activity by students as they master a variety of inner values; the student becomes a true subject in the process of teaching and upbringing. The fourth idea is that the teacher and the upbringer direct and guide the individual activity of the students, but they do not force or dictate their own will to them. Authentic teaching/learning and upbringing come through collaboration by adults with children and adolescents. The fifth idea is that the most valuable methods for students' teaching/learning and upbringing correspond to their development and individual particularities, and therefore these methods cannot be uniform.
>
> (Davydov, 1995, p. 13)

It is important to note that this was written some five years after the fundamental changes had taken place in the former Soviet Union. There were many points in his career when Davydov fell foul of the political scrutiny that existed under the former regime. His emphasis on creativity in the following extract may well have proved somewhat difficult for his political masters at a time when the place of the individual and subjectivity was undervalued and even repressed within the command control consciousness of the past. Here, he discusses his pedagogic contribution to the reform of the Soviet system of education. The key references here are to:

- The development of the whole personality, which always retains a profoundly social characteristic in the Russian language and culture;
- Creative potential – signaling a profound distance from ideologies of determination;
- The emphasis on values;
- The facilitative rather than dominating role of the pedagogue; and
- The need to respond to the diversity of learners with an appropriately diverse range of approaches.

In the recently published "Educational Psychology," Vygotsky announced that, "the fundamental prerequisite of pedagogics inevitably demands an element of individualisation, that is, conscious and rigorous determination of the individualised goals of education for each pupil" (Vygotsky, 1997b, p. 324). This suggestion of responsiveness to diversity rather than imposition of "sameness" in learning and teaching, has still to permeate many practices in the field. Davydov's program advocates pedagogic responsiveness to an individual learner within a framework that is supported by concepts of theoretical knowledge.

Teaching in this way will involve three levels of analysis:

1. A logical analysis of the content of instruction,
2. Psychological analysis of the capabilities of the child in order that the material may be taught in a way that is meaningful to the learner,
3. Pedagogical analysis to identify the teaching procedures.

A curriculum built through these forms of analysis should be dynamic and responsive. As Karpov (2003) reminds us scientific concepts only act as mediators of thinking and problem solving when supported by relevant procedural knowledge. He contrasts Russian approaches, such as those developed by Davydov, with North American guided-discovery pedagogies that he claims serve only to promote empirical learning rather than the theoretical learning that leads to the acquisition of scientific knowledge comprising scientific concepts and relevant procedures.

SOCIAL CONTEXTS FOR LEARNING: SCAFFOLDING

The scaffolding approach has tended to concentrate rather more on distribution across people rather than artifacts or things. Crucially, scaffolding involves simplifying the learner's role rather than the task. In contrast to Developmental Teaching, with its emphasis on the role of appropriate forms of content that will promote development, in scaffolding the overall emphasis is on the creation of a pedagogic context in which combined teacher and learner effort results in a successful outcome. Scaffolding and Developmental Teaching represent fundamentally different degrees of emphasis in the theoretical interpretation and practical implementation of the ZPD.

In an important review of the field, Stone (1998) notes that the term *scaffolding* was originally used as an instructional metaphor in a largely pragmatic and atheoretical manner. He suggests that Cazden (1979) was the first writer to make an explicit reference to Vygotsky's work in connection with the term. Wood, Bruner, and Ross (1976) had previously defined *scaffolding* as a form of adult assistance that enables a child or novice to solve a problem, carry out a task, or achieve a goal that would be beyond his unassisted efforts. They envisaged a process whereby the adult controlled those elements of the task that were initially beyond the learner's capacity thus allowing the learner to complete those that were within existing capabilities.

The way in which combined effort is conceptualized varies as a function of the theoretical metaphors which guide particular authors. For example, Cole and Engeström (1993) invoke the terms of distributed cognition in their portrayal of the requirements for the teaching of reading. They present an image of a teaching system that is "stretched across" other things and people.

> (a) The cognitive processing involved in learning to read is not an individual matter; the requisite cognitive processes are distributed among teacher, pupil, other students, and the cultural artefacts around which they co-ordinate in the activity called teaching/learning to read;
>
> (b) The expected future state, mature reading, must somehow be present at the beginning of instruction as constraints enabling the development

of the to-be-acquired new system of mediation, mature reading. . . . the combined child-adult system . . . can co-ordinate the child's act of reading before the child can accomplish this activity for him-her self.

(Cole & Engeström, 1993, pp. 23–24)

Mehan (1997) reported that ethnomethodological studies of interactional activities arenormative procedures that sustain interaction and the skills and abilities that students must use to appear competent in a classroom. This research serves as an important reminder that nonverbal modalities are functional in scaffolded instruction. The term *scaffolding* could be taken to infer a "one-way" process within the "scaffolder" constructs the scaffold alone and presents it for use to the novice. Newman, Griffin, and Cole (1989) argued that the ZPD is created through negotiation between the more advanced partner and the learner, rather than through the donation of a scaffold as some kind of prefabricated climbing frame. There is a similar emphasis on negotiation in Tharp and Gallimore (1988b), who discussed "teaching as assisted performance," in those stages of the ZPD where assistance is required. The key question here seems to be with respect to where the "hints," "supports," or "scaffold" comes from. Are they produced by "the more capable partner" or are they negotiated? Vygotsky is unclear on this matter.

> Vygotsky never specified the forms of social assistance to learners that constitute a ZPD. . . . He wrote about collaboration and direction, and about assisting children 'through demonstration, leading questions, and by introducing the initial elements of the task's solution.' . . . but did not specify beyond these general prescriptions.   (Moll, 1990, p. 11)

Moll (1990) suggested that the focus of change within the ZPD should be on the creation, enhancement, and communication of meaning through the collaborative use of mediational means rather than on the transfer of skills from the more to less capable partner. Therefore, even within the "scaffolding" interpretation there are fundamental differences. A rigid scaffold may appear little different from a task analysis produced by teaching that has been informed by applied behavior analysis. A negotiated scaffold would arise in a very different form of teaching and may well be associated with collaborative activity as discussed by Moll. From the perspective of Developmental Teaching, it is very unclear as to whether the content of scaffolded instruction would serve a developmental function.

It remains the case that most of Vygotsky's writing tends to focus on the more immediate interactional/interpersonal antecedents of independent or seemingly independent functioning. The first important implication of this for pedagogy is that teaching and assessment should be focused on the potential of the learner, rather than on a demonstrated level of achievement or understanding. The second is that teaching, or instruction, should create the possibilities for development, through the kind of active participation that characterizes collaboration, that should be socially negotiated, and that should entail transfer of control to the learner.

Cazden's (1979) study drew attention to the parallels that exist between parent–child language games and some of the forms of discursive practice that take place in classrooms The promotion of parent–child interaction as a model for teacher–child interaction was also advocated by Langer and Applebee (1986) who identified five key factors in what they considered to be effective scaffolding:

- *ownership* (of the activity to be learned);
- *appropriateness* (to the student's current knowledge);
- *structure* (embodying a 'natural' sequence of thought and action)
- *collaboration* (between teacher and student) and
- *internalization* (via gradual withdrawal of the scaffolding and transfer of control).

It would seem that not all these factors are realized in what may be the dominant forms of classroom practice. Bliss, Askew, and Macrae, (1996) set out to explore and identify scaffolding strategies in three specific primary schooling contexts: design and technology, mathematics, and science. Their claim is that scaffolding specialist knowledge is very difficult in some classrooms. One interpretation of their findings is that much attempted "scaffolding" takes place in a context where there is insufficient understanding of the distinctions that Davydov and Hedegaard make between forms of knowledge. In terms of Vygotsky's original theory, their suggestion is that manipulation of assistance within a ZPD without an understanding of the distinction between scientific and spontaneous concepts is of limited value.

> To imagine that socially constructed knowledge in areas like science, technology or mathematics is everyday knowledge is to misunderstand the purpose of schooling, which is the pupil's initiation into grappling with the theoretical objects of these domains.
>
> (Bliss, Askew, & Macrae, 1996, p. 60)

This echoes Kozulin's (1998) claim that entering formal schooling requires a repositioning with respect to knowledge on the part of the pupils. The skills required for sensitive pedagogic assistance and the understanding of the scientific concepts that constitute the knowledge domain become necessary features of effective teaching and learning that make claims to a Vygotskian root.

Cole and Griffin (1984) mount a strong criticism of the scaffold-ing metaphor based on the extent to which the child's creativity is underplayed. They draw on the work of the Russian physiologist Nicholas Bernstein and A. N. Leontiev. From Bernstein they borrow an emphasis on essential creativity in all forms of living movement, and, borrowing from Leontiev, they pursue the notion of "leading activity." The argument that different settings and activities give rise to "spaces" within the ZPD for creative exploration rather than pedagogic domina-tion is at the heart of their position.

> Adult wisdom does not provide a teleology for child development. Social organization and leading activities provide a gap within which the child can develop novel creative analyses.   (Griffin & Cole, 1984, p. 62)

SOCIAL CONTEXTS FOR LEARNING: RECIPROCAL TEACHING

Brown and Palincsar (1989) and Palincsar and Brown (1984) have devel-oped a cooperative-learning system for the teaching of reading, called *reciprocal teaching*. The teacher and learners assemble in groups of two to seven and read a paragraph together silently. A person assumes the "teacher" role and formulates a question on the paragraph. The group, whose members are playing roles of producer and critic simultaneously, addresses this question. The "teacher" advances a summary, and makes a prediction or clarification, if any is needed. The role of teacher then rotates, and the group proceeds to the next paragraph in the text. The reciprocal teaching method uses a combination of modeling, coaching, scaffolding, and fading to achieve impressive results, with learners show-ing dramatic gains in comprehension, retention, and far transfer over sustained periods.

The reciprocal teaching approach then involves

1. summarizing: identifying and paraphrasing the main idea in the text;
2. questioning: generating: self-questioning about the type of infor-mation that is generally tapped on tests of comprehension and recall;
3. clarifying: discerning when there has been a breakdown in com-prehension and taking the necessary action to restore meaning (e.g., reading ahead, rereading, asking for assistance);
4. predicting: hypothesizing what the structure and content of the text suggest will be presented next (from Palincsar & Brown, 1988).

Palincsar and Brown suggest that strategies such as predicting, questioning, summarizing, and clarifying help readers to anticipate information they will encounter, to integrate what is presented in the text with prior knowledge, to reconstruct prior knowledge, and help teachers to monitor for understanding. Once the children become expert in the use of these skills, they will be of general value in a wide range of contexts. A central issue here is not just that the children are instructed in these skills but also that they may enact them in a context in which particular forms of communication take place. The success of the intervention depends on a broader form of social organization within the classroom.

> Theory and research suggest that these thinking skills be instructed in a manner that promotes expert scaffolding and guided practice in a supportive and collaborative context. Such a context is created when teachers and their students engage in dialogue about text.
>
> (Palincsar & Brown, 1988, p. 58)

This type of approach may be thought of as one in which pupils are required to externalize their self-regulatory practices in order to open them to instruction. Palincsar and Brown (1988) achieved this in the context of acting out problem solving with pupils.

> Pedagogies which do not attend to ways in which understanding develops may, in practice, reconstruct the curriculum subject in such a way that makes real learning more difficult. The scientific concepts of the curriculum subject may be hidden from instruction that is aimed at the production of particular 'performances'. Practices such as reciprocal teaching aim to make explicit those aspects of the curriculum that too often remain tacit for too many learners.

Pupils may cooperate with teachers or more-able peers in an activity that is more complex than they can understand when working on their own.

> Characterizing a relationship as *horizontal* does not exclude the possibility that some members are more capable than others at some given moment. It only means that roles among members are changeable in interaction. Thus the vertical horizontal distinction should be taken as a continuum rather than a dichotomy.
>
> (Hatano & Inagaki, 1991, p. 333)

In reciprocal teaching, the child works with the teacher's understanding of a subject without necessarily being directly taught. Newman, Griffin, and Cole provide an important account of the process of social mediation in learning to divide. They studied division because it provides a clear example of learning in which responsibility is transferred from teacher to learner and then back from the learner to teacher in a series of cycles of increasing understanding and learning control.

> The problem facing the student can be phrased as follows: the student must acquire the concept, 'gazinta' (goes into). At the outset, the child is confronted with the confusing request to say how many times '5 gazinta 27'. Before this time in the arithmetic curriculum, the child has worked on 'number facts', viz., 'five 5s are 25; five 6s are 30' and only 'three 9s' or 'nine 3s' are 27. So, how can 5 'go into' 27? Five can 'go into' 25 or 30; but only 3 or 9 can 'go into' 27! Expert skill in carrying out the procedure actually calls for an initial estimate of the quotient, which is then checked and adjusted in the subsequent steps., the initial step of estimating is a very difficult thing to explain to the novice who does not yet know what it is that one is attempting to estimate!
>
> (Newman et al., 1989)

SOCIAL CONTEXTS FOR LEARNING: PROLEPTIC INSTRUCTION

Prolepsis may occur in reciprocal teaching and many other pedagogic settings. The term refers to a communication that leaves implicit some information that may be provided subsequently. Its literal meaning is the representation of a future act or development as existing. Proleptic instruction may also suggest instruction that takes place in anticipation of competence. Therefore, a learner may be encouraged to participate in an activity, which, as yet, they cannot perform alone. This assumption or anticipation of competence in a social context supports the individual's efforts encourages the learner to make sense of the situation in a powerful way. Here again the emphasis on creativity on the part of the learner is key. Cole (1996) outlines an approach to the teaching of reading known as "Question-Asking-Reading" in which he invokes his emphasis on agency.

> I believe it is useful to conceive of the overall process of learning to read in developmental terms as a process of *re*-mediation, mediating the behaviour of the group and each individual in it in a qualitatively new way. Emphasizing the re in remediation also serves to remind us that the children were not blank slates at the start of instruction.
>
> (Cole, 1996, p. 285)

Reid and Stone (1991) note, what is meant within proleptic instruction is not only determined by the physical context, however, but also depends on the social context of the *adult's intended goal*. Thus, the child is led to infer a new perspective, one that is the *joint product* of the child's own initial perspective and that of the adult.

There is a danger with the use of the term scaffolding that it could become applied so widely and frequently that it loses any meaning beyond some reference to teaching and learning. Given that the term came into use without reference to a particular set of theoretical assumptions, it runs the risk of being appropriated and transformed by almost any set of pedagogic and/or psychological assumptions.

Stone (1998) identifies four key features of the use of scaffolding that also typify reciprocal teaching. These features are useful in that they, at minimum, place some sort of boundary around the use of the term. These features are

1. The recruitment by an adult of a child's involvement in a meaningful and culturally desirable activity beyond the child's current understanding or control;

2. The titration of the assistance provided using a process of "online diagnosis" of the learner's understanding and skill level and the estimation of the amount of support required;

3. The support is not a uniform prescription – it may vary in mode (e.g., physical gesture, verbal prompt, extensive dialogue) as well as in amount;

4. The support provided is gradually withdrawn as control over the task is transferred to the learner.

Because the term *scaffolding* has become overextended in its use, there are a number of others terms that require consideration. Much of the literature focuses on adults, whether they are parents or teachers, as "scaffolders." The literature on *peer tutoring* suggests that this is a serious omission. However, it is also clear that peer tutoring is only effective in specific circumstances. Jonathan Tudge and his colleagues have done much to clarify the potential for peer tutoring within a Vygotskian approach to teaching and learning. Tudge and Rogoff (1989) argue that social interaction does not carry "blanket benefits" and that the circumstances in which social interaction facilitates development need to be carefully specified. They suggest that changes of perspective may be brought about in the free verbal interchange that typifies peer interaction. The central characteristic of effective interaction was seen to be the establishment of intersubjectivity irrespective of whether adults or peers were involved and irrespective of whether the situation was one that embodied Piaget's *cognitive conflict* or Vygotsky's *joint problem solving*.

SOCIAL CONTEXTS FOR LEARNING: COGNITIVE APPRENTICESHIP

The term "cognitive apprenticeship" has been used by Collins (1991) and Collins, Brown, and Newman (1989) among others, to refer to an instructional model informed by the social situation in which an apprentice might work with a master craftsperson in traditional societies. It is also informed by Rogoff and Lave's (1984) work on the way that learning takes place in everyday informal environments. One of the limitations of this model is with respect to the modeling of "ideal" learning environments that may not be attainable within the institutional constraints of schooling.

The cognitive apprenticeship approach proposes that learners should engage in meaningful learning and problem solving while working with authentic problems. This question of authenticity seems to raise key problems. Vygotsky's distinction between the everyday and the scientific would lead to the suggestion that if "authentic problems" in "authentic settings" are to form the content of a curriculum then they should be selected very carefully. Following, Davydov they should be problems that lead to theoretical learning.

The radically situated account of knowledge and learning must be placed within a political analysis of power and control. If not, those who are situated in advantaging contexts will be further advantaged. The cognitive apprentice approach opens the question of the relationship between the schooled and the everyday, and yet, it seems to close the question by attempting to place the schooled in the everyday. This seems to ignore the suggestion that schooling may be capable of helping to transcend the constraints of the everyday. Both scientific and everyday concepts are a necessary part of development.

Hedegaard (1998) extends this argument and proposes three key "anchor" or reference points: (a) everyday life situations that are characteristic to the community; (b) subject matter areas (problem areas that are relevant for society life and that have dominated the difference sciences through time and develop central concepts and procedures of science); and (c) the learning subjects and their development (Hedegaard, 1998, p. 117).

SOCIAL CONTEXTS FOR LEARNING: INSTRUCTIONAL CONVERSATIONS

In their work on instructional conversations, Tharp and Gallimore (1988a, 1988b) propose that teachers should act to "weave together everyday and schooled understanding." The skilled teacher brings, or weaves, together pupil perspectives and understandings with those that she seeks to promote in the classroom. This process builds on pupil prior knowledge and understanding with the ideas and concepts the teacher wishes to explore with them. Here instruction and conversation are woven together. Tharp (1993) has provided a summary of the types of instruction that have been seen to provide assistance to "bring the performance of the learner through the ZPD into an independent capacity" where the "means of assistance are woven into a meaningful dialogue." In the instructional conversation approach parents and teachers are asked to engage in a meaningful instructional dialogue with the child and to help connect their existing understanding with the knowledge and understanding that holds sway in schooling.

SOCIAL CONTEXTS FOR LEARNING: FUNDS OF KNOWLEDGE

Moll and his colleagues (e.g., Moll & Greenberg, 1990; Moll, 1990; Moll, 2000) have taken a similar tack in that they seek to enrich academic understanding with those understandings that have been acquired through participation in communities that have accrued "funds of knowledge." Moll argues that schools should draw on the social and cognitive contributions that parents and other community members can make to children's development. Through anthropologically driven studies of learning in clusters of households much has been learned about the ways in which knowledge is built and acquired in such settings. After-school clubs are used as settings in which the richness of the community knowledge funds can be brought together with the academic purposes of the teaching. The afterschool clubs were designed so that multiple goals could be pursued. The children engaged in meaningful activities in which valued outcomes were achieved. Teachers ensured that academic progress was facilitated in the context of these activities.

Rowlands presents a strident critique of this approach arguing that it fails to incorporate an understanding of Vygotsky's position on epistemology which he attributes to Marx.

> Survival strategies (or "funds of knowledge") of the oppressed cannot be used to facilitate a scientific and objective understanding of the world (this is a Marxist position despite how "politically incorrect" it may sound)! ... A scientific understanding has to be developed from "above" in school; it cannot come from "below", in the everyday experience of having to survive in the world. (Rowlands, 2000, p. 558)

Moll and Greenberg (1990) argue that connections are made between the intellectual resources of home and school. They suggest that scientific concepts *are* to be found in the funds of knowledge that are developed in communities.

> Vygotsky (1987) wrote that in "receiving instruction in a system of knowledge, the child learns of things that are not before his eyes, things that far exceed the limits of his actual and even potential immediate experience" (p. 180). We hardly believe that rote instruction of low-level skills is the system of knowledge that Vygotsky had in mind. We perceive the students' community, and its funds of knowledge, as the most important resource for reorganizing instruction in ways that "far exceed" the limits of current schooling. An indispensable element of our approach is the creation of meaningful connections between academic and social life through the concrete learning activities of the students. We are convinced that teachers can establish, in systemic ways, the necessary social relations outside classrooms that will change and improve what occurs within the classroom walls. These social connections help teachers and students to develop their awareness of how they can use the everyday to understand classroom content and use classroom activities to understand social reality.   (Moll & Greenberg, 1990, pp. 345–346)

SOCIAL CONTEXTS FOR LEARNING: COMMUNITY OF LEARNERS

Brown, Metz, and Campione (1996) report the outcomes of the Community of Learners project (e.g., Brown & Campione, 1990, 1994). This has developed to meet the needs of inner-city children as they engage in science education. The project has been concerned with what should be taught, when it should be taught and how it should be evaluated. In doing so, they have drawn on both Vygotsky and Piaget's work. Piaget's work has informed the design of a developmental science curriculum. They draw on the later functionalist period of Piaget's work rather than the earlier structuralist work, which they see as having led to a consistent underestimation of young learners' capability (Piaget, 1978). Vygotsky's work has informed the design of social contexts for learning. Brown, Metz, and Campione suggest that a learning community is a context within which multiple zones of proximal development are in place simultaneously. It is envisaged that each learner can pursue different sequences and progress through different routes each at their own pace. Therefore, the classroom is seen as a setting in which multiple, overlapping zones of proximal development are supported. This support is made available through the system of practices that make up the Community of Learners project.

The Community of Learners project seeks to promote the formation of discursive practice that is typical of academic discourse in general and scientific discourse in particular. This involves the active promotion of discourse that features constructive discussion, questioning, and criticism as part of its expected and familiar practice. Dialogic participant structures are maintained and supported in face-to-face activities; through print or electronic mail. Importantly, the project seeks to promote the appropriation of such discursive tools in that it is intended that they become part of the thought processes of community members. Minick et al. (1993) argue that within a Vygotskian framework modes of thinking are seen to evolve as integral systems of motives, goals, values, and beliefs that are closely tied to concrete forms of social practice. Brown, Metz, and Campione (1996) suggest that within the Community of Learners project dialogues provide the format for novices to adopt the discourse structure, goals, values, and belief systems of scientific practice. Over time, the community of learners adopts a common voice, a common knowledge base, and a shared system of meaning, beliefs, and activity.

Communities of learners within which communities of discourse evolve are contexts for the constant negotiation of meaning. Brown, Metz, and Campione (1996) also argue that scientific modes of speculation, evidence, and proof become part of the common voice. It is here that they invoke a version of Vygotsky's views on the relationship between scientific and everyday concepts.

> Successful enculturation into the community leads participants to relinquish everyday versions of speech activities having to do with the physical and natural world and replace them with discipline embedded special versions of the same activities.
>
> (Brown, Metz, & Campione, 1996, p. 162)

They suggest that through mutual appropriation, ideas and concepts migrate throughout the community. These ideas may be introduced by any of the participants and may or may not become established within the community. In this way, Brown, Metz, and Campione (1996) describe an intervention that has sought inspiration from Vygotsky for the design and theory of communication and participation. Vygotsky is seen as the inspiration for the design of social sites for learning rather than for the formulation of the content of the curriculum.

Bentley (1998) has proposed that the educational system should look beyond the classroom for social sites for learning. Although well-intentioned, this approach awaits reconciliation with the questions that Vygotsky raised about forms of learning and conceptual development. Moll (1990) and Tharp and Gallimore (1988) have moved some way toward an answer by seeking to connect the everyday development with the schooled development. Their focus has not been on what should count as the "scientific concepts" of schooling. This is the question that Davydov (1988) and Hedegaard (1990) raise as to what sort of content will seek to promote development. The primary distinctions are between tasks in which microgenetic progress may be witnessed and assessed and those activities that serve a genuinely ontogenetic function. One of the many problems associated with this position is that although much time may be expended connecting the everyday development with the schooled development, that which constitutes the schooled development may not embody scientific concepts or the potential for the development of scientific concepts. The formulation of the content, sequence, and criteria of evaluation of the curriculum in school may be subject to many influences and pressures. These pressures may serve immediate political purposes and/or reiterate historical traditions. The extent to which cultural artifacts, such as the school curriculum, are structured with principles of learning and development in mind is open to speculation.

In arguing the case for curriculum design that is informed by Vygotsky's position on conceptual development, I echo the imperatives announced by writers such as Hedegaard and Davydov. The challenge that they in turn face is in finding settings and circumstances in which learners will best participate in appropriate learning experiences.

SOCIAL CONTEXTS FOR LEARNING: THE FIFTH DIMENSION

Michael Cole's work on the after-school educational program that he has named the Fifth Dimension is a good example of an intervention that aims to create sustainable forms of educational activity through collaborative learning with a strong emphasis on play and imagination. The Fifth Dimension aims to sustain a context that can, through the promotion of collaborative learning, create possibilities for children to become motivated and actively involved in their own development.

Nicolopoulou and Cole (1993) showed how sociocultural differences between the broader contexts for learning at Fifth Dimension sites require investigation. Their analysis points to the need to consider the concept of pedagogy at a level beyond the interpersonal level. The broader sociocultural and institutional dimensions of pedagogy are often omitted from the analysis and,therefore, the formulation of what is appropriate. Nicolopoulou and Cole have shown how notionally the same intervention manifests in different ways as a function of broader cultural differences. Yet, so much of the post Vygotskian approach to pedagogy is truncated to operate at the interpersonal level only. Even within one sociocultural setting, some children may need to achieve a balance between different priorities. Different sociocultural contexts may evoke different balances in priority.

SOCIAL CONTEXTS FOR LEARNING: THIRD SPACE PEDAGOGY

Gutierrez and Stone (2000) have used the term script in the analysis of classroom discourse. Their concern is with the way in which official scripts and counterscripts affect learning in the classroom. They are particularly interested in the way in which the discourse of subversion takes place and results in a resistant discourse which serves to create alternative goals and tasks for students who feel marginal within the official script. Using an activity theory approach they analyze the possibilities for a "third space" in which conflict and difference is brought into productive play. Theirs is an attempt to examine the relationship between the interpersonal and the larger community. Lee's (2000) work is suggestive of where this way of conceptualizing the pedagogic task may lead. She has developed an instructional intervention that she terms "cultural modeling," which aims to provide students with explicit strategies for engaging with problems such as those of irony, symbolism, and point of view. Through this modeling the use of language known as "signifying" used in fractions of the African American community can be harnessed to provide support the acquisition of complex skills in the interpretation of literature. Through such modeling, a connection is made between everyday and scientific concepts in what may be seen as a "third pedagogic space."

O'Connor and Michaels (1993) argue that a shared classroom culture is a basic requirement of a context in which students learn to take themselves seriously as learners and see all other students as fellow learners, while fully engaging with the relevant academic content. The creation of such a culture must therefore be a pedagogic intention, which lies beyond a narrow and constrained view of the immediate task demand. It involves the teachers in detailed and demanding coordination of the academic task and social participation structure. Reid summarizes his concerns about the limitations of narrowly construed scaffolding approaches in terms of the wider pedagogic differences that may distinguish between classrooms and schools.

> Careful analyses of the participation structures teachers create in schools not only would reveal the strengths and weaknesses of our scaffolding techniques for bringing about achievement, but also would alert us to possible unintended outcomes, such as the ones just mentioned – disadvantaging students who are unfamiliar with, and unpracticed in using, the particular participation structure; controlling students' responses in ways that lead to under estimation of their communicative competence and abilities; constructing power relations that establish the teacher as sole arbiter of 'truth' and limiting the flow of social interactions among students. By becoming explicit in our thinking bout classroom participant structures, we can learn to use them fairly.   (Reid, 1998, p. 392)

CONCLUSION

Throughout this chapter, I have discussed a range of forms of pedagogic practice that espouse a Vygotskian root or influence. This influence is witnessed in the emphasis on the social dimension of psychological functioning. The notion of the primacy of the social plane in the general genetic law of cultural development drives and directs formulations of pedagogy as it seeks to theorize and describe the key elements of the social plane. With the concept of the ZPD, Vygotsky establishes a position on the way in which learning may serve a developmental function. It is within the ZPD that the interplay between scientific and everyday concepts may be fostered. Vygotsky stressed the importance of appropriate forms of interaction and content if the teaching and learning process is indeed to serve a developmental function rather than a skill-formation function. However, as has been shown in this chapter, the range of interpretations and pedagogic developments of his work have witnessed varying degrees of emphasis on the importance of interaction and the selection of content. Kozulin et al. (2003) open the introduction to their recently published edited volume with the following observation on cultural differences in pedagogic practice.

> What are the differences among American, German, and Japanese classrooms? If we take as a cue the anecdote told by Stigler and Hiebert (1999) in their book *The Teaching Gap*, in a Japanese classroom there are students and there is knowledge and the teacher serves as a mediator between them. In a German classroom there are also knowledge and students, but teachers perceive this knowledge as their property and dispense it to students as they think best. In the American classroom there are teachers and there are students, but the status of knowledge is uncertain.   (Kozulin, 2003, p. 1)

Although it is clear that there is no evidence of a determining effect of culture on the implementation and reformulation of Vygotsky's ideas, there is evidence that suggests that these changes have been shaped by the cultural contexts in which they have emerged. For example, the degree of emphasis within Scandinavian, German, and Russian writing on the selection of appropriate forms of instructional content in pedagogic activity as compared with the much higher level of emphasis placed on interaction in the US, Latin America, and Iberia. Clearly, there is a considerable degree of variation within these cultural contexts. In theoretical terms, one could consider the roots of the variation within cultures in terms of the subject positions. That is, the position that subjects (authors, researchers) have been ascribed is taken up with the field established within the culture. I opened this chapter with a quote from Vygotsky in which he notes the political influence on the formation of pedagogy. When we consider the ways in which Vygotsky has been considered as the primary influence on pedagogic advances, I would venture to suggest that there is evidence to support the assertion that I cited at the opening of this chapter.

> Pedagogics is never and was never politically indifferent, since, willingly or unwillingly, through its own work on the psyche, it has always adopted a particular social pattern, political line, in accordance with the dominant social class that has guided its interests. (Vygotsky, 1997b, p. 348)

The differences in the interpretation of Vygotsky's ideas could be taken as evidence of the same processes of cultural–historical formation that he outlined with reference to child development. There is clearly much to be done if we are to benefit fully from Vygotsky's pedagogic legacy. The logical and pedagogical analysis that developmental teaching requires is underdeveloped, particularly in the west. The reformulation of pedagogic work requires detailed scrutiny of its current state of functioning as well as that of its historical roots. The tensions and dilemmas that would be revealed in such an analysis could constitute the starting points for the development of more advanced forms of pedagogic work.

13 Sociocultural Theory and Education of Children with Special Needs

From Defectology to Remedial Pedagogy

Was the issue of the development and education of children with special needs chosen by Vygotsky, or was it a chance encounter forced by circumstances? We may never be able to find a definitive answer to this question. Vygotsky left no diary, and the testimony of his colleagues does not shed much light on this issue. What is known with certainty is that young Vygotsky's original interests lay in the field of literature and humanities and apparently remained so following his graduation from Moscow University in 1917. The unmerciful reality of everyday life in his hometown of Gomel during the civil war (1918–1922), however, forced everyone – including Vygotsky – to seek any occupation that would make mere survival possible. For Vygotsky, a teacher's job, first at school and then at the Teacher Training College, was such an opportunity. It is apparently under these rather extreme circumstances that Vygotsky encountered the problem of children with special needs for the first time. As the head of the psychological laboratory at the Gomel Teacher Training College, Vygotsky was responsible both for teaching students the techniques of psychological evaluation and actually supervising these evaluations in schools (Van der Veer & Valsiner, 1991; Vygodskaya & Lifanova, 1996, 1999).

This link to the issue of special needs was further strengthened after Vygotsky's move to Moscow in 1924. As with his previous experiences in Gomel, we cannot be sure whether it was Vygotsky's growing interest in special-needs children or the social circumstances that led to his affiliation with the Section of Abnormal Children in the Peoples Education Commissariat of Education. After all, the new post-Revolutionary government was poised to revamp the entire system of education, including special-needs services. In 1926 Vygotsky organized a Medical-Pedagogic Laboratory for the Study of Abnormal Children and in 1929 this laboratory was expanded to become the Experimental Institute of Defectology – currently the Institute of Corrective Pedagogy in Moscow.

Vygotsky's interest in the study and treatment of children with special needs, which started in the early 1920s, continued to the end of his life and career. His paper "The Problem of Mental Retardation" was published posthumously in 1935 (see Vygotsky, 1993). In addition to such general topics as defect and compensation and the sociocultural nature of special needs, Vygotsky also wrote on the education of deaf and blind children, the role of peer interaction for the special-needs child, and the question of "integration" or "mainstreaming" (see Vygotsky, 1983, 1993). Apart from leaving a rich collection of writings, Vygotsky also trained the whole group of psychologists and special education teachers who continued working in the Institute of Defectology after his death in 1934. In many ways, Vygotsky became firmly associated with the field bearing the strange name of "defectology" (*defektologija*).

WHAT IS DEFECTOLOGY?

The term "defeklologija," in Russian, simply means "the study of defects." This term was well-suited to the mechanistic mentality of the 1920s that explicitly compared human beings with mechanisms. If the mechanism is malfunctioning, the defect should be found, classified, and fixed; likewise if the human organism is malfunctioning, the mental or sensorial defect should be identified and corrected. In the Russia of Vygotsky's time, and until the late 1980s, this term covered the following disabilities: the hard of hearing and deaf ("surdo-pedagogica"), the visually impaired and blind ("tiflo-pedagogica"), children with mental retardation ("oligophreno-pedagogica"), and speech- and language-impaired children ("logopedia") (Petrovsky & Yaroshevsky, 1998, p. 364). The field of defectology was comprehensive in the sense that it included diagnosis and treatment as well as research and the university-level training of the specialists called "defectologists."

What was unquestionably unique was the social situation in which Russian defectology found itself in the 1920s. Among the primary victims of the October Revolution and the civil war were children, often orphaned, and almost universally suffering from malnutrition, enforced relocation, and a lack of education. What was difficult for the so-called regular children was twice as hard for children with special needs. The complexity and social interconnectedness of these problems is well-expressed in the very title of the congress convened by the Soviet government in 1920 – The Congress for the Struggle against Child Defectiveness, Homelessness, and Delinquency (McCagg, 1989, p. 41). One may presume that these circumstances could not but influence Vygotsky's perception of special-needs children as a sociocultural rather than an organic or individual developmental phenomenon.

There are certain paradoxical features in Vygotsky's influence on former Soviet and current Russian special education. On the one hand, his influence on theory and research in special education is so significant that a foreign observer would not be able to understand the nature of Russian "defectology" out of the context of Vygotsky's ideas. On the other hand, one would be mistaken to presume that the Soviet practice of education of children with special needs is a living heritage of Vygotsky's thoughts. For political reasons, any open discussion of Vygotsky's ideas was practically impossible from 1936 to the late 1950s (see Kozulin, 1984; van der Veer & Valsiner, 1991). The regimental nature of Soviet education influenced the field of special education. When it once again became fashionable to be called "Vygotskian," some of these regimental–educational principles were presented as coming from the Vygotskian tradition. Thus, it is not surprising that a Western observer was rather disappointed by his firsthand encounter with the Soviet special education system of the early 1990s:

> Rather than the active model of pupil we had come to expect within the neo-Vygotskian practice in England and Wales we observed remarkable passivity on the part of pupils. Children were seated in formal rows of desks with no opportunity for small group interaction or peer-cooperation. Much of the teaching and learning involved drills, repetition and rote learning.   (Daniels & Lunt, 1993, p. 87)

It seems that some of the Vygotskian theoretical principles are still waiting to be implemented not only in the West, but in Russia as well. It has been observed more than once that the path from theoretical innovation to its practical application is particularly thorny in Russia (Lubovsky, 1996).

Although many aspects of defectological research and practice can be mapped into contemporary Western special education with relative ease, these two fields are far from identical. *Defectology* is only roughly equivalent to contemporary Western special education, embracing low-incident disabilities (children with serious organic or sensory impairment and severe developmental delays) and school psychology (mostly in the domain of assessment). Thus, defectology did not include psychopathology, learning disability, or emotional disturbance as known in the West. In Vygotsky's time, the educational ideology that influenced the formation of a specific nomenclature of handicapping conditions was based almost entirely on the organic impairment of the central nervous system and severe sensory deficiency. Children with nonorganic, relatively mild learning disabilities were beyond the realm of Russian defectology until very recently (Gindis, 1986; Sutton, 1988; Suddaby, 1988; Daniels & Lunt, 1993; Smith-Davis, 2000; Malofeev, 2001). Considering the fact that emotionally disturbed and learning-disabled students account for more than half of the special education population in the US (Schulte, Osborn, & Erchul, 1998), the issue of the congruency of Vygotskian defectology with contemporary special education in the West needs to be taken into consideration. Although there has not been a study comparing these two fields, Vygotsky's theoretical and methodological findings can serve as a powerful source of professional inspiration for current and coming generations of special education professionals.

NATURAL AND CULTURAL AXES OF DEVELOPMENT

Vygotsky's contribution to understanding the development of children with special needs is based on two foundations: his general cultural–historical theory of human development (see Vygotsky, 1998) and a special theory that Vygotsky (1993) called the "theory of disontogenesis" (meaning the "theory of distorted development").

Breaking away from the common assumption of his time that disability is mainly biological in nature, Vygotsky suggested that the principal problem of a disability is not the sensory or neurological impairment but its social implications:

> Any physical handicap...not only alters the child's relationship with the world, but above all affects his interaction with people. Any organic defect is revealed as a social abnormality in behavior. It goes without saying that blindness and deafness per se are biological factors; however, teachers must deal not so much with these biological factors by themselves, but rather with their social consequences.
>
> (Vygotsky, 1983, p. 102)

One of the major theoretical innovations brought about by Vygotsky was the distinction between two axes of development: natural and cultural. This schema applies not only to normal development but also problematic development (disontogenesis). The source of the problematic development, therefore, may be both natural and cultural. Along the natural axes, cognitive and social/adaptive functions can be arranged from *retarded* (delayed) functions to *advanced* (highly developed) functions. At the same time, the cultural axis presupposes progression from primitive to highly developed cultural functions. It was

Vygotsky's idea that delays, distortions, and abnormalities in human development may have natural and cultural causes or a combination of both.

Individuals with normal or even highly developed natural abilities, such as spontaneous attention, simple memorization, practical problem solving, phonetic hearing, or imitative behavior, may nevertheless remain deprived of the important symbolic tools offered by their culture. These people, according to Vygotsky, display a syndrome of cultural "primitivity." According to Vygotsky, it is extremely important to distinguish the true sources of the impairment because the outside picture of the impaired performance might be quite similar in the cases of severe cultural "primitivity" and those of organic-based retardation.

Vygotsky referred to the case of a 9-year-old girl (described by Petrova, 1925), who was considered mentally retarded until it was discovered that the girl had never experienced a normal process of linguistic development in either of her two languages, Tartar and Russian. She acquired these languages as the means of immediate communication but no one had mediated to her the meaning of language as a tool of reasoning. 'In one school some children write well, and some draw well. Do all the children in this school write and draw well?' The girl answered: 'How should I know? What I have not seen with my own eyes I cannot explain...'" (Vygotsky, 1993, p. 46).

Another child assessed by Petrova was asked: "How do a tree and a log differ?" The child answered: "I have not seen a tree, I swear I haven't seen one." When shown a linden tree that stands under the window, the child answered: "This is a linden" (Vygotsky, 1993, p. 46). Vygotsky commented that from the point of view of primitive logic the child was right, no one had ever seen "a tree," all we had seen were lindens, chestnuts, ash, and so on. "A tree" is a product of cultural development, when word becomes not only a substitute for concrete objects, but a source of generalizations.

Of course not all culturally "primitive" children are normative in respect to the natural development of their psychological functions. Cultural "primitivity" may enter into different combinations with mental retardation or sensory problems. For example, if special effort is not made and remedial education not offered, deaf children will display many signs of culturally primitive behavior. It is important, however, to remember that underdevelopment of natural functions may be compensated for by acquisition of cultural tools, although even superior development of natural functions, for example, simple memory, cannot guarantee the establishment of higher mental functions that employ cultural tools-mediators. Thus, mentally retarded individuals with good phonetic

Cultural development

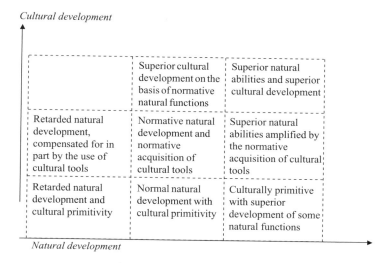

Natural development

FIGURE 13.1. Natural and cultural determinants of development.

hearing and superior imitation abilities may easily acquire a foreign language in its communicative function, skillfully using the entire blocks of learned speech in familiar contexts. The problem is revealed when comprehension of the verbal meanings and reflection on them go beyond immediate situation-embedded communication. Here these individuals reveal their impairment, because they cannot operate with language as an organized system of meanings.

The above diagram in Figure 13.1 presents a schematic view of possible relationships between problems in natural and cultural development.

CULTURAL DIFFERENCE AND CULTURAL DEPRIVATION

For several decades after Vygotsky's death, the cultural aspect of retarded performance seemed to be neglected, both within the Vygotskian school and outside of it. Cross-cultural studies focused on normative behavior and cognition, but the performance of children with special needs was interpreted on an individual level without the involvement of cultural categories. In a sharp departure from this overall tendency, Feuerstein et al. (1979) placed the concepts of cultural difference and cultural deprivation at the very center of their theory of retarded performance. One may hypothesize that a certain affinity of Feuerstein's approach to that of Vygotsky's approach is associated with the similarity of practical tasks facing both psychologists. Vygotsky was designing the special education system in a post-Revolutionary Russia under conditions of sociocultural dislocation and the educational deprivation of large masses of children. Feuerstein was entrusted with finding educational solutions in the 1950s and 1960s for thousands of new immigrant children in Israel, who were also for the most part educationally deprived and dislocated from their familiar sociocultural milieu. In the US and in Western Europe similar problems became recognized much later with an influx of immigrants from the Third World, child victims of regional conflicts, and more recently internationally adopted postinstitutionalized children (Gindis, 1998).

The first finding made by Feuerstein et al. (1979) was that standard psychometric tests are unable to distinguish between children with mental retardation and educationally and socially neglected immigrant children. The second finding made by Feuerstein (1990) concerns the differentiation between two groups of new immigrant children who demonstrated poor results in the standard psychometric tests and were at risk of being placed into special education classes. According to Feuerstein, the first group's problem stems from their difference from Western culture including the culture of psychometric testing. These children, however, had aquired good general learning skills mediated to them in their original culture and, therefore, had a positive prospect for overcoming their initial difficulties and succeeding in adapting to the formal educational system of the new culture. Feuerstein attributed the high learning potential of this *culturally different* group to the sufficient experience of mediated learning received by these children in their original community. The second group was defined by Feuerstein as *culturally deprived*. The cognitive and educational problems of these children originate not so much in their cultural distance from the formal educational culture as in their low learning potential. Feuerstein claimed that the absence of adequate mediated learning in their original culture resulted in the lowered learning potential of this group. One can, of course, be culturally deprived without leaving his or her own culture, but it is the challenge of adaptation to a new culture that clearly revealed the low learning potential of this group.

One may see a clear parallel between Vygotsky's notion of cultural primitivity and Feuerstein's notion of cultural deprivation. Culturally deprived children failed to receive appropriate mediation of their native culture and as a result had to rely almost exclusively on their natural cognitive functions and spontaneous learning skills. Such a scenario fits quite well into the Vygotskian definition of cultural primitivity. Vygotsky, however, placed particular emphasis on the child's appropriation of symbolic tools as a criterion of cultural development. Feuerstein, in turn, focused predominantly on the quality of mediation provided to a

TABLE 13.1. *Matrix of Interactions between Symbolic Tools and Mediated Learning Experience*

A. Mediated learning – adequate. Higher-level symbolic tools available and internalized as psychological tools.	**B.** Mediated learning – adequate. Higher-level symbolic tools unavailable.
C. Higher-level symbolic tools are available but fail to be internalized as psychological tools. Mediated learning is adequate in activities that do not require higher-level symbolic tools.	**D.** Mediated learning insufficient. Higher-level symbolic tools unavailable.

child by the members of his or her extended family and other significant community figures. Kozulin (1998) suggested that these two aspects, *psychological tools* and *mediated learning*, should be integrated into one matrix. For example, in Table 13.1, Field (B) of the matrix corresponds to the case of children who received adequate mediated learning in their native culture but who lack symbolic tools typical for a new or dominant culture. Problems facing these children will depend predominantly on the type and amount of symbolic tools that they have to appropriate and internalize. Field (C) corresponds to the case where the required symbolic tools were present in the child's original culture but failed to be internalized as inner psychological tools. In this case, the main problem is how to turn the symbolic tools already familiar to a child into inner psychological tools.

The question is, however, how to distinguish the *culturally different* children from the *culturally deprived* when the standard test performance of both groups is equally low. Feuerstein proposed that the degree of a child's cognitive modifiability is a differentiating parameter. Children who demonstrated greater responsiveness to a short-term learning of the cognitive principles embedded in the test material were presumed to do this on the basis of the previously mediated learning experience acquired in their native culture. These children, therefore, should be classified as *culturally different* and may rather quickly become integrated into a new school culture. Those children who demonstrate poor responsiveness to short-term learning, and, therefore, lowered cognitive modifiability, are most probably suffering from *cultural deprivation*. Their educators should plan for a long-term remediation process during which these children should first learn how to learn and only later acquire specific knowledge essential in their new cultural context. Referring to the matrix presented in Table 13.1, one may add that the children's modifiability will also depend on the type of psychological tools available to them.

Figures 13.2a and 13.2b show how the evaluation of cognitive modifiability proposed by Feuerstein et al. (1979) may help in deciding whether a given child has an organically impaired performance or is culturally deprived or culturally different. Y, an 11-year-old new immigrant from Ethiopia, was shown the model Rey-Osterrieth Complex Figure and asked to copy it first by looking at the model and then from her immediate memory (see Figure 13.2a). The girl's performance was so inferior that it did not rule out either organic impairment or profound cultural deprivation. However, a relatively short-term (several hours) intervention that included analysis of the model, practice with simpler shapes (square, diamond, etc.), and mediation of the planning strategies resulted in substantial improvement of the girl's performance both in direct copying and drawing from memory (see Figure 13.2b). One may therefore conclude that Y has no organic impairment and that her cognitive modifiability is good enough for successful integration into a regular classroom, provided that she masters a considerable number of symbolic tools and strategies typical of formal education. If Y were culturally deprived, the process of change would be much slower and the outcome would be reached only after a much more intensive mediation (for a detailed description of this and similar cases, see Kaufman and Kozulin, 1999).

VYGOTSKY'S THEORY OF DISONTOGENESIS

Vygotsky's views on the development of children with special needs had been shaped by his polemic with the then-popular quantitative understanding of handicapped development (disontogenesis). The quantitative paradigm presented a mentally retarded child as a normal child minus a certain amount of intelligence and the development of a blind child as normal development minus vision. Vygotsky vigorously argued against this subtractive approach to special-needs children, claiming that "A child whose development is impeded by a defect is not simply a child less developed than his peers but is a child who has developed differently" (Vygotsky, 1993, p. 30).

Vygotsky's model of disontogenesis is based on two major theoretical premises. The first premise is a distinction between primary and secondary defects, and the second premise is the notion of interfunctional relationships in mental development. A primary defect is identified by Vygotsky as an initial sensory, organic, or neurological impairment that influences the development of the child's natural functions

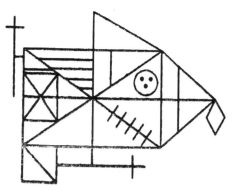

Complex Figure - Model

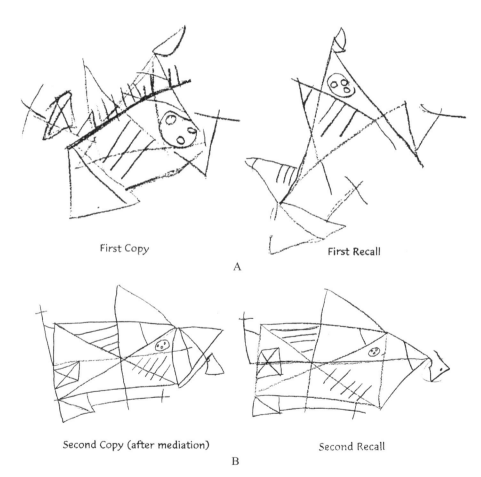

First Copy

First Recall

A

Second Copy (after mediation)

Second Recall

B

FIGURE 13.2. (A) Complex Figure drawing before mediation. (B) Complex Figure drawing after mediation.

341

of perception, memory, communication, and so on. This impairment, however, far from remaining an isolated feature leaves its imprint on the entire structure of the child's development. This secondary influence is both mediated and moderated by the social consequences of the primary defect (on social situation of development see Mahn, 2003).

In the essay "Defect and Compensation," Vygotsky (1993, pp. 52–64) wrote about the "two-sided nature" of a handicap: the underdevelopment or absence of the functions related to an organic defect and formation of an adaptive-compensatory mechanism. He stated that the most efficient compensation for the loss or weakness of natural functions could be achieved through the development of higher psychological functions. Paradoxically, although while what may be impaired are the natural processes (visual, auditory, kinesthetic), the target of intervention is the cultural processes of abstract reasoning, logical memory, voluntary attention, and goal-directed behaviors are the targets of intervention.

Vygotsky believed that unlike attempts at direct compensation, which are limited by the primary defect, *compensatory strategies* are effective because they are based on higher mental processes that may be relatively unaffected by the severity or type of the child's disability. "Cultural development is the main area for compensation of deficiency when further organic development is impossible; in this respect, the path of cultural development is unlimited" (Vygotsky, 1993, p. 169).

Let us consider the case of a child born with mild hemiparesis of the right side of his body. Such a primary neurological defect may, under certain social conditions, evolve into a serious impairment of the whole range of higher mental functions. An initial problem with walking, running, and outdoor games may put such a child at a disadvantage regarding the development of communicative speech, peer interaction, and the psychological mechanisms of role playing. Motor problems with the right hand may prevent him from acquiring writing skills, especially in an educational system that does not recognize left-handed writing as acceptable. At the beginning of primary school, such a child may develop a very negative self-image as a result of both objective learning difficulties and the attitude of peers and teachers. This may result in his being placed in a special educational framework that will further limit his aspirations. Therefore, a primary motor defect may develop into a full-blown secondary psychological defect involving higher verbal functions, problem solving, and personality problems.

However, a supportive social environment and an appropriate compensatory program may help bypass the primary defect and lead the same child to a full mastery of all higher psychological functions. Vygotsky emphasized the role of social mediation and the acquisition of symbolic tools. Vygotsky most probably would have suggested compensating for a child's motor problem by cultivating his verbal functions, teaching him to use a typewriter at a relatively early age, organizing peer interaction around nonmotor activities, and in general by substituting higher cognitive and verbal functions for the impaired motor skills. What the child cannot do by hand, he should be able to do by word.

The second premise of Vygotsky's theory of disontogenesis concerns the interfunctional relationships established during development. This premise comes from Vygotsky's (1986, 1998) general concept of normal (as well as handicapped) development as a process of ever increasing interaction between different psychological functions. Speech, perceptual and motor functions, memory, and problem solving do not develop as separate elements but as functional systems that depend on the acquisition and internalization of symbolic tools. For example, when an educated adult person has to remember something he or she rarely relies on direct memorization – he or she uses an entire complex of verbal and reasoning functions. Disontogenesis, on the one hand, may disrupt this process of system-formation, but on the other hand, it can be compensated via the creation of alternative functional systems.

> Investigative study of the mentally retarded child has revealed that in such a child, interfunctional relationships take shape distinctively and differently in comparison with those that come to light in the development of a normal child. This sphere of psychological development, the change in interfunctional connections and relationships, the change in the internal structure of the psychological system, is the most important area for the compensatory processes in forming [the child's] personality.
> (Vygotsky, 1993, p. 131)

Kozulin (unpublished) observed such a disontogenesis of interfunctional relations in a highly developed adolescent with Down Syndrome. His parents invested an enormous amount of time in the development of their child, who was successfully integrated in a regular classroom, became a fluent reader and writer, and in many other respects demonstrated highly developed cognitive and learning skills. The same adolescent, however, could be seen reading the same text aloud over and over again, under conditions absolutely inappropriate for such an activity. Here, apparently, the functional relations between basic reading skills and the pragmatic aspect of reading failed to be internalized. Under conditions of external contextual "scaffolding" provided by adults, the same reading activity might appear as absolutely appropriate.

Within the context of Vygotsky's paradigm of primary and secondary defects, many symptoms such as behavioral infantilism or primitivism of emotional reactions in individuals with mental retardation are considered to be a secondary handicapping condition because they are acquired in the process of social interaction. If untreated, these conditions may effectively exacerbate the primary disability. Expectations, attitudes, and the general moral atmosphere of a given society influence the access of a child with a disability to sociocultural knowledge, experiences, and the opportunity to participate in shared or joint activities with peers. That is why Vygotsky so passionately insisted on changing the negative societal attitudes toward individuals with disabilities. The search for positive capacities and the creation of quality of life through education and the upbringing of children with disabilities is the trademark of Vygotsky's approach.

Vygotsky emphasized the dynamic nature of disability and argued that constant changes take place both in the structure and content of disontogenesis during the child's development and under the influence of education and remediation. On the one hand, the basic principles of child development, such as the internalization of external cultural activities and symbolic tools in the form of inner psychological processes, are fully applicable to children with disabilities. On the other hand, the development of children with disabilities has major qualitative differences in the means and ways of their internalization of culture. In Vygotsky's view, the core of disabled children's development is the divergence between their natural and social developmental paths. He pointed to two major differences in the development of a child with a disability in comparison with his typically developing peers. These differences are the formation of compensatory strategies (mechanisms) and the emergence of social complications due to the disability ("secondary defect" in his terminology). No effective remediation is possible without an understanding of these qualitative differences.

Vygotsky called for developing a disability-specific profile of the discrepancy between the "natural" and "social" aspects of the development of a child with a particular disability. As the milestones of this profile, he listed the dynamic and forms of socialization, appropriation of psychological tools, and formation and use of compensatory strategies (Vygotsky, 1993, pp. 110–122). Compensatory strategies are by no means mechanical substitutions for impaired functions. Rather they are products of the child's individuality, personal experiences, and what Vygotsky called "the social situation of development" (for further elaboration, see Mann, 2003). Compensatory strategies are aimed at mastering psychological tools and using them to acquire cultural forms of behavior. When the direct way of acquiring psychological tools is blocked (e.g., in the case of blindness), compensatory strategies offer an indirect path to the same goal of cultural development.

The notion of a "disability-specific psychoeducational profile" has been elaborated by a number of Vygotsky's followers in Russia. One was suggested by Lubovsky (1989) and later elaborated by Belopolskaya and Lubovsky (1992). The basis of this model is the relationship between the primary and secondary deficits, as spelled out in Vygotsky's theory of disontogenesis. Belopolskaya and Lubovsky (1992) point to a complex and dialectic interrelationship between primary and secondary disabilities. The same primary defect (organic impairment) may lead to different secondary disabilities, and different primary defects may lead to the same secondary disability. Lubovsky suggested a rather elaborate and complex schema for a disability profile (in relation to mentally retarded students) that includes cognitive, emotional, and motivational components. He also made an interesting and productive attempt to connect his profile with an assessment called "the teaching/learning experiment," one of the forms of dynamic assessment.

Venger (1994) offered his version of disability profile that included three strata or components of disability. The first is composed of individual characteristics of a child. The second stratum consists of those characteristics that are disability-specific or disability dependent. The third includes parameters of social interactions determined by the child's individual and disability-specific characteristics. Venger emphasized that social and cultural interactions influence not only the processes in the third stratum but the two previous strata as well.

THE SOCIOCULTURAL–DEVELOPMENTAL
APPROACH TO REMEDIATION

The essence of Vygotsky's approach to remedial education is in addressing the secondary disability, that is, by countering the negative social consequences of the primary disability. Vygotsky believed that physical and mental impairment could be overcome by creating alternative but essentially equivalent roads for cultural development. By acquiring the psychological tools, disabled children transform their natural abilities into higher mental functions as do their nondisabled peers.

The concept of the internalization of psychological tools has particular importance for the remediation process. In this context, Vygotsky emphasized the dialectic relationship between the means (sign, psychological tool) and the content (meaning) of cultural acquisition. Disability may prevent the child from acquiring psychological tools similar to his or her nondisabled peers, thus requiring different methods of teaching and learning for the appropriation of psychological tools. The sociocultural meaning of the acquired tools remains the same, but they should be delivered via alternative means such as modified signs or specialized psychological tools. In Vygotsky's analysis, the essence of any remedial educational program is in the process of substituting signs while retaining the meaning of the internalization. "Different symbolic systems correspond to one and the same content of education . . . Meaning is more important than the sign. Let us change signs but retain meaning" (Vygotsky, 1983, p. 54).

Vygotsky's vision of the role of symbolic tools for the remediation of specific disability has been fully confirmed by current developments in the field of remedial (special) education and occupational therapy. In addition to such "classical" tools as Braille, sign language, lip-reading, and finger-spelling that were known in Vygotsky's time, a host of new symbolic tools, sophisticated electronic gadgets, and means of mobility have been developed. The crucial question, already formulated by Vygotsky, is how to turn these symbolic or physical means into real tools aimed at changing the disabled child's developmental trajectory.

The process of appropriation of psychological tools is determined by the nature of the disability and correlated modifications of teaching methods. For example, the concept of spontaneous and scientific notions in developing higher forms of reasoning has its specificity in the domain of educational remediation. Everyday (spontaneous) concepts appear as a product of the child's immediate experience. Usually these concepts are unsystematic and contextual. "Scientific" concepts (not necessarily science-related) are the result of specialized learning activity; they are systematic and decontextual. In the course of typical development, there is a dynamic interaction between these two kinds of notions, as analyzed by Vygotsky (1987, pp. 167–240). In the case of children with handicapping conditions (in particular, those with severe sensory impairments), this relationship is atypical. Spontaneous notions are limited, extremely immature and severely distorted (e.g., the case of deaf/blind/mute children or mentally retarded children). In this situation, the meaning and value of scientific notions are increased tremendously, and the teaching methodology must be modified appropriately in comparison with teaching those for whom spontaneous concepts are ordinary facts of their daily lives.

For example, the process of concept formation in blind learners who are integrated into regular schools is dominated by two extremes: abstract verbal notions acquired at school that have little support in the blind learners' experience and very concrete tactile images of the children's immediate environment that possess little potential for generalization and transfer (Gouzman & Kozulin, 2000). As a result the middle ground, that is, everyday concepts that possess a certain degree of generality are underrepresented in the blind learners' cognitive repertoire. The notions and operations that in sighted students appear as a natural outcome of spontaneous daily activities have to be developed in the blind learners in a deliberate way similar to learning scientific concepts.

By tracing Vygotsky's impact on current remediation programs, one may distinguish three broad groups of studies. The first group is a direct continuation of Vygotsky's defectology carried out by his students and his students' students and is represented by the work of Meshcheryakov (1979), Lubovsky (1996), Vlasova (1984), Akhutina (1997), Rubinstein (1979), and others. The second group includes approaches compatible with Vygotsky's vision, but these approaches were developed in the West, mostly independently. The most prominent studies in this group are Feuerstein's mediated learning and cognitive modifiability approach that applied Vygotsky's programs of learning potential assessment (Feuerstein et al., 1980, 1997, 2003), and his Instrumental Enrichment (Feuerstein et al., 1980). The third group includes programs that combine a Vygotskian theoretical basis with mediational, information processing, and other approaches. For this group the work of J. P. Das and his colleagues (Das & Naglieri, 1994; Das & Kendrick, 1997), as well as Haywood, Brooks, Burns (1992) are representative of Vygotsky's work. Certain attempts have also been made to look at the existent remediation programs, such as Feuerstein's "Instrumental Enrichment" through the lens of Vygotsky's theory of psychological tools (Kozulin, 1998, 2003).

One of the most impressive accomplishments of the Russian followers of Vygotsky's defectology was the remediation program for the blind, deaf, and mute children developed by Alexander Meshcheryakov (Meshcheryakov, 1979; Chulkov, Lubovsky, & Martsinovskaia, 1990; Bakhurst & Padden, 1991). It is based on Vygotsky's concept of psychological tools and his belief that "the development of scientific concepts begins with verbal definition" (Vygotsky, 1987, p. 168). Meshcheryakov introduced the notion of "primary gesture" (as an alternative psychological tool for a child who cannot speak, see, and hear). The "primary gesture" originates from the movements that make up the shared/joint activity of the handicapped child and his or her teacher. At first the primary gesture may just reproduce physical activity (e.g., to move their hands upward from knees to waist as part of a "putting on trousers" movement). Later, the primary gesture is simplified and decontextualized by acquiring symbolic meaning (the same abbreviated gesture now means "we go outside"). Finally, it is linked to a dactylic language that makes it possible "to form generalized images that reflect the facts of real life correctly and in depth" (Meshcheryakov, 1979, p. 189).

The concept of psychological tools has also inspired the development of innovative remedial methods in the education of deaf students (Knox & Kozulin, 1989; Berk & Winsler, 1995; Zaittseva, Pursglove, & Gregory, 1999). The specific textbooks, modified curricula, and adapted teaching material developed by the Institute of Corrective Pedagogy in Moscow (formerly the Institute of Defectology) for mentally retarded pupils are examples of effective specialized "psychological tools" presented via mediational techniques (Strebeleva, 2000; Almanah ICP, 2000–2002: electronic version is available at www.ise.iip.net/almanah).

If we turn to a second group of studies, those compatible with the Vygotskian idea of psychological tools but developed independently by Feuerstein et al. (1980, 2003), then the concept of mediation becomes crucial. Nonmediated learning, that is, immediate interaction with the environment through independent observation, trials, contacts, probing, and testing is limited and distorted in a disabled child. Therefore, mediated learning that is conducted through an adult who selects, modifies, and interprets environmental stimuli has a special implication for the disabled child. Remediation, as well as development of higher psychological function in the disabled child, depends on the quality and quantity of mediating activity personalized in a teacher and in the structure and organization of the learning environment. The general principles of mediation are the same for disabled and nonhandicapped students. Instead of focusing exclusively on the delivery of facts and concepts, the human mediator infuses the learning material with intentional teaching strategies and principles. Moreover, the mediator takes care to transfer these cognitive strategies and principles to new learning material and new situations in different content areas. Because not every act of learning influences the child's development, not every act of learning is remedial in itself. To become remedial, learning should appear in the form of a learning activity (see Zuckerman, 2003) that transforms and advances the learner's psychological functions.

Feuerstein and his colleagues (1980) developed a comprehensive system for mediation of general cognitive strategies and skills to special needs students, called "Instrumental Enrichment." The Instrumental Enrichment program includes fourteen booklets of paper-and-pencil exercises that cover such areas as analytic perception, orientation in time and space, comparison, categorization, and so forth. The program is taught individually or to a whole classroom of students by teachers specially trained in the principles of mediated learning and techniques of Instrumental Enrichment. The program proved to be effective in enhancing the cognitive functioning of mentally retarded, learning disabled, and other groups of special needs students (Arbitman-Smith, Haywood, & Bransford, 1984; Kozulin, 2000).

Though Feuerstein et al. (1980) did not use the concept of psychological tools in their theoretical introduction to Instrumental Enrichment, anyone familiar with the program would agree that in practice it offers one of the most systematic schemes of psychological tools (Kozulin, 1998). The unity of psychological tools and mediating the learning experience plays an exceptionally important role in remedial education. "Symbolic tools have a rich educational potential, but they remain ineffective if there is no human mediator to facilitate their appropriation by the learner. By the same token, human mediation that does not involve sophisticated symbolic tools would not help the learner to master more complex forms of reasoning and problem solving" (Kozulin, 2003, p. 35).

It is the unity of psychological tools and teaching based on "mediated learning" that makes remediation effectual. The theoretical integration of the Vygotskian concept of psychological tools with Feuerstein's notion of mediated learning experience served as a basis for concrete intervention programs for culturally different deaf children (Lurie & Kozulin, 1998) and blind students (Gouzman, 2000; Gouzman & Kozulin, 2000).

The third group of remediation studies includes those emerging on the crossroads of Vygotskian ideas and some additional theoretical principles such as information processing. An appropriate example here is J. P. Das's (Das & Kendrick, 1997) methodology for remediation of such "high incidence" disabilities as reading disability. The *Reading Enhancement Program* employs two key Vygotskian concepts: appropriation of psychological tools and social–cultural mediation. It consists of two parts: (1) the global cognitive process-training unit that provides students with a guided opportunity to internalize cognitive strategies and (2) the "bridge unit" that offers training in specific strategies relevant to reading and writing.

Yet another example could be the *Bright Start: Cognitive Curriculum for Young Children* (Haywood, Brooks, & Burns, 1992). The mediation of psychological tools in the context of the zone of proximal development is the essence and major distinctive feature of the program. Although different theories contributed to the creation of *Bright Start*, understanding and practical implementation is more efficiently accomplished from a Vygotskian perspective, according to Gindis's clinical experience. This methodology is designed for use with children who are at high risk of learning failure in the primary grades due to severe deprivation and educational neglect in early childhood (e.g., internationally adopted postinstitutionalized children, Gindis, 2001).

THE PROBLEM OF INCLUSION

One of the "mysterious" aspects of Vygotsky's scientific legacy is his attention to questions that were not relevant at his time but turned out to be of major concern of educators decades after his death. One of those is the issue of "inclusion," which was not even on the agenda of Vygotsky's contemporaries (McCagg, 1989) but became very emotionally charged in the early 1990s in the US. It is difficult to explain why Vygotsky was so passionate in expressing his thoughts on this subject that was outside of the mind-set of both professionals and the public at large. Vygotsky was not able to escape the built-in controversy associated with this issue and readers could become quite confused by him being equally critical of what he called the "unlawful segregation" of the disabled, on the one hand, and the lack of differentiated educational environments for children with special needs, on the other. It took Vygotsky several years to develop his vision for special education that includes "integration based on positive differentiation" (Vygotsky, 1995, pp. 114, 167).

There is both a philosophical and a practical distinction between the concepts of mainstreaming and of inclusion as they are used in contemporary special education in North America. The concept of "mainstreaming" is part of a traditional pattern of special education service delivery. It means that the selective placement of special education students in general education classes is based on their demonstrated ability to function on the same level as the majority of students in that classroom. Usually mainstreaming presupposes a procedure for declassification of a child as a "special needs" case. The child's disability is considered compensated for or remediated to the extent that it does not prevent the child from benefiting from a regular (mainstreamed) curriculum (Stainback, Stainback, & Forest, 1989). Inclusion as an educational concept rejects the idea of special education (with the exception of a small number of cases of severe sensory/physical/mental disability) as a segregated placement. The proponents of this approach believe that a child with a handicap belongs in general education with support services delivered to the child. They may agree with the necessity for the partial or temporary provision of special-needs services outside the general education class if the need arises, but only on a limited basis. Within the inclusion movement, there is also a radical trend called "full inclusion" that insists that all students, regardless of the severity of the handicapping condition, be placed in a regular classroom or program full time, with all services brought to the child in that setting (Fuchs & Fuchs, 1994).

In the early stages of his career as a researcher and an educational administrator, Vygotsky called for "normalization through inclusion" of all children with disabilities, sometimes going to the extreme. Many aspects of his earlier writing had much in common with what is now called "The Full Inclusion Model" or "Regular Classroom Initiative" as described in Lipsky and Gartner (1996). His criticism of the "negative model of special education" as a combination of lowered expectations, a watered-down curriculum, and social isolation sounds very much up to date and is enthusiastically cited by proponents of full inclusion (Fuchs & Fuchs, 1994). Vygotsky argued against what he called "social prejudices against the handicapped" (Vygotsky, 1993, pp. 65–76). This appeal fell on a deaf ears in Stalinist Russia (McCagg, 1989) but was fully appreciated by a broad audience in the US half a century later (Newman & Holzman, 1993).

However, in his later works, Vygotsky expressed the firm conviction that only a truly differentiated learning environment can fully contribute to the development of the higher psychological functions and overall personality of a child with a disability. Special education should be provided in a specially designed setting where the entire staff is able to exclusively serve the individual needs of a child with a disability. It should be a special system that employs its own specific methodologies because students with disabilities require modified and alternative methods of teaching. Students with disabilities need specially trained teachers, a differentiated curriculum, special technological auxiliary means, and simply more time to learn. How realistically can these demands be met in a regular classroom situation? These arguments are used by the proponents of the current (segregated) system of special education in contemporary Russia (Knox & Stevens, 1993; Belopolskaya & Grebennikova, 1997; Smith-Davis, 2000).

This obvious contradiction in Vygotsky's position reflects the inherent controversy over the very notion of inclusion: how to address special needs in a general school environment; how to integrate specialized and generalized teaching methodologies; and how to escape separation in a "closed society" and attend to exceptional individual demands at the same time (see Kauffman & Hallahan, 1995). Summarizing Vygotsky's view on this matter, one can observe that in the process of developing his approach, Vygotsky moved from understanding inclusion as "topographic" (being in the same classroom) and temporal (being in the same classroom at the same time) to developing a sociocultural concept of integration. It is important to understand that although Vygotsky suggested physical separation in specialized day or boarding schools, real integration in his view was supposed to be achieved through similar curriculum content (by providing extra time, adapting specific methods of teaching and providing additional adult mediated assistance) and the appropriation of culturally meaningful psychological tools. He continued to insist on topographical and temporal proximity of special needs and general education students in what he called "political and social activity" (Vygotsky, 1995, pp. 462–467). This idea is similar to what today is called "social mainstreaming." Nonacademic activities such as assemblies, sports, lunchtime, playground games, music, art, and so on provide an opportunity for social learning not only for children with handicapping conditions but also for their nondisabled peers (Kauffman & Hallahan, 1995).

Vygotsky's main premise was that a child with a disability must be accommodated with experiences and opportunities that are as close as possible to the mainstreamed situation, but not at the expense of "positive differentiation." This should be based on the children's potential rather than their current limitations. It was Vygotsky's firm belief that the future of remedial education lies in employing specific methods for achieving mainstreamed social and cultural goals. It is a sad irony that Vygotsky's idea of integration of children with disabilities into the social and cultural life of their communities as a condition of effective rehabilitation and compensation was never realized in his native country (Lubovsky, 1996; Smith-Davis, 2000) but was enthusiastically embraced in US in the last quarter of the twentieth century.

ZONE OF PROXIMAL DEVELOPMENT AND PSYCHOEDUCATIONAL ASSESSMENT

The assessment of children with handicapping conditions has been a socially and politically sensitive and emotionally charged issue for a long time. Dissatisfaction with the existing arsenal of evaluation tools and procedures has spurred the search for more useful alternatives (Feuerstein et al., 1979; Haywood & Tzuriel, 1992). One of the most promising options is the so-called dynamic assessment, of which Vygotsky is rightfully considered to be the "founding father" (Lidz, 1995). Although Vygotsky had no chance to elaborate on specific assessment procedures, his notion of a Zone of Proximal Development (ZPD) forms the theoretical foundation of a group of approaches now commonly recognized as "dynamic assessment" (DA).

Parents and teachers have frequently observed that with the appropriate help and in collaboration with a more experienced partner, a child is capable of more advanced performance than when functioning independently. It was Vygotsky, however, who elevated this otherwise trivial observation to the rank of the scientific paradigm known as ZPD. This is probably the most popular and most discussed of Vygotsky's concepts, one which at the same time remains poorly understood and often misinterpreted (Chaiklin, 2003; see also & del Río & Álvarez, Chapter 11, in this volume).

One apparent reason for difficulty with the notion of the ZPD is that it had been used by Vygotsky in the three interconnected, yet separate, contexts of developmental theory, applied research, and school-based concept-formation studies. The developmental aspect is concerned primarily with the emerging psychological functions of the child. The applied aspect focuses on the difference between the child's individual and aided performance. The concept-formation aspect is related to the interaction between "scientific" and "everyday" concepts in school learning. In addition to the multiplicity of contexts, there is another problematic point – Vygotsky never proposed any specific methodology (in the Western sense of this term) for a study of the ZPD or its use as an assessment technique. He suggested various approaches to a study of emergent psychological functions and various alternatives to standard IQ testing, but not one of them offered a definitive methodological paradigm. Here are two examples of Vygotsky's suggestions:

> We assist each child through demonstration, leading questions, and by introducing elements of the task's solution.
>
> (Vygotsky, 1934/1987, p. 209)

And, describing the action of the examiner,

> We show the child how such a problem must be solved and watch to see if he can do the problem by imitating the demonstration. Or we begin to solve the problem and ask the child to finish it. Or we propose that the child solve the problem that is beyond his mental age by cooperating with another, more developed child or, finally, we explain to the child the principle of solving the problem, ask leading questions, analyze the problem for him, etc.   (Vygotsky, 1934/1998b, p. 202)

One can therefore be true to the word and meaning of Vygotsky's theory of the ZPD, but one cannot follow or deviate from Vygotsky's ZPD assessment methodology for the simple reason that he never spelled it out.

According to Vygotsky, assessment is not an isolated activity that is merely linked to intervention. Assessment, instruction, and remediation can be based on the same universal explanatory conceptualization of a child's development (typical and atypical) and within this model are therefore inseparable. "A true diagnosis must provide an explanation, prediction, and scientific basis for practical prescription" (Vygotsky,

1934/1998, p. 205). Vygotsky made a clear distinction between what he called symptomatic and diagnostic assessment:

> A symptomatic assessment focuses on behaviors and characteristics...that are typical of children of a particular psychological type or developmental stage. In contrast, a diagnostic assessment relies on an explicit explanatory theory of psychological development in an attempt to penetrate the internal causal dynamic and genetic connections that define the process of mental development.   (Vygotsky, 1987, p. 135)

Unlike most norm-based, as well as developmentally based, procedures used in standard assessments, Vygotskian ZPD-based assessments aspire to offer a theory-based diagnostic explanation. Such an explanation is based on the following premises:

1. Vygotsky insisted that assessment of the child's ability to learn through the method of collaborative activity was a better predictor of future cognitive functioning than a measure of independent performance through such measures as traditional IQ tests. His explanation was that the greater number of maturing functions gave the child better opportunities to benefit from school instruction (see Van der Veer & Valsiner, 1991, pp. 336–341, for an elaboration and critique of this claim).

2. The ZPD should be measured in the context of what Vygotsky called either "shared/joint activity" (sovmestnaya deajtelnost) or "collaboration" (sotrudnichestvo), using these terms synonymously. He proposed "that an essential feature of learning is that it creates the zone of proximal development; that is, learning awakens a variety of developmental processes that are able to operate only when the child is interacting with people in his environment and in collaboration with his peers" (Vygotsky, 1935/1978, p. 90).

3. Vygotsky suggested that the "size" of the ZPD was determined by the child's ability to benefit from collaboration with an expert in order to advance the child's performance beyond what was already achieved by nonassisted performance. There is nothing in Vygotsky's texts that suggests that this "size" is a fixed property of the child, remaining constant across age periods. DA should be able to measure the child's ever-changing ability to learn with assistance/guidance as well as to assess the individual "length" of the ZPD.

At the same time, Vygotsky's attitude toward standardized ("static") testing was somewhat inconsistent. On the one hand, he seemed to uncritically accept two major concepts that have been challenged by contemporary science: "mental age" as a psychological construct and the validity of standardized tests as reliable measures of fully developed psychological functions through independent performance. It was rather contradictory that the concept of "mental age," seemingly incompatible with Vygotsky's own theory of child development, was casually used by him in a number of his works. On the other hand, Vygotsky offered one of the most original and insightful critiques of standardized tests. His major objections to standardized tests were that they confused latent capacities with developed abilities; they mixed lower (natural) capability with higher (socially learned) expertise, they had low ecological validity, and they were only marginally relevant to educational processes. He suggested as an alternative the approach based on the notion of the ZPD, focusing on emergent cognitive functions and the child's learning potential.

Not all aspects of the theory of the ZPD found expression in current DA procedures, and not everything that is used in DA is directly derived from Vygotsky's theory. For example, Vygotsky was particularly concerned with assessing the child's readiness for a qualitative change, for a transition to a new age period. As such, his concern was mostly macrodevelopmental (see Chaiklin, 2003). Some of the contemporary DA approaches operate on microdevelopmental level, focusing on a specific function or skill. It would be appropriate to question whether such DA approaches can legitimately be called ZPD-based. Vygotsky's notion of the ZPD is also intimately linked to the appropriation and internalization of psychological tools. Not many of the contemporary DA approaches theoretically acknowledge or operationally use the appropriation of psychological tools as a part of their procedures.

All these difficulties notwithstanding, one can discern a set of assumptions that, on the one hand, unite different DA approaches (whether ZPD-based or not) and, on the other, distinguish them from traditional standardized testing (Kozulin, 1998).

The traditional testing paradigm includes the notions that:

1. The manifest level of functioning reveals the child's inner abilities more or less accurately,
2. Unaided performance is the best format for assessment,
3. The primary goal of testing is to predict future functioning and to classify the child according to level of abilities.

In contrast, DA includes the principles or assumptions that:

1. Cognitive processes are modifiable and an important task of assessment is to ascertain their degree of modifiability, rather

than remain restricted to estimation of the child's manifest level of functioning,

2. Interactive assessment that includes a learning phase provides better insight into the child's learning capacities than unaided performance,

3. The primary goal of assessment is to suggest psychoeducational interventions aimed at the enhancement and realization of the child's latent ability to learn.

Ideally, dynamic testing is intertwined with instruction, and the student's learning ability is observed carefully during the process of learning. The goal of DA is to discover whether and how much the student will change under the influence of scaffolding activities (Tzuriel, 2001). As summarized by Lidz and Elliot (2000): "the essential characteristics of DA are that they are interactive, open ended, and generate information about the responsiveness of the learner to intervention" (Lidz & Elliot, 2000, p. 7). As Lidz (1995) observed, traditional standardized assessment follows the child's cognitive performance to the point of "failure" in independent functioning, but DA in the Vygotskian tradition leads the child to the point of success in joint/shared activity.

Currently available DA procedures are not limited to any single domain (e.g., analogic reasoning), content (e.g., math, language), activity (e.g., testing, teaching), or age. It is a "family" of different procedures that share a set of principles and formats. Sternberg and Grigorenko (2002, pp. 27–28) described the two most common formats of dynamic assessment as "sandwich" design and "cake" design. In the "sandwich" format of dynamic testing, the instruction is given all at once between the pretest and the posttest. In the "cake" format, the instruction is given in graded layers after each test item, in response to the examinee's solution to each test item.

Not all interaction possess the same value for the promotion of child development. Vygotsky himself emphasized the importance of language as a major, if not the primary mechanism of internalization of experiences but was not explicit regarding the details of how best to intervene during the course of the assessment. A number of writers have attempted to fill this gap. For example, Hogan and Pressley (1997) list a number of techniques that describe the various approaches to scaffolding. Others who have attempted to describe the type and nature of assistance provided during the scaffolding process include Tharp and Gallimore (1988) and Gauvain (2001).

One may distinguish two large groups of DA procedures. The primary representative of the first group is Feuerstein's Learning Potential

Assessment Device (LPAD) (Feuerstein et al., 1979, 2003). Feuerstein explicitly rejects the task of prediction and placement as a legitimate goal of DA. For him the only real goal of DA is to identify the child's learning needs to assist in the design of an appropriate remediation strategy. The issue of reliability or validity of assessment instruments seems to be irrelevant in his vision of DA. LPAD is a clinical procedure that emphasizes the flexibility of mediation provided to children in response to their ongoing cognitive performance, repeating the same test when necessary and adding new instruments from the LPAD battery as the children progress in their problem solving. Individual LPAD assessment is time consuming; it is not uncommon for the LPAD assessor to spend ten or fifteen hours working with a child during five to ten assessment sessions. The LPAD procedure was applied with special needs children and adolescents ranging from Down Syndrome, autistic spectrum, and organic brain disorders to learning disabled and regular underachievers (for relevant case studies, see Feuerstein et al., 2003).

DA procedures belonging to the second group are rarely so radical. Guthke and Beckmann (2000), for example, suggested that DA is not an alternative but a supplement to standard assessment. Moreover, DA is often presented as a better way of fulfilling traditional assessment goals, including prediction of the child's future performance and recommendation for placement. The issue of reliability or validity of assessment instruments is of considerable importance for this group of DA procedures (Elliott, 2003).

In different countries, DA appears under different names (Lidz & Elliott, 2000). In Russia, assessment techniques derived from the concept of the ZPD are rarely called "dynamic assessment," though in essence many of them are similar to Western DA approaches. (A review and critical analysis of these methods may be found in Gindis, 1992, and Karpov & Gindis, 2000.) There are at least two DA approaches in Russia that reflect different emphases in methodology and techniques. If the emphasis is on the "assessment," then it is "diagnistika obuchaemosti," translated as "diagnosis of learning aptitude" (Ivanova, 1976). If the emphasis is on teaching and learning in the ZPD, then it would be called "obuchayuchij experiment," translated as "teaching/learning experiment" (Galperin, 1969).

In Soviet and now Russian psychology, the nature of the responsiveness of children to prompts was the basis for differential diagnosis of children with organically based mental retardation and children who were educationally neglected or had temporary delays in cognitive functioning (Gindis, 1986, 1988, 1992). The theoretical development of DA was undertaken, implicitly or explicitly, by a number of prominent

Vygotskians in Russia such as Luria (1961), Elkonin (1977), Galperin (1969), Zaporozhets and Elkonin (1971), Lubovsky (1989), and Venger (1988). The fruitfulness of applying their conceptualizations and methods was convincingly demonstrated by Bodrova and Leong (1996). Certain aspects of DA, such as the emotional/motivational components, were particularly emphasized and elaborated in Russian research, while most Western developers of DA have been focusing on the cognitive aspects of this assessment procedure.

The best-known method of assessing learning aptitude was developed by the Moscow psychologist Anna Ivanova in the early 1970s. An example of Ivanova's diagnostic procedure includes classification of pictures with geometrical designs of different forms, sizes, and colors. The child is asked to sort these cards into groups based on these attributes. In the process of performing this activity, the child received prescribed prompts from the examiner until the assignment was completed. Following this, another set of cards was offered for the same purpose, but this time without the provision of help. The "length" of the ZPD (explicitly associated with learning aptitude) was determined through notation of the quality and quantity of prompts that were needed and the child's ability to transfer the acquired cognitive skills to a new set of similar tasks (Ivanova, 1976). Karpov (1990) observed that these qualitative and quantitative markers of the ZPD may in fact reflect different psychological realities, and, therefore, the use of a "composite" indicator may be misleading.

The "teaching/learning experiment," also theoretically rooted in the concept of the ZPD, was perfected in Russia as a measure of the level of internalization of problem-solving cognitive strategies (Galperin, 1969). Children's ability to move from one level of solving problems to the next is one of the most important characteristics of the process of internalization in their ZPD. In Russian neo-Vygotskian literature, the consecutive levels of internalization are described as visual-motor (actual manipulations with objects), visual-imagery (operations with visual images), and symbolic levels of internalization. In the course of normal development, children progress to increasingly higher levels of internalization of their problem-solving activity (Davydov, 1995). In the "teaching/learning experiment," two characteristics of the child's learning during DA testing are considered as criteria in determining the cross-domain level of internalization of the child's problem-solving activity. These characteristics are (a) the highest initial level (symbolic, visual-imagery, or visual-motor) at which the child is able to understand the algorithm for a new problem-solving process and (b) the highest level at which the child is able to perform a new problem-solving process after planned and prescribed intervention. These characteristics are related to that child's cross-domain ability to learn and transfer new knowledge. One can find a detailed description of the procedure in Karpov and Gindis (2000).

In Russia, the most comprehensive attempt to create a ZPD theory-driven DA is the "diagnostic of learning aptitude" procedure developed by Lubovsky (1989, 1990) and his colleagues (Belopolskay & Lubovsky, 1992). In many ways, their model is similar to the Campione and Brown (1987) "graduated prompts" method. The similarity of these two approaches lies in the measurement and quantification of the amount of help that a child needed to perform a given task. The major differences are related to the elaborated procedures for observing a child's behavior, the detailed descriptions of gradually diminishing adult contribution to a joint/shared activity, and the attention to emotional/motivational aspects.

We must emphasize that in Russia the emotional/motivational aspect of assessment has always been at the center of attention both theoretically (Elkonin, 1977; Zaporozhets & Elkonin, 1971) and practically (Lebedinsky, 1985; Belopolskaya & Lubovsky, 1992). This emphasis can be clearly seen in Elkonin's study of the relationships between cognitively operational and personality-motivational aspects of children's development as well as in Venger's (1988) notion of "sensory standards." Research on internal sources, compared to external sources of motivation, self-esteem, and reaction to success and failure during a DA experimental situation occupied a prominent place in the work of Russian followers of Vygotsky. Belopolskaia and Grebennikova (1997) have differentiated children based on (1) whether motivation was primarily internal or external; (2) whether the children demonstrated the need for moderate or strong stimulation; and (3) whether the children showed well-developed or underdeveloped self-esteem in the experimental situation. One of the most important findings that emerged from the works of Russian psychologists in the early 1980s is that a determining factor in task performance is the nature of the child's "emotional anticipation" of the process of task performance. According to these studies, task performance during DA starts with the appearance of emotional anticipation, which may facilitate or hinder the expression of intellectual abilities (Belopolskaya & Lubovsky, 1992). These and related studies demonstrated that investigating the affective–cognitive content of children's mental activity was useful in developing diagnostic instruments that more fully and accurately assess intellectual abilities and potential, providing more specific information regarding learning problems.

Strebeleva's (2000) system of nonverbal tests developed at the Institute of Corrective Pedagogy in Moscow may serve as a good example of the DA approach relevant to the tasks of special education and preschool learning. Vygotsky's notions of the ZPD as collaboration ("sovmestnaya deyatelnost") and imitation served as a theoretical basis for this system. The test (called *"Early Diagnostic Procedure"* – EDP) consists of ten subtests. Each is presented in a classical test-teach-retest format and includes detailed instructions. The degree of exactness in imitation is measured by assigning points and is considered to reflect the "depth" of the ZPD. According to Strebeleva, this method allows for differentiation between preschoolers with organically based mental retardation and those who are educationally neglected and/or have temporary delays in psychological development. Strebeva's work is one of the first attempts to apply the concept of imitation as the basis of DA in differential diagnostic procedures for children with different degrees of developmental disorder. However, the EDP subtests are quite variable in their degree of difficulty of imitation and appear to address diverse cognitive functions (from elementary visual tracking to rather complex concepts of size, directionality, and object constancy).

The Application of Cognitive Functions Scale (ACFS) by Lidz and Jepsen (2000) may serve as an example of a curriculum-based DA procedure that reflects on Vygotsky's notion of the ZPD and at the same time responds to specific needs and conditions of preschool education in the US. ACFS was developed for children functioning at the level of 3 to 5 year olds. The six scales were designed to represent typical tasks, tapping basic cognitive processes that represent the foundations of learning and that characterize most preschool curricula throughout the US. As a DA procedure, each task is administered first without intervention, then followed immediately with intervention, and finally followed immediately by repetition of (or variation on) the pretest without intervention. The interventions provide mediation for the child through exposure to basic strategies and principles of task solution on materials that differ from the pretests and posttests. The intervention for each task represents instructional strategies relevant to that task. The six tasks of the ACFS include four core scales: *classification, auditory memory, visual memory,* and *sequential pattern completion,* and two supplementary scales: *verbal planning* and *perspective taking.*

The interventions for each of these scales tap the components described as Mediated Learning Experience (MLE) by Feuerstein and his colleagues (Feuerstein, Rand, & Hoffman 1979; Feuerstein et al., 1980), as adapted and elaborated by Lidz (1991, 2002).

The assessor offers intentional intervention, assuming a leadership role while being sensitive to the child's abilities and responses. The assessor's behavior is guided by scripted interventions that provide strategies and principles of task solution intended for generalization from the pretest tasks to the posttest tasks. These interventions include enhancement of the meaning of the task along with proving the transcendence of the child's approach to task solution beyond the current situation.

A Behavior Observation Scale (BOS) accompanies each task and is completed following each pretest and intervention phase of the subtests. The seven dimensions rated on this scale include the following: self-regulation, persistence, frustration tolerance, flexibility, motivation, interactivity, and responsivity. The ACFS yields scores to document the degree to which the child has mastered each of the tasks; summary scores for pretests and posttests as well as change or gain scores between pretests and posttests; and behavior scale ratings. Although these scores are useful for research and monitoring, the more significant value of the ACFS is the possibility of writing descriptive observations of the child in the process of performing each of the tasks independently and in interaction with a mediator.

As with many other aspects of Vygotsky's theoretical legacy, the notion of the ZPD not only serves as a direct source of some DA approaches but (probably more important) also provides a theoretical perspective for the analysis and evaluation of even those DA approaches that have appeared independently and whose original concept lies outside Vygotskian theory. One may only hope that DA methods will find wider application in the practice of special education.

CONCLUSION

Not many theories formulated more than seventy years ago continue to attract attention and provoke controversy. Vygotsky's theory of disontogenesis and his blueprints for remedial pedagogy continue to be in the focus of professional attention. Because of this, we see it befitting to conclude this chapter not with a summary of the past achievements of Vygotskian approach but with a vision of the possible directions in which this approach may develop:

- Further development of the theory of disontegenesis, including research on the dialectic relationship between primary and secondary handicapping conditions, disability-specific "zones of proximal development," the processes of internalization of external cultural activities into internal processes via psychological tools, and mediated learning in relation to high and low incidence disabilities.

- Applied studies aimed at creating disability-specific psychoeducational profiles of different handicapping conditions along with constructing disability-specific sets of psychological tools and disability-specific mediation techniques.
- Perfected "dynamic assessment" procedures for children with handicapping conditions to effectively connect them with remedial methodologies.

14   Putting Vygotsky to Work

The Change Laboratory as an Application of Double Stimulation

INTRODUCTION

This chapter examines Vygotsky's *method of double stimulation* as a basis for formative interventions in the workplace. I argue that double stimulation is radically different from such intervention approaches as the *design experiments* currently discussed in educational research. Double stimulation is, above all, aimed at eliciting new, expansive forms of agency in subjects. In other words, double stimulation is focused on making subjects masters of their own lives.

First, I will present Vygotsky's double stimulation as a theoretical and methodological idea. I will then examine recent notions of "design experiments" and point out some serious limitations in these experiments. Second, I will introduce the Change Laboratory method developed in the Center for Activity Theory and Developmental Work Research and used for ten years in formative interventions in workplaces. Third, I will discuss this method as an application and expansion of double stimulation. Fourth, I will demonstrate the practical implementation of Change Laboratory with an example from a project carried out in Finnish post offices. Fifth, I will conclude the chapter with a discussion of some methodological and theoretical implications of the Change Laboratory method for further development of Vygotskian research, especially as it is applied in the context of the workplace and organizations.

VYGOTSKY'S METHOD OF DOUBLE STIMULATION

In his quest for a new psychology based on cultural mediation of higher mental functions, Vygotsky was very conscious of the need to build a methodology that would correspond to the character of the theory.

> This methodology [study of reactive responses based on the S-R formula], which easily establishes the response movements of the subject, becomes

363

completely impotent, however, when the basic problem is the study of those means and devices that the subject used to organize his behavior in concrete forms most adequate for each given task. In directing our attention to the study of specifically these (external and internal) means of behavior, we must conduct a radical review of the methodology of the psychological experiment itself.   (Vygotsky, 1999, p. 59)

The methodology Vygotsky, Leont'ev, and Luria developed has been characterized by different names. Vygotsky (e.g., 1997a, pp. 68; 1997b, pp. 85–89; 1999, pp. 57–59) used at least the names "experimental-genetic method," "instrumental method," "historical-genetic method," and "method of double stimulation," somewhat interchangeably. In this paper, I will use the "method of double stimulation."

As van der Veer and Valsiner (1991, p. 169) put it, in double stimulation experiments, "the subject is put in a structured situation where a problem exists (...) and the subject is provided with active guidance towards the construction of a new means to the end of a solution to the problem." Vygotsky described the methodology as follows:

> The task facing the child in the experimental context is, as a rule, beyond his present capabilities and cannot be solved by existing skills. In such cases a neutral object is placed near the child, and frequently we are able to observe how the neutral stimulus is drawn into the situation and takes on the function of a sign. Thus, *the child actively incorporates these neutral objects into the task of problem solving.* We might say that when difficulties arise, neutral stimuli take on the function of a sign and from that point on the operation's structure assumes an essentially different character.   (Vygotsky, 1978, p. 74; italics added)

> By using this approach, we do not limit ourselves to the usual method of offering the subject simple stimuli to which we expect a direct response. Rather, we simultaneously offer a *second series of stimuli* that have a special function. In this way, we are able to study the *process of accomplishing a task by the aid of specific auxiliary means;* thus we are also able to discover the inner structure and development of higher psychological processes.

> The method of double stimulation elicits manifestations of the crucial processes in the behavior of people of all ages. Tying a knot as a reminder, in both children and adults, is but one example of a pervasive regulatory principle of human behavior, that of *signification,* wherein people create temporary links and give significance to previously neutral stimuli in the context of their problem-solving efforts. We regard our method as important because it helps to *objectify* inner psychological processes. . . .
>   (Vygotsky, 1978, pp. 74–75)

It is important to note that the second stimuli, the *mediating means*, were not necessarily given to the subjects in any ready-made form.

> In experimental studies, we do not necessarily have to present to the subject a prepared external means with which we might solve the proposed problem. The main design of our experiment will not suffer in any way if instead of giving the child prepared external means, we will wait while he spontaneously applies the auxiliary device and involves some auxiliary system of symbols in the operation. (...) In not giving the child a ready symbol, we could trace the way all the essential mechanisms of the complex symbolic activity of the child develop during the spontaneous expanding of the devices he used. (Vygotsky, 1999, p. 60)

Van der Veer and Valsiner (1991, p. 399) point out the fundamental challenge that this methodology poses to the experimenter who wants to control the experimental situation.

The notion of experimental method is set up by Vygotsky in a methodological framework where the traditional norm of the experimenter's maximum control over what happens in the experiment is a special case, rather than the modal case. The human subject always "imports" a set of *stimulus–means* (psychological instruments) into an experimental setting. These stimulus-means are in the form of signs that the experimenter cannot control externally in any rigid way. Hence, the experimental setting becomes a context of investigation where the experimenter can manipulate the structure of the investigation in order to trigger (but not "produce") the subject's *construction* of new psychological phenomena.

In other words, the subject's *agency* steps into the picture. To fully appreciate the radical potential of the methodology of double stimulation, we need to reconstruct Vygotsky's more general conception of intentionality and agency. Vygotsky described this artifact-mediated nature of intentional action as follows:

> The person, using the power of things or stimuli, controls his own behavior through them, grouping them, putting them together, sorting them. In other words, the great uniqueness of the will consists of man having no power over his own behavior other than the power that things have over his behavior. But man subjects to himself the power of things over behavior, makes them serve his own purposes and controls that power as he wants. He changes the environment with the external activity and in this way affects his own behavior, subjecting it to his own authority. (Vygotsky, 1997a, p. 212)

Vygotsky (1997a, p. 213) pointed out that voluntary action has two phases or "two apparatus." The first phase is the design phase in which the mediating artifact or "the closure part of the voluntary process" is, often painstakingly, constructed. The second phase is the execution phase or "actuating apparatus," which typically looks quite easy and almost automatic, much like a conditioned reflex.

Classic examples of culturally mediated intentionality include devices we construct and use to wake up early in the morning. Vygotsky's examples of voluntary action are mostly focused on individual actors. This must not be interpreted as neglect of collective intentionality. According to Vygotsky's famous principle, higher psychological functions appear twice, first interpsychologically, in collaborative action, and later intrapsychologically, internalized by the individual.

> V. K. Arsen'ev, a well-known researcher of the Ussuriysk region, tells how in an Udeg village in which he stopped during the journey, the local inhabitants asked him, on his return to Vladivostok, to tell the Russian authorities that the merchant Li Tanku was oppressing them. The next day, the inhabitants came out to accompany the traveler to the outskirts. A gray-haired old man came from the crowd, says Arsen'ev, and gave him the claw of a lynx and told him to put it in his pocket so that he would not forget their petition about Li Tanku. The man himself introduced an artificial stimulus into the situation, actively affecting the processes of remembering. Affecting the memory of another person, we note in passing, is essentially the same as affecting one's own memory.
>
> (Vygotsky, 1997a, pp. 50–51)

Vygotsky's colleague A. N. Leont'ev (1932) focused on the social origins of intentional action. He pointed out that signals given by foremen, the rhythmic sounds of a drum, and working songs gave collective work the necessary direction and continuance. The interpsychological origins of voluntary action – and collective intentionality – would thus be found in rudimentary uses of shared external signals, prompts, as well as in reminders, plans, maps, and so forth.

We see the radical potential of double stimulation and mediated intentionality every day in educational practice. Cheating in school is an enlightening example. What does a student do when he or she constructs a cheating slip while preparing for an exam?

The exam questions and the texts one must master are the "first stimuli," or the object, for the student. The cheating device, for example a paper slip, is the "second stimulus," or the mediating tool. The cheating slip is typically a small piece of paper that can be hidden away from the teacher's eyes and on which one writes what one considers to be the most essential information about a topic one expects to be included in the exam questions.

Because the cheating slip is small, it cannot contain too much text. To create a good cheating slip, the student must carefully select the most relevant and useful aspects of the topic and represent them in an economic and accessible way on the slip. Thus, the construction of a cheating slip is truly what Vygotsky described as creating an external auxiliary means for mastering an object. The construction, contents, and use of the cheating slip bring into light and objectify the inner psychological process of preparing for the test. If we get access to the construction, contents, and use of cheating slips, we learn much more about students' learning than merely by reading and grading their exam answers. That is why I occasionally ask my students to prepare cheating slips and to cheat in my exam. Then, at the end of the exam, I collect their slips and the actual answers.

Cheating is an important form of student agency. By creating and using a cheating slip, the student controls his or her own behavior with the help of a tool that he or she made. The hard part is the construction of a good cheating slip – the design phase or the "closure part" of the agentic action. When asked, students often report that the execution part is surprisingly easy. If the slip has been well-prepared, it is often enough that the student merely glances at it – the details seem to follow from memory as if a floodgate had been opened. This is the phenomenon of *instantaneous recollection* or reconstruction of a complex meaningful pattern with the help of a good "advance organizer" (Ausubel, Novak, & Hanesian, 1978; Ausubel, 2000), "orientation basis" (Haenen, 1995; Talyzina, 1981), or "germ cell model" (Davydov, 1990). In other words, learning to cheat well is extremely valuable.

At the same time, cheating is contestation of the given activity of school-going. By constructing and using a cheating slip, the student takes a risk but also creates a new mediating tool for the mastery of the entire testing situation, which is really the core of traditional schooling. This goes far beyond merely quantitatively enlarging or "amplifying" one's memory. Good cheating is a way to beat the system. John Holt gave a vivid picture of the beginnings and inner contradictions of this type of agency when he described how elementary school kids learn to calculate the risk for cheating.

> She knows that in a recitation period the teacher's attention is divided among twenty students. She also knows the teacher's strategy of asking questions of students who seem confused, or not paying attention. She therefore feels safe waving her hand in the air, as if she were bursting to tell the answer, whether she really knows it or not. (...) It is also interesting to note that she does not raise her hand unless there are at least half a dozen other hands up. (Holt, 1964, p. 12)

Agency is constructed and manifested in actions of testing and goes beyond the limits of what is required and allowed. This is what double stimulation is all about. In actions of good cheating, students are making double-stimulation experiments.

DESIGN EXPERIMENTS AND THEIR LIMITS

Design experiments were suggested by Brown (1992) and Collins (1992) to bridge the gap between educational research and practical educational innovation.

> Design experiments ideally result in greater understanding of a learning ecology – a complex, interacting system involving multiple elements of different types and levels – by designing its elements and by anticipating how these elements function together to support learning. Design experiments therefore constitute a means of addressing the complexity that is a hallmark of educational settings.   (Cobb et al., 2003, p. 9)

For Collins, Joseph, and Bielaczyc (2004, p. 33), the methodology of design experiments, or design research, is basically a linear progression of six steps, starting by "implementing a design" and ending by "reporting on design research." Because the process begins with implemention, the making of the design in the first place is not even included in the methodology. Thus, there is no need to consider the issues of who makes the design or what theory or principles are used for the design. In a similar vein, Cobb and his coauthors (2003) seem to take it for granted that it is the researchers who determine the "endpoints" for a design experiment.

> In addition to clarifying the theoretical intent of the experiment, the research team must also specify the significant disciplinary ideas and forms of reasoning that constitute the prospective goals or endpoints for student learning.   (Cobb et al., 2003, p. 11)

The stepwise linear notion of design research is also supported by Bannan–Ritland (2003, p. 22). Cyclic iterations serving the refinement of the design complement but do not challenge the basically linear image. Cobb and coauthors do mention that design experiments that conceived by researchers create discontinuity – but that does not seem to require any further reflection:

> The intent is to investigate the possibilities for educational improvement by bringing about new forms of learning in order to study them. Consequently, there is frequently a significant discontinuity between typical forms of education (these could be studied naturalistically) and those that are the focus of a design experiment.   (Cobb et al., 2003, p. 10)

The emphasis on completeness, finality, and closure may be partly explained by the idea of design experiments as "refinement." The implication is that the researchers have somehow come up with a pretty good model which needs to be perfected in the field.

> Design experiments were developed as a way to carry out formative research to test and refine educational designs based on theoretical principles derived from prior research. This approach of progressive refinement in design involves putting a first version of a design into the world to see how it works. Then, the design is constantly revised based on experience, until *all the bugs* are worked out.
>
> (Collins, Joseph, & Bielaczyc, 2004, pp. 18; emphasis added)

> Design research should always have the dual goals of refining both theory and practice.   (Collins, Joseph, & Bielaczyc, 2004, p. 19)

Collins, Joseph, and Bielaczyc (2004, pp. 18–19) compare educational design research to the design of cars and other consumer products, using *Consumer Reports* as their explict model for evaluation. They do not seem to notice any significant difference between finished mass products and such open-ended, continously coconfigured products as educational innovations (for coconfiguration, see Victor & Boynton, 1998; Engeström, 2004). A strange obsession with "completeness" runs like a red thread through their argument. "Thus, in the jigsaw, all pieces of the puzzle come together to form *a complete understanding*" (Collins, Joseph, & Bielaczyc, 2004, p. 23; emphasis added). What this overlooks is that "one can never get it right, and that innovation may best be seen as a continuous process, with particular product embodiments simply being arbitrary points along the way" (von Hippel & Tyre, 1995, p. 12).

To sum up, in discourse on "design experiments," scholars do not usually ask: Who does the design and why? It is tacitly assumed that researchers make the grand design, teachers implement it (and contribute to its modification), and students learn better as a result. This linear view ignores what sociologists teach us about interventions as contested terrains that are full of resistance, reinterpretation, and surprise from the actors in the design experiment.

> Intervention is an on-going transformational process that is constantly re-shaped by its own internal organisational and political dynamic and by the specific conditions it encounters or itself creates, including the responses and strategies of local and regional groups who may struggle to define and defend their own social spaces, cultural boundaries and positions within the wider power field.

> Crucial to understanding processes of intervention is the need to identify and come to grips with the strategies that local actors devise for dealing with their new intervenors so that they might appropriate, manipulate, subvert or dismember particular interventions.   (Long, 2001, p. 27)

THE CHANGE LABORATORY AS AN APPLICATION
OF DOUBLE STIMULATION

Formative interventions in the Vygotskian sense need to be understood as formation of *critical design agency* among all the parties: researchers, teachers, and students or, respectively, researchers, managers, workers, and clients. Such critical design agency includes the will and courage to say "no" – to challenge the designs offered previously... Students form specific cognitive "endpoints" in complex learning ecologies and actively make sense of and reconfigure the tasks and the context of the tasks among the participants. In other words, what is initially presented as the problem or the task is interpreted and turned into a meaningful challenge several times over in the process of the intervention.

The Change Laboratory method develops work practices by the participants in dialogue and debate among themselves, with their management, with their clients, and – not the least – with the interventionist researchers. It facilitates both intensive, deep transformations and continuous incremental improvement. The idea is to arrange, on the shop floor, a room or space in which there is a rich set of representational tools available for analysis of disturbances and for constructing new models of the work activity. The Change Laboratory method was initially designed to be used by a work team, or a unit, initially with the help of an interventionist. Subsequently, expanded versions of the Change Laboratory method have been developed for the use of two or more organizations or organizational units seeking to enhance their collaboration.

The central tool of the Change Laboratory is a 3×3 set of surfaces for representing the work activity (Figure 14.1). Practitioners participating in the Change Laboratory process face the surfaces and also each other. A scribe is usually appointed from among them, to record intermediate outcomes of the discussion on the three surfaces. One or more researcher-interventionists are present to guide the process. A video projector is important because videotaped work situations are typically used as material in the laboratory sessions. Each session is also videotaped for research and to facilitate the reviewing of critical laboratory events in subsequent sessions.

The horizontal dimension of the surfaces represents different levels of abstraction and theoretical generalization. At one end, the *mirror* surface is used to represent and examine experiences from work practice, particularly problem situations and disturbances, but also novel innovative solutions. Videotaped work episodes as well as photographs, stories, interviews, customer feedback, performance statistics, and so forth, are used as mirror data.

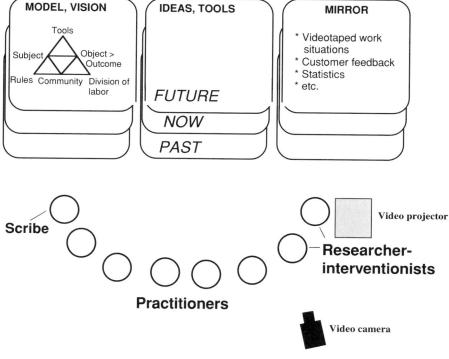

FIGURE 14.1. Prototypical layout of the Change Laboratory.

At the other end, the *model/vision* surface is reserved for theoretical tools and conceptual analysis. The complex triangular model of an activity system (Engeström, 1987, p. 78), displayed schematically in Figure 14.1, is used to analyze the development and interconnections of the work activity under scrutiny. Systemic roots of specific, but recurring problems and disturbances are traced and conceptualized as inner contradictions of the activity system. In addition to the general model of activity system, more specific conceptual models are often used. For instance, in a series of interventions, medical practitioners developed a model for negotiated collaborative care of patients with multiple chronic illnesses in Helsinki. The model itself became the central conceptual tool for further laboratory processes in the field (Engeström, 2001; Engeström, Engeström, & Kerosuo, 2003).

The third surface in the middle is reserved for *ideas and tools*. In analysis of problem situations and in the design of a new model for the work activity, intermediate cognitive tools (Norman, 1993) such as schedules and flowcharts of processes, layout pictures and diagrams of organizational structures, categorizations of interview responses, formulas for calculating costs, (or techniques for idea generation and problem solving (including simulations and role-playing), are often needed. As the participants move between the experiential mirror and the theoretical model/vision, they also produce intermediate ideas and partial solutions to be experimented with and tested. These, too, are represented on the middle surface.

The vertical dimension of the surfaces represents movement in time, between the past, the present, and the future. Work in the Change Laboratory typically starts with the mirror of present problems. It then moves to trace the roots of current trouble by mirroring experiences from the past and by modeling the past activity system. The work then proceeds to model the current activity and its inner contradictions, which enables the participants to focus their transformation efforts on essential sources of trouble. The next step is the envisioning of the future model of the activity, including its concretization by means of identifying "next-step" partial solutions and tools. Subsequently, the stepwise implementation of the new vision is planned and monitored in the Change Laboratory. Such a cycle of expansive learning induced in the Change Laboratory typically takes ten or twelve weekly sessions and one or two follow-up sessions after a few months. One cycle often leads to the next one, and within the cycles there are smaller cycles of problem solving and learning (see Engeström, 1996a).

The Change Laboratory is based on separation and embeddedness simultaneously. It is located in the workplace as close to the shop floor as possible; yet, it is a room protected by walls. The boundaries between Laboratory and practice are made permeable by encouraging movement across them. Practitioners may use the Laboratory space for reflection outside the scheduled sessions. During the sessions, they may go out of the Laboratory space to check the reality on the shop floor. Representations of work are brought into the laboratory from work and are brought out of the laboratory onto the walls of the actual work space. Such shifting of contexts has been found crucial in solving complex problems, such as those involved in the implementation of new machinery on the shop floor.

> A striking feature of the adaptation process was the use of different physical settings for responding to a single problem. In most of the cases studied, engineers needed to investigate the same issue in two different locations (the plant and the lab). They often shifted repeatedly between locations before they could understand and resolve the problem.
> (Tyre & von Hippel, 1993, p. 7; see also Engeström,
> Engeström, & Kärkkäinen, 1995)

What is the similarity between Vygotsky's double stimulation and the Change Laboratory method? In the Change Laboratory method, the original task or "first stimulus" of Vygotskian designs is represented by the *mirror* in which a challenging problem or disturbance is presented by means of experientially powerful examples, often on video. The "first stimulus" needs to be acknowledged and articulated by the participants. This first step is commonly an emotionally charged process in which resistance and denial play an important part.

In Vygotsky's accounts, the "second stimulus" is initially a neutral or ambiguous artifact that is filled with meaning and mediational potential by the acting subject. The notion of "neutral stimulus" is, however, problematic. There are no neutral objects – every artifact has inherent affordances materially and historically inscribed in it. Even an empty sheet of paper is not neutral. It affords or "invites" writing and drawing actions, but it does not afford many other kinds of actions. A closer look at Vygotsky's work reveals that the notion of neutrality is actually not meant to be taken in any absolute sense. Vygotsky repeatedly used the example of experiments related to him by Kurt Lewin:

> In experiments involving meaningless situations, Lewin found that the subject searches for some point of support that is external to him and that he defines his own behavior through this external support. In one set of experiments, for example, the experimenter left the subject and did not return, but observed him from a separate room. Generally, the subject waited for 10–20 minutes. Then, not understanding what he should do, he remained in a state of oscillation, confusion and indecisiveness for some time. Nearly all the adults searched for some external point of support. For example, one subject defined his actions in terms of the striking of the clock. Looking at the clock, he thought: "When the hand moves to the vertical position, I will leave." The subject transformed the situation in this way, establishing that he would wait until 2:30 and then leave. When the time came, the action occurred automatically. By changing the psychological field, the subject created a new situation for himself in this field. He transformed the meaningless situation into one that had a clear meaning. (Vygotsky, 1987, p. 356)

In this case, the "first stimulus" was the problematic task of having to wait without any certainty of a return of the experimenter. To resolve the dilemma, the subject constructed a mediating "second stimulus," namely, the clock as a meaningful sign that would allow the subject to leave. Now the clock was neutral in the sense that it did not initially represent a specific point of time or alerting signal that would relieve the subject. But it did have a culturally pervasive meaningful structure – a display of the progress of hours and minutes. This *general* meaningful structure had to be transformed into a *specific* meaningful sign for the subject and the situation. In other words, what can be used as "second stimulus" is not arbitrary. Instead of using absolute neutrality, it may be more useful to characterize the potential *second stimulus* as something that has culturally appropriate general affordances but also sufficient ambiguity and malleability so that the subject will have to transform it into a situationally effective mediating device by "filling" it with specific contents.

In the Change Laboratory, the initial mediating "second stimulus" is typically a general conceptual model, commonly, but not exlusively, the triangular representation of an activity system (Engeström, 1987, p. 178; see also Figures 14.3 and 14.4). Such a model has a potentially meaningful general structure. However, to invest it with personal sense, it must be explicitly filled by the participants with specific contents that correspond to their assessments of the situation. The activity system model is used to make sense of the built-in contradictions that give rise to the troubles and disturbances depicted in the mirror. This model is also used as a vehicle of time travel, in the construction of a *vision* of the past and the future of the activity system.

In Vygotsky's theory, double stimulation engenders processes that lead to novel solutions, actions, concepts and skills. In the Lewinian experiment on "meaningless situations" described above, the subject literally broke away from an unacceptably dilemmatic, closed situation. Similarly, in Arsen'ev's account from the Udeg village, the villagers' action was an attempt at breaking away from an intolerable, closed framework of exploitation (for the developmental importance of breaking away, see Engeström, 1996b). These examples demonstrate that the formation of new solutions, concepts, and skills in double stimulation is much more than just a cognitive learning achievement. It is a liberating achievement of agency formation, which gives expansive personal and collective meaning to the associated cognitive and cultural learning contents.

In the Change Laboratory, the emerging new solutions and tools are represented on the surface in the middle surface. Breaking away from a dilemmatic and contradictory work situation requires construction of expanded objects, tools, communities, rules, and divisions of labor. In the Change Laboratory, the construction of such new solutions begins by means of articulating, naming, and modeling. These processes may be characterized as *objectification* (Moscovici, 1984) and *stabilization* (Smith, 1998). Breaking away requires stabilization to succeed.

In the Change Laboratory, movement happens in three dimensions. First, the gaze, the intellectual work, and the practical representational work (writing, drawing, etc.) of the participants move horizontally *between the representational surfaces* of the mirror and the model, stopping occasionally in the middle to try and construct new solutions. Second, these processes move *between three layers of time.* And third, the discourse moves *between the participants and their various voices and social languages,* including, minimally, a work team or unit plus one or more researchers/interventionists, and optimally, also representatives of management and clients.

CHANGE LABORATORY IN FINNISH POST OFFICES

The Change Laboratory was first implemented in five pilot post offices of the Finnish Postal Service from February to August, 1996. The project, named *Delivery 2000,* was aimed at redesigning the delivery work of mail carriers. The project was set up and monitored by a tripartite steering group consisting of representatives of management, trade unions, and researcher-interventionists (for a more comprehensive analysis of the project, see Pihlaja, 2005).

The cultural tradition of mail carriers has been a combination of bureaucracy and individualism. The traditional hierarchical organization of the Postal Service has largely precluded innovations from below. Work processes have been meticulously rationalized and measured from above by procedures confirmed through collective bargaining. Individualism, in turn, stems from the fact that individual mail carriers have been free to go as soon as they have finished their individually assigned routes for the day. There has been little incentive for collaborative teamwork.

However, when we started our project, the Finnish Postal Service faced increasing competition from private companies entering the field. There was an urgent need to raise productivity and a looming threat of severe loss of jobs.

All the mail carriers of the five pilot post offices met mostly once a week for four months in their Change Laboratories (called *Room 2000* by the practitioners). Each session was structured around concrete tasks requiring the use of the Change Laboratory surfaces. Figure 14.2 depicts a session in one of them, the post office named Turku 52.

The room in Figure 14.2 was the regular coffee room of the workers, a few feet from the shop floor where the mail was sorted. In the post offices, the available material equipment was minimal: three flip chart stands, felt pens, and a VCR with a TV monitor attached. All the meetings in the five pilot offices were videotaped, as were samples of key work processes (sorting of mail, actual delivery) in each pilot unit at the beginning and at the end of the process. A number of interviews were

FIGURE 14.2. A Change Laboratory session in the post office Turku 52 (the researcher-interventionist sitting third from the left).

made with the workers in each site during the process. The workers also interviewed a number of their clients.

There were three main phases in the process. In the first phase, the workers analyzed the history and the present contradictions of their work activity. Figure 14.3 presents a summary of the results of this phase in the triangular model form used by the workers.

Question marks in the components of the triangle indicate possible contradictions. It was characteristic to the pilot post offices that they characterized their contradictions only in tentative and dilemmatic terms, typically in the form of questions concerning each component on its own rather than as aggravated tensions between components of the activity. After the first phase, the pilots met in a one-day conference where they reported and discussed their intermediate findings. Excerpts from their presentations illuminate the nature of the contradictions.

> We've had lots of good ideas, and we've been thinking that we could do work which is something else than just delivering. We could for example handle some social services, we have quite a lot of old people in our area. But who would train us for that and in what time? And how does it impact the finances, the results; would it bring any revenue?

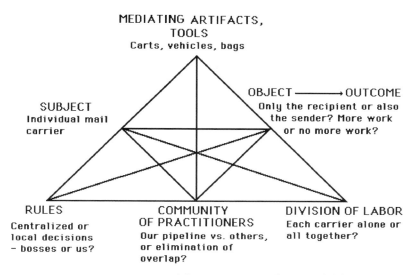

FIGURE 14.3. Summary of the current contradictions of delivery work identified by the mail carriers.

We also had this heated discussion, whether we should expand our object or not.

So it's the old way of thinking, a bureaucrat's way: I'm sitting here and I won't do anything else. I'll go home after I'm done and I don't give a damn about what the others are doing.

Right now it seems that it's becoming a problem, which is in a way also a good thing, namely the increase of advertisement mail.

This internal flexibility, it would mean that the work measurement would be adjustable within our own office. So that when the amounts of mail fluctuate, the real shitty day wouldn't fall on one guy alone, while the others just giggle about it. . . .

There are these so called pipelines [referring to special delivery services and other separate branches of the Postal Services], we do a terrible amount of overlapping work. So for example the special deliveries comes from five kilometers to fetch from us a packet which goes to the house next to us, and takes it there. So that really doesn't make any sense.

The tentative and uncertain tone in the characterization of the contradictions in the Change Laboratories reflected the fact that the Postal Service had had a total monopoly in their field for a long time. There were lots of historically built-in buffers that slowed down and softened the impact of the contradictions experienced in daily work practice.

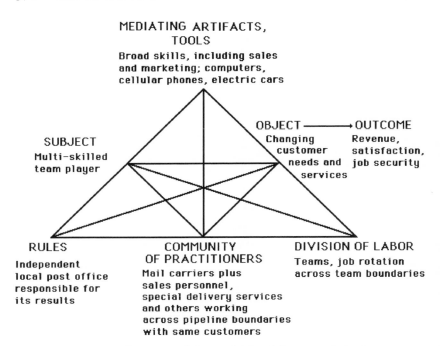

FIGURE 14.4. Summary of the model for delivery work in the year 2000 designed by the workers.

In the second phase of the process, the pilots designed visions for delivery work as it should be organized in the year 2000. The results of this phase are summarized in Figure 14.4.

Figure 14.4 is obviously an idealistic vision. However, the core idea of independent post offices responsible for their own results became a sound guiding principle for the transformation envisioned. While crafting the vision, each pilot also designed a set of first-step solutions and tools to be implemented as local experiments within the next months.

These local experiments had different emphases in the different pilots. Three of the five designed experiments aimed both at introducing teams and also at creating new products and services. Two of the five experiments concentrated on new products and services only.

In the third phase of the process, the experimental solutions were implemented and their impact on revenues, performance, customer satisfaction, and workers' well-being was monitored. Two examples of the new products and services, both pioneered by the Turku 52 pilot office, may be mentioned.

Example 1: The Turku 52 pilot group decided to start selling stamps to the customers at their door, thus saving them the trip to the post office. This had not been the practice in Finnish Postal Service. To put the idea into practice, a pilot group needed to design a brochure advertising the new service to the customers, and an order form for stamps. The pilot group also needed to design and order belt bags for carrying money. They needed to make sure the mail bags were appropriate for carrying stamps. For this concrete solution, the post office had to become a virtual design office for a while. A new set of instruments were created – a step was taken toward a qualitatively new type of instrumentality which involves direct business discussions between the mail carrier and the customers.

Example 2: In the pilot office of Turku 52, the mail carriers designed an entirely new "safety service" for old people living alone in their apartments. The mail carrier would not only drop the mail, he or she would also ring the doorbell and check that everything is all right with the elderly customer. There was rapidly growing need for this type of service due to demographic change in the country. The social services department of the City of Turku quickly endorsed the idea, seeing potential savings in it. The new service was experimentally implemented in the area for which the pilot office was responsible. The experiment attracted nationwide attention in mass media.

These two examples clarify the difference between the process elicited by the Change Laboratory and management consulting approaches such as business process reengineering (BPR). The famous launching slogan of BPR was "Don't automate, obliterate!" (Hammer, 1990), implying that the idea is to radically wipe out unnecessary and wasteful processes. An appropriate slogan for the *Delivery 2000* project would have been: "Don't obliterate, expand!" This implies that new products and new business (e.g., selling stamps, delivering safety services) are built, taking advantage of the existing basic work processes (delivering mail). Such an expansive approach is possible only when instead of mapping and rationalizing the existing processes, one starts by questioning historically the *object* of work: What are we producing and why? (Engeström, Puonti, & Seppänen, 2003).

In each phase of the Change Laboratory process, there was back-and-forth movement between the problems or the first stimuli presented on the *mirror surface* and the conceptual models or the second stimuli worked out on the *model/vision surface* (see Figure 14.1). When a vision for the future organization of work was constructed, the participants were asked to identify practical problems and difficulties that the new model would generate. These were worked out in more detail when the practitioners actually implemented and tested their solutions in practice.

CONCLUSION: LESSONS FOR VYGOTSKIAN STUDIES

In the ten years that have passed after the first Change Laboratory project within the Postal Services, we have conducted dozens of Change Laboratory method intervention studies in various organizations. Variations of the basic Change Laboratory method have been developed, such as *Boundary Crossing Laboratories* between multiple collaborating organizations (e.g., Engeström, Engeström, & Kerosuo, 2003) and *Competence Laboratories* for proactive identification and formation of new competencies on the shopfloor (e.g., Virkkunen & Ahonen, 2004). These studies have generated a very rich database, which, as analyses progress, will yield new insights into the potentials and challenges of expanding Vygotsky's idea of double stimulation to interventionist studies of transformations in work (for some of the analyses, see Engeström, Lompscher, & Rückriem, 2005). At this point, I will take up three such challenges.

The first challenge has to do with the nature of mediation by tools and signs. Previous Vygotskian theorizing and research has mainly focused on a single individual or on two subjects using a single, well-defined mediating tool or artifact. Language as mediator demands a more complex approach – but studies of semiotic mediation have commonly excluded material instruments and tools. In the Change Laboratory, the mediational setup is complex and multilayered both semiotically and instrumentally. Yet the Change Laboratory is temporally and spatially constrained so as to allow the collection of comprehensive fine-grained data by means of videotaping. Analysis of such data forces the researcher to adopt a new view of mediation: instead of using single instruments, tools, or language, one has to analyze a whole interconnected *instrumentality.*

The concept of instrumentality has three implications: (1) The instruments form a system that includes multiple cognitive artifacts and semiotic means used for analysis and design, and straightforward primary tools used in the daily work are brought into the Laboratory for examination, reshaping, and experimentation. (2) In such a dense mediational setting, a set of interconnected new sociocognitive processes are called for and a new mentality is generated. (3) The complexity of the setup means that the instrumentality is constantly evolving; old tools are modified, and new tools are created.

The second challenge stems from the centrality of agency in Vygotsky's theory of double stimulation. If human agency is the central focus, then we need to rethink our standard notions of causality. What kind of interpretive lenses do we need for that? Eskola (1999, p. 111) suggests that the answer lies in three facets: (1) the structure and development

Interpretive Layer	In activity the actor	Takes into account, according to this or that logic, that	If x, then y
			Law, rule
Contradictory Layer	As participant in collective activities	Is driven by contradictory motives	Searching resolution by often unpredictable actions

FIGURE 14.5. Two layers of causality in human action.

of the activity in which the actors are involved, and its meaning to the different actors; (2) the laws and rules that actors take into account in this activity; and (3) the logics used to take part in the activity. Eskola's realistic paradigm focuses on the fact that humans do not merely react as physical objects; they act based on their activities, interpretations, and logics. For the sake of simplicity, I call this the *interpretive layer* of causality.

But there is more to causality in human contexts. Human beings interpret, and they also face contradictions between multiple motives embedded in and engendered by their historically evolving communities and objects. This is the layer that makes humans look irrational and unpredictable (see Engeström, 1989). This adds another layer to human causality. I call it the *contradictory layer* (Figure 14.5).

What is still missing in Figure 14.5 is the human potential for agency, for intentional collective and individual actions aimed at transforming the activity. Thus, I complete the picture by adding an *agentive layer* (Figure 14.6).

Interpretive Layer	In activity the actor	Takes into account, according to this or that logic, that	If x, then y
			Law, rule
Contradictory Layer	As participant in collective activities	Is driven by contradictory motives	Searching resolution by often unpredictable actions
Agentive Layer	As potential individual and collective agent	Takes intentional transformative actions	Inventing and using artifacts to control the action from the outside

FIGURE 14.6. Three layers of causality in human action.

Vygotsky's description of the Lewinian experiment beautifully captures all the three layers of Figure 14.6 in a simplified form. Initially, the subject interpreted the situation as an experiment in which one must follow the rules of the experimenter. When nothing happened, a contradiction emerged between those expected rules and one's quest for meaning; there was a period of confusion, which could lead to unpredictable and "irrational" actions. However, by using an external cultural artifact such as the clock, the subject was able to transform the situation and take agentive action. Notice that agentive action in its rudimentary forms may look like nonaction, or mere resistance – such as leaving the room in the experiment. It is, however, a radically different action from that of, say, passive waiting or "irrational" noisemaking. Translated into the context of collective work activity and the Change Laboratory, the same steps might look like this. Initially, practitioners interpret their work situation as an iron cage where they must do what they are told. As systemic contradictions accumulate in the work activity, repeated dilemmatic problem situations and "impossible tasks" emerge, confusion, stress, and resistance grow, and unpredictable "irrational" actions are likely. By means of external cultural artifacts such as the Change Laboratory instrumentality, a collective effort may be taken to transform the situation by agentive actions. In the Change Laboratory, disturbances and dilemmatic situations, including practitioners' own "irrational" actions engendered by these situations, are reproduced, observed, and reexperienced as "first stimuli." Conceptual models are employed as "second stimuli" to facilitate specific agentive actions of analysis, design, and implementation.

The third challenge is also related to agency. We have extensive experience of generating agentive actions among competent adult practitioners in various workplaces. But can Change Laboratories be useful with children or with underprivileged, marginalized and silenced groups of people? Or will the method turn into a form of paternalistic manipulation if used with such subjects? It seems clear that to take such subjects as equal interlocutors in interventions, the researchers need to learn new ways to listen to and amplify the voices of the subjects (Porter et al. 2005). For example, in the Culture Laboratory, a variation of the Change Laboratory designed for immigrant students, we found that the students' interests were very often expressed in fragmentary and weakly articulated suggestions, which were easily overlooked if the interventionists did not nurture and support the expansion of such suggestions (Teräs, in press).

REFERENCES

INTRODUCTION

Basov, M. Y. (1931). *General foundation of pedology*. Moscow-Leningrad: Gosizdat.

Bernshtein, N. A. (1966). *The psychology of movement and activity*. Moscow: Medical Publishers.

Bernshtein, N. A. (1967). *The coordination and regulation of movements*. Oxford, UK: Pergamon Press

Cole, M. (1996). *Cultural Psychology: A once and future discipline*. Cambridge, MA: Harvard University Press.

Leont'ev, A. N. (1972). On the problem of activity in psychology. *Questions of Psychology, 9*, 4–33.

Luria, A. R. (1979). *The making of mind*. Cambridge, MA: Harvard University Press.

Rubinshtein, S. L. (1957). *Existence and consciousness*. Moscow: Academy of Pedagogical Science.

Uznadze, D. N. (1961). *Experimental basis of the psychology of set*. Tibilisi, Georgia: Academy of Science.

Vygotsky, L. S. (1927/1997a). *The collected works of L. S. Vygotsky. Problems of the theory and history of psychology* (Vol 3). New York: Plenum Press. (Original work published in 1927.)

Vygotsky, L. S. (1934/1962). *Thought and language*. Translated by E. Hanfmann & G.Vakar. Cambridge, MA: MIT Press.

Vygotsky, L. S. (1934/1987). Thinking and speech. In R.W. Rieber & A. S. Carton (Eds.), *The collected works of L. S. Vygotsky. Volume 1: Problems of General Psychology*. New York: Plenum Press.

Vygotsky, L. S. (1997b). *Educational psychology*. Boca Raton, FL: St. Lucie Press. (Originally written 1921–1923.)

Wertsch, J. V. (1995). *Vygotsky: The ambivalent Enlightenment rationalist* (Vol 21). Heinz Werner Lecture Series. Worcester, MA: Clark University Press, pp. 39–62.

Yaroshevsky, M. (1989). *Lev Vygotsky*. Moscow: Progress Publishers.

CHAPTER I

Bailey, D. B., Bruer, J. T., Symons, F. J., & Lichtman, J. W. (2001). *Critical thinking about critical periods*. Baltimore: Paul H. Brookes Publishing Company.

Baldwin, J. M. (1906). *Thought and things* (Vol 1). London: Swan Sonnenschein & Co.

Bauer, R. A. (1955). *Der neue Mensch in der sowjetischen Psychologie*. Bad Nauheim: I. M. Christian-Verlag.

Bekhterev, V. M. (1991). *Ob'ektivnaya psikhologiya*. Moscow: Nauka.

Bekhterev, V. M. (1994). *Izbrannye raboty po sotsial'noy psikhologii*. Moscow: Nauka.

Bekhterev, V. M. (1998). *Suggestion and its role in social life*. New Brunswick, NJ: Transaction Publishers.

Berdyaev, N. A. (1930). V pamyati printsa G. N. Trubetskogo. *Put'*, *21*, 94–96.

Berdyaev, N. A. (1936). V pamyati G. I. Chelpanova. *Put'*, *50*, 56–57.

Blonsky, P. P. (1920). *Reforma nauki*. Moscow: Izdatel'stvo Otdela Narodnogo Prosveshcheniya MSRD.

Blonsky, P. P. (1979). *Izbrannye pedagogicheskie i psikhologicheskie sochineniya*. (2 vols.). Moscow: Pedagogika.

Bogdanchikov, S. A. (1994). Neizvestniy G. I. Chelpanov. *Voprosy Psikhologii*, *1*, 27–35.

Bogdanchikov, S. A. (1996). Pochemu byl uvolen G. I. Chelpanov? *Voprosy Psikhologii*, *1*, 85–96.

Bogdanchikov, S. A. (1998). Nauchno-organizatsionnaya deyatel'nost' G. I. Chelpanova. *Voprosy Psikhologii*, *2*, 126–135.

Botsmanova, M. E., & Guseva, E. P. (1997). Nikolay Aleksandrovich Rybnikov. *Voprosy Psikhologii*, *6*, 96–108.

Brushlinskiy, A. V., & Kol'tsova, V. A. (1994). Sotsial'no-psikhologicheskaya kontseptsiya V. M. Bekhtereva. In V. M. Bekhterev, *Izbrannye raboty po sotsial'noy psikhologii*. Moscow: Nauka, pp. 3–17.

Chelpanov, G. I. (1912). *Mozg i dusha: Kritika materializma i ocherk sovremennykh ucheniy o dushe*. Moscow: Kushnerev.

Chelpanov, G. I. (1913). Ob eksperimental'nom metode v psikhologii. *Novye Idei v Filosofii*, *9*, 12–39.

Chelpanov, G. I. (1915). *Vvedenie v eksperimental'nuyu psikhologiyu*. Moscow: Kushnerev.

Chelpanov, G. I. (1924). *Psikhologiya i markiszm*. Moscow: A. V. Dumnov & Co.

Chelpanov, G. I. (1925). *Ob'ektivnaya psikhologiya v Rossii i Amerike: Refleksologiya i psikhologiya povedeniya*. Moscow: A. V. Dumov & Co.

Chelpanov, G. I. (1926a). *Psikhologiya ili refleksologiya: Spornye problemy psikhologii*. Moscow: Russkiy Knizhnik.

Chelpanov, G. I. (1926b). *Sotsial'naya psikhologiya ili 'uslovnye refleksy'?* Moscow: Russkiy Knizhnik.

Chelpanov, G. I. (1992a). Iz trudov Psikhologicheskogo Instituta. *Voprosy Psikhologii*, *3–4*, 43–46.

Chelpanov, G. I. (1992b). O zadachakh Moskovskogo Psikhologicheskogo Instituta. *Voprosy Psikhologii*, *5*, 41–43.

Ekzemplyarskiy, V. (1992). Georgiy Ivanovich Chelpanov. *Voprosy Psikhologii, 3–4*, 49–50.

Gesell, A. (1928). *Infancy and human growth.* New York: Macmillan.

Gordon, G. O. (1995). Iz vospominaniy o G. I. Chelpanove. *Voprosy Psikhologii, 1*, 84–96.

Kornilov, K. N. (1994). Reaktologiya i marksistskaya psikhologiya. *Voprosy Psikhologii, 2*, 25–27.

Kozulin, A. (1984). *Psychology in Utopia: Toward a social history of Soviet psychology.* Cambridge, MA: MIT Press.

Ladygina-Kohts, N. N. (1923). *Issledovanie poznavatel'nykh sposobnostey shimpanze.* Moscow-Petrograd: Gosudarstvennoe Izdatel'stvo.

Ladygina-Kohts, N. N. (1928a). Recherches sur l'intelligence du chimpanzé. *Journal de Psychologie, 25*, 255–275.

Ladygina-Kohts, N. N. (1928b). *Prisposobitel'nye motornye navyki makaka v usloviyakh eksperimenta: K voprosu o 'trudovykh protsessakh' nizshikh obez'yan.* Moscow: Izdanie Gosudarstvennogo Darvinovskogo Muzeya.

Ladygina-Kohts, N. N. (1930). Les aptitudes motrices adaptives du singe inférieur. *Journal de Psychologie, 27*, 412–447.

Ladygina-Kohts, N. N. (1935). *Ditya shimpanze i ditya cheloveka v ikh instinktakh, emotsiyakh, igrakh, privychkakh i vyrazhitel'nykh dvizheniyakh.* Moscow: Trudy Muzeya.

Ladygina-Kohts, N. N. (1937). La conduite du petit du chimpanzé et de l'enfant de l'homme. *Journal de Psychologie, 34*, 494–531.

Ladygina-Kohts, N. N. (1935, 2002). *Infant chimpanzee and human child.* Oxford: Oxford University Press.

Lipkina, A. I. (1994). Neskol'ko shtrikhov k portretu uchiteley. *Voprosy Psikhologii, 2*, 32–35.

Lomov, B. F., Kol'tsova, V. A., & Stepanova, E. I. (1991). Ocherk zhizni i nauchnoy deyatel'nosti Vladimira Mikhaylovicha Bekhtereva (1857–1927). In V. M. Bekhterev, *Ob'ektivnaya psikhologiya.* Moscow: Nauka, pp. 424–444.

Losskiy, N. O. (1934/1996). O detskom myshlenii. Review of Vygotsky's *Thinking and Speech. Voprosy Psikhologii, 5*, 134–137.

Luria, A. R. (1994). Ob izuchenii reaktsiy i istoricheskom razvitii povedeniya cheloveka. *Voprosy Psikhologii, 2*, 27–32.

Luria, A. R. (2003). *Psikhologicheskoe nasledie.* Moscow: Smysl.

Martsinkovskaya, T. D., & Yaroshevskiy, M. G. (1999). Neizvestnye stranitsy tvorchestva G. I. Chelpanova. *Voprosy Psikhologii, 3*, 99–106.

Mecacci, L. (1977). *Brain and history: The relationship between neurophysiology and psychology in Soviet research.* New York: Brunner/Mazel Publishers.

Myasnikov, V. S. (2002). Gustav Shpet: trudy i gody. In G. Shpet, *Istoriya kak problema logiki: Kriticheskie i metodologicheskie issledovaniya.* Moscow: Pamyatniki Istoricheskoy Mysli, pp. 3–32.

Nikol'skaya, N. A. (1994a). Psikhologo-pedagogicheskie vzglyady G. I. Chelpanova. *Voprosy Psikhologii, 1*, 36–42.

Nikol'skaya, A. A. (1994b). Osnovnye etapy razvitiya nauchnoy deyatel'nosti Psikhologicheskogo Instituta. *Voprosy Psikhologii, 2*, 5–21.

Nikol'skaya, A. A. (1997). A. P. Nechaev: Zhiznenniy i tvorcheskiy Put. *Voprosy Psikhologii*, 2, 100–111.

Petrovsky, A. V. (1984). *Voprosy istorii i teorii psikhologii: Izbrannye trudy*. Moscow: Pedagogika.

Petrovsky, A. V., & Danil'chenko, M. G. (1979). P. P. Blonsky kak pedagog i psikholog. In P. P. Blonsky, *Izbrannye pedagogicheskie i psikhologicheskie sochineniya* (Vol. 1). Moscow: Pedagogika, pp. 8–29.

Rybnikov, N. A. (1994a). Kak sozdavalsya Psikhologicheskiy Institut. *Voprosy Psikhologii*, *1*, 6–16.

Rybnikov, N. A. (1994b). Iz avtobiografii N. A. Rybnikova. *Voprosy Psikhologii*, *1*, 11–16.

Severtsov, A. N. (1922). *Evoliyutsiya i psikhika*. Moscow: Izdanie M. & S. Sabashnikov.

Shapiro, S. A., & Gerke, E. D. (1991). The process of adaptation to environmental conditions in a child's behavior. *Soviet Psychology*, 29(6), 44–90.

Sirotkina, I. E. (1994). Ot reaktsii k zhivomu dvizheniyu: N.A. Bernshteyn v Psikhologicheskom Institute dvadtsatykh godov. *Voprosy Psikhologii*, 4, 16–27.

Strickland, L. H. (1994). Introduction. In L. H. Strickland, *V. M. Bekhterev's collective reflexology. Part 1*. Commack, NY: Nova Science Publishers, pp. xi–xxiv.

Strickland, L. H. (1994). *V. M. Bekhterev's collective reflexology* (Part 1). Commack, NY: Nova Science Publishers.

Talankin, A. A. (1994). O reaktologicheskom iskazhenii marksizma v oblasti psikhologii. *Voprosy Psikhologii*, 2, 22–24.

Troitskiy, M. M. (1885/1995). Sovremennoe uchenie o zadachakh i metodakh psikhologii. *Voprosy Psikhologii*, 4, 93–107.

Umrikhin, V. V. (1994). 'Ideogenez' i 'sotsiogenez' nauki v tvorchestve G. I. Chelpanova. *Voprosy Psikhologii*, *1*, 17–26.

Valsiner, J. (1988). *Developmental psychology in the Soviet Union*. Brighton: Harvester Press Limited.

Valsiner, J. (1994). From energy to collectivity: A commentary on the development of Bekhterev's theoretical views. In L. H. Strickland (Ed.), *V. M. Bekhterev's Collective reflexology*. Commack, NY: Nova Science Publishers, pp. xiii–xxiv.

Valsiner, J., & Van der Veer, R. (1991a). Mikhail Basov: An intellectual biography. *Soviet Psychology*, 29(5), 6–13.

Valsiner, J., & Van der Veer, R. (Eds.). (1991b). Structuring of conduct in activity settings: The contribution of Mikhail Basov. *Soviet Psychology*, 29(5), 3–83; 29(6), 3–90.

Valsiner, J., & Van der Veer, R. (2000). *The social mind: Construction of the idea*. Cambridge, UK: Cambridge University Press.

van der Veer, R. (1996). The concept of culture in Vygotsky's thinking. *Culture and Psychology*, 2, 247–263.

van der Veer, R. (1999). Lev S. Vygotsky. In J. Verschueren, J. O. Östman, J. Blommaert, & C. Bulcaen (Eds.), *Handbook of Pragmatics 1997*. Amsterdam: John Benjamins, pp. 1–15.

van der Veer, R. (2002a). Bekhterev's social psychology. Review of V. M. Bekhterev, Suggestion and its role in social life. *Mind, Culture, and Activity*, 9, 72–74.

van der Veer, R. (2002b). Vygotsky criticized. *Journal of Russian and Eastern European Psychology*, 38, 3–9.

Vucinich, A. (1988). *Darwin in Russian thought*. Berkeley: University of California Press.

Vygotsky, L. S. (1926). Grafika A. Bykhovskogo. In A. Ya. Bykhovsky, *Grafika*. Moscow: Sovremennaya Rossiya, pp. 5–8.

Vygotsky, L. S. (1929a). Geneticheskie korni myshleniya i rechi. *Estvestvoznanie i Marksizm*, 1, 106–134.

Vygotsky, L. S. (1929b). K voprosu ob intellekte antropoidov v svjazi s rabotami W. Köhler'a. *Estvestvoznanie i Marksizm*, 2, 131–153.

Vygotsky, L. S. (1929c/1960). Povedenie zhivotnykh i cheloveka. In L.S. Vygotsky, *Razvitie vysshikh psikhicheskikh funktsiy*. Moscow: APN, pp. 397–456.

Vygotsky, L. S. (1930). Predislovie. In W. Köhler, *Issledovanie intellekta chelovekopodobnykh obez'yan*. Moscow: Izdatel'stvo Kommunisticheskoy Akademii, pp. i–xxix.

Vygotsky, L. S. (1930/1994). Tool and sign. In R. Van der Veer & J. Valsiner (Eds.), *The Vygotsky Reader*. Oxford: Blackwell, pp. 99–174.

Vygotsky, L. S. (1994). The problem of the environment. In R. Van der Veer & J. Valsiner (Eds.), *The Vygotsky Reader*. Oxford: Blackwell, pp. 338–354.

Vygotsky, L. S. (1997a). *Educational psychology*. Boca Raton, FL: St. Lucie Press.

Vygotsky, L. S. (1997b). *The collected works of L. S. Vygotsky. Volume 4. The history of the development of the higher mental functions*. New York: Plenum Press.

Yaroshevskiy, M. G. (1985). *Istoriya psikhologii* (3rd ed.). Moscow: Mysl'.

Yerkes, R. M. (1925). *Almost human*. New York: Century.

Yerkes, R. M., & Petrunkevich, A. (1925). Studies of chimpanzee vision by Ladygina-Kohts. *Journal of Comparative Psychology*, 5, 99–108.

Zhdan, A. N. (1993). Prepodavanie psikhologii v moskovskom universitete. *Voprosy Psikhologii*, 4, 80–93.

Zhdan, A. N. (1995). Moskovskoe psikhologicheskoe obshchestvo (1885–1922). *Voprosy Psikhologii*, 4, 82–92.

CHAPTER 2

Asmus, V. F. (1929). *Ocherki istorii dialektiki v novoi filosofii* [*Essays on the History of Dialectics in Modern Philosophy*]. Progress: Moscow-Leningrad:

Bakhurst, D. (1981). Action, epistemology, and the riddle of the self. *Studies in Soviet Thought*, 24, 185–209.

Bakhurst, D. (1990). Social memory in Soviet thought. In D. Middleton & D. Edwards (Eds.), *Collective Remembering*. London: Sage, pp. 203–226.

Bakhurst, D. (1991). *Consciousness and revolution in Soviet philosophy: From the Bolsheviks to Evald Ilyenkov*. Cambridge, UK: Cambridge University Press.

Bakhurst, D. (1995). Social being and the human essence: An unresolved issue in Soviet philosophy. *Studies in East European Thought*, 47, 3–60.

Bakhurst, D. (1997). Meaning, normativity and the life of the mind. *Language and Communication*, 17(1), 33–51.

Bakhurst, D. (2001a). Tikhij genial'nost' V. A. Lektorskogo [The quiet brilliance of Vladislav Lektorsky]. In *Subjekt, Poznanie, Dejatelnost'. K 70-letiju V. A. Lektorskogo.* Moskva: Izdatel'stvo Kanon, 79–106.

Bakhurst, D. (2001b). Memory, identity, and the future of cultural psychology. In D. Bakhurst & S. Shanker (Eds.), *Jerome Bruner: Language, Culture, Self.* London: Sage, pp. 184–198.

Bibler, V. S. (1975). *Myshlenie kak tvorchestvo [Thinking as creativity].* Moscow: Politizdat.

Bruner, J. (1990). *Acts of meaning.* Cambridge, MA: Harvard University Press.

Davidson, D. (1970/1984). Mental events. In D. Davidson (Ed.), *Essays on Actions and Events.* Oxford: Oxford University Press, pp. 207–225.

Davydov, V. V. (1972). *Vidy obobshcheniya v obuchenii [Types of generalization in instruction].* Moscow: Pedagogika.

Derry, J. (2003). *Vygotsky and his critics: Philosophy and rationality.* Ph.D. Dissertation. University of London.

Derry, J. (2004). The unity of intellect and will: Vygotsky and Spinoza. *Educational Review,* 56(2), 113–120.

Frank, S. L. (1910). *Filosofiia i zhizn'.* St. Petersburg: Zem'lia.

Frank, S. L. (1917/1964). *Dusha cheloveka.* Paris: YMCA Press.

Ilyenkov, E. V. (1960). *The dialectics of the abstract and the concrete in Marx's Capital.* Translated by S. Syrovatkin. Moscow: Progress, 1982.

Ilyenkov, E. V. (1991). Dialektika ideal'nogo [The dialectic of the ideal]. In E. V. Ilyenkov (Ed.), *Filosofiya i kul'tura [Philosophy and Culture].* Moscow: Politizdat, pp. 229–270.

Leibniz, G. (1705/1981). *New essays on human understanding.* Translated and edited by P. Remnant & J. Bennett. Cambridge: Cambridge University Press.

Locke, J. (1690/1975). *An essay concerning human understanding.* Edited by P. Nidditch. Oxford: Oxford University Press.

Mandel'shtam, N. (1970). *Vospominanie. Kniga pervaya.* [Recollections. Book One]. Paris: YMCA Press.

Marx, K. (1845/1968). Theses on Feuerbach. In K. Marx & F. Engels (Eds.) *Selected works in one volume.* London: Lawrence and Wishart.

McDowell, J. (1994). *Mind and World.* Cambridge, MA: Harvard University Press.

Padden, C., & Humphries T. (1988). *Deaf in America: Voices from a culture.* Cambridge, MA: Harvard University Press.

Padden, C., & Humphries T. (2004). *Inside deaf culture.* Cambridge, MA: Harvard University Press.

Sacks, O. (1989). *Seeing voices: A journey into the world of the deaf.* Berkeley: University of California Press.

Sypnowich, C. (2000a). How to live the good life: William Morris's aesthetic conception of equality, *Queen's Quarterly,* 107(3), 391–411.

Sypnowich, C. (2000b). Egalitarianism renewed. In R. Beiner & W. Norman (Eds.), *Canadian political philosophy at the turn of the century: Exemplary Essays.* Oxford U.K.: Oxford University Press, pp. 118–130.

Tomasello, M. (1999). *The cultural origins of human cognition.* Cambridge, MA: Harvard University Press.

Van Der Veer, R. & Valsiner, J. (1991). *Understanding Vygotsky: The quest for synthesis*. Oxford: Blackwell.

Vygotsky, L. S. (1924). The methods of reflexological and psychological investigation. In *The collected works of L. S. Vygotsky* (Vol. 3). New York: Plenum Press, pp. 35–49.

Vygotsky, L. S. (1925a). Consciousness as a Problem for the Psychology of Behaviour. In *The collected works of L. S. Vygotsky* (Vol. 3). New York: Plenum Press, pp. 63–79.

Vygotsky, L. S. (1925b). Principles of social education for the deaf-mute child. In *The collected works of L. S. Vygotsky* (Vol. 2). New York: Plenum Press, pp. 110–121.

Vygotsky, L. S. (1926/1997). *Educational psychology*. Translated by R. Silverman with an introduction by V. V. Davydov. Boca Raton, FL: St. Lucie Press, 1997.

Vygotsky, L. S. (1927). The historical meaning of the crisis in psychology: A methodological investigation. In *The collected works of L. S. Vygotsky* (Vol. 3). New York: Plenum Press, pp. 233–343.

Vygotsky, L. S. (1928a). The blind child. In *The collected works of L. S. Vygotsky* (Vol. 2). New York: Plenum Press, pp. 97–109.

Vygotsky, L. S. (1928b). Defectology and the study of the development of the abnormal child. In *The collected works of L. S. Vygotsky* (Vol. 2). New York: Plenum Press, pp. 164–170.

Vygotsky, L. S. (1930a/1994). The socialist alteration of man. In R. van der Veer & J. Valsiner (Eds.), *The Vygotsky reader*. Oxford: Blackwell, pp. 175–184.

Vygotsky, L. S. (1930b). Preface to Köhler. In *The collected works of L. S. Vygotsky* (Vol. 3). New York: Plenum Press, pp. 175–194.

Vygotsky, L. S. (1930c). The instrumental method in psychology. In *The collected works of L. S. Vygotsky* (Vol. 3). New York: Plenum Press, pp. 85–89.

Vygotsky, L. S. (1931a). Pedology of the adolescent. In *The collected works of L. S. Vygotsky* (Vol. 5). New York: Plenum Press, pp. 1–184.

Vygotsky, L. S. (1931b). *History of the development of the higher mental functions*. In *The collected works of L. S. Vygotsky* (Vol. 4). New York: Plenum Press, pp. 1–251.

Vygotsky, L. S. (1931c). The collective as a factor in the development of the abnormal child. In *The collected works of L. S. Vygotsky* (Vol. 2). New York: Plenum Press, pp. 191–208.

Vygotsky, L. S. (1932). *Lectures on psychology*. In *The collected works of L. S. Vygotsky* (Vol. 1). New York: Plenum Press, pp. 287–373.

Vygotsky, L. S. (1933a). *The teaching about emotions: historical-psychological Studies*. In *The collected works of L. S. Vygotsky* (Vol. 6). New York: Plenum Press, pp. 69–235.

Vygotsky, L. S. (1933b). The problem of consciousness. In *The collected works of L. S. Vygotsky* (Vol. 3). New York: Plenum Press, pp. 129–138.

Vygotsky, L. S. (1934). Thinking and speech. In *The collected works of L. S. Vygotsky* (Vol. 1). New York: Plenum Press, pp. 37–285.

Vygotsky, L. S. (1935). The problem of mental retardation. In *The collected works of L. S. Vygotsky* (Vol. 2). New York: Plenum Press, pp. 220–240.

Vygotsky, L. S. [*SS* 1] (1982a). *Sobranie sochinenii, tom 1: Voprosy teorii i istorii psikhologii* [*The collected works of L. S. Vygotsky. Volume 1: Questions of the theory and history psychology*]. Moscow: Pedagogika.

Vygotsky, L. S. [*SS* 2] (1982b). *Sobranie sochinenii, tom 2: Problemy obshchei psikhologii* [*The collected works of L. S. Vygotsky. Volume 2: Problems of general psychology*]. Moscow: Pedagogika.

Vygotsky, L. S. [*SS* 3] (1983a). *Sobranie sochinenii, tom 3: Problemy razvitiya psikhiki* [*The collected works of L. S. Vygotsky. Volume 3: Problems of the development of mind*]. Moscow: Pedagogika.

Vygotsky, L. S. (1983b). *Sobranie sochinenii, tom 5: Osnovy defektologii* [*The collected works of L. S. Vygotsky. Volume 5: Foundations of defectology*]. Moscow: Pedagogika.

Vygotsky, L. S. [*SS* 4] (1984a). *Sobranie sochinenii, tom 4: Dektskaya psikhologiya* [*The collected works of L. S. Vygotsky.Volume 4: Child psychology*]. Moscow: Pedagogika.

Vygotsky, L. S. [*SS* 6] (1984b). *Sobranie sochinenii, tom 6: Nauchnoe nasledstvo* [*The collected works of L. S. Vygotsky. Volume 6: Scientific legacy*]. Moscow: Pedagogika.

Vygotsky, L. S. (1987). *The collected works of L. S. Vygotsky. Volume 1. Problems of general psychology*. Edited by R. W. Rieber & A. S. Carton. Translated by N. Minick. Prologue by J. S. Bruner. New York and London: Plenum Press.

Vygotsky, L. S. (1993). *The collected works of L S. Vygotsky. Volume: Problems of defectology (abnormal psychology and learning disabilities)*. Edited by R. W. Rieber & A. S. Carton. Translated, with an Introduction, by J. E. Knox & C. B. Stevens. New York and London: Plenum Press.

Vygotsky, L. S. (1997a). *The collected works of L. S. Vygotsky. Volume 3: Problems of the theory and history of psychology*. Edited by R. W. Rieber & J. Wollock. Translated, with an Introduction, by R. van der Veer. Prologue by R. W. Rieber & J. Wollock. New York and London: Plenum Press.

Vygotsky, L. S. (1997b). *The collected works of L. S. Vygotsky. Volume 4: The history of the development of the higher mental functions*. Edited by R. W. Rieber. Translated by M. J. Hall. Prologue by J. Glick. New York and London: Plenum Press.

Vygotsky, L. S. (1998). *The collected works of L. S. Vygotsky. Volume 5: Child psychology*. Edited by R. W. Rieber. Translated by M. J. Hall. Prologue by C. Ratner. New York and London: Plenum Press.

Vygotsky, L. S. (1999). *The collected Works of L. S. Vygotsky. Volume 6: Scientific legacy*. Edited by R. W. Rieber. Translated by M. J. Hall. Prologue by D. Robbins. New York and London: Plenum Press.

Yaroshevsky, M. G. (1984/1999). Epilogue. In R. W, Rieber (Ed.), *The Collected works of L. S. Vygotsky. Volume 6: Scientific legacy*, pp. 245–266.

CHAPTER 3

Blumer, H. (1937). Social psychology. In E. D. Schmidt (Ed.), *Man and Society*. New York: Prentice Hall.

Blumer, H. (1969). *Symbolic interactionism: Perspective and method*. Englewood Cliffs, NJ: Prentice Hall.

Bruner, J. S. (1962). Introduction to L. S. Vygotsky, *Thought and language*. Cambridge, MA: MIT Press.

Bruner, J. S. (1966). *Towards a theory of instruction*. Cambridge, MA: Cambridge University Press.

Cole, M. (1996). *Cultural psychology: A once and future discipline*. Cambridge, MA: Belnap Press.

Davydov, V. V., & Radzikhovskii, L. A. (1985). Intellectual origins of Vygotsky's semiotic analysis. In J. V. Wertsch (Ed.), *Culture, Communication and Cognition: Vygotskian perspectives*. Cambridge, UK: Cambridge University Press.

Edwards, A., Gilroy, P., & Hartley, D. (2002). *Rethinking teacher education: collaborative responses to uncertainty*. London: Routledge/Falmer.

Eldridge, M. (1998). *Transforming experience: John Dewey's cultural instrumentalism*. Nashville, TN: Vanderbilt University Press.

Engeström, Y. (1987). *Learning by expanding: An activity-theoretical approach to developmental research*. Helsinki: Orienta-Konsultit.

Engeström, Y. (1999). Activity theory and individual and social transformation. In Y. Engeström, R. Miettinen, & R.-L. Punamäki (Eds.), *Perspectives on activity theory*. Cambridge, UK: Cambridge University Press.

Garrison, J. (1995). Deweyan pragmatism and the epistemology of contemporary social constructivism. *American Educational Research Journal, 35*(4), 716–740.

Garrison, J. (1996). The unity of the activity: A response to Prawat. *Educational Researcher, 25*(6), 21–23.

Glassman, M. (2001). Dewey and Vygotsky: Society, experience, and enquiry in educational practice. *Educational Researcher, 30*(4), 3–14.

Gredler, M., & Shields, C. (2003). Several bridges too far: A commentary on Richard S. Prawat's "Dewey Meets the 'Mozart of Psychology' in Moscow": The Untold Story. *American Educational Research Journal, 40*(1), 177–187.

Hickman, L. (2001). *Philosophical tools for technological culture: Putting pragmatism to work*. Bloomington: Indiana University Press.

James, W. (1890). *The principles of psychology*. New York: Holt.

James, W. (1971). Does consciousness exist? In R. B. Perry (Ed.), *Essays in radical empiricism and a pluralistic universe*. New York: E. P. Dutton & Co.

Kozulin, A. (1986). The concept of activity in Soviet psychology. *American Psychologist, 41*(3), 264–274.

Lave, J., & Wenger, E. (1991). *Situated Learning: legitimate peripheral participation*. Cambridge, UK: Cambridge University Press.

Leont'ev, A. N. (1981). The problem of activity in psychology. In J. V. Wertsch (Ed.), *The concept of activity in soviet psychology*. Armonk, NY: M. E. Sharpe.

Leont'ev, A. N. (1997). On Vygotsky's creative development. In R. W. Rieber & J. Wollock (Eds.), *The Collected Work of L. S. Vygotsky. Volume 3: Problems of the theory and history of psychology*. New York: Plenum Press.

Lewis, J. D., & Smith, R. L. (1980). *American sociology and pragmatism*. Chicago IL: University of Chicago Press.

Mead, G. H. (1913). The social self. *The Journal of Philosophy, Psychology, and Scientific Methods*, Vol. X. available at: http://varenne.tc.columbia.edu/bib/texts/medoogerg13socsciself.html.

Mead, G. H. (1923). Scientific method and the moral sciences. *International Journal of Ethics, 33*(3), 229–247.

Mead, G. H. (1934). *Mind, self and society*. C. Morris (Ed.). Chicago: University of Chicago Press.

Mead, G. H. (1964). *Selected writings*. A. J. Reck (Ed.). Indianapolis: Bobbs-Merrill Co.

Mead, G. H. (1982). Consciousness, mind, the self and scientific objects. In D. L. Miller (Ed.), *The individual and social self: Unpublished work of George Herbert Mead*. Chicago: University of Chicago Press.

Menand, L. (2001). *The metaphysical club*. London: HarperCollins.

Prawat, R. S. (2000). Dewey meets the "Mozart of psychology" in Moscow: The untold story. *American Educational Research Journal, 37*(3), 663–696.

Prawat, R. S. (2001). Dewey and Peirce, the philosopher's philosopher. *Teachers College Record, 102*(4), 667–721.

Prawat, R. S. (2002). Dewey and Vygotsky viewed through the rearview mirror – and dimly at that. *Educational Researcher, 31*(5), 16–20.

Prawat, R. S. (2003). Full weight of evidence as opposed to selective emphasis: a response to the critique by Gredler and Shields. *American Educational Research Journal, 40*(1), 189–193.

Rieber, R. W., & Wollock, J. (1997). Vygotsky's "crisis," and its meaning today. In R. W. Rieber & J. Wollock (Eds.), *The collected work of L. S. Vygostky. Volume 3: Problems of the theory and history of psychology*. New York: Plenum Press.

Scheffler, I. (1974). *Four Pragmatists: a critical introduction to Peirce, James, Mead and Dewey*. London: Routledge and Kegan Paul.

Valsiner, J., & Van der Veer, R. (1988). On the social nature of human cognition: an analysis of the shared intellectual roots of George Herbert Mead and Lev Vygotsky. *Journal for the Theory of Social Behavior, 18*(1), 117–136.

Valsiner, J. (1998). *The guided mind*. Cambridge MA: Harvard University Press.

Valsiner, J., & Van der Veer, R. (2000). *The social mind*. Cambridge, UK: Cambridge University Press.

van der Veer, R., & Valsiner, J. (1991). *Understanding Vygotsky*. Oxford: Blackwell.

Vygotsky, L. S. (1962). *Thought and language*. Translated by E. Hanfmann & G. Vakar. Cambridge, MA: MIT Press.

Vygotsky, L. S. (1978). *Mind in society*. M. Cole, V. John-Steiner, S. Scribner, & E. Souberman (Eds.), Cambridge MA: Harvard University Press.

Vygotsky, L. S. (1987). Thinking and speech. In R. W. Rieber & A. S. Carton (Eds.), *The collected works of L. S. Vygotsky. Volume 1: Problems of general psychology*. New York: Plenum Press.

Vygotsky, L. S. (1997a). The crisis in psychology. In R. W. Rieber & J. Wollock (Eds.), *The collected work of L. S. Vygostky. Volume 3: Problems of the theory and history of psychology*. New York: Plenum Press.

Vygotsky, L. S. (1997b). Problems of the theory and methods of psychology. In R. W. Rieber & J. Wollock (Eds.), *The collected works of L. S. Vygotsky. Volume 3: Problems of the theory and history of psychology*. New York: Plenum Press.

Vygotsky, L. S. (1997c). Analysis of higher mental functions. In R. W. Rieber (Ed.), *The collected works of L. S. Vygotsky. Volume 4: The History of the Development of Higher Mental Functions*. New York: Plenum Press.

Vygotsky, L. S. (1998a). Problems of child (developmental) psychology. In C. Ratner (Ed.), *The collected works of L. S. Vygotsky. Volume 5: Child psychology*. New York: Plenum Press.

Vygotsky, L. S. (1998b). The pedology of the adolescent. In C. Ratner (Ed.), *The collected works of L. S. Vygotsky. Volume 5: Child psychology*. New York: Plenum Press.

Vygotsky, L. S. (1999). Tool and sign in the development of the child. In R. W. Rieber (Ed.), *The collected works of L. S. Vygotsky. Volume 6: Scientific legacy*. New York: Plenum Press.

Wertsch, J. V. (Ed.). (1985a). *Vygotsky and the social formation of mind*. Cambridge, MA: Harvard University Press.

Wertsch, J. V. (Ed.). (1985b). *Culture, communication, and cognition: Vygotskian perspectives*. Cambridge, UK: Cambridge University Press.

Wertsch, J. V., & Stone, C. A. (1985). The concept of internalization in Vygotsky's account of higher mental functions. In J. V. Wertsch (Ed.), *Culture, communication, and cognition: Vygotskian perspectives*. Cambridge, UK: Cambridge University Press.

CHAPTER 4

Allen, K., Daro, V., & Holland, D. (2002). Becoming an environmental justice activist. In P. C. Pezzullo & R. Sandler (Eds.), *Environmental justice and environmentalism: Contrary or complementary*. Cambridge, MA: MIT Press.

Baldwin, J. M. (1898). *Story of the mind*. New York: D. Appleton & Co.

Bartlett, L. (2005). Identity work and cultural artifacts in literacy learning and use: A sociocultural analysis. *Language and Education, 19*(1), 1–9.

Bartlett, Lesley. (in press). To seem and to feel: Situated identities and literacy practices. *Teachers College Record, 109*(4).

Bakhtin, M. (1981). *The dialogic imagination*. Translated by C. Emerson & M. Holquist. Edited by M. Holquist. Austin: University of Texas Press.

Bakhtin, M. (1990). *Art and answerability*. Translated by V. Liapunov. Edited by M. Holquist & V. Liapunov. Austin: University of Texas Press.

Bhatia, S. (2002). Acculturation, dialogical voices and the construction of the diasporic self. *Theory and Psychology, 12*, 55–77.

Bhatia, S. (2003). Is "integration" the developmental end goal for all immigrants? Redefining "acculturation strategies" from a genetic-dramatistic perspective. In I. Josephs & J. Valsiner (Eds.), *Dialogue and development*. Stamford, CT: Ablex, pp. 198–216.

Bhatia, S., & Ram, A. (2001). Locating the dialogical self in the age of transnational migrations, border crossings and diasporas. Commentary on H. J. M. Hermans' *The dialogical self: Toward a theory of personal and cultural positioning. Culture and Psychology, 7*, 297–309.

Bhatia, S., & Ram, A. (2004). Culture, hybridity, and the dialogical self: Cases from the South Asian diaspora. *Mind, Culture, and Activity, 11*, 224–240.

Blackburn, M. (2003). Losing, finding, and making space for activism through literacy performances and identity work. *Perspectives on Urban Education*, 2(1), 1–19.

Boaler, J., & Greeno, J. (2000). Identity, agency, and knowing in mathematics worlds. In J. Boaler (Ed.), *Multiple perspectives on mathematics teaching and learning*. Westport, CT: Ablex, pp. 171–200.

Bourdieu, P. (1977a). *Outline of a theory of practice*. Translated by R. Nice. Cambridge, UK: Cambridge University Press.

Bourdieu, P. (1977b). The economics of linguistic exchanges. *Social Science Information*, 16, 645–668.

Brumfiel, E. (2005). Materiality, feasts, and figured worlds in Aztec Mexico. In E. Demarrais, C. Gosden, & C. Renfrew (Eds.), *Rethinking materiality*. Cambridge, MA: MacDonald Institute for Archaeological Research.

Burke, P., & Reitzes, D. (1981). The link between identity and role performance. *Social Psychology Quarterly*, 44(2), 83–92.

Burke, P., & Reitzes, D. (1991). An identity theory approach to commitment. *Social Psychology Quarterly*, 54, 239–251.

Cain, C. (1991). Personal stories: Identity acquisition and self-understanding in Alcoholics Anonymous. *Ethos*, 19, 210–253.

Clifford, J. (1988). *The predicament of culture: Twentieth-century ethnography, literature, and art*. Cambridge, MA: Harvard University Press.

Cole, M. (1985). The zone of proximal development: Where culture and cognition create each other. In J. Wertsch (Ed.), *Culture, communication and cognition: Vygotskian perspectives*. New York: Cambridge University Press, pp. 146–161.

Davies, B., & Harré, R. (1990). Positioning: The discursive production of selves. *Journal for the Theory of Social Behavior*, 20, 43–63.

Davies, C. (1999). *Reflexive ethnography: A guide to researching selves and others*. London: Routledge.

Demarath, P. (2003). Negotiating individualist and collectivist futures: Emerging subjectivities and social forms in Papua New Guinean high schools. *Anthropology and Education Quarterly*, 34(2), 136–157.

Edberg, M. (2004). The Narcotrafficker in Representation and Practice: A Cultural Persona from the U.S.-Mexican Border. *Ethos*, 32(2), 257–277.

Eisenhart, M. (1995). The fax, the jazz player, and the self-story teller: How do people organize culture? *Anthropology and Education Quarterly*, 26(1), 3–26.

Erikson, E. H. (1968). *Identity: Youth and crisis*. New York: Norton.

Erikson, E. H. (1980). *Identity and Life Cycle*. New York: Norton.

Ewing, K. (1990). The illusion of wholeness: Culture, self, and the experience of inconsistency. *Ethos*, 18(3), 251–278.

Fields, L. (1995). Constructing local identities in a revolutionary nation: The cultural politics of the artisan class in Nicaragua, 1979–90. *American Ethnologist*, 22(4), 786–806.

Foucault, M. (1978). *Discipline and punish: The birth of the prison*. Translated by A. Sheridan. New York: Pantheon.

Foucault, M. (1988). *Technologies of the self: A seminar with Michel Foucault*. Edited by M. Foucault, L. H. Martin, H. Gutman, & P. H. Hutton. Amherst, MA: University of Massachusetts Press.

Gleason, P. (1983). Identifying identity: A semantic history. *Journal of American History, 69*(4), 910–931.

Goffman, E. (1959). *The presentation of self in everyday life.* Garden City, NJ: Doubleday.

Goffman, E. (1963). *Stigma: Notes on the management of spoiled identity.* Englewood Cliffs, NJ: Prentice-Hall.

Gullestad, M. (2003). 'Mohammed Atta and I': Identification, discrimination, and the formation of sleepers. *European Journal of Cultural Studies, 6,* 529–548.

Harré, R., & Van Langenhove, R. (1991). Varieties of positioning. *Journal for the Theory of Social Behavior, 21,* 391–407.

Hermann, E. (2003). Manifold identifications within differentiations: Shapings of self among relocated Banabans of Fiji. *Focaal – European Journal of Anthropology, 42,* 77–88.

Hermans, H. J. M. (2001). Mixing and moving cultures require a dialogical self. *Human Development, 44,* 24–28.

Hermans, H. J. M., & Kempen, H. (1993). *The dialogical self: Meaning as movement.* San Diego: Academic Press.

Hermans, H. J. M., & Kempen, H. (1998). Moving cultures: The perilous problems of cultural dichotomies in a globalizing society. *American Psychologist, 53,* 1111–1120.

Hervik, P. (2004). The Danish cultural world of unbridgeable differences. *Ethnos, 69,* 247–267.

Hochschild, A. (1983). *The managed heart: Commercialization of human feeling.* Berkeley: University of California Press.

Holland, D. (2003). Multiple identities in practice: On the dilemmas of being a hunter and an environmentalist in the U S. In T. van Meijl & H. Driessen (Eds.), *Multiple identifications and the self.* Special Issue. *Focal: European Journal of Anthropology, 42,* 23–41.

Holland, D., Lachicotte, W., Skinner, D., & C. Cain. (1998). *Identity and agency in cultural worlds.* Cambridge, MA: Harvard University Press.

Holland, D., & Lave, J. (2001). History in person: An introduction. In D. Holland & J. Lave (Eds.), *History in person: Enduring struggles, contentious practice, intimate identities.* Santa Fe: SAR Press, pp. 3–33.

Holland, D., & Leander, K. (2004). Ethnographic studies of positioning and subjectivity: An introduction. *Ethos, 32*(2), 127–139.

Holquist, M. (1990). *Dialogism: Bakhtin and his world.* New York: Routledge.

Hunt, S., Benford, R., & Snow, D. (1994). Identity fields: Framing processes and the social construction of movement identities. In E. Laraña, H. Johnson, & J. Gusfield (Eds.), *New social movements: From ideology to identity.* Philadelphia: Temple University Press, pp. 185–208.

Josephs, I. (1998). Constructing one's self in the city of the silent: Dialogue, symbols, and the role of "as-if" in self-development. *Human Development, 41,* 180–195.

Josephs, I. (2002). "The Hopi in me": The construction of a voice in the dialogical self from a cultural psychological perspective. *Theory and Psychology, 12*(2), 161–73.

Josephs, I., Valsiner, J., & Surgan, S. E. (1999). The process of meaning construction. In J. Brandtstatdter & R. M. Lerner (Eds.), *Action and self-development.* Thousand Oaks, CA: Sage, pp. 257–282.

Lachicotte, W. (2002). Intimate powers, public selves: Bakhtin's space of authoring. In J. Mageo (Ed.), *Power and the self.* New York: Cambridge University Press, pp. 48–66.

Lave, J. (1988). *Cognition in practice: Mind, mathematics, and culture in everyday life.* Cambridge, UK: Cambridge University Press.

Lave, J. (1993). The practice of learning. In S. Chaiklin & J. Lave (Eds.), *Understanding practice: Perspectives on activity and context* (pp. 3–32). Cambridge, UK: Cambridge University Press, pp. 3–32

Lave, J., & Wenger, E. (1991). *Situated learning: Legitimate peripheral participation.* Cambridge, UK: Cambridge University Press.

Leander, K. M. (2002). Locating LaTonya: The situated production of identity artifacts in classroom interaction. *Research in the Teaching of English, 37*(2), 198–250.

Lee, B. (1985). Intellectual origins of Vygotsky's semiotic analysis. In J. Wertsch (Ed.), *Culture, communication and cognition: Vygotskian perspectives.* New York: Cambridge University Press, pp. 66–93.

Lee, B., Wertsch, J., & Stone, A. (1983). Towards a Vygotskian theory of the self. In B. Lee & G. Noam (Eds.), *Developmental approaches to the self.* New York: Plenum Press, pp. 309–341.

Lowe, E. (2003). Identity, activity, and the well-being of adolescents and youth: Lessons from young people in a Micronesian society. *Culture, Medicine, and Psychiatry, 27,* 187–219.

Luria, A. (1981). *Language and cognition.* Edited by J. Wertsch. New York: John Wiley & Sons.

McCall, G. J. (1987). The structure, content, and dynamics of self: continuities in the study of role-identities. In K. Yardley & T. Honess (Eds.), *Self and identity: Psychosocial perspectives.* Chichester: John Wiley & Sons, pp. 133–145.

McCall, G. J., & Simmons, J. L. (1978). *Identities and interactions: An examination of human associations in everyday life.* (revised ed.). New York: Free Press.

Marx, N. (2002). Never quite a native speaker: Accent and identity in the L2 and the L1. *Canadian Modern Language Review, 59*(2), 264–281.

Mattingly, C., Lawlor, M., & Jacobs-Huey, L. (2002). Narrating September 11: Race, gender, and the play of cultural identities. *American Anthropologist, 104*(3), 743–753.

Mead, G. H. (1910). What social objects must psychology presuppose? *Journal of Philosophy, Psychology, and Scientific Methods, 7,* 174–180.

Mead, G. H. (1912). The mechanism of social consciousness. *Journal of Philosophy, Psychology, and Scientific Methods, 9,* 401–406.

Mead, G. H. (1913). The social self. *Journal of Philosophy, Psychology, and Scientific Methods, 10,* 374–380.

Mead, G. H. (1925). The genesis of the self and social control. *International Journal of Ethics, 35,* 251–277.

Mead, G. H. (1934). *Mind, self, and society.* Chicago: University of Chicago Press.

Penuel, W., & Wertsch, J. (1995). Dynamics of negation in the identity politics of cultural other and cultural self: The rhetorical image of the person in developmental psychology. *Culture and Psychology, 1*, 343–359.

Riesman, D. (1953). *The lonely crowd: A study of the changing American character.* Garden City, NJ: Doubleday.

Sarbin, T. (2000). Worldmaking, self and identity. *Culture and Psychology, 6*(2), 253–258.

Satterfield, T. (2002). *Anatomy of a conflict: Identity, knowledge, and emotion in old-growth forests.* Vancouver: University of British Columbia Press.

Sökefeld, M. (1999). Debating self, identity, and culture in anthropology. *Current Anthropology, 40*(4), 417–47.

Steiner, G. (1975). *After Babel: Aspects of language and translation.* New York: Oxford University Press.

Stryker, S. (1968). Identity theory and role performance. *Journal of Marriage and the Family, 30*, 558–64.

Stryker, S. (1980). *Symbolic interactionism: A social structural version.* Menlo Park, CA: Benjamin/Cummings.

Stryker, S. (1987). Identity theory: Developments and extensions. In K. Yardley & T. Honess (Eds.), *Self and identity: Psychosocial perspectives.* Chichester: John Wiley and Sons, pp. 89–103.

Stryker, S. (2000). Identity competition: Key to differential social movement participation? In S. Stryker, T. Owens, & R. White (Eds.), *Self, identity, and social movements.* Minneapolis: University of Minnesota Press, pp. 21–40.

Tappan, M. (1999). Authoring a moral self: A dialogical perspective. *Journal of Constructivist Psychology, 12*, 117–131.

Tappan, M. (2000). Autobiography, mediated action, and the development of moral identity. *Narrative Inquiry, 10*(1), 81–109.

Urrieta, Jr., L. (2003). *Orchestrating the selves: Chicana and Chicano negotiations of identity, ideology, and activism in education.* Unpublished Ph.D. dissertation. University of North Carolina at Chapel Hill.

Urrieta, Jr., L. (2005). "Playing the game" versus "selling out": Chicanas and Chicanos relationship to Whitestream schools. In B. Alexander, B. Anderson, & B. Gallegos, *Performance theories in education: Power, pedagogy, and the politics of identity* (pp. 173–196). Mahwah, NJ: Lawrence Erlbaum and Associates, pp. 173–196.

Valsiner, J. (1998). *The guided mind: A sociogenetic approach to personality.* Cambridge, MA: Harvard University Press.

Valsiner, J. (2002). Forms of dialogical relations and semiotic autoregulation within the self. *Theory and Psychology, 12*(2), 251–265.

Valsiner, J., & van der Veer, R. (1988). On the social nature of human cognition: An analysis of the shared intellectual roots of George Herbert Mead and Lev Vygotsky. *Journal for the Theory of Social Behavior, 18*(1), 117–136.

Van Meijl, T. (n.d.). Multiple identities and the dialogical self: Maori youngsters and the cultural renaissance. Unpublished manuscript, Centre for Pacific and Asian Studies, University of Nijmegen, The Netherlands.

Van Meijl, T., & Driessen, H. (2003). Introduction: Multiple identifications and the self. *Focaal – European Journal of Anthropology, 42*, 17–29.

Vygotsky, L. S. (1978). *Mind in society: The development of higher psychological functions.* Edited by M. Cole, V. John-Steiner, S. Scribner, & E. Souberman. Cambridge, MA: Harvard University Press.

Vygotsky, L. S. (1982). *Sobranie sochinenii: Vol. I. Voprosy teorii i istorii psikhologii.* Moscow: Pedagogika. [English edition, 1997. *The collected works of L. S. Vygotsky. Volume 3: Problems of the theory and history of psychology.* Translated by R. van der Veer. Edited by R. Rieber & J. Wollock. New York: Plenum Press.]

Vygotsky, L. S. (1984a). *Sobranie sochinenii: Vol. 4. Detskaia psikhologia.* Moscow: Pedagogika. [English edition, 1998. *The collected works of L. S. Vygotsky. Volume 5: Child Psychology.* Translated by M. Hall. Edited by R. Rieber. New York: Plenum Press.]

Vygotsky, L. S. (1984b). *Sobranie sochinenii: Vol. 6. Nauchnoe nasledie.* Moscow: Pedagogika. [English edition, 1999. *The collected works of L. S. Vygotsky: Volume 6. Scientific legacy.* Translated by M. Hall. Edited by R. Rieber. New York: Plenum Press.]

Vygotsky, L. S. (1986). *Thought and language* (revised ed.). Translated and edited by A. Kozulin. Cambridge, MA: MIT Press.

Vygotsky, L. S. (1930/1993). *Studies on the history of behavior: Ape, primitive, and child.* Translated and edited by V. Golod & J. Knox. Hillsdale, NJ: Lawrence Erlbaum Associates, Publishers. (Original work published 1930.)

Wertsch, J. V. (1991). *Voices of the mind: A sociocultural approach to mediated action.* Cambridge, MA: Harvard University Press.

Wortham, S. E. F. (2006). *Learning identity: the joint emergence of social identification and academic learning.* New York: Cambridge University Press.

CHAPTER 5

Arendt, H. (1977). *Thinking. The life of the mind. Volume 1.* New York: Harcourt Brace Jovanovich.

Arnheim, R. (1971). *Visual thinking.* Berkeley: University of California Press.

Azmitia, M. (1992). Expertise, private speech, and the development of self-regulation. In R. M. Diaz & L. Berk (Eds.), *Private speech: from social interaction to self-regulation.* Hillsdale, NJ: Lawrence Erlbaum Associates.

Bakhtin, M. M. (1981/2002). *The dialogic imagination: Four essays by M. M. Bakhtin.* Edited by M. Holquist. Translated by C. Emerson & M. Holquist. Austin: University of Texas Press.

Beckner, C. (2003). *Thinking about thinking: Dialectic versus static metaphors for the mind.* Unpublished manuscript. Albuquerque: University of New Mexico, Spring Semester.

Berk, L. (1992). Children's private speech: An overview of theory and the status of research. In R. M. Diaz & L. Berk (Eds.), *Private Speech: From social interaction to self-regulation.* Hillsdale, NJ: Lawrence Erlbaum Associates, Inc.

Berk, L. (1994). Why children talk to themselves. *Scientific American.* Nov. 78–83.

Boroditsky, L., Schmidt, L. A., & Phillips, W. (2003). Sex, syntax, and semantics. In Gertner & Golden-Meadow (Eds.), *Language in mind: Advances in the study of languages and cognition.* Cambridge, MA: MIT Press.

Boroditsky, L. (2001). Does language shape thought? Mandarin and English speakers' conceptions of time. *Cognitive Psychology, 43*, 1–22.

Boroditsky, L. (2000). Metaphoric structuring: Understanding time through spatial metaphors. *Cognition, 75*, 1–28.

Bowerman, M. (1996). The origins of children's spacial semantic categories: Cognitive versus linguistic determinates. In J. J. Gumperz & S. C. Levinson (Eds.), *Rethinking linguistic relativity*. Cambridge, UK: Cambridge University Press.

Bruner, J. (1983). *Child's talk: Learning to use language*. New York: W. W. Norton.

Girbau, D. (2002). Private and social speech in children's dyadic communication in a naturalistic context. *Anuario de psicologia, 33*(3). Barcelona: Universitat of Barcelona, 339–354.

Halliday, M. A. K. (1978). *Language as a social semiotic: The social interpretation of language and meaning*. Baltimore, MD: University Park Press.

Hoijer, H. (1950/1964). Cultural implications of some Navaho linguistic categories. In D. Hymes (Ed.), *Language and culture in society*. New York: Harper and Row.

Ivanov, V. V. (1971). Commentary. *The psychology of art*. Lev Semenovich Vygotsky. Introduction by A. N. Leontiev. Cambridge, MA: MIT Press.

John-Steiner, V. (1992). Private speech among adults. In R. M. Diaz & L. Berk (Eds.), *Private Speech: From social interaction to self-regulation*. Hillsdale, NJ: Lawrence Erlbaum Associates, Inc.

John-Steiner, V., Shank, C., & Meehan, T. (2005). The role of metaphor in the narrative co-construction of collaborative experience. In U. Quasthoff & T. Becker (Eds.), *Narrative Interaction*. Amsterdam: John Benjamin's Publishing Co.

John-Steiner, V., & Tatter, P. (1983). An interactionist model of language development. In B. Bain (Ed.), *The sociogenesis of language and human conduct*. New York: Plenum Press.

Kozulin, A. (1990). *Vygotsky's psychology: A biography of ideas*. Cambridge, MA: Harvard University Press.

Lakoff, G. (1990). *Women, fire, and dangerous things: What categories reveal about women*. Chicago: University of Chicago Press.

Lakoff, G., & Johnson, M. (1999). *Philosophy in the flesh: The embodied mind and its challenge to Western thought*. New York: Basic Books.

Lakoff, G., & Johnson, M. (1989). *More than cool reason: A field guide to poetic metaphor*. Chicago: University of Chicago Press.

Lau, I. Y.-M., Lee, S., & Chiu, C. (2004). Language, cognition and reality: Constructing shared meanings through communication. In M. Schaller & C. S. Crandall (Eds.), *The psychological foundations of culture*. Mahwah, NJ: Lawrence Erlbaum Associates.

Lucy, J. A. (1996). The scope of linguistic relativity: An analysis and review of empirical research. In J. J. Gumperz & S. C. Levinson (Eds.), *Rethinking linguistic relativity*. Cambridge, UK: Cambridge University Press.

Lucy, J. A. (1992). *Language diversity and thought: A reformulation of the linguistic relativity hypothesis*. New York: Cambridge University Press.

Lantolf, J. P., & Appel, G. (1994). Theoretical framework: An introduction to Vygotskian perspectives on second language research. In J. P. Lantolf & G. Appel (Eds.), *Vygotskian approaches to second language research*. Norwood, NJ: Ablex Publishing.

Matuga, J. M. (2004). Situated creative activity: The drawings and private speech of young children. *Creativity Research Journal, 16*, 267–281.

McCafferty, S. G. (1994). The use of private speech by adult ESL learners at different levels of proficiency. In J. P. Lantolf & G. Appel (Eds.), *Vygotskian approaches to second language research*. Norwood, NJ: Ablex Publishing.

Moffett, J. (1981). *Active voice: A writing program across the curriculum*. Montclair, NJ: Boynton/Cook.

Nelson, K. (1986). *Event knowledge: Structure and function in development*. Hillsdale, NJ: Erlbaum.

Pinker, S. (1995). *The language instinct*. New York: Harper Perennial.

Ramirez, J. D. (1992). The functional differentiation of social and private speech: A dialogic approach. In R. M. Diaz & L. Berk (Eds.), *Private Speech: From social interaction to self-regulation*. Hillsdale, NJ: Lawrence Erlbaum Associates, Inc.

Sapir, E. (1931). Conceptual categories in primitive languages. *Science, 74*, 578.

Slobin, D. (1996). From "thought and language" to "thinking for speaking." In J. J. Gumperz & S. C. Levinson (Eds.), *Rethinking linguistic relativity*. Cambridge, UK: Cambridge University Press.

Tomasello, M. (1999). *The cultural origins of human cognition*. Cambridge, MA: Harvard University Press.

van der Veer, R. & Valsiner, J. (1991). *Understanding Vygotsky: A quest for synthesis*. Cambridge, MA: Basil Blackwell, Inc.

Vygotsky, L. S. (1934/1997). The problem of consciousness. In *The collected works of L. S. Vygotsky. Volume 3*. New York: Plenum Press.

Vygotsky, L. S. (1997). The historical meaning of the crisis in psychology: A methodological investigation. In *The collected works of L. S. Vygotsky. Volume 3*. New York: Plenum Press.

Vygotsky, L. S. (1987). *Thinking and speech: Collected works of L. S. Vygotsky, Volume 1*. New York: Plenum Press.

Vygotsky, L. S. (1986). *Thought and language*. Kozulin edition. Cambridge, MA: MIT Press.

Vygotsky, L. S. (1978). *Mind in society: The development of higher psychological processes*. Edited by M. Cole, V. John-Steiner, S. Scribner, & E. Souberman. Cambridge, MA: Harvard University Press.

Vygotsky, L. S., & Luria, A. (1994). Tool and symbol in child development. In R. van der Veer & J. Valisner, (Eds.), *The Vygotsky reader*. Cambridge, MA: Blackwell.

Whorf, B. (1964). A linguistic consideration of thinking. In D. Hymes (Ed.), *Language and culture in society*. New York: Harper and Row.

Woolf, V. (1953). *A writer's diary*. New York: Harcourt Brace Jovanovich.

CHAPTER 6

Brudny, A. A. (1998). *Psychological hermeneutics*. Moscow: Labyrinth.

Cole, M. (1996/1997). *Cultural psychology: A once and future discipline*. Moscow: Cogito-Centre.

Crain, W. (2000). *Theories of development: Concepts and applications*. New Jersey: Prentice Hall.

El'konin D. B. (1995). *Selected works in psychology*. Moscow: "IPP"; Voronezh: NPO "Modec."

Leont'ev, A. N. (1982). Introduction. On Vygotskii's creative path. In L. S. Vygotsky (1982) [Collected works] Moscow: "Pedagogika" Publishers. Volume 1, pp. 9–41.

Leont'ev, A. N. (1983). [Selected psychological works] (Volume 1. Moscow: "Pedagogika" Publishers.

Leont'ev, A. N., & Luria, A. R. (1956). [The psychological views of L. S. Vygotskii]. [Selected psychological investigations]. Moscow: APN RSFSR, pp. 4–36.

Levina, R. E. (1968). L. S. Vygotsky's ideas on planning speech of the child. Issues of Psychology, 4, pp. 105–115.

Lipmann, O., & Bogen, H. (1923). Naive Physik. Leipzig: Verlag von Johan Ambrosius Barth.

Lisina, M. I. (1978). The genesis of the forms of communication in children. In The principle of development in psychology. Moscow: Nauka, pp. 268–294.

Luria, A. R. (1980). Higher cortical functions in man. New York: Basic Books.

Meshcheryakov, B. G. (1998). [Logico-semantic analysis of Vygotsky's conception]. Samara: Samarsk. Gosudarstvennaya Pedagogicheskaya Akademiya.

Meshcheryakov, B. G. (2000). Logico-semantic analysis of Vygotsky's conception. International University of Dubna, Unpublished doctoral dissertation.

Samuhin, N. V., Birnbaum, G. V., & Vygotsky, L. S. (1934). The problem of dementia during Pick's disease. Soviet neurology, psychiatry, and psychological hygiene, 3(6), 97–136.

Shatz, M., & Gelman, R. (1973). The development of communication skills: Modifications in the speech of young children as a function of the listener. Monographs of the Society for Research in Child Development, 38(152), pp. 1–38.

van der Veer R., & Valsiner, J. (1991). Understanding Vygotsky: A quest for synthesis. Oxford: Blackwell.

Vygodskaya, G. I., & Lifanova, T. M. (1996). [Lev Semenovich Vygotskii]. Moscow: "Smysl" Publishers. [See translation in Journal of Russian and East European Psychology, 1999, 37(2,3,4,5).]

Vygotsky, L. S. (1960). [The development of higher mental functions]. Moscow: APN RSFSR.

Vygotsky, L. S. (1982–1984). The Collected Works of L. S. Vyogtsky. Volumes 1–6). Moscow: "Pedagogika" Publishers.

Vygotsky, L. S., & Luria, A. R. (1993). Studies in the history of behavior (Primates, primitive man, the child). Moscow: "Pedagogika" Publishers. Paul M Deutsch Press: Orlando.

Wertsch, J. V. (1991). Voices of the mind. A sociocultural approach to mediated action. Cambridge, MA: Harvard University Press.

CHAPTER 7

Akhutina, T. V. (1975). Neirolingvisticheskii analiz dinamicheskoi afazii [The neurolinguistic analysis of dynamic aphasia]. Moscow: Izdatel'stvo Moskovskogo Gosudarstvennogo Universiteta.

Bakhtin, M. M. (1986). Speech genres & other late essays. Translated by Vern W. McGee. Edited by Caryl Emerson and Michael Holquist. Austin: University Texas Press, pp. 60–102.

Cazden, C. (1981). Performance before competence: Assistance to child discourse in the zone of proximal development. *Quarterly Newsletter of the Laboratory of Comparative Human Cognition, 3*, 5–8.

Cole, M. (1996). *Cultural psychology: A once and future discipline*. Cambridge, MA: Harvard University Press.

Cole, M., & Levitin, K. (2006). Preface. *The autobiography of Alexander Luria: A dialogue with the making of mind*. Mahwah, NJ: Lawrence Erlbaum Associates.

Engestrom, Y. (1987). *Learning by expanding: An activity-theoretical approach to developmental research*. Helsinki: Orieta-Konsultit.

Gibson, J. J. (1979) *The ecological approach to visual perception*. Boston: Houghton Mifflin.

Hutchins, E. (1995). How a cockpit remembers its speeds. *Cognitive Science, 19*, 265–288.

Leont'ev, A. N. (1932). Studies on the cultural development of the child. *Journal of Genetic Psychology, 40*, 52–83.

Luria, A. R. (1975). *Osnovnye problemy neirolingvistiki* [Basic problems of neurolinguistics]. Moscow: Izdatel'stvo Moskovskogo Gosudarstvennogo Universiteta.

Martsinkovskaya, T. D. (1996). Gustav Gustavovich Shpet – life as a creative problem. In Shpet, G. G. (1996). *Psikhologiya sotsial'nogo bitiya: Izbrannye psikhologicheskie trudy* [The psychology of social being: Collected psychological works]. Edited by T. D. Martsinkovskaya. Moscow-Voronezh: Institut prakticheskoi psikhologii.

Nemeth, T. (1997). Gustav Shpet (1879–1937). *The Internet encyclopedia of philosophy*. http://www.iep.utm.edu/.

Peirce, C. S. (1960). *Collected Papers*. Volumes 1–8. Cambridge, MA: Harvard University Press.

Rommetveit, R. (1974). *On message structure: A framework for the study of language and communication*. New York: John Wiley & Sons.

Rommetveit, R. (1979). On the architecture of intersubjectivity. In R. Rommetveit & R. M. Blakar (Eds.), *Studies of language, thought, and verbal communication*. London: Academic Press, pp. 93–108.

Salomon, G. (Ed.). (1993). *Distributed cognitions: Psychological and educational implications*. Cambridge, UK: Cambridge University Press.

Sapir, E. (1921). *Language: An introduction to the study of speech*. New York: Harcourt, Brace and Company.

Shpet, G. G. (1996). *Psikhologiya sotsial'nogo bitiya: Izbrannye psikhologicheskie trudy* [The psychology of social being: Collected psychological works]. Moscow-Voronezh: Institut prakticheskoi psikhologii. Edited by T. D. Martsinkovskaya.

Shpet, G. G. (1927). *Vnutrennyaya forma slova* [The internal form of the word]. Moscow: Gosudarstvennaya Akademiya Khudozhestvennykh Nauk.

Vygodskaya, G. L., & Lifanova, T. M. (1996). *Lev Semënovich Vygotskii: Zhizn', deyatel'nost', shtrikhi, i portrety* [Lev Semënovich Vygotskii: Life, activity, traits, and portraits]. Moscow: Smysl.

Vygotsky, L. S. (1978). *Mind in society: The development of higher psychological processes*. Edited by M. Cole, V. John-Steiner, S. Scribner, and E. Souberman. Cambridge, MA: Harvard University Press.

Vygotsky, L. S. (1981). The instrumental method in psychology. In J. V. Wertsch. (Ed.), *The concept of activity in Soviet psychology*. Armonk, NY: M. E. Sharpe, pp. 134–143.

Vygotsky, L. S. (1982). *L. S. Vygotskii. Sobranie sochinenii. Tom pervyi. Problemy teorii I istorii psikhologii* [*The collected works of L. S. Vygotsky. Volume 1: Problems of theory and history*]. Moscow: Pedagogika.

Vygotsky, L. S. (1987). *The collected works of L. S. Vygotsky. Volume 1: Problems of general psychology. Including the Volume Thinking and speech*. Edited and Translated by N. Minick. New York: Plenum.

Wertsch, J. V. (1985). *Vygotsky and the social formation of mind*. Cambridge, MA: Harvard University Press.

Wertsch, J. V. (1998). *Mind as action*. New York: Oxford University Press.

Wertsch, J. & Kazak, S. (in press). Saying more than you know in instructional settings. In T. Koschmann (Ed.). *Theorizing practice*. Mahwah, NJ: Lawrence Erlbaum.

Zinchenko, V. P. (2000). *Mysl' i slovo Gustava Shpeta*. [The sense and word of Gustav Shpet]. Moscow: Izdatel'stvo YRAO.

CHAPTER 8

Arnold, M. A. (1874/1924). *Literature and dogma: An essay towards a better apprehension of the Bible*. London: J. Murray.

Bacon, F. (1620/1960). *The new organum and related writings*. New York: Macmillan.

Backhurst, D. (1990). *Consciousness and revolution in Soviet philosophy: From the Bolsheviks to Evald Ilyenkov*. New York: Cambridge University Press.

Bergson, H. (1911/1983). *Creative evolution*. New York: H. Holt.

Bruner, J. S. (1962). Introduction. In L. S. Vygotsky (Ed.), *Thought and language*. Cambridge, MA: MIT Press.

Cole, M. (1996). *Cultural psychology: A once and future discipline*. Cambridge, MA: Harvard University Press.

Cole, M. (2006). Culture and cognitive development in phylogenetic, historical and ontogenetic perspective. In D. Kuhn & R. Siegler (Eds.), (W. Damon & R. Lerner, Series Eds.), *Handbook of Child Psychology: Volume 2. Cognition, Perception, and Language*. (6th ed.). Hoboken, NJ: Wiley, pp. 636–86.

Cole, M., & Engeström, Y. (1993). A cultural-historical approach to distributed cognition. In G. Salomon (Ed.), *Distributed Cognition: Psychological and Educational Considerations*. Cambridge, UK: Cambridge University Press, pp. 1–46.

Cole, M., & Scribner, S. (1977). Cross-cultural studies of memory and cognition. In R. V. Kail, Jr. & J. W. Hagen (Eds.), *Memory in cognitive development*. Hillsdale, NJ: Erlbaum.

D'Andrade, R. (1986). Three scientific world views and the covering law model. In D. Fiske & R. A. Shweder (Eds.), *Metatheory in the social sciences*. Chicago: University of Chicago Press.

de Waal, F. (2001). *The ape and the sushi master: Cultural reflections by a primatologist*. London: Allen Lane.

Donald, M. (1991). *The making of the modern mind*. Cambridge, MA: Harvard University Press.

Engeström, Y. (1993). Developmental studies of work as a testbench of activity theory. In S. Chaiklin & J. Lave (Eds.), *Understanding Practice: Perspectives on Activity and Context*. Cambridge, UK: Cambridge University Press.

Geertz, C. (1973). *The interpretation of Cultures*. New York: Basic Books.

Goody, J. (1977). *The domestication of the savage mind*. Cambridge, UK: Cambridge University Press.

Graham, L. R. (1972). *Science, philosophy, and human behavior in the Soviet Union*. New York: Columbia University Press.

Herder, J. (1803/1966). *Outlines of a philosophy of the history of man*. New York: Bergman Publishers. (First published in English, 1803.)

Herodotus (1945). *The history of Herodotus*. New York: E. P. Dutton.

Hodgen, M. T. (1964). *Early anthropology in the sixteenth and seventeenth centuries*. Philadelphia: University of Pennsylvania Press.

Ilyenkov, E.V. (1977). The concept of the ideal. In *Philosophy in the USSR: Problems of dialectical materialism*. Moscow: Progress.

Jaensch, E. (1930). *Eidetic imagery and typological methods of investigation; their importance for the psychology of childhood, the theory of education, general psychology, and the psychophysiology of human personality*. New York: Harcourt, Brace.

Jahoda, G. (1992). *Crossroads between culture and mind: Continuities and change in theories of human nature*. New York: Harvester/Wheatsheaf.

Jahoda, G. (1999). *Images of savages*. London: Routledge, 1999.

Judd, C. H. (1926). *The psychology of social institutions*. New York: Macmillan.

Leontiev, A. N. (1981). The problem of activity in psychology. In J.V. Wertsch (Ed.), *The concept of activity in Soviet Psychology*. White Plains, NY: Sharpe.

Levy-Bruhl L. (1910/1926). The problem of activity in psychology. In J. V. Wertsch (Ed.), *The concept of activity in Soviet Psychology*. White Plains, NY: Sharpe.

Luria, A. R. (1976). *Culture and cognitive development*. Cambridge, MA: Harvard University Press.

Luria, A. R., & Vygotsky, L. S. (1930/1993). *Studies on the history of behavior: ape, primitive, and child*. Hillsdale, NJ: Erlbaum.

Medin, D. K., & Atran, S. (2004). The native mind: Biological categorization and reasoning in development and across cultures. *Psychological Review, 111*(4), 960–983.

Meshcheriakov, B. G. (2000). Vygotsky's conception: A logico-semantic analysis. *Journal of Russian and East European Psychology, 38*(2), 34–55.

Morgan, L. H. (1878/1963). *Ancient society, or, Researches in the lines of human progress from savagery through barbarism to civilization*. Cleveland: World Pub. Co.

Nettle, D., & Romaine, S. (2000). *Vanishing voices: The extinction of the world's languages*. Oxford: Oxford University Press.

Plotkin, H. (2001). Some elements of a science of culture. In E. Whitehouse (Ed.), *The debated mind: Evolutionary psychology versus ethnography*. New York: Berg, pp. 91–109.

Schedrovitsky, P. (2003, July). *Tragedy of L. Vygotsky, prince of psychology*. Retrieved from http://www.russ.univer/chairs/schedrov/prince.htm on February 27, 2005.

Scribner, S. (1985). Vygotsky's uses of history. In J. V. Wertsch (Ed.). *Culture, communication, and cognition: Vygotskian perspectives.* New York: Cambridge University Press.

Scribner, S., & Cole, M. (1981). *The psychology of literacy.* Cambridge, MA: Harvard University Press.

Thurnwald, R. (1922). Psychologie des primitiven Menschen. In I. G. Kafka (Ed.), *Handuch der vergleichenden Psychologie. Band 1.* Munich: Verlag von Ernst Reinhardt.

Tylor, E. B. (1865/1964). *Researches into the early history of mankind and the development of civilization.* Edited reprint. Chicago: University of Chicago Press.

Tulviste, P. (1999). Activity as an explanatory principle in cultural psychology. In S. Chaiklin & M. Hedegaard (Eds.), *Activity Theory and Social Practice.* Aarhus, Denmark: Aarhus University Press, pp. 66–78.

Valsiner, J. (1988). *Developmental psychology in the Soviet Union.* Bloomington: Indiana University Press.

Valsiner, J. (1998). *The guided mind: A sociogenetic approach to personality.* Cambridge, MA: Harvard University Press.

van der Veer, R. (2002). Vygotsky criticized. *Journal of Russian and Eastern European Psychology, 38*(6), 3–9.

van der Veer, R., & Valsiner, J. (1991). *Understanding Vygotsky: A Quest for Synthesis.* Cambridge, MA: Harvard University Press.

van der Veer, R. (1996). The conept of culture in Vygotsky's thinking. *Culture and Psychology, 2*(3), 247–263.

Von Humboldt, W. F. (1836/1999). On language: on the diversity of human language construction and its influence on the mental development of the human species. New York: Cambridge University Press.

Wertsch. J. V. (1998). *Mind as action.* London: Oxford University Press.

Wertsch, J. V. (1993). Introduction. In A. R. Luria & L. S. Vygotsky (Eds.), (1930/1993) *Studies on the History of Behavior: Ape, Primitive, and Child.* Hillsdale, NJ: Erlbaum.

Wertsch, J. V. (1985). *Vygotsky and the social formation of mind.* Cambridge, MA: Harvard University Press.

Wertsch, J. V., & Tulviste, P. (1992). L. S. Vygotsky and contemporary developmental psychology. *Developmental Psychology, 28*(4), 548–557.

Zinchenko, V. P. (1985). Vygotsky's ideas about units for the analysis of mind. In J. V. Wertsch (Ed.), *Culture, Communication, and Cognition: Vygotskian Perspectives.* Cambridge, UK: Cambridge University Press, pp. 94–118.

CHAPTER 9

Akhmatova, A. (1977). *Stikhi, perepiska, vospominaniia, iconografía.* Ann Arbor: Ardis.

Aristotle. (1996). *Poetics.* Harmondsworth, UK: Penguin Classics.

Arsenyev, A. S. (1993). *O tvorcheskoj sud'be S. L. Rubinshteina* [On the creativity and fate of S. L. Rubinstein]. *Voprosy filosofii* [*Problems of philosophy*]. (No. 5.). Moscow: Nauka.

Bakhtin, M. M. (1994). *Raboty 1920-kh godov* [Works from the 1920s]. Kiev: NEXT.

Bakhtin, M. M. (1994a). *Problemy tvorchestva Dostoevskogo* [Problems of Dostoevsky's creative poetics]. Kiev: NEXT.

Bernshtein, N. A. (1966). *Ocherki po fiziologii dvizhenij i fiziologii aktivnosti* [Essays on the physiology of movement and the physiology of activation]. Moscow: Medetsina.

Bibikhin, V. V. (2001). *V poiskakh suti slova* [In search of the essence of word]. *Slovo i sobytie* [Word and event]. Moscow: Editorial USSR.

Eliot, T. S. (1930). *Ash-Wednesday*. New York, London, G. P. Putnam's Sons.

Eliot, T. S. (1942). *Little Gidding*. London, Faber and Faber.

Gal'perin, P. Ya. (1998). *Psihologiya kak ob'ektivnaya nauka* [Psychology as objective science]. Moscow-Voronezh: Institut Prakticheskoi Psihologii.

Gordeeva, N. D., & Zinchenko, V. P. (1982). *Funktsional'naya struktura deistviya* [The functional structure of action]. Moscow: MGU.

Gordeeva, N. D., & Zinchenko, V. P. (2001). Rol'refleksii v postroenii predmetnogo deistviya [The role of reflection in the construction of object-oriented action]. *Chelovek [Man]* (No. 6). Moscow: Nauka.

Gumilev, N. S. (1989). The word. In *Stikhotvoreniia i poemy* Moscow: Sovremennik.

Hadamard, J. (1970). *Issledovanie psikhologii processa izobreteniya v matematike* [Research in psychology on the process of invention in mathematics]. Moscow: Sovetskoye Radio.

Humboldt, W. (1984). *Izbrannye trudy po yazykoznaniyu* [Collected works in linguistics]. Moscow: Progress.

Lashley, K. S. (1964). *Brain mechanisms and intelligence: a quantitative study of injuries to the brain*. New York: Hafner.

Luria, A. R. (1982). Posleslovie [Afterword]. In L. S. Vygotsky. *Sobranie sochinenii* [*The collected works of L. S. Vyogtsky. Volume 2.*] Moscow: Pedagogika.

Mamardashvili, M. K. (2000). *Estetika myshleniya* [The aesthetics of thinking]. Moscow: Moskovskaya Shkola Politicheskih Issledovanii.

Mandel'shtam O. (1987). *Slovo i kul'tura* [Word and Culture]. Moscow: Sovetskii Pisatel'.

Meshcheryakov, B. G. (2000). *L.S. Vygotsky: Motsart ili Lyuter?* [L. S. Vygotsky: Mozart or Luther?]. *Chelovek [Man]* (No.1). Moscow: Nauka.

Meshcheryakov, B. G., & Zinchenko, V. P. (2000). *Kul'turno-istoricheskaya psikhologiya: Vchera, segodnya, zavtra* [Cultural–historical psychology: Yesterday, today, tomorrow]. *Zhurnal Voprosy psihologii [Journal Problems of Psychology]*. 2.

Ortega y Gassett, J. (1997). *Razmyshleniya o "Don-Kihote"* [Reflections on "Don Quijote"]. Saint Petersburg: Estetika. Filosofia Kul'turi.

Pasternak, B. L. (1990). *Perepiska Borisa Pasternaka* [The correspondence of Boris Pastenak]. Moscow: Khudozhestvennaya Literatura.

Plato *Plato's Sophist: Part II of The Being of the Beautiful*. (1984). Chicago: University of Chicago Press. (Translated by Seth Benardete).

Portnov, A. I. (1999). Filosofiya yazyka G. G. Shpeta [Shpet's philospohy of language]. In G. G. Shpet. *Vnutrennyaya forma slova* [The inner form of word]. Ivanovo: MGU.

Potebnya, A. A. (1976). *Estetika i poetika* [Aesthetics and Poetics]. Moscow: Iskusstvo.

Potebnya, A. A. (1999). *Sobranie trudov. Mysl' i yazyk* [Collected works. Thought and language]. Moscow.: Labirint.

Shpet, G. G. (1914). *Yavlenie i smysl* [Phenomenon and sense]. Moscow: Germes.

Shpet, G. G. (1989). *Sochineniya* [Works. Moscow: Pravda.

Shpet, G. G. (1994). *Filosofskie etyudy* [Philosophical essays]. Moscow: Progress.

Shpet, G. G. (1996). *Psikhologiya sotsial'nogo bytiya* [The psychology of social being]. Moscow-Voronezh: Institut Practicheskoi Psihologii.

Shpet, G. G. (1999). *Vnutrennyaya forma slova* [The inner form of word]. Ivanovo: MGU.

Ukhtomsky, A. A. (1978). *Izbrannie trudy* [Collected works]. Leningrad: Nauka.

Volkov, N. N. (1977). *Kompozitsiya v zhivopis* [Composition in painting]. Moscow: Iskusstvo.

Vygodskaya, G. L., & Lifanova, T. M. (1996). *Lev Semenovich Vygotsky: Zhizn.' Deyatel'nost.' Shtrihi k portretu* [Lev Semenovich Vygotsky. Life. Activity. Touches to the portrait]. Moscow: Smisl, Academia.

Vygotsky, L. S. (1982–1984). *Sobranie sochinenii v 6 tomakh* [Collected works in 6 volumes]. Moscow: Pedagogika.

Vygotsky, L. S. (1987). *Psikhologiya iskusstva* [The psychology of art]. Moscow: Iskusstvo

Vygotsky, L. S. (1991). *Pedagogicheskaya psikhologiya* [Pedagogical psychology]. Moscow: Pedagogika.

Weber, Max. (1978). *Economy and society.* Berkeley: University of California Press.

Wertheimer, M. (1987). *Produktivnoe myshlenie* [Productive thinking]. Moscow: Progress.

Zaporozhets, A. V. (1986). *Izbrannie psikhologicheskie trudy* [Collected psychological works]. Volumes 1–2. Moscow: Pedagogika.

Zhinkin, N. I. (1998). *Yazyk. Rech'. Tvorchestvo.* [Language. Speech. Creativity]. Moscow: Labirint.

Zinchenko, V. P. (1981). Idei L. S. Vygotskogo o edinitsakh analiza psikhiki [L.S. Vygotsky's ideas on units of analysis of the mind]. *Psikhologicheskii zhurnal* [Psychological Journal], 2.

Zinchenko, V. P. (1996). Intuitsiya N.A. Bernshteina: Dvizhenie – zhivoe sushch-estvo. K 100-letiyu N.A. Bernshteina [Bernshtein's intuition: Movement is a living being. Bernshtein's 100th anniversary]. *Zhurnal Voprosy psikhologii* [*Journal Problems of psychology*], 6.

Zinchenko, V. P. (1996). Ot klassicheskoi k organicheskoi pskihologii. K 100-letiyu L.S. Vygotskogo [From classical to organic psychology. Vygotsky's 100th anniversary]. *Zhurnal Voprosy psikhologii* [*Journal Problems of Psychology*], 5, 6.

Zinchenko, V. P. (1998). *Psikhologicheskaya pedagogika. Chast' 1 Zhivoe znanie* 2-e izdanie [Psychological pedagogy. Part 1. Living knowledge. (2nd ed.]. Samara: Samarskii Gosudarstvennii Pedagogicheskii Universitet.

Zinchenko, V. P. (2000). *Mysl' i slovo Gustava Shpeta* [The thought and word of Gustav Shpet]. Moscow: Universitet Rossiiskoi Akademii Obrazovaniya.

Zinchenko, V. P. (2003). Teoreticheskii mir psikhologii [The theoretical world of psychology]. *Zhurnal Voprosy pskihologii [Journal Problems of Psychology]*, 5.

Zinchenko, V. P. & Vergiles, N. Yu. (1969). *Formirovanie zritel'nogo obraza* [The formation of the visual image]. Moscow: MGU.

Zinchenko, V. P. & Mamardashvili, M. K. (1977). Problema ob'ektivnogo metoda v psikhologii [The problem of objective method in psychology]. *Voprosy filosofii. [Problems of Philosophy]*, 7. Moscow: Nauka.

CHAPTER 10

Bruner, J. S., Olver, R. R., & Greenfield, P. H. (1966). *Studies in cognitive growth.* New York: Wiley.

Bruner, J. S. (1986). *Actual minds, possible worlds.* Cambridge, MA: Harvard University Press.

Cole, M. (1996). *Cultural psychology: A once and future discipline.* Cambridge, MA: Belknap Press of Harvard University Press.

Corsaro, W. A. (1997). *The sociology of childhood.* Thousand Oaks, CA: Pine Forge Press.

Davydov, V. V. (1982). *Ausbildung der Lerntätigkeit* [Development of Learning Activity]. In V. V. Davydov, J. Lompscher, & A. K. Markova (eds.), *Ausbildung der Lerntätigkeit bei Schülern.* Berlin: Volk und Wissen, pp. 14–27.

Davydov, V. V. (1988). Problems of developmental teaching. *Soviet Education*, 30(8), 6–97.

Davydov, V. V. (1972/1990). *Types of generalization in instruction: Logical and psychological problems in the structuring of school curricula* (Soviet studies in mathematics education, Volume 2. Edited by J. Kilpatrick. Translated by J. Teller. Reston, VA: National Council of Teachers of Mathematics. (Original work published 1972.)

Davydov, V. V. (1993). The influence of L. S. Vygotsky on education, theory, research and practice. *Educational Researcher, 23*, 12–21.

Davydov, V. V. (1998). L. S. Vygotsky and reform of today's school. *Journal of Russian and East European Psychology, 36*, 83–101.

Davydov, V. V., & Markova, A. K. (1983). A concept of educational activity for schoolchildren. *Soviet Psychology, 21*, 50–76.

El'konin, D. B. (1978/1988). *Legens psykologi.* Translated by J. Hansen. Moscow: Sputnik. (Original work published 1978.)

El'konin, D. B. (1999). Toward the problem of stages in the mental development of children. *Journal of Russian and East European Psychology, 37*(6), 11–30.

Hedegaard, M.* (1984). *Lege – lære.* Copenhagen: BUPLs forlag.

Hedegaard, M.* (1990). The zone of proximal development as basis for instruction. In L. C. Moll. (Ed.), *Vygotsky and education: Instructional implications and applications of sociohistorical psychology.* Cambridge, UK: Cambridge University Press, pp. 349–371.

Hedegaard, M.* (2002). *Learning and child development: A cultural-historical study.* Aarhus: Aarhus University Press.

---

* This author has also published as M. Stenild.

Heidbreder, E. (1952). Toward a dynamic theory of cognition. *Psychological Review, 59,* 461–472.

Hundeide, K. (2005). Sociocultural tracks of development, opportunity situations and access-skills. *Culture and Psychology, 11* (2), 241–261.

Kravtsov, G., & Berezlizhkovskaya, E. L. (1999). The education of pre-school children. In M. Hedegaard & J. Lompscher (Eds.), *Learning activity and development.* Aarhus: Aarhus University Press.

Iljenkov, E. V. (1977). The concept of the ideal. In *Philosophy in the USSR.* Moscow: Progress Publishers.

Leontiev, A. N. (1978). *Activity, consciousness, and personality.* Englewood Cliffs, NJ: Prentice-Hall.

Luria, A. R. (1976). *Cognitive development: Its cultural and social formation.* Cambridge, MA: Harvard University Press.

Nelson, K. (1974). Concept, word, and sentence. Interrelationship in acquisition and development. *Psychological Review, 81,* 267–285.

Nelson, K. (1977a). Cognitive development and the acquisition of concepts. In R. C. Anderson, R. J. Spiro, & M. E. Montague (Eds.), *Schooling and the acquisition of knowledge.* New York: Wiley.

Nelson, K. (1977b). The conceptual basis for naming. In J. Macnamara (Ed.), *Language, learning, and thought.* New York: Academic Press.

Nelson, K. (1995). From spontaneous to scientific concepts: Continuities and discontinuities from childhood to adulthood. In L. Martin, K. Nelson, & E. Tobach (Eds.), *Sociocultural psychology: Theory and practice of doing and knowing.* New York: Cambridge University Press.

Nelson, K. (1996). *Language in cognitive development. The emergence of the mediated mind.* Cambridge, UK: Cambridge University Press.

Pintrich, P. R., Marx, R. W., & Boyle, R. A. (1993). Beyound conceptual change: The role of motivational beliefs and classroom contextual factors in the process of conceptual change. *Review of Educational Research, 63,* 167–199.

Rogoff, B. (2003). *The cultural nature of human development.* Oxford: Oxford University Press.

Scribner, S., & Cole, M. (1981). *The psychology of literacy.* Cambridge, MA: Harvard University Press.

Stenild, M.* (1978). Concept learning. A microgenetic analysis examined in relation to intention, action, experience, and language. *Communication and Cognition, 11,* 249–265.

Wartofsky, M. (1979). *Models – Representations and the scientific understanding.* Dordrecht and Boston: D. Reidel.

Vygotsky, L. S. (1962). *Thought and language.* Cambridge, MA: MIT Press.

Vygotsky, L. S. (1978). *Mind in society.* Cambridge, MA: Harvard University Press.

Vygotsky, L. S. (1987). Thinking and speech. *The collected works of L. S. Vygotsky. Volume 1: Problems of the theory and history of psychology.* Translated by M. Hall. In R. W. Rieber. (Ed.). New York: Plenum Press, pp. 39–285.

* This author has also published as M. Hedegaard.

Vygotsky, L. S. (1997). The instrumental method in psychology. *The collected work of L.S. Vygotsky, Vol. 3. Problems of the theory and history of psychology.* Translated by M. Hall. In R. W. Rieber (Ed.). New York: Plenum Press, pp. 85–89.

Vygotsky, L. S. (1930/1998a). Development of thinking and formation of concepts in the adolescent. Translated by M. Hall. In R. W. Rieber. (Ed.), *The collected works of L. S. Vygotsky. Volume 5: Child psychology.* New York: Plenum Press, pp. 29–82. (Original work published 1930.)

Vygotsky, L. S. (1931/1998b). Problems of child (developmental) psychology. *The collected works of L. S. Vygotsky. Volume 5: Child psychology.* Translated by M. Hall. In R. W. Rieber (Ed.), New York: Plenum Press, pp. 187–319. (Original work written 1931.)

CHAPTER 11

Bernshtein, N. A. (1966). *Orcherki po fisiologuii dvizhenii i fisiologuii aktivnosti (Essays on the phisiology of movements and the fisiology of activation).* Moscow: Meditzina.

Binet, A. (1903). *L'étude éxperimentale de l'intelligence.* Paris: Schleicher.

Cazden, C. (1981). Performance before competence: Assistance to child discourse in the zone of proximal development. *Quarterly Newsletter of the Laboratory of Comparative Human Cognition, 3*(1), 5–8.

Claparède, E. (1973). *L'éducation functionelle.* Neuchâtel: Delachaux et Niestlé.

Cobb, P. (1998). Learning from distributed theories of intelligence. *Mind, Culture and Activity, 5*(3), 187–204.

Cole, M. (1985). The Zone of Proximal Development: Where culture and cognition create each other. In J. V. Wertsch (Ed.), *Culture, communication and cognition: Vygotskian perspectives.* Cambridge, UK: Cambridge University Press, pp. 146–161.

Cole, M. (1997). *Culture and Cognitive Science.* http://lchc.ucsd.edu.People/Localz/MCole/santabar.html.

Cordón, F. (1990). *Tratado evolucionista de biología. Historia natural de la acción y experiencia.* Madrid: Aguilar.

Damasio, A. (2000). *The feeling of what happens: Body and emotions in the making of consciousness.* New York: Harcourt Brace.

del Río, P. (1990). La Zona de Desarrollo Próximo y la Zona Sincrética de Representación: El espacio instrumental de la mediación social. *Infancia y Aprendizaje, 51–52,* 191–244.

del Río, P. (2002). The external brain: Eco-cultural roots of distancing and mediation. *Culture and Psychology, 8*(2), 233–265.

del Río, P., & Álvarez, A. (1995). Tossing, praying and reasoning: The changing architectures of mind and agency. In J. V. Wertsch, P. deldr Riío & A. Álvarez (Eds.), *Sociocultural studies of mind.* Cambridge, UK: Cambridge University Press, pp. 215–247.

del Riío, P., & Álvarez, A. (1999). La puesta en escena de la realidad cultural. Una aproximación histórico-cultural al problema de la etnografía audiovisual. *Revista de Antropología Social, 8,* 121–136.

del Riío, P., & Álvarez, A. (2002). From activity to directivity. The question of involvement in education. In G. Wells & G. Claxton (Eds.), *Learning for life in the 21st Century: Sociocultural perspectives on the future of education* (pp. 59–72). Oxford: Blackwell.

Elkonin, B. D. (1994). Historical crisis of childhood: Developing D. B. Elkonin's concept. In A. Álvarez & P. del *Río* (Eds.), *Explorations in Sociocultural Studies, vol IV. Education as cultural construction.* Madrid: Fundación Infancia y Aprendizaje, pp. 47–51.

Galperin, P. (1978/1992). Stage by stage formation as a method of psychological investigation. *Journal of Russian and East European Psychology,* 30(4), 61–80.

Gibson, J. J. (1979). *The ecological approach to visual perception.* Boston: Houghton Mifflin.

Gombrich, E. H. (1989). *The story of art.* New York: Phaidon Press.

Hutchins, E. (1995). *Cognition in the wild.* Cambridge, UK: Cambridge University Press.

Janet, P. (1937). Les conduites sociales. In *XIeme Congrès International de Psychologie,* Paris.

Jennings, H. S. (1906). *Behaviour of the lower organisms.* New York.

Koffka, K. (1935). *Principles of Gestalt Psychology.* New York: Harcourt Brace.

Lave, J., & Wenger, E. (1991). *Situated Learning.* Cambridge, UK: Cambridge University Press.

Leont'ev, A. N. (1975). *Deiatel'nost, soznanie, lichnost.* Moscú: Izdatel'stvo Polichiteskoi Literaturi.

Leont'ev, A. N. (1981). The problem of activity in psychology. In J. V. Wertsch (Ed.), *The concept of activity in Soviet psychology.* Armonk, NY: Sharpe, pp. 37–71.

Lewin, K. (1926). Vorsatz, Wille Und Bedürfnis – Untersuchungen zur Handlungs- und Affekt-Psychologie. *Psychologische Forschung,* 4, 1–39.

Lewin, K. (1936). *Principles of topological psychology.* New York: McGraw-Hill.

Lorenz, K. (1993). *La ciencia natural del hombre. "El manuscrito de Rusia" (1944–1948).* Barcelona: Tusquets.

Luria, A. R. (1979). *The making of mind.* Cambridge, MA: Harvard University Press.

McLuhan, M. (1964). *Understanding media: The extensions of man.* New York: McGraw-Hill.

Moll, L. C. (1990). *Community knowledge and classroom practice. Combining resources for literacy instruction.* Tucson: The University of Arizona.

Moll, L. C. (2005). Reflections and possibilities. In N. González, L. C. Moll & C. Amanti (Eds.), *Funds of Knowledge.* Mahwah, NJ: Lawrence Erlbaum, pp. 275–287.

Rogoff, B. (1990). *Aprenticeship in thinking.* New York: Oxford University Press.

Spencer, H. (1887). *The factors of Organic Evolution,* London: Williams & Norgate.

Turvey, N. T., & Shaw, R. (1977). The primacy of perceiving: An ecological reformulation of perception for understanding memory. In Lars-Göran Nielson (Ed.), *Perspectives on memory research: Essays in honor of Uppsala University's 500th anniversary.* Uppsala: Uppsala University Press.

van der Veer, R., & Valsiner, J. (1991). *Understanding Vygotsky. A quest for synthesis.* Cambridge, MA and Oxford, UK: Blackwell.

von Uexküll, J. (1909). *Umwelt und Innenleben der Tiere.* Berlin: J. Springer.

von Uexküll, J. (1926). *Theoretical Biology.* London: Kegan Paul.

von Uexküll, J. (1934). *Der Mensch und die Natur.* Bern: Francke A.G.

Vygotsky, L. S. (1926). *Pedagoguicheskaia Psijologia. Kratki Kurs.* Moscow: Rabotnik Prosveshchenia.

Vygotsky, L. S. (1926/1982/1990). Prólogo a la edición rusa del libro de E. Thorndike "Principios de enseñanza basados en la psicología". En A. Álvarez & P. del Río (Eds.), *L. S. Vygotski. Obras Escogidas, Vol. I. Problemas teóricos y metodológicos de la psicología.* Translated by José María Bravo. Madrid: Visor Distribuciones, pp. 143–162.

Vygotsky, L. S. (1927/1982/1990). El significado histórico de la crisis de la psicología. Una investigación metodológica. In A. Alvarez & P. del Rio (Eds.), *L. S. Vygotski. Obras Escogidas, Vol. I. Problemas teóricos y metodológicos de la psicología.* Translated by José María Bravo). Madrid: Visor Distribuciones, pp. 257–407.

Vygotsky, L. S. (1930/1984). Orudie i znak v razvitie rebenka [Tool and sign in the development of the child]. In M. G. Yaroshevski (Ed.), *L. S. Vygotsky. Sobranie Sochinenii, Tom 6. Nauchnoe Nasledstvo.* Moscow: Pedagogika, pp. 5–90.

Vygotsky, L. S. (1930/1984/1999). Tool and sign in the development of the child. In R. W. Rieber (Ed.), *The collected works of L. S. Vygotsky. Volume 6. Scientific Legacy.* Translated by Marie Hall). New York: Kluwer/Plenum, pp. 3–68.

Vygotsky, L. S. (1933/1982/1990). El problema de la conciencia. In A. Álvarez & P. del, Río (Eds.), *L. S. Vygotski. Obras Escogidas, Vol. I. Problemas teóricos y metodológicos de la psicología.* Translated by José María Bravo). Madrid: Visor Distribuciones, pp. 119–132.

Vygotsky, L. S. (1934/1956). *Izbrannie psikhologicheskie issledovaniya.* Moscú: Akademii Pedagogicheskikh Nauk.

Vygotsky, L. S. (1934/1982/1987). Thinking and Speech. In R. W. Rieber & A. S. Carton (Eds.), *The collected works of L. S. Vygotsky. Volume 1: Problems of general psychology.* Translated by Norris Minick. New York and London: Plenum, pp. 3–68.

Vygotsky, L. S. (1934/1982/1993). Pensamiento y lenguaje. In A. Álvarez & P. del, Río (Eds.), *L. S. Vygotsky Obras Escogidas, Vol. II. Problemas de psicología general.* Translated by José María Bravo. Madrid: Visor Distribuciones, pp. 9–348.

Vygotsky, L. S. (1935). Dinamika umstvennogo razvitija shkol'nika v svjazi s obucheniem. In *Umstvennoe razvitie detej v processe obuchenija.* Moscow-Leningrad: Uchpedgiz, pp. 33–52.

Vygotsky, L. S. (1978a). Interaction between learning and development. In M. Cole, V. John-Steiner, & E. Souberman (Eds.), *Mind in society: The development of higher psychological processes.* Cambridge, MA: Harvard University Press, pp. 79–91.

Vygotsky, L. S. (1978b). Tool and symbol in child development. In M. Cole, V. John-Steiner, & E. Souberman (Eds.), *Mind in society: The development of higher psychological processes.* Cambridge, MA: Harvard University Press, pp. 19–30.

Vygotsky, L. S. (1980). Fragmento de los apuntes de L. S. Vygotski para unas conferencias de psicología de los párvulos. In B. D. Elkonin (Ed.), *Psicología del juego*. Madrid: Phaedos, pp. 269–276.

Vygotsky, L. S. (1981). The genesis of higher mental functions. In J. V. Wertsch (Ed.), *The concept of activity in Soviet psychology*. Armonk, NY: Sharpe, pp. 144–188.

Vygotsky, L. S., & Luria, A. (1994). Tool and symbol in child development. In R. van der Veer & J. Valsiner (Eds.), *The Vygotsky Reader*. Oxford, UK: Basil Blackwell, pp. 99–176.

Wallon, H. (1934). *Les origines du caractère chez l'enfant*. Paris: Presses Universitaires de France.

Wells, G. (1999). *Dialogic inquiry: Towards a sociocultural practice and theory of education*. New York: Cambridge University Press.

Wertsch, J. V. (1985). *Vygotsky and the social formation of mind*. Cambridge, MA: Cambridge University Press.

Zaporozhets, A. V. (1959). *Razvitie proizvol'nykh dvizhenii (The development of voluntary movements)*. Moscow: Izdatel'stvo Akademii Pedagogicheskikh Nauk RSFSR.

Zaporozhets, A. V. (Ed.). (1967). *Vospratie i deistvie (Perception and Action)*. Moscow: Prosveschenie.

Zazzo, R. (1968). *Conduites et Conscience, vol 1. Psychologie de l'enfant et méthode génétique*. Nêuchatel: Delachaux et Niestlé.

Zinchenko, V. P. (1985). Vygotsky and units for the analyisis of mind. In J. V. Wertsch (Ed.), *Culture, Communication and Cognition. Vygotskyan perspectives*. Cambridge, UK: Cambridge University Press, pp. 94–118.

CHAPTER 12

Bentley, T. (1998). *Learning beyond the classroom: Education for a changing world*. London: Demos and Routledge.

Bernstein, B. (1999). Official knowledge and pedagogic identities. In F. Christie (Ed.), *Pedagogy and the Shaping of Consciousness: Linguistic and Social Processes*. London: Cassell.

Bliss, J., Askew, M., & Macrae, S. (1996). Effective teaching and learning: Scaffolding revisited. *Oxford Review of Education, 22*(1), 37–61.

Brown, A. L., & Campione, J. C. (1990). Communities of learning thinking, or a context by any other name. In D. Kuhn (Ed.), *Developmental perspectives on teaching and learning thinking skills. Volume 21: Contributions in Human Development*. Basel: Karger.

Brown, A. L., & Campione, J. C. (1994). Guided discovery in a community of learners. In K. McGilly (Ed.), *Integrating cognitive theory and classroom practice: Classroom lessons*. Cambridge, MA: MIT Press/Bradford Books, pp. 229–272.

Brown, A. L., Metz, K. E., & Campione, J. C. (1996). Social interaction and individual understanding in a community of learners: The influence of Piaget and Vygotsky. In A. Tryphon & J. Voneche (Eds.), *Piaget-Vygotsky: The Social Genesis of Thought*, Hove: Psychology Press.

Brown, A. L., & Palincsar, A. S. (1989). Guided co-operative learning and individual knowledge acquisition. In L. B. Resnick (Ed.), *Knowing, learning, and instruction: Essays in Honor of Robert Glaser*. Hillsdale, NJ: Erlbaum, pp. 393–451.

Cazden, C. B. (1979). Peekaboo as an instructional model: Discourse development at home and at school. *Papers and reports on child language development*, 17. Palo Alto, CA: Stanford University, Department of Linguistics.

Chaiklin, S. (2003). The Zone of Proximal Development, In Vygotsky's analysis of Learning and Instruction. In A. Kozulin, B. Gindis, V. Ageyev, & S. Miller (Eds.), *Vygotsky's Educational Theory in Cultural Context*. Cambridge, UK: Cambridge University Press.

Cole, M. (1996). *Cultural Psychology: A once and future discipline*. Cambridge, MA: Harvard University Press.

Cole, M., & Engeström, Y. (1993). A cultural-historical approach to distributed cognition. In G. Salomon (Ed.), *Distributed cognitions: Psychological and educational considerations*. New York: Cambridge University Press.

Collins, A. (1991). Cognitive apprenticeship and instructional technology. In L. Idol & B. F. Jones (Eds.), *Educational values and cognitive instruction: Implications for reform*. Hillsdale, NJ: Erlbaum.

Collins, A., Brown, J. S., & Newman, S. E. (1989). Cognitive apprenticeship: Teaching the crafts of reading, writing and mathematics. In L. B. Resnick (Ed.), *Knowing, learning and instruction: Essays in honor of Robert Glaser*. Hillsdale, NJ: Erlbaum, pp. 453–494.

Davydov, V. V. (1988). Problems of developmental teaching: the experience of theoretical and experimental psychological research. *Soviet Education, 20*(8), 3–87; (9), 3–56; (10), 2–42.

Davydov, V. V. (1990). The content and unsolved problems of activity theory. Paper presented May 22, 1990 at the 2nd International Congress on Activity theory, Lahti, Finland.

Davydov, V. V. (1993). *Current efforts at restructuring Russian education*. Paper presented at the annual meeting of the American Educational Research Association, Atlanta, Georgia, April, 1993.

Davydov, V. (1995). The influence of L. S. Vygotsky on education theory, research and practice. *Educational Researcher, 24*, 12–21.

Griffin, P., & Cole. M. (1984). Current activity for the future: The zo-ped. In B. Rogoff & J. V. Wertsch (Eds.), *Children's learning in the zone of proximal development*. San Francisco: Jossey-Bass.

Gutierrez, K. D., & Stone, L. D. (2000). Synchronic and diachronic dimensions of social practice: An emerging methodology for cultural–historical perspectives on literacy learning. In C. D. Lee & P. Smagorinsky (Eds.), *Vygotskian Perspectives on Literacy Research: Constructing Meaning Through Collaborative Inquiry*. Cambridge, UK: Cambridge University Press.

Hedegaard, M. (1990). How instruction influences children's concepts of evolution. *Mind, Culture, and Activity, 3*, 11–24.

Hedegaard, M., Chaiklin, S. (1990). Review of Davydov. V. V. (1986/1990). *Quarterly Newsletter of the Laboratory of Comparative Human Cognition, 12*(4), 153–154.

Hedegaard, M. (1998). Situated learning and cognition: Theoretical learning of cognition. *Mind Culture, and Activity*, 5(2), 114–126.

Hatano, G., & Inagaki, K. (1991). Sharing Cognition through Collective Comprehension Activity. In L. B. Resnick, J. M. Levine, & S. D. Teasley (Eds.), *Perspectives on Socially Shared Cognition*, Washington, DC: American Psychological Association.

Ivic, I. (1989). Profiles of educators: Lev S. Vygotsky (1896–1934). *Prospects, XIX*, (3) 427–436.

Karpov, Y. (2003). Development through the life span: A neo-Vygotskian perspective. In A. Kozulin, V. S. Ageyev, S. M. Miller, & B. Gindis (Eds.), *Vygotsky's Theory of Education in Cultural Context*. New York: Cambridge University Press.

Kozulin, A. (1996). A literary model for psychology. In D. Hicks (Ed.), *Discourse, Learning and Schooling*. Cambridge, UK: Cambridge University Press.

Kozulin, A., Gindis, B., Ageyev, V. S., Miller, & S. M. (2003). Introduction: Scociocultural theory and education: Students teachers and knowledge. In A. Kozulin, B. Gindis, V. Ageyev & S. Miller (Eds.), *Vygotsky's Educational Theory in Cultural Context*. Cambridge, UK: Cambridge University Press.

Langer, J. A., & Applebee, A. N. (1986). Reading and writing instruction: Toward a theory of teaching and learning. In E. Z. Rothkopf (Ed.), *Review of Research in Education, 13*. Washington, DC: American Educational Research Association, pp. 171–194.

Lee, C. D. (2000). Signifying in the Zone of Proximal Development. In C. D. Lee & P. Smagorinsky (Eds.), *Vygotskian Perspectives on Literacy Research: Constructing meaning through Collaborative Inquiry*. Cambridge, UK: Cambridge University Participant structures.

Mehan, H. (1997). Students' interactional competence in the classroom. In M. Cole, Y. Engestrom, & O. Vasquez (Eds.), *Mind, Culture and Activity: Seminal papers from the Laboratory of Comparative Human Cognition*. Cambridge, UK: Cambridge University Press.

Minick, N. (1987). The development of Vygotsky's thought: An introduction. In R. W. Rieber & A. S. Carton (Eds.), *The collected works of L. S. Vygotsky. Volume 1*. New York: Plenum Press.

Minick, N., Stone, C. A., & Forman, E. A. (1993). Introduction: Integration of individual, social and institutional processes in accounts of children's learning and development. In E. A. Forman, N. Minick, & C. A. Stone (Eds.), *Contexts for learning: sociocultural dynamics in children's development*. Oxford: Oxford University Press, pp. 3–16.

Moll, L. C. (1990). Introduction. In L. C. Moll (Ed.), *Vygotsky and education. Instructional implications and applications of sociohistorical psychology*. Cambridge, UK: Cambridge University Press, pp. 1–27.

Moll, L. C., & Greenberg, J. B. (1990). Creating zones of possibilities: combining social contexts for instruction. In Luis C. Moll (Ed.), *Vygotsky and Education. Instructional Implications and Applications of Sociohistorical Psychology*. Cambridge, UK: Cambridge University Press, pp. 319–348.

Moll, L. C. (2000). Inspired by Vygotsky: Ethnographic experiments in education. In C. D. Lee & P. Smagorinsky (Eds.), *Vygotskian Perspectives on Literacy*

Research: Constructing meaning through Collaborative Inquiry. Cambridge, UK: Cambridge University Press, pp. 256–269.

Newman, D., Griffin, P., & Cole, M. (1989). *The construction zone: Working for cognitive change in school.* Cambridge, UK: Cambridge University Press.

Nicolopoulou, A., & Cole, M. (1993). Generation and transmission of shared knowledge in the culture of collaborative learning: The fifth dimension, its play-world, and its institutional contexts. In E. A. Forman, N. Minick, & C. Addisondr Stone (Eds.), *Contexts for Learning. Sociocultural Dynamics in Children's Development.* New York: Oxford University Press, pp. 283–314.

O'Connor, C., & Michaels, S. (1993). Aligning academic task and participation status through revoicing: Analysis of a classroom discourse strategy. In *Anthropology and Education Quarterly, 24*(4), 318–335.

Palincsar, A., & Brown, A. L. (1984). Reciprocal teaching of comprehension-fostering and comprehension-monitoring activities. *Cognition and Instruction, 1*(2), 117–175.

Palincsar, A. S., & Brown, A. L. (1988). Teaching and practicing thinking skills to promote comprehension in the context of group problem solving. *Remedial and Special Education, 9*(1), 53–59.

Piaget, J. (1978). *Recherches sur la generalisation.* Paris: Presses Universitaires de France.

Reid, D. K. (1998). Scaffolding: A broader view. *Journal of Learning Disabilities, 31*(4), 386–396.

Reid, D. K., & Stone, C. Addison. (1991). Why is cognitive instruction effective? Underlying learning mechanisms. *Remedial and Special Education, 12*(3).

Rogoff, B., & Lave, J. (Eds.). (1984). *Everyday cognition: Its development in social context.* Cambridge, MA: Harvard University Press, pp. 95–116.

Stone, C. A. (1998). The metaphor of scaffolding: its utility for the field of Learning disabilities. *Journal of Learning Disabilities, 31*(4), 344–364.

Rowlands, S. (2000). Turning Vygotsky on his head: Vygotsky's "scientifically based method" and the socioculturalist's "social other." *Science and Education, 9,* 537–575.

Stigler, J. W., & Hiebert, J. (1999). *The teaching gap: Best ideas from the world's teachers for improving education in the classroom.* New York: Free Press.

Tharp, R. G. (1993). Institutional and social context of educational practice and reform. In E. A. Forman, N. Minick, & C. A. Stone (Eds.), *Contexts for learning: sociocultural dynamics in children's development.* Oxford: Oxford University Press, pp. 268–282.

Tharp, R. G., & Gallimore, R. (1988a). *Rousing minds to life: Teaching, learning, and schooling in social context.* Cambridge, UK: Cambridge University Press.

Tharp, R. G., & Gallimore, R. (1988b). Rousing schools to life. *American Educator, 13*(2), 20–25, 46–52.

Tudge, J. R. H., & Rogoff, B. (1989). Peer influences on cognitive development: Piagetian and Vygotskian perspectives. In M. H. Bornstein & J. S. Bruner (Eds.), *Intercation in Human Development.* Hillsdale, NJ: Lawrence Erlbaum, pp. 145–171.

van der Veer, R. (1994). The concept of development and the development of concepts education and development. In L. S. Vygotsky,'s *Thinking and Speech European Journal of Psychology Of Education, 9*(4), 293–300.

Vygotsky, L. S. (1978). *Mind in society: The development of higher psychological processes*. Edited and Translated by M. Cole, V. John-Steiner, S. Scribner, & E. Souberman. Cambridge, MA: Harvard University Press.

Vygotsky, L. S. (1987). *The of L. S. Vygotsky. Volume 1: Problems of general psychology*, including the volume *Thinking and speech*. Edited by R. W. Rieber & A. S. Carton. Translated by N. Minick. New York: Plenum Press.

Vygotsky, L. S. (1997a). *The collected works of L. S. Vygotsky. Volume 3: Problems of the theory and history of psychology*. Edited by R. Rieber & J. Wollock (Ed.). Translated by R. van der Veer. London: Plenum Press.

Vygotsky, L. S. (1997b). *Educational psychology*. Boca Raton, FL: St. Lucie Press. (Originally written 1921–1923.)

Vygotsky, L. S. (1998). *The collected works of L. S. Vygotsky. Volume 5: Child psychology*. Edited by R. Rieber. Translated by M. J. Hall. London: Plenum Press.

Wardekker, W. L. (1998). Scientific concepts and reflection. *Mind, Culture, and Activity*, 5(2), 143–154.

Wood, D., Bruner, J. C., & Ross, G. (1976). The role of tutoring in problem solving. *Journal of Child Psychology and Psychiatry*, *17*, 89–100.

CHAPTER 13

Akhutina, T.V. (1997). The remediation of executive functions in children with cognitive disorders: The Vygotsky–Luria neuropsychological approach. *Journal of Intellectual Disability Research*, *41*(2), 144–151.

Almanah (2000–2002). Publication of the Institute of Corrective Pedagogy, Moscow. Available at: www.ise.iip.net/almanah.

Arbitman-Smith, R., Haywood, C., & Bransford, J. (1984). Assessing cognitive change. In P. Brooks, R. Sperber, & C. McCauly (Eds.), *Learning and cognition in the mentally retarded*. Mahwah, NJ: Erlbaum, pp. 433–471.

Bakhurst, D., & Padden, C. (1991). The Meshcheryakov experiment: Soviet work on the education of blind/deaf children. *Learning and Instruction*, *1*, 201–215.

Belopolskay, N. L., & Lubovsky, V. I. (1992). Differentsial'no-psikhologicheskaia diagnostika deteei s intellektualnoi nedastatochnost'iu [Differential psychological diagnostics of children with cognitive deficiency]. *Psikhologichesky Zhurnal*, *4*, 98–97.

Belopolskaya, N. L., & Grebennikova, N. V. (1997). Neuropsychology and psychological diagnosis of abnormal development. In E. L. Grigorenko, P. M. Ruzgis, & R. J. Sternberg (Eds.), *Russian psychology: Past, present, and future*. Commack, NY: Nova Academic Press, pp. 155–179.

Berk, L., & Winsler, A. (1995). *Scaffolding children's learning: Vygotsky and early childhood education*. Washington, DC: National Association for the Young Children.

Bodrova, E., & Leong, D. J. (1996). *Tools of the mind: The Vygotskian approach to early childhood education*. Columbus, OH: Merrill.

Campione, J. C., & Brown, A. L. (1987). Linking dynamic assessment with school achievement. In C. S. Lidz (Ed.), *Dynamic assessment: An interactional approach to evaluating learning potential*. New York: Guilford, pp. 82–113.

Chaiklin, S. (2003). The Zone of Proximal Development in Vygotsky's analysis of learning and instruction. In A. Kozulin, B. Gindis, V. Ageyev, & S. Miller, (Eds.), *Vygotsky's educational theory in cultural context.* New York: Cambridge University Press, pp. 39–64.

Chulkov, V. N., Lubovsky, V. I., & Martsinovskaia, E. N. (Eds.). (1990). *Differentsirovannyi podkhod pri obuchennii i vospitan sleoglukhikry detei* [Differentiative approaches to the teaching and upbringing of deaf-blind children]. Moscow: Academia Pedagogicheskikh Nauk.

Daniels, H., & Lunt, I. (1993). Vygotskian theory and special education practice in Russia. *Educational Studies, 19*(1), 79–89.

Das, J. P., & Kendrick, M. (1997). PASS Reading Enhancement Program: A short manual for teachers. *Journal of Cognitive Education, 5*(3), 193–208.

Das, J. P., Naglieri, J. A., Kirby, J. R. (1994). *Assessment of cognitive processes: The PASS theory of intelligence.* MA: Allyn and Bacon.

Davydov, V. V. (1995). The influence of L. S. Vygotsky on education theory, research, and practice. *Educational Researcher, 24*(3), 12–21.

Elkonin, D. (1977). Toward the problem of stages in the mental development of the child. In M. Cole (Ed.), *Soviet developmental psychology.* White Plains, NY: M. E. Sharpe, pp. 538–563.

Elliott, J. (2003). Dynamic assessment in educational settings. *Educational Review, 55*, 15–32.

Feuerstein, R. (1990). The theory of structural cognitive modifiability. In B. Presseisen (Ed.), *Learning and thinking styles: Classroom interaction.* Washington, DC: National Education Association, pp. 68–134.

Feuerstein, R., Rand, Y., & Hoffman, M. (1979). *Dynamic assessment of retarded performer.* Baltimore, MD: University Park Press.

Feuerstein, R., Rand, Y., Hoffman, M., & Miller, R. (1980). *Instrumental Enrichment.* Baltimore, MD: University Park Press.

Feuerstein, R., & Gross, S. (1997). The Learning Potential Assessment Device. In D. Flanagan et al. (Eds.), *Contemporary intellectual assessment: Theories, tests, and issues.* New York: Guilford Press.

Feuerstein, R., Rand, Y., Falik, L., & Feuerstein, R. A. (2003). *Dynamic assessment of cognitive modifiability.* Jerusalem: ICELP Press.

Fuchs, D., & Fuchs, L. (1994). Inclusive school movement and the radicalization of special education reform. *Exceptional Children, 60*, 294–309.

Galperin, P. Y. (1969). Stages in the development of mental acts. In M. Cole & I. Maltzman (Eds.), *A handbook of contemporary Soviet psychology.* New York: Basic Books, pp. 34–61.

Gauvain, M. (2001). *The social context of cognitive development.* New York: Guilford.

Gindis, B. (1986). Special education in the Soviet Union: Problems and perspectives. *Journal of Special Education, 20*(3), 375–383.

Gindis, B. (1988). Children with mental retardation in the Soviet Union. *Mental Retardation, 26*(6), 381–384.

Gindis, B. (1992). Successful theories and practices from Russia: Can they be adopted in the United States? *AAMR News and Notes, 5*(6), 3–5.

Gindis, B. (1998). Navigating uncharted waters: School psychologists working with internationally adopted post-institutionalized children. *Communiqué* (National Association of School Psychologists) September (Part 1) 27(1), 6–9 and October (Part 2) 27(2), 20–23.

Gindis, B. (2001). Detecting and remediating the cumulative cognitive deficit in school age internationally adopted post-institutionalized children. *The Post: Parent Network for the Post-Institutionalized Child,* 271–276.

Gouzman, R., & Kozulin, A. (2000). Enhancing cognitive skills in blind learners. *The Educator, 12,* 20–29.

Gouzman, R. (2000). The Instrumental Enrichment program for the blind learners. *The Educator, 12,* 30–37.

Grigorenko, E. L., Ruzgis, R. M., & Sternberg, R. J. (Eds.). (1997). *Russian psychology: Past, present, and future.* Commack, NY: Nova Academic Press, pp. 155–179.

Guthke, J., & Beckmann, J. (2000). Learning test concept and dynamic assessment. In A. Kozulin & Y. Rand (Eds.), *Experience of mediated learning.* Oxford: Elsevier Scientific, pp. 175–190.

Haywood, H. C., & Tzuriel, D. (1992). *Interactive assessment.* New York: Springer-Verlag.

Haywood, H. C. Brooks, P. H., & Burns, S. (1992). *Bright Start: Cognitive curriculum for young children.* Watertown, MA: Charles Bridge Publishers.

Hogan, K., & Pressley, M. (Eds.). (1997). *Scaffolding student learning: Instructional approaches and issues.* Cambridge, MA: Brookline Books.

Ivanova, A. Ya. (1976). *Obuchaemost kak printsip otsenki ymstvennogo pazvitia u detei* [Learning aptitude as a diagnostic method in cognitive development of children]. Moscow, Pedagogika.

Karpov, Y. V., & Gindis, B. (2000). Dynamic assessment of the level of internalization of elementary school children's problem solving activity. In C. S. Lidz & J. G. Elliott (Eds.), *Dynamic Assessment: Prevailing models and applications.* Amsterdam: Elsevier Science, pp. 133–154.

Karpov, Y. V. (1990). Obuchaemost kak characteristika umstvennogo razvitia [Learning aptitude as an indicator of cognitive development]. *Psikhologia, 14*(2), 3–16.

Kauffman, J. M., & Hallahan, D. P. (1995). *The illusion of full inclusion.* Austin, TX: Pro-Ed.

Kaufman, R., & Kozulin, A. (1999). Case studies. In R. Feuerstein and associates, (Eds.), *Educational intervention with new immigrant students from Ethiopia: Final report.* Jerusalem: ICELP & The Jewish Agency.

Knox, J., & Kozulin, A. (1989). The Vygotskian tradition in Soviet psychological study of deaf children. In W. O. McCagg & L. Siegelbaum (Eds.), *The disabled in the Soviet Union.* Pittsburgh, PA: University of Pittsburgh Press, pp. 63–84.

Knox, J., & Stevens, C. (1993). Vygotsky and Soviet Russian Defectology: An Introduction. In R. W. Rieber & A. S. Carton (Eds.), *The collected works of L. S. Vygotsky. Volume 2: The fundamentals of defectology (abnormal psychology and learning disabilities).* New York: Plenum Press, pp. 1–28.

Kozulin, A. (1984). *Psychology in Utopia: Toward a social history of Soviet psychology.* Cambridge, MA: MIT Press.

Kozulin, A. (1986). Vygotsky in Context. In L. S. Vygotsky (Ed.). *Thought and Language* (pp. xi–lxi), (rev. edition). Cambridge, MA: MIT Press.

Kozulin, A. (1990). *Vygotsky's psychology: A biography of ideas.* Cambridge, MA: Harvard University Press.

Kozulin, A. (1998). *Psychological tools: A sociocultural approach to education.* Cambridge, MA: Harvard University Press.

Kozulin, A. (2000). Diversity of Instrumental Enrichment applications. In A. Kozulin & Y. Rand (Eds.), *Experience of mediated learning.* Oxford: Elsevier Scientific, pp. 257–273.

Kozulin, A. (2003). Psychological tools and mediated learning. In A. Kozulin, B. Gindis, V. Ageyev, & S. Miller (Eds.), *Vygotsky's Educational Theory in Cultural Context.* New York: Cambridge University Press, pp. 15–38.

Kozulin, A., & Presseisen, B. Z. (1995). Mediated learning experience and psychological tools: Vygotsky's and Feuerstein's perspectives in a study of student learning. *Educational Psychologist, 30*(2), 67–76.

Lebedinsky, V. V. (1985). *Narushchenia v psikhicheskom razvitii u detei* [Disorders in Children's Psychological Development]. Moscow: MGU Press.

Lidz, C. S., & Elliott, J. (Eds.). (2000). *Dynamic assessment: Prevailing models and applications.* Oxford: Elsevier Science.

Lidz, C. S. (1991). *Practitioner's guide to dynamic assessment.* New York: Guilford.

Lidz, C. S. (1995). Dynamic assessment and the legacy of L.S. Vygotsky. *School Psychology International, 16*(2), 143–153.

Lidz, C. S. (2000). The Application of Cognitive Functions Scale (ACFS): An example of curriculum-based dynamic assessment. In C. S. Lidz & J. G. Elliott (Eds.), *Dynamic Assessment: Prevailing Models and Applications.* Amsterdam: Elsevier Science, pp. 407–239.

Lidz, C. S. (2002). Mediated Learning Experience (MLE) as a basis for an alternative approach to assessment. *School Psychology International, 23*(1), 68–84.

Lipsky, D., & Gartner, A. (1996). Inclusion, school restructuring, and the remaking of American society. *Harvard Educational Review, 66,* 762–796.

Lubovsky, V. I. (1989). *Psikhologicheskie problemy diagnostiki anormalnogo razvitia detei* [Psychological issues in diagnosis of children with abnormal development]. Moscow: Pedagogika Press.

Lubovsky, V. I. (1990). Psikhologicheskii Experiment v Differentcialnoi Diagnistike Umstvennoi Otstalosti [Psychological experiment in differential diagnosis of mental retardation in children]. *Defectology, 6,* 3–16.

Lubovsky, V. I. (1996). L. S. Vygotsky i spetcialnaya psikhologia. [L. S. Vygotsky and special psychology]. *Voprosy Psikhologii, 6,* 118–125.

Luria, A. R. (1961). An objective approach to the study of the abnormal child. *Journal of the American Orthopsychiatric Association, 31,* 1–16.

Lurie, L., & Kozulin, A. (1998). The Instrumental Enrichment cognitive intervention program with deaf Ethiopian immigrant children in Israel. In A. Weisel

(Ed.), *Issues unresolved: New perspectives on language and deaf education*. Washington, DC: Gallaudet University Press, pp. 161–170.

Mahn, H. (2003). Periods in child development: Vygotsky's perspective. In A. Kozulin, B. Gindis, V. Ageyev, & S. Miller (Eds.), *Vygotsky's educational theory in cultural context*. New York: Cambridge University Press, pp. 119–137.

Malofeev, N. N. (2001). Specialnoe Obuchenie v Rossii I Zagranistei [Special Education in Russia and Abroad] (Publication of the Institute of Corrective Pedagogy). Moscow: Pechatnyi Dvor.

McCagg, W. O. (1989). The origins of defectology. In W. O. McCagg & L. Siegel-baum (Eds.), *The Disabled in the Soviet Union*. Pittsburgh, PA: University of Pittsburgh Press, pp. 27–58.

Meshcheriakov, A. (1979). *Awakening to life: Forming behavior and mind in deaf-blind children*. Translated by K. Judelson. Moscow: Progress Publishing.

Newman, F., & Holzman, L. (1993). *Lev Vygotsky: Revolutionary scientist*. London & New York: Routledge Press.

Petrova, A. (1925). Peti-primitivy [Primitive children]. In M. O. Gurevich (Ed.), *Voprosy pedologii I detskoi psikhonevrologii* [Problems of pedology and child psychoneurology]. Moscow: Zhizn I Znanie.

Petrovsky, A., & Yaroshevsky, M. (1998). Kratki Psickologicheskii Slovar [Brief Psychological Encyclopedia], Rostov-na-Dony, Russia: Fenix.

Presseisen, B., & Kozulin A. (1994). Mediated learning: The contribution of Vygotsky and Feuerstein in theory and practice. In M. Ben-Hur (Ed.), *On Feuerstein's Instrumental Enrichment*. Palatine, IL: IRI/Skylight Publishing, pp. 121–156.

Rubinshtein, S. Ya. (1979). *Psikhologia umstvenno otstalogo shkolnika* [Psychology of a mentally retarded student]. Moscow: Prosvecshenie Press.

Schulte, A., Osborn, S., Erchul, W. (1998). Effective special education: A United States dilemma. *School Psychology Review, 27*(1), 66–77.

Smith-Davis, J. (2000). People with disabilities in Russia: Progress and prospects. In K. Keith & R. Schalock (Eds.), *Cross-Cultural Perspectives on Quality of Life*. Washington, DC: AAMR.

Stainback, S., Stainback, W., & Forest, M. (1989). *Educating all students in the mainstream of regular education*. Baltimore: Brookes Publishing Co.

Sternberg, R. J., & Grigorenko, E. L. (2002). *Dynamic testing: The nature and measurement of learning potential*. New York: Cambridge University Press.

Strebeleva, E. A. (2000). Rannyia diagnostika umstvennoi otstalosti [Procedures for early diagnosis of mental retardation] (Institute of Corrective Pedagogy, Moscow). *Almanah, 2*, 2–11. Retrieved January 9, 2002 from: www.ise.iip.net/almanah/2/sto9.htm.

Suddaby, A. (1998). Children with Learning Difficulties. In J. Riordan (Ed.), *Soviet education: The gifted and the handicapped*. London: Routlege, pp. 76–87.

Sutton, A. (1988). Special Education for Handicapped Pupils. In J. Riordan (Ed.), *Soviet education: The gifted and the handicapped*. London: Routlege, pp. 88–102.

Tharp, R. G., & Gallimore, R. (1988). *Rousing minds to life: Teaching, learning, and schooling in social context*.

Tzuriel, D. (2001). *Dynamic assessment of young children.* New York: Kluwer Academic/ Plenum Publishers.

van der Veer, R., & Valsiner, J. (1991). *Understanding Vygotsky: A quest for synthesis.* Oxford: Basil Blackwell.

Venger, A. L. (1994). Structura psychologicheskogo syndroma [Structure of psychological syndrome]. *Voprosy Psichologii, 4,* 82–92.

Venger, L. A. (1988). The origin and development of cognitive abilities in preschool children. *International Journal of Behavioral Development, I(2),* 147–153.

Vlasova, T. A. (1984). *Otbor detei v vspomogatelny shkolu* [Screening children for special schools]. Moscow: Pedagogika.

Vygodskaya, G. L., & Lifanova, T. M. (1999). Life and works of L. S. Vygotsky. *Journal of Russian and East European Psychology, 37(2),* 23–81, 37(3), 3–31.

Vygodskaya, G., & Lifanova, T. A (1996). *Lev Semenovich Vygotsky: Igo Zhizn i Dejtelnost. Shtrikhi K Portrery* [Lev Semenovich Vygotsky: His life and work. Brush strokes of the portrait]. Moscow: Smysl.

Vygotsky, L. S. (1983). *Sobraniye sochinenii* [Collected works], Volume 5. Moscow: Pedagogika.

Vygotsky, L. S. (1995). *Problemy defectologii* [Problems of defectology]. Moscow: Prosvecshenie.

Vygotsky, L. (1986). *Thought and language* (rev. ed.). Cambridge, MA: MIT Press.

Vygotsky, L. S. (1987). *The collected works of L. S. Vygotsky. Volume 1: Problems of general psychology.* Translated by Norris Minick. Edited by R. W. Rieber & A. S. Carton. New York: Plenum Press.

Vygotsky, L. S. (1993). *The collected works of L. S. Vygotsky. Volume 2: The fundamentals of defectology (abnormal psychology and learning disabilities).* Translated by J. E. Knox & C. B. Stevens. Edited by R. W. Rieber & A. S. Carton. New York: Plenum Press.

Vygotsky, L. S. (1998). *The collected works of L. S. Vygotsky. Volume 5: Child psychology.* Edited by R. W. Rieber. New York: Plenum Press.

Zaitseva, G., Pursglove, M., & Gregory, S. (1999). Vygotsky, sign language, and the education of deaf pupils. *Journal of Deaf Studies and Deaf Education, 4(1),* 9–15.

Zaporozhets, A. V., & Elkonin, D. B. (Eds.) (1964/1971). *The psychology of preschool children.* Cambridge, MA: MIT Press. (Original work published 1964.).

Zuckerman, G. (2003). The learning activity in the first years of schooling. In A. Kozulin, B. Gindis, V. Ageyev, & S. Miller (Eds.), *Vygotsky's educational theory in cultural context.* New York: Cambridge University Press, pp. 177–199.

CHAPTER 14

Ausubel, D. P. (2000). *The acquisition and retention of knowledge: A cognitive view.* Dordrect: Kluwer.

Ausubel, D. P., Novak, J. D., & Hanesian, H. (1978). *Educational psychology: A cognitive view.* New York: Holt, Rinehart, and Winston.

Bannan-Ritland, B. (2003). The role of design in research: The integrative learning design framework. *Educational Researcher, 32,* 21–24.

Brown, A. L. (1992). Design experiments: Theoretical and methodological challenges in creating complex interventions in classroom settings. *Journal of the Learning Sciences, 2,* 141–168.

Cobb, P., Confrey, J., diSessa, A., Lehrer, R., & Schauble, L. (2003). Design experiments in educational research. *Educational Researcher, 32,* 9–13.

Collins, A. (1992). Toward a design science of education. In E. Scanlon & T. O'Shea (Eds.), *New directions in educational technology.* Berlin: Springer, pp. 77–97.

Collins, A., Joseph, D., & Bielaczyc, K. (2004). Design research: Theoretical and methodological issues. *The Journal of the Learning Sciences, 13,* 15–42.

Davydov, V. V. (1990). *Types of generalization in instruction: Logical and psychological problems in the structuring of school curricula.* Reston, VA: National Council of Teachers of Mathematics.

Engeström, Y. (1987). Learning by expanding: An activity-theoretical approach to developmental research. Helsinki: Orienta-Konsultit.

Engeström, Y. (1989). The cultural–historical theory of activity and the study of political repression. *International Journal of Mental Health, 17*(4), 29–41.

Engeström, Y. (1991). Developmental work research: Reconstructing expertise through expansive learning. In M. I. Nurminen & G. R. S. Weir (Eds.), *Human jobs and computer interfaces.* Amsterdam: Elsevier Science Publishers.

Engeström, Y. (1992). Interactive expertise: Studies in distributed working intelligence. University of Helsinki, Department of Education. Research Bulletin 83.

Engeström, Y. (1993). Developmental work research as a testbench of activity theory: The case of primary care medical practice. In S. Chaiklin & J. Lave (Eds.), *Understanding practice: Perspectives on activity and context.* Cambridge, UK: Cambridge University Press, pp. 64–103.

Engeström, Y. (1996a). Developmental work research as educational research: Looking ten years back and into the zone of proximal development. *Nordisk Pedagogik, 16,* 131–143.

Engeström, Y. (1996b). Development as breaking away and opening up: A challenge to Vygotsky and Piaget. *Swiss Journal of Psychology, 55,* 126–132.

Engeström, Y. (2001). Expansive learning at work: Toward an activity theoretical reconceptualization. *Journal of Education and Work, 14*(1), 133–156.

Engeström, Y. (2004). New forms of learning in co-configuration work. *Journal of Workplace Learning, 16,* 11–21.

Engeström, Y., Engeström, R., & Kerosuo, H. (2003). The discursive construction of collaborative care. *Applied Linguistics, 24,* 286–315.

Engeström, Y., Engeström, R., & Kärkkäinen, M. (1995). Polycontextuality and boundary crossing in expert cognition: Learning and problem solving in complex work activities. *Learning and Instruction, 5,* 319–336.

Engeström, Y., Lompscher, J., & Rückriem, G. (Eds.). (2005). *Putting activity theory to work: Contributions from developmental work research.* Berlin: Lehmanns Media.

Engeström, Y., Puonti, A., & Seppänen. L. (2003). Spatial and temporal expansion of the object as a challenge for reorganizing work. In D. Nicolini, S. Gherardi, & D. Yanow (Eds.), *Knowing in organizations: A practice-based approach.* Armonk: Sharpe, pp. 286–315.

Eskola, A. (1999). Laws, logics, and human activity. In Y. Engeström, R. Miettinen & R.-L. Punamäki (Eds.), *Perspectives on activity theory.* Cambridge, UK: Cambridge University Press, pp. 107–114.

Haenen, J. (1995). *Pjotr Gal'perin: Psychologist in Vygotsky's footsteps.* Hauppauge: Nova Science Publishers.

Hammer, M. (1990). Reengineering work: Don't automate, obliterate! *Harvard Business Review, 68*(4), 104–112.

von Hippel, E., & Tyre, M. J. (1995). How learning by doing is done: Problem identification in novel process equipment. *Research Policy, 24,* 1–12.

Holt, J. (1964). *How children fail.* New York: Dell.

Leont'ev, A. N. (1932). The development of voluntary attention in the child. *Journal of Genetic Psychology, 40,* 52–81.

Long, N. (2001). *Development sociology: Actor perspectives.* London: Routledge.

Moscovici, S. (1984). The phenomenon of social representations. In R. M. Farr & S. Moscovici (Eds.), *Social representations.* Cambridge, UK: Cambridge University Press, pp. 118–136.

Norman, D. A. (1993). *Things that make us smart.* Reading: Addison-Wesley.

Pihlaja, J. (2005). *Learning in and for production: An activity-theoretical study of the historical development of distributed systems of generalizing.* Helsinki: University of Helsinki, Department of Education.

Porter, J., Aspinall, A., Parsons, S., Simmonds, L., Wood, M., Culley, G., & Holroyd, A. (2005). Time to listen. *Disability and Society, 20,* 575–585.

Smith, B. C. (1998). *On the origin of objects.* Cambridge, MA: MIT Press.

Talyzina, N. F. (1981). *The psychology of learning: Theories of learning and programmed instruction.* Moscow: Progress.

Teräs, M. (in press). Intercultural learning and hybridity in the Culture Laboratory. PhD dissertation. Helsinki: Department of Education, University of Helsinki.

Tyre, M. J., & von Hippel, E. (1995). *Locating adaptive learning: The situated nature of adaptive learning in organizations.* Working Paper no. 90–93. The International Center for Research on the Management of Technology. Sloan School of Management, Massachussets Institute of Technology.

van der Veer, R., & Valsiner, J. (1991). *Understanding Vygotsky: A quest for synthesis.* Oxford: Blackwell.

Victor, B., & Boynton, A. C. (1998). *Invented here: Maximizing your organization's internal growth and profitability.* Boston: Harvard Business School Press.

Virkkunen, J., & Ahonen, H. (2004). Transforming learning and knowledge creation on the shop floor. *International Journal of Human Resources Development and Management, 4,* 57–72.

Vygotsky, L. S. (1978). *Mind in society: The psychology of higher mental functions.* Cambridge, MA: Harvard University Press.

Vygotsky, L. S. (1987). Lectures on psychology. In *The collected works of L. S. Vygotsky. Volume 1. Problems of general psychology.* New York: Plenum.

Vygotsky, L. S. (1997a). The history of the development of higher mental functions. In *The collected works of L. S. Vygotsky. Volume 4: The history of the development of higher mental functions.* New York: Plenum, pp. 1–26.

Vygotsky, L. S. (1997b). The instrumental method in psychology. In *The collected works of L. S. Vygotsky. Volume 3: Problems of the theory and history of psychology.* New York: Plenum.

Vygotsky, L. S. (1999). Tool and sign in the development of the child. In *The collected works of L. S. Vygotsky. Volume 6: Scientific legacy.* New York: Kluwer/Plenum.

INDEX

364, 366, 367, 373, 374, 377, 379,
381, 392, 396, 406, 423, 424
meanings, 110, 227
pure, 218, 219
real, 258, 260, 296
and signs, 99
and tools, 167
observable, 125, 135, 223
behavior, 40, 43, 135
observation, 14, 36, 38, 40, 48, 90, 98,
107, 116, 140, 214, 215, 227, 251,
266, 272, 297, 330, 348, 352
ontic, 229, 230, 236
ontogenesis, 10, 48, 156, 167, 223, 310
individual, 281
ontogeny, 159, 203, 209, 211
of imitation, 105
ontological, 215, 218, 229, 230, 231
spheres, 229
operational, 230, 237, 302, 308, 359
meanings, 226, 231
operations, 14, 98, 139, 143, 162, 169,
175, 176, 179, 182, 193, 200, 223,
226, 242, 250, 259, 260, 280, 281,
292, 293, 294, 296, 298, 302, 315,
365
psychological, 226, 299
operators, 14, 280, 281, 290, 291, 293,
301, 302
cultural, 14, 288
opportunities, 344, 349
opposition, 33, 106, 110, 127, 135,
179, 183, 185, 213, 215, 243, 252
activity in, 128
order, 3, 84, 97, 124, 125, 138, 142,
165, 179, 233, 311
social, 122, 190
organic, 178, 195, 230, 284, 334, 335,
336, 340, 342, 345, 357, 407
organization, 11, 27, 71, 84, 85, 87, 91,
103, 110, 111, 112, 113, 116, 143,
148, 181, 182, 183, 184, 197, 199,
208, 257, 285, 290, 294, 297, 299,
302, 320, 321, 348, 364, 369, 372,
375, 379, 424
social, 96
orientation, 255, 263, 273, 348

original, 1, 157, 165, 166, 244
origins, 16, 24, 31, 48, 58, 80, 94, 99,
133, 161

paradox, 64, 164, 169, 223, 234, 237,
238, 277, 334
Parmenides, 215
participant, 134
structures, 327, 330
participation, 2, 6, 7, 12, 15, 28, 102,
112, 113, 114, 115, 118, 119, 120,
121, 122, 124, 140, 141, 146, 148,
151, 187, 215, 219, 237, 238, 239,
246, 253, 260, 262, 265, 267, 269,
271, 272, 273, 275, 287, 294, 303,
307, 311, 319, 322, 325, 327, 328,
329, 330, 344, 370, 372, 373, 374,
375, 379, 391, 396, 397
passions, 65, 236, 237, 261
passive, 39, 121, 146, 159, 168, 169,
382
Pasternak, 24, 240
path, 56, 62, 71, 120, 122, 146, 156,
196, 293, 300, 334, 342, 345,
401
developmental, 182
pathogenesis, 10, 156
paths
developmental, 278, 344, 346
patterns, 16, 33, 106, 142, 143, 186,
203, 307, 331, 350, 360, 367
institutional, 148
Paulhan, 226
Paustovsky, 24
Pavlov, 4, 25, 26–28, 29, 31, 35, 37, 38,
40, 43, 46, 48, 289, 290
Pavlovian, 27, 290
pedagogic, 252, 307, 308, 316, 319, 329
interaction, 15
practices, 15
pedagogical, 265
analysis, 331
pedagogy, 15, 16, 61, 72, 99, 276, 307,
308, 309, 312, 313, 316, 317, 318,
320, 322, 323, 329, 330, 331, 361,
397, 407, 413
Pedersen, 39